¿Qué hay de nuevo?

Adelante and En camino

The first Spanish program completely designed for the middle grades

¡Ven conmigo!

Adelante (Level 1A)
En camino (Level 1B)   *or*   ¡Ven conmigo! (Level 1)

¡Ven conmigo! (Level 2)

¡Ven conmigo! (Level 3)

ADELANTE and *EN CAMINO* articulate directly into Level 2 of *¡Ven conmigo!* and provide everything a student needs to succeed.

Structure for the Middle Grades

ADELANTE and *EN CAMINO* are designed for the way middle school students learn.

- Chapters focus on specific communicative goals that help students develop their listening, reading, writing, speaking, and cultural skills.

- A variety of well-sequenced activities give middle school students the practice they need.

- Pair and group assignments are broken into progressive, easy-to-follow steps.

- The proficiency-oriented approach carefully recycles and spirals instruction so students can build skills with confidence.

Active Learning

Middle school learners require engaging, relevant activities. *ADELANTE* and *EN CAMINO* provide a wealth of motivational instruction.

- Audio, video, and CD-ROM presentations show students how to use language in a cultural context.

- Features encourage middle school learners to investigate cultural, cross-cultural, and interdisciplinary connections.

- A range of imaginative pair and group activities involve extensive student-to-student interaction.

- A wide variety of oral and written projects, games, and realia stimulate students to think and create in Spanish.

Integrated Technology

ADELANTE and EN CAMINO feature the most extensive technology package available for middle school learners.

- *Audiocassettes* and *Audio Compact Discs* provide songs and listening activities for every chapter section.

- For every chapter, the *Video* and *Videodisc Program* presents:

  - a two-part story that models the language and culture students will learn in the chapter

  - a video connection that introduces the communicative goal of each chapter section

  - native speaker interviews that encourage students to think about cultural similarities and differences

  - footage that presents cultural vignettes to help students visualize abstract concepts

  - music videos, commercials, news reports, and other authentic video from Spanish-speaking television

- The *CD-ROM Program* gives students interactive practice with the language and cultural features of each chapter.

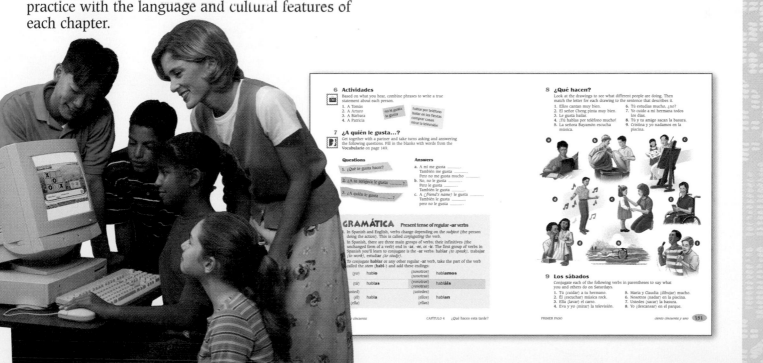

> If you give students a variety of media exposure, you increase what they're going to retain. My eighth graders are coming out of eighth grade far more fluent because of the variety of media exposure they get.
>
> — David Makepeace, Livonia Junior/Senior High School, Livonia, New York

Resources for Middle School

ADELANTE and *EN CAMINO* offer a wide
assortment of instructional options that ensure
success with all types of students and teaching
situations.

- The *Annotated Teacher's Edition* provides:
  - detailed suggestions on ways to integrate technology
    and print resources with lessons
  - presentation and practice ideas for different types
    of learners
  - creative suggestions for TPR, games, oral and written
    portfolios, homework, and hands-on projects
  - suggestions for native speakers
- A *Lesson Planner* contains lesson plans for each chapter
  section with suggestions for block scheduling.
- *Teaching Transparencies* include vocabulary presentations
  and situations for each chapter section.
- *Activities for Communication* feature a variety of communicative activities and realia geared to the interests
  of middle school students.
- The *Grammar and Vocabulary Workbook* augments
  instruction with carefully structured exercises.
- The *Practice and Activity Workbook* has a variety of
  writing activities, readings, and exercises specifically
  structured for middle school learners.
- The *Testing Program*, *Alternative Assessment Guide*, and
  Test Generator offer extensive assessment options.

An *Exploratory Guide
with Copying Masters*
has theme-centered
lesson plans and
resources to help you
use *ADELANTE* and
EN CAMINO in an
exploratory class.

¡Una perspectiva
totalmente nueva!

CAPÍTULO 6 Segundo paso

- Video Progra
  cassette 1; V
  pp. 1–2
- Videodisc Prog
  Videodisc 1A;
  Guide, pp. 1–3
- Practice and Act
  pp. 1–4

Resources

For correlated print a
visual materials, see *A
Teacher's Edition*, p. T

2 Lesson Planner

48 Grammar and Vocabulary Workboo

101L

HOMEWORK SUGGESTIONS   CHA

HOLT
FOREIGN
LANGUAGES

DESTINATION:
COMMUNICATION

¡Ven conmigo!®

Adelante

Holt Spanish Level 1A

Annotated
Teacher's Edition

Nancy A. Humbach
Oscar Ozete

HOLT, RINEHART AND WINSTON
Harcourt Brace & Company

Austin • New York • Orlando • Atlanta • San Francisco • Boston • Dallas • Toronto • London

In the *Annotated Teacher's Edition:*

Photography Credits

Abbreviations used: (t) top, (b) bottom, (c) center, (l)left, (r), right, (i) inset, (bkgd) background.
All pre-Columbian symbols by EclectiCollections/HRW.
All photos by Marty Granger/Edge Video Productions/HRW except:
Front Cover: (bl), Townsend P. Dickinson/Comstock; (br), Dallas and John Heaton/Westlight; (bkgd), © Robert Fried; (c), Joe Viesti/Viesti Associates, Inc. **Front Matter:** Page T1, (cr); T2, (bl), (cr); T3 (bl); T4, (bl), (tr), Sam Dudgeon/HRW Photo; T22 (tc), Stuart Cohen/Comstock; T23 (tl), Christine Galida/HRW Photo; (bc), Peter Van Steen/HRW Photo; T24 (cl), Richard Hutchings/HRW Photo; T32 (br), T43 (c), Michelle Bridwell/Frontera Fotos; T51 (b), Michelle Bridwell/HRW Photo; T55 (bc), Michelle Bridwell/ Frontera Fotos; T61 (b), Sam Dudgeon/HRW Photo. **Preliminary Chapter:** Page T66 (bl), S. Howell/Gamma Liaison, (br) Culver Pictures, Inc. **Location Opener—Spain:** Page15D (c), David R. Frazier Photolibrary. **Chapter Two:** Page 57J (br), Sam Dudgeon/HRW Photo. **Location Opener—Mexico:** Page 97D (b), Jorge Nuñez/Latin Focus. **Location Opener—Florida:** Page 183B (br), Latin Focus; 183C (cl), Tony Arruza; 183D (b), Steve Ferry/P & F Communications.

Illustration Credits
All art, unless otherwise noted, by Holt, Rinehart & Winston.
Preliminary Chapter: Page T71, Deborah Haley Melmon/Sharon Morris Associates.
Chapter One: Page 15C, GeoSystems. **Chapter Two:** Page 57F, Eldon Doty/Pat Hackett. **Chapter Three:** Page 97C, GeoSystems; 101F, Elizabeth Brandt; 101I, Michael Morrow; 101J, Deborah Haley Melmon/Sharon Morris Associates. **Chapter Four:** 141E, Edson Campos; 141F, Deborah Haley Melmon/Sharon Morris Associates, 141K, Eva Vagretti Cockrille. **Chapter Five:** 183C, GeoSystems; 187J, Deborah Haley Melmon/Sharon Morris Associates. **Chapter Six:** 227F, Edson Campos; 227H, Lori Osiecki; 227J, Fian Arroyo/Dick Washington.

In the *Pupil's Edition:*

Acknowledgments
For permission to reprint copyrighted material, grateful acknowledgment is made to the following sources:
Banco Central de Cuenca: Excerpts and illustrations from "Calendario de Eventos" from *60 Aniversario de la Fundación del Banco Central de Cuenca, Antiguo Hospital San Vicente de Paul,* June–July 1988.
Bayard Revistas-Súper Júnior: Excerpts and illustrations from "¡Anímate a escribir!" from *Súper Júnior,* no. 22–23, July–August, 1996. Copyright © 1996 by Súper Júnior Bayard Revistas, Hispano Francesa de Ediciones, S.A.
Cines Lumiere: Advertisement for "Cines Lumiere" from *Guía El País,* no. 57, December 27, 1990.
Club de Tenis Las Lomas: Advertisement for "Club de Tenis Las Lomas" from *Guía El País,* no. 57, December 27, 1990.
Editorial Atlántida, S.A.: Videocassette cover from *Billiken presenta: Mundo Marino.* Jacket cover from *La isla del terror* by Tony Koltz, illustrations by Ron Wing. Photograph from "Empezar con todo" from *Billiken: Diccionario Escolar,* primera entrega, no. 3765, March 9, 1992. Copyright © 1992 by Editorial Atlántida, S.A. Illustration on page 34 from *Billiken de Regalo: Almanaque 1997,* no. 4016, December 30, 1996. From "Deportes en el agua" by Alejandra Becco from *Billiken,* February 17, 1992. Copyright © 1992 by Editorial Atlántida, S.A.
Editorial Eres: Illustration "Regresa a clases" from *Eres,* December 16, 1993. Copyright © 1993 by Editorial Eres.
Editorial Everest, S.A.: Front cover and text from *Everest enciclopedia ilustrada de los animales, Tomo I: Mamíferos* by Dr. Philip Whitfield. Copyright © by Editorial Everest, S.A.
Editorial Televisa, S.A.: Adapted from *Tele*Guía,* año 42, no. 2159, December 25–31, 1993. Copyright ©1993 by Editorial Television, S.A. From "La Chica Sándwich" from *Tú internacional,* año 14, no. 1, January 1993. Copyright ©1993 by Editorial América, S.A. Header and adapted excerpts from "línea directa" from *Tú internacional,* año 14, no. 6, June 1993. Copyright ©1993 by Editorial América, S.A.
Emecé Editores España, S.A.: Illustration and text from jacket cover for *50 cosas que los niños pueden hacer para salvar la tierra* by The Earth Works Group.
Gativideo S.A.: Videocassette cover from *Las nuevas aventuras de Mofli* by Gativideo.
Hotel Agua Escondida: Advertisement for Hotel Agua Escondida.
Instituto Municipal de Deportes, Ayuntamiento de Madrid: Advertisement for "Piscina Municipal Aluche" from the "En Forma" section from *Guía El País,* no. 57, December 27, 1990.
Metro Vídeo Española, S.L.: Videocassette cover from *Los dinosaurios. Su descubrimiento.*
The Quintus Communications Group: Excerpts from "Diez cosas curiosas para hacer en la Pequeña Habana" from *Miami Mensual,* año 13, no. 3, March 1993. Copyright © 1993 by The Quintus Communications Group.

ANNOTATED TEACHER'S EDITION CREDITS

Contributing Writers

Dr. Marjorie E. Artzer
Northern Kentucky University
Highland Heights, KY

Jackie Moase-Burke
Language Arts Oakland Schools
Clinton Township, MI

Pablo Muirhead Montesinos
Shorewood Intermediate School
Milwaukee, WI

Jacqueline Hall-Muirhead
Pius XI High School
Milwaukee, WI

The following people researched and wrote culture features:

Mildred Cancel-García
Austin, TX

Mary Nichols
Austin, TX

Mariángeles LaPointe
Austin, TX

Amy Propps
Austin, TX

Field Test Participants

Bill Braden
South Junior High School
Boise, ID

Paula Critchlow
Indian Hills Middle School
Sandy, UT

Frances Cutter
Convent of the Visitation School
St. Paul, MN

Carlos Fernández
Sandy Creek High School
Tyrone, GA

Maureen Fischer
Marian Catholic High School
Chicago Heights, IL

Jan Holland
Lovejoy High School
Lovejoy, GA

Nancy Holmes
Marian Catholic High School
Chicago Heights, IL

Gloria Holmstrom
Emerson Junior High School
Yonkers, NY

K. A. Lagana
Ponus Ridge Middle School
Norwalk, CT

Michelle Mistric
Iowa High School
Iowa, LA

Rubén Moreno
Aycock Middle School
Greensboro, NC

Fred Pratt
San Marcos High School
San Marcos, TX

Regina Salvi
Museum Junior High School
Yonkers, NY

Lorraine Walsh
Lincoln Southeast High School
Lincoln, NE

Reviewers

Dr. Edward D. Allen
Ohio State University
Columbus, OH

Daniel J. Bender
Adlai Stevenson High School
Lincolnshire, IL

Marie Carrera Lambert
Iona College
New Rochelle, NY

Dr. June Carter
The University of Texas
Austin, TX

Myrtress G. Eddleman
Carver High School
Birmingham, AL

Rubén Garza
James Bowie High School
Austin, TX

Joseph N. Harris
Poudre School District
Fort Collins, CO

Stephen L. Levy
Roslyn Public Schools
Roslyn, NY

Laura Olson
Austin Waldorf School
Austin, TX

Carmen Reyes
Jonesboro High School
Jonesboro, GA

Dr. Yolanda Russinovich Solé
The University of Texas
Austin, TX

Brian A. Souza
Plymouth South High School
Plymouth, MA

Elena Steele
Clark County School District
Las Vegas, NV

Dora Villani
John F. Kennedy High School
Bronx, NY

Jo Anne S. Wilson
J. Wilson Associates
Glen Arbor, MI

Professional Essays

Technology as a Tool in the Foreign Language Classroom
Cindy A. Kendall
Williamston High School
Williamston, MI

Standards for Foreign Language Education
Robert LaBouve
Board of National Standards in Foreign Language Education
Austin, TX

Teaching Culture
Nancy A. Humbach
Miami University
Oxford, OH

Dorothea Bruschke
Parkway School District
Chesterfield, MO

Using Portfolios in the Foreign Language Classroom
Jo Anne S. Wilson
J. Wilson Associates
Glen Arbor, MI

Learning Styles and Multi-Modality Teaching
Mary B. McGehee
Louisiana State University
Baton Rouge, LA

New Perspectives for Native Speakers
Cecilia Rodríguez-Pino
New Mexico State University
Las Cruces, NM

AUTHORS

Nancy A. Humbach
Miami University
Ms. Humbach collaborated in the development of the scope and sequence and video material, and created activities and culture features.

Dr. Oscar Ozete
University of Southern Indiana
Dr. Ozete collaborated in the development of the scope and sequence, reviewed all Pupil's Edition material, and wrote grammar explanations.

CONTRIBUTING WRITERS

Dr. Pennie Nichols-Alem
Baton Rouge, LA
Dr. Nichols-Alem wrote the **Enlaces.**

Susan Peterson
The Ohio State University
Columbus, OH
Mrs. Peterson selected realia for readings and developed reading activities.

CONSULTANTS

John DeMado
John DeMado Language Seminars
Washington, CT

Dr. Ingeborg R. McCoy
Southwest Texas State University
San Marcos, TX

Jo Anne S. Wilson
J. Wilson Associates
Glen Arbor, MI

REVIEWERS

Susan Campbell
Lisha Kill Middle School
Albany, New York

Rocco Fuschetto
Northside Middle School
Muncie, Indiana

Gabriela Gándara
Austin, TX

Ester García
Coral Gables Senior High
Coral Gables, FL

Francisco González-Soldevilla
Mast Academy
Miami, FL

Gretchen Hatcher
Foley Senior High School
Foley, AL

Sheila D. Landre
Turlock Junior High School
Turlock, CA

Steve Lucero
Arrowview Middle School
San Bernardino, CA

Mary Luzzi
Lisha Kill Middle School
Albany, NY

Marta Meacham
Bethlehem Central High School
Delmar, NY

Joanne Micale
Lisha Kill Middle School
Albany, NY

Linda Nass
Farnsworth Middle School
Guilderland, NY

Francisco Perea
Austin, TX

Gail Saucedo
Coronado Middle School
Coronado, CA

Barbara Sawhill
The Noble and Greenough School
Dedham, MA

Lois Seijo
Churchville Middle School
Elmhurst, IL

Teresa Shu
Austin, TX

Paula Twomey
Ithaca High School
Ithaca, NY

Cristina Villarreal
Houston, TX

FIELD TEST PARTICIPANTS

We express our appreciation to the teachers and students who participated in the field test. Their comments were instrumental in the development of this program.

Bill Braden
South Junior High School
Boise, ID

Paula Critchlow
Indian Hills Middle School
Sandy, UT

Gloria Holmstrom
Emerson Junior High School
Yonkers, NY

K.A. Lagana
Ponus Ridge Middle School
Norwalk, CT

Rubén Moreno
Aycock Middle School
Greensboro, NC

Regina Salvi
Museum Junior High School
Yonkers, NY

TO THE STUDENT

Some people have the opportunity to learn a new language by living in another country. Most of us, however, begin learning another language and getting acquainted with another culture in a classroom with the help of a teacher, classmates, and a book. To use your book effectively, you need to know how it works.

Adelante *(Let's get started)* is the first book in a series called *¡Ven conmigo!* It's organized to help you learn about the Spanish language and about the cultures of people who speak Spanish. A Preliminary Chapter presents some basic concepts in Spanish and offers some strategies for learning a new language. This is followed by six chapters and three Location Openers. Each of these six chapters and each Location Opener follow the same pattern.

Adelante takes you to three different Spanish-speaking locations. Each location you visit is introduced with photos and information on four special pages called the Location Openers. You can also see these locations on video and on CD-ROM.

The two Chapter Opener pages at the beginning of each chapter tell you about the chapter theme and goals. These goals outline what you learn to do in each section of the chapter.

De antemano *(Getting started)* This part of the chapter is an illustrated story that shows you Spanish-speaking people in real-life situations, using the language you'll learn in the chapter. You also might watch this story on video.

Primer, Segundo, and **Tercer paso** *(First, Second, Third Part)* After **De antemano,** the chapter is divided into three sections called **pasos.** At the beginning of each **paso,** there is a reminder of the goals you'll aim for in this part. Within the **paso,** you will find boxes called **Así se dice** *(Here's how to say it)* that give the Spanish expressions you'll need to communicate. You'll also find boxes called **Vocabulario** that list new vocabulary you'll need to know and that you'll be responsible for on the Chapter Test. Along with the new expressions and vocabulary words, you'll need to learn certain structures. These structures are provided in the **Gramática** and **Nota gramatical** boxes. To learn all the new expressions, vocabulary, and grammar,

there are several fun activities to practice what you're learning. These activities help you develop your listening, speaking, reading, and writing skills. By the end of each **paso,** you'll have met your goal.

Panorama cultural *(Cultural Panorama)* On this page of the chapter, you'll read interviews with Spanish-speaking people around the world. They'll talk about themselves and their lives, and you can compare their culture to yours. You can watch these interviews on video or listen to them on audiocassette or CD. You can also watch them on a computer using the CD-ROM program, then check to see if you've understood by answering some questions.

Nota cultural *(Culture Note)* Within each chapter, there are culture notes to give you more information about the culture of Spanish-speaking people. These notes might tell you interesting facts, describe common customs, or offer other information that will help you understand what's expected of you if you visit a Spanish-speaking area.

Encuentro cultural *(Cultural Encounter)* This culture section is found in every even-numbered chapter. A native Spanish-speaker will host a first-hand encounter with some aspect of Spanish-speaking culture. You can also watch this section on the video.

Enlaces *(Links)* These pages link the study of Spanish-speaking culture with other subjects you might be studying at school, such as social studies, science, or math.

Vamos a leer *(Let's read)* You'll find the reading section after the three **pasos**. The readings, which are related to the chapter theme, will help you develop your reading skills in Spanish. The **Estrategia** in each chapter will give you helpful strategies to improve your reading comprehension.

iv

Repaso *(Review)* These review pages give you the chance to practice what you've learned in the chapter. You'll improve your listening and reading skills and practice communicating with others. You'll also practice what you've learned about culture. A special section called **Vamos a escribir** in Chapters 3–6 will help you develop writing skills and strategies.

A ver si puedo *(Let's see if I can . . .)* This page at the end of the chapter is just for you. It will help you check what you've learned without your teacher's help. A series of questions, followed by short activities, will help you decide how well you can do on your own. Page numbers beside each section will tell you where to go for help if you need it.

Throughout each chapter, certain special features provide extra tips and reminders. **Sugerencia** *(Suggestion)* offers helpful study hints to help you succeed in a foreign language class. **¿Te acuerdas?** *(Do you remember?)* reminds you of grammar and vocabulary you may have forgotten. **Vocabulario extra** *(Extra Vocabulary)* gives you some extra words to use when talking about yourself and your own special interests. These words will not appear on the quizzes and test unless your teacher chooses to include them.

Vocabulario *(Vocabulary)* You'll find a Spanish-English vocabulary list on the last page of the chapter. The words are grouped by the **paso** they're in. These are the words that will be required on the quizzes and tests.
You'll also find Spanish-English and English-Spanish vocabulary lists at the end of the book. The words you'll need to know for the quizzes and tests will be in bold face type.

Also, at the end of your book, you'll find more helpful material, such as:
- a summary of the expressions you'll learn in the **Así se dice** boxes
- a summary of the grammar you'll study
- additional vocabulary words you might want to use
- a grammar index to help you find where grammar structures are introduced

Adelante Let's get started on an exciting trip to new cultures and a new language!

EXPLANATION OF ICONS IN ADELANTE

Throughout *Adelante* you'll see these symbols, or icons, next to activities. They'll tell you what you'll probably do with that activity. Here's a key to help you understand the icons.

Listening Activities
This icon means that this is a listening activity. You'll need to listen to the tape, the CD, or your teacher in order to complete the activity.

CD-ROM Activities
Whenever this icon appears, it lets you know that there's a related activity on the *Interactive CD-ROM Program.*

Writing Activities
When you see this icon, it means that the activity is a writing activity. The directions may ask you to write words, sentences, paragraphs, or a whole composition.

Pair Work Activities
Activities with this icon are designed to be completed with a partner. Both you and your partner are responsible for completing the activity.

Group Work Activities
If an activity has this icon next to it, you can expect to complete it with two or three of your classmates. Each person in the group is responsible for a share of the work.

v

PARA MEJOR APRENDER EL ESPAÑOL

How best to learn Spanish

LISTEN

It's important to listen carefully in class. Take notes and ask questions if you don't understand, even if you think your question seems a little silly. Other people are probably wondering the same thing you are. You won't be able to understand everything you hear at first, but don't feel frustrated. You're actually absorbing a lot even when you don't realize it.

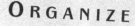

ORGANIZE

Your memory is going to get a workout, so it's important to get organized. Throughout the textbook you'll see learning tips (**Sugerencias**) that can improve your study skills. For starters, here's a hint: see things with your mind. Associate each new word, sentence, or phrase with an exaggerated or unusual mental picture. For example, if you're learning the word **regla** *(ruler)*, visualize an enormous ruler on an enormous desk as you practice saying a sentence with the word.

EXPAND

Increase your contact with Spanish outside of class in every way you can. You may be able to find someone living near you who speaks Spanish. It's easy to find Spanish-language programs on TV, on the radio, or at the video store. Many magazines and newspapers in Spanish are published or sold in the United States. Don't be afraid to read, watch, or listen. You won't understand every word, but that's okay. You can get a lot out of a story or an article by concentrating on the words you do recognize and doing a little intelligent guesswork.

SPEAK

Practice speaking Spanish aloud every day. Talking with your teachers and classmates is an easy and fun way to learn. Don't be afraid to experiment. Your mistakes will help identify problems, and they'll show you important differences in the way English and Spanish "work" as languages.

PRACTICE

Learning a foreign language is like learning to ride a bicycle or play an instrument. You can't spend one night cramming and then expect instantly to be able to ride or play the next morning. You didn't learn English that way either! Short, daily practice sessions are more effective than long, once-a-week sessions. Also, try to practice with a friend or a classmate. After all, language is about communication, and it takes two to communicate.

CONNECT

Some English and Spanish words have common roots in Latin, and the two languages have influenced each other, so your knowledge of English can give you clues about the meaning of many Spanish words. Look for an English connection when you need to guess at unfamiliar words. You may also find that learning Spanish will help you in English class!

HAVE FUN!

Above all, remember to have fun! The more you try, the more you'll learn. Besides, having fun will help you relax, and relaxed people learn better and faster. **¡Buena suerte!** *(Good luck!)*

ANNOTATED TEACHER'S EDITION

Contents

Adelante *Contents*

Come along—to a world of new experiences!

Adelante offers you the opportunity to learn the language spoken by millions of people in the many Spanish-speaking countries around the world. Let's find out about the countries, the people, and the Spanish language.

CAPÍTULO PRELIMINAR

vii

¡Ven conmigo a España!

CAPÍTULO 1

¡Mucho gusto! 20

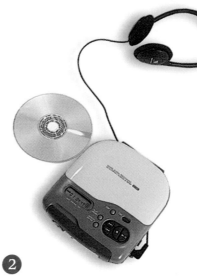

CAPÍTULO ②

¡Organízate!...... 58

¡Ven conmigo a México!

VISIT THE HISTORIC CITIES OF CUERNAVACA AND
MEXICO CITY WITH FOUR MEXICAN TEENAGERS AND—

Talk about things you like and
explain why • CAPÍTULO 3

Discuss what you and others do
during free time • CAPÍTULO 4

CAPÍTULO 3

Nuevas clases, nuevos amigos . . . 102

x

CAPÍTULO 4

¿Qué haces esta tarde?...... 142

xi

T17

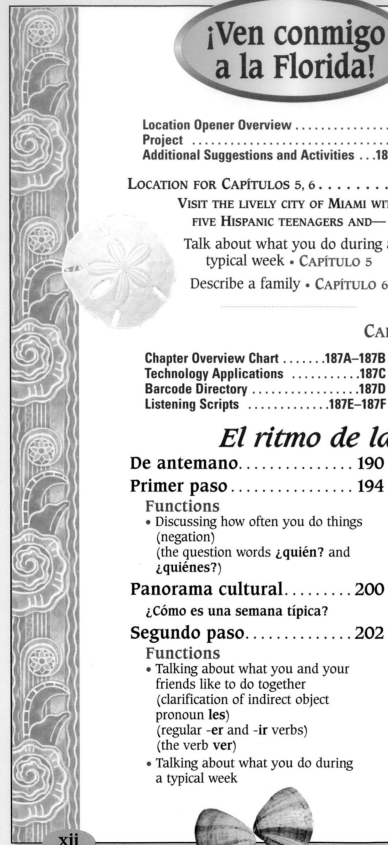

¡Ven conmigo a la Florida!

LOCATION FOR CAPÍTULOS 5, 6 184

VISIT THE LIVELY CITY OF MIAMI WITH
FIVE HISPANIC TEENAGERS AND—

Talk about what you do during a
typical week • CAPÍTULO 5

Describe a family • CAPÍTULO 6

CAPÍTULO ❺

El ritmo de la vida 188

CAPÍTULO ⑥

Entre familia *228*

CULTURAL REFERENCES

Home and Family Life

Special Days

Sports

Telephone

Transportation

Vacation

Variation in the Spanish Language

Sayings and Expressions

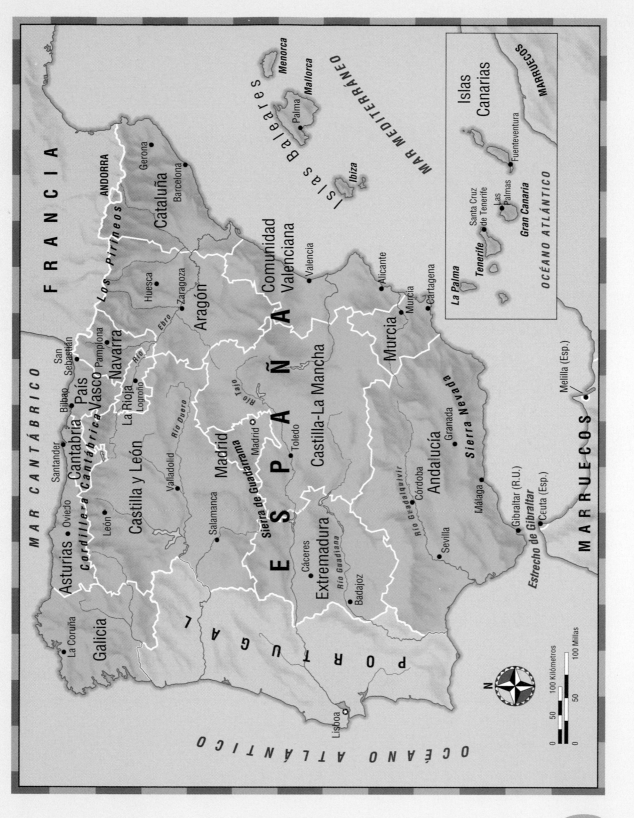

FRANCIA

MARRUECOS

Islas Canarias

OCÉANO ATLÁNTICO

La Palma
Tenerife
Santa Cruz de Tenerife
Las Palmas
Gran Canaria
Fuenteventura

MAR CANTÁBRICO

Menorca
Mallorca
Palma
Islas Baleares
Ibiza

MAR MEDITERRÁNEO

Gerona
Cataluña
Barcelona

ANDORRA

Los Pirineos

San Sebastián
Pamplona
Navarra
Huesca
Zaragoza
Aragón
Río Ebro
Río
La Rioja
Logroño
País Vasco
Bilbao
Cantabria
Santander
Cordillera Cantábrica
Oviedo
Asturias
León
Castilla y León
Valladolid
Río Duero
Salamanca
Sierra de Guadarrama
Madrid
Madrid
Río Tajo
Toledo
Castilla-La Mancha

E S P A Ñ A

Comunidad Valenciana
Valencia
Alicante
Murcia
Murcia
Cartagena

Cáceres
Extremadura
Río Guadiana
Badajoz

Córdoba
Andalucía
Río Guadalquivir
Granada
Sierra Nevada
Sevilla
Málaga

Gibraltar (R.U.)
Estrecho de Gibraltar
Ceuta (Esp.)

Melilla (Esp.)

M A R R U E C O S

La Coruña
Galicia

P O R T U G A L

Lisboa

OCÉANO ATLÁNTICO

N

100 Kilómetros
100 Millas
50
50

xvii

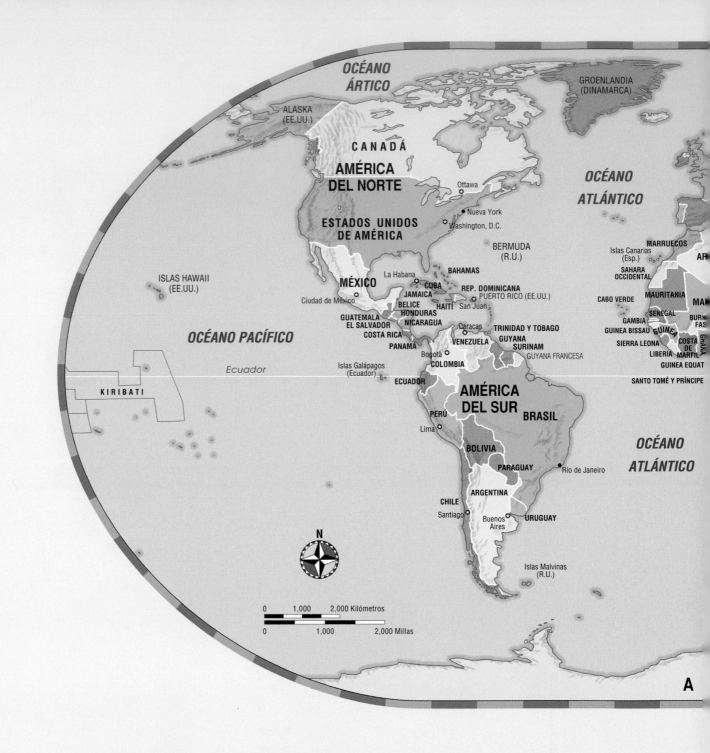

OCÉANO
ÁRTICO

GROENLANDIA
(DINAMARCA)

ALASKA
(EE.UU.)

CANADÁ

AMÉRICA
DEL NORTE

OCÉANO

ATLÁNTICO

Ottawa

ESTADOS UNIDOS
DE AMÉRICA

Nueva York
Washington, D.C.

BERMUDA
(R.U.)

Islas Canarias
(Esp.)

MARRUECOS

AR

ISLAS HAWAII
(EE.UU.)

La Habana

MÉXICO

Ciudad de México

BAHAMAS

CUBA
JAMAICA

REP. DOMINICANA
PUERTO RICO (EE.UU.)

San Juan

SAHARA
OCCIDENTAL

CABO VERDE

MAURITANIA

MA

BELICE
HONDURAS

HAITÍ

GAMBIA

SENEGAL

BURK
FAS

GUATEMALA
EL SALVADOR

NICARAGUA

OCÉANO PACÍFICO

COSTA RICA

PANAMÁ

Caracas

TRINIDAD Y TOBAGO

VENEZUELA

GUYANA

SURINAM

GUYANA FRANCESA

GUINEA BISSAU

SIERRA LEONA

GUINEA

LIBERIA

COSTA
DE
MARFIL

GHANA

Bogotá

COLOMBIA

GUINEA EQUAT.

Ecuador

Islas Galápagos
(Ecuador)

SANTO TOMÉ Y PRÍNCIPE

KIRIBATI

ECUADOR

AMÉRICA
DEL SUR

BRASIL

PERÚ

Lima

BOLIVIA

OCÉANO

ATLÁNTICO

PARAGUAY

Río de Janeiro

ARGENTINA

CHILE

Santiago

URUGUAY

Buenos
Aires

N

Islas Malvinas
(R.U.)

0	1,000	2,000 Kilómetros

0	1,000	2,000 Millas

A

xviii

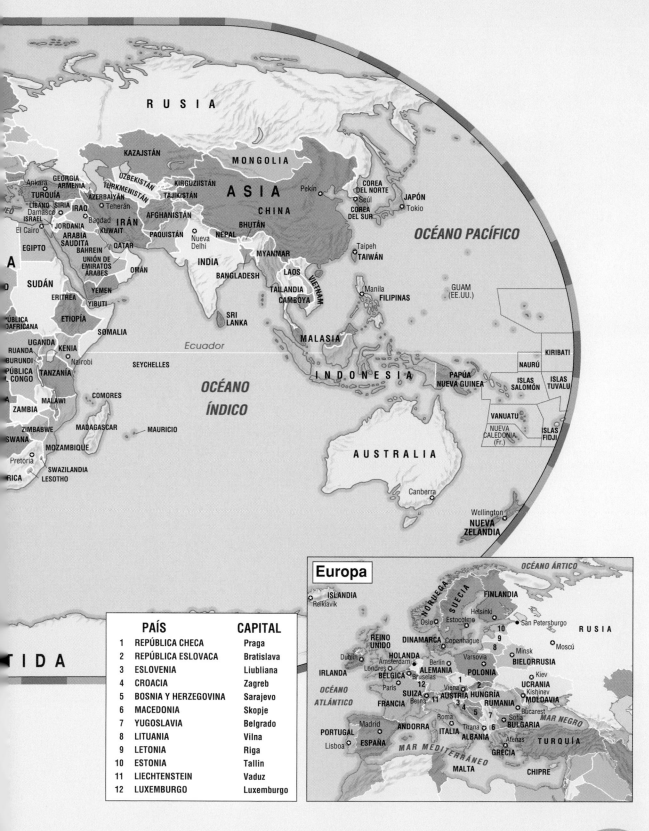

RUSIA

KAZAJSTÁN

MONGOLIA

ASIA

GEORGIA
ARMENIA
TURQUÍA
ANKARA
LÍBANO
SIRIA IRAQ
ISRAEL
Damasco
JORDANIA
El Cairo
EGIPTO
ARABIA
SAUDITA
BAHREIN
UNIÓN DE
EMIRATOS
ÁRABES
YEMEN
SUDÁN
ERITREA
YIBUTI
...ÚBLICA
...OAFRICANA
ETIOPÍA
UGANDA
SOMALIA
RUANDA
BURUNDI
KENIA
Nairobi
...PÚBLICA
...L CONGO
TANZANÍA
ZAMBIA
MALAWI
COMORES
ZIMBABWE
MADAGASCAR
MAURICIO
SWANA
MOZAMBIQUE
Pretoria
RICA
SWAZILANDIA
LESOTHO

UZBEKISTÁN
TURKMENISTÁN
AZERBAIYÁN
KIRGUZIISTÁN
TAJIKISTÁN
Teherán
IRÁN
Bagdad
KUWAIT
QATAR
OMÁN
AFGHANISTÁN
PAQUISTÁN
Nueva
Delhi
NEPAL
BHUTÁN
INDIA
BANGLADESH
MYANMAR
LAOS
TAILANDIA
CAMBOYA
VIETNAM
SRI
LANKA
MALASIA

CHINA
Pekín
COREA
DEL NORTE
Seúl
COREA
DEL SUR
JAPÓN
Tokio
Taipeh
TAIWÁN

OCÉANO PACÍFICO

GUAM
(EE.UU.)
Manila
FILIPINAS

Ecuador

SEYCHELLES

OCÉANO
ÍNDICO

INDONESIA

KIRIBATI

NAURÚ
ISLAS
SALOMÓN
ISLAS
TUVALU

PAPÚA
NUEVA GUINEA

VANUATU
NUEVA
CALEDONIA
(Fr.)
ISLAS
FIDJI

AUSTRALIA

Canberra

Wollington
NUEVA
ZELANDIA

TIDA

	PAÍS	CAPITAL
1	REPÚBLICA CHECA	Praga
2	REPÚBLICA ESLOVACA	Bratislava
3	ESLOVENIA	Liubliana
4	CROACIA	Zagreb
5	BOSNIA Y HERZEGOVINA	Sarajevo
6	MACEDONIA	Skopje
7	YUGOSLAVIA	Belgrado
8	LITUANIA	Vilna
9	LETONIA	Riga
10	ESTONIA	Tallin
11	LIECHTENSTEIN	Vaduz
12	LUXEMBURGO	Luxemburgo

Europa

OCÉANO ÁRTICO

ISLANDIA
Reikiavik
NORUEGA
SUECIA
FINLANDIA
Oslo
Estocolmo
Helsinki
San Petersburgo
10
9
8
Minsk
Moscú
RUSIA
REINO
UNIDO
DINAMARCA
Copenhague
HOLANDA
Amsterdam
Dublín
IRLANDA
Londres
BÉLGICA
Bruselas
Berlín
ALEMANIA
Varsovia
POLONIA
Kiev
BIELORRUSIA
UCRANIA
Kishinev
MOLDAVIA
OCÉANO
ATLÁNTICO
Paris
FRANCIA
SUIZA
Berna
12
11
Viena
AUSTRIA
HUNGRÍA
1
3
4
5
2
RUMANIA
Bucarest
MAR NEGRO
Roma
7
Sofia
BULGARIA
6
PORTUGAL
Lisboa
Madrid
ESPAÑA
ANDORRA
ITALIA
Tirana
ALBANIA
GRECIA
Atenas
TURQUÍA
MAR MEDITERRÁNEO
MALTA
CHIPRE

xix

T27

América del Sur

MAR DE LAS ANTILLAS

OCÉANO ATLÁNTICO

América Central

Cartagena
Maracaibo
Caracas
VENEZUELA
Medellín
Orinoco
Ciudad Bolívar
COLOMBIA
Bogotá

GUYANA
SURINAM
Georgetown
Paramaribo
Cayena
GUYANA
FRANCESA

Islas
Galápagos
(Ecuador)

Quito
ECUADOR
Guayaquil
Cuenca

Cordillera

Río Putumayo

Río

Manaus
Amazonas

Ecuador

Belén

B R A S I L

Recife

PERÚ
Lima
Andes
Cuzco

de los

Salvador

Lago
Titicaca
La Paz
BOLIVIA
Sucre

Brasilia

Cordillera de los

PARAGUAY
Asunción

Paraná

San Pablo
Río de Janeiro

OCÉANO

Trópico de Capricornio

PACÍFICO

CHILE
Tucumán

ARGENTINA
Córdoba
Valparaíso
Santiago
Mendoza
Buenos Aires

Andes

URUGUAY
Montevideo

Río de la Plata

OCÉANO

ATLÁNTICO

N

0   500   1.000 Kilómetros

0   500   1.000 Millas

Cordillera de los

Bariloche

Estrecho de Magallanes

Islas
Malvinas
(R.U.)

Andes

Punta Arenas
Tierra del Fuego

Cabo de
Hornos

XX

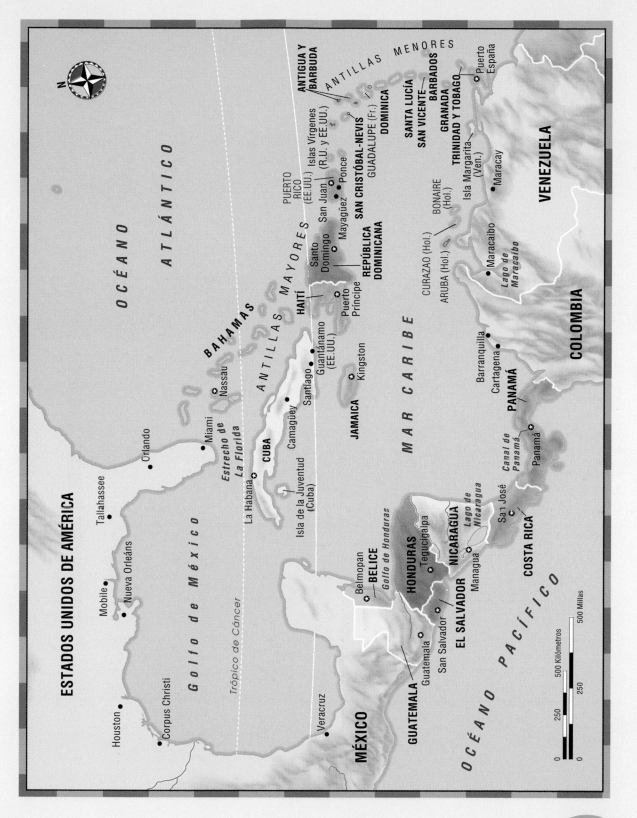

ESTADOS UNIDOS DE AMÉRICA

OCÉANO ATLÁNTICO

OCÉANO PACÍFICO

MÉXICO

Golfo de México

MAR CARIBE

Houston

Corpus Christi

Mobile

Nueva Orleáns

Tallahassee

Orlando

Miami

Veracruz

Trópico de Cáncer

Estrecho de La Florida

BAHAMAS

Nassau

La Habana

Isla de la Juventud (Cuba)

CUBA

Camagüey

Santiago

Guantánamo (EE.UU.)

Golfo de Honduras

Belmopan

BELICE

Guatemala

GUATEMALA

San Salvador

EL SALVADOR

HONDURAS

Tegucigalpa

Managua

NICARAGUA

Lago de Nicaragua

San José

COSTA RICA

PANAMÁ

Canal de Panamá

Panamá

JAMAICA

Kingston

ANTILLAS MAYORES

HAITÍ

Puerto Príncipe

Santo Domingo

REPÚBLICA DOMINICANA

PUERTO RICO (EE.UU.)

San Juan

Mayagüez

Ponce

Islas Vírgenes (R.U. y EE.UU.)

SAN CRISTÓBAL-NEVIS

GUADALUPE (Fr.)

DOMINICA

ANTIGUA Y BARBUDA

ANTILLAS MENORES

SANTA LUCÍA

SAN VICENTE

BARBADOS

GRANADA

TRINIDAD Y TOBAGO

Puerto España

Isla Margarita (Ven.)

Maracay

CURAZAO (Hol.)

BONAIRE (Hol.)

ARUBA (Hol.)

Maracaibo

Lago de Maracaibo

VENEZUELA

COLOMBIA

Barranquilla

Cartagena

ANTILLAS

N

xxi

T29

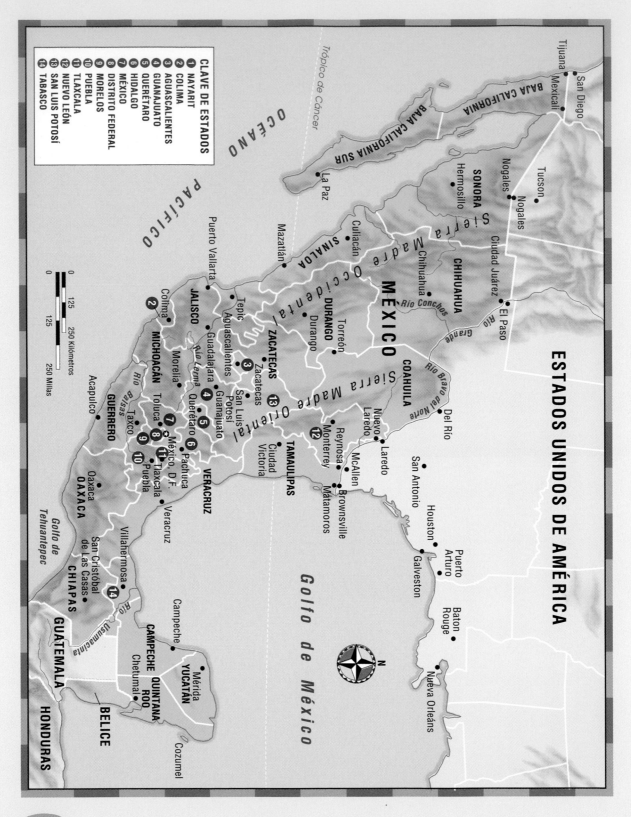

ESTADOS UNIDOS DE AMÉRICA

CLAVE DE ESTADOS
1. NAYARIT
2. COLIMA
3. AGUASCALIENTES
4. GUANAJUATO
5. QUERÉTARO
6. HIDALGO
7. MÉXICO
8. DISTRITO FEDERAL
9. MORELOS
10. PUEBLA
11. TLAXCALA
12. NUEVO LEÓN
13. SAN LUIS POTOSÍ
14. TABASCO

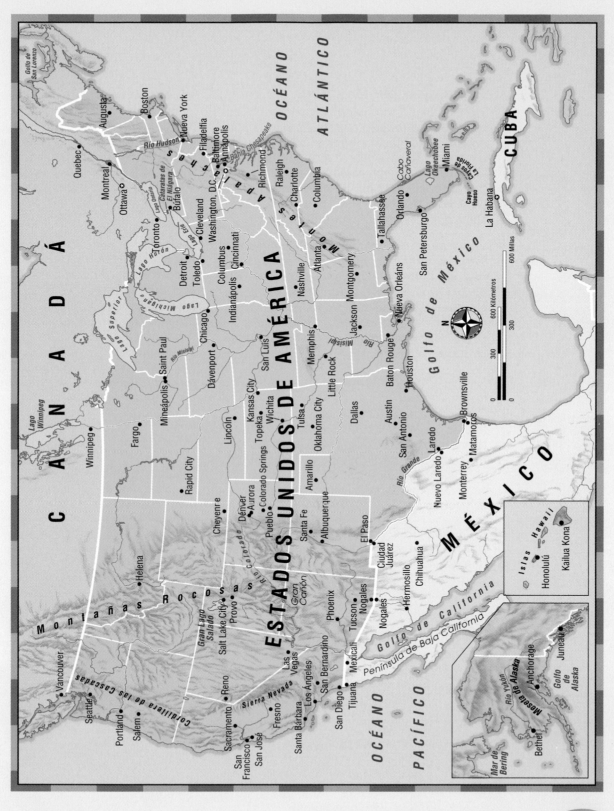

Golfo de San Lorenzo
OCÉANO ATLÁNTICO
CUBA

CANADÁ

Augusta
Boston
Quebec
Nueva York
Montreal
Río Hudson
Ottawa
Filadelfia
Baltimore
Annapolis
Cataratas de
El Niágara
Washington, D.C.
Bahía Chesapeake
Richmond
Lago Ontario
Toronto
Búfalo
Raleigh
Charlotte
Columbia
Lago Erie
Cleveland
Lago Hurón
Detroit
Columbus
Cincinnati
Atlanta
Tallahassee
Orlando
Cabo Cañaveral
Lago Okeechobee
Miami
San Petersburgo
Cayos de La Florida
Cayo Hueso
La Habana

Lago Superior
Toledo
Indianápolis
Nashville
Montgomery
Cabos de La Florida

Lago Michigan
Chicago
Memphis
Jackson
Nueva Orleáns
Golfo de México

Saint Paul
Mineápolis
Río Misisipi
Dávenport
San Luis
Little Rock
Baton Rouge
Houston
Río Misisipi

Lago Winnipeg
Fargo
Lincoln
Kansas City
Wichita
Tulsa
Oklahoma City
Dallas
Austin
San Antonio
Brownsville

Winnipeg
Rapid City
Topeka
Amarillo
Laredo
Nuevo Laredo
Matamoros

ESTADOS UNIDOS DE AMÉRICA

Cheyenne
Denver
Aurora
Pueblo
Colorado Springs
Santa Fe
Albuquerque
El Paso
Monterrey

Río Colorado
Helena
Gran Cañón
Ciudad Juárez

MÉXICO

Montañas Rocosas
Gran Lago Salado
Salt Lake City
Provo
Phoenix
Tucson
Nogales
Nogales
Hermosillo
Chihuahua

Vancouver
Cordillera de las Cascadas
Reno
Las Vegas
San Bernardino
Los Ángeles
Mexicali
Tijuana
Península de Baja California
Golfo de California

Seattle
Portland
Salem
Sacramento
San José
San Francisco
Fresno
Santa Bárbara
San Diego
Sierra Nevada

OCÉANO PACÍFICO

N
600 Millas
600 Kilómetros
300
300
0
0

Islas Hawaii
Honolulú
Kailua Kona

Río Yukón
Meseta de Alaska
Anchorage
Juneau
Golfo de Alaska
Bethel
Mar de Bering

T31

TO THE TEACHER

In recent years, we have seen significant advances in modern foreign language curriculum practices:

1 *a redefinition of the objectives of foreign language study involving a commitment to the development of proficiency in the four skills and in cultural awareness;*

2 *a recognition of the need for longer sequences of study;*

3 *a new student-centered approach that redefines the role of the teacher as facilitator and encourages students to take a more active role in their learning;*

4 *the inclusion of students of all learning abilities.*

The new Holt, Rinehart and Winston foreign language programs take into account not only these advances in the field of foreign language education, but also the input of teachers and students from around the country. ♦

Principles and Practices

As nations become increasingly interdependent, the need for effective communication and sensitivity to other cultures becomes more important. Today's youth must be culturally and linguistically prepared to participate in a global society. At Holt, Rinehart and Winston, we believe that proficiency in more than one language is essential to meeting this need.

The primary goal of the Holt, Rinehart and Winston foreign language programs is to help students develop linguistic proficiency and cultural sensitivity. By interweaving language and culture, our programs seek to broaden students' communication skills while deepening their appreciation of other cultures.

♦♦♦

We believe that all students can benefit from foreign language instruction. We recognize that not everyone learns at the same rate or in the same way; nevertheless, we believe that all students should have the opportunity to acquire language proficiency to a degree commensurate with their individual abilities.

Holt, Rinehart and Winston's foreign language programs are designed to accommodate all students by appealing to a variety of learning styles.

♦♦♦

We believe that effective language programs should motivate students. Students deserve an answer to a question they often ask: "Why are we doing this?" They need to have goals that are interesting, practical, clearly stated, and attainable.

Holt, Rinehart and Winston's foreign language programs promote success. They present interesting content in manageable increments that encourage students to achieve the functional objectives.

We believe that proficiency in a foreign language is best nurtured by programs that encourage students to think critically and to take risks when expressing themselves in the language. We also recognize that students should strive for accuracy in communication. While it is imperative that students have a knowledge of the basic structures of the language, it is also important that they go beyond the simple manipulation of forms.

Holt, Rinehart and Winston's foreign language program reflects a careful progression of activities that guides students from comprehensible input of authentic language through structured practice to creative, personalized expression. This progression, accompanied by consistent re-entry and spiraling of functions, vocabulary, and structures, provides students with the tools and the confidence to express themselves in their new language.

♦♦♦

Finally, we believe that a complete program of language instruction should take into account the needs of teachers in today's increasingly demanding classrooms.

At Holt, Rinehart and Winston, we have designed programs that offer practical teacher support and provide resources to meet individual learning and teaching styles.

USING THE PUPIL'S EDITION

¡Ven conmigo!
Adelante

Adelante *offers an integrated approach to language learning. Presentation and practice of functional expressions, vocabulary, and grammar structures are interwoven with cultural information, language-learning tips, and realia to facilitate both learning and teaching. The technology, audiovisual materials, and additional print resources integrated into each chapter allow instruction to be adapted to a variety of teaching and learning styles.* ◆

¡Ven conmigo! Adelante Level 1A

Adelante consists of a preliminary chapter that introduces students to Spanish and the Spanish-speaking world, followed by six instructional chapters. Below is a description of the various features in *Adelante* and suggestions on how to use them in the classroom. While it is not crucial for students to cover all material and do all activities to achieve the goals listed at the beginning of each chapter, the material within each chapter has been carefully sequenced to enable students to progress steadily at a realistic pace to the ultimate goal of linguistic and cultural proficiency. As presenter, facilitator, and guide, you will determine the precise depth of coverage, taking into account the individual needs of each class and the amount and type of alternative instructional material to be used from the *Adelante* program.

Setting the Scene . . .

In *Adelante* chapters are arranged in groups of two, with each pair of chapters set in a different Spanish-speaking location. Each new location is introduced by a **Location Opener**, four pages of colorful photos and background information that can be used to introduce the region and help motivate students.

The two-page **Chapter Opener** is intended to pique students' interest and focus their attention on the task at hand. It is a visual introduction to the theme of the chapter and includes a brief description of the topics and situations students will encounter, as well as a list of objectives they will be expected to achieve.

Starting Out . . .

Language instruction begins with **De antemano**, comprehensible input that models language in a culturally authentic setting. Whether presented on video or as a reading accompanied by the audiocassette or compact disc recording, the highly visual presentation—in **fotonovela** format—ensures success as students practice their receptive skills and begin to recognize some of the new functions and vocabulary they will encounter in the chapter. Following **De antemano** is a series of activities that can be used to help guide students through the story and to check comprehension.

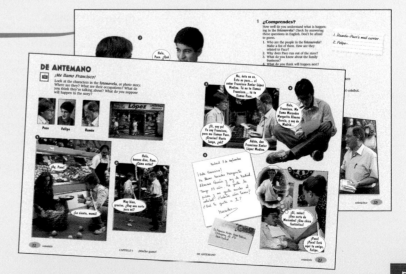

Building Proficiency Step by Step . . .

Primer, **Segundo**, and **Tercer paso** are the three core instructional sections where the greater part of language acquisition will take place. The communicative goals in each chapter center on the functional expressions presented in **Así se dice** boxes. These expressions are supported and expanded by material in the **Vocabulario**, **Gramática**, and **Nota gramatical** sections. Activities immediately following these features are designed to practice recognition or to provide closed-ended practice with the new material. Activities then progress from controlled to open-ended practice where students are able to express themselves in meaningful communication. Depending on class size, general ability level, and class dynamics, you may wish to proceed sequentially through all activities in a chapter, supplementing presentation or practice at various points with additional materials from *Adelante,* or you may proceed more quickly to open-ended pair and group work.

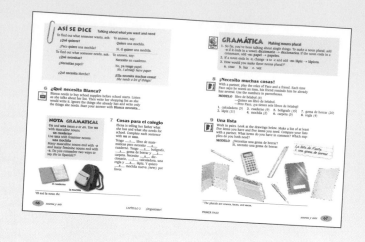

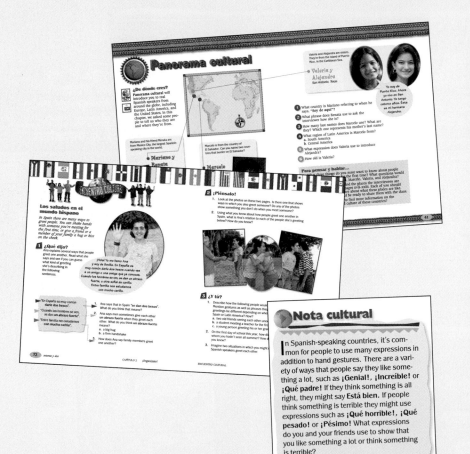

Discovering the Culture . . .

Cultural information has been incorporated throughout the chapter wherever possible. There are also three types of culture features to help students develop an appreciation and understanding of the cultures of Spanish-speaking countries.

Panorama cultural presents spontaneous interviews conducted in various countries in the Spanish-speaking world on a topic related to the chapter theme. The interviews may be presented on video or done as a reading supplemented by the audiocassette or compact disc recording. Culminating activities on this page may be used to verify comprehension and encourage students to think critically about the target culture as well as their own.

Encuentro cultural introduces students to people, places, and customs throughout the Spanish-speaking world and invites them to compare and contrast the target culture with their own. The presentation may be done through the use of video or as a reading.

Nota cultural provides short presentations of both "big C" and "little c" culture that can be used to enrich and enliven activities and presentations at various places throughout each chapter.

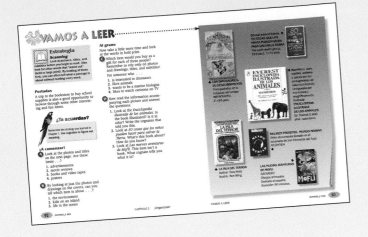

Understanding Authentic Documents . . .

Vamos a leer presents reading strategies that help students understand authentic Spanish-language documents and literature. The reading selections vary from advertisements to letters to short stories or poems in order to accommodate different interests and familiarize the students with different styles and formats. The accompanying activities progress from prereading to reading and postreading tasks and are designed to develop students' overall reading skills and challenge their critical thinking abilities.

Targeting Students' Needs . . .

In each **paso** these special features may be used to enhance language learning and cultural appreciation.

Sugerencia suggests effective ways for students to learn a foreign language.

Vocabulario extra presents optional vocabulary related to the chapter theme. These words are provided to help students personalize activities; students will not be required to produce this vocabulary on the Chapter Quizzes and Test.

The dictionary in the back of this book can be a helpful tool as you learn Spanish. For example, some of the words in **Letra y sonido** might be new to you. A dual-language dictionary will usually have the Spanish to English section first, followed by the English to Spanish section. Try looking up the word **isla** in the back of the book. Begin with the Spanish-English Vocabulary section that starts on page 281. Look in the alphabetized **i** section (ignore the article **la** when checking alphabetical order) and write down what **isla** means. Now look up the word **carpeta**. Does it mean what you might think it does?

VOCABULARIO EXTRA

un disco compacto   *CD*
un estante   *bookshelf*
una pecera   *fish bowl*
una planta   *plant*
un tocador de discos compactos   *CD player*
un videojuego   *videogame*

LETRA Y SONIDO

A. The Spanish vowels (**a, e, i, o, u**) are pronounced clearly and distinctly. Learn to pronounce them by mimicking the recording or your teacher.

1. **a**: as in *father*, but with the tongue closer to the front of the mouth

| Ana | cámara | amiga | tarea | llama |

2. **e**: as in *they*, but without the *y* sound

| este | eres | noche | excelente | café |

3. **i**: as in *machine*, but much shorter

| íntimo | isla | legítimo | Misisipi | día |

4. **o**: as in *low*, but without the *w* sound

| hola | moto | años | dónde | color |

5. **u**: as in *rule*

| fruta | uno | fútbol | único | música |

B. **Dictado**
Ana has just met several new friends in Madrid and is practicing the new phrases she has heard. Write what you hear.

C. **Trabalenguas**
¡A, e, i, o, u! Arbolito del Perú, ¿cómo te llamas tú?

Letra y sonido

At the end of each **Tercer paso** is **Letra y sonido**, a recorded pronunciation feature that explains sounds and spelling rules. Pronunciation is practiced using vocabulary words that contain the targeted sounds. In a dictation exercise that follows, students hear and write sentences using the targeted sounds and letters. The last part of this feature, the **trabalenguas**, gives students an additional opportunity to practice the targeted sounds in amusing and challenging tongue twisters.

Interdisciplinary Connections

Enlaces is an interdisciplinary feature that links the learning of Spanish to other subjects students might be studying. Each **Enlaces** presents further aspects of Spanish-speaking culture and relates them to an academic subject. It encourages students to apply what they learn in other classes to the acquisition of a second language and culture.

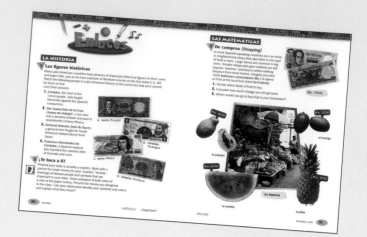

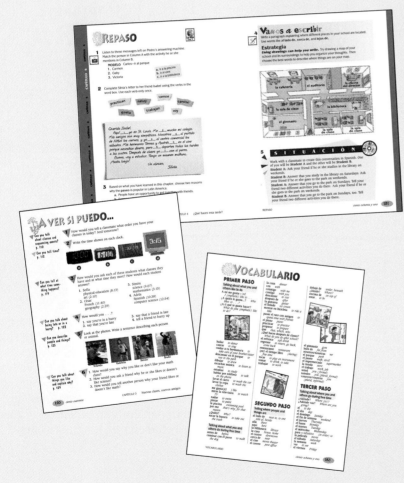

Wrapping it All Up . . .

Repaso, at the end of each chapter, gives students the opportunity to review what they have learned and to apply their skills in new communicative contexts. Beginning in Chapter 3, **Repaso** contains **Vamos a escribir**, a process-writing feature that provides students with guided writing activities as well as strategies to further develop their writing skills. Focusing on all four language skills as well as cultural awareness, **Repaso** can help you determine whether students are ready for the Chapter Test.

A ver si puedo... follows **Repaso** and is a checklist that students can use on their own to see if they have achieved the goals stated in the Chapter Opener. Each communicative function is paired with one or more activities for students to use as a self-check. Page references are given for students who need to return to the chapter for review.

Vocabulario presents the chapter vocabulary grouped by **paso** and arranged according to communicative function or theme. This list represents the active words and expressions that students will be expected to know for the **Paso** Quizzes and Chapter Test.

ANCILLARIES

¡Ven conmigo! **Adelante**

The **Adelante** *Spanish program offers a state-of-the-art ancillary package that addresses the concerns of today's teachers. Because foreign language teachers work with all types of students, the activities in our ancillaries accommodate all learning styles. The variety of activities provided in the* ¡Ven conmigo! *ancillary materials are both innovative and relevant to students' experiences.* ◆

Technology Resources

Adelante and **En camino** are the first Spanish programs to offer technology resources specifically designed for students in the middle grades. Interviews with young adolescent native speakers and an **Encuentro cultural** feature enhance a highly effective video program. The cultural interviews are incorporated in the middle school *Interactive CD-ROM Program* with appropriate activities and with vocabulary support in the online reference section. For a detailed description of all the technology resources available with *Adelante*, see pages T40–T41.

Grammar and Vocabulary Workbook

The *Grammar and Vocabulary Workbook* re-presents all major grammar points and offers additional focused practice with the structures, words, and phrases targeted in each **paso**. Instruction lines and exercise items have been revised to ensure that students in Grades 6–9 will be able to follow directions and succeed at these important practice activities whether they are done in class or at home. Suggestions for using these activities as homework can be found in the Chapter Interleaf pages of the *Annotated Teacher's Edition*. The *Grammar and Vocabulary Workbook Teacher's Edition* contains the same pages as the workbook plus a convenient, easy-to-use answer key at the back.

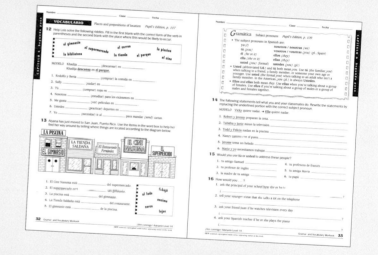

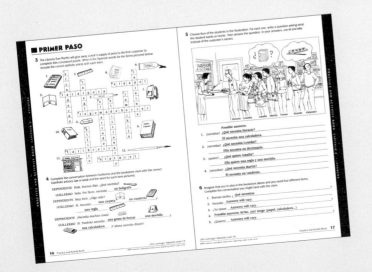

Practice and Activity Book

The *Practice and Activity Book* is filled with a variety of activities that provide further practice with the functions, grammar, and vocabulary presented in each **paso**. Additional reading, culture, and journal activities for each chapter give students the opportunity to apply the reading and writing strategies they've learned in relevant, personalized contexts. The Practice and Activity Book reinforces many of the same concepts practiced in the Grammar and Vocabulary Workbook and provides opportunities to use them in more open-ended, creative contexts. *The Practice and Activity Book Teacher's Edition* contains the same pages as the student edition plus overprinted answers for convenient use.

Listening Activities

This component contains all print material associated with the *Audio Program*. Student Response Forms for Textbook Listening Activities and scripts and answers appear here for convenient use.

Additional Listening Activities provide students with a unique opportunity to actively develop their listening skills in a variety of authentic contexts. They appear here as activity masters with scripts and answers.

Each chapter contains a song culturally or thematically related to the chapter or location. The lyrics for each of these songs are provided with each chapter's listening material.

Audio Assessment Items are integrated into the **Paso** Quizzes and Chapter Tests, and the scripts and answers for these items complete the *Listening Activities* component.

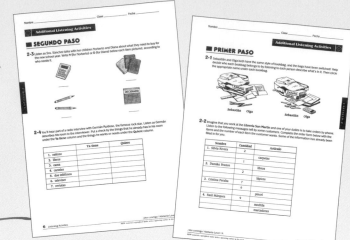

Activities for Communication

Oral communication is the most challenging language skill to develop and test. The *Adelante Activities for Communication* book is designed to help facilitate students' development of listening and speaking skills through pair activities in which students communicate in a variety of life-like situations and contexts. The Communicative Activities offer information-gap tasks in which students rely on a partner to fill in the gaps, and the Situation Cards offer opportunities for interviews and role-playing.

This component also contains **Realia** pages, which reproduce real documents to provide students with additional reading and language practice. Included with the **Realia** are teacher suggestions and student activities.

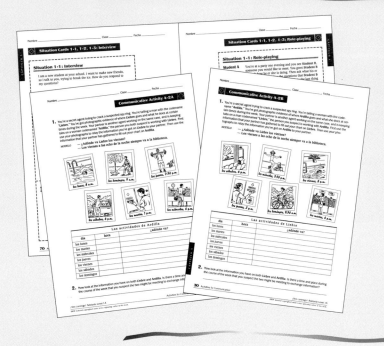

Testing Program

The *Testing Program* encourages students to work toward realistic, communicative goals.

• Three **Quizzes** per chapter (one per **paso**); each **Quiz** includes a listening, reading, and writing section, and very often a culture section

• Each **Chapter Test** includes listening, reading, writing, and culture sections and a score sheet for easy grading. Selected sections of each Chapter Test can be corrected on ScanTron®

• One **Speaking Test** per chapter

• One **Midterm** and one **Final Exam**

Also included in the *Testing Program* are scripts and answers to the **Paso Quizzes, Chapter Tests, Midterm,** and **Final Exam.**

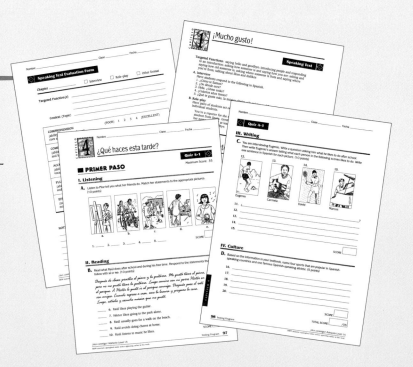

Alternative Assessment Guide

The *Alternative Assessment Guide* describes various testing and scoring methods. This guide also includes **Portfolio Assessment** suggestions and rubrics as well as suggestions for **Performance Assessment**.

Exploratory Guide

The *Exploratory Guide* provides suggestions and techniques for teaching an exploratory class using *Adelante* and *En camino*'s wealth of materials, such as the *Video* and *Audio Programs*, the *Interactive CD-ROM Program*, the *Teaching Transparencies*, and a host of workbook materials.

Teaching Transparencies

Colorful teaching transparencies benefit all students, and the visual learner in particular, by adding variety and focus to your daily lesson plans. Situations, Vocabulary, and Maps allow you to present and practice vocabulary, culture, and a variety of communicative functions. Each transparency in the *Teaching Transparencies* package comes with a copying master as well as suggestions to practice four skills and culture. In addition to the teaching suggestions that accompany the transparencies, numerous other activities, projects, and games using the maps can be found throughout the *Annotated Teacher's Edition.*

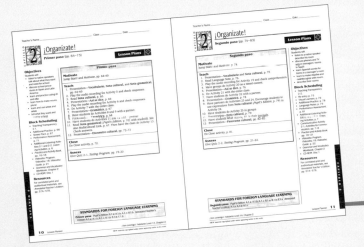

Lesson Planner

The *Lesson Planner* contains chapter-by-chapter suggestions on how to structure the daily lesson for optimal pacing and effectiveness. Each chapter's Lesson Plan guides the teacher through the program's cycle of presentation, practice, and assessment. Specific suggestions for block scheduling give the teacher the option of expanding the material as needed. In addition, all lesson material is correlated to the Standards for Foreign Language Learning and can readily be adapted to document weekly or monthly progress.

Native Speaker Activity Book

The *¡Ven conmigo!* Level 1 *Native Speaker Activity Book* includes suggestions and activities designed to address the needs of the native speakers in your Spanish class. It includes reading, writing, and speaking tasks for native speakers to complete, rounding out their Spanish language learning. *The Teacher's Edition* contains an answer key at the back.

Test Generator

The *¡Ven conmigo!* Level 1 *Test Generator's* user-friendly software, which enables you to create customized practice sheets, quizzes, and tests for each chapter in *¡Ven conmigo!,* is available for IBM® PC and compatibles and Macintosh® computers.

Adelante Video and Audio Programs bring the textbook to life and introduce your students to people they will encounter in every chapter of the Pupil's Edition. The video and audio programs feature native speakers of Spanish in realistic, interesting situations. ◆

VIDEO TECHNOLOGY

Adelante *Video Program*

Video is an ideal medium for providing authentic input needed to increase proficiency in Spanish. Both informative and entertaining, the episodes of the *Video Program* provide rich visual clues to aid comprehension and motivate students to learn more.

The *Video Program* is fully integrated and correlates directly with the *Adelante Pupil's Edition:*

Location Opener A narrated collage of images from regions of the Spanish-speaking world expands students' acquaintance with the geography and people presented in each Location Opener.

De antemano The introductory dialogue or story in each chapter is a videotaped dramatic episode based on the chapter theme. It introduces the targeted functions, vocabulary, and grammar of the chapter, in addition to re-entering material from previous chapters in new contexts. Since this video episode corresponds directly with the **De antemano** and the chapter, it can be used as a general introduction to the chapter, as a chapter review, and as a visual support for presenting the elements of the lesson.

A continuación These continuations of the dramatic episodes provide high-interest input that helps motivate students and offers additional opportunities to expand on what they have learned. **A continuación** continues the story and resolves the dramatic conflict that was created in **De antemano.** Designed to facilitate proficiency by providing additional comprehensible input, this episode offers an extended presentation of the chapter material and re-enters functions, vocabulary, and structures from previous chapters.

Panorama cultural Authentic interviews with native speakers of Spanish bring the Spanish-speaking world to life as real people talk about themselves, their country, and their way of life. Each interview topic is thematically related to the chapter.

Encuentro cultural A tour guide from one of the many Spanish-speaking locations of *Adelante* introduces students to people, places, and customs.

Videoclips Students will enjoy the authentic footage from Spanish and Latin American television: music videos, commercials, and more. These short segments of video give students confidence as they realize that they can understand and enjoy material that was produced for native speakers of Spanish!

Adelante *Video Guide*

Adelante Video Guide provides background information together with suggestions for presentation and pre- and postviewing activities for all portions of the *Video Program.* In addition, the *Video Guide* contains reproducible student activity sheets as well as a transcript and synopsis of each episode and supplementary vocabulary lists.

¡VEN CONMIGO! LEVEL 1

Videodisc Program and Guide

¡Ven conmigo! Level 1 Videodisc Program presents in videodisc format all the authentic footage, interviews, and dramatic episodes presented in the *¡Ven conmigo! Level 1 Video Program.* Additional cultural and geographic material further enrich your students' experience. Barcodes provide instant access to all material and facilitate efficient integration of video resources into each lesson. Key barcodes are provided in the *Adelante Level 1A Annotated Teacher's Edition.* Teaching suggestions, activity masters, and a complete barcode directory are provided in the *¡Ven conmigo! Level 1 Videodisc Guide.*

AUDIO TECHNOLOGY

Adelante *Audio Program*

Audio is another ideal medium for providing authentic input needed to increase language proficiency. The activities in the **Audio Program** allow students to focus their attention on the sound of the language while at the same time accomplishing authentic real-life linguistic tasks.

The *Audio Program,* available in both audiocassette and compact disc format, is fully integrated and correlates directly with the following sections of *Adelante Pupil's Edition:*

De antemano The **De antemano** as it appears in the *Pupil's Edition* is an abridged version of the video episode. The *Audio Program* contains the soundtrack of the video episode edited to match **De antemano** to bring the page to life and to give students an opportunity to practice pronunciation.

Textbook Listening Activities Each chapter contains various listening activities that give students aural practice with the chapter's linguistic functions and communicative goals. These listening activities integrate previous chapter material with new structures being taught in the chapter.

Panorama cultural Audio recordings of these authentic interviews are contained in the *Audio Program.* The interviews are on separate tracks on the Audio CDs for convenient random access.

Adelante *Listening Activities*

Adelante Listening Activities contains all print material related the *Audio Program* including Student Response Forms, scripts and answers for the Textbook Listening Activities, copying masters for the Additional Listening Activities, and song lyrics.

CD-ROM TECHNOLOGY

Adelante *and* En camino *Interactive CD-ROM Program*

CD-ROM technology offers students an opportunity to interact with the target language and culture in new and exciting ways. This medium brings together print, graphics, video, and audio to provide a language-learning experience that is both enjoyable and challenging. Simulated real-life tasks provide a realistic context for language learning and will appeal to students with a variety of learning styles.

The **Interactive CD-ROM Program** is correlated to both *Adelante* and *En camino* to offer students a complete interactive language-learning experience.

Location Opener

The **¡Ven conmigo a… !** presentations include a travelogue movie about specific locations around the Spanish-speaking world. The map on the right-hand side of the screen contains a map of the featured country and buttons that control the different portions of the travelogue. After students have watched the travelogue presentation, they use what they have learned to complete a related activity.

En contexto

Students complete a lifelike conversation with a video character that targets the chapter functions, vocabulary, and grammar in meaningful, realistic contexts. Students choose the best response based on a series of audio and visual prompts. When students choose the correct response, the conversation continues. If students answer incorrectly, feedback will then help guide them.

¡A escoger! This multiple-choice activity practices vocabulary, grammar concepts, functional expressions, or culture. Students respond to each item based on what they see or hear.

¿Cuál es? In this game students organize words and phrases according to two or more categories.

Imagen y sonido In the presentation mode of this activity, students identify and pronounce vocabulary and/or functional expressions by exploring an image. The test mode evaluates students' aural recognition of vocabulary words and expressions.

Patas arriba In this activity, students will sequence words into sentences or sentences into paragraphs or dialogues.

¿Qué falta? This activity makes use of a familiar game, Tic Tac Toe, to practice vocabulary or grammar. Students can play with each other or against the computer.

¡Super memoria! This activity gives students an opportunity to practice vocabulary, grammar concepts, functional expressions, or culture by matching sound or text with images.

Panorama cultural

Each **Panorama cultural** screen includes six QuickTime™ movies with interviews of students from around the Spanish-speaking world as well as multiple-choice comprehension questions.

Speaking and Writing

¡A hablar! and **¡A escribir!** provide both guided and open-ended speaking and writing tasks that combine the functions, vocabulary, grammar, and culture of each chapter. These sections can be used for self evaluation, for peer evaluation, or assessment by the teacher.

En voz alta and **¡Exprésate!** These features allow students to record and write original assignments. Suggestions for assignments are included in every chapter of the *CD-ROM Teacher's Guide.*

Reference Sections

Vocabulary The vocabulary reference section provides a glossary of Spanish-English and English-Spanish words and expressions. Students can access this online reference at any time.

Grammar The grammar reference section provides a summary of the grammar concepts presented in *¡Ven conmigo!* Students can access this online reference at any time.

Help This section guides users through the mechanics of the program. Students may access this online reference at any time to find information about navigation, control panels, directions for activities, and file storage and retrieval.

¡VEN CONMIGO!

CD-ROM Teacher's Guide

The *CD-ROM Teacher's Guide* will help you integrate the CD-ROM program and its components into your lesson plan. It contains detailed descriptions that walk you through each section of the program, correlations to the chapter, suggestions for assessment options, student checklists, and rubrics to evaluate students' written and oral work.

The **Adelante** *Annotated Teacher's Edition is designed to help you meet the increasingly varied needs of today's students by providing an abundance of suggestions and strategies. The* **Annotated Teacher's Edition** *includes the pages of the* **Pupil's Edition** *with teacher annotation, side column teacher text with video references and barcodes, notes, suggestions, answers, and additional activities, as well as icon annotations that correlate each presentation to a corresponding ancillary. The* **Annotated Teacher's Edition** *also inludes interleafed pages with scripts, suggestions for use of technology, projects, games, and homework suggestions before each chapter.* ◆

Using the Location Opener and Location Opener Interleaf

In the interleaf and side column extension of each student page you will find background information about the photographs and settings. In addition, teaching suggestions help you motivate students to learn more about the history, geography, and culture of Spanish-speaking countries.

Using the Chapter Interleaf

The chapter interleaf includes a chapter overview correlation chart for teaching resources, *Pupil's Edition* listening scripts, and suggestions for homework, the use of technology, projects, and games.

The **Chapter Overview** chart outlines at a glance the functions, grammar, culture, and re-entry items featured in each **paso.** A list of corresponding print and audiovisual resource materials for each section of the chapter is provided to help integrate media and print ancillaries into your lessons. The pronunciation, reading, interdisciplinary, and review features for each chapter are also referenced, as are a variety of assessment and portfolio options.

The **Technology Applications in the Classroom** page provides a variety of suggestions on how to effectively implement the various technology components that accompany *Adelante.*

The **Barcode Directory** reproduces the barcodes from the *Level 1 ¡Ven conmigo! Videodisc Program* in one convenient location. You will also find the relevant barcodes strategically placed in the side column of each chapter at their precise point of use.

Textbook Listening Activities Scripts provide the scripts of the chapter listening activities for reference or for use in class. The answers to each activity are provided below each script for easy reference.

Projects propose extended four-skills activities based on the chapter theme and content. **Projects** suggestions are provided to give students the opportunity to personalize the information they've learned in the chapter. Individual projects offer students the chance to explore topics related to the chapter theme that are of interest to them. Group and cooperative learning projects encourage students to work together to apply what they've learned in the chapter by creating a poster, brochure, or report, often accompanied by an oral presentation.

Games provide students with informal, entertaining activities in which they can apply and reinforce the functions, structures, vocabulary, and culture of the chapter. Games appeal to a variety of learners and encourage teamwork and cooperation among students of different levels and learning styles.

Answers to Chapter Activities contains answers to selected activities from the chapter.

Homework Suggestions provide a list of assignments from the *Pupil's Edition, Grammar and Vocabulary Workbook, Practice and Activity Book,* and *Interactive CD-ROM Program* that would be appropriate

for students to do as homework. Each suggestion is correlated to a specific presentation from the chapter.

Using the Side-Column Teacher Text

Side-column teacher text gives point-of-use suggestions and information to help you make the most of class time. The side-column style of the *Annotated Teacher's Edition* also conveniently presents barcodes, video references, and activity answers together on the same page with the *Pupil's Edition* page.

Teaching Cycle

For each **paso,** a logical instructional sequence includes the following steps to enable you to

- **Jump Start!** your students with an individual writing activity that focuses their attention on previously learned material while they wait for class to begin.

- **Motivate** students by introducing the topic in a personalized and contextualized way.

- **Teach** the functions, vocabulary, structures, and culture with a variety of approaches.

- **Close** each **paso** with activities that review and confirm the communicative goals.

- **Assess** students' progress with a quiz and/or performance assessment activity. **Performance Assessment** suggestions provide an alternative to pen and paper tests and give you the option of evaluating students' progress by having them perform communicative, competency-based tasks. These may include teacher-student interviews, conversations, dialogues, or skits that students perform for the entire class. These tasks can also be recorded or videotaped for evaluation at a later time.

- **Portfolio** icons signal activities that are appropriate for students' oral or written portfolios. They may include lists, posters, letters, journal entries, or taped conversations or skits. A variety of suggestions are provided within each chapter so that you can work with your students to select the activities that would best document their strengths and progress in the language. Portfolio information, including checklists and suggestions for evaluation, are provided in the *Alternative Assessment Guide,* which also contains suggestions for the expansion of the two designated portfolio activities from the *Pupil's Edition.* In each Chapter Overview, these two activities are listed under "Portfolio Assessment" (one written and one oral). The portfolio suggestions will help students further develop their oral and written language skills, often in the context of real-life situations. For a discussion of portfolio creation and use, see *Using Portfolios in the Foreign Language Classroom,* pages T52–T53.

For Individual Needs

Suggestions under the following categories provide alternative approaches to help you address students' diverse learning styles.

- **Visual, Auditory, Tactile, and Kinesthetic Learners** benefit from activities that accommodate their unique learning styles.
- **Slower Pace** provides ideas for presenting material in smaller steps to facilitate comprehension.
- **Challenge** extends activities into more challenging tasks that encourage students to expand their communicative skills.

Native Speakers

Native speakers benefit from the various projects and activities that validate their individual culture and language. They are encouraged to share their knowledge of Spanish regionalisms and culture with non-native Spanish-speaking students.

Native-speaker activities are designed to highlight the skills and culture of native speakers and channel their input to the advantage of the entire class. The in-class activities and out-of-class assignments for native speakers often integrate family and community into the students' learning experience. Native speaker work lends authenticity to Spanish-language instruction and guides students toward a comprehensive understanding of the Spanish-speaking world. For more information on native speakers, see the essay *New Perspectives for Native Speakers* by Cecilia Rodríguez-Pino on pages T56–T57.

Making Connections

To help students appreciate their membership in a global society, suggestions for linking Spanish with other disciplines, their community, and other cultures appear under several categories:

- **Math... Geography... Health... Science... History... Language** and **Arts Links** relate the chapter topic to other subject areas, and make Spanish relevant to the students' overall academic experience.
- **Multicultural Links** provide students the opportunity to compare and contrast

their language and culture with those of Spanish-speaking countries and other parts of the world.

- **Community... Family Links** encourage students to seek opportunities for learning outside of the classroom by interacting with neighbors and family members. These suggestions also call on students to share their learning with their family and community.

Developing Thinking Skills

Thinking Critically helps students develop their higher-order thinking skills with suggestions to extend activities beyond an informational level. It increases comprehension of language and cultures and helps students exercise and develop higher-order thinking skills.

Establishing Collaborative Learning

Cooperative Learning allows students to work together in small groups to attain common goals by sharing responsibilities. Students are accountable for setting group objectives, completing the assignment, and ensuring that all group members master the material. Working together in cooperative groups allows students to take an active role in the classroom, to develop more confidence as they contribute to the success of the group, and to experience less anxiety by working in small groups. Cooperative learning enables students to improve interpersonal communication skills by encouraging them to listen to and respect other opinions.

Total Physical Response (TPR) techniques reinforce structures and vocabulary visually and kinesthetically. They are active-learning exercises that encourage students to focus on class interaction while learning Spanish.

Teaching Vamos a leer

Teacher's notes and suggestions in **Vamos a leer** offer prereading, reading, and postreading skills. Background information and useful terms related to the reading are provided as well.

ADELANTE AND EN CAMINO IN THE MIDDLE GRADES

Middle-grade teachers can readily describe the excitement they feel when students are able to make complex connections for the first time, and are so fired up about what they are learning that sparks fly. Teachers at these grade levels delight in their students' wonderful curiosity about and openness to others. They can also describe the challenges of teaching students who can't seem to sit still, who want to hang out with friends all the time, and who are painfully self-conscious.

Increased understanding of this exciting age group, a well-designed curriculum and textbook, and appropriate classroom management approaches can maximize teaching fun and effectiveness, greatly decrease teacher frustration, and enhance the students' experiences in a multitude of ways.

Characteristics of the Middle-Grades Learner

Young adolescents undergo tremendous physical and mental growth. This is a time when they undertake the important tasks of forming a personal identity, acquiring social skills, establishing personal autonomy, and developing discipline.

This is also a time of rapid cognitive growth. Around the age of twelve, most students begin a gradual transition from concrete operations (the ability to think logically about real experiences) to formal operations (the ability to think reflectively, to reason, and to consider complex issues). For the majority of students, this highly unique and individual process may continue until age 15. An integrated curriculum that involves students in global thinking and interdisciplinary learning furthers the higher-order thinking skills that the students are beginning to develop. A task-focused curriculum that organizes content around themes or issues increases student engagement in learning and leads to increased skill and understanding. It recognizes effort and progress, utilizing portfolios and other authentic assessment tools.

As formal thinking skills develop, the middle-grades student is able to consider the thoughts of others and to perceive him or herself as the object of others' attention. While this means the student now lives in a broader and more interesting world, the student can also feel alone, unsure, and self-conscious. These feelings can manifest themselves as intense egocentrism and self-consciousness, qualities that the teacher needs to understand and work with creatively. It is generally more effective with young adolescent learners to provide cooperative group learning opportunities while avoiding singling out students. This helps maintain an atmosphere of emotional safety and high motivation while facilitating the development of autonomy and self-confidence.

The middle-grades teacher needs to assist students in increasing their concentration span, improving self discipline, and beginning to think about long-term goals. Because young adolescents have a relatively short attention span, an ideal curriculum should provide for diversity in both presentation and practice. It should also provide opportunities for students to move around in non-disruptive ways and work in a variety of groups.

Increased understanding of this exciting age group, a well-designed curriculum and textbook, and appropriate classroom management approaches can maximize teaching fun and effectiveness and enhance students' learning experiences.

Curriculum Materials in the Middle-Grades

A well-constructed set of curriculum materials should take advantage of students' thirst for peer interactions and their willingness to learn. The ideal program builds on students' strengths with concrete, contextualized learning activities, gradually offering more opportunities to challenge students and stretch their skills into new areas of development. This can be accomplished in a variety of ways: by strategically introducing abstract topics that require creativity and flexibility, by making connections with other disciplines, and by providing as many opportunities as possible to apply new learning in authentic, life-like settings. The well-designed curriculum should also address the special characteristics of the middle-grade learner and allow the teacher to turn students' preoccupations into assets.

Using Adelante in the Middle Grades

Levels 1A and 1B of the Holt Spanish program have been designed to accomplish two major goals. First, *Adelante* and *En camino* were specifically created to address the unique needs and interests of young adolescents with a rich and highly diverse program that engages students' interest and promotes enthusiasm for learning at various stages of development. Second, *Adelante* and *En camino* teach the full scope and sequence of *¡Ven conmigo!* Level 1, allowing students who have completed Levels 1A and 1B to continue successfully with *¡Ven conmigo!* Level 2.

Adelante and *En camino* capitalize on young adolescents' interest in peer interaction and physical activity by building in a wide selection of projects, games, and pair and group activities. A variety of TPR (Total Physical Response) suggestions are included in the *Annotated Teacher's Edition*.

High-interest themes (such as sports, food, shopping, and friendships) and geographic locations integrate the audio, video, and text, and workbook content. Short learning units called **pasos** allow for frequent assessment. The testing program, oriented to the specific needs of the middle grades learner, includes **paso** quizzes, chapter tests, speaking tests, and authentic assessment tools such as portfolios and performance-based activities. A structured approach to peer assessment is included to further profit from students' interest in peer interaction.

Each proficiency-oriented learning unit flows from concrete, closed-ended activities to more abstract, open-ended activities.

These offer opportunities for students to interact with a variety of realia and other multisensory input. This progression solidifies the active use of language and generates opportunities to employ newly emerging cognitive skills.

Global thinking is inspired through a variety of program features. **Enlaces** tie the theme or location of the chapter to other disciplines, encouraging students to draw together thoughts and ideas from different sources and to use their background knowledge. **Encuentro cultural** and **Panorama cultural** furnish an opportunity for students to relate to the interests, thoughts, and priorities of young adolescents in the Spanish-speaking world. Students are encouraged to think reflectively about their own lives and interests in comparison to their counterparts in other parts of the world. **Notas culturales** present high-interest cultural information and again invite students to make connections and comparisons.

References

Irvin, Judith L. *Cognitive Growth During Early Adolescence: The Regulator of Developmental Tasks.* Middle School Journal. September 1995.

Irvin, Judith, L. *Developmental Tasks of Early Adolescence: How Adult Awareness Can Reduce At-Risk Behavior.* The Clearing House Vol. 69 (4). March/April 1996.

Raven, Patrick T. and Wilson, Jo Anne S. *Focus on Teaching Foreign Languages in the Middle Grades: A Summary Statement from the Central States Conference.* Central States Conference on the Teaching of Foreign Languages. April, 1997.

ADELANTE

Adelante *supports the middle-grades teacher in the following ways:*

◆ Engages students with Spanish-speaking adolescents through new video, audio, and CD-ROM programs.

◆ Promotes skill development with both print and technology resources.

◆ Provides appealing, age-appropriate reading selections.

◆ Instructs students on the process of writing.

◆ Relates language learning to other disciplines.

Adelante *also builds on young adolescents' growing social skills by*

◆ Providing diverse pair, group, and cooperative learning experiences.

◆ Offering a wide variety of games, projects, and activities.

◆ Including peer assessment of writing.

◆ Building connections with the lives of young adolescents in Spanish-speaking countries.

Adelante *supports appropriate classroom management strategies in the following ways:*

◆ Provides suggestions for how to modify activities for different types of learners.

◆ Includes portfolio management.

◆ Offers lesson-planning suggestion for traditional or block-scheduling.

◆ Provides materials and suggestions for building an exploratory Spanish course.

TECHNOLOGY IN THE FOREIGN LANGUAGE CLASSROOM

BY CINDY A. KENDALL

Many remember when overhead projectors and audiocassettes were on the cutting edge. Today's foreign language teachers and their students are discovering new technological applications that make teaching and learning more exciting and effective. Teachers are integrating these technologies into their classes and fundamentally changing the way students learn languages.

The wealth of technological possibilities available to foreign language teachers, such as multimedia computer software, videodiscs, and the Internet, is more sophisticated than ever. This wider range of technological possibilities offers new challenges. In order to use technology effectively, teachers must become familiar with the resources available and understand how the use of technology can enhance language learning.

What role does technology play in the foreign language classroom?

Technology is a powerful tool in the foreign language classroom because it combines visual, auditory, and cultural input and allows for the simultaneous practice of listening, speaking, reading, and writing skills. It can help the instructor reach the five goals of the Standards for Foreign Language Learning: Communication, Culture, Connections, Comparisons, and Community.

The versatility, immediacy, and interactive nature of technology make studying a foreign language more relevant and meaningful to students. Through technology, students can "visit" countries where the target language is spoken and listen to and interact with native speakers. On the Internet, students can perform tasks in the target language at World Wide Web sites created in target-language countries. Technology makes the notion of the global village a reality for today's foreign language students.

In addition, technology helps the teacher work with students of differing skills and learning styles. Technology-based instruction offers teachers and students the flexibility of working as a class, in small groups, or as individuals.

What technological resources are available?

Overhead Projection
The overhead projector, a long-time companion in the classroom, provides a way to effectively combine visual and auditory practice. Transparencies can be an alternative to writing on the chalkboard, and have the added advantage of permitting the teacher to write presentations in advance that can be used over and over.

Audio
Foreign language instructors are familiar with the use of audiocassettes as part of students' listening comprehension practice, and know all too well some common problems with this format: the loss of time in cueing the appropriate segment and wear and tear on the audiocassette. Audio compact discs enable the teacher to cue the desired track quickly and deliver the same content with much greater ease. Other benefits of compact discs include higher-quality recordings and longer product shelf life.

Video and Videodisc
Video technology offers multiple benefits to teachers and is increasingly becoming a standard part of the curriculum system. Videos that are shot on location and feature native speakers in real settings can supply linguistically and culturally authentic input and facilitate comprehension with richer contexts, while at the same time reinforcing new language and structures. The use of video has progressed beyond simply watching. Videos and the print-matter guides that often accompany them give teachers ideas to motivate students, to provide comprehensible input, and to review material. By watching videoclips of interviews, ads, music performances, and other authentic target-language programming, students get a taste of the "real" foreign language. Videodiscs have brought a new and welcome dimension of video technology into the classroom. Like audio compact discs, videodiscs provide superior sound and images, a more durable physical medium, and quick random access using a barcode scanner.

Multimedia Software
Interactive CD-ROM programs are easy-to-use computer software programs that deliver large amounts of sound and images along with text. In the most effective CD-ROM programs, students not only hear and see language in action, but interact with it as well. This powerful learning tool weaves listening, reading, speaking, writing, and culture into a tapestry of realistic situations that motivates students to

practice and communicate in the foreign language. As an added benefit for busy teachers, CD-ROM technology requires little or no training and is virtually foolproof. No matter how many students use the disk, it is impossible to erase the program or write over it.

CD-ROM technology gives teachers flexibility in several areas. They can work with students as a whole class, in small groups, or individually; they can use the program at any phase of the lesson cycle; and they can easily help students with varied learning strengths and styles.

Internet

The Internet is an electronic resource that offers unmatched potential for connecting the foreign language classroom to the outside world. The World Wide Web (WWW) is a treasure trove of authentic materials that can bring target-language cultures into the classroom on a daily basis. By connecting to the Internet and using WWW resources, teachers can overcome the difficulties inherent in teaching a foreign language in an English-speaking country and provide students with experiences they would otherwise not have. Students can find out what is playing at the movies in Buenos Aires or what the hours of operation are at the Prado Museum; they might read the latest headlines in Santiago de Chile or get information about the Spanish royal family; or they can scan weather reports in Puerto Rico or soccer scores in Mexico. They can also download audio now; thanks to this new resource, accessing international music and broadcasts is easier than ever.

What implications does increased use of technology have for teachers and students?

Both teachers and students benefit in many ways from the growing variety of technological tools available for use in and out of the classroom. Students are more motivated to learn, and motivated students are easier to teach. The variety of formats the teacher can now offer makes it much easier to address individual learning styles in classrooms that have grown increasingly diverse.

New technologies also facilitate classroom management in many ways. Software programs can help the teacher build more effective presentations using less time and energy. Multimedia programs can often give students immediate feedback, track their progress through different types of assignments, and make accurate records management much easier for the teacher.

Along with their many benefits, teachers will find that new technologies also bring new responsibilities. Teachers who have used magazine articles and books understand the need to review such materials to be sure content is appropriate and will naturally apply similar standards to CD-ROM programs and to Internet activities. In addition, activities that put students in contact with the public on the Internet make it imperative that teachers set standards and communicate clearly with both parents and students about what is acceptable and safe.

As students move into working more independently with creative technologies both as individuals and in groups, teachers may also need to modify their strategies for monitoring students' work to maintain accountability and to make sure students are getting the most out of their time with each medium. Teachers may want to re-examine how they assess students; performance assessment and portfolio assessment offer opportunities for students to demonstrate their increasing skill in the language and can help prepare them for the kinds of proficiency tests that are becoming more common at checkpoints or as exit requirements.

Properly used, new technology tools can bring the language to life for students and make teachers' work easier and more effective. Teachers are learning new skills and adapting their approaches to classroom management and assessment. Students are also learning "how to learn" with these new resources, and the rewards can be great.

ADELANTE

Adelante's *technology package facilitates presentation, practice, review, and assessment in the following ways:*

Video and Videodisc Programs

◆ Provide high-interest stories, interviews, and travelogues shot on location.

◆ Are fully integrated into each corresponding section of the *Pupil's Edition*.

Audio Program

◆ Allows students ample practice in every chapter listening to native speakers.

◆ Is available on audio CDs for ease of use.

Interactive CD-ROM Program

◆ Provides interactive, authentic, multi-sensory practice with corrective feedback.

◆ Practices each chapter's functions, grammar, vocabulary, and culture.

◆ Offers an online teacher management system to insure student accountability.

Teaching Transparencies

◆ Present situations, vocabulary, and maps that practice key concepts and skills.

Test Generator

◆ Allows teachers to create and print alternate tests and make short practice tests.

Adelante's *planning tools facilitate the integration of technology in the following ways:*

Pupil's Edition

◆ Indicates for both teacher and student when CD-ROM activities are available.

Annotated Teacher's Edition

◆ Includes convenient barcodes for use with the *Videodisc Program* and a quick guide to technology resources for each chapter.

Ancillaries

◆ Include a teacher's guide for every technology component.

◆ Include a *Lesson Planner* that suggests appropriate places to integrate technology.

STANDARDS FOR FOREIGN LANGUAGE LEARNING

BY ROBERT LABOUVE

Development of Foreign Language Standards

In 1989 educational reform in the United States took on an entirely different look when state and national leaders reached consensus on six national educational goals for public schools. In 1994 a new law, *Goals 2000: Educate America Act,* endorsed these six goals and added two more. The most important national goal in the law for foreign language educators is Goal Three, which establishes a core curriculum and places foreign languages in that core. As a result of this consensus on national goals, the federal government encouraged the development of high standards in the core disciplines.

We must first define "standards" in order to fully understand the rationale for their development. Content standards ask: What should students know and be able to do? Content standards have recently been developed by the American Council on the Teaching of Foreign Languages, the American Association of Teachers of French, the American Association of Teachers of German, and the American Association of Teachers of Spanish and Portuguese.

Performance standards ask: How good is good enough? Opportunity-to-learn standards ask: Did the school prepare all students to perform well? There is a growing consensus that states and local districts should address the last two types of standards.

A task force of foreign language educators began work on the standards in 1993 by establishing specific foreign language goals. They then set content standards for each goal. The task force sought feedback from the foreign language profession through an extensive dissemination program and produced a draft of the standards document for introduction at a number of sites around the United States during the 1994–1995 school year. The final version, published in 1996, incorporated suggestions from the sites where the standards were introduced and reaction from volunteer reviewers and the field in general.

While the standards are world class, they are realistic and attainable by most students. The task force also realized that the general set of goals and standards would have to be made language specific in a curriculum development process and that continuing staff development would be essential.

FOREIGN LANGUAGE GOALS AND STANDARDS

Communication Communicate in Languages Other Than English	**Standard 1.1**	Students engage in conversations, provide and obtain information, express feelings and emotions, and exchange opinions.
	Standard 1.2	Students understand and interpret written and spoken language on a variety of topics.
	Standard 1.3	Students present information, concepts, and ideas to an audience of listeners or readers on a variety of topics.
Cultures Gain Knowledge and Understanding of Other Cultures	**Standard 2.1**	Students demonstrate an understanding of the relationship between the practices and perspectives of the culture studied.
	Standard 2.2	Students demonstrate an understanding of the relationship between the products and perspectives of the culture studied.
Connections Connect with Other Disciplines and Acquire Information	**Standard 3.1**	Students reinforce and further their knowledge of other disciplines through the foreign language.
	Standard 3.2	Students acquire information and recognize the distinctive viewpoints that are only available through the foreign language and its cultures.
Comparisons Develop Insight into the Nature of Language and Culture	**Standard 4.1**	Students demonstrate understanding of the nature of language through comparisons of the language studied and their own.
	Standard 4.2	Students demonstrate understanding of the concept of culture through comparisons of the cultures studied and their own.
Communities Participate in Multilingual Communities at Home and Around the World	**Standard 5.1**	Students use the language both within and beyond the school setting.
	Standard 5.2	Students show evidence of becoming life-long learners by using the language for personal enjoyment and enrichment.

Impact of the Standards

The goals and standards describe a K–12 foreign language program for *all* students, presenting languages, both modern and classical, as part of the core curriculum for every student, including those whose native language is not English. Broad goals establish the basic framework of the language program. The proposed content standards set for these goals describe what students should know and be able to do in a language. The chart shows how the standards are arrayed alongside the goals.

The first two goals in this expanded language program describe today's typical school language program. The last three are often identified by teachers as important, but are not always implemented. The standards-based program moves beyond an emphasis on skills to a redefinition of the language program itself.

Sample progress indicators are provided for Grades 4, 8, and 12 as examples of what students can do to meet the standards and accomplish the goals of the language program. A higher level of performance will be expected as students progress from one benchmark grade to another. For example, Standard 1.1 at Grade 4 suggests that students can "ask and answer questions about such things as family, school events, and celebrations in person or via letters, e-mail, or audio and video tapes," but Standard 1.1 at Grade 12 suggests that students can "exchange, support, and discuss their opinions and individual perspectives with peers and/or speakers of the target language on a variety of topics dealing with contemporary and historical issues."

While there is an assumption that foreign language goals and standards will have a great impact upon the states and local districts, the national standards themselves are voluntary. Clearly, standards will influence instruction and curriculum development in districts that choose to align their language programs with the national standards. Assessment programs will most likely begin to reflect the influence of the standards. The standards will also have an impact on the preparation of future teachers.

A curriculum based on the standards will encourage students to take responsibility for their learning by making the language curriculum coherent and transparent to them. Students will know from the beginning what they should be able to do when they exit the program and can judge for themselves how they are progressing, especially at Grades 4, 8, and 12.

The standards will direct instruction in the classroom by providing curriculum developers and teachers with a broad framework upon which to construct the expanded language program. Standards for each goal will ensure that no goal is treated informally or left to chance. Teachers who use the content standards should play a critical role in their district by deciding how good is good enough for students who exit the program.

The standards will also have a significant impact on the demand for sequential, cross-disciplinary materials for a K–12 language program. Another challenge will be the development of new technologies.

Probably the greatest benefit that national standards may bring will be in the area of making possible articulation that is horizontal (linking languages to other disciplines) and vertical (grade to grade, school to school, and school to college). Language teachers will join their English and social studies colleagues in helping students become language-competent, literate citizens of the world.

A language program that is at once coherent and transparent to students and others will provide all language educators a basis for reaching consensus about their expectations on what students should know and do. To those of us who feel that foreign language education is basic education for all students, the national standards document should become a strong advocate for languages in the curriculum of every school and for the extended sequences of study presented by the goals and standards. This makes it easier for language educators to present a rationale for foreign languages in the curriculum.

To order *Language Learning: Preparing for the 21st Century,* please contact the project office:

National Standards in
Foreign Language Education
c/o ACTFL
6 Executive Plaza
Yonkers, NY 10701-6801
(914) 963-8830
FAX: (914) 963-1275

ADELANTE

Adelante supports the Foreign Language Goals and Standards in the following ways:

The Pupil's Edition

◆ Encourages students to take responsibility for their learning by providing clearly defined chapter objectives.

◆ Provides pair- and group-work activities in which students use the target language in a wide range of settings and contexts.

◆ Offers culture activities and questions that develop students' insight and encourage observational and analytic skills.

The Annotated Teacher's Edition

◆ Provides a broad framework for developing a foreign language program and offers specific classroom suggestions for reaching students with various learning styles.

◆ Offers ideas for multicultural and multidisciplinary projects as well as community and family links that encourage students to gain access to information both at school and in the community.

The Ancillary Program

◆ Provides students with on-location video footage of native speakers interacting in their own cultural and geographic context.

◆ Includes multiple options for practicing new skills and assessing performance, including situation cards, portfolio suggestions, speaking tests, and other alternatives.

◆ Familiarizes students with tasks they will be expected to perform on exit exams.

By Nancy A. Humbach and Dorothea Bruschke

Ask students what they like best about studying a foreign language. Chances are that learning about culture, the way people live, is one of their favorite aspects. Years after language study has ended, adults remember with fondness the customs of the target culture, even pictures in their language texts. It is this interest in the people and their way of life that is the great motivator and helps us sustain students' interest in language study.

We must integrate culture and language in a way that encourages curiosity, stimulates analysis, and teaches students to hypothesize and seek answers to questions about the people whose language they are studying. Teaching isolated facts about how people in other cultures live is not enough. This information is soon dated and quickly forgotten. We must go a step beyond and teach students that all behavior, values, and traditions exist because of certain aspects of history, geography, and socio-economic conditions.

There are many ways to help students become culturally knowledgeable and to assist them in developing an awareness of differences and similarities between the target culture and their own. Two of these approaches involve critical thinking, that is, trying to find reasons for a certain behavior through observation and analysis, and putting individual observations into larger cultural patterns. ◆

First Approach: Questioning

The first approach involves questioning as the key strategy. At the earliest stages of language learning, students begin to learn ways to greet peers, elders, and strangers, as well as the use of **tú** and **usted.** Students need to consider questions such as: "How do Spanish-speaking people greet each other? Are there different levels of formality? Who initiates a handshake? What's considered a good handshake?" Each of these questions leads students to think about the values that are expressed through word and gesture. They start to "feel" the other culture and, at the same time, understand how much of their own behavior is rooted in their cultural background.

Magazines, newspapers, advertisements, and television commercials are all excellent sources of cultural material. For example, browsing through a Spanish magazine, one finds an extraordinary number of advertisements for health-related products. Could this indicate a great interest in staying healthy? Reading advertisements can be followed up with viewing videos and films, or with interviewing native speakers or people who have lived in Spanish-speaking countries to learn about customs involving health. Students might want to find answers to questions such as: "How do Spanish speakers treat a cold? What is their attitude toward fresh air? toward exercise?" This type of questioning might lead students to discover that we view health matters and the curative properties of food and exercise differently. As in this country, many of the concepts have their roots in the traditions of the past.

An advertisement for a refrigerator or a picture of a Spanish or Latin American kitchen can provide an insight into practices of shopping for food. Students first need to think about the refrigerator at home, take an inventory of what is kept in it, and consider when and where their family shops. Next, students should look closely at a Spanish or Latin American refrigerator. Is it smaller? What could that mean? (Shopping takes place more often, stores are within walking distance, and people eat more fresh foods.)

Food wrappers and containers also provide good clues to cultural insight. For example, laundry detergent is packaged in small plastic bags in many Spanish-speaking countries. Further, instead of "blue-white" cleaning properties, a "red-white" is preferred and considered the epitome of clean. Because of the lack of paper board for boxes, the humidity in many areas, the use for hand laundry, and shopping habits, plastic bags are a more practical form of packaging.

We must integrate culture and language in a way that encourages curiosity, stimulates analysis, and teaches students to hypothesize.

Second Approach: Associating Words with Images

The second approach for developing cultural understanding involves forming associations of words with the cultural images they suggest. Language and culture are so closely related that one might actually say that language is culture. Most words, especially nouns, carry a cultural connotation. Knowing the literal equivalent of a word in another language is of little use to students in understanding this connotation. For example, **relación** cannot be translated simply as relationship, **comida** as food, or **paseo** as walk. The Spanish phrase **dar un paseo,** for instance, carries with it such social images as people out walking with friends or family, sitting in a sidewalk café, seeing people and being seen by others. In Spanish-speaking countries, "to go for a walk" often means something entirely different than it does for North Americans.

When students have acquired some sense of the cultural connotation of words—not only through teachers' explanations but, more importantly, through observation of visual images—they start to discover the larger underlying cultural themes, or what is often called "deep culture."

These larger cultural themes serve as organizing categories into which individual cultural phenomena fit to form a pattern. Students might discover, for example, that Spanish speakers, because they live in much more crowded conditions, have a great need for privacy (cultural theme), as reflected in such phenomena as fences or walls around property, and curtains on windows. Students might also discover that love of nature and the outdoors is an important cultural theme, as indicated by

such phenomena as flower boxes and planters in public places—even on small traffic islands—well-kept public parks in every town, and people going for a walk or going hiking.

As we teach culture, students learn to recognize elements not only of the target culture but also of their American cultural heritage. They see how elements of culture reflect larger themes or patterns. Learning what constitutes American culture and how that information relates to other people throughout the world can be an exciting journey for a young person.

As language teachers, we are able to facilitate that journey into another culture and into our own, to find our similarities as well as our differences from others. We do not encourage value judgments about others and their culture, nor do we recommend adopting other ways. We simply say to students, "Other ways exist. They exist for many reasons, just as our ways exist due to what our ancestors have bequeathed us through history, traditions, values, and geography."

USING PORTFOLIOS IN THE FOREIGN LANGUAGE CLASSROOM

By Jo Anne S. Wilson

The communicative, whole-language approach of today's foreign language instruction requires assessment methods that parallel the teaching and learning strategies in the proficiency-oriented classroom. We know that language acquisition is a process. Portfolios are designed to assess the steps in that process. ◆

What Is a Portfolio?

A portfolio is a purposeful, systematic collection of a student's work. A useful tool in developing a student profile, the portfolio shows the student's efforts, progress, and achievements for a given period of time. It may be used for periodic evaluation, as the basis for overall evaluation, or for placement. It may also be used to enhance or provide alternatives to traditional assessment measures, such as formal tests, quizzes, class participation, and homework.

Why Use Portfolios?

Portfolios benefit both students and teachers because they

- **Are ongoing and systematic.** A portfolio reflects the real-world process of production, assessment, revision, and reassessment. It parallels the natural rhythm of learning.

- **Offer an incentive to learn.** Students have a vested interest in creating the portfolios, through which they can showcase their ongoing efforts and tangible achievements. Students select the works to be included and have a chance to revise, improve, evaluate, and explain the contents.

- **Are sensitive to individual needs.** Language learners bring varied abilities to the classroom and do not acquire skills in a uniformly neat and orderly fashion. The personalized, individualized assessment offered by portfolios responds to this diversity.

- **Provide documentation of language development.** The material in a portfolio is evidence of student progress in the language learning process. The contents of the portfolio make it easier to discuss their progress with the students as well as with parents and others.

- **Offer multiple sources of information.** A portfolio presents a way to collect and analyze information from multiple sources that reflects a student's efforts, progress, and achievements in the language.

Portfolio Components

The foreign language portfolio should include both oral and written work, student self-evaluation, and teacher observation, usually in the form of brief, non-evaluative comments about various aspects of the student's performance.

Portfolios offer a more realistic and accurate way to assess the process of language teaching and learning.

The Oral Component

The oral component of a portfolio might be an audio- or videocassette. It may contain both rehearsed and extemporaneous monologues and conversations. For a rehearsed speaking activity, give a specific communicative task that students can personalize according to their individual interests (for example, ordering a favorite meal in a restaurant). If the speaking activity is extemporaneous, first acquaint students with possible topics for discussion or even the specific task they will be expected to perform. (For example, tell them they will be asked to discuss a picture showing a sports activity or a restaurant scene.)

The Written Component

Portfolios are excellent tools for incorporating process writing strategies into the foreign language classroom. Documentation of various stages of the writing process—brainstorming, multiple drafts, and peer comments—may be included with the finished product.

Involve students in selecting writing tasks for the portfolio. At the beginning levels, the tasks might include some structured writing, such as labeling or listing. As students become more proficient, journals, letters, and other more complicated writing tasks are valuable ways for them to monitor their progress in using the written language.

Student Self-Evaluation

Students should be actively involved in critiquing and evaluating their portfolios and monitoring their own progress. The process and procedure for student self-evaluation should be considered in planning the contents of the portfolio. Students should work with you and their peers to design the exact format. Self-evaluation encourages them to think about what they are learning (content), how they learn (process), why they are learning (purpose), and where they are going in their learning (goals).

Teacher Observation

Systematic, regular, and ongoing observations should be placed in the portfolio after they have been discussed with the student. These observations provide feedback on the student's progress in the language learning process.

Teacher observations should be based on an established set of criteria that has been developed earlier with input from the student. Observation techniques may include the following:
• Jotting notes in a journal to be discussed with the student and then placed in the portfolio
• Using a checklist of observable behaviors, such as the willingness to take risks when using the target language or staying on task during the lesson
• Making observations on adhesive notes that can be placed in folders
• Recording anecdotal comments, during or after class, using a cassette recorder.

Knowledge of the criteria you use in your observations gives students a framework for their performance.

How Are Portfolios Evaluated?

The portfolio should reflect the process of student learning over a specific period of time. At the beginning of that time period, determine the criteria by which you will assess the final product and convey them to the students. Make this evaluation a collaborative effort by seeking students' input as you formulate these criteria and your instructional goals.

Students need to understand that evaluation based on a predetermined standard is but one phase of the assessment process; demonstrated effort and growth are just as important. As you consider correctness and accuracy in both oral and written work, also consider the organization, creativity, and improvement revealed by the student's portfolio over the time period. The portfolio provides a way to monitor the growth of a student's knowledge, skills, and attitudes and shows the student's efforts, progress, and achievements.

How to Implement Portfolios

Teacher-teacher collaboration is as important to the implementation of portfolios as teacher-student collaboration. Confer with your colleagues to determine, for example, what kinds of information you want to see in the student portfolio, how the information will be presented, the purpose of the portfolio, the intended purposes (grading, placement, or a combination of the two), and criteria for evaluating the portfolio. Conferring among colleagues helps foster a departmental cohesiveness and consistency that will ultimately benefit the students.

The Promise of Portfolios

The high degree of student involvement in developing portfolios and deciding how they will be used generally results in renewed student enthusiasm for learning and improved achievement. As students

compare portfolio pieces done early in the year with work produced later, they can take pride in their progress as well as reassess their motivation and work habits.

Portfolios also provide a framework for periodic assessment of teaching strategies, programs, and instruction. They offer schools a tool to help solve the problem of vertical articulation and accurate student placement. The more realistic and accurate assessment of the language learning process that is provided by portfolios is congruent with the strategies that should be used in the proficiency-oriented classroom.

LEARNING STYLES AND MULTI-MODALITY TEACHING

BY MARY B. MCGEHEE

The larger and broader population of students who are enrolling in foreign language classes brings a new challenge to foreign language educators, calling forth an evolution in teaching methods to enhance learning for all our students. Educational experts now recognize that every student has a preferred sense for learning and retrieving information: visual, auditory, or kinesthetic. Incorporating a greater variety of activities to accommodate the learning styles of all students can make the difference between struggle and pleasure in the foreign language classroom. ◆

Accommodating Different Learning Styles

A modified arrangement of the classroom is one way to provide more effective and enjoyable learning for all students. Rows of chairs and desks must give way at times to circles, semicircles, or small clusters. Students may be grouped in fours or in pairs for cooperative work or peer teaching. It is important to find a balance of arrangements, thereby providing the most comfort in varied situations.

Since visual, auditory, and kinesthetic learners will be in the class, and because every student's learning will be enhanced by a multisensory approach, lessons must be directed toward all three learning styles. Any language lesson content may be presented visually, aurally, or kinesthetically.

Visual presentations and practice may include the chalkboard, charts, posters, television, overhead projectors, books, magazines, picture diagrams, flash cards, bulletin boards, films, slides, or videos. Visual learners need to see what they are to learn. Lest the teacher think he or she will never have the time to prepare all those visuals, Dickel and Slak (1983) found that visual aids generated by students are more effective than ready-made ones.

Auditory presentations and practice may include stating aloud the requirements of the lesson, oral questions and answers, paired or group work on a progression of oral exercises from repetition to communication, tapes, CDs, computer sound recordings, dialogues, and role-playing. Jingles, catchy stories, and memory devices using songs and rhymes are good learning aids. Having students record themselves and then listen as they play back the recording allows them to practice in the auditory mode.

Kinesthetic presentations entail the students' use of manipulatives, chart materials, gestures, signals, typing, songs, games, and role-playing. These lead the students to associate sentence constructions with meaningful movements.

A Sample Lesson Using Multi-Modality Teaching

A multi-sensory presentation on greetings might proceed as follows.

For Visual Learners
As the teacher begins oral presentation of greetings and introductions, he or she simultaneously shows the written forms on transparencies, with the formal expressions marked with an adult's hat, and the informal expressions marked with a baseball cap.

The teacher then distributes cards with the hat and cap symbols representing the formal and informal expressions. As the students hear taped mini-dialogues, they hold up the appropriate card to indicate whether the dialogues are formal or informal. On the next listening, the students repeat the sentences they hear.

Incorporating a greater variety of activities to accommodate the learning styles of all students can make the difference between struggle and pleasure in the foreign language classroom.

For Auditory Learners
A longer taped dialogue follows, allowing the students to hear the new expressions a number of times. They write from dictation several sentences containing the new expressions. They may work in pairs, correcting each other's work as they "test" their own understanding of the lesson at hand. Finally, students respond to simple questions using the appropriate formal and informal responses cued by the cards they hold.

For Kinesthetic Learners

For additional kinesthetic input, members of the class come to the front of the room, each holding a hat or cap symbol. As the teacher calls out situations, the students play the roles, using gestures and props appropriate to the age group they are portraying. Non-cued, communicative role-playing with props further enables the students to "feel" the differences between formal and informal expressions.

Helping Students Learn How to Use Their Preferred Mode

Since we require all students to perform in all language skills, part of the assistance we must render is to help them develop strategies within their preferred learning modes to carry out an assignment in another mode. For example, visual students hear the teacher assign an oral exercise and visualize what they must do. They must see themselves carrying out the assignment, in effect watching themselves as if there were a movie going on in their heads. Only then can they also hear themselves saying the right things. Thus, this assignment will be much easier for the visual learners who have been taught this process, if they have not already figured it out for themselves. Likewise, true auditory students, confronted with a reading/ writing assignment, must talk themselves through it, converting the entire process into sound as they plan and prepare their work. Kinesthetic students presented with a visual or auditory task must first break the assignment into tasks and then work their way through them.

Students who experience difficulty because of a strong preference for one mode of learning are often unaware of the degree of preference. In working with these students, I prefer the simple and direct assessment of learning styles offered by Richard Bandler and John Grinder in their book *Frogs into Princes,* which allows the teacher and student to quickly determine how the student learns. In an interview with the student, I follow the assessment with certain specific recommendations of techniques to make the student's study time more effective.

It is important to note here that teaching students to maximize their study does not require that the teacher give each student an individualized assignment. It does require that each student who needs it be taught how to prepare the assignment using his or her own talents and strengths. This communication between teacher and student, combined with teaching techniques that reinforce learning in all modes,

can only maximize pleasure and success in learning a foreign language.

References

Dickel, M.J. and S. Slak. "Imaging Vividness and Memory for Verbal Material." *Journal of Mental Imagery* 7, i (1983):121–126.

Bandler, Richard, and John Grinder. *Frogs into Princes.* Real People Press, Moab, UT. 1978.

ADELANTE

Adelante accommodates different learning styles in the following ways:

The Pupil's Edition

◆ Presents basic material in audio, video, and print formats.

◆ Includes role-playing activities and a variety of multi-modal activities, including an extensive listening strand and many art-based activities.

The Annotated Teacher's Edition

◆ Provides suggested activities for visual, auditory, and kinesthetic learners as well as suggestions for slower-paced learning and challenge activities.

◆ Includes Total Physical Response activities.

The Ancillary Program

◆ Provides additional reinforcement activities for a variety of learning styles.

◆ Presents a rich blend of audiovisual input through the video, audio, and CD-ROM programs, and through transparencies and copying masters.

NEW PERSPECTIVES FOR NATIVE SPEAKERS

BY CECILIA RODRÍGUEZ-PINO

Spanish teachers often simultaneously teach two groups of students whose learning needs are markedly different. The first group, the majority, for whom most curricula are developed, are English-proficient but at a beginner's level in Spanish. The second group consists of students whose proficiency in English varies but who already speak Spanish, often quite proficiently. From their own experience they already understand a great deal about the Spanish language and the cultures of Spanish speakers. Many schools have not yet set up Spanish for Native Speakers (SNS) sections with specialized curricula that would build on these students' linguistic and cultural strengths. As a result, in some schools native speakers who want to study Spanish are enrolled in courses where Spanish is taught as a foreign language. Addressing their learning needs thus becomes the particular challenge of the teacher, who must create and implement supplemental classroom materials. ◆

Types of Native Spanish Speakers

The greatest number of native Spanish speakers in the classroom are Spanish-speaking immigrants and American students of Hispanic descent. Many immigrants have been uprooted from their native countries and find themselves in a new and foreign environment without the skills to communicate. Often they must struggle to adapt to mainstream sociocultural norms and values. Psychological adjustment, cultural integration, and the acquisition of new communicative skills are daily concerns for them. Building teacher-student and peer-peer learning relationships may be harder for such students.

American students of Hispanic descent are often bilingual. Some are highly proficient in both written and oral Spanish, but many are proficient to varying degrees, depending on the circumstances, topics, tasks, and informal situations. These students reflect the various socio-economic classes of society and speak a wide range of Spanish dialects. Research indicates that the dialect they speak affects how they are viewed at school. When they speak a "standard" variety of Spanish or are from an educated class, as are many Cuban Americans in Florida, reactions to them are usually positive. But when Spanish speakers are from a rural background, speak a "non-standard" dialect, or come from a non-literate background, reactions in school are often negative. Attempting to modify their dialect can be detrimental to their linguistic and social development.

Linguistic Needs

Native Spanish speakers need to retrieve any Spanish they may have lost, maintain the competency they already have, and expand their knowledge and skills in Spanish.

The problem of native language loss is receiving much attention in the profession. Children appear to lose production skills more quickly than they lose comprehension ability. Thus retrieval efforts should focus on production. Rapid changes in society and in the patterns by which Spanish is transmitted from one generation to the next account for much of students' language loss. Word borrowing and code switching to English may also account for language loss. These practices are not unique to bilingual students in the United States; they are common linguistic phenomena, observed wherever languages are in contact. A native speaker may switch from Spanish to English when referring to activities generally associated with the dominant culture—even when the speaker is perfectly familiar with the relevant Spanish vocabulary. Efforts to eradicate code switching may harm students' linguistic and social development.

Affective Needs

Native Spanish-speaking students bring to class much valuable cultural and linguistic experience. Cultural opportunities need to be provided for them through which they can express their knowledge of their own particular Spanish-speaking culture and gain a greater overview of other Spanish-speaking communities and countries. They need to understand that their heritage, language, culture, dialect, and individual abilities are valuable to society. As teachers we must respect and value the different languages and dialects our students speak, and we must create an instructional context in which students will develop positive attitudes toward their own ethnic group and their own ethnic identity.

An SNS Program Approach

A task-based, whole-language approach is recommended. Receptive and productive skills can be developed through culturally meaningful activities whose contexts are community, school, home, and self. These activities can be carried out in conjunction with textbook thematic units. Such an approach creates a student-centered classroom in which the teacher acts as a facilitator connecting students to the bilingual community.

Expanding Receptive Skills

Students should perform activities in which they listen to their native language in a broad range of formal and informal contexts, from simple topics to complex ones. Audio- or videotaped versions of stories, songs, documentaries, speeches, or debates can be adapted for class assignments. Guest speakers from the community are extremely valuable resources for presentations or interviews on the chapter topic.

Students should have access to diverse, authentic reading materials from the popular culture as well as from more formal subject areas. Chicano, Cuban, Dominican, Colombian, Nicaraguan, Honduran, Panamanian, and Puerto Rican writings—which are underrepresented in the mainstream literary canon—can play an important role in instilling in students a sense of pride and awareness of their cultural heritage. Students relate well to literature written by contemporary Hispanic authors who have had experiences similar to the students' in the United States. For example, they might read the short story "Desde que se fue," from the collection *Madreselvas en flor* by literary prize-winning Chicano author Ricardo Aguilar-Melantzón, about growing up in a bilingual setting.

Developing Productive Skills

Oral history projects, ethnographic interviews, sociolinguistic surveys, dialogue journals, letter writing, and other purposeful authentic activities are effective techniques that focus on interactions among students, teacher, and community. These kinds of activities give students the opportunity to develop individual strengths and to explore their language and culture in a community context.

Classroom Environment

We can change the classroom space itself to create an environment that recognizes the prestige of the students' language and cultural heritage. Using a brief questionnaire, the teacher can find out the students' backgrounds and then display relevant posters, travel brochures, art, literature, or historical information. Students can contribute captioned photographs depicting cultural events and family traditions, so that the bulletin board reflects their personal view of the Spanish-speaking world rather than just the teacher's perspective.

Individual Assessment and Evaluation

Individual assessment at the beginning of the year should be based primarily on content so that students' errors are not the main focus. Use content, organization, and language as criteria for evaluating speaking and writing. In evaluating students' work for the year, take into account how students have broadened their functional range. This requires students to be responsible for the concepts that are essential to comprehension and production. A writing portfolio is a valuable component of the evaluation process. Oral presentations of ethnographic and sociolinguistic projects are contextualized activities for evaluating speaking.

PROFESSIONAL REFERENCES

This section provides information about resources that can enrich your Spanish class. Included are addresses of Spanish and Latin American government offices, pen pal organizations, subscription agencies, and many others. Since addresses change frequently, you may want to verify them before you send your requests. ◆

Pen pal organizations

For the names of pen pal groups other than those listed below, contact your local chapter of AATSP. There are fees involved, so be sure to write for information.

Student Letter Exchange
(League of Friendship)
211 Broadway, Suite 201
Lynbrook, NY 11563
(516) 887-8628

World Pen Pals
1694 Como Avenue
St. Paul, MN 55108
(612) 647-0191

Embassies and consulates

Addresses and phone numbers of embassies and consulates for Spanish-speaking countries are available in most U.S. city telephone directories. All are available in the directory for Washington, D.C.

Periodicals

Subscriptions to the following cultural materials are available through jobbers or directly from the publishers. See also the section on Subscription Services.

- **Blanco y negro,** a general interest weekly magazine in Spain
- **Eres,** a Mexican magazine for teens
- **El País,** a major daily newspaper in Spain

- **Hispanic,** an English-language magazine about Hispanics in the U.S.
- **La Prensa,** a major daily paper in Argentina
- **Tú internacional,** a magazine for teens published in several Spanish-speaking countries
- **México desconocido,** a cultural and environmental magazine about Mexico

Cultural agencies

For historical and tourist information about Spanish-speaking countries, contact:

Tourist Office of Spain
666 Fifth Avenue
New York, NY 10022
(212) 265-8822

Intercultural exchange

CIEE Student Travel Services
205 East 42nd St.
New York, NY 10017
(888) 268-6245

American Field Service
198 Madison, 8th Floor
New York, NY 10016
(212) 299-9000

Professional organizations

The American Council on the Teaching of Foreign Languages (ACTFL)
6 Executive Plaza
Yonkers, NY 10701
(914) 963-8830

American Association of Teachers of Spanish and Portuguese (AATSP)
Butter-Hancock Hall #210
University of Northern Colorado
Greeley, CO 80639
(970) 351-1090

Subscription services

Spanish-language magazines can be obtained through subscription agencies in the United States. The following companies are among the many which can provide your school with subscriptions:

EBSCO Subscription Services
P.O. Box 1943
Birmingham, AL 35201-1943
(205) 991-6600

Continental Book Company
8000 Cooper Ave., Bldg. 29
Glendale, NY 11385
(718) 326-0560

Miscellaneous

Gessler Publishing Company, Inc.
10 E. Church Ave.
Roanoke, VA 24011
(800) 456-5825

- Foreign language periodicals

The International Film Bureau
332 South Michigan Ave.
Chicago, IL 60604-4382
(312) 427-4545

- Foreign language videos for sale and/or rent

Américas
Organization of American States
17th and Constitution Ave. NW
Room #307
Washington, D.C. 20006
(202) 458–3000

- Magazine available in English or Spanish text

A BIBLIOGRAPHY FOR THE SPANISH TEACHER

¡Ven conmigo!
Adelante

This bibliography is a compilation of resources available for professional enrichment. ◆

Selected and annotated list of readings

I. Methods and Approaches

Cohen, Andrew D. *Assessing Language Ability in the Classroom, 2/e.* Boston, MA: Heinle, 1994.

• Assessment processes, oral interviews, role-playing situations, dictation, and portfolio assessment.

Hadley, Alice Omaggio. *Teaching Language in Context, 2/e.* Boston, MA: Heinle, 1993.

• Language acquisition theories and models and adult second language proficiency.

Krashen, Stephen, and Tracy D. Terrell. *The Natural Approach: Language Acquisition in the Classroom.* New York: Pergamon, 1983.

• Optimal Input Theory: listening, oral communication development, and testing.

Oller, John W., Jr. *Methods That Work: Ideas for Language Teachers, 2/e.* Boston, MA: Heinle, 1993.

• Literacy in multicultural settings, co-operative learning, peer teaching, and computer-assisted instruction.

Shrum, Judith L., and Eileen W. Glisan. *Teacher's Handbook: Contextualized Language Instruction.* Boston, MA: Heinle, 1993.

• Grammar, testing, using video texts, microteaching, case studies and daily plans.

II. Second-Language Theory

Krashen, Stephen. *The Power of Reading.* New York: McGraw-Hill, 1994.

• Updates Optimal Input Theory by incorporating the reading of authentic texts.

Liskin-Gasparro, Judith. *A Guide to Testing and Teaching for Oral Proficiency.* Boston, MA: Heinle, 1990.

• Oral proficiency through interview techniques and speech samples.

Rubin, Joan, and Irene Thompson. *How To Be a More Successful Language Learner, 2/e.* Boston, MA: Heinle, 1993.

• Psychological, linguistic, and practical matters of second-language learning.

III. Video and computer-assisted instruction

Altmann, Rick. *The Video Connection: Integrating Video into Language Teaching.* Boston, MA: Houghton Mifflin, 1989.

• Diverse strategies for using video texts to support second- language learning.

Dunkel, Patricia A. *Computer-Assisted Language Learning and Testing.* Boston, MA: Heinle, 1992.

• CAI and computer-assisted language learning (CALL) in the foreign language classroom.

Kenning, M. J., and M. M. Kenning. *Computers and Language Learning: Current Theory and Practice.* New York, NY: E. Horwood, 1990.

• Theoretical discussions and practical suggestions for CAI in second-language development.

IV. Teaching Native Speakers

Aguilar-Melantzón, Ricardo. "Desde que se fue."

• Produced for Teaching Spanish to Southwest Hispanic Students, National Endowment for the Humanities Summer Conference, Cecilia Rodríguez-Pino, project director. Las Cruces: New Mexico State University, 1993. Available through Spanish for Native Speakers Program, New Mexico State University. Audiotape of short story narrated by author.

Merino, Barbara J., Henry T. Trueba, and Fabián A. Samaniego. *Language and Culture in Learning: Teaching Spanish to Native Speakers of Spanish.* London, England: Falmer Press, 1993.

Rodríguez-Pino, Cecilia, and Daniel Villa. "A Student-Centered Spanish for Native Speakers Program: Theory, Curriculum Design and Outcome Assessment." *In Faces in a Crowd: The Individual Learner in Multisection Courses.* Edited by Carol A. Klee. American Association of University Supervisors Series. Boston, MA: Heinle, 1994.

Valdés, Guadalupe. "The Role of the Foreign Language Teaching Profession in Maintaining Non-English Languages in the United States." In *Northeast Conference Reports: Languages for a Multicultural World in Transition.* Edited by Heidi Byrnes. Lincolnwood, IL: National Textbook, 1992.

SCOPE AND SEQUENCE: SPANISH LEVEL 1A

Capítulo Preliminar: ¡Adelante!

- Map of the Spanish-speaking world
- El español—¿Por qué?
- ¿Sabías?
- ¿Los conoces?

Getting started with Spanish:

- ¿Cómo te llamas?, Los acentos
- El alfabeto, Los cognados
- Frases útiles
- Los colores
- El calendario
- Los números

Capítulo 1: ¡Mucho gusto!

LOCATION: SPAIN

Functions:

- Saying hello and goodbye
- Introducing people and responding to an introduction
- Asking how someone is and saying how you are
- Asking and saying how old someone is
- Asking where someone is from and saying where you're from
- Talking about likes and dislikes

Grammar:

- Punctuation marks
- Pronouns tú and yo
- Soy, eres, and es
- Asking questions
- Nouns and definite articles

Culture:

- First and last names in Spanish
- First names and Catholicism
- Saint's Days
- Greetings
- Handwriting in Spanish-speaking countries
- Snack foods in Spain
- ¿De dónde eres?

Re-entry:

- Accents (from Capítulo preliminar)
- Numbers 0–30 (from Capítulo preliminar)

Capítulo 2: ¡Organízate!

LOCATION: SPAIN

Functions:

- Talking about what you want or need
- Telling what's in your room
- Talking about what you need and want to do

Grammar:

- Indefinite articles un and una
- Noun plurals
- Plural indefinite articles
- Subject pronouns él and ella
- Plurals of ¿cuánto? and mucho
- Identifying infinitives

Culture:

- Extended family
- School uniforms
- Apartments in Spain/Sharing TV set
- Exclamations
- Los saludos
- ¿Qué necesitas para el colegio?

Re-entry:

- Subject pronouns: tú and yo (from Capítulo 1)
- Definite articles: el and la (from Capítulo 1)
- Talking about likes and dislikes (from Capítulo 1)
- Numbers 0–30 (from Capítulo preliminar)
- Using cognates (from Capítulo preliminar)

Capítulo 3: Nuevas clases, nuevos amigos

LOCATION: MEXICO

Functions:

- Talking about classes and sequencing events
- Telling time
- Telling at what time something happens
- Talking about being late or in a hurry
- Describing people and things
- Talking about things you like and explaining why

Grammar:

- Plural definite articles los and las
- Telling time with ser
- The preposition de
- The verb ser for descriptions
- Adjective agreement
- Tag questions

Culture:

- Class schedules in Spanish-speaking countries
- Grades in Spanish-speaking countries
- The siesta
- Titles of respect
- ¿Cómo es un día escolar típico?

Re-entry:

- Present tense of tener
- Numbers 0–99
- School supplies
- Forming questions
- Present tense of tener
- Noun-adjective agreement
- Forms of necesitar and querer
- Talking about likes and dislikes
- Question formation with ¿cómo?

Capítulo 4: ¿Qué haces esta tarde?

LOCATION: MEXICO

Functions:

- Talking about what you and others like to do
- Talking about what you and others do during free time
- Telling where people and things are
- Talking about where you and others go during free time

Grammar:

- Present tense of regular -ar verbs
- con, conmigo, contigo
- Relative pronoun que
- The verb estar
- Subject pronouns
- The verb ir
- Days of the week

Culture:
- Hispanic athletes
- Referring to or greeting friends
- Sights and activities in Cuernavaca
- **tú** and **usted**
- **Un recorrido de la Plaza de las Armas**
- **¿Te gusta pasear con tus amigos?**

Re-entry:
- Present tense of **tener**
- Present tense of **gustar**
- Subject pronouns **yo, tú, él, ella**
- Describing with **ser**
- Telling time
- Days of the week

Capítulo 5: El ritmo de la vida
LOCATION: FLORIDA

Functions:
- Discussing how often you do things
- Talking about what you and your friends like to do together
- Talking about what you do during a typical week
- Giving today's date
- Talking about the weather

Grammar:
- Negation
- The question words **¿quién?** and **¿quiénes?**
- The pronoun **les**
- **-er** and **-ir** verbs
- The formula for giving today's date

Culture:
- Leisure-time activities
- Meeting places
- The seasons of the year in South America
- **¿Cómo es una semana típica?**

Re-entry:
- Present tense of regular **-ar** verbs
- Negation with **no**
- **¿quién?**
- **gustar**
- Subject pronouns
- Days of the week

Capítulo 6: Entre familia
LOCATION: FLORIDA

Functions:
- Describing a family
- Describing people
- Discussing things a family does together
- Discussing problems and giving advice

Grammar:
- Possessive adjectives
- the verbs **hacer** and **salir**
- The personal **a**
- The verb **deber**
- The verb **poner**
- Present tense of **decir: dice**

Culture:
- Diminutive names
- El Compadrazgo
- **La importancia de la familia hispana**
- **¿Cuántos son en tu familia?**

Re-entry:
- **hay**
- Possessive adjectives
- Demonstrative adjectives
- Use of **de**
- Colors
- Descriptions of people
- Pastimes/hobbies
- **¿con qué frecuencia?**
- Adjective agreement
- Forming questions with **¿cómo?** and **¿cuántos?**

Capítulo Puente: En camino
(REVIEW)

Functions:
- Greeting others; saying what you have
- Talking about what you do and when; describing people and places
- Talking about how often you do things; talking about your family

Grammar:
- The verbs **estar**, **ser**, and **tener**
- Indirect object pronouns
- Using **hay**
- Possessive adjectives
- Telling time
- Present tense of regular -**ar**, -**er**, and -**ir** verbs
- Adjective agreement
- The verbs **hacer, salir, poner, deber,** and **ir**

Re-entry:
- The Bridge Chapter is a global review of Level 1A

Capítulo 7: ¿Qué te gustaría hacer?
LOCATION: ECUADOR

Functions:
- Talking on the telephone
- Extending and accepting invitations
- Making plans
- Talking about getting ready
- Turning down an invitation and explaining why

Grammar:
- **e** to **ie** stem-changing verbs
- **pensar** + infinitive and **ir** + **a** + infinitive
- Reflexive verbs (infinitives only)
- Expressions with **tener**

Culture:
- Telephone greetings
- Modes of transportation
- **¿Qué haces para conocer a un nuevo estudiante?**

Re-entry:
- Invitations: **gustar**
- Days of the week
- Future expressions: **hoy, mañana,** etc.
- Expressions of frequency
- The verb **tener**

Capítulo 8: ¡A comer!
LOCATION: ECUADOR

Functions:
- Talking about meals and food
- Commenting on food
- Making polite requests
- Ordering dinner in a restaurant
- Asking for and paying the bill in a restaurant

Grammar:
- The verb **encantar** and indirect object pronouns
- **o** to **ue** stem-changing verbs
- **Ser** and **estar** with food
- Expressions with **tener**
- **Así se dice:** Indirect object pronouns **nos** and **me**
- **otro**
- **Así se dice:** Indirect object pronoun **le; quisiera**

Culture:
- Names of fruits and vegetables
- Main meal of the day
- Eating out in Ecuador
- Table manners
- Dinner and snacks
- Types of foods
- **La comida en el mundo hispanohablante**
- **¿Cuál es un plato típico de tu país o región?**

Re-entry:
- Expressing likes and dislikes
- Present tense of regular and **e** to **ie** stem-changing verbs
- Times of day
- **estar** versus **ser**
- Expressions with **tener**
- Numbers 200–100,000
- Question words **¿qué?** and **¿cuánto?**

Capítulo 9: ¡Vamos de compras!
LOCATION: TEXAS

Functions:
- Talking about giving gifts
- Asking for and giving directions downtown
- Commenting on clothes
- Making comparisons
- Expressing preferences
- Asking about prices and paying for something

Grammar:
- Indirect object pronouns **le** and **les**
- Use of **ser** to tell what something is made of
- Making comparisons: **más... que, menos... que, tan... como**
- Using the demonstrative adjectives **este** and **ese**

Culture:
- Specialty stores in Spain
- Personal care and dress in Spanish-speaking countries
- Currencies in Spanish-speaking countries
- **¿Estás a la moda?**

Re-entry:
- **ir** + **a** + infinitive for planning
- Describing family
- Talking about locations
- Talking about where things are
- Present tense of **ser** for description
- Numbers 0–100,000

Capítulo 10: Celebraciones
LOCATION: TEXAS

Functions:
- Talking about what you're doing right now
- Asking for and giving an opinion
- Asking for help and responding to requests
- Telling a friend what to do
- Talking about past events

Grammar:
- Present progressive
- Informal commands

- Preterite tense of regular -ar verbs
- Direct object pronouns **lo** and **la**

Culture:
- **Día del santo**
- **La quinceañera**
- Traditional holiday foods
- **El Paseo del Río**
- **¿Qué hacen ustedes para celebrar?**

Re-entry:
- **estar**
- Dates, months, seasons
- Extending, accepting, and turning down invitations
- **tú** versus **usted**
- Household chores
- Days of the week
- Question words **¿quién?** and **¿quiénes?**
- Free-time activities
- Places

Capítulo 11: Para vivir bien
LOCATION: PUERTO RICO

Functions:
- Making suggestions and expressing feelings
- Talking about moods and physical condition
- Saying what you did
- Talking about where you went and when

Grammar:
- **¿Te acuerdas?**: the verb **dormir**
- Present tense of **sentirse**
- The verb **doler** with **me, te, le**
- The verb **jugar** in the preterite
- The verb **ir** in the preterite

Culture:
- Body parts in common expressions
- Baseball in Spanish-speaking countries
- Sports in Spanish-speaking countries
- **¿Qué deporte practicas?**

Re-entry:
- **e** to **ie** stem-changing verbs
- Food vocabulary
- Expressions of frequency
- Definite articles
- **estar +** condition
- **o** to **ue** stem-changing verbs
- Use of preterite tense to discuss past events
- Sports

Capítulo 12: Las vacaciones ideales
LOCATION: PUERTO RICO (REVIEW)

Functions:
- Talking about what you do and like to do every day; making future plans
- Discussing what you would like to do on vacation
- Saying where you went and what you did on vacation

Grammar:
- **e** to **ie** and **o** to **ue** stem-changing verbs
- Verbs followed by an infinitive
- Uses of **ser** and **estar**
- Uses of the preterite

Culture:
- **¿Adónde vas y qué haces en las vacaciones?**

Re-entry:
- Chapter 12 is a global review of Chapters 1–11.

Capítulo 1: Mis amigos y yo
LOCATION: ANDALUCÍA (REVIEW)

Functions:
- Introducing yourself and others
- Describing people
- Talking about what you and others do
- Saying what you like and don't like

Grammar:
- Present tense of **tener**
- Adjective agreement
- Present tense of regular verbs
- Indirect object pronouns with verbs like **gustar**

Culture:
- Description of appearance of Hispanics
- **¿Quién es americano?**
- Planning evening activities in Spain
- **¿Qué es un buen amigo?**
- **cafeterías**

Re-entry:
- Chapter 1 reviews Spanish taught in *¡Ven conmigo! Level 1.*

Capítulo 2: Un viaje al extranjero
LOCATION: ANDALUCÍA (REVIEW)

Functions:
- Talking about how you're feeling
- Making suggestions and responding to them
- Saying if something has already been done
- Asking for and offering help
- Describing your city or town

Grammar:
- The verb **estar**
- Preterite of -**ar** verbs
- Present tense of **querer** and **poder**

Culture:
- Extended family living together
- **¿En dónde te gustaría vivir?**
- Celsius vs. Fahrenheit

Re-entry:
- Chapter 2 reviews Spanish taught in *¡Ven conmigo! Level 1.*

Capítulo 3: La vida cotidiana
LOCATION: VALLE DE MÉXICO

Functions:
- Talking about your daily routine
- Talking about responsibilities
- Complaining
- Talking about hobbies and pastimes
- Saying how long something has been going on

Grammar:
- Reflexive verbs and pronouns
- **e** to **i** stem change in **vestirse**
- Adverbs ending in -**mente**
- Direct object pronouns: **lo, la, los, las**
- **hace** + quantity of time + **que** + present tense

Culture:
- **¿Cuál es tu profesión?**
- Household chores
- Expressions of agreement
- Popular free-time activities among teenagers

Re-entry:
- Verbs of personal grooming
- Adverbs of time and place
- Vocabulary of hobbies and pastimes
- Making excuses
- Vocabulary of hobbies and pastimes
- Question formation

Capítulo 4: ¡Adelante con los estudios!
LOCATION: VALLE DE MÉXICO

Functions:
- Asking for and giving opinions
- Giving advice
- Talking about things and people you know
- Making comparisons
- Making plans

Grammar:
- **deberías** vs. **debes**
- **ser** + adjective to describe people
- **estar** + adjective to describe location
- Present tense of the verb **conocer**
- Direct object pronouns

Culture:
- School levels in Mexico
- Cost of university education in Latin America

- ¿Qué haces después del colegio?
- ¿Cuándo asistes a clases?

Re-entry:
- School subjects
- **para** (in order to) + infinitive
- **ser** vs. **estar**
- Comparisons: **más... que**
- **ir** + **a** + infinitive

Capítulo 5: ¡Ponte en forma!
LOCATION: TEXAS

Functions:
- Talking about staying fit and healthy
- Telling someone what to do and not to do
- Making excuses

Grammar:
- Preterite of the verb **dormir**
- Preterite of regular -**er** and -**ir** verbs
- Informal commands
- Irregular informal commands
- Preterite of **poder**
- Reflexives with verbs of emotion

Culture:
- Student responses about health habits in Spanish-speaking countries
- Vending machines in high schools
- Snack foods in Spanish-speaking countries
- **Garnachas, antojitos y bocadillos**
- **¿Qué haces para mantenerte en forma?**

Re-entry:
- Preterite of regular -**ar** verbs
- Informal commands
- Spelling changes in verbs that end in -**car**, -**gar**, -**zar**
- Reflexive verbs

Capítulo 6: De visita en la ciudad
LOCATION: TEXAS

Functions:
- Asking for and giving information
- Relating a series of events
- Ordering in a restaurant

Grammar:
- Present tense of **saber**
- **saber** vs. **conocer**
- Preterite forms of **pedir, servir, traer**

Culture:
- San Antonio
- **¿Cómo llegas al colegio?**
- Birthday celebrations

Re-entry:
- Direct object pronouns
- **poder**
- The preterite for listing events
- Food vocabulary

Capítulo 7: ¿Conoces bien tu pasado?
LOCATION: EL CARIBE

Functions:
- Talking about what you used to do
- Saying what you used to like and dislike
- Describing what people and things were like
- Using comparisons to describe people

Grammar:
- The imperfect tense of -ar, -er, -ir verbs
- The imperfect tense of **ir** and **ver**
- Spelling change of **o** to **u** and **y** to **e** to avoid vowel repetition
- Imperfect of **ser** to describe people and things
- The imperfect of **hay**
- **tan** + adjective/adverb + **como**

Culture:
- **Lo mejor de lo antiguo**
- Public services in Latin American cities
- **dichos**
- **¿De quién es esta estatua?**

Re-entry:
- The preterite
- Talking about likes and dislikes using the preterite
- Comparisons: **más/menos** + adjective + **que**
- Complaining
- Descriptive adjectives

Capítulo 8: Diversiones
LOCATION: EL CARIBE

Functions:
- Describing a past event
- Saying why you couldn't do something
- Reporting what someone said

Grammar:
- Adjectives with **-ísimo/a**
- Superlatives
- Verbs with prepositions
- Using **mientras** in the past
- Preterite of **decir**

Culture:
- **El Yunque** and **el coquí**
- **¿Cuáles son las fiestas más importantes de tu ciudad o país?**
- Holidays and festivals in Spanish-speaking countries

Re-entry:
- Describing things
- Describing what you did
- The imperfect tense
- The preterite

Capítulo 9: ¡Día de mercado!
LOCATION: LOS ANDES

Functions:
- Asking for and giving directions
- Asking for help in a store
- Talking about how clothes look and fit
- Bargaining in a market

Grammar:
- Formal commands with **usted, ustedes**

Culture:
- **En la ventanilla tres, por favor**
- Clothing and shoe sizes
- **¿Dónde compras tu comida?**
- Expressions for shopping
- Mural art

Re-entry:
- Numbers
- **ser** + **de** + material
- Clothing material and pattern
- Direct and indirect objects

Capítulo 10: ¡Cuéntame!
LOCATION: LOS ANDES

Functions:
- Setting the scene for a story
- Continuing and ending a story
- Talking about the latest news
- Reacting to news

Grammar:
- The preterite vs. the imperfect
- Preterite of **oír, creer, leer, caerse**
- The preterite and the imperfect to tell a story

Culture:
- **¿Te sabes algún cuento?**
- A Chilean folk tale
- An Ecuadorean legend
- **Mafalda** comic strip
- **la Llorona**

Re-entry:
- Reflexive verbs

- Preterite of **ser** and **tener**
- Weather expressions

Capítulo 11: Nuestro medio ambiente
LOCATION: CALIFORNIA

Functions:
- Describing a problem
- Talking about consequences
- Expressing agreement and disagreement
- Talking about obligations and solutions

Grammar:
- Negative words
- **si** clauses in present tense
- **nosotros** commands

Culture:
- The rain forest
- **¿Qué haces para el medio ambiente?**
- Environmental programs
- **el medio ambiente**
- San Diego and Tijuana

Re-entry:
- Affirmative and negative words
- Giving an opinion
- Cognates
- Informal commands

Capítulo 12: Veranos pasados, veranos por venir
LOCATION: CALIFORNIA (REVIEW)

Functions:
- Exchanging the latest news
- Talking about where you went and what you did
- Telling when something happened
- Saying how you feel about people
- Describing places
- Saying when you're going to do something

Grammar:
- The subjunctive mood

Culture:
- Baja California
- **¿Cómo celebran el fin de cursos?**
- **viaje de curso**

Re-entry:
- Chapter 12 is a global review of Chapters 1–11, *Level 2.*

Capítulo 1: ¡Qué bien lo pasé este verano!
LOCATION: LA CORUÑA, SPAIN (REVIEW)

Functions:
- Expressing interest, indifference, and displeasure
- Asking for information
- Describing yourself and others

Grammar:
- Stem-changing verbs in the present tense
- The present tense
- The preterite
- **y** and **o** before vowels
- Adjectives
- **saber** vs. **conocer**

Culture:
- Vacation activities of students from Costa Rica, Spain, and Miami
- Seafood in Spain
- The sport **parapente**

Re-entry:
Chapters 1 and 2 are a global review of *¡Ven conmigo! Levels 1* and *2*

Capítulo 2: Por una vida sana
LOCATION: LA CORUÑA, SPAIN (REVIEW)

Functions:
- Asking for and giving advice
- Talking about taking care of yourself

Grammar:
- Informal commands
- Irregular informal commands
- Reflexive verbs
- The imperfect

Culture:
- Regional languages of Spain
- Work schedules in Spain
- Health habits of people in Spain and Latin America
- Socializing with friends in Spain

Re-entry:
Chapters 1 and 2 are a global review of *¡Ven conmigo! Levels 1* and *2*

Capítulo 3: El ayer y el mañana
LOCATION: CARACAS, VENEZUELA

Functions:
- Talking about what has happened
- Expressing and supporting a point of view
- Using conversational fillers
- Talking about future events
- Talking about responsibilities

Grammar:
- The present perfect
- **lo que**
- The future tense

Culture:
- Today's technology in the Spanish-speaking world
- The role of oil in the Venezuelan economy
- The past and present of Caracas

Re-entry:
- Electrical appliances
- Object pronouns
- **todavía, ya, alguna vez**
- Affirmatives and negatives
- Comparisons of equality and inequality
- **vamos a** + infinitive
- Supporting opinions

Capítulo 4: Alrededor de la mesa
LOCATION: CARACAS, VENEZUELA

Functions:
- Talking about how food tastes
- Talking about unintentional events
- Asking for help and requesting favors

Grammar:
- **se** with unintentional events
- **por** and **para**
- Double object pronouns

Culture:
- The **sobremesa**
- Ways of getting assistance from service personnel
- Foods and holiday dishes of Venezuela
- Favorite foods of typical students from Miami, Quito, and Caracas
- The **causa picante**

Re-entry:
- Ordering a meal
- Making excuses

- Commands
- Pronouns with commands
- The suffix **-ísimo**

Capítulo 5: Nuestras leyendas
LOCATION: GUADALAJARA, MEXICO

Functions:
- Expressing qualified agreement and disagreement
- Reporting what others say and think
- Talking about hopes and wishes

Grammar:
- Impersonal **se**
- The subjunctive to express hopes and wishes
- Subjunctive of **ir, ser, dar**

Culture:
- la "**leyenda negra**"
- Aztec pictographs
- The legends "**La llorona**" and "**La carreta sin bueyes**"
- The legend of Quetzalcóatl
- The legend "**El Quetzal**"

Re-entry:
- Verbs followed by an infinitive

Capítulo 6: El arte y la música
LOCATION: GUADALAJARA, MEXICO

Functions:
- Introducing and changing a topic of conversation
- Expressing what needs to be done
- Expressing an opinion
- Making suggestions and recommendations
- Turning down an invitation

Grammar:
- Gender of some words ending in -**a** and -**o**
- Irregular **yo** forms in the present subjunctive
- The use of **que** with the subjunctive
- **nosotros** commands

Culture:
- The murals of Orozco
- The role of murals in Mexico
- How some Hispanic students express themselves through art
- Musical instruments

- Mexican pop music star Luis Miguel
- Life and works of Frida Kahlo

Re-entry:
- The use of the infinitive vs. the subjunctive
- Formation of the subjunctive
- **ir, ser,** and **dar** in the subjunctive
- Comparisons

Capítulo 7: Dime con quién andas
LOCATION: BUENOS AIRES, ARGENTINA

Functions:
- Expressing happiness and unhappiness
- Comforting someone
- Making an apology

Grammar:
- The subjunctive with expressions of feelings
- Reflexive verbs for reciprocal actions
- The present perfect subjunctive
- The subjunctive with the unknown or nonexistent

Culture:
- The use of **vos**
- Cafés
- The Organization of American States
- The popularity of movies
- The popularity of soccer
- How Spanish-speaking teenagers solve interpersonal problems

Re-entry:
- The use of the infinitive vs. the subjunctive
- Irregular subjunctive
- Past participle forms
- Present perfect subjunctive
- Affirmative and negative words
- Subjunctive forms

Capítulo 8: Los medios de comunicación
LOCATION: BUENOS AIRES, ARGENTINA

Functions:
- Expressing doubt and disbelief
- Expressing certainty
- Talking about possibility and impossibility
- Expressing surprise

Grammar:
- the subjunctive after expressions of doubt and disbelief
- **por** in fixed expressions

- The subjunctive after impersonal expressions

Culture:
- The communications network in Argentina
- How commercials affect our attitudes and behavior
- Newsstands in Buenos Aires

Re-entry:
- Uses of **se**

Capítulo 9: Las apariencias engañan
LOCATION: NUEVA YORK

Functions:
- Talking about your emotional reaction to something
- Expressing disagreement
- Expressing an assumption
- Making hypothetical statements

Grammar:
- The subjunctive after certain conjunctions
- The subjunctive with expressions of denial and disagreement
- The conditional

Culture:
- Hispanics in the United States
- Impressions Spanish-speaking people have of the United States
- Spanish-language media in New York

Re-entry:
- The subjunctive

Capítulo 10: La riqueza cultural
LOCATION: NUEVA YORK

Functions:
- Talking about accomplishments
- Talking about future plans
- Expressing cause and effect
- Expressing intention and purpose

Grammar:
- Verbs after prepositions
- The subjunctive with **para que**

Culture:
- Hispanics in New York City
- How Spanish-speaking students view themselves
- **La Sociedad Hispánica de América**
- **El Ballet Hispánico de Nueva York**

Re-entry:
- The subjunctive with certain conjunctions
- The present perfect

- Reflexive pronouns
- The conditional
- The subjunctive

Capítulo 11: El mundo en que vivimos
LOCATION: COSTA RICA

Functions:
- Pointing out problems and their consequences
- Talking about how you would solve a problem
- Talking about hypothetical situations

Grammar:
- The past subjunctive

Culture:
- Environmental issues facing North and Central America
- Literacy in Costa Rica
- Political stability in Costa Rica
- Conservation in Costa Rica

Re-entry:
- Impersonal **se**
- Talking about consequences
- The conditional
- The preterite

Capítulo 12: Mis planes para el futuro
LOCATION: COSTA RICA (REVIEW)

Functions:
- Talking about former jobs and goals
- Talking about future career plans
- Giving advice and making recommendations about work

Grammar:
- Preterite and imperfect
- Future tense and **ir a** + infinitive
- The subjunctive
- Personal **a** before certain pronouns
- The past subjunctive

Culture:
- Universities in Costa Rica
- Plans some Hispanic students have for the future
- Employment in Costa Rica
- Ecotourism in Costa Rica
- Formality in the Spanish-speaking world

Re-entry:
- Chapter 12 is a global review of Chapters 1–11, *Level 3.*

¡Adelante! pp. T74–15

CHAPTER OVERVIEW

The following material introduced in the **Capítulo preliminar** is presented again for testing in the chapters cited.

TEXTBOOK LISTENING ACTIVITIES SCRIPTS

¿CÓMO TE LLAMAS? pp. 6–7

The script is the same as the list of names in the *Pupil's Edition*, pp. 6–7

3 Nombres en español p. 7

Marta	Miguel	Cristóbal
Claudia	Luisa	Gregorio
Margarita	Isabel	Antonio
Andrés		

EL ALFABETO pp. 8–9

A	a de águila	N	ene de naranja
B	be de bandera	Ñ	eñe de castañuelas
C	ce de ciclismo	O	o de oso
CH	che de chaleco	P	pe de piñata
D	de de dinero	Q	cu de quetzal
E	e de ensalada	R	ere de toro
F	efe de fruta	RR	erre de burro
G	ge de geografía	S	ese de salvavidas
H	hache de helicóptero	T	te de teléfono
I	i de iguana	U	u de uvas
J	jota de jabón	V	ve de violín
K	ka de karate	W	doble ve de Walter
L	ele de lámpara	X	equis de examen
LL	elle de llanta	Y	i griega de yate
M	eme de máscara	Z	zeta de zapatos

6 Por teléfono p. 9

1. Pe, a, u, ele, a; Paula
2. I, ge, ene, a, ce, i, o; Ignacio
3. Jota, o, ere, ge, e; Jorge
4. Eme, a, ere, te, a; Marta
5. A, de, ere, i, a, ene, a; Adriana
6. Che, a, ere, o; Charo

FRASES ÚTILES PARA ESCUCHAR p. 10

Abran el libro (en la página 20), por favor.
Levántense, por favor.
Siéntense, por favor.
Levanten la mano.
Bajen la mano.
Escuchen con atención.
Repitan.
Saquen una hoja de papel.
Silencio, por favor.
Miren la pizarra.

8 Simón dice p. 10

1. Simón dice, "levántense, por favor".
2. Simón dice, "siéntense".
3. Simón dice, "saquen una hoja de papel".
4. Simón dice, "levanten la mano".
5. Bajen la mano.
6. Simón dice, "bajen la mano".
7. Miren la pizarra.
8. Simón dice, "repitan después de mí: ¡Gracias!"

PARA DECIR p. 11

Buenos días.	¿Puedo ir por mi libro?
Buenas tardes.	No entiendo.
¿Cómo se dice... en español?	No sé.
	¿Puede repetir, por favor?
¿Cómo se escribe?	Perdón.
Más despacio, por favor.	Tengo una pregunta.

17 Números de teléfono p. 14

1. Me llamo Nicolás Guillén y mi número de teléfono es el 4-7-3-0-0-1-6.
2. Me llamo Juana Gómez Berea. Mi número de teléfono es el 3-9-1-2-3-4-6.
3. Soy Miguel Campos Romero. Mi número de teléfono es el 7-4-5-0-8-1-2.
4. Soy Cristina García. Mi número de teléfono es el 5-1-0-5-7-2-4.

¡Adelante!
PROJECTS

LAS INTENCIONES CUENTAN

Students will consider their reasons for studying Spanish and set personal goals for the year. Students will share their ideas with the class through creative poster or brochure presentations. You may wish to have students make a brochure to include in their individual Portfolios. (See pages T52–T53.) This project should be completed in English unless you have fluent native speakers. It may be assigned as either an individual or small-group assignment.

Materials students may need

- ◆ Poster board
- ◆ Scissors
- ◆ Tape
- ◆ Travel brochures
- ◆ Construction paper
- ◆ Glue
- ◆ Magazines

Introduction

Have students address the following questions:

- **Motivation**—Why are you learning Spanish? Where could you use the Spanish you will learn? To be able to talk to Spanish speakers you know? Where could you travel to speak Spanish? What country would you like to visit?
- **Objectives**—What would you like to learn in Spanish this semester? (For example, to write a postcard to a Spanish-speaking pen pal.) What words would you like to learn to say?
- **Long-term Application**—Would you like to be able to converse with friends or relatives in Spanish? to write a letter or make a phone call in Spanish?

Sequence

1 Discuss the importance of being clear about personal objectives and goals for language learning. Mention that their perceptions are likely to change throughout the learning process. You may want to share with students your own learning experience. Explain what inspired you to study another language. Recount how your motivation, objectives, and the ways you used your second language unfolded over the years.

2 Describe the project and assign dates for oral presentations. Write project questions on the board, or distribute a project assignment sheet. Be sure to set a firm time limit for presentations.

3 Go over project questions and elicit a few sample answers from the class. If no one has any ideas at first, you might suggest a few of these examples.
   a. Motivation—need to learn a language for high school or college; have Spanish-speaking friends or relatives
   b. Objectives—carry on simple conversations in Spanish; write letters to a Spanish-speaking pen pal; get a good grade in this class
   c. Long-Term Application—talk to Spanish-speaking friends or relatives; travel in Spanish-speaking countries

4 Emphasize that students should be specific about motivation, objectives, and goals. Give students time in class to brainstorm and organize their thoughts.

5 Students create posters based on personal motivations, objectives, and goals. Suggest that they include information on culture, food, work opportunities, and so forth. Encourage students to be as expressive as they wish, using words, photos, and drawings. This can be done in class or at home. Students present their posters or brochures to the class, explaining their reasons for studying Spanish. Students may then select some of the personal goals as class goals.

Grading the project

Because of the personal nature of this project, grading should focus on completion, presentation, and effort.

Suggested point distribution (total = 100 points):

Completion of assignment	**30**
Poster/Brochure	**40**
Effort	**10**
Presentation	**10**
Teamwork (if done as a group)	**10**

EL MUNDO HISPANOHABLANTE

*Making a map of the Spanish-speaking world is a great way to learn the names of the countries and capitals in Spanish. Students identify a Spanish-speaking country by its shape, then find information concerning principal cities and geographical features. They can then relate these locations to the people they will see and hear in the video. A variety of items can be attached to this map as the semester goes by, including pictures of the characters from the **fotonovela**, or small symbols for the items reported about each country in the second half of this project.*

Materials students may need

◆ Large roll of paper
◆ Scissors
◆ Glue or tape
◆ Library Resources
◆ Markers

Sequence

Part 1: Create a **World Map** highlighting Spanish-speaking countries

1 Enlarge a blank, outline map of the countries where Spanish is spoken to make individual maps of each country on standard or legal size paper. You may want to use the Copying Masters of the maps from the *Teaching Transparencies.* Include all the Spanish-speaking countries in South and Central America, the Caribbean, Mexico, and Spain. (You may also include Equatorial Guinea and the Philippines). Do not identify the countries. Pass out the outline maps to pairs of students.

2 Students must identify their individual country, locate its capital, and label both in Spanish on their map. They can use the maps on pages xvii–xxiii. Then have them indicate the capital with a star, draw in mountains, major rivers, and write the names of other cities in Spanish.

TEACHER NOTE

You may wish to assign step two as homework, if students work individually. Set a date for students to bring in their country maps and attach them to the world map in the classroom.

Part 2: **Country Report**

3 Allow pairs or small groups to choose a country for a class report. The project should be flexible enough to allow for individual differences, as well as creative abilities. Stress hands-on action in this activity.

4 Students could make a travel video with two students playing travel guide and tourist respectively. This can be done outside of class, during school with the school's video equipment, or as a class skit. The guide should point out major points of interest and special cultural customs, songs, dances, history, or traditional foods. Students may want to consult travel books for information.

5 Native speakers may choose to demonstrate a dance, teach a song, or bring in traditional foods and explain their importance. One student could explain while the others demonstrate. It is important that the native speakers have the choice whether or not to play this informational role so that they feel comfortable sharing with the class.

6 Other possibilities: students perform skits about the history of the country they have chosen, create a commercial for a Spanish-speaking country, or present cultural customs or other features of the countries to the class. If your school has the technology, have your class design a web page about Latin America using the information they have researched. Allow students to be creative in how they present their country report and have them submit their topics to you for approval.

7 In conjunction with student reports, offer each group suggestions for research. Suggest they call the local consulate or a travel agent to request posters or ask for any free information. Also, they might ask local folklore groups to perform for the class. Check with these contacts beforehand to make sure they are willing to interact with students.

8 Allow library research time. Remind students to check all resources for information, including the Internet.

Grading the project

Suggested Point Distribution (total = 100 points):

Map Identifications	35
Appearance	15
Originality	25
Oral presentation	25

CAPÍTULO
PRELIMINAR

¡Adelante!
GAMES

TEACHER NOTE

Simulations and playful learning activities can be effective teaching tools, lowering students' anxieties and aiding language acquisition. For games to be most beneficial, the atmosphere needs to be fun and relaxed—the students should look forward to doing the activity. Games can be cooperative rather than competitive. Here are some suggestions to help you incorporate games in your lesson plan:

- Games should be played in Spanish as much as possible. Ground rules may be explained in English, as necessary.
- Keep games simple so that a minimum of class time is spent explaining the rules.
- Involve students as scorekeepers or referees, to help with classroom management.
- Choose games that practice comprehension or production in meaningful contexts.
- Identify your teaching objective. Is the game for recognition only? Is it to improve student production, to recycle previously presented material, to practice a particular skill, or to develop higher-order thinking skills?
- Always set a time limit. If you stick to announced time limits, students will help each other stay on task.
- When you find a game that both you and your students respond to well, recycle it in new contexts throughout the year. This will give students a sense of security and continuity and reduce set-up time.

ALFABETO

This game helps students recognize and produce letters in Spanish.

Procedure

1 Write some randomly chosen letters on the board or on a transparency.

2 Ask students recognition questions, such as ¿**Es una "ere"?**

3 Students respond with thumbs up or thumbs down, or by holding up a **sí** or **no** card. Board races are appropriate at this level of recognition as well.

4 Dictate words letter by letter. Try including names of famous people, students' first or last names, your school mascot, or local sports stars. Have students write the words on the board or on paper. Write the words on a transparency so students can check their answers.

¿DERECHA O IZQUIERDA?

This is a game to practice the alphabet, as well as introduce words for left and right. It may be played in small or large groups.

Procedure

1 A group leader stands in the middle of the circle of chairs.

2 The leader says **a la izquierda,** points to a person, and begins counting to 10 in Spanish. That person must say the name of the person to the left and spell it using the Spanish alphabet before the leader counts to 10.

3 If the leader points to a person and says **a la derecha,** that person must say the name of the person to his or her right and spell it.

4 If the person fails to say the letters correctly, he or she takes the role of leader and goes to the center of the circle. The former leader takes the empty chair.

5 You may decide to allow the game to continue until all students have had a turn to be the leader, or you may limit it to only five different leaders.

COLORES

This game is good for visual and tactile learners.

Materials students may need
◆ Colored construction paper
◆ Scissors

Preparation
1 Have students cut colored construction paper into 16 squares by folding it in half three times, unfolding it, and cutting along the folds.
2 Students pass out one square of the color to each student.

Procedure
1 Have students begin by pointing out the colors in Spanish to his or her partner.
2 Then have students arrange the papers left to right or top to bottom on their desks in the order you name the colors.
3 Finally, at the end of the game, students write the Spanish word for the color on their pieces of construction paper to use them as flash cards.

NÚMEROS

This game is good to help students practice recognizing numbers.

Procedure
1 Have students listen as you say various combinations of numbers.
2 Then ask comprehension questions such as: "**Uno-tres-cinco-siete,** even or odd?" "**Nueve-ocho-siete-seis,** forward or backward?"
3 Dictate a series of numbers and have students say or write the next number in the series.

CHALLENGE
Have students solve simple arithmetic problems using numerals as you read the problems to them in Spanish. They will need to know **más** (+), **menos** (−), **por** (×), **dividido por** (÷), and **es/son** (=).

NÚMEROS EN LÍNEA

This game gives students practice understanding and saying numbers in Spanish.

Preparation
Have students prepare index cards with numbers written out as words.

Procedure
1 Randomly pass out cards to students.

2 Instruct students to line up in numerical order in complete silence, then read off their numbers.
3 Repeat the lineup with even numbers (**pares**) on one side of the room and odd numbers (**nones, impares**) on the other or (**del 30 al uno**), or (**por dos**) reading off their cards again after the lineup.

¡Adelante!

VIDEO INTEGRATION

Adelante LEVEL 1A
Video Program,
Videocassette 1, 1:17–4:51 OR
¡Ven conmigo! LEVEL 1
Videodisc Program,
Videodisc 1A

Search 1, Play To 5865

The video for the Preliminary Chapter introduces your students to some of the people they will view in the rest of the program. Some are the actors in the **fotonovelas** found in **De antemano**, and others are people interviewed on the street for the **Panorama cultural.** Play the video now to give your students an introduction to the Spanish language.

MOTIVATING ACTIVITIES

• Ask students: What comes to mind when you think of the Spanish-speaking world? Which states have Spanish names? (Colorado, Florida, Montana, Nevada, California) Can you think of cities with Spanish names? (San Francisco, San Antonio, Boca Raton)

• Ask students to name any movies or TV shows in which Spanish is spoken. Ask if they know of celebrities who have a Hispanic heritage. (Selena, Rosie Perez, Emilio Estevez)

¡Adelante!

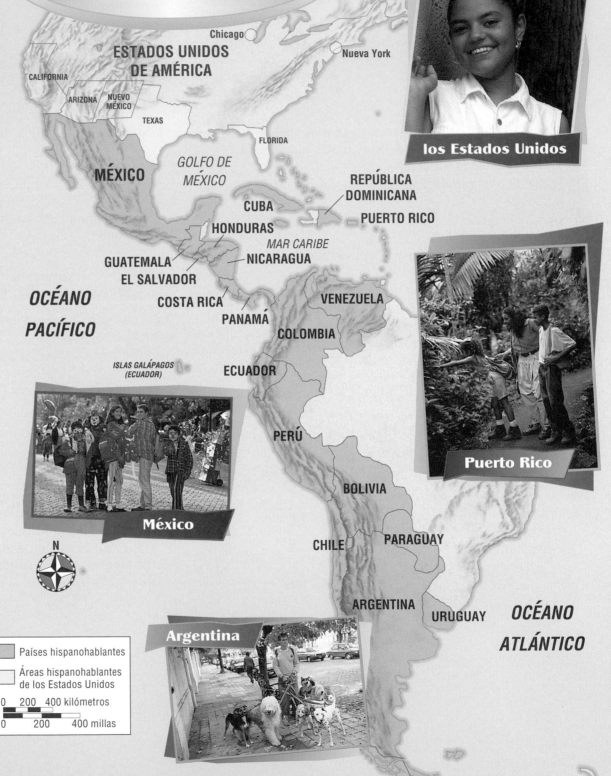

los Estados Unidos

Chicago
ESTADOS UNIDOS DE AMÉRICA
Nueva York
CALIFORNIA
ARIZONA
NUEVO MÉXICO
TEXAS
FLORIDA
MÉXICO
GOLFO DE MÉXICO
REPÚBLICA DOMINICANA
CUBA
PUERTO RICO
HONDURAS
MAR CARIBE
GUATEMALA
NICARAGUA
EL SALVADOR
COSTA RICA
PANAMÁ
VENEZUELA
OCÉANO PACÍFICO
COLOMBIA
ISLAS GALÁPAGOS (ECUADOR)
ECUADOR
PERÚ
BOLIVIA
CHILE
PARAGUAY
ARGENTINA
URUGUAY
OCÉANO ATLÁNTICO

Puerto Rico

México

Argentina

☐ Países hispanohablantes
☐ Áreas hispanohablantes de los Estados Unidos

0   200   400 kilómetros
0   200   400 millas

N

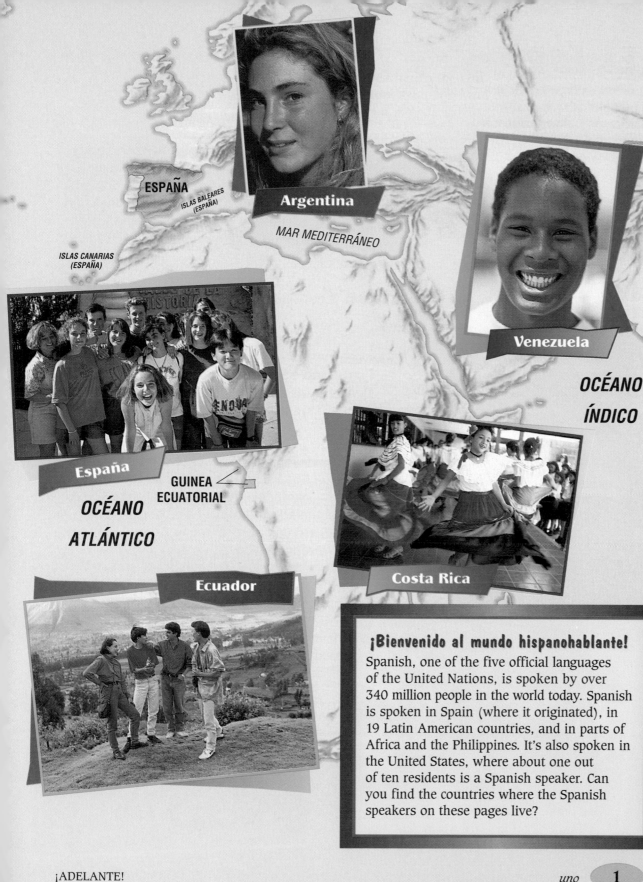

ESPAÑA

ISLAS BALEARES
(ESPAÑA)

MAR MEDITERRÁNEO

Argentina

ISLAS CANARIAS
(ESPAÑA)

Venezuela

OCÉANO
ÍNDICO

España

GUINEA
ECUATORIAL

OCÉANO
ATLÁNTICO

Costa Rica

Ecuador

¡Bienvenido al mundo hispanohablante!

Spanish, one of the five official languages of the United Nations, is spoken by over 340 million people in the world today. Spanish is spoken in Spain (where it originated), in 19 Latin American countries, and in parts of Africa and the Philippines. It's also spoken in the United States, where about one out of ten residents is a Spanish speaker. Can you find the countries where the Spanish speakers on these pages live?

PHOTO FLASH!

Some photos on this page are of people that your students will view in the videos. Some are actors who play characters in the **fotonovelas**, and others are people interviewed on the street in numerous Spanish-speaking countries.

HISTORY LINK

Guinea Ecuatorial *(Equatorial Guinea)* is a country on the west coast of Africa. The territory that the country now occupies was ceded to Spain by Portugal in 1778. Spanish is its official language and is spoken mainly in schools and government offices. In Equatorial Guinea each ethnic group also speaks its own language, such as Fang or Bubi.

HISTORY LINK

The Spanish began colonizing the Philippines in 1565 and ruled the islands until 1898, when they lost control to the United States in the Spanish-American War. They named the islands after King Philip II (**Felipe II**). The Spanish legacy is still felt throughout the region.

1

EL ESPAÑOL—¿POR QUÉ?

There are many reasons for learning to speak Spanish.
Which of these reasons is most important to you?

Parque El Retiro en Madrid, España

Each language has its own personality. To really get to know someone, you have to speak that person's language. Someday you may travel to a Spanish-speaking country. Whatever your reason for going, you'll get a lot more out of your stay if you can speak the language.

You're living in one of the major Spanish-speaking countries right now—the United States! Learning Spanish can open up a whole new world of information, entertainment, and adventure. Spanish-language movies, books, videos, magazines, TV shows, and music are all around you.

One of the best reasons for studying Spanish is for satisfaction. Studying another language is a challenge to your mind. And you get a great feeling of accomplishment the first time you have a conversation in Spanish!

Playa en Chile

Festival en la Calle Ocho en Miami

Colegio en Cuernavaca, México

¿SABÍAS...?

Spanish language and culture are important parts of our national history. As you begin your study of Spanish, you should be aware that . . .

▼ the Spanish were among the first European explorers in what is today the United States.

▼ the Spaniards founded St. Augustine (**San Agustín**), Florida, the first European settlement in the United States, in 1565.

▼ parts of the U.S. once belonged to Mexico.

▼ Spanish is the second most frequently spoken language in the U.S.

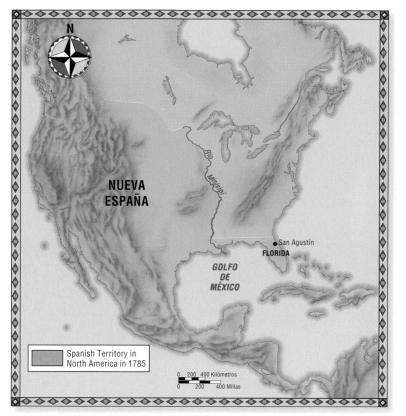

NUEVA ESPAÑA

GOLFO DE MÉXICO

San Agustín
FLORIDA

Spanish Territory in North America in 1785

0   200   400 Kilómetros
0   200   400 Millas

1 Herencia hispana   Answers will vary. Possible answers below:

Working in small groups, discuss the following topics. Share your findings with the class.

1. Many cities in the U.S. have Spanish names. Name four cities that you know of with Spanish names. (Hint: Many begin with San, Los, and Las.)
2. Many foods common in the U.S. come from Spanish-speaking countries. List two foods from a Spanish-speaking country that you've eaten or have heard of.
3. Using the maps on pages xvii–xxiii, name two Spanish-speaking countries that you've heard something about. Choose one country and list at least two things you know about it.
4. Can you name three famous Spanish-speaking people? They can be a movie star, a singer, an athlete . . .

1. Los Angeles, San Diego, San Antonio, Albuquerque, Santa Fe, Las Vegas, San Francisco   2. taco, enchilada, burrito, salsa, chocolate, tortilla, fajita
3. Answers will vary.   4. Antonio Banderas, Gloria Estefan, Sergi Bruguera, Jennifer López

¡ADELANTE!

tres 3

BACKGROUND

St. Augustine, Florida, was founded in 1565 by Pedro Menéndez de Avilés, a Spaniard. It is considered the first permanent European settlement in what is today the United States. St. Augustine is on the northeastern coast of Florida just south of Jacksonville.

HISTORY LINK

In 1848 the Mexican Congress signed **el Tratado de Guadalupe Hidalgo,** ending the Mexican-American War. With this treaty Mexico ceded to the United States more than one-third of Mexico's total territory—the present-day states of Texas, California, Arizona, New Mexico, Nevada, Utah, and part of Colorado.

SUGGESTION

1 You may wish to make this an overnight assignment.

LANGUAGE NOTE

The word **chocolate** came into Spanish from Nahuatl, an indigenous language spoken in central and western Mexico. **Xocolatl** (*sho-ko-la-tul*), meaning *bitter water,* is the Nahuatl word for a drink made from the cacao plant. The Aztec nobility drank it without sugar. Today, there are over one million native Nahuatl speakers in Mexico.

¿LOS CONOCES? PA p. 1 Act. 1

Spanish speakers from all over the world have made valuable contributions in science, sports, politics, and the arts.

Miguel de Cervantes y Saavedra (1547–1616) was the author of *Don Quixote*, one of the great works of Spanish literature. He wrote very realistic stories about life in Spain at the end of the 16th century.

Mariano Rivera (b. 1969), from Panama City, Panama, is a pitcher for the New York Yankees. He helped his team win the 1996 World Series.

Simón Bolívar (1783–1830), born in Caracas, Venezuela, led a brilliant struggle against Spanish colonialism that helped win independence for most of South America. Today he is honored as **el Libertador**, The Liberator.

La Reina Isabel (Isabel I of Spain; 1451–1504) helped unite what is today modern Spain by marrying Fernando, King of Aragon. We know her best for paying for Columbus's voyage to the New World.

Frida Kahlo (1907–1954), a Mexican artist, is most famous for the paintings she made of herself. Like her husband, the famous painter and muralist Diego Rivera, Frida Kahlo painted the history and political life of her country.

Rigoberta Menchú (b. 1959), a Guatemalan Quiché woman, won the 1992 Nobel Prize for speaking out against the inhumane treatment of the indigenous people of Central America.

Desiderio (Desi) Arnaz (1917–1986), a native of Cuba, is best known as Ricky Ricardo on the 1950s TV show *I Love Lucy*. The 3-camera system he created for *I Love Lucy* set the standard for television filming and is still used today.

Arantxa Sánchez Vicario (b. 1971) is one of Spain's hottest tennis stars. She has won both the French and U.S. Opens. With over eight tournament titles, she is well on her way to being one of the world's leading tennis players.

¡ADELANTE!

HISTORY LINK

A memorable figure in Mexican history is Benito Pablo Juárez (1806–1872). Mexicans regard him as one of their greatest presidents, much as Americans regard Abraham Lincoln. During his presidency (1861–1872) he was responsible for leading the campaign that ended French occupation in Mexico. Today Mexicans celebrate **el Cinco de mayo** to commemorate this.

SCIENCE LINK

A noted figure in science is Spanish engineer Juan de la Cierva (1895–1936). His invention of the hinged flapping rotor blade and autogyro set the stage for the development of the modern-day helicopter.

¿CÓMO TE LLAMAS?

PA p. 1 Act. 2

Cass. 1A
CD 1 Tr. 1

Here are some common names from Spanish-speaking countries. Choose a name for yourself from the list if you wish. Script is the list of names on these two pages.

Me llamo Teresa.

Adela

Alicia (Licha)

Ana, Anita

Ángela, Angélica

Beatriz

Carmen

Catalina (Cata)

Claudia

Cristina (Tina)

Daniela

Dolores (Lola)

Elena (Nena)

Graciela (Chela)

Inés

Isabel (Isa)

Juana

Luisa

Margarita

María

Marisol (Mari)

Marta

Mercedes (Merche)

Natalia

Paloma

Pilar

Rosario (Charo)

Sara

Susana

Teresa

Verónica (Vero)

Me llamo Ema.

2 Mis amigos

Find and write Spanish names from pages six and seven that match the names of at least six of your family members, friends, or classmates. Check to see that you've written the accents in the correct places.

Answers will vary, see names on these pages.

CAPÍTULO PRELIMINAR ¡Adelante!

Alberto
Alejandro (Alejo)
Andrés
Antonio (Toño)
Carlos
Cristóbal
Diego
Eduardo (Lalo)
Francisco (Paco)
Gregorio
Guillermo
Ignacio (Nacho)
Jaime
Jesús (Chuy)
Jorge

José (Pepe)
Juan
Julio
Lorenzo
Luis
Manuel
Mario
Miguel
Pablo
Pedro
Rafael (Rafa)
Ricardo
Roberto (Beto)
Santiago
Tomás

Me llamo Pablo.

Me llamo César.

GAME

4 Have students line up in alphabetical order according to their chosen Spanish name. They are only allowed to say their Spanish name and are not allowed to speak in English.

CHALLENGE

After reviewing these two pages of Spanish names, have students go around a circle saying Spanish names in alphabetical order. For example, if the first student says Alberto, then the next would say Beatriz, the third Carmen, and so on.

CULTURE NOTE

It is very popular in the Dominican Republic to give children Russian names. (Vladimir, Katirina, Ivan, Tavia) It is also popular to give children name of countries and cities. (América, Venecia, Roma, Australia)

LANGUAGE NOTE

An **apodo** is an affectionate nickname, such as **el gallo**, or **la rubia**, which is frequently given to fellow students in school.

3 Nombres en español Script on p. T69

Cass. 1A
CD 1 Tr. 2

Listen to a series of names in Spanish and repeat them aloud after the speaker. Try to guess the English equivalent of each one. Does your name have an equivalent in Spanish?

4 Me llamo...

Form a name chain in your row. The first person turns to a classmate and asks his or her name. That person answers with a chosen name in Spanish, and then asks the next person's name. Keep going to the end of the row.

MODELO —¿Cómo te llamas?
—Me llamo Carlos.
¿Cómo te llamas?

Los acentos

You may have noticed the accent mark (´) and the tilde (~) on letters in the name chart. They're used to help you pronounce the words correctly. You'll learn more about these and other special marks, including the upside-down question mark and exclamation point, in Chapter 1.

MOTIVATING ACTIVITY
To build confidence, help students identify the Spanish cognates such as **ciclismo**, **ensalada**, **examen**, or **violín**.

SUGGESTION
• Before students try to produce the sounds themselves, have them point to the corresponding letter and picture as they listen to the **Alfabeto** on Audiocassette 1A or Audio CD 1 Track 3.
• A recitation of the alphabet in Spanish is on the Preliminary Chapter segment of the video.

AUDITORY LEARNERS
Students may like to chant rhymes or make up rap tunes to learn the correct sounds. **(A-E-I-O-U, Yo me llamo María. ¿Cómo te llamas tú?)** As their vocabulary increases, encourage students who respond well to this approach to revise their rhymes to include new words.

NATIVE SPEAKERS
Have native speakers begin a notebook in which they write down words that are commonly misspelled. Have them focus on the following letters or combinations of letters, one page for each: *b, ce, ci, ge, gi, h, j, ll, s, v, z.* Point out that the pronunciation of a word will help them spell it, but words with these letters must be memorized.

EL ALFABETO

Script on p. T67
Cass. 1A CD 1 Tr. 3
PA p. 2 Act. 3

The Spanish alphabet isn't quite the same as the English one. What differences do you notice? Listen to the names of the letters and repeat after the speaker.

Although **ch** and **ll** have been officially dropped from the Spanish alphabet, dictionaries and glossaries published before 1994 will continue to show them as separate entries.

águila

bandera

ciclismo

chaleco

dinero

ensalada

fruta

geografía

helicóptero

iguana

jabón

karate

lámpara

llanta

5 Los cognados
Cognates are words in Spanish and English that look similar. Although they're pronounced differently, they often have the same meaning—but not always! For example, **asistir** means *attend,* not *assist.* There are seven cognates in this ad. Can you find them?

correspondencia, inteligente, sincera, sociable, música, teléfono, televisión

☛ **Busco amigo por correspondencia**
Me llamo Catalina. Soy inteligente, sincera y muy sociable. Me gusta leer, escuchar música, hablar por teléfono y mirar televisión.

M máscara

N naranja

Ñ castañuelas

O oso

P piñata

Q quetzal

R toro

RR burro

S salvavidas

T teléfono

U uvas

V violín

W Walter

X examen

Y yate

Z zapatos

6 ## Por teléfono Script on p. T67

Cass. 1A
CD 1 Tr. 4

Imagine that you work as a receptionist answering the phone.
Listen as six Spanish speakers spell their names for you. Write
each name as you hear it spelled.

7 ## ¿Cómo se escribe...?

Spell each of the following items to your partner, in Spanish. Your
partner will write each word as you spell it. Switch roles when
you're done. Answers will vary.

1. your first name   2. your last name   3. the name of your school

¡ADELANTE!

nueve **9**

SUGGESTIONS

• Dictate the spelling of words
and have students find them
in the illustrations.

• Dictate a list of items for students to remember on a trip
to the grocery store. (**jabón,
fruta, naranja, uvas, dinero**)

CHALLENGE

6 Spell students' last names
out loud in Spanish and ask
them to raise their hands when
they recognize their own names.

SUGGESTION

7 Teach students **con
mayúscula**. Point out that
names are capitalized in
Spanish just as they are in
English. Teach **con acento** or
lleva acento as well. (**eme
con mayúscula, a, ere, i con
acento, a: María**)

LANGUAGE NOTES

• Although the **Real Academia**
deleted the letters *ch* and *ll*
from the alphabet, many dictionaries still have separate
entries for these letters.
The vocabulary lists in this
book follow the new rules,
with *ch* and *ll* in sequence:
"*ce...ch...ci*" and "*li...ll...lo.*"

• Although in the Americas *rr*
is commonly recognized as
a separate letter, the **Real
Academia** does not officially
recognize it.

TPR Play **Frases útiles** on Audiocassette 1A Audio CD 1 Track 5. Or pronounce the commands for students yourself. Practice having students carry out the commands as you say them.

GAMES

Mímica Have students play charades. One student acts out a phrase without speaking and the other students guess what the phrase is in Spanish.

Tiritas Divide the class into groups of three to five. Have the groups write each word in the phrases on a separate scrap of paper (one per piece of paper). Have students scramble the scraps. With books closed, dictate the phrases while students arrange the scraps to form the Spanish phrases. The first group to get the correct answer gets a point.

ADDITIONAL PRACTICE

8 Play **Simón dice**. Have students take turns being **Simón**. See Script page T67.

Answers to Activity 9

1. Siéntense, por favor.
2. Silencio, por favor.
3. Abran el libro.
4. Saquen una hoja de papel.
5. Escuchen con atención.
6. Levántense, por favor.

FRASES ÚTILES

PA p. 2 Act. 4

Para escuchar   Script on p. T67

Here are some phrases you'll probably hear regularly in Spanish class. Learn to recognize them and answer appropriately.

Cass. 1A
CD 1 Tr. 5

Miren la pizarra.

Abran el libro (en la página 20), por favor.	*Open your books (to page 20), please.*
Levántense, por favor.	*Please stand up.*
Siéntense, por favor.	*Please sit down.*
Levanten la mano.	*Raise your hands.*
Bajen la mano.	*Put your hands down.*
Escuchen con atención.	*Listen closely.*
Repitan.	*Repeat.*
Saquen una hoja de papel.	*Take out a sheet of paper.*
Silencio, por favor.	*Silence, please.*
Miren la pizarra.	*Look at the chalkboard.*

8 Simón dice   Script on p. T67

Listen to some commands and do what the person says, such as raising your hand or opening your book. Respond only if the speaker says **Simón dice**.

Cass. 1A
CD 1 Tr. 6

9 ¿Qué dice?

Get together with a partner and find the phrase from the list that Mrs. Mercado, the new Spanish teacher, would use in the following situations.   Answers in side column

1. She wants the students to sit down.
2. She wants everyone to be quiet.
3. She wants everyone to open their books.
4. She wants everyone to take out a sheet of paper.
5. She wants everyone to listen carefully.
6. She wants everyone to stand up.

Para decir

Script on p. T67

Cass. 1A
CD 1 Tr. 7

Here are some phrases that you'll need to use often. Learn as many as you can and use them when they're appropriate.

Tengo una pregunta.

Buenos días.	*Good morning.*
Buenas tardes.	*Good afternoon.*
¿Cómo se dice... en español?	*How do you say . . . in Spanish?*
¿Cómo se escribe...?	*How do you spell . . .?*
Más despacio, por favor.	*Slower, please.*
¿Puedo ir por mi libro?	*Can I go get my book?*
No entiendo.	*I don't understand.*
No sé.	*I don't know.*
¿Puede repetir, por favor?	*Can you repeat, please?*
Perdón.	*Excuse me.*
Tengo una pregunta.	*I have a question.*

10 ¿Qué haría?

What would Mr. García, the Spanish teacher, do if one of his students said each of the following? Match each item with an appropriate answer.

1. Más despacio, por favor. c
2. Tengo una pregunta. e
3. No entiendo. b
4. ¿Puede repetir, por favor? d
5. ¿Cómo se dice *Good morning* en español? a

a. He would say **Buenos días**.
b. He would explain the lesson another way.
c. He would speak slower.
d. He would repeat what he just said.
e. He would ask what the question is.

11 Situaciones

What would you say in the following situations? Choose your responses from the list above. Answers in side column

1. You see your teacher at the store one afternoon.
2. You don't understand the directions.
3. Your teacher is talking too fast.
4. You don't know the answer.
5. You'd like to ask a question.
6. You need to hear something again.

ADDITIONAL VOCABULARY

Para escuchar If you use an overhead transparency instead of a chalkboard, you may wish to teach the phrase **Miren la transparencia**. Another command you may find helpful is **¡Libros al suelo!**

Para decir Additional phrases you may wish to teach your students are **¿Qué quiere decir...?**; **No oigo**; **¿Puedo ir al baño?**; **¿Puedo ir a la oficina?**

Answers to Activity 11

1. Buenas tardes.
2. No entiendo.
3. Más despacio, por favor. / ¿Puede repetir, por favor?
4. No sé.
5. Tengo una pregunta.
6. ¿Puede repetir, por favor?

11

LOS COLORES

PA p. 3
Act. 7

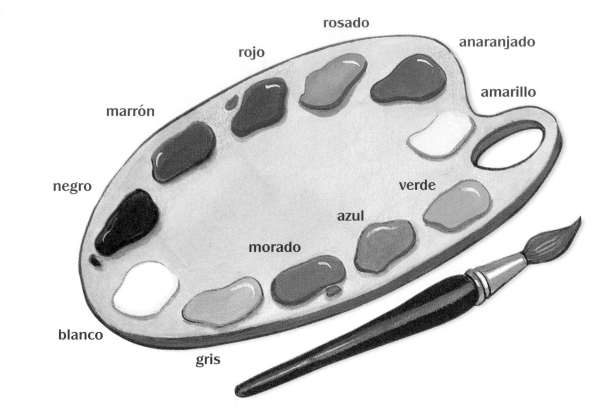

rosado

rojo

anaranjado

amarillo

marrón

negro

verde

azul

morado

blanco

gris

SUGGESTIONS

- Let students be creative in the colors they say but ask them to explain their choices. For example, leaves may be red, orange, or yellow in the fall and strawberries have a green stem and black spots.

- For personalization, point to various clothing items worn by students as you say the corresponding color.

- Ask students to name the colors of various classroom items. To evaluate listening comprehension, have students respond **cierto** or **falso** to your statements about colors in the room. For example, **El libro _Adelante_ es amarillo. (cierto)**

- Some of your students may be colorblind (unable to distinguish between two or more of the colors red, green, and blue). With a colorblind student, you should stress color associations (fruits, plants, holidays) rather than color distinctions.

ADDITIONAL VOCABULARY

café; pardo _brown_
(café) claro _light (brown)_
(azul) oscuro _dark (blue)_
oro _gold_
plata _silver_

12 Colores típicos

What colors come to mind when you think of the following things? Say them in Spanish. Answers will vary. Possible answers:

1. a zebra blanco, negro
2. the sky azul, blanco, gris
3. coffee marrón
4. a banana amarillo, verde, negro
5. grape juice morado
6. a tire negro
7. a traffic light rojo, amarillo, verde
8. grass verde
9. a strawberry rojo
10. a pumpkin anaranjado
11. a cloudy day gris, blanco
12. snow blanco

13 ¿Qué cosas son de este color?

Get together with a partner. For each of the following colors, name three things that are that color. Answers will vary. Possible answers:

1. azul blueberries, the sky, bluebirds
2. rojo cherries, fire engines, cardinals
3. morado grapes, violets, eggplants
4. negro coal, newsprint, the night sky
5. verde celery, spinach, grass
6. amarillo the sun, squash, lemons

EL CALENDARIO

PA p. 3 Act. 8

Los días de la semana

enero semana 1			
1	lunes	5	viernes
2	martes	6	sábado
3	miércoles	7	domingo
4	jueves		

14 ¿Qué día es?

If **el lunes** is *Monday*, what days do you think the following are?

1. el jueves Thursday
2. el viernes Friday
3. el miércoles Wednesday

Which days in Spanish are the following?

4. Sunday el domingo
5. Tuesday el martes
6. Saturday el sábado

Los meses del año

PA p. 4 Act. 9

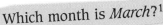
Which month is *March*?[1]

la primavera
· marzo
· abril
· mayo

el invierno
· diciembre
· enero
· febrero

el verano
· junio
· julio
· agosto

el otoño
· septiembre
· octubre
· noviembre

15 ¿En qué mes estamos?

Talk to your partner about what months of the year and what season it might be when these things happen. Answers will vary. Possible answers:

1. It snows outside.
2. People celebrate Thanksgiving.
3. You and your friends go swimming.
4. You don't have school.
5. Leaves fall off the trees.
6. It rains a lot outside.

---

[1]*March* is **marzo**.

1. diciembre, enero, febrero, el invierno
2. noviembre, el otoño
3. junio, julio, agosto, el verano
4. junio, julio, agosto, el verano
5. septiembre, octubre, noviembre, el otoño
6. marzo, abril, mayo, la primavera

¡ADELANTE!

trece **13**

LOS NÚMEROS

PA p. 4 Act. 10

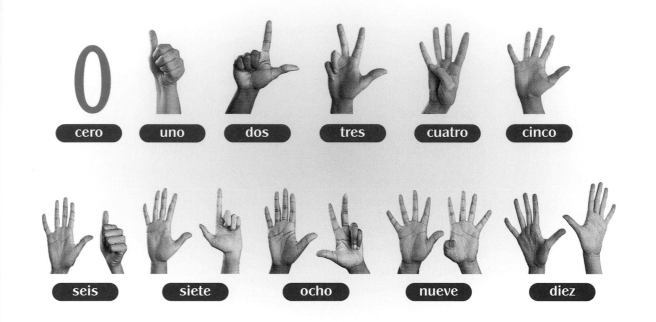

cero   uno   dos   tres   cuatro   cinco

seis   siete   ocho   nueve   diez

16 Números de todos los días

What numbers come to mind when you look at each of the following items? Make up your own for the last item.

1. a pair of tennis shoes dos
2. your fingers cinco, diez
3. a tricycle tres
4. a pack of soft drink cans seis
5. an octopus ocho
6. a rectangle cuatro
7. a week siete
8. ¿? Answers will vary.

17 Números de teléfono

Script on p. T69

Cass.1A
CD 1 Tr. 8

Listen as four Spanish speakers tell you their telephone numbers. Based on what you hear, match each speaker's name with the right number.

1. Nicolás   3. Miguel
2. Juana   4. Cristina

Miguel
745-08-12

Juana
391-23-46

Cristina
510-57-24

Nicolás
473-00-16

Del once al treinta

11 once   **16** dieciséis   **21** veintiuno   **26** veintiséis

12 doce   **17** diecisiete   **22** veintidós   **27** veintisiete

13 trece   **18** dieciocho   **23** veintitrés   **28** veintiocho

14 catorce   **19** diecinueve   **24** veinticuatro   **29** veintinueve

15 quince   **20** veinte   **25** veinticinco   **30** treinta

18 Datos importantes

Use numbers in Spanish to give the following information.

                                              Answers will vary.

1. your age
2. your telephone number and area code
3. your zip code
4. the number of students in your row

19 Placas y permisos en México

Your partner will read a number or name a color from these license stickers and plates. If you hear a number, name a color from the license plate that has that number, and vice versa. Switch roles after four or five tries.   *Answers will vary.*

MODELO   —¿QZB 7829?
                  —Verde.
                  —¡Sí!

997 FEV   DF 99 MEX

(a)

QZB 7829   MEX MEX

(b)

996 FEP   DF 99 MEX

(c)

KZY 8762   DF MEX

(d)

15

BACKGROUND

19 Items **a.** and **c.** are registration stickers that change yearly. Item **b.** is a license plate from the State of Mexico, and item **d.** is from Tamaulipas. Cars keep the same plates for ten years. Registration stickers are placed on the inside of the windshield. Cars from Mexico City and surrounding areas have to show that they have passed the six-month smog inspection. Cars must also have a sticker (not shown in text, but on the Level 1 *Videodisc Program*) for pollution control. It is called **la calcomanía** or **el engomado** and says **Hoy No Circula**. This sticker designates the day of the week when the car may not be driven.

PRINT	MEDIA

Adelante LEVEL 1A

CD-ROM Teacher's Guide
◆ Location 1, p. xxxiv

Video Guide
◆ Activity Masters and Teaching Suggestions, pp. 3–4

Interactive CD-ROM Program
◆ Disc 1

Video Program
◆ Videocassette 1

¡Ven conmigo! LEVEL 1

Videodisc Guide
◆ Activity Masters and Teaching Suggestions, pp. 4–6
◆ Additional Stills, p. 5

Videodisc Program
◆ Videodisc 1A

The **acueducto de Segovia** is an example of Roman engineering in Spain. Built in the second century BC, this structure is made up of interlocking granite blocks that are held in place without mortar. It carried water to the city until modern times.

Segovia aqueduct

Search Frame 42693

The **Castillo de Alcázar**, in Segovia, was constructed as a fortress in the 12th century. When it was restored after a 19th-century fire, some of the most decorative elements of the castle were added, making it look more like a fairy-tale castle than a fortress.

Castillo de Alcázar

Search Frame 45155

El Templo de la Sagrada Familia in Barcelona was begun as a neo-Gothic construction in 1882 and was taken over by Antonio Gaudí y Cornet in 1891. Gaudí's plan for the cathedral included towers that resembled trees and vines instead of traditional pillars. Gaudí passed away at an early age in 1926, but the cathedral is still under construction to this day.

Sagrada Familia

Search Frame 9463

Every year in March, Valencia celebrates **las Fallas**, a tradition dating back to the Middle Ages when carpenters burned wood shavings in bonfires to honor Saint Joseph, patron saint of woodworkers. The tradition evolved into current celebrations in which huge satirical structures of wood, papier mâché, and cardboard are constructed and eventually burned.

Fallas in Valencia

Search Frame 8409

Many cities in Spanish-speaking countries have a central square called the **plaza mayor**. Children, teens and older people, gather in the **plaza** to walk and talk. In Madrid, **la Plaza Mayor** is a popular meeting place for people of all ages.

Plaza Mayor

Search Frame 9077

The following Web sites contain additional information on Spain. Since addresses and content change frequently, you might want to preview them before attempting to access them in class.

Spain Online magazine
http://www.spainonline.com

Free Internet Encyclopedia
http://clever.net/cam/encyclopedia.html

El país Spanish news
http://www.elpais.es

PROJECT

✂ EL ARTE ÁRABE

Many buildings in southern Spain show Arabic influence in their designs and ornamentation. The elaborate geometric figures of the Alhambra are a good example. Explain to students that the designs don't include people or animals as the Islamic religion forbids the portrayal of human or animal figures. Have students draw one of the geometric patterns portrayed on the walls of the Alhambra.

Materials students may need

- ◆ Drawing paper
- ◆ Drawing compass (to make circles)
- ◆ Pencils, pens, and colored markers
- ◆ Rulers

Sequence

1. Present students with pictures of the **Alhambra** from an encyclopedia or reference book. Show students several examples of the geometric patterns.

2. Point out that the patterns are repeated geometric shapes. Many patterns are based upon a circle, using the center point as the anchor for a particular shape.

3. Have each student choose one figure they would like to draw and make a pattern for the shape that is repeated.

Challenge

The following is an example of a more complex pattern of geometric shapes from the Alhambra. For a challenge, have students make the three patterns for the design, trace the outline of the geometrical shapes on paper, and color them in. Hint: Have students trace the shape that looks like a three-legged starfish first, and then trace the star and hexagon shapes.

Grading the project

Suggested point distribution (total = 100 points):

Overall appearance	**25**
Neatness	**25**
Creativity	**25**
Artistic design	**25**

¡Ven conmigo a España!

LOCATION OPENER CHAPTERS 1, 2 (cont.)

Using the Map
- Have students find the capital of Spain. (Madrid)
- Have students identify the other country occupying the Iberian Peninsula. (Portugal) Explain that the Portuguese language is related to Spanish and is similar in many ways.
- Have students identify Spain's neighbors to the north, west, and south. (France, Andorra, Portugal, Morocco)
- Have students find the areas on the map where other languages of Spain are spoken.
- Have students locate Gibraltar. Ask them if they have heard of the Rock of Gibraltar, a large limestone mass that occupies most of Gibraltar's 2.3 square miles. You may want to point out that Gibraltar has been a British possession since 1713.
- Point out the short distance between Spain and Morocco. A distance of only 8 miles separates the Spanish town of Algeciras from the coast of North Africa. (about one hour by ferry)
- Point out Ceuta, part of Spain that is in Africa.

Thinking Critically
Ask students what language the majority of the people in the U.S. speak. Then tell them we speak English because England colonized the U.S. Have them compare and contrast what would have happened had the French colonized. Have students think about that for a moment. Then ask students if they know what language is spoken in most of Latin American countries. If they can tell you Spanish, have them think about why. Tell them that it's because Spain colonized most of Latin America.

History Link
The North Africans who conquered Spain in the early 700s were Muslims (**musulmanes**), followers of Islam. These Arabic-speaking people brought with them very sophisticated science, mathematics, architecture, culture, and medicine.

Slower Pace
Have students study the photograph of the Segovia castle on pages 16–17. Ask them to describe what they see. Lead a discussion about the differences between what is portrayed in the photo and the land, buildings, and culture in the city where they live.

NATIVE SPEAKER
Ask native speakers if they know about some customs or regional idioms from Spain. Some examples are **Vale** for *OK,* **patata** for **papa**. What are some other examples that students know?

Language Notes

- In 1492, the Catholic kings reconquered the remaining Moorish territories on the Iberian Peninsula and expelled the Jewish people. Many fled to the Balkans and Israel. Today, those people (Sephardic Jews) still speak a Castilian-like language called Ladino. It contains many elements of 15th-century Castilian that are no longer present in today's Spanish. For example, **hijo** is *fijo,* **hablar** is *fablar,* and **ahora** is *agora*. Like Yiddish, Ladino is written using the Hebrew alphabet.

- Many words in the Spanish language that begin with **al-** are Arabic in origin:

alcalde (m.)	*mayor, judge*	**almohada**	*pillow*
almacén (m.)	*store*	**alquilar**	*to rent*
alfombra	*rug*	**albóndiga**	*meatball*

- Just as U.S. English differs from British English, so too does Latin American Spanish differ from Peninsular Spanish. Furthermore, the varieties of Spanish spoken in countries within Latin America differ from each other in both vocabulary and pronunciation.

Culture Note

Madrid, the capital of Spain, has many attractions to keep a tourist busy. One can sit and enjoy a **tortilla española** in a café, row boats on the lake in the **Parque del Retiro,** visit the fashionable shops downtown, or spend a quiet afternoon in the world-renowned **Museo del Prado**.

Multicultural Link

Have students name some annual celebrations from your area. (Thanksgiving, New Year's, etc.) Ask students if they are familiar with annual celebrations in other countries. This is an opportunity for students of other backgrounds to share their heritage with the class. Ask students if they have ever heard of the Running of the Bulls. It is a celebration known as **El Día de San Fermín** in Pamplona where it is held every July. Bulls are set loose in the streets, where only the most daring try to outrun them without getting hurt.

¡Ven conmigo a España!

VIDEO INTEGRATION

Adelante LEVEL 1A
Video Program,
Videocassette 1, 4:52–7:26 OR
¡Ven conmigo! LEVEL 1
Videodisc Program,
Videodisc 1A

Search 5865, Play To 10545

MOTIVATING ACTIVITY

Before students open their books, have them brainstorm about what they think Spain is like. Then have them compare their guesses to what they see in the photographs on pages 16–19.

BACKGROUND

The word **alcázar** means *fortified palace* or *fortress* in Arabic. The **Castillo de Alcázar** in Segovia was constructed as a fortress in the 13th century. In 1474, **la Princesa Isabel** left the **Alcázar** to be crowned the queen of Castile. In the 16th century, the tower was used as a state prison. The **Castillo de Alcázar** is one of 1,400 castles and palaces in Spain.

Segovia has one of the best-preserved Roman aqueducts. The aqueduct was used to bring water to the city from the **Río Frío**. It is almost 100 feet tall at its highest point. The Romans built this aqueduct around 50 A.D.

16

CAPÍTULOS 1 Y 2

The *Castillo de Alcázar* in Segovia, Spain, is more than 700 years old.

¡Ven conmigo a España!

España

Population: more than 39,000,000

Area: 504,788 kms^2 (194,898 sq. mi.). Spain is larger than California, but smaller than Texas.

Capital: Madrid; population: about 3 million

Government: constitutional monarchy (King Juan Carlos I since 1975), with an elected parliament

Industries: food products, automobiles, steel, ships, textiles

Monetary unit: peseta

Main languages: Spanish, Catalan, Basque, Galician

USING THE ALMANAC

- **Government:** The king serves as Spain's head of state. Although he does not have a direct role in running the government, he is an advisor.

- **Main Languages:** Although Castilian Spanish (**el castellano**) is the official language, there are also three other major languages. Catalan (**el catalán**) is spoken in the region around Barcelona; Basque (**el vasco**), also called Euskera, is spoken in the region around Bilbao, and Galician (**el gallego**) is spoken in the northwest region of Spain bordering Portugal.

diecisiete 17

USING THE PHOTO ESSAY

❶ In mountainous northern Spain people enjoy many outdoor sports such as white water rafting, hiking, climbing, and camping.

❷ The Costa Brava is a beautiful coastal zone north of Barcelona with steep cliffs, small coves, and finely grained sand. People from all over the world come to enjoy its beaches.

❸ The Pyrenees Mountains (**los Pirineos**) stretch over 270 miles with a maximum width of about 100 miles. They form the boundary between France and Spain. Only Switzerland surpasses Spain as Europe's most mountainous country. The **Pico de Aneto** in Aragon is the tallest peak in the Pyrenees, at 11,169 feet. This peak is as tall as 11 Empire State buildings.

MOTIVATING ACTIVITY

Can students think of any regions in the United States that have large mountains? (the Colorado Rockies, the Adirondacks, the Appalachians)

ESPAÑA

What comes to mind when you think of Spain? Spain is known for its beautiful architecture and rich cultural history dating back tens of thousands of years. The different regions of Spain have distinct landscapes and cultures. Many of these regions still retain their own languages.

▲ **Aventuras en los ríos**
The swift waters and rugged terrain in northern Spain are ideal for white water rafting adventures.

◄ **Las playas de la Costa Brava**
The beaches of the Costa Brava in northeastern Spain are very popular.

Esquiar en los Pirineos ►
The Pyrenees Mountains form a natural border separating Spain from the rest of Europe. Abundant snowfall on the higher peaks makes them an excellent location for winter sports.

Chapters 1 and 2 will introduce you to some students who live in Madrid, the capital of Spain. Located in the center of the country, Madrid is a large, modern city of about three million people. Both visitors and **madrileños** *(the residents of Madrid) love to explore the city's cultural treasures, parks, and cafés.*

▲ **Los parques de Barcelona**
Barcelona, like many cities in Spain, has beautiful parks where families and friends go to relax.

El baile flamenco ▶
This young woman is wearing a traditional costume of Andalucía. Costumes like these are often worn to dance flamenco, a music and dance tradition that originated with the gypsies in southern Spain.

❹ One of the most famous parks in Barcelona is Güell Park, which was designed by Antonio Gaudí, a Catalonian architect (1852–1926). It has curved benches, decorative staircases, and a breathtaking view of the city.

❺ **Flamenco**, a lively tradition in **Andalucía,** is a dance of complex rhythms that involves acoustic guitar, hand-clapping, clicking castanets, and heel-stomping. The art of flamenco is a prime example of the blend of cultures that occurred in Spain. Experts continue to debate about the exact contributions of Andalusian popular songs, gypsy rhythms, Jewish laments, and Arabic style to the development of flamenco. While it is true that much of Andalusian food, culture, and architecture is the result of 800 years of Moorish influence, it is only part of the story for the flamenco song, dance, and guitar tradition.

MOTIVATING ACTIVITY
Play *Pin the Flag on Spain.* Mount an enlarged copy of the world map on pages xviii–xix or project Map Transparency 2 (**Europa y las Américas**) on the wall. Have students tape a small flag of Spain in the appropriate place on the map. For an advanced challenge, students can pin a flag on other Spanish-speaking countries.

CHAPTER OVERVIEW

De antemano pp. 22–25	¡Me llamo Francisco!			
	FUNCTIONS	**GRAMMAR**	**CULTURE**	**RE-ENTRY**
Primer paso pp. 26–33	• Saying hello and goodbye, p. 27 • Introducing people and responding to an introduction, p. 29 • Asking how someone is and saying how you are, p. 31	• **Gramática**: Punctuation marks, p. 30 • **Gramática**: Subject pronouns **tú** and **yo**, p. 32	• **Nota cultural**: First and last names in Spanish, p. 26 • **Nota cultural**: First names and Catholicism, p. 27 • **Nota cultural**: Saint's Days, p. 30 • **Nota cultural**: Greetings, p. 33	• Accents (from **Capítulo preliminar**)
Segundo paso pp. 34–39	• Asking and saying how old someone is, p. 35 • Asking where someone is from and saying where you're from, p. 38	• **Nota gramatical: Soy, eres**, and **es**, p. 38 • **Nota gramatical**: Asking questions, p. 39	• **Nota cultural**: Handwriting in Spanish-speaking countries, p. 34 • **Panorama cultural**: ¿De dónde eres?, pp. 40–41	• Numbers 0–30 (from **Capítulo preliminar**)
Tercer paso pp. 42–49	• Talking about what you like and don't like, p. 43	• **Gramática**: Nouns and definite articles, p. 46	• **Nota cultural**: Snack foods in Spain, p. 42	

Letra y sonido	p. 49	The vowels	**Dictado**: Textbook Audiocassette 1A	
Enlaces	p. 50	**Las ciencias sociales y la geografía**		
Vamos a leer	pp. 52–53	**Categorías**	**Reading Strategy**: Using cognates	
Review	pp. 54–57	**Repaso**, pp. 54–55	**A ver si puedo...**, p. 56	**Vocabulario**, p. 57

Assessment

TESTING PROGRAM
- **Primer paso**, Quiz 1-1, pp. 1–2
- **Segundo paso**, Quiz 1-2, pp. 3–4
- **Tercer paso**, Quiz 1-3, pp. 5–6
- Assessment Items, Audiocassette 4A OR Audio CD 1 Tracks 28–30

- **Chapter Test**, pp. 7–12
- Assessment Items, Audiocassette 4A OR Audio CD 1 Tracks 31–32

Alternative Assessment
Portfolio Assessment
ANNOTATED TEACHER'S EDITION
- **Written: Repaso** Activity 5, p. 55
- **Oral**: Activity 33, p. 48
ALTERNATIVE ASSESSMENT GUIDE, p. 12

PRINT	MEDIA

Adelante LEVEL 1A

Pupil's Edition, pp. 20–57

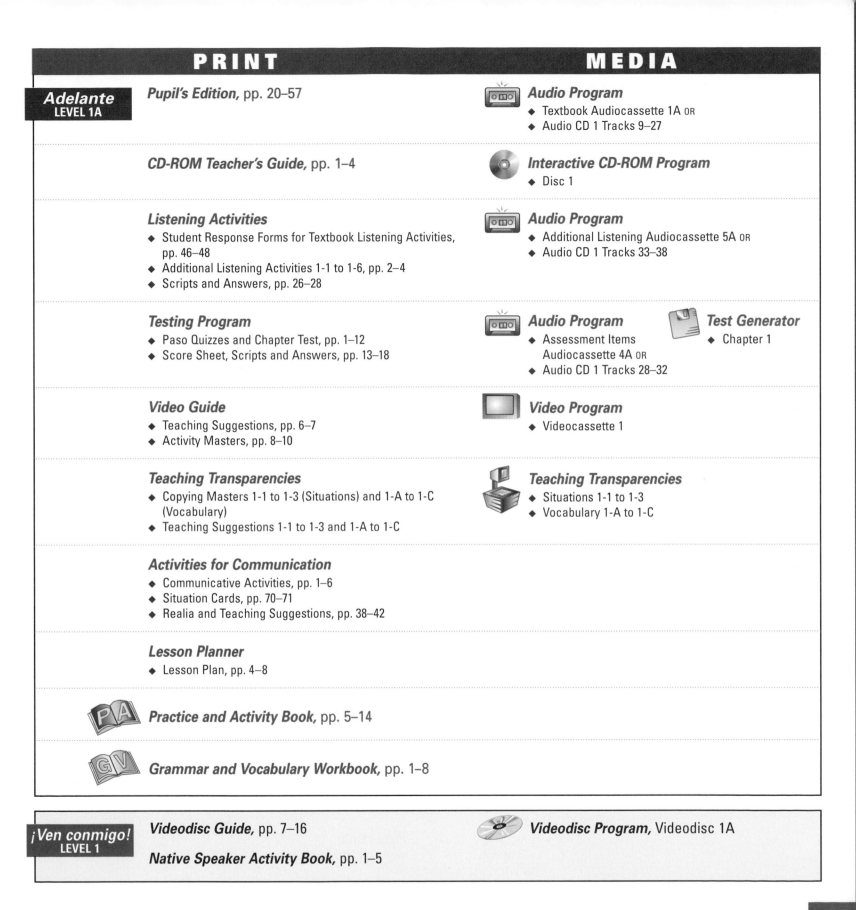 **Audio Program**
- Textbook Audiocassette 1A OR
- Audio CD 1 Tracks 9–27

CD-ROM Teacher's Guide, pp. 1–4

Interactive CD-ROM Program
- Disc 1

Listening Activities
- Student Response Forms for Textbook Listening Activities, pp. 46–48
- Additional Listening Activities 1-1 to 1-6, pp. 2–4
- Scripts and Answers, pp. 26–28

Audio Program
- Additional Listening Audiocassette 5A OR
- Audio CD 1 Tracks 33–38

Testing Program
- Paso Quizzes and Chapter Test, pp. 1–12
- Score Sheet, Scripts and Answers, pp. 13–18

Audio Program
- Assessment Items Audiocassette 4A OR
- Audio CD 1 Tracks 28–32

Test Generator
- Chapter 1

Video Guide
- Teaching Suggestions, pp. 6–7
- Activity Masters, pp. 8–10

Video Program
- Videocassette 1

Teaching Transparencies
- Copying Masters 1-1 to 1-3 (Situations) and 1-A to 1-C (Vocabulary)
- Teaching Suggestions 1-1 to 1-3 and 1-A to 1-C

Teaching Transparencies
- Situations 1-1 to 1-3
- Vocabulary 1-A to 1-C

Activities for Communication
- Communicative Activities, pp. 1–6
- Situation Cards, pp. 70–71
- Realia and Teaching Suggestions, pp. 38–42

Lesson Planner
- Lesson Plan, pp. 4–8

Practice and Activity Book, pp. 5–14

Grammar and Vocabulary Workbook, pp. 1–8

¡Ven conmigo! LEVEL 1

Videodisc Guide, pp. 7–16

Videodisc Program, Videodisc 1A

Native Speaker Activity Book, pp. 1–5

¡Mucho gusto!

TECHNOLOGY APPLICATIONS IN THE CLASSROOM

For a complete list of the media resources and their accompanying print matter guides, see page 19B.

DE ANTEMANO pp. 22–25

Video

- Show *¡Me llamo Francisco!* See *Video Guide* pp. 5–6, 8.

Audio

- Play the **fotonovela** to practice pronunciation.

PRIMER PASO pp. 26–33

Video

- Show the **paso** opener to model greetings and introductions.

Audio

- Use Textbook Listening Activity 5 to practice greetings.
- Use Textbook Listening Activity 8 to practice introductions.
- (Challenge) Additional Listening Activities 1-1 and 1-2 practice introducing people and subject pronouns **tú** and **yo.** Use them after the grammar practice on page 32.

Transparencies

- Use Situation Transparency 1-1 to present and practice activities using the teaching suggestions. Students can do the CD-ROM activities as a follow-up.

CD-ROM

- Activities 1 and 2 practice saying hello and goodbye, introducing someone, and saying how someone is doing.

SEGUNDO PASO pp. 34–39

Video

- Show the **paso** opener to model saying someone's age and where someone is from.

Audio

- Use Textbook Activity 20 to practice saying how old someone is.
- Use Textbook Activity 23 to practice saying where someone is from.
- (Challenge) Additional Listening Activities 1-3 and 1-4 practice numbers and countries of origin. Use them after the **Primer paso.**

Transparencies

- Use Vocabulary Transparency 1-2 to practice saying how old someone is and where someone is from. Students can do the CD-ROM as a follow-up.

CD-ROM

- Activity 3 practices numbers.
- Activity 4 practices the verb **ser.**
- After completing the **paso,** have students do Activity 5 as a review.

PANORAMA CULTURAL pp. 40–41

Audio

- Play the **Panorama cultural** as students read along. Remind students they might not be able to understand all of what each person says, but they should try to recognize words and deduce global meanings.

Video

- Show the interviews to students. See *Video Guide* pp. 5–10.

CD-ROM

- Have students do the **Panorama cultural** activity for Chapter 1 after showing them the video.

TERCER PASO pp. 42–49

Video

- Show the **paso** opener to model saying what people like and don't like.

Audio

- Use Textbook Activities 28–29 to practice saying what people like and dislike.
- Textbook Activity 32 practices nouns and definite articles.
- (Challenge) Additional Listening Activities 1-5 and 1-6 practice vocabulary for things that people enjoy.

Transparencies

- Vocabulary Transparency 1-3 practices nouns and definite articles. Use it after presenting the phrases for discussing likes and dislikes.

CD-ROM

- After presenting the vocabulary on pp. 44–45, have students do Activity 6.

REPASO pp. 54–55

Video

- Replay *¡Me llamo Francisco!* and ask students to point out exchanges in which the characters perform the functions targeted in this chapter.

CD-ROM

- Have students do the **En contexto** to practice introducing themselves and talking about their likes and dislikes.

Test Generator

- Make a short practice test to help students prepare for the Chapter Test.

 **Videodisc Guide** ◆ pp. 7–16

¡Mucho gusto!
BARCODE DIRECTORY

 CAPÍTULO **1**

DE ANTEMANO

Barcodes A and B access **De antemano** and **A continuación** in their entirety. Subsequent barcodes show individual scenes. The barcode numbers correspond to the scene numbers as they appear in **De antemano**.

¡Me llamo Francisco! **A**
Search 10545, Play To 17810

¡Ay, Paco! **1**
Search 11010, Play To 12955

Hola, buenos días... **2**
Search 12955, Play To 13350

No, ésta no... **3**
Search 13350, Play To 14269

Hola, me llamo... **4**
Search 14270, Play To 15638

¡Sí, señor! **5**
Search 15638, Play To 16830

Hola, Paco. **6**
Search 16830, Play To 17046

Oye, ¿qué es...? **7**
Search 17046, Play To 17255

¿Una chica? ¿Cómo...? **8**
Search 17255, Play To 17810

¡Me llamo Francisco!
(a continuación) **B**
Search 17810, Play To 27260

VIDEOCLIPS

This is a promotional piece about Colombia. You may want to preview it before showing it to students.

Colombia
Search 31050, Play To 39278

PASO OPENERS

Each **paso** begins with a re-presentation of a scene from **De antemano** that models targeted functions, vocabulary, and grammar.

Hola, buenos días... **1** p. 26
Search 12955, Play To 13350

¡Sí, señor! **3** p. 42
Search 15638, Play To 16830

Hola, me llamo... **2** p. 34
Search 14270, Play To 15638

PANORAMA CULTURAL

¿De dónde eres?
These barcodes access supplementary interviews that do not appear in the textbook. Not all barcodes are listed here. For a complete listing of supplemental interviews, see the *Level I Videodisc Guide*, p. 8.

Ivette, Puerto Rico **1**
Search 28186, Play To 28316

Miguel, España **2**
Search 28317, Play To 28524

Sandra, Venezuela **3**
Search 28525, Play To 28607

Manolo, Texas **4**
Search 29000, Play To 29180

Laura y Jacó, España **5**
Search 29482, Play To 29845

Honry, El Salvador **6**
Search 29946, Play To 30101

María Luisa, Ecuador **7**
Search 30102, Play To 30251

Eduardo, México **8**
Search 30747, Play To 30886

Raquel, Nicaragua **9**
Search 30887, Play To 31014

All interviews **10**
Search 27260, Play To 31050

¡Mucho gusto!
TEXTBOOK LISTENING ACTIVITIES SCRIPTS

For Student Response Forms, see Listening Activities pp. 46–49

PRIMER PASO pp. 26–33

5 Saludos y despedidas p. 27

1. — Hasta luego, Miguel Ángel. Tengo que irme.
   — ¡Chao, Alicia!
2. — Hola Santiago.
   — ¿Qué tal, Miguel Ángel?
3. — Buenos días, don Alonso.
   — Hola, Miguel Ángel.
4. — Adiós, Mariana.
   — Sí, hasta mañana, Miguel Ángel.
5. — Buenas tardes, doña Luisa. ¿Cómo está?
   — Buenas tardes. Estoy bien, gracias.
6. — Bueno, tengo clase.
   — ¡Hasta luego, David!

Answers to Activity 5

1. Alicia: leaving	4. Mariana: leaving
2. Santiago: arriving	5. Doña Luisa: arriving
3. Don Alonso: arriving	6. David: leaving

8 ¿Cómo respondes? p. 29

1. Mucho gusto.
2. Me llamo Abel. ¿Y tú? ¿Cómo te llamas?
3. Éste es mi amigo. Se llama Felipe.
4. Ésta es Evita, la estudiante del programa internacional.
5. Encantada.
6. Soy la señora Rivas.

Answers to Activity 8

1. Igualmente.	4. ¡Mucho gusto!/Encantado/a
2. Me llamo...	5. Igualmente.
3. ¡Mucho gusto!/Encantado/a	6. Encantado/a/¡Mucho gusto!

12 ¿Cómo estás? p. 31

1. SARA   ¿Cómo estás, Daniel?
   DANIEL   Ay, muy mal.
2. SARA   ¿Qué tal, Marta?
   MARTA   Más o menos, Sara. ¿Y tú?
3. SARA   Buenos días, Elena. ¿Cómo estás?
   ELENA   Estoy muy bien, gracias, Sara.
4. SARA   Hola, José Luis. ¿Qué tal?
   JOSÉ LUIS Pues, muy bien, Sara. ¿Y tú?
5. SARA   Buenas tardes, Carlos. ¿Cómo estás?
   CARLOS   ¡Excelente!
6. SARA   ¿Qué tal, Juan?
   JUAN   Pues, estoy muy mal, amiga, muy mal.

Answers to Activity 12

bien	regular	mal
Elena	Felipe (modelo)	Daniel
José Luis	Marta	Juan
Carlos		

SEGUNDO PASO pp. 34–39

20 Edades p. 37

DANIEL   Ésta es Marisa y tiene catorce años. Éste es José.

ADRIANA ¿Cuántos años tiene?

DANIEL   Tiene seis años.

ADRIANA ¿Y éste? ¿Cómo se llama?

DANIEL   Se llama David. Tiene once años.

ADRIANA ¿Y ésta?

DANIEL   Se llama Anita. Tiene veinticinco años.

ADRIANA ¿Y éste?

DANIEL   ¡Éste es Daniel! ¡Sí, soy yo! En esta foto tengo un año.

Answers to Activity 20

a. Marisa	c. Anita	e. José
b. Daniel	d. David	

23 ¿De dónde es? p. 38

1. — Es Gabriela, ¿no?
   — Sí, es Gabriela. Es de Buenos Aires, Argentina.
2. — ¿Y ésta es Maricarmen?
   — Sí, es Maricarmen y es de Santiago de Chile.
3. — ¿De dónde es David?
   — David es de Madrid, España.
4. — ¿Cómo te llamas?
   — Me llamo Antonio y soy de Quito, Ecuador.
5. — ¿Y tú? Eres Laura, ¿verdad?
   — Sí, Laura Alicia, encantada. Yo soy de San José, Costa Rica.
6. — ¿De dónde es Pedro?
   — Pedro es de Bogotá, Colombia.

Answers to Activity 23

1. Gabriela: **b** Es de Buenos Aires, Argentina.
2. Maricarmen: **d** Es de Santiago de Chile.
3. David: **a** Es de Madrid, España.
4. Antonio: **c** Es de Quito, Ecuador.
5. Laura: **f** Es de San José, Costa Rica.
6. Pedro: **e** Es de Bogotá, Colombia.

TERCER PASO pp. 42–49

28 Planes p. 43

CARLOS ¿Te gusta el voleibol?

ELENA Bueno, no. No me gusta mucho.

CARLOS ¿Te gusta la pizza?

ELENA No, no me gusta.

CARLOS Oye, ¿te gusta la música pop?

ELENA Pues, no me gusta.

CARLOS Bueno, entonces, ¿qué te gusta?

ELENA A ver... ¿te gusta la comida mexicana?

CARLOS Sí, me gusta.

ELENA ¡Estupendo! A mí también me gusta. ¿Te gusta el restaurante El Mercado?

CARLOS Mmm..., no, no me gusta mucho.

ELENA Ah, bueno...

Answers to Activity 28

1. voleibol—Elena doesn't like it.
2. pizza—Elena doesn't like it.
3. la música pop—Elena doesn't like it.
4. la comida mexicana—Carlos and Elena both like it.
5. el restaurante El Mercado—Carlos doesn't like it.

29 Una fiesta p. 45

AMIGO ¿Te gustan los deportes?

DIANA Sí, me gusta el béisbol. Y me gusta mucho el tenis. No me gusta mucho la natación.

AMIGO Bueno, y ¿qué comida te gusta?

DIANA Mmm, no me gusta la fruta. Me gusta la comida italiana. Y la ensalada. ¡Me gusta mucho la ensalada!

AMIGO Y a ti te gusta bastante la música, ¿verdad?

DIANA Sí, me gusta la música pero no me gusta el jazz. Me gusta más la música rock.

Answers to Activity 29

Answers will vary. Possible answers:

el béisbol, la comida italiana, la ensalada, la música rock

LETRA Y SONIDO p. 49

For the scripts for Parts A and C, see page 49. The dialogue for Part B is below.

B. Dictado

— Buenos días, Marta. ¿Qué tal?
— Muy bien, Ana. ¿Cómo estás?
— Bien. Bueno, tengo que irme.
— Hasta luego.
— Chao.

REPASO pp. 54–55

1 p. 54

MODELO Me llamo Mariana Castillo. Soy de España. Tengo quince años y me gusta mucho la música pop. No me gusta el tenis.

— Hola. Me llamo <u>Liliana Rivera</u>. Soy de <u>Santiago de Chile</u> y tengo <u>dieciséis años</u>. Me gusta mucho <u>el tenis</u> pero no me gusta hacer <u>la tarea</u>.

— Hola, ¿qué tal? Soy <u>Pablo García</u>. Soy de <u>Monterrey, México</u>, y tengo <u>quince años</u>. Me gusta mucho <u>el inglés</u>. No me gusta <u>la música clásica</u>, pero <u>la música rock</u>, sí.

¡Mucho gusto!
PROJECTS

COLLAGE

In this activity students will create picture collages of some of their favorite things to use as visual support when they introduce themselves and say how old they are in Spanish. Suggest to students that they consider saving the collage in their portfolios.

Materials students may need

- ◆ Poster board
- ◆ Glue
- ◆ Old magazines
- ◆ Photos
- ◆ Removable tape or paper clips
- ◆ Scissors

Sequence

1. Ask students what they are interested in when they meet a new friend. What do they want to find out or know about someone new?

2. Working individually, students make a list in English of what things they like and don't like. For Spanish vocabulary, students can refer to the Additional Vocabulary on pp. 275–280.

3. Students write sentences in Spanish about their likes and dislikes.

4. Students find pictures in magazines or make their own drawings to illustrate their likes and dislikes.

5. Students may mount their illustrations above or around the text on a large sheet of paper. Paper clips or small pieces of removable tape are helpful to hold the illustrations in place until they decide on the final layout.

6. Have students peer-edit their Spanish captions and make corrections before final mounting.

7. Student arrange their illustrations with the appropriate descriptions and rehearse the collage presentation.

Grading the project

Suggested point distribution (total = 100 points):

Completion of all steps	15
Self or peer-edit	30
Visual presentation	15
Grammar	25
Pronunciation	15

NOTE

You may suggest that students save the collages in their Portfolio (see pp. T52–T53). If the projects are for the Portfolio, tell students beforehand to save their English notes, the first draft of the Spanish text, and the final draft of the Spanish text.

FAMILY LINK

Students may show their projects to a family member or a friend who is not taking Spanish. Ask students if they are able to make themselves understood by showing the pictures and Spanish text.

TEACHER NOTE

Keep in mind when giving assignments that entail the disclosure of personal information that some students and their families may consider family matters private. In some cases, you may want to give students the option of discussing a make-believe family.

PASSPORT

In this activity students will create a passport for themselves or for an imaginary person. Passports are recognized worldwide as a form of identification. Have students discuss when and where they might use a passport and why they think passports are important. Have them do research to find out how they would go about getting a passport (where they would go, what forms they might need, and how long they would need to wait).

Materials students may need

◆ A recent photo of themselves
◆ A pocket size notebook
◆ Pens or markers
◆ Stickers or ink pad and stamps
◆ Old magazines
◆ Construction paper
◆ Tape
◆ Glue
◆ Scissors

Sequence

To create their passports, students may use a cutout from a magazine if they are making a passport for an imaginary person. Students may also wish to draw their own portraits. Explain that passport photos must be a headshot. Students should then choose a country of origin.

1 Have students design a cover for their passport. It should display the name of the country and an official seal or emblem. If a student chooses an actual country, you may wish to have him or her do library research to find out what its official seal looks like.

2 Remind students that their passport should contain blank pages at the back for visas.

3 Have students prepare a sketch of the body of their passport before beginning. They should use expressions from this chapter in place of words like **nombre** (**me llamo...**), **edad** (**tengo...años**), and **nacionalidad** (**soy de...**).

4 Students first make a rough draft for peer review in which they sketch the images they plan to use and the way they plan to use them. Students exchange rough drafts for peer review and then turn in revised drafts for teacher review and suggestions.

5 Students complete the final draft leaving several blank pages at the end for visas. The idea of the passport can continue. Students can design their own stickers and stamps as they progress through different locations of *¡Ven conmigo!*

FAMILY LINK

If a family member or guardian has a passport, students may wish to compare their own passport to that one. They may also wish to invite them to bring their passport in to show the class. Or they could ask other teachers or school personnel if they have a passport.

Grading the project

Suggested point distribution (total = 100 points):

Creativity **15**
Appearance. **25**
Originality **25**
Peer-editing. **15**
Accurate use of chapter expressions **20**

LAS FICHAS

A good beginning project for any foreign language class is to create flash cards. They may be used at home, in groups, or in class for games and review.

Materials students may need

◆ An index card box or sealable plastic pencil bag
◆ Index cards
◆ Pens or markers
◆ Old magazines

1 One set of cards could include pictures of things students like in order to practice **"me gusta"**.

2 Another set could have questions on one side of the card and an appropriate answer on the other. For Chapter 1, include greetings, goodbyes, introductions, or any of the functional expressions from the chapter.

3 Vocabulary from each **paso** should be included on the cards. Point out that using a picture on one side and the Spanish vocabulary word on the other will stimulate their visual recall, helping them to remember more.

Grading the project

Flash cards may be placed in students' portfolios.

Suggested point distribution: (total = 100 points):

Originality and design **25**
Spelling **25**
Variety of vocabulary and expressions **25**
Grammar **25**

¡Mucho gusto!
GAMES

¿DÓNDE ESTÁ?

*The objective of this game is to familiarize students with Spanish-speaking countries and their major cities. This may be played after the **Panorama cultural** on pages 82–83.*

Materials you may need

- ◆ Wall map of the world or a globe
- ◆ Slips of paper
- ◆ Container for folded slips of paper

Procedure

On each slip of paper, write the name of a major city or country in which Spanish is spoken. Divide the class into two teams, Team A and Team B. Choose one student to be the scorekeeper. A member of Team A draws a name from the container and says to a member of Team B, **¿Dónde está _____?** A member of Team B must point to the country or city on the map within ten seconds. If he or she is unsuccessful, the turn goes to Team A. If successful, Team A receives the point. If neither is successful, then the teacher or another student supplies the correct information and neither team scores. Team B then draws a new slip of paper and the game continues. The team with the most points wins.

¿QUÉ TE GUSTA?

This word scramble can be played to quickly review vocabulary presented in Chapter 1.

Procedure

Students unscramble seven words from the chapter vocabulary list to find the answer to the question **¿Qué te gusta?** Students place one letter in each blank to form the words. Students then arrange the circled letters to unscramble the answer to the question **¿Qué te gusta?**

Materials you may need

- ◆ Chapter vocabulary list
- ◆ Pencils or pens
- ◆ Copy of word scramble

ME GUSTA LA

Ⓟ I Z Z A ZAZPI
F R U T Ⓐ ARFTU
E N S A Ⓛ A D A NSAEALAD
T E L E V I Ⓢ I Ó N STIVNIÓLEE
C L A S Ⓔ ESLAC
M A Ⓝ A N A ANAMÑA
C Ⓞ M I D A DCIMOA
SOLUCIÓN: ME GUSTA EL E S P A Ñ O L .

PONGA

This game, which is played exactly like Bingo®, gives students the opportunity to practice numbers in Spanish while enjoying a familiar game. Use it to practice the numbers on page 36.

Materials students may need

- ◆ Index cards or cardboard
- ◆ Permanent ink pen
- ◆ Paper scraps

Procedure

Students prepare their own PONGA card by drawing a card similar to a Bingo® card on a sheet of paper. Cards should have five horizontal spaces and five vertical spaces. Students write a number between 0 and 30 in each space on the card. Read a number between 0 and 30 in Spanish and record it. Students cover or cross off numbers as they are

191 GAMES   CHAPTER 1

called. When a player has marked off an entire row of numbers, he or she says "PONGA," then reads the numbers back to the teacher in Spanish. If the numbers are correct, that student is the winner. You may want to laminate the cards and reuse them with future classes. Students can use paper scraps to cover the numbers (if they have been written on before lamination) or write with a water-based marker.

P	O	N	G	A
12	9	30	27	0
20	15	4	2	7
1	23	18	25	18
17	13	5	16	3

DERECHA / IZQUIERDA

This is a game to practice the alphabet, as well as to introduce the vocabulary for left and right. It may be played in small or large groups.

Procedure

A group leader stands in the middle of the circle. He or she points to a person and says **izquierda** and begins counting. That person must say the name of the person to his or her left and spell it before the leader counts off the full circle. If the leader points to a person and says **derecha,** that person must say the name of the person to his or her right and spell it. If the person fails to say the letters correctly, he or she takes the role of leader and comes to the center of the circle. The former leader takes the empty chair.

NÚMEROS EN LÍNEA

Preparation

Have students prepare index cards with numbers written out as words in Spanish.

Materials students may need

◆ Index cards   ◆ Markers

Procedure

Randomly pass out cards to students. Instruct students to line up in numerical order in complete silence, then read off their numbers.

Repeat the lineup with even numbers (**pares**) on one side of the room and odd numbers (**nones, impares**) on the other. Or, ask them to line up in reverse order (**del 30 al 1**), or by every other number (**por dos**). Again, ask students to read off their number after they've lined up.

LA PAPA CALIENTE

Make a **"papa caliente"** using a battery operated alarm clock in a small box. Be sure to make the box top removable and choose an alarm or timer that ticks loudly.

Materials you may need

◆ A small box   ◆ A battery-operated alarm clock

Procedure

When students enter the classroom, pass the **"papa"** to one of the students with the instructions, "I have just handed you a timer set to go off at any moment. If you're holding it when it does you're out of the game." The only way you can get rid of it is to correctly introduce yourself to someone else, say where you're from, and find out that person's name and where he or she is from. Then, you may give that person the **"papa."** Continue the game until the timer goes off, then reset as often as needed until all of the students have taken part in the activity.

¡Mucho gusto!
ANSWERS TO CHAPTER 1 ACTIVITIES

Answers not listed here appear on corresponding pupil pages. Listening activity answers appear with the Scripts for this chapter on pages 19E–19F.

SEGUNDO PASO   pp. 34–39

21 Answers will vary. Possible answers:
1. Tiene cinco años.
2. Tiene dieciocho años.
3. Tiene trece años.
4. Tiene doce años.
5. Tiene diecinueve años.
6. Tiene dieciséis años.
7. Tiene diez años.

24
1. María Luisa es de Honduras.
2. Daniel es de Perú.
3. Patricia es de El Salvador.
4. Fabiola es de Ecuador.
5. Esteban es de Paraguay.
6. Yo soy de...

TERCER PASO   pp. 42–49

30 Answers will vary. Possible answers:
1. deportes - Me gusta la natación. No me gusta el baloncesto.
2. comida - Me gusta la comida mexicana. No me gusta la pizza.
3. música - Me gusta el jazz. No me gusta la música pop.
4. clases - Me gusta la clase de español. No me gusta la tarea.

32 Answers will vary. Possible answers:
1. Me llamo...
2. Estoy bien, gracias.
3. Tengo... años.
4. No, no me gusta el béisbol.

VAMOS A LEER   pp. 52–53

A Answers will vary. Possible answers:
Videos
Natura
Arte
Música
Humor
Al grano

B
1. Trivia
2. Tecnología
3. Humor
4. Tu Estilo Personal
5. Arte
6. Música
7. Pasatiempos
8. Ecología
9. Videos
10. Natura

Cognados falsos
real—*royal* not *real*
grupo—*group*
ropa—*clothes* not *rope*
disgusto—*displeasure* not *disgust*
sopa—*soup* not *soap*
The words **real, disgusto, ropa,** and **sopa** are false cognates.

A VER SI PUEDO...   p. 56

1 Answers will vary. Possible answers:
1. Buenos días, señor/a.
2. Bueno, tengo clase.
3. Hasta mañana.

2 Answers will vary. Possible answers:
1. Me llamo...
2. Mucho gusto; Encantado/a.
3. Igualmente.

3 Answers will vary. Possible answers:
1. ¿Qué tal?; ¿Cómo estás?
2. Bien; Regular.

4 Answers will vary. Possible answers:
1. ¿Cuántos años tienes?
2. Tengo ... años.
3. Juan tiene ... años.

5 Answers will vary. Possible answers:
1. Soy de Minnesota.
2. ¿De dónde eres?
3. Juan es de Puerto Rico.

6 Answers will vary. Possible answers:
1. ¿Te gusta el voleibol? Sí, me gusta...; No me gusta...
2. ¿Te gusta el béisbol?
3. ¿Te gusta la comida italiana?
4. ¿Te gusta la música pop?
5. ¿Te gusta el baloncesto?

HOMEWORK SUGGESTIONS

CAPÍTULO 1

Chapter Section	Presentation	Homework Options
Primer paso	**Así se dice,** p. 27	*Pupil's Edition,* p. 28, #6 *Grammar and Vocabulary,* p. 1, #1
	Así se dice, p. 29	*Pupil's Edition,* p. 29, #9 *Practice and Activity Book,* p. 6, #4 *Grammar and Vocabulary,* p. 1, #2
	Así se dice, p. 31	*Pupil's Edition,* p. 32, #13 *Practice and Activity Book,* p. 7, #5–6 *Grammar and Vocabulary,* p. 3, #6–7 *CD-ROM,* Disc 1, Chapter 1, #2
	Gramática, p. 30	*Grammar and Vocabulary,* p. 2, #3–5
	Gramática, p. 32	*Practice and Activity Book,* p. 8, #7–8 *Grammar and Vocabulary,* p. 4, #8–10
Segundo paso	**Así se dice,** p. 35	*Practice and Activity Book,* p. 9, #10
	Vocabulario, p. 36	*Practice and Activity Book,* p. 9, #9 *Grammar and Vocabulary,* p. 5, #11–13 *CD-ROM,* Disc 1, Chapter 1, #3
	Así se dice, p. 38	*Practice and Activity Book,* p. 10, #13
	Nota gramatical, p. 38	*Grammar and Vocabulary,* p. 6, #14
	Nota gramatical, p. 39	*Pupil's Edition,* p. 39, #25–26 *Practice and Activity Book,* p. 10, #12 *Grammar and Vocabulary,* p. 6, #15 *CD-ROM,* Disc 1, Chapter 1, #4
Tercer paso	**Así se dice,** p.43	*Practice and Activity Book,* p. 11, #14
	Vocabulario, pp. 44–45	*Grammar and Vocabulary,* p. 7, #16–17 *CD-ROM,* Disc 1, Chapter 1, #6
	Gramática, p.46	*Practice and Activity Book,* pp. 11–12, #15–17 *Grammar and Vocabulary,* p. 8, #18–20

¡Mucho gusto!

MOTIVATING ACTIVITY
Ask students the following: What do you say to someone you've just met? What would you write in a letter introducing yourself to a pen pal? How would your greetings differ if you were meeting someone face to face as opposed to introducing yourself by mail?

PHOTO FLASH!
① Pilar and Eva are from the province of Ciudad Real, in the region of Castilla-La Mancha. The girls have just finished dancing a **jota**, a traditional Castilian dance. The girls danced in a city park in Madrid to a chorus of traditional songs sung by other park visitors. Such impromptu performances are not unusual in Spain, where many people learn the traditional songs and dances of their region as children and dance them at parties and festivals throughout their lives.

THINKING CRITICALLY
Ask students to observe from the background where each photo might have been taken. (restaurant, park, city street) What clues tell where the photos were taken?

CAPÍTULO

1

¡Mucho gusto!

FRANCISCO

RAMON

MERCE

① **Me llamo Pilar. Soy de Ciudad Real. Ésta es mi amiga Eva.**

The start of a new school year means seeing old friends but also meeting some new ones. What's the first day of school like for you? What things do you look forward to?

In this chapter you will learn

- to say hello and goodbye; to introduce people and respond to an introduction; to ask how someone is and say how you are
- to ask and say how old someone is; to ask where someone is from and say where you're from
- to talk about what you like and don't like

And you will

- listen as people introduce themselves and tell their names, ages, and where they're from
- read a **fotonovela** and a letter from a pen pal
- write a short letter introducing yourself to a pen pal
- find out how Spanish speakers greet one another and introduce themselves

② Hola, soy yo. Soy Ana. ¿Qué tal?

③ ¿Te gusta el voleibol?

TEACHER NOTE
Some activities suggested in the *Annotated Teacher's Edition* ask students to contact various people and organizations in the community. It is advisable to request parental permission for these activities. In some cases, you may also want to obtain permission from the parties the student will be asked to contact.

FOCUSING ON OUTCOMES
- Have students read the list of objectives for this chapter, then match the first three learner outcomes to a photo. (Photo 1: introductions; photo 2: saying hello and asking how someone is; photo 3: talking about likes and dislikes.)
- Have students identify as many English expressions as possible to say hello and goodbye. When would they use each expression? What gesture, if any, do they use with these greetings? (a handshake, a kiss, a hug)

PHOTO FLASH!
② Ask students to guess what the girl in this photo is saying and who she's speaking to. Ask students why someone might need to make telephone calls from a telephone booth. Point out that although almost every household in the U.S. has a telephone, telephone service in Spain and Latin America is much more expensive and fewer people have telephones.

CAPÍTULO 1

VIDEO INTEGRATION

***Adelante* LEVEL 1A**
Video Program,
Videocassette 1, 7:27–11:30 OR
***¡Ven conmigo!* LEVEL 1**
Videodisc Program,
Videodisc 1A

Search 10545, Play To 17810

TEACHER NOTE
The **fotonovela** is an abridged version of the video episode.

VIDEO SYNOPSIS
Paco is waiting for Ramón, the mail carrier, to bring a letter from his new pen pal. Paco sees Ramón coming and runs through his parents' fruit and vegetable store. Paco bumps into his mother, apologizes, and goes to get the letter. The mailman pretends not to have a letter for Paco because the letter is addressed to "Francisco," Paco's full name. Back in his room, Paco reads the letter and daydreams about his pen pal. Then Paco's friend Felipe stops by for a visit.

MOTIVATING ACTIVITY
Ask students if they have ever anxiously awaited a call or letter. How did they feel?

SUGGESTION
Refer to page T58 for names and addresses of pen pal organizations. Have students begin corresponding with a pen pal throughout the year.

DE ANTEMANO
Reminder: Read the highest bubble first.

Cass. 1A
CD 1 Trs. 9–10

¡Me llamo Francisco!

Look at the characters in the **fotonovela**, or photo story. Where are they? What are their occupations? What do you think they're talking about? What do you suppose will happen in the story?

p. 5
Acts. 1–2

Paco   Felipe   Ramón

22   *veintidós*

CAPÍTULO 1   ¡Mucho gusto!

22

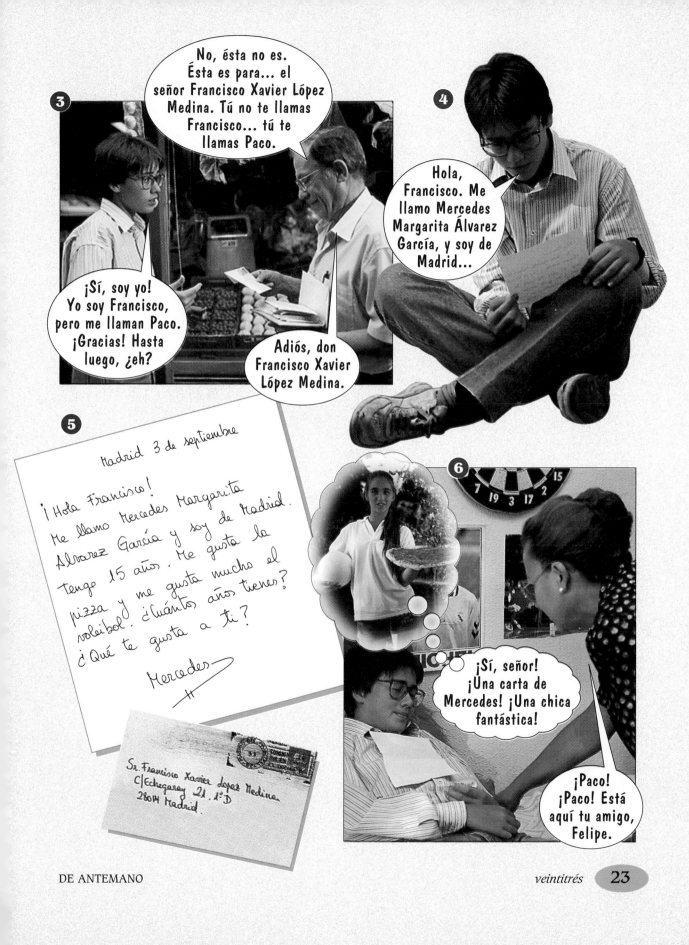

PRESENTATION

Have students scan the speech bubbles and find up to eight words whose meaning they think they can guess. Point out that **pizza** and **voleibol** are cognates (words that are similar in two languages). Tell students that looking and listening for cognates will help them understand. Then discuss each of the following:

1. What do you think the following words or phrases mean? **¡Buenos días! ¿Cómo estás? ¡Hola!**

2. What do you think Paco is expecting from Ramón? Can you guess what word means *letter*?

3. What kinds of things do you think Mercedes is telling Paco in her letter?

4. Play the video or audio recording a second time, then break the class into pairs for students to practice reading the dialogues and role-playing the parts of the different characters. As you circulate, check pronunciation.

CHALLENGE

5 Using the letter as a model, have students write a similar letter about themselves or about an alter ego.

23

LANGUAGE NOTE

Characters in this video episode speak with a Spanish accent. Point out that through the *Video Program* they will hear many accents from around the Spanish-speaking world.

NATIVE SPEAKERS

Explain to native speakers from Latin America that Spaniards have an additional sound in the language, similar to the *th* in the English word *think*. Model how Spaniards would distinguish between these word pairs: **casa** *(ka sa)*, **caza** *(ka tha)*; **siento** *(syen to)*, **ciento** *(thyen to)*, **coser** *(ko ser)*, **cocer** *(ko ther)*

VIDEO INTEGRATION

Adelante LEVEL 1A
Video Program,
Videocassette 1, 11:31–16:45 OR
¡Ven conmigo! LEVEL 1
Videodisc Program,
Videodisc 1A

Search 17810, Play To 27260

VIDEO SYNOPSIS

In *A continuación,* Paco and Felipe go to meet Mercedes, Paco's pen pal. She arrives at the pizzeria with her friend Juanita. Paco and Mercedes know each other from school as Paco and Merche. They finally realize that they are one another's pen pal under their full names, Francisco and Mercedes.

24

1 ¿Comprendes?

How well do you understand what is happening in the **fotonovela**? Check by answering these questions in English. Don't be afraid to guess.

1. Who are the people in the **fotonovela**? Make a list of them. How are they related to Paco?
2. Why does Paco run out of the store?
3. What do you know about the family business?
4. What do you think will happen next?

2 Cortesías

Match the English phrase to the Spanish phrase the characters use in the **fotonovela**.

1. Hello. f
2. Good morning! c
3. I like volleyball a lot. b
4. My name is . . . a
5. Thank you. e
6. Goodbye. d

a. Me llamo...
b. Me gusta mucho el voleibol.
c. ¡Buenos días!
d. Adiós.
e. Gracias.
f. Hola.

3 ¡Soy yo!

Find the sentences in the **fotonovela** and fill in the blanks.

PACO ¿Hay una ___1___ para mí?

RAMÓN No, ésta no es. Esta carta es para ___2___ .

PACO ¡Sí, soy yo! Yo ___3___ Francisco pero me llaman Paco.

RAMÓN ___4___ , don Francisco Xavier López Medina.

1. carta
2. el señor Francisco Xavier López Medina
3. soy
4. Adiós

1. Ramón-Paco's mail carrier

2. Felipe-

1. Ramón, Paco's mail carrier; Felipe, Paco's friend; Mamá, Paco's mother; Paco, main character
2. To see if the mail carrier has a letter for him.
3. They operate a fruit and vegetable store.
4. Paco will tell Felipe about his new pen pal Mercedes.

SUGGESTIONS

1 Have students work with a partner. Allow approximately five minutes for pairs to prepare answers to the questions. Review with the entire class.

2 You might ask students to write the Spanish expressions in Activity 2. In the early stages of language acquisition, copying is a valid writing activity. Assure students that it is normal for the skills of speaking and writing (productive skills) to develop more slowly than the skills of listening and reading (receptive skills). Allow time for students to develop their receptive skills before asking them to speak and write sentences of their own creation. Not all students will develop their productive skills at the same pace.

COOPERATIVE LEARNING

Once students have seen the video twice and have had the chance to practice the dialogue, divide them into groups of three or four. Have each team appoint a scribe. Allow about eight to ten minutes for them to complete exercises 2 and 3; the scribe will record the group's answers. At the end of the allotted time, have groups exchange their answers and correct them as a class. Everyone in the group will earn the same grade. Repeat this type of activity after watching subsequent videos. Stress teamwork.

VIDEO INTEGRATION

Adelante LEVEL 1A

Video Program,
Videocassette 1, 8:48–9:01 OR
¡Ven conmigo! LEVEL 1

Videodisc Program,
Videodisc 1A

Search 12955, Play To 13350

JUMP START!

Have students refer to the **fotonovela** on pages 22–24 and write all of the expressions they can find to greet someone and to say goodbye.

SUGGESTIONS

• After reading the **Nota cultural**, ask volunteers to say what their last name would be if they used this naming convention. To create a comfortable and nonthreatening atmosphere, it is best to ask only volunteers to provide such personal examples.

• As an additional challenge, ask students where their last name would be listed in the phone book using both parents' last names. (It would be listed by the first letter of their father's last name: Smith Anderson, Smith Brown, Smith Cole, Smith Davis, etc.)

PRIMER PASO

Saying hello and goodbye; introducing people and responding to an introduction; asking how someone is and saying how you are

4 ¿Qué pasa?

What greeting does the mail carrier use in this photo? How does Paco answer? Put the following phrases in the correct order.

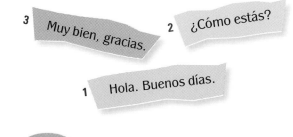

3 Muy bien, gracias.

2 ¿Cómo estás?

1 Hola. Buenos días.

Nota cultural

Spaniards and Latin Americans often use both their first and middle names. They also generally use two last names: first the father's (in Paco's case, López) and then the mother's maiden name (for Paco, it's Medina). In the phone book, Paco's name would be listed under "**L**" as **López Medina, Francisco.** What would your full name be in a Spanish-speaking country?

ASÍ SE DICE
Saying hello and goodbye

CD-ROM
Disc 1

To greet someone, say:

¡Hola! *Hello!*

Buenos días, señor. *Good morning, sir.*

Buenas tardes, señorita. *Good afternoon, miss.*

Buenas noches, señora. *Good evening/Good night, ma'am.*

To say goodbye to someone, say:

Adiós.	*Goodbye.*
Bueno, tengo clase.	*Well, I have class.*
Chao.	*'Bye.*
Hasta luego.	*See you later.*
Hasta mañana.	*See you tomorrow.*
Tengo que irme.	*I have to go.*

PA
p. 6
Act. 3

GV
p. 1
Act. 1

1-1

5 Saludos y despedidas
Script and answers on p. 19E

Cass. 1A
CD 1 Tr. 11

Miguel Ángel talks with various people throughout his day. Listen and decide if each person he speaks with is leaving or arriving.

MODELO —¡Hola, Miguel Ángel!
—Buenos días, señora López. *(arriving)*

1. Alicia
2. Santiago
3. don Alonso
4. Mariana
5. doña Luisa
6. David

Recuerdo del bautizo de
María Magdalena Montoya Ramírez
13 de mayo de 1998
Padrinos: José Antonio Muñoz Ruiz y
Ana María Cervantes Banderas

Nota cultural

Many people in Spain and Latin America are Roman Catholic. This influences the names that families give their children. Common first names are José and Juan Pablo for males, María José and Magdalena for females. Many girls' names commemorate the Virgin Mary: Ana María and María del Socorro. Some common Jewish names include Miriam and Ester for girls and Isaac and Jacobo for boys. Islamic names include Ómar and Ismael for boys and Jasmín and Zoraida for girls. Do you know the origin of your first name?

☀ MOTIVATE

Ask pairs of volunteers to demonstrate in front of the class how they greet people. Have them do this as if they were greeting close friends of the same or opposite sex, parents, grandparents, the school principal, a small child, or a new student in school.

☀ TEACH

**PRESENTATION
ASÍ SE DICE**

TPR Model the expressions using appropriate gestures and expressions. Then call out the new functional phrases. Students show comprehension by acting out the phrases. (You say, **¡Hasta luego!** and students pretend to leave, wave, etc.)

SUGGESTION
5 Discuss the value of being a good listener. Play the recording, then verify answers with students. Play the recording again and have them repeat the Spanish. Encourage them to imitate the pronunciations they hear as closely as possible.

6 ¡Buenos días!

How would you say hello or goodbye to the following people? How would they respond to your greetings? Choose your phrases from **Así se dice** on page 27. Answers will vary. Possible answers in side column

7 Entre clases

Work with a partner. Imagine you just ran into each other in the hall between classes. Greet each other briefly. Tell your partner you have to go and then say goodbye. Switch roles and have the conversation again. This time use different expressions.

MODELO

TÚ	¡Hola!
TU AMIGO/A	¡Buenos días!
TÚ	Bueno, tengo clase.
TU AMIGO/A	¡Hasta luego!

Answers will vary. Possible answers:
—¡Hola!
—¡Hola!
—Tengo clase. ¡Adiós!
—Hasta luego.

ASÍ SE DICE

Introducing people and responding to an introduction

To introduce yourself, say:

Me llamo... *My name is . . .*

Soy... *I am . . .*

¿Y tú? ¿Cómo te llamas?
And you? What's your name?

To introduce others, say:

Éste es mi amigo...
This is my (male) friend . . .

Ésta es mi amiga...
This is my (female) friend . . .

Se llama... *His/Her name is . . .*

To respond to an introduction, say:

¡Mucho gusto! *Nice to meet you!*

Encantado/a.[1]
Delighted to meet you.

To respond to **Mucho gusto** or **Encantado/a,** say:

Igualmente. *Same here.*

PA
p. 6
Act. 4

GV
p. 1
Act. 2

1-1

PRESENTATION
ASÍ SE DICE
Walk around the room greeting various students, using the suggested phrases. Encourage students to respond using the appropriate expression. Ask several students **¿Cómo te llamas?** As they respond, shake each student's hand and reply **¡Mucho gusto!** or **Encantado/a.** Then introduce them to the class by saying **Éste/a es** or **Se llama.** Ask for student volunteers to model the phrases.

8 **¿Cómo respondes?** Script and answers on p. 19E

Cass. 1A
CD 1 Tr. 12

Look over the **Así se dice** section above. Then listen as some people at a party introduce themselves to you. Use the phrases in the box to answer what each person says. You will use some phrases more than once.

> **Igualmente.** **Me llamo...**
> **¡Mucho gusto!** **Encantado/a.**

SUGGESTION
9 For additional practice, students can go back to **Así se dice** and copy words and phrases or make picture flash cards. As a follow-up, or to correct the activity, have groups of three read the completed dialogue to the class.

9 **Te presento a...**

A friend wants to introduce you to a new student. Work with two other classmates to act out the conversation with words and phrases you've learned. Then change roles and try it again.

CHRIS   Hola.

LUPE   ___1___ Hola.

CHRIS   Ésta es mi amiga Patricia.

LUPE   ___2___, Patricia. Mucho gusto

PATRICIA   Igualmente. ¿Y tú? ¿Cómo te llamas?

LUPE   Me ___3___ Lupe. llamo

CHRIS   Bueno, ___4___ clase. Tengo que irme. tengo

LUPE   Hasta ___5___. luego

PATRICIA   ___6___. Answers will vary. Possible answer: Adiós.

---

[1] If you're male, use **Encantado.** If you're female, use **Encantada.**

PRESENTATION
GRAMÁTICA

Point out to students that the inverted question and exclamation marks used in Spanish signal the tone of a sentence before you start to read it. Explain that Spanish accent marks are part of the spelling of the words, and that accent marks sometimes change the meaning of a word. (**qué** = *what* **que** = *that*). Ask students how many of these new punctuation marks they can find in the **Así se dice** boxes on pages 27 and 29.

SUGGESTION

10 This pair-work activity is best done orally. Allow approximately three minutes for students to complete this activity.

CHALLENGE

10 Have students create their own dialogues and perform them for the class. They should change the setting (school, outside, home, or at the mall). After a pair has presented their dialogue, ask the class to paraphrase what they said.

GV

p. 2
Acts. 3–5

GRAMÁTICA   Punctuation marks

1. Questions and exclamations in Spanish begin and end with punctuation. Spanish uses upside-down punctuation marks to begin a question (¿) and an exclamation (¡). Questions and exclamations end with question marks (?) and exclamations (!).

   ¿Cómo te llamas?   **¡Mucho gusto!**

2. An accent mark is sometimes needed over a vowel (**á, é, í, ó, ú**). This shows which syllable is stressed.

3. The mark on the **ñ** (as in **mañana**) is called the **tilde**. It indicates the sound *ny* as in *canyon*.

10   Mini-situaciones

What would you say in the following situations? First find the words and phrases you need in **Así se dice**. Then, with a partner, act out each mini-situation. Be sure to use gestures to make your dialogue more authentic.   Answers will vary. Possible answers:

1. A friend introduces you to a new student. ¡Mucho gusto!; Hola; Me llamo...
2. You want to ask a classmate what his or her name is. ¿Cómo te llamas?
3. You've just been introduced to your new Spanish teacher. Mucho gusto.
4. Your new counselor has just said **"Mucho gusto."** Igualmente.
5. You want to introduce your friend Ana to your partner. Ésta es mi amiga Ana.
6. You want to say "His name is Daniel." Se llama Daniel.

Nota cultural

Roman Catholics in Latin America and Spain celebrate the feast day of the Christian saint they are named after. Spanish speakers have a celebration on their birthday, and often a second celebration on their Saint's Day. For example, a girl named Susana might celebrate her **Día de Santo** on August 11 in honor of St. Susan. How many of the saints' names in this calendar do you recognize?

ASÍ SE DICE

Asking how someone is and saying how you are

To find out how a friend is, ask:

¿Cómo estás? *How are you?*   ¿Qué tal? *How's it going?*

¿Y tú? *And you?*

CD-ROM Disc 1

Your friend might say:

Estoy (bastante) bien, gracias.
I'm (pretty) well, thanks.

Yo también. *Me too.*

Estupendo/a. *Great.*

Excelente. *Great.*

Regular. *Okay.*

Más o menos. *So-so.*

(Muy) mal. *(Very) bad.*

¡Horrible! *Horrible!*

pp. 7–8
Acts. 5–8

pp. 3–4
Acts. 6–7

1-1

PRESENTATION
ASÍ SE DICE
Model these expressions, and have students repeat after you, imitating your gestures. (**regular**—thumb up; **horrible**—thumb down; **más o menos**—hand rocking side to side with palm down; **estupendo** and **excelente**—emphatic gestures)

11   ¿Qué tal?

Look at the faces on the right and decide how the characters might answer the greeting ¿Cómo estás? ¿Qué tal? Match the letter of each face to a phrase below. You may use some of the faces more than once.

1. Estoy bien, gracias. b
2. Estoy horrible. d
3. Estoy mal. a

4. Regular, ¿y tú? c
5. Estupendo. b
6. Más o menos. c

a   **b**

c   **d**

SUGGESTION
11 Draw faces on the chalkboard or on flashcards to practice the new vocabulary. Have students call out an appropriate response to a smiling face, a sad face, etc.

VISUAL LEARNERS
• Use gestures or sketch visual cues on index cards to represent each functional phrase.

• If students are developing their own flash cards, they should make some representing the phrases in **Así se dice.** They can use the cards to verify comprehension and also for pair and small-group practice.

12   ¿Cómo estás?   Script and answers on p. 19E

Cass. 1A
CD 1 Tr. 13

As each friend tells Sara how he or she is, write the person's name under the appropriate heading. The names are listed in the box below.

MODELO   —Buenas tardes, Felipe. ¿Qué tal?
—Regular, gracias. ¿Y tú?

bien   regular   mal
Felipe

Juan   Carlos   Sara
José Luis   Elena
Marta   Daniel

COOPERATIVE LEARNING

13 Divide the class into groups of three. Assign one student to be the scribe and two to be performers. Each group should agree on the correct responses to the items in Activity 13. The group should make up a conversation, combining several of the verbal exchanges in an original dialogue. The students assigned to perform may use cue cards in presenting to the class but should avoid reading word for word.

PRESENTATION

GRAMÁTICA

TPR Write several sentences on the board or on a transparency using **tú** or **yo**. Put students in groups of two. Students read each sentence and point to themselves when they say **yo**, and to their partner when they say **tú**. Point out the accent mark on **tú**.

NATIVE SPEAKERS

Point out to native speakers from Latin America, who might be used to using the second person singular pronoun **vos**, that **vos** is not used throughout the entire Spanish-speaking world. They should also be familiar with the pronoun **tú** and its forms.

---

13 ¿Cómo contestas? 🏠

Work with your partner to practice saying and answering the following phrases. Answers will vary. Possible answers:

1. ¡Hola! ¿Qué tal? Bien, gracias.
2. Ésta es mi amiga Charín. Mucho gusto, Charín.
3. ¿Cómo estás? Regular.
4. Soy Eduardo Robledo. ¿Y tú? Me llamo...
5. ¡Hasta luego! Adiós.

GV
p. 4
Acts.
8–10

GRAMÁTICA — Subject pronouns **tú** and **yo**

1. Use the pronoun **yo** to refer to yourself. In Spanish, **yo** *(I)* is not capitalized except at the beginning of a sentence. Use **tú** *(you)* when you're talking to another student, to a friend, or to someone who is about your own age. Notice that **tú** has an accent.

2. In Chapter 4 you'll learn a different pronoun to use when speaking to someone older than you or to a stranger. You'll also discover that subject pronouns like these aren't used as often in Spanish as in English.

14 ¿Tú o yo?

Which pronoun (**tú** or **yo**) is understood but not stated in each sentence?

MODELO ¿Cómo estás? (tú)

1. ¿Cómo te llamas? tú
2. Me llamo Mercedes Margarita. yo
3. Soy Francisco. yo
4. ¿Cómo estás, Francisco? tú
5. Estoy bien, gracias. yo
6. ¿Estás bien, Merche? tú

15 ¿Quién es?

Imagine it's the first day of school in Madrid and several people are introducing themselves. Fill in the blanks with the pronouns **tú** or **yo** to complete the students' conversation.

—___1___ te llamas Enrique, ¿no? Tú

—Sí, ___2___ me llamo Enrique. yo

—Yo me llamo Raquel. ¿Y ___3___? tú
¿Cómo te llamas?

—Me llamo Sandra. ¿Cómo estás?

—Estoy bien. ¿Y ___4___? tú

—Bien, gracias. Bueno, tengo clase. ¡Adiós!

16 Charla

Mercedes is talking to a new classmate. Using words or phrases you've learned, write their conversation.   Answers will vary. Possible answers:

MERCEDES   *greets her friend* ¡Hola, Elena! ¿Qué tal?

ELENA   *responds and introduces her friend Pedro* Muy bien, Mercedes. Éste es mi amigo Pedro.

MERCEDES   *says it's nice to meet Pedro* Mucho gusto, Pedro.

PEDRO   *responds and asks Mercedes how she is* Igualmente. ¿Cómo estás?

MERCEDES   *responds and says she has class* Muy bien, gracias, pero tengo clase.

ELENA   *says she also has to go* Sí, yo tengo que irme.

ALL   *say goodbye* ¡Adiós! ¡Hasta luego!

Nota cultural

In Spanish, there are many informal ways to greet friends and ask how they're doing. You might hear **¿Qué pasa?** *(What's happening?)* and **¿Qué hay?** or **¿Qué tal?** *(What's up?)*. Other greetings include **¿Qué onda?** and **¿Qué hubo?** or **¿Qué húbole?**, as well as **¡Epa, 'mano!** What do you say when you greet your friends?

VIDEO INTEGRATION

Adelante LEVEL 1A

Video Program,
Videocassette 1, 9:32–10:17 OR

¡Ven conmigo! LEVEL 1

Videodisc Program,
Videodisc 1A

Search 14270, Play To 15638

SUGGESTION

Show the video without sound. Ask students if they remember what's happening in the story at this point.

JUMP START!

Have students use Mercedes' letter as a model. They should rewrite it and personalize it.

17 Have a discussion with students asking what they would write to a pen pal. What would they tell about themselves? What would they want to ask their pen pal?

SEGUNDO PASO

Asking and saying how old someone is; asking where someone is from and saying where you're from

> Madrid 3 de septiembre
>
> ¡Hola Francisco!
> Me llamo Mercedes Margarita
> Alvarez García y soy de Madrid.
> Tengo 15 años. Me gusta la
> pizza y me gusta mucho el
> voleibol. ¿Cuántos años tienes?
> ¿Qué te gusta a ti?
>
> Mercedes

> Sr. Francisco Xavier López Medina
> C/ Echegaray 21. 1.º D
> 28014 Madrid.

Nota cultural

Handwriting in Spanish-speaking countries is slightly different from handwriting in the U.S. Note the **m, s, p,** and **z** in Mercedes' letter. Also, look at the number one (written with a tail) in the letter and on the envelope. What other differences can you find? Share your findings with the class.

17 ### ¿Qué escribe ella?

Find and copy the phrases Mercedes uses . . .

1. to tell Francisco how old she is Tengo 15 años.
2. to tell him where she's from Soy de Madrid.
3. to ask him how old he is ¿Cuántos años tienes?

ASÍ SE DICE
Asking and saying how old someone is

To ask how old someone is, say:	To answer, say:
¿Cuántos años tienes? *How old are you?*	**Tengo... años.** *I'm . . . years old.*
¿Cuántos años tiene? *How old is (he/she)?*	**Tiene... años.** *(He/She) is . . . years old.*

PA
p. 9
Act. 10

CD-ROM Disc 1

1-2

18 Conversación

Using the dialogue bubbles, rewrite the dialogue on your paper, putting the sentences in the correct order. Answers in side column.

5 Tengo trece años. ¿Y tú?

4 Igualmente. ¿Cuántos años tienes?

1 ¡Hola! Me llamo Lupe. ¿Cómo te llamas?

2 Me llamo Raúl.

7 ¡Chao!

3 Mucho gusto.

6 Tengo doce años. Bueno, tengo clase. ¡Adiós!

PRESENTATION

VOCABULARIO

Have all students stand. Give a foam ball or some other light object to a student and ask him or her to begin the count with **uno**. The student then tosses the ball to another student and sits down. The student who caught the ball calls out the next number in the sequence, throws the ball to a classmate, and sits down. Continue the game until all students are seated. As you repeat the game, vary the rules by setting time limits of 45–60 seconds or by having students count by twos or threes.

GAME
¿Cuántos años tienes?

Write numbers out as numerals or as words on flashcards. Give one to each student and have students pretend that the number represents their age. Students then put themselves in order according to age by asking **¿Cuántos años tienes?**

CHALLENGE
19 Teach students the phrase **Pienso en un número entre uno y treinta** and the words **más**, and **menos**. Then play a guess-the-number game with the class, or have the students play the game with a partner.

PA p. 9 Act. 9

VOCABULARIO

GV p. 5 Acts. 11–13

1-A

Los números del 0 al 30

cero   uno   dos   tres

cuatro   cinco   seis   siete

ocho   nueve   diez

11 once	**12** doce	**13** trece	**14** catorce
15 quince	**16** dieciséis	**17** diecisiete	**18** dieciocho
19 diecinueve	**20** veinte	**21** veintiuno	**22** veintidós
23 veintitrés	**24** veinticuatro	**25** veinticinco	**26** veintiséis
27 veintisiete	**28** veintiocho	**29** veintinueve	**30** treinta

---

19 Número secreto

You and a partner should each write five secret numbers between 0 and 30. Then take turns trying to guess each other's numbers in Spanish, one number at a time. If a guess is wrong, your partner will say **más** to mean higher, or **menos** to mean lower. Keep trying until you guess right. Answers will vary.

20 Edades

Script and answers on p. 19E

Cass. 1A
CD 1 Tr. 14

Daniel is showing Adriana pictures in the family album. Listen as he tells how old each relative is. Then match the correct picture to the age he gives.

Marisa   José   David

Anita   Daniel

a

b

c

d

e

21 ¿Cuántos años tienen?

Daniel has some other cousins whose ages he's not sure about. Read the information given. Then write a sentence telling how old each cousin probably is.   Answers on p. 19K

MODELO   Chela just learned how to walk.
Tiene un año.

1. Miguel just started kindergarten.
2. Teresa graduated from high school last spring.
3. Lalo just started eighth grade.
4. Rosario just started seventh grade.
5. Diego started college last year.
6. Raquel just got her driver's license.
7. Gabriela is in fifth grade.

22 Presentaciones

Introduce yourself to the two classmates sitting closest to you. Greet them and ask each one's name and age. Then introduce your two new friends to the class.   Answers will vary.

CHALLENGE
Have students call out in Spanish the number of students in the classroom, the number of windows in the room, the number of desks, the number of certain objects in the rooms, and so on.

SLOWER PACE
22 Before having the students break into groups, briefly review expressions for introductions, how people are, and ages on pages 29, 31, and 35.

SUGGESTION
22 Have students create imaginary names and origins for themselves. You also may point to Spanish-speaking countries on a map and have students answer that they are from that country by saying **Soy de...**

ADDITIONAL PRACTICE
22 As homework, have students interview at least three people (school staff, faculty members, or other students). Have them ask the three people their names and their country of origin. The students will draw a picture of the people they interview and write captions underneath. For example, **Ésta es la señora Corrales. Es de California** or **Éste es Nico. Es de El Salvador.**

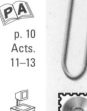

p. 10
Acts.
11–13

1-2
CD-ROM
Disc 1

ASÍ SE DICE

Asking where someone is from and saying where you're from

To find out where someone is from, ask:

> **¿De dónde eres?**
> *Where are you from?*

To answer, say:

> **Soy de los Estados Unidos.**
> *I'm from the United States.*

> **¿De dónde es...?**
> *Where is . . . from?*

> **Es de...**
> *(She/He) is from . . .*

---

23 ¿De dónde es? Script and answers on p. 19F

Cass. 1A
CD 1 Tr. 15

You'll overhear students talking at a party. Match the name of the person with the sentence that tells where he or she is from.

1. Gabriela
2. Maricarmen
3. David
4. Antonio
5. Laura
6. Pedro

a. Es de Madrid, España.
b. Es de Buenos Aires, Argentina.
c. Es de Quito, Ecuador.
d. Es de Santiago de Chile.
e. Es de Bogotá, Colombia.
f. Es de San José, Costa Rica.

España

Ecuador

Costa Rica

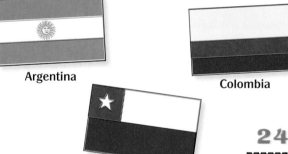

Argentina

Colombia

Chile

NOTA GRAMATICAL

CD-ROM
Disc 1

GV
p. 6
Act. 14

The words **soy, eres,** and **es** are all forms of the verb **ser,** which is one way to say *to be* in Spanish. When talking about where someone is from, use these forms.

24 Nuevos amigos

You're writing a letter to your pen pal in Madrid about some new students in your school. Write a sentence that tells your pen pal what country each student is from.

MODELO Juana – España
Juana es de España.

1. María Luisa – Honduras
2. Daniel – Perú
3. Patricia – El Salvador
4. Fabiola – Ecuador
5. Tú – Paraguay
6. Yo – ¿? Answers on p. 19K

NOTA GRAMATICAL

So far, you've asked questions using several different words.

¿Cómo estás?

¿Cómo te llamas?

¿Cuántos años tienes?

¿De dónde eres?

To ask questions like these, put the question word at the beginning of the sentence. These question words have accents.

GV
p. 6
Act. 15

¿Cuántos años tienes?

25 El comienzo de una amistad

It's the first day of school for Ana, a new student at a school in Madrid. Complete the following sentences with the correct word.

ANA   Buenos días. ¿___1___ (Cómo/Cuántos) estás? Cómo

FEDERICO Bien, ¿y tú?

ANA   Regular. Oye, soy Ana. Y tú, ¿___2___ (de dónde/cómo) te llamas? cómo

FEDERICO Me llamo Federico. Tú no eres de aquí, ¿verdad? ¿___3___ (Cuántos/De dónde) eres? De dónde

ANA   Soy de Andalucía. ¿___4___ (Cuántos/Cómo) años tienes? Cuántos

FEDERICO Tengo trece años. ¿Y tú?

ANA   Yo tengo trece años también.

26 Una encuesta

A Imagine that you're listening to Javier as he's being interviewed over the phone for a survey. Below are the answers Javier gave. Match the correct question to the answer he gave.

1. Bien, gracias. c
2. De Madrid. d
3. Catorce. a
4. Javier Francisco González. b

B Next, take a survey in your class. Ask three students these same questions. Are there any similarities? differences?

a. ¿Cuántos años tienes?

b. ¿Cómo te llamas?

c. ¿Cómo estás?

d. ¿De dónde eres?

VIDEO INTEGRATION

Adelante LEVEL 1A
Video Program,
Videocassette 1, 16:47–18:45

TEACHER NOTES

- Each **Panorama cultural** section consists of authentic video interviews shot on location in different parts of the Spanish-speaking world. The *Video Program* and *Level 1 Videodisc Program* include numerous interviews in addition to those featured in the Pupils Edition. See *Level 1A Video Guide* and *Level 1 Videodisc Guide* for activity masters and teaching suggestions.

- Remind students that cultural material may be included in the Quizzes and Chapter Test.

- The language of the people interviewed represents informal, unrehearsed speech. Occasionally, text has been edited for clarity.

Panorama cultural

CD-ROM Disc 1

Cass. 1A
CD 1 Trs. 16–19

¿De dónde eres?

Panorama cultural will introduce you to real Spanish speakers from around the globe, including Europe, Latin America, and the United States. In this chapter, we asked some people to tell us who they are and where they're from.

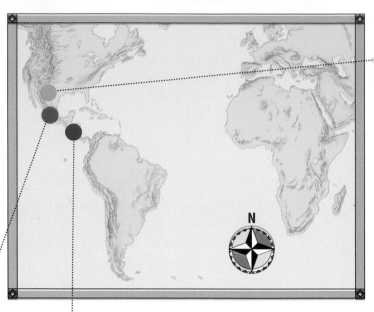

N

Mariano and his friend Renata are from Mexico City, the largest Spanish-speaking city in the world.

Marcelo is from the country of El Salvador. Can you name two countries that border on El Salvador?

● Mariano y Renata
Ciudad de México, México CD 1 Tr. 17

● Marcelo
San Salvador, El Salvador
CD 1 Tr. 18

Me llamo Mariano Mañón Talamantes. Tengo trece años. Soy de aquí, de México. Ella se llama Renata.

Hola. ¿Qué tal?

Mi nombre es Marcelo Antonio Comedo Valencia, y yo vengo de El Salvador en Centroamérica.

Valeria and Alejandra are sisters. They're from the island of Puerto Rico, in the Caribbean Sea.

Valeria y Alejandra

San Antonio, Texas

CD 1 Tr. 19

Yo soy de Puerto Rico. Ahora yo vivo en San Antonio. Yo tengo catorce años. Ésta es mi hermana Alejandra.

1 What country is Mariano referring to when he says, **"Soy de aquí"**? México

2 What phrase does Renata use to ask the interviewer how she is? ¿Qué tal?

3 How many last names does Marcelo use? What are they? Which one represents his mother's last name? two; Comedo Valencia; Valencia

4 What region of Latin America is Marcelo from?
a. South America
b. Central America

5 What expression does Valeria use to introduce Alejandra? Ésta es mi hermana Alejandra.

6 How old is Valeria? 14 years old

Para pensar y hablar... Answers will vary.

A. What three things do you most want to know about people when you meet them for the first time? What questions would you ask Mariano, Renata, Marcelo, Valeria, and Alejandra?

B. Work with a partner to find the places the interviewees are from. Use the maps on pages xvii–xxiii. Each of you should write three ideas you have about what these places are like. Compare your ideas, and be ready to share them with the class.

C. Where would you turn to find more information on the geography, history, and culture of these countries?

41

VIDEO INTEGRATION

Adelante LEVEL 1A
Video Program,
Videocassette 1, 10:18–10:57 OR
¡Ven conmigo! LEVEL 1
Videodisc Program,
Videodisc 1A

Search 15638, Play To 16830

JUMP START!
Have students answer the following questions in writing:
¿Cómo te llamas? ¿De dónde eres? ¿Cuántos años tienes?

SUGGESTION
Write the letter on the board or on a transparency leaving out the following words: **15, pizza, voleibol,** and **Mercedes.** Have students rewrite the letter filling in the missing words with their own information.

TERCER PASO

Talking about what you like and don't like

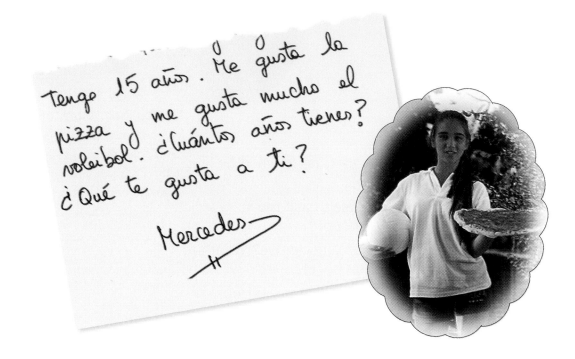

Tengo 15 años. Me gusta la pizza y me gusta mucho el voleibol. ¿Cuántos años tienes? ¿Qué te gusta a ti?

Mercedes

27 ¿Qué te gusta?

Complete the questions asking Mercedes what she likes. Use the words from the box.

1. ¿Te gusta el __voleibol__ ?
2. Me __gusta__ mucho el voleibol.
3. ¿Te gusta la __pizza__ ?
4. Sí, __me__ gusta mucho la pizza.

me	voleibol
gusta	pizza

Nota cultural

Spain has many pizzerias and fast food restaurants. These foods are popular but not traditional. One type of traditional fast food in Spain is **tapas**. **Tapas** can include marinated olives, meatballs, mussels, snails, anchovies, cheese, a serving of Spanish **tortilla** (omelet with potatoes), and many other foods. Snacks are particularly important in Spain as dinner is served late, often after 9 P.M. Have you tasted any of the foods that are traditionally served as **tapas**?

ASÍ SE DICE   Talking about what you like and don't like

To find out what a friend likes, ask:

¿Qué te gusta?
What do you like?

Your friend might answer:

Me gusta la comida mexicana.
I like Mexican food.

Me gusta mucho el tenis.
I like tennis a lot.

No me gusta la natación.
I don't like swimming.

¿Te gusta el fútbol?
Do you like soccer?

Sí, pero me gusta más el béisbol.
Yes, but I like baseball more.

PA
p. 11
Act. 14

1-3

28 Planes   Script and answers on p. 19F

Cass. 1A
CD 1 Tr. 20

Elena and her cousin Carlos are making plans for her visit to the city next weekend. As you listen to them talk, take notes about which items Elena likes and doesn't like by writing the number of the photo under the categories **Me gusta** or **No me gusta**. Is there anything she and Carlos both like?

1. el voleibol

4. la comida mexicana

2. la pizza

5. el restaurante El Mercado

3. la música pop

TERCER PASO

cuarenta y tres   **43**

☀ **MOTIVATE**

Write *Food, Sports,* and *School* as column heads across the top of a transparency. Ask students to name some things in English that they like and dislike in each category. Write their responses under the category heads. Have students fill in the Spanish equivalents after the presentation of the **Vocabulario** on pages 44–45.

☀ **TEACH**

PRESENTATION

ASÍ SE DICE

Model pronunciation and sentence construction with **gustar.** Then, using the transparency from MOTIVATE, point to a word and mime whether or not you like the item using **(No) me gusta...** and the Spanish equivalent of the activity.

SUGGESTION

28 Have students take on the identity of either Carlos or Elena and write a paragraph about themselves based on what they heard.

44

P A   p. 12   Acts. 16–17

1-B

CD-ROM Disc 1

VOCABULARIO

Los deportes

el fútbol

el béisbol

el voleibol

la natación

el baloncesto

el tenis

el fútbol norteamericano

Las clases

¿Qué tal?

Shakespeare

el español

la tarea

la clase de inglés

La música

el jazz

la música

la música clásica

MOZART

la música de...

la música pop/rock

La comida

la cafetería

| la pizza | la fruta | la ensalada | la comida mexicana | la comida china | el chocolate |

la comida italiana   *Italian food*

29 Una fiesta   Script and answers on p. 19F

You're in charge of planning a party for Diana. Listen as a friend asks Diana what she likes and doesn't like. Take notes. Then, based on your list, name one sport, one food, and one kind of music you would include in a party to please her.

Cass. 1A
CD 1 Tr. 21

VISUAL LEARNERS
Have students make review cards for new vocabulary. They can draw or paste pictures of sports, food, or school-related items on the face of each card and write the Spanish word on the back of the card.

SUGGESTION
You might want to play **¿Qué te gusta?** from page 19I at this time.

PA p. 11 Act. 15

GV p. 8 Acts. 18–20

GRAMÁTICA   Nouns and definite articles

All the vocabulary words on pages 44–45 are nouns—words used to name people, places, and things. As you can see, all the nouns in the list have **el** or **la** *(the)* before them. Most nouns ending in **–o** (and nouns referring to males) are called *masculine*. Most nouns ending in **–a** (and nouns referring to females) are called *feminine*. When learning new nouns, always learn the definite article that goes with the noun at the same time.

MASCULINE NOUNS: **el amigo, el tenis**

FEMININE NOUNS: **la amiga, la natación**

30 Gustos personales

Get together with two classmates. For each category listed, write a sentence stating one thing in the category that you like and another that you don't like. Be sure to use the correct definite article (**el** or **la**) in your sentence. Compare answers with the others in your group. Are there any similarities? differences?

MODELO   deportes   Answers on p. 19K
  1. **Me gusta el tenis.**
  2. **No me gusta el fútbol.**

a. deportes   **b.** comida   **c.** música   **d.** clases

VOCABULARIO EXTRA

el arte   *art*
las arvejas   *peas*
la carne asada   *roast beef*
el ciclismo   *cycling*
la coliflor   *cauliflower*
el espagueti   *spaghetti*
la biología   *biology*
la lucha libre   *wrestling*
la historia   *history*
el taller   *shop*

31 La nueva estudiante

Felipe is interviewing the new student from Managua, Nicaragua, for the Spanish newspaper. Take the role of the new student and write his or her part.   Answers will vary. Possible answers:

FELIPE ¡Hola! Me llamo Felipe. ¿Cómo te llamas?

ESTUDIANTE 1. ¡Mucho gusto! Me llamo...

FELIPE ¿Cómo estás?

ESTUDIANTE 2. Estoy bien, gracias.

FELIPE ¿Y cuántos años tienes?

ESTUDIANTE 3. Tengo doce años.

FELIPE El fútbol es muy popular en Nicaragua. ¿Te gusta el fútbol?

ESTUDIANTE 4. No, no me gusta el fútbol.

FELIPE Personalmente, me gusta más el béisbol. ¿Te gusta el béisbol también?

ESTUDIANTE 5. Sí, me gusta el béisbol también.

FELIPE Bueno, gracias y hasta luego.

ESTUDIANTE 6. Adiós .

32 ¡Mucho gusto!

Work with a partner and take turns playing the roles of two new friends, Pilar and Miguel. Use the photos as a cue to answer each other's questions about your name, age, where you're from, and what kinds of things you like. Then switch roles.
Answers on p. 19K

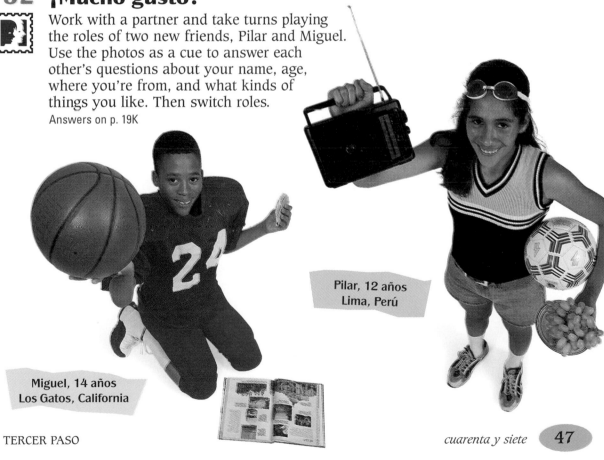

Pilar, 12 años
Lima, Perú

Miguel, 14 años
Los Gatos, California

TERCER PASO

ADDITIONAL PRACTICE
32 Have students use cutouts from magazines or drawings to create a collage of the things they like and don't like. They can use their collages instead of the photos in the textbook to interview one another.

33 ¡Entrevista!

Interview a classmate. Find out your partner's name, age, and where he or she is from. Also find out at least three things your partner likes and doesn't like. Be prepared to act out your interview for the class. Answers will vary.

¿Cómo te llamas?

¿Cuántos años tienes?

¿De dónde eres?   ¿Qué te gusta?

¿Qué no te gusta?

Arantxa Sánchez Vicario

34 ¿Qué les gusta a las estrellas?

Make a list of three famous people and write what you think they probably would like and not like. Then share your list with your partner. Are your lists similar? Are there any differences?

MODELO   1. A _____ le gusta el tenis.
A _____ no le gusta el baloncesto.
Answers will vary.

35 En mi cuaderno

Write a letter to a pen pal. Introduce yourself and give your age and where you're from. List three or four things that you like and don't like. Then ask your pen pal at least three questions. Keep a copy of this letter in your journal. Answers will vary.

Querido amigo / Querida amiga,

Me llamo . . .   Tengo . . .
Me gusta . . .   pero no . . .

También me . . .   pero . . . más

Con abrazos,

LETRA Y SONIDO

Script on p. 19F

Cass. 1A
CD 1
Trs. 22–26

A. The Spanish vowels (**a, e, i, o, u**) are pronounced clearly and distinctly. Learn to pronounce them by mimicking the recording or your teacher.

1. **a:** as in *father,* but with the tongue closer to the front of the mouth

Ana	cámara	amiga	tarea	llama

2. **e:** as in *they,* but without the *y* sound

este	eres	noche	excelente	café

3. **i:** as in *machine,* but much shorter

íntimo	isla	legítimo	Misisipi	día

4. **o:** as in *low,* but without the *w* sound

hola	moto	años	dónde	color

5. **u:** as in *rule*

fruta	uno	fútbol	único	música

B. Dictado

Ana has just met several new friends in Madrid and is practicing the new phrases she has heard. Write what you hear.

C. Trabalenguas

¡A, e, i, o, u! Arbolito del Perú, ¿cómo te llamas tú?

SUGERENCIA

The dictionary in the back of this book can be a helpful tool as you learn Spanish. For example, some of the words in **Letra y sonido** might be new to you. A dual-language dictionary will usually have the Spanish to English section first, followed by the English to Spanish section. Try looking up the word **isla** in the back of the book. Begin with the Spanish-English Vocabulary section that starts on page 281. Look in the alphabetized **i** section (ignore the article **la** when checking alphabetical order) and write down what **isla** means. Now look up the word **carpeta**. Does it mean what you might think it does?

AUDITORY LEARNERS

Tongue twisters and songs can help students focus on pronunciation. The tongue twister that practices vowel pronunciation can be a helpful mnemonic device for students.

SUGGESTION

It's important for students to develop dictionary skills. Develop in students the habit of cross-referencing the words they look up by looking up the English to Spanish translation then checking the Spanish to English translation of the same word.

☀ CLOSE

Conduct a short question-and-answer session in which students say what they like and don't like. They should use as much of the vocabulary from this **paso** as possible.

☀ ASSESS

QUIZ 1-3
Testing Program, pp. 5–6
Audio Program,
Audiocassette 4A OR
Audio CD 1 Track 30

PERFORMANCE ASSESSMENT

In pairs, have students role-play a situation where one is a famous sports figure and the other is a reporter. The reporter asks questions about the star's likes and dislikes (sports and food vocabulary) and the star answers the questions.

The **Enlaces** pages are an interdisciplinary feature. It links the study of Spanish and Spanish-speaking culture with other subjects that students might be studying. These subjects include social studies, mathematics, science, literature, and history.

PRESENTATION

Ask students the following questions: What is a census? Why does the government conduct a census every ten years? What useful information do they find out in a census? How would they use that information?

ADDITIONAL PRACTICE

2 As a class wrap-up activity, make a chart for the entire class based on the information gathered from the small groups. List all the countries mentioned by the students. Then make a chart of the different backgrounds of students in the class.

CIENCIAS SOCIALES

1 ¿De dónde son?

Did you know that over 25 million people of Spanish-speaking origin live in the United States? What countries do they come from? Use the information in the pie chart to complete these sentences.

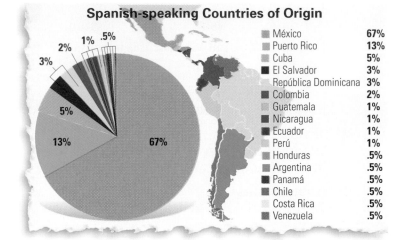

Spanish-speaking Countries of Origin

■ México	**67%**
■ Puerto Rico	**13%**
■ Cuba	**5%**
■ El Salvador	**3%**
■ República Dominicana	**3%**
■ Colombia	**2%**
■ Guatemala	**1%**
■ Nicaragua	**1%**
■ Ecuador	**1%**
■ Perú	**1%**
■ Honduras	**.5%**
■ Argentina	**.5%**
■ Panamá	**.5%**
■ Chile	**.5%**
■ Costa Rica	**.5%**
■ Venezuela	**.5%**

1. Most Spanish speakers in the United States are from ———. Mexico

2. The three largest Spanish-speaking groups in the United States come from ———, ———, and ———. Mexico, Puerto Rico, Cuba

3. The largest group of Central American Spanish speakers comes from ———. El Salvador

4. The largest group of South American Spanish speakers comes from ———. Colombia

2 ¿De dónde somos?

Work in groups of five. Find out what countries each student and his or her parents, grandparents, or great-grandparents came from. First decide who takes the following roles: Answers will vary.

- Interviewer: asks the question about countries
- Note taker: writes down everyone's answers
- Mathematician: adds up the number of people from each country
- Artist: draws the countries (see the world map in the front of the book, pp. xviii–xix)
- Presenter: tells the class about the list of countries and the maps

GEOGRAFÍA

3 Mira el mapa

Read the clues below aloud to your partner. Identify where each Spanish-speaking student lives. Use the maps in the beginning of the book on pages xvii through xxii to figure out what country each student is describing.

Norte

Oeste  *Este*

Sur

I'm from South America. My country doesn't have a border next to an ocean. Peru and Chile are to the west and to the east is Brazil. To the south is Argentina. **Bolivia**

Me llamo Carolina. Vivo en América del Sur. ¿De dónde soy?

I'm from a country in Central America. To the north is Mexico and to the east, Belize. To the south are El Salvador and the Pacific Ocean. **Guatemala**

Me llamo Alberto. Vivo en Centroamérica. ¿De dónde soy?

I'm from the Spanish-speaking half of an island between Cuba and Puerto Rico. It's in the Caribbean Sea. Haiti is the other half of the island. **La República Dominicana**

Me llamo Paloma. Vivo en Europa. ¿De dónde soy?

Me llamo Graciela. Vivo en el Caribe. ¿De dónde soy?

I'm from Europe. They speak Portuguese in the country to the west. To the east is the Mediterranean Sea. **España**

ENLACES

cincuenta y uno 51

VAMOS A LEER

Estrategia
Cognates
Spanish shares many words with English. Words with similar meanings and spellings in both languages are called *cognates**. Recognizing cognates can help you understand more Spanish words.

¡A comenzar!

Ⓐ These headlines are from different Spanish-language magazines. Find five Spanish/English cognates. Compare your list with a classmate's and discuss the English meaning of each headline. Look up any words you're not sure of in the dictionary beginning on page 281. Answers on p. 19K

Al grano   Answers on p. 19K

Ⓑ The following are descriptions of articles from these magazines. In which magazine would you look to find the following information?

1. interesting facts about famous personalities
2. the latest in compact disc players
3. jokes and riddles
4. mural paintings in East Los Angeles
5. the new album by a Spanish rap group
6. suggestions about what to do on your next free Saturday
7. how to organize your school to do a neighborhood cleanup
8. reviews of movies to watch at home
9. building a birdhouse

Cognados falsos

Ⓒ Some words look the same but don't mean the same thing in both languages. For example, **vaso** means *drinking glass,* not *vase.* List a similar English word for each Spanish word below. Then look up the Spanish words in the Spanish-English dictionary beginning on page 281 to see what they actually mean. How many are false cognates? Answers on p. 19K

real	**disgusto**
grupo	**sopa**
ropa	**teatro**

---

* So-called false cognates can be misleading. For example, **librería** means *bookstore,* not *library.*

VAMOS A LEER

cincuenta y tres **53**

☼ READING

🤝 COOPERATIVE LEARNING

B Put students in groups of four. Ask them to choose a discussion leader, a scribe, a proofreader, and an announcer (or assign these roles). Give students three to five minutes to complete Activity C. Monitor the groups' work as you walk around. Help students as necessary. At the end of the activity, call on the announcer to read the group's results. Remind students that they will receive a common group grade. This will keep each person on task and engaged in the total process.

☼ POSTREADING

SUGGESTION

C After doing Activities A and B, have students brainstorm to find as many English-Spanish cognates as they can in three minutes. Review their lists as a class. Clarify the meaning of any **cognados falsos** *(false cognates)*.

NATIVE SPEAKERS

Ask native speakers to bring in Spanish-language magazines or newspaper clippings. Preview the reading materials for age-appropriate content. Then have students look for cognates.

TEACHER NOTE

For additional reading, see *Practice and Activity Book*, page 13.

The **Repaso** reviews and integrates all four skills and culture in preparation for the Chapter Test.

SUGGESTION

Before beginning the **Repaso**, have students turn to page 21 and review the chapter objectives. Ask them if they feel they have learned what was intended. Proceed through the **Repaso** activities. Encourage both group and individual work.

ADDITIONAL PRACTICE

1 Have students create a third card and fill it out for themselves. Then have students fill out a card for a partner, to practice asking in the **tú** form and reporting in the **él** or **ella** form.

TEACHER NOTE

The **¡A hablar!**, **¡A escribir!**, and **En contexto** sections from the CD-ROM provide students with an excellent opportunity to integrate and practice chapter material.

REPASO

1

Cass. 1A
CD 1
Tr. 27

Imagine that you work for a pen pal service. Your job is to complete a set of cards with information left by the clients on the answering machine. One card has been done for you as an example. Create two other cards and fill them in as you listen to the messages.   Script and answers on p. 19F

NOMBRE: Mariana Castillo
ORIGEN: Es de España.
EDAD: Tiene 15 años.
LE GUSTA: la música rock
NO LE GUSTA: el tenis

2
Read the following letter from a client looking for a pen pal (**amigo por correspondencia**). Then decide which of the three candidates in Activity 1 would be a good pen pal for him. Base your decision on what they like and don't like.   Pablo García would be a good match because they both like rock music and neither one likes classical music.

Hola. Busco un amigo por correspondencia. Me llamo José Luis Bazán. Tengo trece años y soy de Guatemala. Me gusta mucho el fútbol y el béisbol. También me gusta la música rock, pero no me gusta la música clásica.

3
Make a chart of what you like and don't like for each of the categories in the word box. Present your information on a poster. Share with the class. Look at the **Vocabulario** on pages 44–45 for help.   Answers will vary.

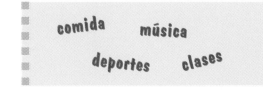

comida   música

deportes   clases

4 What is Andrés López Medina's father's last name? What is his mother's last name? Can you explain the system of last names to someone who has not studied Spanish? Write your answer out and present it to the class.

	LOPEZ - 89
LOPEZ MATEOS, N. - Galileo, 21	
» **MATEOS, J.** - Alonso Cano, 33	248 9093
» **MATUTE, R.** - Giralda, 204	730 1883
» **MAYORAL, A.** - Palencia, 101	775 8964
» **MAYORAL, C.** - Luis Buñuel, 12	263 3276
» **MEDIAVILLA, P.** - Embajadores, 78	437 1806
	711 8419
LOPEZ MEDINA, A. - Av. S. Eloy, 301	
» **MEDINA, F.** - Amor Hermoso, 69	472 4932
» **MEDINA, R.** - Echegaray, 21	326 3771
» **MEDINA, T.** - Av. Valle, 35	775 8964
» **MEDRANO, A.** - Cerro Blanco, 14	464 7691
	558 2220
LOPEZ MEGIA, J. - Bolivia, 35	
» **MEIRA, L.** - Libertad, 45	471 4936
	792 2039

Father's last name: López; Mother's last name: Medina

5 The editor of your Spanish class newspaper has asked you to come up with a standard questionnaire for interviewing new students. Create an interview form that asks for their name, age, where they're from, and what they like and don't like. Then try your questionnaire out on a classmate.   Answers will vary.

¿Cómo te llamas?	¿Cómo estás?	¿Cuántos años tienes?	¿De dónde eres?
1.			
2.			

6

S I T U A C I Ó N

You've been asked to introduce the new student from Ecuador to your class. Role play the scene with a partner, using the information given. Be sure to ask for his or her name and age, where he or she is from, and several things that he or she likes and doesn't like. Then introduce your new friend to the class.

ECUADOR TENIS Y SQUASH CLUB

Esta tarjeta da al socio derecho de ingresar al Club a sus instalaciones y a la utilización de servicios.
En caso de pérdida notificar al Ecuador Tenis y Squash Club.

Nombre **MARIA LORENA**
VITALI SÁNCHEZ
Socio **ESPECIAL** nº **12-911**
Fecha Nac. **13-08-1987**

María Lorena Vitali Sánchez
Firma

📁 **PORTFOLIO**
5 **Written** Activity 5 may be used as a Portfolio entry. For Portfolio suggestions, see *Alternative Assessment Guide,* p. 12.

This page is intended to help students prepare for the Chapter Test. It is designed for the students to work on their own initiative and consists of a brief checklist of the major points covered in the chapter. The students should be reminded that this is only a checklist and does not necessarily include everything that will appear on the Chapter Test.

TEACHER NOTE

As this Chapter Test may be the first foreign-language test your students will take, you may wish to give them some tips on test preparation. Point out that this is a skills test, not a knowledge test. Cramming will not help them because memorization is not what they will be tested on. Communicating is what language is about, so it is a good idea for students to study together. For example, they could re-read the **fotonovela** aloud, taking turns playing the character's roles. Then they could identify vocabulary and phrases in the characters' lines from the presentations in the chapter. You may also want to refer them to page vi for language study tips.

¡A VER SI PUEDO...

Answers on p. 19K

▼ Can you say hello and goodbye? p. 27

▼ Can you introduce people and respond to an introduction? p. 29

▼ Can you ask how someone is and say how you are? p. 31

▼ Can you ask and say how old someone is? p. 35

▼ Can you ask where someone is from and say where you're from? p. 38

▼ Can you talk about what you like and don't like? p. 43

1 How would you greet or say goodbye to these people?

1. the principal before class
2. a classmate as the bell rings
3. a friend at the end of the school day

2 What would you say in the following situations?

1. The new Spanish teacher asks your name.
2. You've just been introduced to Juan, the new student from Spain.
3. Juan has just said, "Mucho gusto."

3 Juan has just joined your class and you want to get to know him. How would you . . .?

1. ask him how he's doing
2. tell him how you're doing

Juan Fernández Jiménez

4 How would you . . .?

1. ask Juan how old he is
2. tell him how old you are
3. tell your friend how old Juan is

5 Can you . . .?

1. tell Juan where you're from
2. ask him where he's from
3. tell your friend where Juan is from

6 You'd like to ask Juan to do something with you on Saturday, but you don't know what he likes. Ask him if he likes these things, and tell him which ones you like.

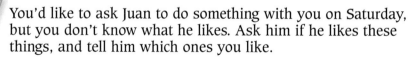

1. volleyball
2. baseball
3. Italian food
4. pop music
5. basketball

VOCABULARIO

PRIMER PASO

Saying hello and goodbye

Adiós. *Goodbye.*
Buenas noches. *Good night.*
Buenas tardes. *Good afternoon.*
Bueno, tengo clase. *Well, I have class (now).*
Buenos días. *Good morning.*
Chao. *'Bye.*
Hasta luego. *See you later.*
Hasta mañana. *See you tomorrow.*
¡Hola! *Hello!*
señor *sir, Mr.*
señora *ma'am, Mrs.*
señorita *miss*
Tengo que irme. *I have to go.*

Introducing people and responding to an introduction

¿Cómo te llamas? *What's your name?*
Encantado/a. *Delighted to meet you.*
Ésta es mi amiga. *This is my friend.* (to introduce a female)
Éste es mi amigo. *This is my friend.* (to introduce a male)
Igualmente. *Same here.*
Me llamo... *My name is . . .*
Mucho gusto. *Nice to meet you.*
Se llama... *His/Her name is . . .*
Soy... *I am . . .*
¿Y tú? *And you?* (familiar)

Asking how someone is and saying how you are

¿Cómo estás? *How are you?* (to ask a friend)
Estoy (bastante) bien, gracias. *I'm (pretty) well, thanks.*
Estupendo/a. *Great./Marvelous.*
Excelente. *Great./Excellent.*
Gracias. *Thanks.*
Horrible. *Horrible.*
Más o menos. *So-so.*

(Muy) mal. *(Very) bad.*
¿Qué tal? *How's it going?*
Regular. *Okay.*
tú *you* (informal)
¿Y tú? *And you?*
yo *I*
Yo también. *Me too.*

SEGUNDO PASO

Asking and saying how old someone is

¿Cuántos años tiene? *How old is (he/she)?*
¿Cuántos años tienes? *How old are you?*
el número *number*
Tengo ... años. *I'm . . . years old.*
Tiene ... años. *He/She is . . . years old.*

Asking where someone is from and saying where you're from

¿De dónde eres? *Where are you from?*
¿De dónde es? *Where is he/she from?*
Es de... *He/She is from . . .*
ser *to be*
Soy de... *I'm from . . .*

Numbers 0–30

See p. 36

TERCER PASO

Talking about what you like and don't like

el baloncesto *basketball*
el béisbol *baseball*
la cafetería *cafeteria*
el chocolate *chocolate*
la clase de inglés *English class*
la comida mexicana/italiana/china *Mexican/Italian/Chinese food*
el *the*
la ensalada *salad*
el español *Spanish*
la fruta *fruit*
el fútbol *soccer*
el fútbol norteamericano *football*
el jazz *jazz*
la *the*
más *more*
Me gusta... *I like . . .*
Me gusta más... *I prefer . . .*
mucho *a lot*
la música clásica/pop/rock *classical/pop/rock music*
la música de... *music by . . .*
la natación *swimming*
no *no*
No me gusta... *I don't like . . .*
pero *but*
la pizza *pizza*
¿Qué te gusta? *What do you like?*
sí *yes*
la tarea *homework*
¿Te gusta...? *Do you like . . .?*
el tenis *tennis*
el voleibol *volleyball*

KINESTHETIC LEARNERS
Place actual objects as well as plastic replicas, drawings, and pictures in a box. Have students take an item and use the name of the item in a Spanish phrase or sentence.

TEACHER NOTE
Adelante presents the Spanish spelling of **voleibol**. If you prefer the spelling **volibol** used in the Americas, be aware that the spelling in the testing program is **voleibol**.

CHAPTER 1 ASSESSMENT

CHAPTER TEST
- *Testing Program*, pp. 7–12
- *Audio Program*, Assessment Items, Audiocassette 4A OR Audio CD 1

SPEAKING TEST
- *Testing Program*, p. 112

TEST GENERATOR
Chapter 1

ALTERNATIVE ASSESSMENT
Performance Assessment
You might want to use the **Situación** on page 55 as a cumulative performance assessment activity.

Portfolio Assessment
ANNOTATED TEACHER'S EDITION
- **Written: Repaso** Activity 5, p. 55
- **Oral:** Activity 33, p. 48
ALTERNATIVE ASSESSMENT GUIDE, p. 12

CAPÍTULO 2

¡Organízate!

CHAPTER OVERVIEW

De antemano pp. 60–63	¡Mañana es el primer día de clases!			
	FUNCTIONS	**GRAMMAR**	**CULTURE**	**RE-ENTRY**
Primer paso pp. 64–71	• Talking about what you want or need, p. 66	• **Así se dice: Quiero, Quieres,** p. 66 • **Gramática:** Noun plurals, p. 67; Plural indefinite articles, p. 68 • **Notas gramaticales:** Indefinite articles, p. 66; Subject pronouns, **él** and **ella,** p. 70	• **Nota cultural:** Extended family, p. 63 • **Nota cultural:** School uniforms, p. 65 • **Encuentro cultural: Los saludos,** pp. 72–73	• Subject pronouns: **tú** and **yo** (from **Capítulo 1**) • Definite articles: **el** and **la** (from **Capítulo 1**)
Segundo paso pp. 74–81	• Saying what's in your room, p. 76	• **Así se dice:** Using **hay,** p. 76 • **Gramática:** Agreement of **mucho** and **¿cuánto?,** p. 78	• **Nota cultural:** Apartments in Spain/Sharing TV set, p. 75 • **Nota cultural:** Exclamations, p. 79 • **Panorama cultural: ¿Qué necesitas para el colegio?,** pp. 82–83	• Talking about likes and dislikes (from **Capítulo 1**) • Numbers 0–30 (from **Capítulo preliminar**)
Tercer paso pp. 84–89	• Talking about what you need and want to do, p. 85	• **Así se dice: Necesitar, querer** + infinitive, p. 85 • **Nota gramatical:** Identifying infinitives, p. 86	• **Realia:** Spanish currency, p. 88	• Numbers 0–30 (from **Capítulo preliminar**) • Using cognates (from **Capítulo 1**)

Letra y sonido	**p. 89**	The letter **d**	**Dictado:** Textbook Audiocassette 1B/Audio CD 2	
Enlaces	**pp. 90–91**	**La historia y las matemáticas**		
Vamos a leer	**pp. 92–93**	**Portadas**	**Reading Strategy:** Reading titles	
Review	**pp. 94–97**	**Repaso,** pp. 94–95	**A ver si puedo...,** p. 96	**Vocabulario,** p. 97

Assessment

TESTING PROGRAM
• **Primer paso,** Quiz 2-1, pp. 19–20
• **Segundo paso,** Quiz 2-2, pp. 21–22
• **Tercer paso,** Quiz 2-3, pp. 23–24
• Assessment Items, Audiocassette 4A OR
• Audio CD 2 Tracks 17–19

• **Chapter Test,** pp. 25–32
• Assessment Items, Audiocassette 4A OR
• Audio CD 2 Tracks 20–21

Alternative Assessment
Portfolio Assessment
ANNOTATED TEACHER'S EDITION
• **Written: Repaso** Activity 2, p. 94
• **Oral: A ver si puedo...** Activity 2, p. 96
ALTERNATIVE ASSESSMENT GUIDE, p.13

PRINT   MEDIA

Pupil's Edition, pp. 58–97

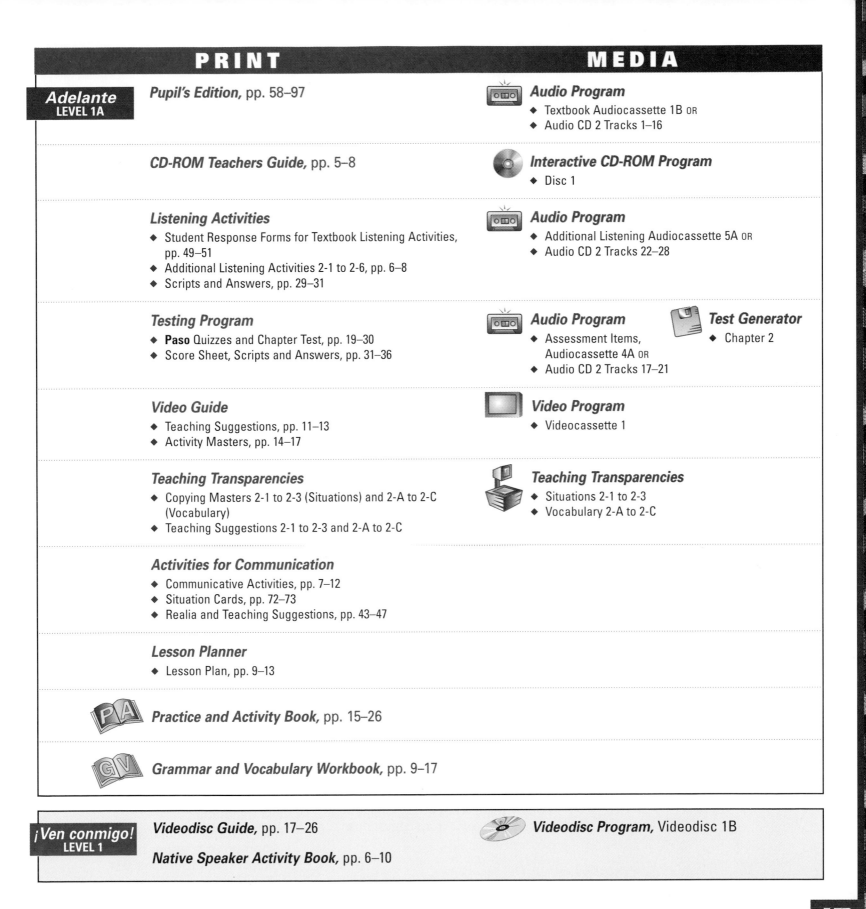

Audio Program
- Textbook Audiocassette 1B OR
- Audio CD 2 Tracks 1–16

CD-ROM Teachers Guide, pp. 5–8

Interactive CD-ROM Program
- Disc 1

Listening Activities
- Student Response Forms for Textbook Listening Activities, pp. 49–51
- Additional Listening Activities 2-1 to 2-6, pp. 6–8
- Scripts and Answers, pp. 29–31

Audio Program
- Additional Listening Audiocassette 5A OR
- Audio CD 2 Tracks 22–28

Testing Program
- **Paso** Quizzes and Chapter Test, pp. 19–30
- Score Sheet, Scripts and Answers, pp. 31–36

Audio Program
- Assessment Items, Audiocassette 4A OR
- Audio CD 2 Tracks 17–21

Test Generator
- Chapter 2

Video Guide
- Teaching Suggestions, pp. 11–13
- Activity Masters, pp. 14–17

Video Program
- Videocassette 1

Teaching Transparencies
- Copying Masters 2-1 to 2-3 (Situations) and 2-A to 2-C (Vocabulary)
- Teaching Suggestions 2-1 to 2-3 and 2-A to 2-C

Teaching Transparencies
- Situations 2-1 to 2-3
- Vocabulary 2-A to 2-C

Activities for Communication
- Communicative Activities, pp. 7–12
- Situation Cards, pp. 72–73
- Realia and Teaching Suggestions, pp. 43–47

Lesson Planner
- Lesson Plan, pp. 9–13

Practice and Activity Book, pp. 15–26

Grammar and Vocabulary Workbook, pp. 9–17

Videodisc Guide, pp. 17–26

Videodisc Program, Videodisc 1B

Native Speaker Activity Book, pp. 6–10

¡Organízate!

TECHNOLOGY APPLICATIONS IN THE CLASSROOM

For a complete list of the media resources and their accompanying printmatter guides, see page 57B.

DE ANTEMANO pp. 60–63

Video

• Show *¡Mañana es el primer día de clases!* See *Video Guide* pp. 11–16 for synopsis, teaching suggestions, and activity masters.

Audio

• Play the **fotonovela** for students to read along or for pronunciation practice.

PRIMER PASO pp. 64–71

Video

• Show the **paso** opener to model saying what people want or need.

Audio

• Use Textbook Listening Activities 5 and 6 to practice saying what people want or need.

• Use Additional Listening Activities 2-1 and 2-2 to practice talking about items that people want or need.

Transparencies

• Use Vocabulary Transparency 2-1 to present and practice activities using the teaching suggestions. Use the CD-ROM activities as a follow-up.

CD-ROM

• Activity 1 practices saying what someone wants or needs.

• Activity 2 practices singular and plural nouns and indefinite articles.

ENCUENTRO CULTURAL pp. 72–73

Video

• Play the video without sound and ask students to indicate when they see non-verbal greetings. Then show the video with sound to see if students can identify the phrases associated with each non-verbal greeting.

SEGUNDO PASO pp. 74–81

Video

• Show the **paso** opener to model describing the contents of a room. Have students read along.

Audio

• Use Textbook Activity 19 to practice bedroom contents vocabulary.

• Use Additional Listening Activities 2-3 and 2-4 to practice items found in someone's bedroom as a challenge.

Transparencies

• Vocabulary Transparency 2-B contains bedroom contents vocabulary. Use the CD-ROM as a follow-up.

CD-ROM

• Activity 3 practices bedroom and classroom vocabulary.

• Activity 4 practices **mucho** and **cuánto.**

PANORAMA CULTURAL pp. 82–83

Audio

• Play the **Panorama cultural** as students read along.

Video

• Show the interviews to students. See *Video Guide* for suggestions.

CD-ROM

• Have students do the **Panorama cultural** activity for Chapter 2.

TERCER PASO pp. 84–89

Video

• Show the **paso** opener to model saying what people need and want to do. Have students read along.

Audio

• Use Textbook Activity 32 to practice saying what people need to do.

• Use Additional Listening Activities 2-5 and 2-6 to practice numbers and talking about what people need and want to do.

Transparencies

• Situation Transparency 2-3 depicts things that people need or want to do. Use it after presenting the phrases needed to discuss these activities.

CD-ROM

• After presenting the vocabulary on p. 86, have students do Activity 5.

• After completing the **paso,** have students do Activity 6 to review numbers.

REPASO pp. 94–95

Video

• Replay the **fotonovela** and ask students to point out when characters perform this chapter's functions.

CD-ROM

• In **En contexto** students discuss the first day of classes with a new friend from Spain.

Test Generator

• Use the Test Generator to make a short practice test to help students prepare for the chapter test.

DE ANTEMANO

Barcodes A and B access the **De antemano** dramatic episode in its entirety. Subsequent barcodes show individual scenes. The barcode numbers correspond to the scene numbers as they appear in the **De antemano**.

¡Mañana es el primer día de clases! **A**
Search 1, Play To 8875

Abuela... **1**
Search 450, Play To 1812

Ah, lo siento... **2**
Search 1813, Play To 3673

Sí, sí... **3**
Search 3674, Play To 3889

Paco, mira... **4**
Search 3890, Play To 4219

Y ves... **5**
Search 4220, Play To 4359

Aquí tienes... **6**
Search 4360, Play To 5044

Abuela, ¡ya estoy listo! **7**
Search 5045, Play To 6970

Bueno, no necesito... **8**
Search 6971, Play To 8236

Bueno, Paco... **9**
Search 8327, Play To 8548

¡El dinero! **10**
Search 8572, Play To 8875

¡Mañana es el primer día de clases! (a continuación) **B**
Search 8875, Play To 22810

VIDEOCLIPS

This clip is a public service announcement designed to promote literacy. You may want to preview it before showing it to students.

Alfabetismo

Search 30860, Play To 32149

PASO OPENERS

Each **paso** begins with a re-presentation of a scene from the dramatic episode that models targeted functions, vocabulary, and grammar.

Bueno, no necesito... **1** p. 64
Search 6971, Play To 8236

Ah, lo siento... **3** p. 84
Search 1813, Play To 3673

Paco tiene... **2** p. 74
Search 9850, Play To 11260

PANORAMA CULTURAL

¿Qué necesitas para el colegio?

These barcodes access supplementary interviews that do not appear in the book. Not all barcodes are listed here. For a complete listing of supplemental interviews, see the *Videodisc Guide,* p. 18.

Paulina, Ecuador **1**
Search 24374, Play To 24542

Brenda, México **5**
Search 26517, Play To 27169

Jimena, Argentina **2**
Search 24543, Play To 24906

Johnny, Venezuela **6**
Search 27170, Play To 27493

Fabiola, Venezuela **3**
Search 24907, Play To 26191

Ángel, Venezuela **7**
Search 29022, Play To 29886

Tomás, Texas **4**
Search 26192, Play To 26516

Carlos, México **8**
Search 29887, Play To 30860

¡Organízate!

TEXTBOOK LISTENING ACTIVITIES SCRIPTS

For Student Response Forms, see Listening Activities pp. 49–51

PRIMER PASO   pp. 64–71

5 Arturo y Sumiko   p. 65

ARTURO   Para las clases, necesito unas gomas de borrar, cuadernos y libros, claro. Tú, ¿qué necesitas?

SUMIKO   Necesito lápices y cuadernos, y una regla nueva.

Answers to Activity 5

una mochila
unos cuadernos—A, S
unos lápices—S
un libro—A
un diccionario
un bolígrafo
una calculadora
una carpeta
una regla—S
papel
unas gomas de borrar—A

6 ¿Qué necesita Blanca?   p. 66

Necesito papel, una calculadora, lápices y una carpeta. Ya tengo una mochila, varios cuadernos, los libros y los bolígrafos.

Answers to Activity 6

Blanca necesita papel, una calculadora, lápices y una carpeta.

SEGUNDO PASO   pp. 74–81

19 ¿Qué hay?   p. 76

En mi cuarto hay dos camas. También tengo un escritorio y un armario. Tengo tres revistas y dos carteles. También hay una radio y dos sillas.

Answers to Activity 19

dos camas
tres revistas
dos carteles
dos sillas

32 Victoria y Tomás necesitan...   p. 86

Primero les digo lo que necesito hacer yo. Necesito organizar mi cuarto, poner la ropa en el armario y encontrar mi mochila. Necesito hacer muchas cosas. Mi hermano Tomás también necesita hacer muchas cosas. Él necesita ir al centro comercial para comprar una mochila nueva, pero primero necesita hacer la tarea.

Answers to Activity 32

1. B
2. T
3. T
4. V
5. V
6. V
7. T

For the scripts for Parts A and C, see page 89. The script for Part B is below.

B. Dictado

Quiero ir de compras. Necesito varias cosas: diez lápices, una calculadora, dos cuadernos y un diccionario. No necesito bolígrafos; ya tengo cinco. Y carpetas, ya tengo cuatro. ¿Qué más? Ah sí, ¡necesito el dinero!

1 p. 94

Para las clases necesitas muchas cosas. Necesitas una mochila, cuatro cuadernos, cinco carpetas, diez bolígrafos, seis lápices y un diccionario.

Answers to Repaso Activity 1

a. cuatro cuadernos
b. un diccionario
c. diez bolígrafos
d. cinco carpetas
e. seis lápices
f. una mochila

¡Organízate!

PROJECTS

DESEOS Y NECESIDADES

*This activity allows for written production while calling for higher-order thinking skills as students determine their wants and needs. Students are to set up a budget for **deseos y necesidades** as if they, or some imaginary person, were going to boarding school. If they wish, native speakers can share insights with you and the class.*

Introduction

Initiate a short discussion in English concerning the role the media (television, radio, movies, etc.) play in determining who we should be and how we should look. Encourage them to discuss how they determine what they really need.

Materials students may need

◆ Exchange rate information   ◆ Pencils or pens
◆ Budget example   ◆ Graph paper

Sequence

1 Students use the currency exchange rate to determine how many **pesetas** they can buy for 20 dollars and how many they can buy for 100 dollars.

2 Students list their wants and needs and find out their respective prices in dollars, then convert the prices of those items to **pesetas.**

3 Students list all the items they need to buy in their 20-dollar scenario and all the items they want to buy in their 100-dollar scenario.

4 You may decide to have students work on this project individually, entirely outside of class, or in groups that prepare a single budget to present to the class.

5 Assign a date for the rough draft, which may be peer reviewed in pairs for corrections, then specify a final date to present budgets for partners to evaluate orally.

6 The final written copy and the partner evaluation are turned in to the teacher.

Grading the project

Suggested point distribution (total = 100 points):

Vocabulary use. **40**
Creativity and appearance **20**
Correct exchange rate. **10**
Oral presentation **30**

EL REGRESO A CLASES

*In this activity, students will use all four skills to create full-page magazine ads in Spanish. The theme of students' ads may be "Back to School" (**El regreso a clases**). Have students discuss how advertising affects what they decide to buy. Ask them what types of advertising they prefer and have them identify ways in which advertisers target certain consumer groups at certain times of the year.*

Introduction

Tell students they will be able to use the vocabulary they have learned for school supplies and classroom items to create their ads. Ask them to make the ads appealing but accurate for the back-to-school theme. Help students brainstorm the key information an ad should contain: product name, benefits to the consumer, price, and when to buy it.

Materials students may need

◆ Large sheets of paper   ◆ Tape
◆ Old magazines   ◆ Scissors
◆ Exchange rate information   ◆ Markers
◆ Internet access   ◆ Glue

Sequence

1 Have students work individually or in groups. To create their ads, they need pictures of vocabulary items listed on page 97. Students cut pictures out of magazines or draw the items and list a price in **pesetas** at the current exchange rate. Have students research the exchange rate in a recent national newspaper or on the Internet.

2 Describe the project and assign a date for the rough draft. Assign a date for them to complete the ad and a date for oral presentations. Distribute a project assignment sheet and post a copy in the classroom, or write the assignment on the board.

3 If they will be working in groups, give students time in class to brainstorm and organize their ideas. Monitor their progress frequently.

4 Have students complete their first drafts for peer review and suggestions before turning them in.

5 Students complete the final drafts, present their ads to the class, and submit their written ads to the teacher.

FAMILY LINK

If students have worked individually on the project, they may also wish to present their ads to their families. Have them ask family members if they would buy the product based on the information in the ad. Why or why not?

Grading the project

Suggested point distribution (total = 100 points):

Chapter vocabulary use in ad	40
Creativity and appearance	20
Correct exchange rate	10
Oral presentation	30

NOTES

- You may wish to devote bulletin board space to finished products.
- Students may want to put their ads in their individual portfolios.
- Oral presentations may be recorded on audio- or videotape.

EL DINERO

*The following activity introduces students to the different monetary units used in Spanish-speaking countries. You may wish to have students refer to the **Enlaces** section on page 90 to introduce some currencies used in other countries.*

Materials students may need

- Encyclopedias
- Internet information (see page 15A)
- Paper or poster board
- Actual currency (optional)

Sequence

1 Point out the opportunity to learn new Spanish words, as well as interesting historical and cultural information about different countries through this research project.

2 Have students conduct library or Internet research on a particular currency.

3 Each student produces a poster with a visual replica of the country's money large enough for the class to see and a report on that currency.

4 Students look for the following information:
- the color of the bill
- who is pictured on the bill
- why the person pictured is important
- the names of any monuments on the bill
- the current exchange rate

5 Remind students that all labels must be in Spanish.

Grading the project

Suggested point distribution (total = 100 points):

Historical information	40
Creativity and appearance	20
Located currency reproduction	10
Oral presentation	30

NOTES

Some bulletin board space may be devoted to the finished products. You may decide to put their ads in students individual portfolios. Oral presentations may be videotaped.

CAPÍTULO 2

¡Organízate!

GAMES

LA TORRE DE BLOQUES

This game is good for learners with high visual/spatial intelligence. It promotes memory and Spanish-speaking skills.

Materials students may need

◆ Building blocks

Procedure

1. The object of the game is to make the highest stack of blocks without the tower falling over.

2. Students should sit in a circle on the floor or around a table with a bucket of blocks. Each block must go on top of the previous block.

   Before each student adds a block he or she must tell the group what all the students before him or her said in the same order without making a mistake and add a statement of his or her own. For example:

RAFAEL	Necesito un bolígrafo. *(Adds a block)*
VICENTE	Rafael necesita un bolígrafo y yo necesito papel. *(Adds a block)*
CARMELA	Rafael necesita un bolígrafo, Vicente necesita papel y yo necesito un lápiz. *(Adds a block)*

3. Have students continue until they use all the blocks or the tower falls.

EL CUARTO IMAGINARIO

This game may be played in pairs with students sitting back to back, or as a game show with groups of students in front of the classroom and the rest of the class as the audience. It is designed to review indefinite articles and vocabulary from this chapter. It also introduces students to new vocabulary in a meaningful setting.

Materials students may need

◆ Paper
◆ Pens or pencils
◆ Chapter vocabulary lists
◆ Large spinner (for game show)
◆ Index cards with dollar amounts

Procedure 1

Pair work:

1. Have two students each prepare a list of items that might be found in their imaginary rooms. They may include any of the vocabulary items from the Preliminary Chapter through Chapter 2, as well as cognates the teacher may suggest, or an item they locate the meaning for in the dictionary. (They must explain to their partners.)

2. Sitting back to back with a partner, one student must guess if an item is found in his partner's imaginary room. For example ¿**Tienes un armario?**

3. His or her partner responds with a **sí** or **no**. For every correct answer, the person guessing receives 10 points.

4. Then, the roles are reversed and the other student will ask about the items in his or her partner's imaginary room.

Procedure 2

Game show:

1. A large spinner with dollar amounts written in Spanish is handy for a variety of game shows, or you may have the game show host draw index cards with dollar amounts.

2. Divide students into groups and choose a moderator for the game show **El cuarto imaginario.**

3. Each team chooses a name and must prepare a list of items as indicated above. Each team member will contribute at least one item to the list.

4. The moderator then introduces the show and chooses two groups at a time to compete.

5. Team members sit back to back, and the moderator announces the value of each answer, **Por diez dólares, ¿qué hay en el cuarto imaginario?**

6 Each team member guesses one at a time the items selected by the other team, who will answer with **sí** or **no**.

7 This game promotes creative thinking because the correct answer is up to the individuals who make the list of items in the imaginary room.

8 Encourage students to be as original as possible. Mention a few cognates and personalized vocabulary items in the chapters to get them started, such as:

un cartel de (favorite actor, actress, musician, or band)

un reloj

una fotografía de (favorite actor, actress, musician, or band)

una alfombra (color)

una guía telefónica

SOBRE LA MESA

This game allows students to work in teams and to practice vocabulary from Chapter 2.

Materials you may need

◆ As many items from **Vocabulario** on page 65 as possible

Procedure

1 Place the items on a table or desk and cover them with a cloth. Divide students into teams.

2 Have all students gather around the table as you remove the cloth. Give students two minutes to study the items on the table. At the end of two minutes, replace the cloth and have them regroup into their teams. They are to make a list in Spanish of as many of the items as they can remember.

3 You many wish to provide students with a second look if they need to add to their lists. The teams with the most correct list wins.

Challenge

Remove one or two of the items and hide them. Students must then say which items are missing. This can also be played as a team activity.

LA BÚSQUEDA

*This game is a scavenger hunt to reinforce the vocabulary of Chapter 2, and to re-enter colors from the **Capítulo preliminar**. It will work best in classrooms where the students have access to common supplies.*

Materials students may need

◆ Six or more different types of common school supplies

Procedure

1 Divide the class into small groups. Each group should make up a list of classroom supplies for another group. Tell them that lists should be as realistic as possible, but may include colors and numbers as modifiers as well. The items on the list are restricted to vocabulary from the chapter that is available in the classroom. (**una calculadora, dos lápices amarillos, una mochila roja, dos carpetas...**)

2 Have groups exchange lists and allow time for a scavenger hunt for the items on their list. At the end of the time limit (five minutes, for example), have groups show their supplies while reading off the list. The group that has found the most items on its list is the winner.

¡Organízate!

ANSWERS TO CHAPTER 2 ACTIVITIES

Listening activity answers appear on Scripts pages 57E–57F. Answers to all other activities appear on corresponding pupil pages.

PRIMER PASO   pp. 64–71

8
1. Quiero una calculadora.
   Pero Paco, ya tienes tres calculadoras.
2. Necesito unos lápices.
   Ya tienes once lápices.
3. Quiero unos cuadernos.
   Ya tienes nueve cuadernos.
4. Necesito una mochila.
   Ya tienes dos mochilas.
5. Necesito unos bolígrafos.
   Ya tienes quince bolígrafos.
6. Necesito una carpeta.
   Ya tienes cinco carpetas.
7. Necesito unas gomas de borrar.
   Ya tienes veinte gomas de borrar.
8. Necesito una regla.
   Pero ya tienes cuatro reglas.

15 Answers will vary. Possible answers:
1. Necesito un diccionario, un bolígrafo y unos papeles.
2. Necesito una carpeta y un cuaderno.
3. Necesito papel, unas marcadoras, pintura y un pincel.
4. Necesito una calculadora.
5. Necesito una mochila.
6. Necesito un diccionario.
7. Necesito un bolígrafo.
8. Necesito papel, un lápiz, una goma de borrar y un marcador.

SEGUNDO PASO   pp. 74–81

20 Answers will vary. Possible answers:

En el cuarto de Débora y en mi cuarto hay	veinte sillas
	una puerta
	un reloj
una mesa	cinco ventanas
una silla	**En la clase no hay**
una puerta	un armario
un reloj	un televisor
una ventana	una cama
En la clase hay	una radio
veinte mesas	una lámpara

21 Answers will vary. Possible answers:
1. En el cuarto de Débora hay tres revistas.
2. Débora tiene cuatro lápices.
3. En el cuarto de Débora hay una silla.
4. Débora tiene una cama.
5. Débora tiene un reloj.

TERCER PASO   pp. 84–89

34 Answers will vary. Possible answers:
1. Necesita comprar un reloj.
2. Necesita organizar el cuarto.
3. Necesita comprar un diccionario de español.
4. Necesita ir a la librería.
5. Necesita conocer a nuevos amigos.
6. Necesita comprar ropa.
7. Necesita comprar una lámpara.
8. Necesita comprar zapatillas de tenis.

35 Answers will vary. Possible answers:
1. ¿Quieres comprar un reloj?
2. ¿Quieres organizar el cuarto?
3. ¿Quieres comprar un diccionario de español?
4. ¿Quieres ir a la librería?
5. ¿Quieres conocer a nuevos amigos?
6. ¿Quieres comprar ropa?
7. ¿Quieres comprar una lámpara?
8. ¿Quieres comprar zapatillas de tenis?

A VER SI PUEDO...   p. 96

1
1. Juanita, ¿necesitas unos bolígrafos y papel?
   Sí, necesito unos bolígrafos y papel.
2. Paco, ¿necesitas una calculadora?
   No, no necesito una calculadora.
3. Felipe, ¿necesitas unos cuadernos?
   Sí, necesito unos cuadernos.

2
1. ¿Cuánto papel necesitas?
2. ¿Cuántos libros necesitas?
3. ¿Cuántas reglas necesitas?
4. ¿Cuántos cuadernos necesitas?
5. ¿Cuántas carpetas necesitas?
6. ¿Cuántos lápices necesitas?

3
¿Tienes un armario en tu cuarto?
¿Tienes una cama en tu cuarto?
¿Tienes un estéreo en tu cuarto?
¿Tienes un televisor en tu cuarto?

4
1. Necesita organizar su cuarto. Quiero organizar mi cuarto.
2. Necesita poner las zapatillas en el armario. Quiero poner las zapatillas en el armario.
3. Necesita comprar unos cuadernos. Quiero comprar unos cuadernos.
4. Necesita conocer a muchos nuevos amigos. Quiero conocer a muchos nuevos amigos.
5. Necesita comprar zapatillas de tenis. Quiero comprar unas zapatillas de tenis.

Chapter Section	Presentation	Homework Options
Primer paso	**Vocabulario,** p. 65	*Grammar and Vocabulary,* p. 9, #1–2
	Así se dice, p. 66	*Practice and Activity Book,* p. 17, #5
	Gramática, p. 67	*Grammar and Vocabulary,* p. 11, #5–6 *Practice and Activity Book,* p. 18, #7 *CD-ROM,* Disc 1, Chapter 2, #2
	Gramática, p. 68	*Pupil's Edition,* pp. 68–69, #10, 12 *Grammar and Vocabulary,* p. 12, #7–8 *Practice and Activity Book,* p. 18, #8
	Nota gramatical, p. 70	*Grammar and Vocabulary,* p. 13, #9–10
Segundo paso	**Vocabulario,** p. 75	*Pupil's Edition,* p. 75, #18 *Grammar and Vocabulary,* p. 14, #11–12 *Practice and Activity Book,* p. 19, #9 *CD-ROM,* Disc 1, Chapter 2, #3
	Así se dice, p. 76	*Pupil's Edition,* p. 76, #19 *Practice and Activity Book,* p. 19, #9–10
	Gramática, p. 78	*Pupil's Edition,* p. 78, #23 *Grammar and Vocabulary,* p. 15, #13 *Practice and Activity Book,* pp. 20–21, #11–13 *CD-ROM,* Disc 1, Chapter 2, #4
Tercer paso	**Así se dice,** p. 85	*Pupil's Edition,* p. 85, #30 *Practice and Activity Book,* p. 22, #14–15 *CD-ROM,* Disc 1, Chapter 2, #5
	Vocabulario, p. 86	*Pupil's Edition,* pp. 86–87, #33–34 *Practice and Activity Book,* pp. 22–24, #16–18 *Grammar and Vocabulary,* p. 16, #14
	Nota gramatical, p. 86	*Grammar and Vocabulary,* p. 16, #15
	Vocabulario, p. 88	*Pupil's Edition,* pp. 88–89, #37–38 *Practice and Activity Book,* p. 24, #19 *Grammar and Vocabulary,* p. 17, #16–17

¡Organízate!

MOTIVATING ACTIVITIES

- Ask students what they do to get ready to go back to school and what they usually need to buy. What do they keep from year to year and what do they have to buy each year?

- Have students list in English the items in the photo that they need for school. In pairs, have them compare their lists. Students should refer to the lists at the end of the chapter to see what they've learned.

PHOTO FLASH!

① Ask students if they know any words in English ending in **-ería**. Try to get them to come up with pizzeria. Tell them that **papel** means paper and ask them to try to figure out what a **papelería** is. What other products would they expect to find in a **papelería?**

RE-ENTRY

Ask students how the girl in the photo would tell her friend that she likes her new notebook. How would she ask if he likes it?

AUDITORY LEARNERS

Ask students to point to the items in the photo as you read aloud: **fotos, mapas, diccionarios,** and **globos.** Point out that some of these are cognates.

CAPÍTULO 2

¡Organízate!

① **Necesito dos libros. ¿Qué necesitas tú?**

What do you usually do to get ready for school each year? Like Paco, you may need to take a look around your room, get things organized, and make a list of the school supplies you'll need.

In this chapter you will learn

- to talk about what you want and need
- to say what's in your room
- to talk about what you need and want to do

And you will

- listen to people talk about what they need, what they have in their rooms, and what they need to do
- read about some videos and books you might find interesting
- write a list of the things in someone's room
- find out how Spanish-speaking students prepare for the school year
- find out how Spanish speakers around the world greet people

② ¡Hombre! Necesitas organizar tus cosas.

③ ¿Qué hay en tu cuarto?

59

FOCUSING ON OUTCOMES

Explain to students that in this chapter they will be learning to communicate to others what they need and want. Have them read the learner outcomes and match them to the photos. (Photo 1: talking about what you need. Photo 2: talking about what you need to do. Photo 3: saying what's in your room.) Ask students to think of several items they want at the beginning of a new school year and several more they really need.

PHOTO FLASH!

② This photo is taken from the video episode for Chapter 2. **Abuela** tells Paco that his room is a mess and that he needs to put his things away before he goes shopping.

ADDITIONAL VOCABULARY

almohada *pillow*
manta, frazada *blanket*
sobrecama *bedspread*
cortinas *curtains*
cuadro *picture, portrait*
animal (m.) de peluche/un peluche *stuffed animal*
alfombra *carpet*
cómoda *dresser*
espejo *mirror*

 VIDEO INTEGRATION

Adelante LEVEL 1A
Video Program,
Videocassette 1, 23:35–28:31 OR

¡Ven conmigo! LEVEL 1
Videodisc Program,
Videodisc 1B

Search 1 , Play To 8875

TEACHER NOTE

The **fotonovela** is an abridged version of the video episode.

VIDEO SYNOPSIS

Paco explains to his grandmother that he needs to buy school supplies. His grandmother tells him to straighten his room first and gives him money to buy what he needs. While straightening his room, Paco discovers that he doesn't really need everything he thought he did. His grandmother tells him to buy only what he needs. But then Paco can't find the money.

MOTIVATING ACTIVITY

Have students predict what is going to happen in the **fotonovela.**

 CULTURE NOTE
In Spanish-speaking countries fewer teenagers have part-time jobs or receive allowances. Therefore, they need to ask their parents for spending money.

DE ANTEMANO

Cass. 1B
CD 2 Trs. 1–2

¡Mañana es el primer día de clases!

Look at the pictures in the **fotonovela.** Who are the characters? Where are they? Is there a problem? What are the clues that tell you this?

p. 15
Acts. 1–2

Paco

Abuela

1

Abuela... ¡Abuela!... ¿Abuela?

Ta...ta...da...da...

2

Ah, lo siento, Paco, ¿qué necesitas?

Pues, abuela... mañana es el primer día de clases y necesito muchas cosas.

Necesito una mochila... unos cuadernos... unos lápices... libros... papel... bolígrafos... una calculadora, un diccionario y unas zapatillas de tenis.

3

Sí, sí. Ven conmigo, Paco. ¡Ven conmigo!

4 Paco, mira. ¡Tu cuarto es un desastre! Primero... organiza tu cuarto.

Aquí tienes el dinero, pero para las cosas que necesitas.

5 Y ves, ya tienes lápices.

6 Gracias, abuelita. Pero... ¿organizar mi cuarto?

7 Abuela ¡ya estoy listo!

Bueno, no necesito lápices... ni necesito bolígrafos. Y ya tengo una calculadora. Pero no tengo mucho papel... y necesito más cuadernos.

8 Necesito también unas zapatillas de tenis. Y necesito una mochila.

61

PRESENTATION

Play the video or audio recording for students as they follow along in their books. Then read the **fotonovela** frame by frame, modeling the language while students repeat after you. Encourage students to guess meaning from context and visual clues. Students need not master structures and vocabulary at this point as they will be presented and practiced in the **pasos**.

KINESTHETIC LEARNERS

Pick up or point to the following items in the classroom: **mochila, cuaderno, lápiz, libro, papel, bolígrafo, calculadora, diccionario, zapatillas de tenis.** Then ask students to show you each article by picking it up or pointing it out. (**Muéstrame una calculadora.**) To review names and personalize the activity, ask ¿**Quién tiene una calculadora?** Then have students ask other students the question.

TEACHER NOTE

Throughout ¡**Ven conmigo!**, students learn vocabulary variants (such as **zapatillas de tenis**) that are appropriate to the chapter's geographical setting. If you prefer another local term, be aware that the *Testing Program* calls for forms presented in the *Pupil's Edition*.

LANGUAGE NOTES

• The word **goma** means both *eraser* and *rubber*. Use **borrador** for a chalkboard eraser.

• In some countries such as Puerto Rico, **bulto** is used for *backpack* and in Spain **lapicero** means *pen*. In South America, **carpeta** is also used to mean *notebook*.

THINKING CRITICALLY

Ask students to think of different possible endings for the **fotonovela** episode.

VIDEO INTEGRATION

Adelante LEVEL 1A

Video Program,
Videocassette 1, 28:32–36:16 OR

¡Ven conmigo! LEVEL 1

Videodisc Program,
Videodisc 1B

Search 8875, Play To 22810

VIDEO SYNOPSIS

In ***A continuación,*** Paco looks for the missing money. His grandmother comes in and is shocked at the mess. Paco calls Felipe and they go shopping together. First they visit a stationery store, next a shoe store, and finally a music store, where Paco buys a gift for his grandmother.

1 ¿Comprendes?

Check your understanding of the **fotonovela**. Choose the best answer to each question.

These activities check for global comprehension only. Students should not yet be expected to produce language modeled in **De antemano**.

1. Where does the story take place?
   a. Paco's school
   (b) Paco's house

2. What does Paco's grandmother tell him to do?
   (a) clean his room
   b. do his homework

3. At the end of the scene, which items does Paco find out that he does <u>not</u> need?
   a. an eraser and a ruler
   (b) pencils and pens

4. How does the scene end?
   a. Paco makes a phone call.
   (b) Paco can't find his money.

2 ¿Cierto o falso?

Based on the **fotonovela**, respond to each statement with **cierto** (true) or **falso** (false).

1. Mañana es el primer día de clases. cierto
2. Paco no necesita más cuadernos. falso
3. Paco no necesita más lápices. cierto
4. La abuela organiza el cuarto de Paco. falso
5. Paco necesita unas zapatillas de tenis. cierto

3 ¿Listos?

Complete the following paragraph about Paco with the correct words from the box.

Ay, ¡mañana es el primer día de ___1___! Bueno, no ___2___ lápices ni necesito bolígrafos, y ya tengo una ___3___. Pero no tengo mucho ___4___ y necesito más cuadernos. Y también necesito unas ___5___ de tenis. Ahora, ¿dónde está el dinero?

5 **zapatillas**   2 **necesito**

1 **clases**   3 **calculadora**

4 **papel**

Nota cultural

It's common for extended families to live together in Spain and Latin America. Like Paco, many young people grow up in homes with parents, grandparents, and even an aunt or uncle. What are the advantages and disadvantages of living with many relatives? How does this compare with your family or your friends' families?

COOPERATIVE LEARNING

1 through **3** Have students work through these exercises together in groups of two to four. Their answers should be identical. This means they need to agree upon their answers. Let them know that you will randomly choose only one sheet from each group. Every member will receive the grade from the sheet.

CHALLENGE

2 If a statement is false, students should change it to make it true.

SUGGESTIONS

1 Ask for volunteers to ask and answer questions. Have the class indicate whether answers are correct with thumbs up or thumbs down.

2 Write the words and phrases that make up these sentences on magnetic or felt board strips. Then ask students to manipulate the sentences to change negative sentences into positive ones and vice-versa.

ADDITIONAL PRACTICE

Have partners make a shopping list for Paco. The list should include only the items he decides he needs after he has straightened his room. Ask students how much money Paco will have to spend on his school supplies. Ask pairs to compare their lists.

VIDEO
INTEGRATION

Adelante LEVEL 1A

Video Program,
Videocassette 1, 27:28–28:09 OR
¡Ven conmigo! LEVEL 1

Videodisc Program,
Videodisc 1B

Search 6971, Play To 8236

SUGGESTION

As students watch the video, ask them to identify an expression other than **necesito** that implies something Paco needs. (**No tengo mucho papel.**)

JUMP START!

Have students make two columns in their notebooks. They should read **Paco tiene** and **Paco no tiene**. Based on the **fotonovela,** students complete these columns with the different school supplies Paco has and does not have.

NATIVE SPEAKERS

For some native speakers **carpeta** might mean *desk,* for others it might mean *carpet.* Point out that **el pupitre** is also used for *desk* and that **la alfombra** is standard for *carpet.*

Ask students which items in the word box for Activity 4 are things they need for school. Ask if there is anything they still need.

PRIMER PASO

Talking about what you want and need

4 La lista de Paco

Look at the word box. List the five school supplies that Paco mentions in the photo above. calculadora, lápices, papel, cuadernos, bolígrafos

libros   calculadora   bolígrafos   regla

papel   cuadernos   lápices

VOCABULARIO

Cosas para el colegio en la librería...

una mochila

una calculadora

un cuaderno

un lápiz

un libro

un diccionario

un bolígrafo

una regla

una goma de borrar

una carpeta

papel

5 Arturo y Sumiko

Cass. 1B
CD 2 Tr. 3

Follow the instructions to find out about Arturo and Sumiko's shopping trip. Script and answers on p. 57E

a. Make sure you have a separate piece of paper with a list of the eleven school supplies shown above.
b. Then, listen as Arturo and Sumiko talk about the supplies they need for school.
c. Write an **A** by every item Arturo needs and an **S** by every item Sumiko needs.
d. Finally, circle the item that both Arturo and Sumiko need.

🌐 Nota cultural

To prepare for school, many students in Spanish-speaking countries buy pens and notebooks just as you do. However, many of these students also need to buy school uniforms. You'll notice photos of students wearing school uniforms as you work with this book. Do you or any of your friends wear a uniform to school? What are some good things and bad things about school uniforms?

☀ TEACH

PRESENTATION

VOCABULARIO

Fill a backpack with objects from the **Vocabulario** and walk into class. Sit at an empty desk and model the pronunciation of each item by saying **Tengo...** as you take them out. Once you are done, practice asking students ¿**Tienes...?** Have them respond with **Sí, tengo...** or **No, no tengo...** Ask them to hold up the supplies in order to verify that their answers are correct.

SUGGESTION

Have students follow up by doing *CD-ROM,* Activity 1, an **Imagen y sonido** activity.

THINKING CRITICALLY

After students have read the **Nota cultural,** ask them why students might wear a uniform. Explain that students in many countries wear uniforms and that uniforms help provide a form of equality among all students. This is especially important in countries with big disparities between the rich and the poor.

CD-ROM
Disc 1

PA
p. 16
Act. 3

GV
p. 9
Acts. 1–2

2-A

pp. 16–17
Acts. 4–5

2-1

ASÍ SE DICE
Talking about what you want and need

To find out what someone wants, ask:	To answer, say:
¿Qué quieres?	**Quiero** una mochila.
¿Paco quiere una mochila?	Sí, él **quiere** una mochila.
To find out what someone needs, ask:	To answer, say:
¿Qué necesitas?	**Necesito** un cuaderno.
¿Necesitas papel?	No, **ya tengo** papel. *No, I already have paper.*
¿Qué necesita Merche?	**¡Ella necesita muchas cosas!** *She needs a lot of things!*

PRESENTATION
ASÍ SE DICE
Say **quiero (un libro)** and prompt students to give you the item. Then reverse it by taking an item from a student's desk and asking **¿Quieres (un libro)?** and prompting the student to answer with **Sí, quiero (un libro).** Then ask the class **¿(Student's name) quiere un libro?** Prompt the class to answer. Repeat the activity with **necesitar.**

NOTA GRAMATICAL
Write a list of nouns without articles on the board and have students provide **un** or **una.** Make sure they understand that **un** and **una** mean *a* or *an,* and that **un** replaces **el** and **una** replaces **la.** Encourage students to guess when they're not sure of the appropriate article.

---

6 ¿Qué necesita Blanca? Script and answers on p. 57E

Cass. 1B
CD 2 Tr. 4

Blanca needs to buy school supplies before school starts. Listen as she talks about her list. Then write her shopping list as she would write it. Ignore the things she already has and write only the things she needs. Start your answer with **Blanca necesita...**

ADDITIONAL PRACTICE
6 Set up a classroom store. Ask some students to be clerks and the rest to be shoppers. Give each clerk a list of the supplies they have for sale. The list can be the same for each clerk. Give shoppers a list of supplies that they need. Have the shoppers compare their list with the supplies they actually have in order to determine what they need and what they already have.

---

p.10
Acts. 3–4

NOTA GRAMATICAL

Un and **una** mean *a* or *an.* Use **un** with masculine nouns.
un cuaderno
Use **una** with feminine nouns.
una mochila
Many masculine nouns end with **-o** and many feminine nouns end with **-a.** Do you remember two ways to say *the* in Spanish?[1]

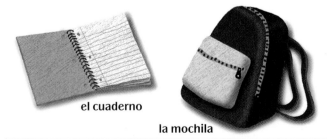

el cuaderno

la mochila

---
[1]**El** and **la** mean *the.*

7 Cosas para el colegio
Elena is telling her father what she has and what she needs for school. Complete each sentence with **un** or **una.**

Tengo ___1___ libro de matemáticas pero necesito ___2___ cuaderno. Tengo ___3___ bolígrafo, ___4___ goma de borrar y ___5___ carpeta. Necesito ___6___ diccionario, ___7___ calculadora, una regla y ___8___ lápiz. Y quiero ___9___ mochila nueva *(new),* por favor.

1. un	**4.** una	**7.** una
2. un	**5.** una	**8.** un
3. un	**6.** un	**9.** una

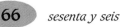

CD-ROM Disc 1

GRAMÁTICA   Making nouns plural

PA
p. 18
Act. 7

GV
p.11
Acts. 5–6

1. So far, you've been talking about single things. To make a noun plural, add -**s** if it ends in a vowel: **diccionario** → **diccionarios.** If the noun ends in a consonant, add -**es**: **papel** → **papeles.**
2. If a noun ends in -**z**, change -**z** to -**c** and add -**es**: **lápiz** → **lápices.**
3. How would you make these nouns plural?[1]

    a. cruz   b. luz   c. vez

8 ¡Necesito muchas cosas!

With a partner, play the roles of Paco and a friend. Each time Paco says he wants an item, his friend reminds him he already has several. Use the numbers in parentheses.   Answers on p. 57K

MODELO   libro de béisbol (6)
            —Quiero un libro de béisbol.
            —Pero Paco, ¡ya tienes seis libros de béisbol!

1. calculadora (3)   **3.** cuaderno (9)   **5.** bolígrafo (15)   **7.** goma de borrar (20)
2. lápiz (11)   **4.** mochila (2)   **6.** carpeta (5)   **8.** regla (4)

9 Una lista

Work in pairs. Look at the drawings below. Make a list of at least five items you have and five items you need. Compare your lists with a partner. What items do you have in common? Which supplies do you both need? Answers will vary.

MODELO   ¿Necesitas una goma de borrar?
            Sí, necesito una goma de borrar.

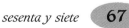

La lista de Marta
1. una goma de borrar

---

[1] The plurals are **cruces, luces,** and **veces.**

PRESENTATION
GRAMÁTICA
Ask students to make plural each of the vocabulary items on page 65. Practice by holding up one or more of the items on the list and asking students to say **un** or **una.**

MULTICULTURAL LINK
Have students interview exchange students or others who have studied in Spanish-speaking countries. Ask if students in those countries follow the same kind of schedule as students in your school. Do they stay in the same room all day? How does this affect what they bring to school? Do students wear uniforms? If there are no exchange students in your school, your students might ask these questions of pen pals. See page T58 for pen pal information.

SLOWER PACE
8 Before students join their partner, have them write the words for the numerals describing how many items Paco has. Allow them to use the written responses as they role-play Paco and his friend.

CD-ROM
Disc 1

PA
p. 18
Act. 8

GV
p. 12
Acts. 7–8

GRAMÁTICA Indefinite articles (un, una, unos, unas)

1. You've already learned that **un** and **una** mean *a* or *an*. **Unos** and **unas** mean *some* or *a few*. This chart shows how the four forms of the indefinite article are used.

	SINGULAR	PLURAL
MASCULINE	un bolígrafo	unos bolígrafos
FEMININE	una mochila	unas mochilas

2. Use **unos** with a masculine plural noun. When referring to a group that includes both males and females, the masculine plural is used (**unos estudiantes**).

3. In a negative sentence, **un, una, unos,** and **unas** are often dropped.
   ¿Necesitas unos bolígrafos?   No, no necesito bolígrafos.

10   Hablando con Felipe 🏠

It's the first day of school. Complete Paco and Felipe's phone conversation. Use the correct indefinite article (**un, una, unos,** or **unas**) with each missing word.

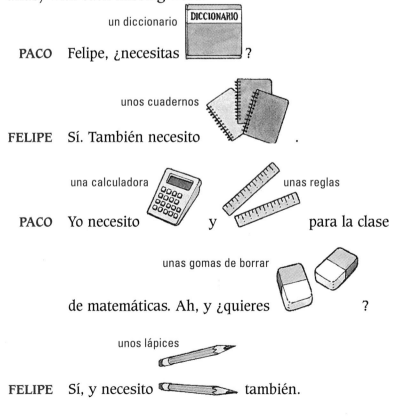

un diccionario

PACO   Felipe, ¿necesitas [DICCIONARIO] ?

unos cuadernos

FELIPE   Sí. También necesito   .

una calculadora   unas reglas

PACO   Yo necesito   y   para la clase

unas gomas de borrar

de matemáticas. Ah, y ¿quieres   ?

unos lápices

FELIPE   Sí, y necesito   también.

VISUAL LEARNERS
Have students label their school supplies by copying the words for them onto adhesive labels or onto strips of paper, then affixing them to the corresponding item. The class can also do this for other objects in the room.

ADDITIONAL PRACTICE
Divide students into groups of four. Explain that they will be setting up their own **tienda.** They need to come up with a name and a sign for their **tienda.** There should be two people working and two people shopping. After each pair has three exchanges, they should switch roles. Students will buy and sell different class supplies using the vocabulary they already know.

11 ¿Qué necesitas?

What school supplies do you need for your classes? With a partner, take turns asking each other what you need for the following classes. Name at least two items.

MODELO   la clase de arte
—¿Qué necesitas para la clase de arte?
—Necesito unos lápices y una goma de borrar.

1. la clase de español   un bolígrafo y un cuaderno
2. la clase de matemáticas   una regla y una calculadora
3. la clase de inglés   un cuaderno y un diccionario
4. la clase de historia   una carpeta y un cuaderno
5. la clase de ciencias   una lupa y un microscopio
6. la clase de computación   una computadora y un cuaderno

VOCABULARIO
EXTRA

la computadora   *computer*
la enciclopedia   *encyclopedia*
la lupa   *magnifying glass*
el microscopio   *microscope*

12 ¿Dónde está la mochila?

Paco lost his new backpack with all his school supplies in it. Help him out by making a list of at least five things he needs to replace. Remember that he'll need more of some items than others, so tell him exactly how many you think he needs.

MODELO   Necesitas diez lápices.

Necesitas tres cuadernos, cinco bolígrafos, una calculadora, una mochila y una regla.

GV
p.13
Acts. 9–10

NOTA GRAMATICAL

In Chapter 1 you learned to use the subject pronoun **yo** when talking about yourself and **tú** when talking to another student or someone your own age. When you want to talk about someone else, use **él** to mean *he* and **ella** to mean *she*.

Él necesita una mochila.

Ella necesita una calculadora.

13 ¿Él o ella?

Complete each of the sentences with **él** or **ella,** as appropriate.

MODELO ¿Felipe? ¿Qué tiene ═══════? **(él)**

1. ¿Paco? ═══════ ya tiene papel. Él
2. ¿Merche? ═══════ quiere una mochila. Ella
3. ¿Leticia? No, ═══════ no necesita un cuaderno. ella
4. ¿Juan Antonio? ¿Qué quiere ═══════? él
5. ¿Noemí? Sí, ═══════ necesita bolígrafos. ella
6. ¿Ignacio? ═══════ no necesita lápices. Él
7. ¿Verónica? ═══════ ya tiene unas gomas de borrar. Ella

14 Memoria

Work in groups of three. Each person takes turns saying one school supply he or she needs. Next, everyone says what the person on the right needs, using **tú**. Then all say what the other person in the group needs, using **él** or **ella**. Answers will vary.

MODELO Yo necesito una carpeta.
Tú necesitas unos papeles. (*to* the person on your right)
Ella necesita un lápiz. (*about* the person on your left)

15 ¿Qué necesitas para...?

Get together with a partner. Take turns saying what items you need to do the activities listed below. Use the items in the **Vocabulario** on page 65 and the words in the **Vocabulario extra** box. Answers on p. 57K

MODELO   to do math homework
Necesito un libro, un papel, una calculadora, una goma de borrar y una regla.

1. to write a report
2. to carry loose papers
3. to make a poster for art class
4. to add up some numbers
5. to carry your books
6. to look up unknown words
7. to write in your journal
8. to make a birthday card for your friend

VOCABULARIO EXTRA

el lápiz de color   *colored pencil*

el marcador   *marker*

el pincel   *paintbrush*

la pintura   *paint*

16 Comparaciones

Look at the school supplies that Anabela and Juan have in the photos. Take turns describing to your partner what Juan and Anabela have or need. You may also say something about an item they both have or an item they both need. Each of you should say at least three things about the photos. Answers will vary. Possible answers below:

MODELO   1. **Anabela tiene una carpeta. Juan necesita una carpeta.**
          2. **Juan necesita unos lápices de color y Anabela necesita unos lápices de color también.**

1. Juan tiene una regla. Anabela necesita una regla.
2. Juan tiene un libro. Anabela necesita un libro.
3. Anabela tiene un diccionario. Juan necesita un diccionario.

PRIMER PASO

setenta y uno **71**

GAME

Dibujos To review material from this **paso**, divide the class into two teams. Be sure to keep a record of each item for scoring. Ask the first player from team one to go to the board. Show the student a vocabulary word. The student draws a picture of the word and his or her team says the word in Spanish, including the correct definite article (**el** or **la**). The team has one minute to draw and guess the word before the opposing team may try. The successful team gets the point. Repeat with the other team, but this time ask for indefinite articles. Alternate teams and definite and indefinite articles.

ASSESS

QUIZ 2-1
Testing Program, pp. 19–20
Audio Program,
Audiocassette 4A OR
Audio CD 2 Track 17

PERFORMANCE ASSESSMENT

List on the board ten school supplies that students typically bring to school, and have students copy it. Put these ten supplies in a backpack. Then take out an item, and at the same time call out a number (**uno** for the first item, **diez** for the last). Ask students to write the number you call next to the name of the item on the list they copied.

VIDEO INTEGRATION

Adelante LEVEL 1A
Video Program,
Videocassette 1, 36:45–39:06

TEACHER NOTE
Even-numbered chapters have an **Encuentro cultural,** in which a young Spanish speaker introduces students to a variety of customs and cultural themes from around the Spanish-speaking world. The textbook pages are coordinated with a video presentation.

PRESENTATION
Have your students think about the ways people greet one another in our culture. Point out that they greet friends in quite a different way than they greet teachers, parents, or adults they don't know. How do they greet people their own age that they're meeting for the first time? What do they think are some of the factors that determine how two people will greet one another? (age, gender, circumstances, familiarity, etc.)

ENCUENTRO CULTURAL

Los saludos en el mundo hispano

In Spain there are many ways to greet people. You can shake hands with someone you're meeting for the first time, or give a friend or a member of your family a hug or kiss on the cheek.

1 ¿Qué dijo?
Ana explains several ways that people greet one another. Read what she says and see if you can guess what kind of greeting she's describing in the following sentences.

¡Hola! Yo me llamo Ana y soy de Sevilla. En España es muy común darle dos besos cuando ves a un amigo o una amiga que ya conoces. Cuando los hombres se ven, se dan un abrazo fuerte, u otra señal de cariño. Entre familia nos saludamos con mucho cariño.

▶ "En España es muy común **darle dos besos**".

▶ "Cuando los hombres se ven, se dan **un abrazo fuerte**".

▶ "Entre familia nos saludamos **con mucho cariño**".

1. Ana says that in Spain **"se dan dos besos"**. What do you think that means? two kisses

2. Ana says men sometimes give each other **un abrazo fuerte** when they greet each other. What do you think **un abrazo fuerte** means?
   (a.) a big hug
   b. a firm handshake

3. How does Ana say family members greet one another? with a lot of affection

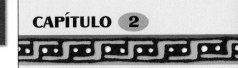

2 ¡Piénsalo!

1. Look at the photos on these two pages. Is there one that shows ways in which you also greet someone? Do any of the photos show something you don't do when you meet someone?

2. Using what you know about how people greet one another in Spain, what is Ana's relation to each of the people she's greeting below? How do you know?

1. Answers will vary. Possible answers:
   Do: hugging, shaking hands, or kissing cheek
   Don't: kiss friends on the cheek

2. The woman and young man are close friends or relatives. The older man is an acquaintance or someone Ana has just met.

3 ¿Y tú?

1. Describe how the following people would greet each other. Mention gestures as well as phrases they might use. Would the greetings be different depending on whether the people were in Spain or Latin America? How? Answers will vary. Possible answers:
   a. two old friends seeing each other unexpectedly two kisses (one kiss in Latin America) or a big hug
   b. a student meeting a teacher for the first time shake hands
   c. a young person greeting his or her grandparent kisses and hugs

2. On the first day of school this year, how did you greet friends whom you hadn't seen all summer? How did you greet teachers you knew? Answers will vary.

3. Imagine two situations in which you might need to know how Spanish speakers greet each other. Answers will vary. Possible answers: meeting a foreign exchange student from a Spanish-speaking country; studying abroad in a Spanish-speaking country

ENCUENTRO CULTURAL

setenta y tres 73

THINKING CRITICALLY

2 Have students imagine that they're writing an etiquette guide for exchange students from Spain or Latin America who will be attending their school. Have them write a short section on the do's and don'ts of greetings in their community, including information such as how to greet friends, family, teachers, and new people.

CHALLENGE

3 For an added challenge, have students mention phrases that people might use to greet each other in these three situations.

   Using what they now know about greetings, have your students discuss how Spanish-speaking teens might behave under the same circumstances.

MULTICULTURAL LINK

Have students research ways to greet people in other cultures, particularly non-Western cultures. The richest source of information for them will probably be people from other countries and in other language communities.

SUGGESTION

Show the video sequence of Paco greeting Merche or show other footage of Spanish-speaking people greeting one another to illustrate culturally appropriate displays of affection.

VIDEO INTEGRATION

Adelante LEVEL 1A
Video Program,
Videocassette 1, 29:04–29:50 OR
¡Ven conmigo! LEVEL 1
Videodisc Program,
Videodisc 1B

Search 9850, Play To 11260

JUMP START!

Ask students to list the school supplies they have either in their backpacks, their desks, or their lockers. (**En mi mochila tengo...**)

SUGGESTION

17 This scene from the video shows Paco and his grandmother in his room. Have students watch the scene or look closely at the photo to determine what Paco has and doesn't have.

☀ MOTIVATE

- Ask students to envision their ideal room; have several students describe the way they see it. How do they envision their own rooms when they get to high school?

- Ask students to jot down five things they consider essential for any student's room. Tally the number of times each item is listed, and put the most frequently listed items first when introducing this lesson.

SEGUNDO PASO

Saying what's in your room

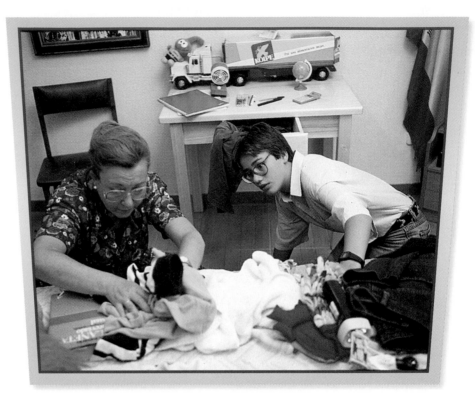

17 ¿Qué hay en el cuarto de Paco?

Look at the photo. Find three items from the choices below that are in the photo above. Then write a sentence saying what Paco has in his room. Begin your sentence with **Paco tiene...**

una calculadora

una mochila

el dinero

un libro

un lápiz

unos bolígrafos

un cuaderno

Answers will vary.
Possible answer:
Paco tiene una calculadora, unos bolígrafos y un cuaderno.

 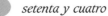

El cuarto de Débora

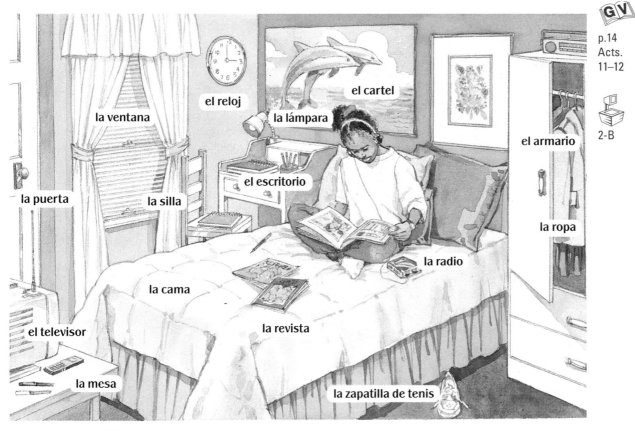

el reloj

el cartel

la ventana

la lámpara

el armario

el escritorio

la puerta

la silla

la ropa

la radio

la cama

el televisor

la revista

la mesa

la zapatilla de tenis

GV
p.14
Acts.
11–12

2-B

18 En mi cuarto tengo...

List five items from Débora's room that you have in your room. How many of each item do you have?

MODELO Tengo una cama, un armario, una radio, dos ventanas y tres carteles.

Answers will vary.

Nota cultural

In Spain, most people live in **pisos** *(apart- ments)* in cities or towns. Bedrooms are often smaller, and sisters or brothers will sometimes have to share a room. Generally, the family shares a single TV and a single phone. It's not common for younger family members to have a TV or phone of their own. What's positive and negative about sharing a TV or phone with the family?

PA
p. 26
Acts.
21–22

☀ TEACH

PRESENTATION

VOCABULARIO

Prepare a set of photos of the items in the **Vocabulario** and tape them to one side of the board. Label the other side **Mi cuarto ideal.** As you describe your ideal room by calling out each item, have a student get up and move that item to the other side of the board. Afterwards, have students turn to the Chapter Opener on page 58 and answer the question **¿Qué hay en su cuarto?**

18 Some students may not have their own room. Allow all students to give imaginary answers. Tell them the impor- tant thing is to practice the new vocabulary.

RE-ENTRY

Have students describe **El cuarto de Débora,** using an indefinite article for each vocabulary item.

PA
p. 19
Act. 10

2-2

ASÍ SE DICE — Saying what's in your room

To find out what there is in someone's room, ask:

To answer, say:

¿Qué hay en tu cuarto?

Tengo una mesa y dos sillas **en mi cuarto.** *I have a table and two chairs in my room.*

¿Qué hay en el cuarto de Paco?
What is there in Paco's room?

Hay libros y cuadernos **en su cuarto.** *There are books and notebooks in his room.*

¿Tienes un televisor?
Do you have a TV set?

No, **no tengo** televisor.

¿Qué tiene Merche **en su cuarto?**
What does Merche have in her room?

Merche **tiene** unos carteles y una radio **en su cuarto.**

PRESENTATION
ASÍ SE DICE

Draw a picture of a room on a transparency and describe it. (**En el cuarto hay una cama, una silla...**) Then ask students personalized questions about their rooms. (**Pepe, ¿tienes una ventana en tu cuarto?**) Put students at ease by assuring them that their answers can refer to an imaginary or an ideal room.

VISUAL LEARNERS
19 Label vocabulary items found in your classroom to help students remember the words.

LANGUAGE NOTE
Las zapatillas de tenis is the common term for *tennis shoes* in Spain. In other countries the words **los zapatos de tenis** and **los tenis** are common.

MUSIC LINK
To the tune of a favorite song, students can write their own lyrics describing their **cuarto ideal**. (Here's an example using the tune of **La bamba: En mi cuarto hay mesas, tengo yo una cama, una ventana, una lámpara grande.**)

---

19 ¿Qué hay? [H] Script and answers on p. 57E

Cass. 1B
CD 2 Tr. 5

First read the list of items below. Then, listen as Julio describes what's in his room. Julio has more than one of some items. Use the list to help you write the four items he says he has several of. For each of the four items you have listed, write how many he has.

1. una cama
2. una mesa
3. un reloj
4. una silla
5. una revista
6. una lámpara
7. un escritorio
8. una radio
9. un armario
10. ropa

tres revistas

20 En la sala de clase

Which of the things in Débora's room are also found in your classroom? Make two lists. The first one shows how many there are (**hay**) of each item in Débora's room and in your classroom. The second list shows which items there aren't any of (**no hay**) in your classroom. Answers on p. 57K

hay	no hay
una ventana	un armario

21 Describir el cuarto

Look at the drawing on page 75. With your partner, take turns telling him or her how many of each item Débora has in her room. Find four items that she has in her room. Start with **En el cuarto de Débora hay...** or **Débora tiene...** Your partner should also find four different items to tell you about.

Answers on p. 57K

VOCABULARIO
EXTRA

el estéreo *stereo*

el teléfono *telephone*

la videocasetera *VCR*

22 Un cuarto perfecto

Look at the photo of this bedroom. Imagine that it's your room and write a sentence describing it. Begin your description with **En mi cuarto hay...** Answers will vary. Possible answers below:

En mi cuarto hay una cama, una radio, muchos carteles, una ventana y un reloj.

ADDITIONAL PRACTICE
21 Display Teaching Transparency 2-2 to give students more practice saying what's in a room.

SLOWER PACE
22 Pair students with different abilities beforehand. Have one student write what the other one dictates.

VISUAL LEARNERS
Have students draw a floor plan of their **cuarto ideal,** including images of the things that are in it. Their plans should be large, labeled, and in color. As a challenge, have them present their plan to the class and describe what's in the room.

PRESENTATION GRAMÁTICA

Point out that ¿cuánto/a? and mucho/a are used when referring to things we can't count or usually don't count. (¿Cuánto papel hay en el escritorio? Hay mucho. ¿Cuánta fruta hay en la mesa? Hay mucha.) ¿Cuántos/as and muchos/as are used when we can count the items to which we refer. (¿Cuántos relojes hay en la escuela? ¿Cuántas lámparas hay en la sala? Hay muchas.)

SUGGESTION

Have students do *CD-ROM,* Activity 4, a multiple-choice activity to practice the **Gramática**.

ADDITIONAL PRACTICE

• Have one partner ask the other questions about his or her room. (**¿Cuántas ventanas hay en tu cuarto?**) Partners should take turns asking questions.

• For a journal entry suggestion for Chapter 2, see *Practice and Activity Book,* p. 76.

CD-ROM Disc 1

pp. 20–21
Acts. 11–13

p. 15
Acts. 13

GRAMÁTICA
Agreement of **mucho** and **cuánto** with nouns

1. Many nouns and adjectives have the following endings:

	SINGULAR	PLURAL
MASCULINE	-o	-os
FEMININE	-a	-as

Making the endings of adjectives and nouns match is called *agreement in gender* (masculine/feminine) and *number* (singular/plural).

2. **¿Cuánto?** and **¿Cuánta?** mean *how much?* **¿Cuántos?** and **¿Cuántas?** mean *how many?* Like other adjectives, **¿cuánto?** matches the noun it describes.

   ¿Cuánt**as** carpet**as** necesitas?
   ¿Cuánt**os** bolígraf**os**?
   ¿Cuánt**o** papel?
   ¿Cuánt**a** tarea tienes?

3. The forms of **mucho** mean *a lot, much,* or *many*. Like **cuánto, mucho** changes to match the noun it modifies.

   No necesito much**as** carpet**as**, pero necesito much**os** bolígraf**os**.
   Tengo much**a** tar**ea**.

---

23 ¿Cuántas cosas tengo?

Patricia has just moved to a new town, and her classmate David wants to know more about her. Complete their conversation using forms of **cuánto** and **mucho**.

DAVID ¿Te gusta el colegio? ¿__1__ clases tienes? Cuántas
¿Hay mucha tarea?

PATRICIA Me gusta el colegio. Tengo siete clases y sí, ¡hay __2__ tarea! mucha

DAVID ¿Te gusta tu cuarto? ¿Hay __3__ ventanas? muchas

PATRICIA No hay __4__ ventanas. Sólo *(only)* hay una. muchas

DAVID ¿__5__ carteles hay? ¿Y cuántos libros tienes? Cuántos

PATRICIA Tengo muchos carteles y __6__ libros. Pero David... muchos
no tengo __7__ amigos. muchos

DAVID Ay, Patricia... ¡yo soy tu amigo!

24 David y Patricia

Now try acting out the roles of Patricia and David. Use the dialogue from the previous activity as a script.

25 Comparación de cuartos

Work with a partner. Imagine that one of you is staying in the **Hotel Dineral** and the other is staying in the **Hotel Pocovale**. Pretend that you're talking to each other on the telephone, comparing your rooms. Tell your partner four things that are in your room, then list four things that are not there. Answers in side column

MODELO —En mi cuarto hay dos camas.
—No tengo televisor.

Hotel Dineral

Hotel Pocovale

Nota cultural

In Spanish-speaking countries, it's common for people to use many expressions in addition to hand gestures. There are a variety of ways that people say they like something a lot, such as **¡Genial!**, **¡Increíble!** or **¡Qué padre!** If they think something is all right, they might say **Está bien.** If people think something is terrible they might use expressions such as **¡Qué horrible!**, **¡Qué pesado!** or **¡Pésimo!** What expressions do you and your friends use to show that you like something a lot or think something is terrible?

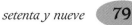
¡Esta música es genial!

LANGUAGE NOTE
25 Point out that when saying, "There isn't a . . . ," the indefinite article is often omitted: **No hay televisor.**

CULTURE NOTE
Additional phrases for expressing that something is impressive include **¡Qué chévere!** (Venezuela), **¡Fenomenal! ¡Bárbaro!** (Spain), **¡Bacán!** (Peru and Ecuador).

Answers to Activity 25

Answers will vary. Possible answers:

Hotel Pocovale
1. En mi cuarto hay un teléfono, pero no hay una radio.
2. En mi cuarto hay una ventana grande.
3. Tengo dos lámparas.
4. Tengo una silla pero no tengo una mesa.

Hotel Dineral
1. En mi cuarto tengo una mesa y cuatro sillas.
2. En mi cuarto no hay una radio, pero tengo un televisor.
3. En mi cuarto hay una cama grande, pero no tengo videocasetera.

NATIVE SPEAKERS

26 Native speakers might want to use the conditional form of **haber (habría)** or some other verb form in this activity. Encourage them to use **hay** as well. Also point out that the forms of **haber** are good words to include in their spelling notebook of words that begin with silent *h*.

TEACHER NOTE

The Additional Vocabulary that begins on page 275 is not presented or tested as active vocabulary. It gives students a chance to expand their vocabulary and use it creatively in open-ended activities.

Answers to Activity 26

Answers will vary. Possible answers:

En la sala de clase ideal de mi grupo hay diez computadoras y un televisor.

Hay una radio.

Hay muchos carteles y hay muchas ventanas.

26 La sala de clase ideal

Work with two classmates to find out what items would be in the ideal classroom. List at least six items. Be prepared to tell the class what kind of classroom your group would have.

MODELO En la sala ideal de mi grupo (*my group*) hay...

Answers in side column

una pecera

una planta

un videojuego

VOCABULARIO EXTRA

un disco compacto   *CD*

un estante   *bookshelf*

una pecera   *fish bowl*

una planta   *plant*

un tocador de discos compactos   *CD player*

un videojuego   *videogame*

un disco compacto

un tocador de discos compactos

un estante

¿Te acuerdas?

Look on pages 65 and 75 for more ideas of what to put in your ideal classroom. See also additional vocabulary on pages 275–280.

Robertín

Rosa

Magdalena

27 ¿Quién es?

With a partner, make a list with three columns. At the top of the columns, write the names **Rosa, Robertín,** and **Magdalena.** Then decide which person in the photos is best described by each statement and write the number of the sentence in that column. Choose the answer you think is best.   Answers will vary. Possible answers:

1. Tengo catorce años.
2. Tengo un diccionario inglés-español.
3. Tengo cinco años.
4. Necesito una mochila.
5. Tengo ocho años.
6. Tengo una calculadora.
7. En mi cuarto, hay una muñeca *(a doll).*
8. Quiero un teléfono en mi cuarto.
9. Tengo lápices de color.

Rosa	Robertín	Magdalena
3, 7, 9	4, 5	1, 2, 6, 8

28 El cuarto de mis sueños

Choose a photo or drawing of your ideal room from a magazine, or draw a room yourself. Then write a description of it, including how many of various things you have.

MODELO   En mi cuarto ideal hay dos carteles...   Answers will vary.
Possible answer:
En mi cuarto ideal hay un televisor, un estéreo y treinta discos compactos...

SUGERENCIA

Try making Spanish labels for things you use every day at school and at home (your school supplies, things in your room, etc.). This way, every time you look at an item you'll be reminded of how to say it in Spanish. And don't forget to include **el** and **la** to remind you of which words are masculine and which ones are feminine.

SEGUNDO PASO

ochenta y uno 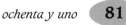 **81**

VIDEO INTEGRATION

Adelante LEVEL 1A
Video Program,
Videocassette 1, 39:08–42:08

TEACHER NOTES

• See *Video Guide* for suggestions on different ways to use this versatile resource in the classroom and for activities related to the **Panorama cultural**.

• Remind students that cultural material may be included in the Quizzes and Chapter Test.

• The language of the people interviewed represents informal, unrehearsed speech. Occasionally, text has been edited for clarity.

MOTIVATING ACTIVITY

Using the new vocabulary from Chapter 2, have students list the supplies necessary for school. Write their suggestions on the board or on a transparency.

PRESENTATION

Have students watch the video without looking at the written interview. Have them recall the supplies that they heard named. Check the items off the list from the Motivating Activity. Then have students read the interviews while listening to the videotape a second time and check the answers that were given.

Panorama cultural

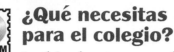

¿Qué necesitas para el colegio?

In this chapter, we asked some people what they need to buy before the school year starts.

Cass. 1B
CD 2 Trs. 6–9

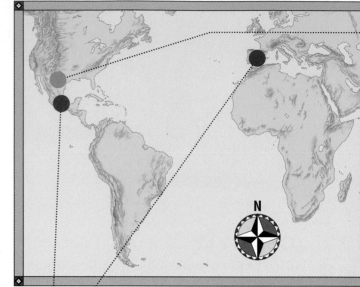

What does Héctor say he needs for school? What does he already have?

Bárbara likes to shop at the mall for school supplies. Is this similar to how you get ready to go back to school? What does she need to buy?

● **Héctor**
Ciudad de México, México
CD 2 Tr. 8

[Necesito] un uniforme. Lo que tengo es un diccionario, ...un cuaderno, un marcador color verde, un lápiz y una pluma.

● **Bárbara**
Sevilla, España
CD 2 Tr. 7

Necesito comprar una mochila, unos colores, ...dos bolígrafos, un sacapuntas y unas tijeras.

Do you buy any of the same supplies that Jorge does?

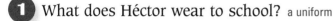

Jorge

San Antonio, Texas CD 2 Tr. 9

Normalmente tengo que comprar una mochila, cuadernos, también bolígrafos, lápices y una carpeta... mi libro de francés... y también mi calculadora gráfica.

1 What does Héctor wear to school? a uniform

2 How many things does Héctor have to write with? What are they? three: a marker, a pencil, and a pen

3 How does Bárbara carry her school supplies? a backpack

4 Bárbara mentions having to buy **colores** and **tijeras** *(scissors)*. What class does she probably have? art

5 What language class does Jorge have? French

6 What tells you that Jorge takes math? calculator

Para pensar y hablar... Answers will vary.

A. What supplies do you need to buy for school? Are they the same as those mentioned by Bárbara, Héctor, and Jorge? Explain.

B. Héctor mentions having to buy a uniform. Design your ideal school uniform. What would it look like?

CULTURE NOTE
Schools in Latin American countries often don't provide as many materials as schools in the United States do. For example, you might point out that many schools in Spain and Latin America require uniforms and that often the students must purchase them. It's common for students to have to purchase their books because schools don't always provide them.

CHALLENGE
Play the interviews and have students listen for words they don't recognize. See if it's clear to them what **marcador, tijeras,** and **sacapuntas** are.

83

VIDEO INTEGRATION

Adelante LEVEL 1A
Video Program,
Videocassette 1, 24:40–25:36 OR
¡Ven conmigo! LEVEL 1
Videodisc Program,
Videodisc 1B

Search 1813, Play To 3673

JUMP START!
Display Teaching Transparency 2-2. Give students five minutes to describe the room, listing as many items as they can.

☀ MOTIVATE

Ask students to list in English the things they need to do *(make the bed, do the dishes,* etc.), and a list of things they want to do *(watch a movie, go out for lunch,* etc.)

TERCER PASO

Talking about what you need and want to do

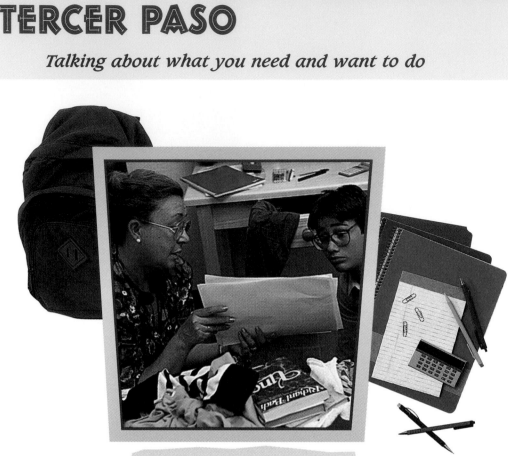

¿Qué necesita comprar Paco?

29 Las compras de Paco
Look at the choices below. Find the four items that Paco can most likely buy at a bookstore. unos libros, unos cuadernos, papel, una mochila

una pizza   un chocolate   papel

unos libros   unas zapatillas de tenis

una mochila   unos cuadernos

84 *ochenta y cuatro*

ASÍ SE DICE

Talking about what you need and want to do

p. 22
Acts.
14–15

To find out what someone needs to do, ask:

¿Qué necesitas hacer?

¿Y qué necesita hacer Paco?

To answer, say:

Necesito organizar mi cuarto.
I need to organize my room.

Necesita ir a la librería.
He needs to go to the bookstore.

2-3

To find out what someone wants to do, ask:

¿Qué quieres hacer?

¿Y qué quiere hacer Merche?

No sé, pero no quiero hacer la tarea.
I don't know, but I don't want to do homework.

Quiere ir a la pizzería.

30 ¿Necesitas o quieres?

Find Miguel's answer to each of his grandmother's questions.

Preguntas

1. ¿Necesitas cuadernos? c
2. ¿Qué cosas necesitas hacer? b
3. ¿Qué quieres comprar? a
4. ¿Necesitas dinero? d

Respuestas

a. Quiero comprar unas zapatillas de tenis.
b. Necesito organizar mi cuarto.
c. No, no necesito cuadernos.
d. Sí, ¡necesito mucho!

31 Tú y tu abuela

With a partner, act out the roles of a student and his or her grandmother. Use the dialogue from the previous activity. Then switch roles and this time try to use different phrases.

TEACH

**PRESENTATION
ASÍ SE DICE**

Model the expressions in **Así se dice** for correct pronunciation and intonation. Have students repeat after you. Then give them one minute to role-play the first exchange with a partner. After the minute, ask them to report what they found out about their partner using the third person forms as shown in **Así se dice**.

SUGGESTION

31 Check students' answers to Activity 30 before students role-play.

CHALLENGE

To model the concept of first, second, and third person, count off students in groups of three. Have them model the expressions in **Así se dice** according to the following model:

JUAN **María, ¿qué necesita Pablo?**

MARÍA **No sé. Pablo, ¿qué necesitas?**

PABLO **Necesito un cuaderno.**

MARÍA **Juan, Pablo necesita un cuaderno.**

PRESENTATION

VOCABULARIO

Model the pronunciation of the phrases and have students repeat after you. Then ask the class **¿Necesitas poner la ropa en el armario?** Have the class answer all together first, then call on some individual students. Next practice **¿Quieres ir al centro comercial esta tarde?** and **¿Quieres comprar muchas cosas? ¿Necesitas muchas cosas o solamente *quieres* muchas cosas?** Then have students practice using the new phrases in pairs.

AUDITORY LEARNERS

32 After writing the answers, have students check answers orally in pairs, asking each other what the various people need. (**¿Qué necesita hacer Victoria? Necesita comprar una mochila.**) Ask them how well prepared they think both **Victoria** and **Tomás** are.

Answers to Activity 33

Answers will vary. Possible answers:
1. Necesito organizar mi cuarto.
2. Quiero ir a clase.
3. Necesito comprar un diccionario de español.
4. Quiero encontrar el dinero.
5. Necesito hacer la tarea para mañana.

VOCABULARIO

PA
pp. 22–24
Acts.
16–18

GV
p. 16
Act. 14

2-C

Necesito...

poner la ropa en el armario   **encontrar** el dinero primero

NOTA GRAMATICAL

Comprar, poner, conocer, and **ir** are infinitives. The infinitive is the form of the verb found in a dictionary. There are three kinds of infinitive endings in Spanish: **-ar, -er,** and **-ir.**

GV
p. 16
Act. 15

Quiero...

ir al centro comercial   **conocer** a muchos nuevos amigos   **comprar** muchas cosas

---

32 **Victoria y Tomás necesitan...** Script and answers on p. 57F

Cass. 1B
CD 2 Tr. 10

First, read the list of things to do. Listen as Victoria lists seven things she and Tomás need to do before Monday. For each item, write **V** if it's something Victoria needs to do, or write **T** if it's something Tomás needs to do. Write **B** if it's something they both need to do.

1. hacer muchas cosas
2. ir al centro comercial
3. comprar una mochila
4. organizar el cuarto
5. encontrar la mochila
6. poner la ropa en el armario
7. hacer la tarea

33 **Mis planes**

Write five sentences telling what you plan to do this week. Use verbs from the first column with phrases from the second. Start each sentence with **Necesito...** or **Quiero...** Compare your sentences with a partner's.

Answers in side column

poner
hacer
comprar
organizar
ir
encontrar

mi cuarto
a clase
la tarea para mañana
el dinero
un diccionario de español
mi libro en la mochila

34 Problemas

The following people need your help. Write what each person needs to do, wants to buy, or where each one needs to go. Use as many new expressions as you can.   Answers on p. 57K

MODELO   Mingo's clothes are scattered all over his room.
   Necesita poner la ropa en el armario.

1. Juanita never knows what time it is.
2. Isabel can't find tomorrow's homework in her cluttered room.
3. Rafael is trying to build his vocabulary for Spanish class.
4. Diego is out of pens, pencils, and paper.
5. Inés is new in town and feeling lonely.
6. María doesn't have enough clothes.
7. Jorge's room is too dark.
8. Adelaida is not prepared for physical education.

35 ¿Qué necesitas hacer?

Work in pairs. Tell your partner what each person in Activity 34 needs to do. Then find out if your partner wants or needs to do the same things. Answer your partner's questions. Switch roles after number four.   Answers on p. 57K

MODELO   —Diego necesita ir a la librería. ¿Y tú? ¿Quieres ir a la librería?
   —Sí, quiero ir a la librería. Necesito cuadernos.

36 El anuncio

Work with your group to design an ad for school supplies. Have a member of your group draw a picture of the product. Then label your product and write the price. Share your ad with the class.

¡Claro!
Porque ya puedes encontrar tu
superpaquete ERES

Con:
2 cuadernos de rayas
1 cuaderno de cuadros
1 libreta

Hay dos modelos:
el **ecológico** y...

reglas $3.50

SUGGESTION

35 Have students imagine that they're getting ready to go back to school. Ask them **¿Necesitas comprar muchas cosas?** If they answer **sí**, then ask **¿Qué necesitas comprar?** If they answer **no**, ask them **¿Qué tienes ya?** Next have them imagine that they're packing their backpacks the night before school starts. Ask **¿Qué necesitas poner en la mochila?**

ADDITIONAL PRACTICE

The packing activity from **Suggestion** (above) can be used in groups of two to four, with one student asking questions and the others answering. The role of questioner alternates.

KINESTHETIC LEARNERS

Prepare a set of cards with vocabulary and expressions from **Así se dice** as well as some with punctuation marks written on them. Have students line up in order to form sentences according to cues you call out. (Example: You say, **"No tengo papel."** Students line up to form the sentence **Necesitas comprar papel.**)

PA
p. 22
Act. 19

GV
p. 17
Acts.
16–17

PRESENTATION

VOCABULARIO

 Count out loud by two's from 20 to 30, writing the numbers on the board as you say them. From 30 on, model the first number in each series (30, 40, 50, etc.) and have students continue until the next series is reached. Then play **PONGA** (see page 15J) to further practice the numbers. Students should prepare their **PONGA** cards with numbers from 31 through 100.

ADDITIONAL PRACTICE

37 Introduce the word **mil** (one thousand), and have students use play money to practice shopping and counting in **pesetas**.

CULTURE NOTE

People in Spanish-speaking countries don't use personal checks as often as people in the United States. In Mexico many people pay their utility bills with personal checks, but in Spain bills are usually paid by direct withdrawal. Cash is universally accepted, and most stores also accept credit cards, especially in larger cities.

Answers to Activity 37

1. Tengo treinta y dos pesetas.
2. Tengo ciento cincuenta y cinco pesetas.
3. Tengo ciento once pesetas.

VOCABULARIO

¿Cuánto es en dólares?

31 treinta y uno	**40** cuarenta	**101** ciento uno
32 treinta y dos	**50** cincuenta	**102** ciento dos
33 treinta y tres	**60** sesenta	**103** ciento tres
34 treinta y cuatro	**70** setenta	...
35 treinta y cinco	**80** ochenta	...
36 treinta y seis	**90** noventa	...
...	**100** cien	**199** ciento noventa y nueve

Uno at the end of a number changes to **un** before a masculine noun and **una** before a feminine noun: **veintiún dólares** *(dollars)*, **veintiuna pesetas.**

37 ¿Cuánto tienes?

Indicate how much money you have, using the Spanish words for the numbers. Answers in side column

MODELO (38 pesetas)
—Tengo treinta y ocho pesetas.

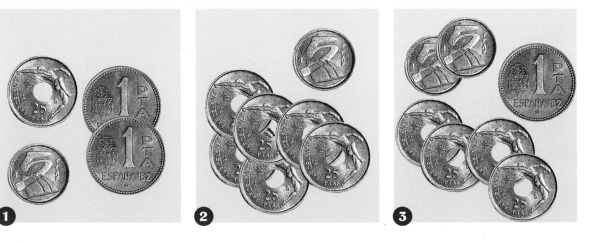

❶   ❷   ❸

38 ¿Cuántos años tiene?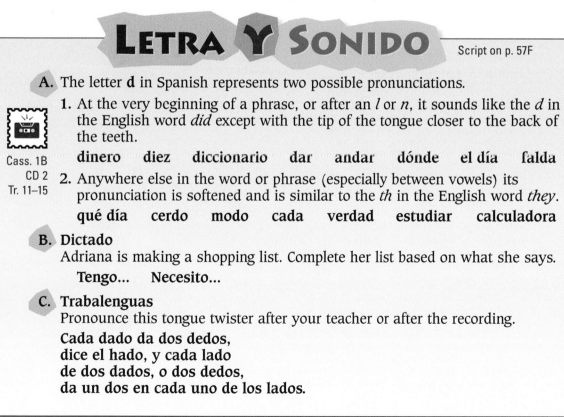

Write a sentence giving the ages of the following people, following the **Modelo**. If you don't know, you'll have to ask! If you can't ask, just guess.   Answers will vary.

MODELO   your uncle
         Él tiene treinta y dos años.

1. your parent or guardian
2. your principal
3. the person sitting next to you
4. a TV star
5. the President
6. a grandparent or elderly person
7. the person in your family nearest your age
8. your favorite singer or musician

39 En mi cuaderno

Do you need to get more organized? In your journal, write a paragraph about what you need to do this week. Include at least four things you need to do and where you need to go.

LETRA Y SONIDO

Script on p. 57F

Cass. 1B
CD 2
Tr. 11–15

A. The letter **d** in Spanish represents two possible pronunciations.

1. At the very beginning of a phrase, or after an *l* or *n*, it sounds like the *d* in the English word *did* except with the tip of the tongue closer to the back of the teeth.

   dinero   diez   diccionario   dar   andar   dónde   el día   falda

2. Anywhere else in the word or phrase (especially between vowels) its pronunciation is softened and is similar to the *th* in the English word *they*.

   qué día   cerdo   modo   cada   verdad   estudiar   calculadora

B. **Dictado**
   Adriana is making a shopping list. Complete her list based on what she says.

   Tengo...   Necesito...

C. **Trabalenguas**
   Pronounce this tongue twister after your teacher or after the recording.

   **Cada dado da dos dedos,
   dice el hado, y cada lado
   de dos dados, o dos dedos,
   da un dos en cada uno de los lados.**

NATIVE SPEAKERS
Have native speakers write the tongue twister in the **Letra y sonido** as you dictate it. After they have finished, ask them to look at the text to correct their work.

CLOSE

Set up a **papelería** in the classroom with a variety of classroom objects "for sale" at various prices. Ask students to take the role of salesclerk and shopper and to practice buying items in the store.

ASSESS

QUIZ 2-3
Testing Program, pp. 23–24
Audio Program,
Audiocassette 4A OR
Audio CD 2 Track 19

PERFORMANCE ASSESSMENT
Write **organizar el cuarto** on a sheet of paper. Students are to describe the steps that need to be accomplished to complete the task. This can be done orally, or in writing.

PRESENTATION
Begin by asking students questions about the United States dollar. What color is it? (green) Are all bills the same color? (yes) Whose pictures are on the various bills? Have they seen the new designs for some of the bills? What do they think of them?

HISTORY LINKS
• **La Reina Isabel** *(Queen Isabella)* of Spain sent the explorer **Cristóbal Colón** *(Christopher Columbus)* west in search of India. Most Europeans didn't know about the American continents until he reached them by sailing west in 1492. Today, the currencies in both Costa Rica and El Salvador are named **colón** in his honor.
• **Sor Juana Inés de la Cruz** **(Juana de Asbaje y Ramírez)** was a very intelligent woman who lived in colonial Mexico. At that time, women were not allowed to attend universities. Juana's mother opposed her desperate plan to go to the university disguised as a man. Because of her passion for learning, Sor Juana abandoned her life in the courts of the Viceroy of Mexico to pursue studies in math, geometry, science, philosophy, and literature as a nun.

Enlaces

LA HISTORIA

1 Las figuras históricas

Many Latin American countries have pictures of important historical figures on their coins and paper bills, just as we have a picture of Abraham Lincoln on the five-dollar U.S. bill. Match the following people in Latin American history to the currencies that were named for them or that carry their pictures.

1. **Lempira**, the chief of the Lenca people, who fought heroically against the Spanish conquerors. d

2. **Sor Juana Inés de la Cruz (Juana de Asbaje)**, a nun who was a devoted scholar and poet in seventeenth-century Mexico. c

3. **General Antonio José de Sucre**, a general who fought for South American independence from Spain. a

4. **Francisco Hernández de Córdoba**, a Spanish explorer who founded the colonial cities of Granada and León. b

a. **sucre:** Ecuador

b. **córdoba:** Nicaragua

c. **peso:** México

d. **lempira:** Honduras

2 ¡Te toca a ti!

Pretend your state is actually a country. Work with a partner to create money for your "country." Include drawings of famous people and symbols that are important in your state. Draw examples of both sides of a coin or the paper money. Present the money you designed to the class. Can your classmates identify your symbols and colors and explain what they mean?

LAS MATEMÁTICAS

3 De compras (Shopping)

In most Spanish-speaking countries you can shop in neighborhood shops that specialize in one type of food or item. Large stores are common in big cities. Smaller shops and open markets are still popular, however, and they're within walking distance from most homes. Imagine you have 1500 **bolívares venezolanos (Bs.)** to spend on fruit at the local fruit stand (**la frutería**). *Answers will vary.*

1. Decide which kinds of fruit to buy.
2. Calculate how much change you will get back.
3. Where would you go to buy fruit in your hometown?

(Bs. 1500)

Bs. 230

el mango

Bs. 400

la papaya

Bs. 500

La frutería

Bs. 370

la sandía

la piña

HISTORY LINK
Simón Bolívar was a leader who helped many regions of South America win their independence from Spain. The **bolívar** is the national currency in Venezuela and the **boliviano** is the monetary unit of Bolivia.

MATH LINK
Have students look up exchange rates for the Mexican **peso** on the Internet or in a national newspaper. Show them a school supply advertisement from a local newspaper and have them figure out what the school supplies would cost in **pesos**.

THINKING CRITICALLY
Remind students that a store that sells paper (**papel**) is called a **papelería,** and that a store that sells books (**libros**) is called a **librería.** Have students guess what a store is called that sells shoes (**zapatos**), flowers (**flores**), and watches (**relojes**). (**zapatería, florería, relojería**)

 CULTURE NOTE
In many Spanish-speaking countries people grow fruit trees in their backyards. They grow fruits like **mango, guanábana, limón,** and **tamarindo.**

91

READING STRATEGY
Using pictures, titles, and subtitles before reading.

☀ PREREADING

MOTIVATING ACTIVITY
Ask students to brainstorm the names of any books and movies from other countries that they might be familiar with.

☀ READING

TEACHING SUGGESTION
C Ask students to choose three of the items. What kinds of people would like these as gifts? (**50 cosas que los niños pueden hacer para salvar la tierra:** people who are interested in nature, animals, oceans, recycling)

THINKING CRITICALLY
Ask students what they think they could learn from each of the items. Other than what the titles say, what information might be included?

___

Answers to C

1. Los dinosaurios; su descubrimiento
2. Enciclopedia ilustrada de los animales
3. Mundo marino
4. Las nuevas aventuras de Mofli

Estrategia
Scanning
Look at pictures, titles, and subtitles before you begin to read. Also look for other words that "stand out" (bold or large print). By looking at these first, you can often tell what a passage is about without reading every word.

Portadas

A trip to the bookstore to buy school supplies is also a good opportunity to browse through some other interesting and fun items.

¿Te acuerdas?

Remember the strategy you learned in Chapter 1. **Use cognates to figure out meaning.**

¡A comenzar!

A Look at the photos and titles on the next page. Are these items . . .?

1. advertisements   no
2. movie reviews   no
3. books and video tapes   yes
4. posters   no

B By looking at just the photos and drawings on the covers, can you tell which item is about . . .?

1. the environment
2. kids on an island
3. life in the ocean

1. 50 cosas que los niños pueden hacer para salvar la Tierra
2. La isla del terror
3. Mundo marino

Al grano

Now take a little more time and look at the words in bold print.

C Which item would you buy as a gift for each of these people? Remember to rely only on photos and drawings, titles, and subtitles!

For someone who . . .

1. is interested in dinosaurs
2. likes animals
3. wants to be a marine biologist
4. likes to watch cartoons on TV
Answers in side column

D Now read the information accompanying each picture and answer the questions.

1. Look at the *Enciclopedia ilustrada de los animales.* Is the book illustrated? Is it in color? Write the cognates that told you this.
2. Look at *50 cosas que los niños pueden hacer para salvar la Tierra.* What's this book about? How do you know?
3. Look at *Las nuevas aventuras de Mofli.* This item isn't a book. What cognate tells you what it is?

1. Yes, the book is illustrated and is in color. The cognates are *ilustrada* and *color*.
2. The book is about 50 things that children can do to save the Earth. The number 50, the picture of the planet Earth, and the English phrase, *The earth works group* provide the clues.
3. Video.

Educar para el futuro. ▶
**50 COSAS QUE LOS
NIÑOS PUEDEN HACER
PARA SALVAR LA TIERRA**
The earth works group.
Ed Emecé. 1.110 ptas.

▲ **LOS DINOSAURIOS.
SU DESCUBRIMIENTO**.
Transportados en la
máquina del tiempo.
METROVIDEO.
2.495 ptas.

◀ Mamíferos, aves,
reptiles, anfibios
y peces son los
protagonistas de
esta enciclopedia
compuesta por
tres tomos y
magníficamente
ilustrada.
**ENCICLOPEDIA
ILUSTRADA
DE LOS ANIMALES**
Ed. Everest 2.900
ptas. cada tomo.

BILLIKEN PRESENTA: MUNDO MARINO
Video documental filmado en el
oceanario de San Clemente del Tuyú.
ATLÁNTIDA

◀

▲ **LA ISLA DEL TERROR**
Author: Tony Koltz
Ilustró: Ron Wing

**LAS NUEVAS AVENTURAS
DE MOFLI**
GATIVIDEO
Dibujos animados.
Doblada al español.
Duración: 90 minutos.

▶

The exchange rate of the dollar
and the **peseta** varies. Check
the current exchange rate in
the newspaper and have students compute the cost of
each book and video in dollars
and cents. Do the prices seem
reasonable?

☀ **POSTREADING**

SUGGESTION
Ask students to think about
their favorite book. What is the
title? What do they like about
the book? Can they tell from the
title what the book is about?

NATIVE SPEAKERS
Ask native speakers to bring in
a favorite Spanish language
book or video. You may want
to preview the materials that
students bring in for age-
appropriate content. See if
non-native speakers can determine what it is about by reading the title. Then ask native
speakers to describe its contents and why they like it.

CAPÍTULO 2 CAPÍTULO 2 CAPÍTULO 2 CAPÍTULO 2 CAPÍTULO 2 CAPÍTULO 2 CAPÍTULO 2 CAPÍTULO 2 CAPÍTULO 2

The **Repaso** reviews and integrates all four skills and culture in preparation for the Chapter Test.

ADDITIONAL PRACTICE

1 After they complete the first activity, have students pair up. Students should list five items they need including how many of each without discussing it with the partner. After completing their lists, one partner reads his or her list aloud. The other partner should listen and write down the items mentioned. Then, the student who read aloud should check the answers. After checking the answers students should switch roles.

📁 PORTFOLIO

2 **Written** Suggest that students write a paragraph about a member of their own family or a fictional family using vocabulary and functions learned in this chapter. A complete paragraph should include the following: what the person likes, what he or she needs or wants to buy, and places he or she needs or wants to go. For Portfolio suggestions, see the *Alternative Assessment Guide*, page 13.

 **REPASO**

 CD-ROM Disc 1

Script and answers on p. 57F

1

Cass. 1B
CD 2
Tr. 16

Imagine that it's the first day of school and your Spanish teacher is telling you what supplies you will use for the year. Based on what he tells you, how many of each item do you need? Write the numbers as words.

a. cuaderno   d. carpeta
b. diccionario   e. lápiz
c. bolígrafo   f. mochila

2 With a partner, look at the photos and match each statement below to the person who made it. Make up a description for the remaining photo.

1. Tengo veintiocho años. Me gusta la música clásica y tengo muchos discos compactos. ¿Quién soy? d
2. Me gusta ir al centro comercial. Necesito zapatillas de tenis. Tengo quince años. ¿Quién soy? c
3. Me gusta ir al centro comercial. Necesito un libro, pero primero necesito encontrar mi dinero. Tengo cuarenta años. ¿Quién soy? b

3 It's time to go shopping for school supplies! Write a conversation that you might have with a parent. Say two things you want and two things you need. Imagine what the parent would say to answer. Write at least four lines for each character. Be sure to use **quiero** and **necesito**. Answers will vary.

4 Your homeroom class has raised $150 for improvements to the local community center. You and your partner should each write a list of items you want to buy. Tell your partner how you would spend the money. Start your sentence with **Quiero comprar...** Work together to produce one list that includes items from both lists. Answers will vary.

una silla	$10.00	un cartel	$3.00	una radio	$40.00
una mesa	$20.00	un voleibol	$15.00	un reloj	$20.00
una lámpara	$15.00	un televisor	$100.00		

5 What would Enrique, a 13-year-old living in Spain, do to greet his uncle? What would Alicia, an 11-year-old living in Paraguay, do to greet a friend?
Enrique will give his uncle a hug. Alicia would kiss her friend once on the cheek.

6

S I T U A C I Ó N

Get together with two or three classmates. Imagine that you're students from different Spanish-speaking countries, with new names and ages. Introduce yourself to the group in Spanish. Ask your partners questions about where they're from, what things they have in their room, what they like and don't like, and what they want to do this weekend.

SUGGESTION
3 After they create their individual written dialogues, have students pair up. One partner takes the role of the student and the other of the parent. The partners choose which dialogue to perform first. After performing the first partner's dialogue, they switch roles and perform the other one.

VISUAL LEARNERS
4 Have students list the items before beginning this activity. If possible, label items in the classroom with prices.

CHALLENGE
In pairs, each student thinks of two things he or she needs and a reason why it might be difficult to get. Students describe the problem and what they need using chapter vocabulary. (**No tengo dinero. Necesito un cuaderno.**) The partner should then offer a solution, also using the phrases and vocabulary from the chapter. (**Necesitas ir al banco. Necesitas comprar un cuaderno.**) After one partner has presented two problems and the other has presented two solutions, have students switch roles.

This page is intended to help students prepare independently for the Chapter Test. It is a brief checklist of the major points covered in the chapter. Students should be reminded that this is only a checklist and does not necessarily include everything that will appear on the Chapter Test.

📁 PORTFOLIO

Oral Suggest that students record their dialogue from this activity as an oral Portfolio entry. For other Portfolio suggestions, see the *Alternative Assessment Guide*, p. 13.

ADDITIONAL PRACTICE

Place as many items from the **vocabulario** as possible on a desk in the middle of the room where all students can see them. Divide the class in two. Begin by holding up a pencil and pointing to one half of the class. They should respond by saying **¡Un lápiz!** Then hold up a pen and point to the other half of the class. They should respond **¡Un bolígrafo!** Continue until students have practiced the vocabulary words.

A VER SI PUEDO...

▼ Can you talk about what you want and need? p. 66

1 How would you ask these students if they need the items listed? How would the students answer? Answers on p. 57K

MODELO Adriana / some pencils (no)
Adriana, ¿necesitas unos lápices?
No, no necesito lápices.

1. Juanita / some pens and paper (sí)
2. Paco / a calculator (no)
3. Felipe / some notebooks (sí)

2 Tomorrow is the first day of class. Ask a friend how much or how many he or she needs of each item. How would your friend answer? Answers on p. 57K

1. paper   4. notebooks
2. books   5. folders
3. rulers   6. pencils

▼ Can you say what's in your room? p. 76

3 1. Describe your ideal room and include the items pictured below. Answers on p. 57K
2. You want to ask a friend if he or she has these items in his or her room. Write the question you would use.

▼ Can you talk about what you need and want to do? p. 85

4 Paco isn't very well prepared for the first day of class. How would you say he needs to do the following things? How would you say you want to do the same things? Answers on p. 57K

1. to straighten up his room
2. to put his tennis shoes in the closet
3. to buy some notebooks
4. to meet some new friends
5. ¿?

VOCABULARIO

PRIMER PASO

Talking about what you want and need

el bolígrafo   *ballpoint pen*
Bueno...   *Well . . .*
la calculadora   *calculator*
la carpeta   *folder*
el colegio   *high school*
el cuaderno   *notebook*
el diccionario   *dictionary*
él   *he*
ella   *she*
la goma de borrar   *eraser*
el lápiz   *pencil*
la librería   *bookstore*
el libro   *book*
la mochila   *book bag, back-pack*
necesita   *he/she needs*
necesitar   *to need*
necesitas   *you need*
necesito   *I need*
el papel   *paper*
querer (ie)   *to want*
quiere   *he/she wants*
quieres   *you want*
quiero   *I want*
la regla   *ruler*
un   *a, an* (masc. sing.)
una   *a, an* (fem. sing.)
unas   *some, a few* (fem. pl.)
unos   *some, a few* (masc. pl.)
ya   *already*

SEGUNDO PASO

Saying what's in your room

el armario   *closet*
la cama   *bed*
el cartel   *poster*
¿cuánto/a?   *how much?*
¿cuántos/as?   *how many?*
el cuarto   *room*
el escritorio   *desk*
hay   *there is, there are*
la lámpara   *lamp*
la mesa   *table*
mi   *my*
mucho/a   *a lot (of); a lot*
muchos/as   *many, a lot of*
la puerta   *door*
¿Qué hay en...   *What's in . . .?*
la radio   *radio*
el reloj   *clock; watch*
la revista   *magazine*
la ropa   *clothing*
la silla   *chair*
su   *his; her*
el televisor   *TV set*
tener (ie)   *to have*
tengo   *I have*
tiene   *he/she has*
tienes   *you have* (familiar)
tu   *your* (familiar)
la ventana   *window*
las zapatillas
   de tenis   *tennis shoes*
   (Spain)

TERCER PASO

Talking about what you need and want to do

el centro
   comercial   *shopping mall*
comprar   *to buy*
conocer   *to get to know (someone)*
la cosa   *thing*
el dinero   *money*
el dólar   *dollar*
encontrar (ue)   *to find*
hacer   *to do, to make*
ir   *to go*
No sé.   *I don't know.*
nuevos amigos   *new friends*
organizar   *to organize*
la pizzería   *pizzeria*
poner   *to put*
primero   *first*

Numbers 31–199
See p. 88

¡Ven conmigo a México!

LOCATION OPENER CHAPTERS 3, 4

PRINT	MEDIA

Adelante LEVEL 1A

CD-ROM Teacher's Guide
◆ Location 2, p. 9

Video Guide
◆ Activity Masters and Suggestions, pp. 18–19

Interactive CD-ROM Program
◆ Disc 1

Video Program
◆ Videocassette 1

¡Ven conmigo! LEVEL 1

Videodisc Guide
◆ Activity Masters and Suggestions, pp. 27–29
◆ Additional Stills, p. 28

Videodisc Program
◆ Videodisc 2A

Teotihuacán, which means *the place where people become gods* in Nahuatl, was already an ancient ruin when the Spaniards arrived. According to myth, the gods met here to create the sun and the moon. A huge pyre was built, and the brave god Nanahuatzin threw himself without fear into the fire and became the sun. The god Tecciztecatl, who had boasted of his bravery, hesitated before casting himself into the flames. He became the pale moon.

The two great pyramids—the Pyramid of the Sun (**la pirámide del sol**) and the Pyramid of the Moon (**la pirámide de la luna**)—are the most prominent structures in Teotihuacán. The Pyramid of the Sun stands 215 feet tall. The smaller Pyramid of the Moon is 147 feet tall.

Teotihuacán

Search Frame 3500

Taxco is a colonial silver-mining town about 70 miles southwest of Mexico City and is the oldest mining town in North America. The entire town was declared a national monument by the Mexican government—making it illegal to construct buildings that are not in the same style as existing ones.

Taxco

Search Frame 3044

The Central Library of the **Universidad Nacional Autónoma de México** (UNAM) has a stone mosaic designed by Juan O'Gorman in 1950 to symbolize the history of Mexican culture. In the mosaic, O'Gorman used such materials as stone, colored cement, tile, and blown glass.

Mural at UNAM

Search Frame 31190

Mexico has about 6,320 miles (10,170 kms) of coastline. By comparison, the continental United States has only 4,993 miles (8,035 kms). Many Mexican coastal cities such as **Acapulco**, **Cancún**, and **Puerto Vallarta**, have become important tourist destinations because of their comfortable climate and attractive beaches.

Coastline

Search Frame 1372

The following Web sites contain additional information on Mexico. Since addresses and content change frequently, you might want to preview them before attempting to access them in class.

México (University of Guadalara site)
http://mexico.udg.mx/

Worldview Highlight Events in Mexico City (Worldview Systems site)
http://bin-1.gnn.com/bus/wview/cityhigh/ch1mex.html

Secretaría de Turismo de México (links to people, places, and events)
http:/mexico-travel.com/sectur/ sectur_esp.html

PROJECTS

MAPA DE PRODUCTOS E INDUSTRIAS

This activity introduces students to industries and agricultural products of Mexico that are mentioned in the Almanac Box. Students will produce a map that illustrates the products and their location within Mexico.

Introduction

Mexico is a land rich in natural resources and agricultural products. Talk with students about the importance of natural resources and the development of new industries. Ask students if they know of any major crops that come from Mexico. Ask students if anyone has visited Mexico and has seen the landscape and agriculture. Explain that students will be looking for information about products that come from Mexico and that they will be making a map to illustrate their findings.

Materials students may need

- ◆ Poster board
- ◆ Overhead transparencies
- ◆ Markers—fine and wide tip
- ◆ Transparency pens
- ◆ Rulers, pencils

Sequence

1. Divide students into groups of four. Within each group, assign the roles of Librarian, Cartographer, Researcher, and Reporter.

2. Groups draw a map outline of Mexico. They produce a list of agricultural products and locate on the map where they are grown. Students list natural resources of Mexico that have contributed to the growth of industry and illustrate them on the map.

3. The group Librarian is in charge of getting materials for the group; The Cartographer is in charge of drawing the outline map; the Researcher is in charge of researching and illustrating products mentioned in the Almanac on page 99; and the Reporter explains the findings to the class.

4. Groups may produce overhead transparencies to teach the class. Other groups may produce large posters that can be displayed in the classroom and later used as a teaching tool and a reference to the economy of Mexico.

Grading the project

Suggested point distribution (total = 100 points):

Map	30
Content	30
Oral presentation	30
Group effort	10

¡Ven conmigo a México!

LOCATION OPENER CHAPTERS 3, 4 (cont.)

Using the Map

Refer students to the map of Mexico on page xxii to answer the following questions.

1 Have students point out countries that border Mexico. (the United States, Guatemala, Belize)

2 Have students point out **el D.F.** (**Teotihuacán** is about 30 miles from **el D.F.**)

3 Have students locate **Monterrey,** an important industrial center.

4 Have students locate **Guadalajara,** an important agricultural and industrial center.

5 Have students locate **Acapulco, Cozumel, Mazatlán,** and **Puerto Vallarta.** Ask if they have visited these popular places.

HISTORY LINK

According to legend, the god Huitzilopochtli told the Aztecs to establish their capital, **Tenochtitlán,** where they saw an eagle perched on a cactus with a serpent in its mouth. They saw this on an island in the middle of Lake Texcoco, a large salt lake surrounded by volcanic peaks. Some parts of Tenochtitlán, now Mexico City, were built on artificial garden-islands known as **chinampas,** which also provided much of the city's food supply. The Spanish conquerors were astounded at how developed Tenochtitlán was and took over the city for their own capital. Ask students to say where there is a famous salt lake in the United States. (Utah)

Culture Notes

El día de las madres (el 10 de mayo), in Mexico is a day the entire extended family comes together to celebrate. Family members serenade the mother from beneath her window in the early hours of the morning. They sing **Madrecita querida** and other songs honoring mothers. The mother also receives flowers and presents from her children and grandchildren. The family eats a late afternoon meal called a **merienda,** inlcuding dishes like **mole de pollo** or **mole de puerco con arroz y frijoles.**

Guadalajara is the lively capital of Jalisco. It's famous for preserving its traditional Mexican culture of **mariachis,** folk dances, and Orozco murals. José Clemente Orozco, a famous Mexican muralist, was born in Guadalajara, and he painted several huge murals on buildings in his home town.

Geography Link

Tell students that many buildings in Mexico City are very slowly sinking because the Spanish built Mexico City over the Aztec city, **Tenochtitlán,** which had been constructed on artificial islands on Lake Texcoco. The Spanish drained the lake, and Mexico City expanded out onto the flat plains, which had formerly been a muddy lake bed. As the city's population grew, and as more water was taken from wells, the ground underneath some parts of the city became compressed. As a result, many buildings have begun to sink. The soft soils of the former lake bed are especially unstable during earthquakes. This is why destruction from earthquakes can be so dramatic in Mexico City.

Multicultural Link

Explain to students the difference between the Egyptian pyramids and those in the Americas. In the Americas, pyramids have steps, flat tops, and were used as temples. In Egypt, they have smooth sides, pointed tops, and were used as tombs and monuments.

ART LINK

Ask students if they know what a mural is. (a large picture painted on a wall or a ceiling) Can they describe a mosaic? (pictures or designs made by inlaying small bits of colored stone, glass, tile, etc., in mortar) Who are some famous Mexican muralists? (Diego Rivera, José Clemente Orozco, David Siqueiros)

Multicultural Link

The Olmecs are noted for their contribution to the development of the calendar. Ask students what other ancient cultures developed calendars. (Egyptian, Babylonian, Roman, Arabs, Aztecs, Chinese) Ask them why they think calendars are important. Why do we need calendars?

Thinking Critically

Ask students to think about why most of Latin America is Spanish-speaking. Help them draw a parallel between North and South America. (The British colonized the north; the Spanish, the south.)

Multicultural Link

Ask students if they know about traditional dances from any other country such as Scotland, India, Ghana, or folk dances from the United States.

Thinking Critically

Ask students to compare Chapultepec Park to a park they know. Do both parks have many trees? Are they near water? Do people like to go there to relax? If students don't know of a park, have them go to the library or media center to get information.

SCIENCE LINK

Have students get some information on earthquakes to find out what causes them. Have them find out where in the Americas earthquakes occur. (California, Alaska, Chile, Nicaragua, Costa Rica, etc.) If you live in an area subject to earthquakes, have students review how to prepare for one and what to do if one strikes. Tell students that some words for earthquake in Spanish are **el terremoto, el temblor,** and **el sismo.**

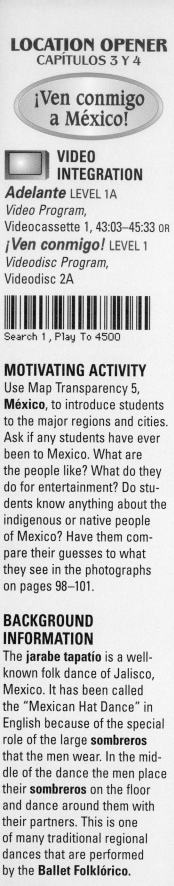

¡Ven conmigo a México!

VIDEO INTEGRATION

Adelante LEVEL 1A
Video Program,
Videocassette 1, 43:03–45:33 OR
¡Ven conmigo! LEVEL 1
Videodisc Program,
Videodisc 2A

Search 1 , Play To 4500

MOTIVATING ACTIVITY
Use Map Transparency 5, **México**, to introduce students to the major regions and cities. Ask if any students have ever been to Mexico. What are the people like? What do they do for entertainment? Do students know anything about the indigenous or native people of Mexico? Have them compare their guesses to what they see in the photographs on pages 98–101.

BACKGROUND INFORMATION
The **jarabe tapatío** is a well-known folk dance of Jalisco, Mexico. It has been called the "Mexican Hat Dance" in English because of the special role of the large **sombreros** that the men wear. In the middle of the dance the men place their **sombreros** on the floor and dance around them with their partners. This is one of many traditional regional dances that are performed by the **Ballet Folklórico**.

¡Ven conmigo a México!

Estos jóvenes bailan el "jarabe tapatío", un baile típico en México.

USING THE ALMANAC

- **La bandera:** The emblem in the center of the flag commemorates the legend of the founding of **Tenochtitlán**, the Aztec capital and the site of present-day Mexico City.

- **Capital:** Mexico City may be referred to simply as **México;** as **México, Distrito Federal;** or in casual speech as **el D.F.**

- **República federal:** Mexico is composed of 31 states and a federal district.

- **Industrias: acero** *steel;* **plata** *silver;* **productos químicos** *chemicals;* **electrodomésticos** *electrical household appliances;* **caucho** *rubber*

- **Cosechas principales: algodón** *cotton;* **café** *coffee;* **trigo** *wheat;* **arroz** *rice;* **caña de azúcar** *sugarcane*

- **Idiomas:** Spanish is the official language of Mexico, but many people speak native languages entirely unrelated to Spanish, especially in the rural areas of **Oaxaca, Chiapas, Michoacán,** and **Yucatán.** The main indigenous languages are **maya, mixteco, náhuatl, otomí, purépecha,** and **zapoteca.**

México

Population: 96,000,000

Size: Three times as large as the state of Texas. Mexico has nearly 6,000 miles (10,000 km) of coastline.

Capital: Mexico City; population; more than 20,000,000

Monetary unit: nuevo peso

Government: federal democratic republic

Industries: steel, silver, chemicals, textiles, petroleum, tourism

Important crops: corn, cotton, coffee, wheat, rice, fruits, vegetables

Languages: Spanish, more than fifty native languages

noventa y nueve 99

USING THE PHOTO ESSAY

1 In Oaxaca you can find indigenous black pottery and Spanish-style green-glazed pottery. Also for sale in the **mercados** are weavings, textiles, filigree jewelry, ceramics, sculptures, baskets, and colorful native dresses called **huipiles**. **Oaxaca** is a Zapotec word. The *x* is pronounced like the *x* in **México**.

2 Masks are used for more than just wall decoration in Mexico. They have been used in religious ceremonies since long before the Spanish arrived. Currently, masks are used in many celebrations throughout the year, such as **Carnaval**, **Semana Santa**, and **Corpus Christi**, as well as in local festivals. People use them to act out the stories of the celebrations. Masks are usually made of papier mâché or wood. **Guerrero**, **Oaxaca**, and **Michoacán** are the states where most masks are made.

3 **El Parque de Chapultepec** is a favorite spot for Mexicans, especially on Sunday afternoons. It covers 40 square miles. Chapultepec has an amusement park, three lakes, and eight museums, including the famous **Castillo de Chapultepec**, where the president lived until 1940. In Nahuatl, the language of the Aztecs, **chapultepec** means *grasshopper hill.*

☀MEXICO

Mexico is a nation rich in natural resources, culture, and history. The diverse population includes indigenous, or native, people and those whose ancestors came from Europe, Africa, the Middle East, and Asia.

CD-ROM
Disc 1

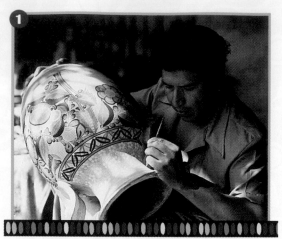

▲ **Los mercados de Oaxaca**
The markets of Oaxaca are excellent places to find colorful pottery, weavings, jewelry, ceramics, and baskets.

◄ **Máscaras especiales para las fiestas**
There are many festivals in Mexico. During some festivals, people wear hand-painted masks. What festivals and special community events are there where you live?

**El Parque de ►
Chapultepec**
In Mexico, parks are favorite spots to see friends, get exercise, have a picnic, or read a book. The largest and best known is Chapultepec Park in Mexico City.

In Chapters 3 and 4 you will meet several students who live in Cuernavaca, the capital of the Mexican state of Morelos. People from all over the world come to Cuernavaca to study Spanish. Young people from Mexico City come to Morelos for fun-filled weekends of water sports, shopping, and visiting historical sites like the **Palacio de Cortés**.

4 Piñatas are used in a traditional Mexican party game, especially around Christmastime. **Piñatas** are containers in the shape of animals or other figures and are filled with confetti, fruit, nuts, coins, candy, and toys. Blindfolded children take turns hitting the **piñata** with a stick until it breaks open. Then the children rush to catch the **piñata** contents as they fall. Traditionally **piñatas** were made of clay, but now they're usually made of papier mâché.

ART LINK
Have the class get together and make a **piñata** for a classroom celebration.

5 Charreadas are rodeo-like competitions popular in western Mexico. The male horsemen, called **charros,** wear suits made of doeskin or velvet with a short jacket known as a **bolero,** and riding pants with gold or silver buttons down the sides. The **charras** wear a feminine version of the **charro** suit, and the **amazonas** wear long, colorful dresses.

▲ Las piñatas
Piñatas are very popular at children's parties. Piñatas are made of papier mâché and filled with candy.

▲ La charrería
These women are dressed in the typical *amazona* costume worn at Mexican *charrería*, or rodeo, festivals. The biggest rodeo rings in Mexico are in Mexico City and Guadalajara.

CAPÍTULO
3

Nuevas clases, nuevos amigos
CHAPTER OVERVIEW

De antemano pp. 104–107	¡Bienvenida al colegio!			

	FUNCTIONS	**GRAMMAR**	**CULTURE**	**RE-ENTRY**
Primer paso pp. 108–115	• Talking about classes and sequencing events, p. 110 • Telling time, p. 112	• **Nota gramatical:** Plural definite articles **los** and **las,** p. 109 • **Gramática:** Telling time, p. 113	• **Nota cultural:** Class schedules, p. 108 • **Nota cultural:** Grades, p. 110 • **Nota cultural:** The **siesta,** p. 115 • **Panorama cultural:** ¿Cómo es un día escolar típico?, pp. 116–117	• Present tense of **tener** • Numbers 0–99 • School supplies • Forming questions
Segundo paso pp. 118–123	• Telling at what time something happens, p. 119 • Talking about being late or in a hurry, p. 122	• **Nota gramatical:** The preposition **de,** p. 121	• **Nota cultural:** Regional vocabulary for objects, p. 121	• Present tense of **tener** • Noun-adjective agreement • Forms of **necesitar** and **querer**
Tercer paso pp. 124–133	• Describing people and things, p. 125 • Talking about things you like and explaining why, p. 129	• **Nota gramatical:** The verb **ser,** p. 126 • **Gramática:** Adjective agreement, p. 127 • **Nota gramatical:** Tag questions, p. 131	• **Nota cultural:** Titles of respect, p. 124	• Talking about likes and dislikes • Question formation with ¿cómo?

Letra y sonido p. 133	The letters *g, h,* and *j*	**Dictado:** Textbook Audiocassette 2A/Audio CD 3
Enlaces pp. 134–135	Time zones and the 24-hour clock	
Vamos a leer pp. 136–137	**Calificaciones y horarios**	**Reading Strategy:** Using background knowledge
Review pp. 138–141	**Repaso,** pp. 138–139	**A ver si puedo...,** p. 140 **Vocabulario,** p. 141

Assessment

TESTING PROGRAM
• **Primer paso,** Quiz 3-1, pp. 37–38
• **Segundo paso,** Quiz 3-2, pp. 39–40
• **Tercer paso,** Quiz 3-3, pp. 41–42
• Assessment Items, Audiocassette 4A or Audio CD 3 Tracks 18–20

• **Chapter Test,** pp. 43–48
• Assessment Items, Audiocassette 4A or
• Audio CD 3 Tracks 21–22

• **Midterm Exam,** pp. 115–120
• *Audio Program,* Assessment Items: Audiocassette 4A or Audio CD 3 Tracks 23–24

Alternative Assessment
Portfolio Assessment
ANNOTATED TEACHER'S EDITION
• **Written:** Activity 43, p. 132
• **Oral:** Activity 39, p. 130
ALTERNATIVE ASSESSMENT GUIDE, p. 14

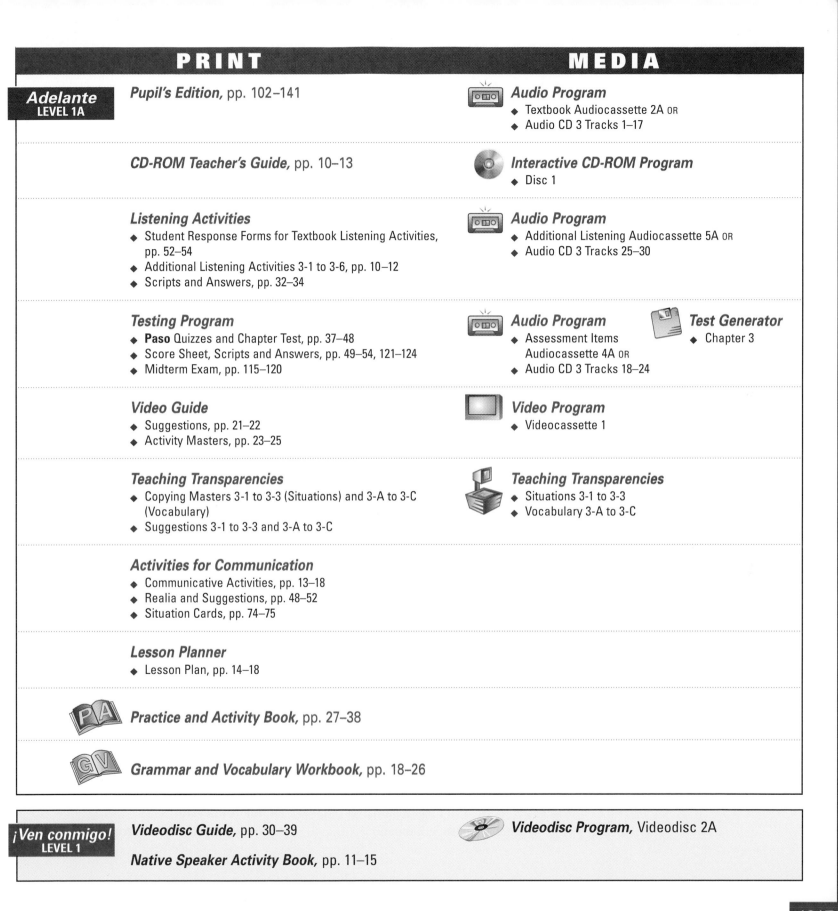

PRINT	MEDIA

Adelante
LEVEL 1A

Pupil's Edition, pp. 102–141

Audio Program
- Textbook Audiocassette 2A OR
- Audio CD 3 Tracks 1–17

CD-ROM Teacher's Guide, pp. 10–13

Interactive CD-ROM Program
- Disc 1

Listening Activities
- Student Response Forms for Textbook Listening Activities, pp. 52–54
- Additional Listening Activities 3-1 to 3-6, pp. 10–12
- Scripts and Answers, pp. 32–34

Audio Program
- Additional Listening Audiocassette 5A OR
- Audio CD 3 Tracks 25–30

Testing Program
- **Paso** Quizzes and Chapter Test, pp. 37–48
- Score Sheet, Scripts and Answers, pp. 49–54, 121–124
- Midterm Exam, pp. 115–120

Audio Program
- Assessment Items Audiocassette 4A OR
- Audio CD 3 Tracks 18–24

Test Generator
- Chapter 3

Video Guide
- Suggestions, pp. 21–22
- Activity Masters, pp. 23–25

Video Program
- Videocassette 1

Teaching Transparencies
- Copying Masters 3-1 to 3-3 (Situations) and 3-A to 3-C (Vocabulary)
- Suggestions 3-1 to 3-3 and 3-A to 3-C

Teaching Transparencies
- Situations 3-1 to 3-3
- Vocabulary 3-A to 3-C

Activities for Communication
- Communicative Activities, pp. 13–18
- Realia and Suggestions, pp. 48–52
- Situation Cards, pp. 74–75

Lesson Planner
- Lesson Plan, pp. 14–18

Practice and Activity Book, pp. 27–38

Grammar and Vocabulary Workbook, pp. 18–26

¡Ven conmigo!
LEVEL 1

Videodisc Guide, pp. 30–39

Videodisc Program, Videodisc 2A

Native Speaker Activity Book, pp. 11–15

For a complete list of the media resources and their accompanying print matter guides, see page 101B.

DE ANTEMANO   pp. 104–107

Video
• Show or play *¡Bienvenida al colegio!* See *Video Guide* pp. 20–25.

Audio
• Play **fotonovela** for students to read along or for pronunciation practice.

PRIMER PASO   pp. 108–115

Video
• Show the **paso** opener to model talking about classes, sequencing events, and telling time. Have students listen for the **paso** functions.

Audio
• Use Textbook Listening Activity 5 to practice talking about class schedules.
• Use Textbook Listening Activities 10 and 15 to practice telling time.
• Use Additional Listening Activities 3-1 and 3-2 to practice class schedules and telling time.

Transparencies
• Use Situation Transparency 3-1 to present and practice saying what classes people have using the teaching suggestions. Students can do CD-ROM Activity 3 as a follow-up.

CD-ROM
• Activity 1 practices telling time and sequencing events.
• Activity 2 practices telling time.
• Activity 3 practices school subjects.

PANORAMA CULTURAL   pp. 116–117

Audio
• As a prelistening activity, have students brainstorm words or phrases they're likely to hear based on the topic.
• Play the **Panorama cultural** on Textbook Audiocassette 2A or Audio CD 3 Tracks 6–9.

Video
• Show the interviews to students. See *Video Guide* pp. 20–25.

CD-ROM
• Have students do the **Panorama cultural** activity for Chapter 3.

SEGUNDO PASO   pp. 118–123

Video
• Show the **paso** opener to model talking about at what time something happens and talking about being late or in a hurry. Tell students to listen for the **paso** function.

Audio
• Use Textbook Activity 19 to practice telling at what time something happens.
• Use Additional Listening Activities 3-3 and 3-4 to practice saying when something happens. Students can do CD-ROM Activity 1 as a follow-up.

Transparencies
• Teaching Transparency 3-2 practices telling at what time something happens.

CD-ROM
• Activity 4 practices saying at what time something happens.

TERCER PASO   pp. 124–133

Video
• Show the **paso** opener to model describing and talking about things people like and why they like them. Tell students to listen for the **paso** function.

Audio
• Use Textbook Activity 39 to practice talking about things people like.
• Additional Listening Activity 3-5 practices describing people, and Activity 3-6 practices talking about things people like.

Transparencies
• Teaching Transparency 3-3 practices describing things.

CD-ROM
• After presenting the phrases for describing people and things and expressing what people like and dislike, have students do Activity 5.
• After completing the **paso**, have students do Activity 6.

REPASO   pp. 138–139

Video
• Replay *¡Bienvenida al colegio!* and ask students to point out exchanges in which the characters perform the functions from this chapter.

CD-ROM
• Have students do the **En contexto** activity, in which students discuss classes, school schedules, and how to do well in school, with a new friend.

Test Generator
• Use the Test Generator to make a short practice test.

DE ANTEMANO

Barcodes A and B access **De antemano** and **A continuación** in their entirety. Subsequent barcodes show individual scenes. The barcode numbers correspond to the scene numbers as they appear in **De antemano**.

¡Bienvenida al colegio! **A**
Search 4500, Play To 14390

Bueno, ya son... **1**
Search 5840, Play To 7683

Muchachos, buenos días... **2**
Search 7684, Play To 8621

Me llamo María Inés... **3**
Search 8622, Play To 9478

Sí, la capital... **4**

Fernando, ¿cómo es... **5**
Search 12071, Play To 13180

Señor Rodríguez, una... **6**
Search 13181, Play To 14039

¡Ay, no! **7**
Search 14040, Play To 14390

¡Bienvenida al colegio!
(a continuación) **B**
Search 14390, Play To 23875

VIDEOCLIPS

This clip is an ICE ad for lower phone rates. You may want to preview it before showing it to students.

ICE
Search 29320, Play To 30872

PASO OPENERS

Each **paso** begins with a re-presentation of a scene from the dramatic episode that models targeted functions, vocabulary, and grammar.

Bueno, ya son... **1** p. 108
Search 5840, Play To 7683

Sí, la capital... **2** p. 118
Search 9479, Play To 12070

Fernando, ¿cómo es... **3** p. 124
Search 12071, Play To 13180

PANORAMA CULTURAL

¿Cómo es un día escolar típico?
These barcodes access supplementary interviews that do not appear in the book. Not all barcodes are listed here. For a complete listing of supplemental interviews, see the *¡Ven conmigo!* Level 1 *Videodisc Guide*, p. 31.

Mario, Costa Rica **1**
Search 24633, Play To 24966

Natalie, Venezuela **2**
Search 24967, Play To 25521

Ómar, Argentina **3**
Search 25996, Play To 26343

Ángela, Costa Rica **4**
Search 26679, Play To 26972

Gala, Argentina **5**
Search 26973, Play To 27460

Juan, México **6**
Search 27461, Play To 27745

Lucila, Argentina **7**
Search 28666, Play To 29375

For Student Response Forms, see Listening Activities pages 52–54.

PRIMER PASO   pp. 108–115

5 ¡Tenemos la misma clase!   p. 109

— Hola, Lupita. ¿Qué tal?

— Hola, Álvaro. ¿Cómo estás?

— Bien, ¿y tú?

— Bueno, más o menos. Es el primer día de clase y ya tengo mucha tarea.

— ¿Qué clases tienes?

— Tengo ciencias, francés, arte, matemáticas, computación, educación física e historia con el profesor Maldonado. ¿Qué clases tienes tú?

— Yo tengo historia con la profesora Vásquez, álgebra, biología, computación y geografía.

— ¿A qué hora tienes clase de computación?

— A la una menos cinco.

— ¡Qué bien! Estamos en la misma clase, entonces.

— ¡Ay, no, llegamos tarde!

— ¡Vamos!

Answer to Activity 5

They have their computer science (**computación**) class together.

10 El reloj   p. 112

1. — Oye, Bernardo, ¿qué hora es?
   — Son las dos y media.

2. — Bernardo, dime, ¿qué hora es?
   — Son las tres y cuarto.

3. — No tengo reloj, Bernardo. ¿Qué hora es?
   — Son las seis.

4. — ¿Qué hora es, por favor?
   — Es la una y cuarto.

5. — Ahora, ¿qué hora es?
   — Son las diez. Vete a jugar.

6. — Bueno, Geraldo. ¡Despiértate!
   — ¿Qué hora es?
   — Son las ocho.

7. — Ya es tarde.
   — Pero, Bernardo, ¿qué hora es?
   — Son las ocho y media.

8. — Bernardo, ¿qué hora es?
   — Son las cuatro. ¡Vamos al parque!

Answers to Activity 10

1. h   2. f   3. g   4. a   5. c   6. e   7. b   8. d

15 ¿Qué clase tengo ahora?   p. 114

1. Ya son las nueve y cuarto. Tengo la clase de arte.

2. Ahora tengo ciencias sociales. Son las ocho y venticinco.

3. Son las once y cuarenta. Por fin tengo almuerzo.

4. ¡Ya es la una! Tengo clase de matemáticas.

5. Ya son las dos menos cinco. Tengo educación física.

6. Son las tres menos cuarto. Tengo la clase de francés.

7. ¿Son las diez y cinco? ¡Tengo geografía!

Answers to Activity 15

1. d, arte
2. g, ciencias sociales
3. b, almuerzo
4. f, matemáticas
5. c, educación física
6. e, francés
7. a, geografía

SEGUNDO PASO   pp. 118–123

19 Horarios   p. 119

1. Necesito ir a clase. ¿Qué hora es?

2. ¿A qué hora es el descanso?

3. Necesito organizar mi cuarto. ¿Ya son las tres?

4. ¿A qué hora es el almuerzo?

5. ¿A qué hora necesitas ir a la clase de inglés?

6. Quiero ir al centro comercial. ¿Qué hora es?

Answers to Activity 19

1. b   2. b   3. a   4. b   5. a   6. b

39 Patricia y Gregorio p. 130

— Hola, Patricia, soy Gregorio. ¿Cómo estás?

— Muy bien. ¿Y tú?

— Bien. Oye, ¿qué haces esta tarde? Hay una fiesta a las ocho.

— ¡Ay, no, una fiesta no, por favor! No me gustan las fiestas. Pero me gustan los partidos de fútbol.

— Este, pues... No me gustan los partidos de fútbol. No son interesantes. Pero, a ver... me gustan los videojuegos. ¿A ti te gustan?

— Los videojuegos no me gustan. Bueno, Gregorio, ¿te gustan los partidos de tenis?

— Es que no me gustan los deportes. Pero me gustan los conciertos.

— ¡Ay, sí! Me encantan los conciertos. ¿Qué música te gusta? ¿Te gusta la música rock?

— Sí, me gusta la música rock. ¡Vamos a un concierto!

Answers to Activity 39

1. cierto   **2.** falso   **3.** falso   **4.** cierto

For the scripts for Parts **A** and **C**, see page 133. The script for Part **B** is below.

B. Dictado

Necesito una goma de borrar y una regla en matemáticas. En geografía, necesito un bolígrafo y un cuaderno.

1 p. 138

1. MIGUEL Mañana tengo la clase de geografía a las diez y cuarto.

2. EDGARDO Y yo tengo la clase de arte a las once en punto. Me gusta la clase de arte porque el profesor es muy cómico.

3. MIGUEL Yo tengo almuerzo a las doce menos diez. ¿A qué hora es tu descanso?

4. EDGARDO El descanso es a la una y cuarto.
    MIGUEL ¿Y a qué hora es el examen de ciencias?

5. EDGARDO El examen de ciencias es a las dos y veinte.

Answers to Repaso Activity 1

1. c   **2.** d   **3.** b   **4.** a   **5.** e

Nuevas clases, nuevos amigos

PROJECTS

MI DICCIONARIO

Making a Spanish picture dictionary is an easy and entertaining way to review and increase vocabulary. Encourage students to seek out words for those things they're most interested in learning. Invite them to be creative by drawing their own pictures or using magazine cutouts. They can look at the alphabet presentation on pages 8–9 for a sample. For any words that your students are unable to find in their own dictionaries, encourage them to consult other resources, such as dictionaries in the library, or suggest that they ask native speakers.

Materials students may need

◆ Spiral notebook or notebook paper ◆ Scissors

◆ Old magazines ◆ Glue

◆ English-Spanish dictionary ◆ Markers

Sequence

1 This project may be done individually or in groups.

2 If students work in groups, each group could be assigned to research a particular category for a class dictionary. If students work individually, specify a minimum number of categories and words.

3 Suggest a table of contents similar to the Additional Vocabulary on pages 275–277. Include categories such as:

Nombres comunes (suggest they find names other than those in this book)

Frases útiles

Me gusta/Me gustan

No me gusta/No me gustan

Mi casa

Mi cuarto

La clase de español

España

México

Para describir a la gente

Para describir las cosas

4 Review basic dictionary skills by looking at different types of dictionary entries in an English-Spanish dictionary.

5 Go over all abbreviations to make sure students can identify nouns, verbs, and adjectives. Alert students to the basic problems associated with finding words in the dictionary. Discourage literal translations, and always have them cross-reference any new words they find.

6 Once students have chosen categories and entries and have found illustrations for them, they should design the pages. Allow for individual creativity.

Grading the project

Suggested point distribution (total = 100 points):

Dictionary format **15**

Neatness **20**

Accuracy of definitions **15**

Spelling **15**

Originality **20**

Number of words included **15**

UN FOLLETO PARA ESTUDIANTES

In this activity students will create a brochure of their school or town. This project may be done in class or as an outside assignment. Tell students to imagine that they are creating the brochures for a foreign exchange program. Exchange students in Spanish-speaking countries will use the information in the brochures to decide where in the United States they would like to live and attend school.

Materials students may need

◆ Old magazines ◆ Scissors

◆ Old newspapers ◆ Glue or tape

◆ Construction paper ◆ Colored markers

◆ A camera

Sequence

1 Students obtain pictures to illustrate the brochure. They may draw them, take photos, or cut pictures from magazines and newspapers. Each group decides which pictures to use.

2 Students prepare a short written description in Spanish of each picture used. Each student is responsible for writing at least one description. Review the **Vocabulario** on page 141.

3 Groups design a preliminary two-page layout in which they indicate where pictures and descriptions will go.

4 Each group member proofreads the group's layout for accuracy. Option: Groups might critique each other's work at this point.

5 Groups glue or tape pictures on construction paper and write descriptions by the pictures. Groups also design a cover and a title for their brochures.

6 Each student reads the descriptions she or he has written to the class.

Grading the project

Suggested point distribution (total = 100 points):

Brochure content	40
Correct vocabulary and grammar	20
Originality	20
Oral presentation	20

TEACHER NOTE

If your class has a pen pal program, students might send the brochure to their pen pals' school and ask for one in return.

MI HORARIO ESCOLAR

This project enables students to review the school-related vocabulary and compare their school schedules with those of students from Mexico. They will prepare a poster that illustrates a weekly schedule for a student in the United States and a poster that illustrates a weekly schedule for a Mexican student.

Introduction

Discuss the differences between academic schedules for students in Mexico and for your own students. In the United States, do students attend the same classes each day? In Mexico, do students attend the same classes each day? How many subjects does a typical student take in the U.S.? How may subjects does a typical Mexican student take? Discuss the advantages or disadvantages of each system.

Materials students may need

◆ Colored poster board   ◆ Meter sticks
◆ Markers

Sequence

1 Divide students into pairs. One will be the Artist, the other will be the Writer. Each pair of students should think of an ideal schedule to put into draft form. The Writer will write a draft of the schedule that they have created. Students should refer to the **Vocabulario** on page 141. Each draft should include:
- the days of the week
- times from the beginning to the end of the school day (to represent class periods or blocks)
- at least six to eight class subjects

2 The Artist will prepare the chart and transfer the information from the draft to a poster (preferred) or to an overhead transparency.

3 Each pair will present its schedule to the class, pointing out the differences and similarities between class schedules in the United States and Mexico.

Grading the project

Suggested point distribution (total = 100 points):

Overall appearance, neatness	30
Information and content	20
Accuracy of information, spelling, gender correctness	30
Group participation and cooperation	20

CAPÍTULO 3

Nuevas clases, nuevos amigos
GAMES

DE SÍLABAS A PALABRAS

This game provides an opportunity to practice pronunciation. It can also be used to review vocabulary from this or any chapter.

Materials you may need

- ◆ An ample supply of unruled index cards
- ◆ Pens or markers

Preparation

Review the definition of a syllable as a short unit of speech. Every syllable contains at least one vowel sound, and at least one or more consonant sounds. Break up the vocabulary words from the chapter into syllables and have the students write each syllable on an index card using large letters. For example, make three cards for **mar - ca - dor**, two cards for **com - prar,** etc.

Procedure

1 Shuffle the cards and pass them out among students.

2 Either the teacher or a selected student says **de sílabas a palabras.**

3 Give the students a specific amount of time (one minute) to find other people with whom they can form a word.

4 Tell students to call out **¡Palabra!** when they have formed a word.

5 The group must say their word in unison as you point to them.

6 Students who are not in a word group may clap, tap with a pen or pencil, or use their fingers to count syllables as they repeat the words.

7 Collect all the index cards, shuffle them, and redistribute them to play again.

¿QUÉ HORA ES?

The following game practices telling time. It's easy to set up and can be used by pairs of students or by small groups to practice telling time.

Materials you may need

- ◆ Paper plates
- ◆ Brads (metal clasps available at most office supply stores)
- ◆ Markers
- ◆ Index cards

Preparation

Have students write various times on the index cards in Spanish. They should use a variety of times including full hours, half hours, quarter hours, before and after the hour, as well as special expressions such as:

La hora de la clase de español
La hora de ir a la escuela
¡Ahora!

Procedure

1 Place index cards face down.

2 Have one student draw an index card with a specific time.

3 First the student must read the time aloud and set the clock to the correct time.

4 If the clock is set correctly the student wins one point.

PALABRAS REVUELTAS

This game is especially good for tactile learners. The objective is for students to be able to construct at least five Spanish words from scrambled letters.

Materials you may need

10 small squares of paper for each student

Procedure

1 Divide the class into two teams.

2 Each person on the team looks up a Spanish word from the **Vocabulario** on page 141 and writes the letters that make up that word on squares of paper, one letter per square.

3 Then they scramble their letters.

4 Ask for members from each team to exchange their letters.

5 Students try to immediately arrange the letters in the correct order.

6 The student who unscrambles his or her word before his or her opponent wins a point for his or her team.

CADENA

This game, which helps students review vocabulary, is good for auditory learners.

Procedure

1 Have all students stand up.

2 Begin by saying **Este semestre tengo geografía.**

3 The first student then says **Este semestre tengo geografía y física.**

4 The second student repeats what has already been said, adding a new school subject to the sentence.

5 When someone says the "chain" incorrectly, he or she sits down.

6 This sequence continues until no one can add any more school subjects to the sentence. Then begin a new sentence, such as **Me gusta el arte.**

7 The winners are the last three students to be left standing.

¿ES LA HORA?

*This game is especially good for auditory learners. The objective is for students to be able to distinguish between **a las** and **son las**.*

Preparation

Prepare twenty to thirty flashcards with questions in Spanish about time. For example, **¿A qué hora es la clase de español?** or **Compro el almuerzo. ¿Qué hora es?**

Procedure

1 Divide the class into two teams. Allow them to pick a name for their team.

2 Hand the representative from first team a card with a question. They ask the representative from the second team the question, and he or she must answer correctly using **a las...** or **son las...**

3 Then have a representative from Team 2 ask a question. Have the team representatives change every question so that everyone can participate.

Answers to listening activities appear on pages 101E–101F. Answers to all other activities appear on corresponding pupil pages.

PRIMER PASO   pp. 108–115

9 Answers will vary. Possible answers:
(1A) Hola, ¿qué tal?
(2A) Estoy bien. ¿Cómo estás?
(1B) Bien, gracias. ¿Qué clases tienes este semestre?
(2B) Tengo el francés, la biología y la geografía. ¿Qué clases tienes hoy?
(1C) Primero tengo la clase de español. Luego tengo la computación.
(2C) Me gusta la clase de biología.
(1D) Bueno, tengo que irme. Hasta luego.
(2D) Adiós.

SEGUNDO PASO   pp. 118–123

20 1. —¿A qué hora es la clase de matemáticas?
   —Es a las once menos veinticinco de la mañana.
2. —¿A qué hora es la clase de computación?
   —Es a las dos y diez de la tarde.
3. —¿A qué hora es la clase de educación física?
   —Es a las cuatro menos veinte de la tarde.
4. —¿A qué hora es la clase de francés?
   —Es a las doce menos diez de la mañana.
5. —¿A qué hora es la clase de arte?
   —Es a la una y media de la tarde.
6. —¿A qué hora es la clase de geografía?
   —Es a las ocho y veinticinco de la mañana.

22 Answers will vary. Possible answers:
STUDENT 1   Hola, ¿cómo estás?
STUDENT 2   Muy bien. ¿Y tú?

STUDENT 1   Bien, gracias. ¿De dónde eres?
STUDENT 2   Soy de Cuernavaca. ¿Qué clases tienes este semestre y a qué hora son?
STUDENT 1   Tengo geografía y francés. La clase de geografía es a las nueve y la clase de francés es a las diez.

27 Answers will vary. Possible answers:
—Hola, Marcos, ¿cómo estás?
—Muy bien. ¿Y tú?
—Más o menos. ¿Cómo es tu clase de francés?
—Es buena, pero tengo que irme.
—Y ¿cómo es el profesor?
—Es simpático, pero tengo mucha prisa. Estoy atrasado.
—Bueno, hasta luego.

TERCER PASO   pp. 124–133

36 Answers will vary. Possible answers:
1. —¿Cómo es tu libro de ciencias sociales?
   —Es grande pero interesante.
2. —Oye, ¿cómo es la comida en la cafetería?
   —Mira, es buena.
3. —Oye, ¿cómo es la clase de inglés?
   —Mira, es aburrida, pero me gusta.
4. —Oye, ¿cómo es la tarea de español?
   —Bueno, hay mucha, pero es fácil.
5. —¿Cómo son tus amigos?
   —Son muy simpáticos.
6. —Oye, ¿cómo es la música de...?
   —Es buena.

ENLACES   pp. 134–135

1 1. Son las cuatro de la tarde.
2. Son las cinco de la mañana.
3. Son las tres y media de la tarde.
4. Son las ocho y cuarto de la noche.

VAMOS A LEER   pp. 136–137

B 1. report cards
2. report cards
3. report cards and schedules
4. schedules
5. report cards and schedules
6. neither
7. report cards
8. neither
9. report cards and schedules

C 1. her conduct
2. Óscar: 8.8; Juana: 9
3. Óscar
4. Óscar

D 1. Gloria: 9; Óscar: 8; Juana: 10
2. Answers will vary.
3. A las siete y media.

REPASO   pp. 138–139

2 1. La clase de español de Gabriela es a las doce y media. La clase de español de Martín es a las trece y media.
2. Gabriela tiene primero la clase de ciencias sociales. Martín tiene primero la clase de francés.
3. Después del almuerzo Gabriela tiene la clase de español. Después del almuerzo Martín tiene la clase de ciencias sociales.

A VER SI PUEDO...   p. 140

5 Answers will vary. Possible answers:
Yolanda es inteligente y morena.
Gabriela es alta y rubia.
Simón es joven y cómico.
Bruto es grande y simpático.

Chapter Section	Presentation	Homework Options
Primer paso	**Vocabulario**, p. 109	*Grammar and Vocabulary*, p. 18, #1–2 *CD-ROM*, Disc 1, Chapter 3, #3
	Nota gramatical, p. 109	*Grammar and Vocabulary,* p. 19, #3–5
	Así se dice, p. 110	*Pupil's Edition*, pp. 110–111, #6–8 *Practice and Activity Book*, pp. 28–29, #4, 6
	Así se dice, p. 112	*Practice and Activity Book*, p. 30, #7 *CD-ROM*, Disc 1, Chapter 3, #1
	Gramática, p. 113	*Pupil's Edition*, pp. 113–115, #12–14, 17 *Grammar and Vocabulary*, p. 20, #6–7 *CD-ROM*, Disc 1, Chapter 3, #2
Segundo paso	**Así se dice**, p. 119	*Pupil's Edition*, p. 120, #20
	Vocabulario, p. 119	*Practice and Activity Book*, pp. 31–32, #9–10 *Grammar and Vocabulary*, p. 21, #8–9
	Nota gramatical, p. 121	*Grammar and Vocabulary*, p. 22, #10–11
	Así se dice, p. 122	*CD-ROM*, Disc 1, Chapter 3, #4 *Pupil's Edition*, pp. 122–123, #24–26 *Practice and Activity Book*, pp. 32–33, #11–12
Tercer paso	**Así se dice**, p. 125	*Pupil's Edition*, p. 125, #29 *Practice and Activity Book*, p. 35, #15
	Vocabulario, p. 125	*Pupil's Edition*, pp. 127–128, #33–34, 37 *Practice and Activity Book*, pp. 35–36, #16–17, 19 *CD-ROM*, Disc 1, Chapter 3, #6
	Nota gramatical, p. 126	*Grammar and Vocabulary*, p. 23, #12–13
	Gramática, p. 127	*Grammar and Vocabulary*, p. 25, #17
	Así se dice, p.129	*Pupil's Edition*, p. 129, #38 *Practice and Activity Book*, pp. 36, #18 *CD-ROM*, Disc 1, Chapter 3, #5
	Vocabulario, p. 130	*Grammar and Vocabulary*, p. 26, #18–19

Nuevas clases, nuevos amigos

MOTIVATING ACTIVITIES

• Ask students to list in English what they might say to each other on the first day of a new school year. What might they ask new and old friends?

• Have students briefly discuss the classes they have this year and which they anticipate to be the best, hardest, most useful, most enjoyable, or most interesting.

• Ask students how they think they would feel about starting the year in a new school. Would they be excited about making new friends, or would they miss their old school?

FOCUSING ON OUTCOMES

Have students look at the chapter outcomes and match them with the three photos. (Photo 1 represents describing people and things; photo 2 represents telling at what time something happens, telling time, and talking about class schedules; and photo 3 represents talking about class schedules.) Point out to students that many of the people they meet are at school, and much of their time is spent there, so it is important to be able to talk about these things.

CAPÍTULO

3 Nuevas clases, nuevos amigos

① **Mis compañeros de clase son simpáticos.**

For Spanish-speaking students, a new school year means getting used to a new class schedule. It means finding out what new classes, teachers, and classmates are like. Best of all, the new school year means seeing old friends and meeting new ones. What is the beginning of the new school year like for you?

In this chapter you will learn

- to talk about classes and to sequence events; to tell time
- to tell at what time something happens; to talk about being late or in a hurry
- to describe people and things; to talk about things you like and explain why

And you will

- listen to conversations about classes and hear descriptions of people
- read class schedules and report cards from Spanish-speaking countries
- write a paragraph describing your classes, teachers, and friends
- find out about what students in Spanish-speaking countries study

② **¿A qué hora es la clase?**

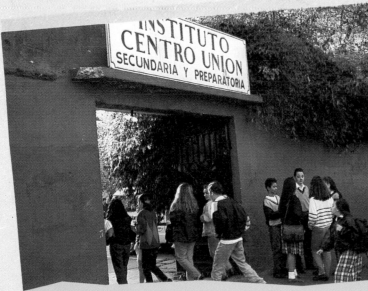

③ **Tenemos clase de ciencias a las siete y media.**

103

103

NATIVE SPEAKERS

If any of your students have lived in or visited Mexico, ask them if they would be willing to share some of their experiences. Ask them how Mexico is similar to the United States. What foods are similar? Which stores do the two countries have in common? Which sports are the same? What are Mexican schools like compared with those in the United States? Are there more or fewer classes each day? Is the schedule the same or a bit different? How many students are there in a class?

TEACHER NOTE

You may wish to assign your students the Additional Vocabulary on **asignaturas,** pp. 275–277.

VIDEO INTEGRATION

Adelante LEVEL 1A
Video Program,
Videocassette 1, 45:34–51:03 OR
¡Ven conmigo! LEVEL 1
Videodisc Program,
Videodisc 2A

Search 4500, Play To 14390

TEACHER NOTE
The **fotonovela** is an abridged version of the video episode.

VIDEO SYNOPSIS
Claudia is starting the year at a new school. She meets the school principal, who introduces her to the students in her first class. While they wait for their teacher to arrive, Claudia talks with her new acquaintances. The students are friendly, and one is particularly mischievous.

MOTIVATING ACTIVITY
Divide students into small groups. Have students use the photos to predict what is going to happen in the **fotonovela.** Ask them to make their predictions by answering questions based on *who? how old? what? where?* and *why?* This may be done in English or in Spanish, depending on students' proficiency, but remember that your main purpose is to engage the students' interest and focus their attention on the **fotonovela.**

DE ANTEMANO

Cass. 2A
CD 3 Trs. 1–2

¡Bienvenida al colegio!

Look at the photos that accompany the story. Where and when do you think these scenes are taking place? What clues tell you this? What do you think will happen in the story?

PA
p. 27
Acts. 1–2

María Inés, Fernando y Claudia   **Director Altamirano**   **Profesor Romanca**

DIRECTOR Bueno, ya son las ocho menos cinco. Aquí tienes el horario. Ahorita tienes clase de ciencias sociales... y a las ocho y cincuenta tienes clase de francés. El descanso es a las nueve y cuarenta...

DIRECTOR   Muchachos, buenos días. Ella es una compañera nueva. Se llama Claudia Obregón Sánchez. Es de la Ciudad de México.

MARÍA INÉS   Me llamo María Inés.

FERNANDO   Y yo soy Fernando. Encantado. Y ¡bienvenida a Cuernavaca!

MARÍA INÉS   Eres de la Ciudad de México, ¡ay, qué padre! Hay muchas cosas interesantes allá, ¿no?

CLAUDIA   Sí, la capital es muy divertida. Mira, me gusta ir al parque... visitar los museos... y también me gusta mucho jugar al basquetbol.

FERNANDO   Miren, ya son las ocho. ¿Dónde está el profesor? Está atrasado.

PRESENTATION

Have students follow along as you read the captions or play the audio recording. Next, have students repeat the dialogue after you. In their same groups from the Motivating Activity, encourage students to guess the meaning of the captions. Ask groups to revise their original predictions. Play the video and then have students describe what is happening in each frame of the **fotonovela**.

LANGUAGE NOTE

Explain some colloquial words in the **fotonovela** that might be unfamiliar to students.
¡Qué padre!   *Cool!*
¡Mira!   *Look!* or *Hey!*
¡Híjole!   *Gosh!*

SUGGESTIONS

• Point out that **bienvenida** in the title refers to Claudia, and that **bienvenido** changes in gender and number depending on who is being addressed.

• After students read the **fotonovela,** ask them if they have ever been in a similar situation (a new student in another country or simply in a new school). If so, how did they handle it? What were some of the differences they found?

ADDITIONAL PRACTICE

Have students scan the text in the **fotonovela** for ten cognates. On this page, they should be able to recognize **clase**, **horrible**, **favorita**, **exámenes**, **profesor/a**, **estudiar**.

THINKING CRITICALLY

Have students try to guess what will happen to María Inés. What is her teacher, Profesor Romanca, likely to say to her? How might she respond to what he says?

VIDEO INTEGRATION

Adelante LEVEL 1A

Video Program,
Videocassette 1, 51:04–56:20 OR
¡Ven conmigo! LEVEL 1

Videodisc Program,
Videodisc 2A

Search 14390, Play To 23875

VIDEO SYNOPSIS

When the story continues, María Inés receives an extra assignment from the teacher. The friends meet after school in the courtyard, and Claudia meets more of María Inés's and Fernando's friends.

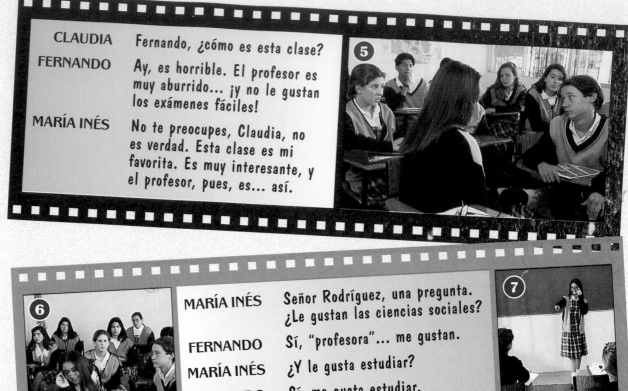

CLAUDIA Fernando, ¿cómo es esta clase?

FERNANDO Ay, es horrible. El profesor es muy aburrido... ¡y no le gustan los exámenes fáciles!

MARÍA INÉS No te preocupes, Claudia, no es verdad. Esta clase es mi favorita. Es muy interesante, y el profesor, pues, es... así.

MARÍA INÉS Señor Rodríguez, una pregunta. ¿Le gustan las ciencias sociales?

FERNANDO Sí, "profesora"... me gustan.

MARÍA INÉS ¿Y le gusta estudiar?

FERNANDO Sí, me gusta estudiar.

MARÍA INÉS Entonces, ¿por qué no le gusta estudiar las ciencias sociales?

¡Ay, no!

1 ¿Comprendes?

Check your understanding of the **fotonovela** by answering these questions.

These activities check for global comprehension only. Students should not yet be expected to produce language modeled in **De antemano**.

1. What time is it when the story begins? How do you know?
   a. 7:55 *(circled)*   because director Altamirano states the time and the
   b. 8:00   clock shows 7:55
2. What do you think the principal is discussing with Claudia?
   a. the bus schedule
   b. her class schedule *(circled)*
3. What kind of photographs is Claudia showing Fernando and María Inés?
   a. pictures of Mexico City *(circled)*
   b. pictures of Cuernavaca
4. What do María Inés and Fernando think of this class?
   a. Fernando really likes it and María Inés thinks it's awful.
   b. Fernando thinks it's horrible and María Inés thinks it's interesting. *(circled)*
5. The **fotonovela** ends with . . .
   a. María Inés walking into the wrong classroom.
   b. the teacher walking in while María Inés is imitating him. *(circled)*

2 ¿Quién es?

Match the name of the person with the sentence that describes him or her.

1. María Inés d
2. Claudia a
3. Fernando b
4. el señor Romanca c

a. Ella es de la Ciudad de México.
b. A él no le gusta la clase de ciencias sociales.
c. Es el profesor de ciencias sociales.
d. A ella le gusta la clase de ciencias sociales.

3 ¡Opiniones!

Using the **fotonovela** as a guide, complete this conversation between two students with the words from the box.

—Tengo la clase de ___1___ a las ocho. No me ___2___ la clase. ¡Es ___3___ y los exámenes son difíciles!
—¿Ah, sí? Pues, es mi clase ___4___. ¡Es muy ___5___!

> interesante   gusta
> horrible   favorita
> ciencias sociales

1. ciencias sociales
2. gusta
3. horrible
4. favorita
5. interesante

SUGGESTION

1 Have students review questions with a partner. Then ask for volunteers to answer the questions. Ask the class to use thumbs up if the answer is correct and thumbs down if the answer is incorrect.

ADDITIONAL PRACTICE

2 Put words and phrases that make up the following sentences on sentence strips or a felt board, and have students move the words to make the false sentences true and correct false ones.

Fernando es de la Ciudad de México.
La compañera nueva se llama María Inés.
La clase es de matemáticas.
María Inés es la profesora de la clase.
Señor Romanca es el profesor de la clase.

JUMP START!

Write the following questions on the board and have students write their answers.

¿Qué necesitas para el colegio?

¿Cuántos cuadernos necesitas?

¿Cuántas carpetas necesitas?

¿Tienes una calculadora?

¿Tienes muchos bolígrafos?

 CULTURE NOTE
Point out that a **siesta** isn't necessarily a nap. It can be just some time to relax. Also, in larger cities, it may be some extra time to commute to and from home for the midday meal. Nine-to-five schedules without a **siesta** are increasingly common.

PRIMER PASO

Talking about classes and sequencing events; telling time

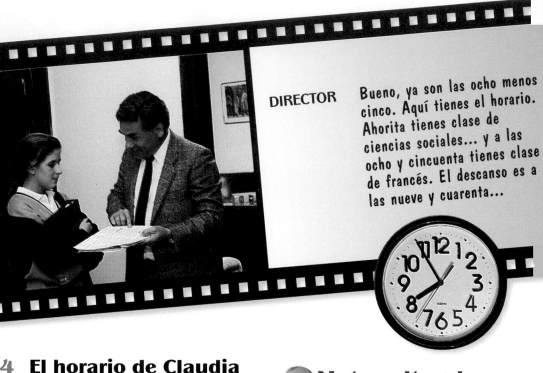

DIRECTOR: Bueno, ya son las ocho menos cinco. Aquí tienes el horario. Ahorita tienes clase de ciencias sociales... y a las ocho y cincuenta tienes clase de francés. El descanso es a las nueve y cuarenta...

4 El horario de Claudia

Help Claudia complete part of her class schedule.

Claudia Obregón Sánchez

7:55 – la clase de _ciencias sociales_

8:50 – la clase de _francés_

9:40 – _____ _descanso_

Nota cultural

Some students in Spanish-speaking countries go home for lunch and a **siesta** (*nap* or *rest*) in the middle of the school day. They then go back to school in the afternoon. These students may not get out of school for the day until 4:30 or 5:00. Other students attend school only in the morning, while a second group of students attends school only in the afternoon. What do you think the ideal school schedule is? Why?

VOCABULARIO

CD-ROM Disc 1

PA p. 28 Act. 3

GV p. 18 Acts. 1–2

3-A

¿Qué materias estudias?   *What subjects are you studying?*

el francés

la geografía

las matemáticas

el almuerzo

la educación física

el arte

las ciencias

el descanso

la computación

las ciencias sociales

NOTA GRAMATICAL

With nouns referring to more than one thing, like **libros** or **clases**, use **los** or **las**. **Los** is for masculine nouns. **Las** is for feminine nouns. Both words mean *the.*

Tengo **los** libros.

¿Tienes **las** gomas de borrar?

Also use **los** when referring to a group of people that includes both males and females.

Los profesores son de México.

PA p. 29 Act. 5

GV p. 19 Acts. 3–5

5 ¡Tenemos la misma clase!

Cass. 2A
CD 3 Tr. 3

Script and answers on p. 101E

Listen to Álvaro and Lupita discuss their new class schedules. What class do they have together?

Álvaro	Lupita

☀ MOTIVATE

Ask students what their favorite and least favorite subjects are. As they mention different subjects, respond with **Entonces te gusta.../no te gusta...**

☀ TEACH

PRESENTATION

VOCABULARIO

Have students scan the vocabulary for recognition. Then ask **¿Quién tiene clase de arte?** Ask for a show of hands. Repeat for the other subjects. Continue by asking individuals if they like certain subjects.

TEACHER NOTE

Teach students some extra vocabulary for classes, such as: **el coro** *choir*, **la banda** *band*, **la orquesta** *orchestra*, and **el taller** *shop*.

PRESENTATION

NOTA GRAMATICAL

Remind students that nouns in Spanish are either masculine or feminine. Review **el** and **la** and introduce **los** and **las**. Ask students to call out the appropriate article for objects you hold up. (**carpeta, cuadernos, bolígrafo,** etc.) Vary the number and gender of objects you hold up.

109

pp. 28–29
Acts. 4, 6

CD-ROM Disc 1

ASÍ SE DICE Talking about classes and sequencing events

To find out what classes a friend has, ask:

Your friend might answer:

¿Qué clases tienes este semestre?
What classes do you have this semester?

Bueno, **tengo** matemáticas, inglés, español y ciencias sociales.

¿Qué clases tienes hoy?
What classes do you have today?

Primero tengo geografía, **después** computación y **luego** francés.
First I have geography, afterwards computer science, and then French.

¿Y cuándo tienes un día libre?
And when do you have a day off?

¡Mañana, por fin, tengo un día libre!
Tomorrow, at last, I have a day off!

6 ¿Qué clase tiene primero?

Alma is talking about her class schedule with a friend. Read the conversation. Then list the items in the box in the order she'll need them, based on her schedule. Label the first item she'll need number one, and the last item she'll need number five.   Answers in side column

—Primero tengo la clase de matemáticas.

—¿Y después tienes la clase de geografía?

—Sí, y después del almuerzo, tengo educación física. Luego tengo la clase de ciencias.

—Y por último tienes la clase de arte, ¿verdad?

> zapatillas de tenis
> lápices de color
> un mapa de México
> libro de biología
> una calculadora

p. 38
Act. 21

Nota cultural

How would you feel if you got a score of 18 on a test? In Peru, this would actually be a high grade, equivalent to a 90. Peruvian schools use a scale of 1 to 20, with 11 the lowest passing score. Mexican schools use a scale of 1 to 10, with 6 as passing. What would your grades be if you went to school in Peru? In Mexico?

AÑO	ASIGNATURAS	EDUCACION BASICA						Calificación Definitiva
		1o Lapso Calif.	Inas.	2o Lapso Calif.	Inas.	3o Lapso Calif.	Inas.	
9no	Castellano	12		11		11		11
	Biología	14		12		10		12
	Inglés	18		16		16		17
	Geografía de Venezuela	13		12		13		13
	Cátedra Bolivariana	14		10		11		12
	Química	16		10		12		13
	Física	11		15		15		14
	Matemáticas	10		10		13		11
	Educación Física	05		14		11		10
	Psicopedagogía	15		16		17		16
	Computación	11		12		13		12
	Sorámbo	10		13		13		12
						12		12

7 Primero tiene...

Complete this description of Eduardo's weekly morning schedule using the words below. Two answers are interchangeable. Answers in side column

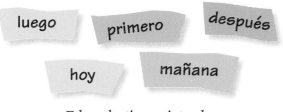

luego   primero   después

hoy   mañana

Eduardo Bello González			
	LUNES	MARTES	MIÉRCOLES
8:00	Matemáticas	Matemáticas	Matemáticas
9:00	Ciencias Sociales	Ciencias Sociales	Ciencias Sociales
10:00	descanso	descanso	descanso
10:30	Computación	Educación Física	Computación
11:30	Ciencias	Ciencias	Ciencias
12:30	almuerzo	almuerzo	almuerzo
1:00	Francés	Arte	Francés
2:00	Español	Español	Español

___1___ Eduardo tiene siete clases.
___2___ tiene la clase de matemáticas con la profesora Lares. ___3___ tiene las ciencias sociales y un descanso.
___4___ tiene la computación, las ciencias y el almuerzo. ___5___ tiene educación física a las 10:30 y arte a la 1:00.

8 El día de Julia

First, rewrite Julia's schedule, putting everything in order. Then write three things that *you* do showing the order in which you do them. Use the words from Activity 7 to write your sentences, and put them in order with **primero, luego,** and **después**. Personalized answers will vary.

a. Luego tengo descanso. 3
b. Después del descanso tengo arte. 4
c. Primero tengo ciencias. 1
d. ¡Por fin no tengo más clases! 5
e. Después de ciencias tengo 2 español.

9 Pues, tengo...

Get together with a partner. Create a conversation in which you greet one another and find out what classes you each have and in what order you have them. Use words like **primero, luego,** and **después.** Follow the guide below. Answers will vary. Possible answers on p. 101K

Tú	Tu compañero/a
Greet your friend.	Respond to your partner's greeting and ask how he or she is doing.
Respond that you're doing well. Ask what class he or she has this semester.	Answer your partner's question. Ask your partner what classes he or she has today.
Tell your partner what class you have first and then what you have afterwards.	Tell your partner which class you like.
Say goodbye.	Say goodbye.

EN MI CUADERNO

7 Have students write a description of their class schedule in their journals. Ask them to use the adverbs **primero, después, luego,** and **por fin** for sequencing the classes. For an additional journal entry suggestion for Chapter 3, see *Practice and Activity Book,* p. 77.

MATH LINK

7 Take a poll to find out how many students have other classes in common. Ask the class for a show of hands as you ask questions like **¿Quién tiene geografía?** Write the results on the board. Have students use the results to create a bar graph labeled in Spanish.

CULTURE NOTE

Students in Spain often receive comments instead of number or letter grades: **sobresaliente, bien, suficiente, suspendido,** or **deficiente.**

SLOWER PACE

9 You might want to write days of the week on the board and have students structure their conversation around them. (**¿Qué clases tienes hoy?** or **¿Qué clases tienes mañana?**)

Answers to Activity 7
1. Hoy
2. Primero
3. Luego *or* Después
4. Luego *or* Después
5. Mañana

p. 30
Act. 7

ASÍ SE DICE   Telling time

To find out what time it is, ask:

¿Qué hora es?

To answer, say:

Son las ocho.
It's eight o'clock.

Son las once y media.
It's 11:30.

Es la una y cuarto.
It's 1:15. (It's a quarter after one.)

¡Ay! ¿Ya son las tres?
Yikes! Is it already three o'clock?

Sí, es tarde. ¡Vamos!
Yes, it's late. Let's go!

10 El reloj

Bernardo is babysitting today. You'll hear his brother at different times throughout the day asking him what time it is. Match each time mentioned with the correct clock below.   Scripts and answers on p. 101E

GRAMÁTICA Telling time

1. To tell the hour (except for times around 1:00), use **Son las...** plus the hour.

   Son las ocho. *It's 8:00.*

2. For times after the hour, follow this pattern:

   Son las siete y cuarto. *It's a quarter after seven.*
   Son las ocho y veinticinco. *It's 8:25.*
   Son las once y media. *It's 11:30.*

3. For times before the hour, say:

   Es la una menos veinte.
   It's twenty minutes to one.
   Son las doce menos cuarto.
   It's a quarter to twelve.
   Son las ocho menos diez.
   It's ten minutes to eight.

4. For times including 1:00, use **Es la una...**

   Es la una y veinte. *It's 1:20.*

PA
p. 30
Act. 8

GV
p. 20
Acts. 6–7

PRESENTATION GRAMÁTICA

Before beginning this section, prepare large flashcards. On each card write a time, such as 3:00. As you hold up each card, have students tell you whether to use **son las** or **es la**. Say the time with them: **Son las tres.** Next, show the cards one at a time and have the class tell you the time in unison in Spanish. Students can do *CD-ROM*, Activity 2 as a follow up.

11 ¿Qué hora es?

With a partner, take turns asking and telling each other what time it is on each watch.

1. Son las tres y media.
2. Son las doce menos veinte.
3. Son las cinco.
4. Son las diez y cuarto.
5. Son las seis y cinco.
6. Son las diez menos cinco.

SUGGESTION

11 Tell students there are different ways to tell time. For example, instead of saying **Son las ocho menos diez**, they may say **Son las siete y cincuenta** for 7:50. You may point out that director Altamirano in **De antemano** uses **a las ocho y cincuenta** rather than **a las nueve menos diez** when he tells Claudia about the class schedule.

12 La hora

Read the sentences and match each one with the correct time.

1. Son las diez menos cinco. c
2. Son las ocho y cuarto. e
3. Son las nueve menos diez. a
4. Son las siete menos seis. d
5. Es la una menos cuarto. b

a. 8:50
b. 12:45
c. 9:55
d. 6:54
e. 8:15

13 Relojes

Draw a clock that corresponds to each of the times given below.
Then copy the time in words below your drawing.

1. Son las once menos cuarto. `10:45`   4. Son las diez menos veinte. `9:40`
2. Son las cuatro. `4:00`   5. Es la una y media. `1:30`
3. Son las tres y media. `3:30`   6. Son las dos menos diez. `1:50`

14 ¿Qué hora es cuando...?

Generally, what time is it when . . .?   Answers will vary. Possible answers below

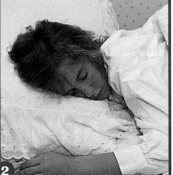

Son las siete de la tarde.

Son las once de la noche.

Son las siete de la mañana.

Es la una de la tarde.

Son las siete y media de la mañana.

Son las doce de la tarde.

15 ¿Qué clase tengo ahora?   Scripts and answers on p. 101E

Cass. 2A
CD 3 Tr. 5

Imagine that you're talking with your new friend Alberto about a typical school day. Listen as he tells you about his schedule. Write the class that he has for each of the times listed.

MODELO   —Son las doce y diez. Tengo la clase de computación.
(h, computación)

a. 10:05   c. 1:55   e. 2:45   g. 8:25
b. 11:40   d. 9:15   f. 1:00   h. 12:10

Nota cultural

In Spanish-speaking countries, especially those with warmer climates, you might find that people's schedules are a little different from yours. A **siesta** after lunch makes it possible for people to eat dinner later and stay up later, too. The **siesta** is a time when stores and businesses close for around two hours at noon. They then stay open a little later in the evening. The dinner hour is also later, usually between 8:00 and 10:00. In many areas, however, this is changing. Many businesses are now open from 9:00 to 5:00. Do you think a **siesta** is a good idea? Why or why not?

☀ CLOSE

17 Ask students comprehension questions, such as, **¿Qué clase tiene primero, Adela?; ¿Cuántas clases tiene Martín hoy?**; or **¿Cuántas clases tiene Martín mañana?** Then, ask several students the same questions about their own schedules, **¿Qué clase tienes primero?; ¿Cuántas clases tienes hoy?**; or **¿Cuántas clases tienes mañana?** Next, assign pairs in which students write and perform a dialogue based on this conversation between Adela and Martín.

☀ ASSESS

QUIZ 3-1
Testing Program, pp. 37–38
Audio Program,
Assessment Items,
 Audiocassette 4A OR
Audio CD 3 Track 18

PERFORMANCE ASSESSMENT
In pairs, have students describe their schedules to each other as they would to a new friend. They should tell which classes they have at what time and indicate the order of their classes using **primero, después, luego,** and **por fin.** Have students present their dialogues to the class or record them on audiocassette or videocassette.

16 Son las...

Take turns reading each item to your partner and asking and answering what time it is. More than one time may be appropriate for some items. Create your own item for number 6.

MODELO   Tienes clase de matemáticas. → Son las nueve menos diez.

1. Es la hora del almuerzo.
2. Necesitas hacer la tarea.
3. Necesitas ir al colegio.
4. Hay un descanso.
5. Tienes la clase de español.
6. ¿?

Answers will vary.
Possible answers:
1. Son las doce de la tarde.
2. Son las cuatro de la tarde.
3. Son las ocho de la mañana.
4. Son las dos y media de la tarde.
5. Son las diez de la mañana.

17 Las clases

Adela and Martín are talking before school in the morning. Show the order of their conversation by writing the letters of each item in the correct order.

3 **a.** —Primero tengo la clase de matemáticas. Luego tengo la clase de ciencias a las nueve y media. Y tú, ¿cuántas clases tienes hoy?

2 **b.** —Estoy bien, Adela. ¿Qué clase tienes primero?

4 **c.** —Yo tengo seis clases hoy. Mañana tengo siete porque tengo educación física. Oye, Adela, ¿qué hora es?

6 **d.** —¡Ay! Es tarde. Tengo clase. ¡Vamos!

1 **e.** —Hola, Martín. ¿Cómo estás?

5 **f.** —Son las ocho menos cuarto.

VIDEO INTEGRATION

Adelante LEVEL 1A
Video Program,
Videocassette 1, 56:22–59:17

TEACHER NOTES

- See the *Video Guide* for activities related to **Panorama cultural**.

- Remind students that cultural information may be included in the Quizzes and the Chapter Test.

- The language of the people interviewed represents informal, unrehearsed speech. Occasionally, text has been edited for clarity.

MOTIVATING ACTIVITY

Ask students what a typical school day is like for them. What times do their classes start? What electives can they take? What subjects do they like? What do they do after class?

PRESENTATION

Have students look at the interviews to find five words about schedules, five words about classes and one about an elective.

Panorama cultural

¿Cómo es un día escolar típico?

In this chapter, we asked some students at what time they usually go to school, what they do after class, and which classes they like.

Cass. 2A
or CD 3
Trs. 6–9

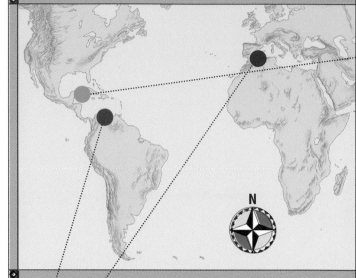

N

Rodrigo's school day starts at 5:45 A.M., and he has several classes. What is a typical day at your school like?

● **Rodrigo**
*San Miguel,
Costa Rica*
CD 3 Tr. 7

[Tengo] español, estudios, ciencias, matemáticas, agricultura y religión. [Mi clase favorita es] ciencias.

In Spain, students almost always go home for lunch. They sometimes have an hour and a half.

● **Elizabeth**
Sevilla, España
CD 3 Tr. 8

Voy desde las nueve de la mañana hasta las dos del mediodía y luego voy a mi casa a comer.

As soon as she gets to school, Renata greets her teachers. Do you say hello to your teachers when you begin the school day?

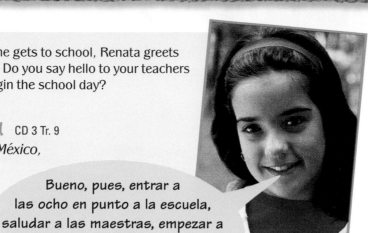

Renata CD 3 Tr. 9
*Ciudad de México,
México*

Bueno, pues, entrar a las ocho en punto a la escuela, saludar a las maestras, empezar a trabajar en matemáticas, después en español, después en ciencias naturales y geografía.

1. How many classes does Rodrigo have? 6

2. What classes does Rodrigo take that you don't? Answers will vary.

3. Elizabeth starts school much later than Rodrigo. What time does she start? She starts at 9:00 A.M.

4. At 2:00 P.M., Elizabeth goes _____ for lunch.
   (a.) home
   b. to the cafeteria

5. What time does Renata start school?
   a. around 8:00 A.M.
   (b.) at 8:00 on the dot

6. What classes do you have in common with Renata? Answers will vary.

Para pensar y hablar... Answers will vary.

A. Which student has classes or a school routine most like yours? Explain.

B. In a group of three or four, talk about a normal day at school. What do you like about the class schedule at your school? What would you change about it if you could?

THINKING CRITICALLY
Lead a class discussion comparing the school schedules of the students in the **Panorama cultural** with the students in your class. Which classes do your students have in common with the students interviewed and which classes are different? Are your students allowed to go home for lunch? Do they begin the day as early as Rodrigo? Would they like to begin at 6:00 A.M. if they could leave school for the day at 1:00 P.M.?

NATIVE SPEAKERS
• Have native speakers look for words with *s, ci, h,* and *z* in the **Panorama cultural** interviews. They should find two with *s,* one with *ci* (**ciencias**), one with *h* (**hasta**), and one with *z* (**empezar**). Have them add these words to their spelling notebook.

• Preguntas adicionales:
1. ¿Dónde almuerzas durante la semana?
2. ¿Te gustaría ir a tu casa para almorzar?
3. ¿A qué hora empiezan tus clases?
4. ¿Con qué clase preferirías empezar, y por qué?

VIDEO INTEGRATION

Adelante LEVEL 1A
Video Program,
Videocassette 1, 48:20–49:46 OR
¡Ven conmigo! LEVEL 1
Videodisc Program,
Videodisc 2A

Search 9479, Play To 12070

JUMP START!

Write the following questions on the board or on a transparency and have students write their answers:

¿Qué materias tienes este semestre?
¿Qué clases tienes hoy?
¿Qué clase tienes ahora?
¿Qué hora es?

SUGGESTION

Ask students what happens if they are late to a class. What are some of the reasons they might be late? What are some reasons a teacher might be late?

☀ MOTIVATE

Ask students when they need to know at what time something starts. (to watch a TV program or to get to a movie or concert on time) Are they ever late? When do they feel the need to hurry to get somewhere? In this **paso** they will learn to talk about these things in Spanish. Have them list three things for which they need to know the starting time.

SEGUNDO PASO

Telling at what time something happens; talking about being late or in a hurry

CLAUDIA Sí, la capital es muy divertida. Mira, me gusta ir al parque... visitar los museos... y también me gusta mucho jugar al basquetbol.

FERNANDO Miren, ya son las ocho. ¿Dónde está el profesor? Está atrasado.

18 ¿Dónde está el profesor?

Answer the questions according to what Fernando says.

1. ¿Qué hora es?
   a. 7:55
   b. 8:00

2. ¿Está en la clase el profesor?
   a. Sí, ya está en la clase.
   b. No, no está en la clase.

3. ¿Quién está atrasado?
   a. el profesor
   b. Fernando

Una plaza en la Ciudad de México

ASÍ SE DICE
Telling at what time something happens

PA
p. 31
Act. 9

To find out at what time something happens, ask:

¿A qué hora es la clase?
At what time is the class?

¿A qué hora es el almuerzo?

To answer say:

(Es) a las tres de la tarde.
(It's) at three in the afternoon.

¡Es ahora! Son las doce **en punto.**
It's now! It's twelve o'clock on the dot.

VOCABULARIO

PA
pp. 31–32
Act. 10

GV
p.21
Acts. 8–9

de la mañana
in the morning (A.M.)

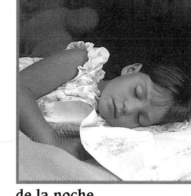

de la tarde
in the afternoon (P.M.)

de la noche
in the evening (P.M.)

---

19 Horarios
Script and answers on p. 101E

Cass. 2A
CD 3 Tr. 10

Two new students are discussing their daily schedules. Listen to each question. Then choose the best answer for each question.

1. a. Es la una de la mañana.
   b. Son las ocho de la mañana.

2. a. A las siete de la mañana.
   b. A las doce y media de la tarde.

3. a. Sí, son las tres de la tarde.
   b. Sí, son las tres de la mañana.

4. a. A las seis de la tarde.
   b. A las doce menos cuarto.

5. a. A la una y cuarto de la tarde.
   b. A las dos de la mañana.

6. a. Son las tres de la mañana.
   b. Son las cinco de la tarde.

☀ TEACH

PRESENTATION
ASÍ SE DICE
Create a list in Spanish of upcoming school-related activities. Make a calendar and enter the activities and the times they start. Ask students to practice asking a partner what time an event takes place.
—¿A qué hora es el partido de fútbol?
—A las siete.

VOCABULARIO
Using the new vocabulary items, ask students when they have different classes:
—Julia, ¿a qué hora tienes la clase de arte?
—Tengo arte a las dos y media de la tarde.

ADDITIONAL PRACTICE
To practice the vocabulary, ask students questions and have them clarify whether the activity takes place in the morning, afternoon, or evening. **¿Practicas el fútbol a las cinco? ¿A las cinco de la mañana o de la tarde? (A las cinco de la tarde.)**

🌐 CULTURE NOTE
Throughout a great deal of the Spanish-speaking world, the idea of the afternoon is a little different. The afternoon for many Spanish speakers can be as late as 7:00 P.M.

20 La tele

Complete the conversation between Sandra and Juan Carlos with the words from the word box. One word will be used more than once. Use the TV schedule to help you.

1. gusta
2. qué
3. siete
4. después
5. a las
6. a qué hora
7. de la noche
8. gusta

SANDRA   A mí me ___1___ *Beetlejuice*.

JUAN CARLOS   ¿A ___2___ hora es?

SANDRA   A las ___3___. Y ___4___ de *Beetlejuice* es *Batman*.

JUAN CARLOS   Es ___5___ siete y media, ¿no? Y ¿___6___ es *Intriga Tropical*?

SANDRA   A las ocho ___7___. ¿Te gusta *Intriga Tropical*?

JUAN CARLOS   Sí, me ___8___ mucho.

de la noche   gusta   a qué hora

qué   después   a las   siete

Jueves
DIC.30 NOCHE

7:00 **5** BEETLEJUICE. Dibujos animados.
NOCHE **7** ALF. Comedia.
9 ESPECIAL MUSICAL. Variedades. "Timbiriche".
11 HOY EN LA CULTURA Entrevista especial a Octavio Paz. Premio Nobel de Literatura y Orgullo de México. Conducción: Sari Bermúdez.
7:30 **7** ¡LLEVATELO! Concursos para toda la familia, con Paco Stanley y Gabriela Ruffo.
5 BATMAN. Dibujos animados.
7 SALVADO POR LA CAMPANA. Aventuras.
11 EL HOMBRE Y LA INDUSTRIA. Reportajes. Juventud.
13 SEÑORA. Telenovela.
22 POR AQUI PUEDEN PASAR. Animación infantil. Cuentos alrededor del mundo: Rumpelstikin.
7:50 **22** ENCUADRE. Cartelera cinematográfica. Con Leonardo García Tsao y Nelson Carro.
8:00 **4** LOS INTOCABLES. Aventuras policíacas.
5 INTRIGA TROPICAL. Aventuras de un ex-agente antinarcóticos y su socia detective. Rob Stewart "Nick Slaughter", Carolyn Dunn "Sylvie Girard", Pedro Armendáriz "Lt. Carrillo".
7 LOS SIMPSONS Dibujos animados.
9 LOLITA AYALA, FERNANDO SCHWARTZ. Muchas Noticias.

21 ¿A qué hora es la clase?

With a partner, take turns asking each other when these classes meet. Use the times given for each course. Answers on p. 101K

MODELO   ¿A qué hora es la clase de ciencias?
A las nueve menos cuarto de la mañana.

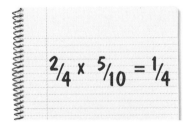

1. 10:35 de la mañana

2. 2:10 de la tarde

3. 11:50 de la mañana

4. 3:40 de la tarde   **5.** 1:30 de la tarde

6. 8:25 de la mañana

22 Entrevista

Get together with a classmate. Imagine that you've just met. Exchange greetings and then find out the following information about each other. After you've interviewed each other, write down each other's schedules. Answers on p. 101K

a. how each of you is feeling today
b. where each of you is from
c. what classes you each have today and at what time they meet

PA
p. 33
Act. 13

GV
p. 22
Acts.
10–11

NOTA GRAMATICAL

In Spanish, to show that something belongs to someone, use **de**.

> **los zapatos de David**
> *David's shoes*
>
> **las clases de Eva**
> *Eva's classes*

De combines with **el** to form the contraction **del**.

> el perro **del** profesor
> *the teacher's dog*
>
> la directora **del** colegio
> *the school's director*

Nota cultural

In Spain, sneakers are referred to as **zapatillas de tenis**. In Latin America, they're called **zapatos de tenis**. In fact, the word **zapatillas** means slippers in Latin America. Spanish sometimes has more than one word for an object, depending on the country. English is like this, too. For example, in England an elevator is called a lift. Can you think of other examples in English where there is more than one word for something?

PRESENTATION

NOTA GRAMATICAL

First, have the students read the grammar explanation. Then walk around the class and pick up various objects. Ask for volunteers to answer questions such as **¿De quién es este libro?** Elicit answers such as **Es el libro de Beth** or **Es de Beth.**

SUGGESTION

22 Have students work in pairs, or suggest that students alternate asking questions around their circle of three. Each student will then have an opportunity to both ask and answer questions. Students may need an example of an interview dialogue:

—¿Cómo estás? —Estoy bien. ¿De dónde eres? —Soy de aquí.
—A las ocho ¿qué clase tienes? —Tengo la clase de arte a las ocho.

23 Una encuesta

With your partner, take turns completing the sentences below. Be ready to report your and your partner's choices to the class. Answers will vary.

MODELO   LUIS   Mi actor favorito es Andy García.
              TÚ   El actor favorito de Luis es Andy García.

1. Mi actor favorito es...
2. Mi actriz *(actress)* favorita es...
3. Mi libro favorito es...

4. Mi deporte favorito es...
5. Mi color favorito es...
6. Mi programa de televisión favorito es...

FAMILY LINK

Ask students to get together with someone at home and write out that person's daily schedule. Does the person do the same things at the same time every day, or does his or her schedule vary? Have students report their findings to the class, describing in Spanish a typical day in a family member's life. Remind them that they can substitute an imaginary family member if they wish.

pp. 32–33
Acts. 11–12

ASÍ SE DICE   Talking about being late or in a hurry

To tell someone you are late, say:

Estoy atrasada. *(if you're female)*

Estoy atrasado. *(if you're male)*

To tell someone you are in a hurry, say:

Tengo prisa.

To say that someone else is late, say:

La profesora de biología **está atrasada.**

El director del colegio **está atrasado.**

To tell a friend to hurry up, say:

¡Date prisa!

24 ¡Date prisa!

Everyone's running late today! Match the correct photo to each caption below.

a   b   c   d

1. ¡Ay! Son las nueve y cuarto. Estoy atrasado. c
2. Buenas tardes, señor Altamirano. Tengo prisa porque la clase de ciencias sociales es a la una. b
3. ¿Estás atrasado, Julio? ¿A qué hora tienes clase? a
4. ¡Date prisa, Claudia! También quiero ir al centro comercial. d

25 ¡Es tarde!

Leopoldo left his watch at home and is having a hard day.
Complete the conversation below.

son	hora
	clase
prisa	atrasado

LEOPOLDO La ___1___ de español es a   clase
las dos. ¿Qué ___2___ es?   hora

CARLA Ya ___3___ las dos y cinco.   Son

LEOPOLDO ¡Ay! Estoy ___4___.   atrasado

CARLA ¡Date ___5___!   prisa

26 Los planes 🏠

Luisa and Juan are talking on the telephone. Write Juan's part of
the conversation. You might also want to draw a picture of Juan
on a piece of paper and write his answers to her questions beside
your picture as in the drawing of Luisa.

Answers will vary.
Possible answers:
—Sí, me gusta la comida
mexicana.
—Es a las siete de la noche.
—Sí, a las siete en punto.
—Bueno, hasta luego.

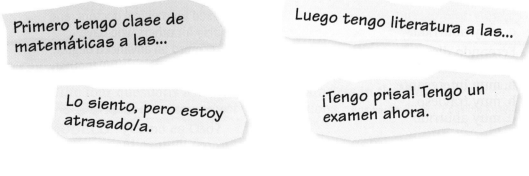

¿Te gusta la comida mexicana?

A mí también. Oye, ¿a qué hora es la fiesta de Mónica?

¿A las siete en punto?

Tengo que irme. Estoy atrasada. ¡Chao!

Luisa

27 Lo siento, no tengo tiempo.

Imagine that you and your partner have just run into each other
at a shopping mall. Write a conversation in which one of you
keeps on talking about his or her schedule while the other tries to
end the conversation. Practice the conversation with your partner.   Answers on p. 101K

Primero tengo clase de matemáticas a las...

Luego tengo literatura a las...

Lo siento, pero estoy atrasado/a.

¡Tengo prisa! Tengo un examen ahora.

VISUAL LEARNERS
26 Write sentences on
paper strips that reflect both
sides of the conversation. Test
student comprehension by mix-
ing up the sentences and having them put the sentences in
the correct order.

☀ CLOSE

Ask your students: **¿A qué hora
es la clase de español?, ¿A
qué hora es el almuerzo?,** or
**Tienes la clase de español a
las ocho. Son las ocho y
media. ¿Estás atrasado/a?** Use
Teaching Transparency 3-2 and
Teaching Transparency 3-A to
further review the material
from this **paso**.

☀ ASSESS

QUIZ 3-2,
Testing Program, pp. 39–40
Audio Program,
Assessment Items,
Audiocassette 4A OR
Audio CD 3 Track 19

**PERFORMANCE
ASSESSMENT**
Make up an age-appropriate
TV schedule and pass out a
copy to each student. Have
students work in pairs to prepare a dialogue in which one
asks the times of various programs, which the other student
provides. Students are to present their dialogues to the
class or record them on an
audio- or videocassette.

GV
p. 26
Acts.
18–19

3-C

VOCABULARIO

el baile

el concierto

los deportes

el examen
(pl. los exámenes)

la fiesta

la novela

el partido de...

el videojuego

39 Patricia y Gregorio Script and answers on p. 101F

Cass. 2A
CD 3 Tr. 11

Patricia and Gregorio have just met at school. First, read the true and false statements about their conversation. Then, listen to Patricia and Gregorio as they try to decide what to do. Based on their conversation, respond to these statements with **cierto** or **falso.**

1. A Patricia no le gustan las fiestas.
2. A Gregorio le gustan los partidos de fútbol porque son interesantes.
3. A Patricia no le gustan los conciertos.
4. A Gregorio le gusta la música rock.

VOCABULARIO

First, have pairs of students look at the drawings and read the captions. Then have them interview their partners about their likes and dislikes. Have them use the new vocabulary to ask questions: **¿Te gustan los conciertos? ¿Te gustan los bailes?** After the interview, have them report their findings to the class in Spanish: **Le gustan los bailes...**

 PORTFOLIO

39 Oral Have students role-play the following situation: Two students are discussing their school schedules and activities. One asks the other what classes he or she has, and whether he or she likes them. The second replies, giving the reason for liking or disliking the classes. They should also ask about favorite and least favorite activities. For Portfolio suggestions, see *Alternative Assessment Guide,* p. 14.

NOTA GRAMATICAL

p. 34
Act. 14

One way of asking a question is by adding **¿no?** or **¿verdad?** to the end of a sentence. These are called *tag questions.*

La clase es difícil, **¿no?**
The class is difficult, isn't it?

Te gustan las fiestas, **¿verdad?**
You like parties, don't you?/ right?

¡Una Fiesta de Cumpleaños!

40 ¿Por qué te gusta? Answers will vary.

Take turns asking each other whether or not you like the things in the list below. When your partner answers, ask "why?" and listen to the reason. Use the adjectives from the word box in your explanation.

MODELO —Te gustan los bailes, ¿no?
—Sí, me gustan mucho.
—¿Por qué?
—Porque son divertidos.

1. la música pop
2. los exámenes
3. el basquetbol
4. las fiestas
5. los deportes
6. los videojuegos
7. el tenis

antipático/a   bueno/a
cómico/a   difícil
divertido/a   fácil   malo/a
interesante   simpático/a
nuevo/a

41 La fiesta de cumpleaños Answers will vary.

You're helping your friend plan a birthday party. Ask your partner at least four questions to try to find out what activities he or she might like at the party. Use tag questions like **¿no?** and **¿verdad?** in two of your questions. Then reverse roles.

MODELO —Te gusta la música popular, ¿verdad?
—Sí, me gusta la música popular en inglés y en español.

PRESENTATION

NOTA GRAMATICAL
Model the use of tag questions verbally and on the board. For example, **Paul Rodríguez es cómico, ¿verdad?** or **Homer Simpson es muy delgado, ¿no?** You may wish to play the section of the video where María Inés models the use of **¿no?** or point out her question in **De antemano** on page 105. See barcode below.

Search 7684, Play To 8621

SLOWER PACE

40 If students are having trouble remembering vocabulary, put pictures of famous people on the board and number each one. Ask students to write a list of adjectives for each picture. It may be helpful for them to associate an image with adjectives. Then, have them check their adjective endings to be sure the form is correct.

42 Soy...

 Form a group of five. On a sheet of paper, write a detailed description of yourself. In your description, include your age, what kind of person you are, what you look like, and things you like and don't like. Don't include your name, and try to disguise your handwriting. Fold your paper in half. Shuffle all the papers. Each group member picks one paper, reads it aloud and tries to guess who it is. If you get your own paper, pick **again**. Answers will vary.

43 De visita

A Imagine that you're a student at the **Instituto Centro Unión** in Cuernavaca, Mexico. Prepare a list of at least six questions that you can use to interview students from the U.S. who are visiting your class. Write at least one question about each of the following.

how old he or she is
—¿Cuántos años tienes?

what classes he or she has this semester
—¿Qué clases tienes este semestre?

what his or her friends are like
—¿Cómo son tus amigos?

what he or she likes
—¿Qué te gusta?

what his or her teachers are like
—¿Cómo son tus profesores?

what he or she doesn't like
—¿Qué no te gusta?

B Now work with a partner and decide who will play the student from Cuernavaca and who will be a student from the U.S. Interview your partner using the questions you've prepared. Then switch roles.

¿Cuál es tu profesor favorito?

¿Por qué?

Pues, mi profesor favorito es el profesor Romanca.

Porque es muy bueno.

44 En mi cuaderno

In your journal, write seven or eight sentences about what you need and want to do at different times tomorrow. Include such items as going to class, doing homework, and going shopping. Use **necesito** and **quiero**.   Answers will vary.

MODELO   Mañana necesito hacer la tarea de inglés a las cuatro y media. También quiero...

LETRA Y SONIDO

Script on p. 101F

Cass. 2A
CD 3
Trs. 12–16

A. 1. **h:** The letter **h** in Spanish is always silent.

   hora   ahora   héroe   Hugo   hijo   hospital

2. **j:** The letter **j** in Spanish represents a sound that has no matching sound in English. It's pronounced like the *h* in the English word *house,* but much stronger.

   jugar   jefe   ají   joven   pasaje   caja   juego

3. **g:** The letter **g** before the vowels **e** and **i** has the same sound as the letter *j* in the examples above.

   gente   general   geografía   gimnasio   corregir   agitar

4. Before the vowels **a, o,** and **u** the letter **g** is pronounced like the *g* in the English word *go.*

   ángulo   tengo   gusto   mango

   Between vowels this sound is much softer.

   haga   agua   agotar   mucho gusto

5. The **g** is pronounced "hard," like the *g* in *get,* when it's part of **gue** or **gui.**

   guerra   llegué   guitarra   guía

B. Dictado

   Jimena describes for us what she needs in two of her classes. Write what Jimena is saying.

C. Trabalenguas

   La gente de San José generalmente juega a las barajas con ganas de ganar.

EN MI CUADERNO

44 For an additional Chapter 3 journal entry suggestion, see *Practice and Activity Book,* page 77.

ADDITIONAL PRACTICE

44 Have student brainstorm first, to think of vocabulary for what they need and want to do.

☀ CLOSE

Hold up photos of famous people clipped from magazines. Ask students to describe the people. For example, while holding a photo of a famous athlete, ask: **¿Quién es? ¿Cómo es él/ella? ¿Es alto/a? ¿Es guapo/a? ¿moreno/a? ¿simpático/a? ¿Qué le gusta a él/ella? ¿Le gustan los deportes?** Repeat with various photos to review a variety of adjectives.

☀ ASSESS

QUIZ 3-3
Testing Program, pp. 41–42
Audio Program,
Assessment Items,
   Audiocassette 4A OR
   Audio CD 3 Track 20

PERFORMANCE ASSESSMENT

Bring in ads from a magazine for students to critique. What do they like about the ad? (**Me gustan los colores. Son bonitos.**) What would they change? (**No me gusta el hombre. No es cómico.**)

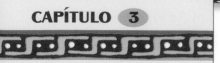

LAS MATEMÁTICAS/LA GEOGRAFÍA

1 ¿Qúe hora es?

Look at the time zone map and note how many hours difference there is between different areas of the world. Next look at the times and places in the questions below. For each item, say what time it is in the Latin American country given.   Answers on p. 101K

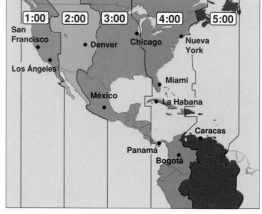

MODELO   Son las cuatro de la tarde en Miami. ¿Qué hora es en Caracas?

The time zone map shows it's one hour later in Caracas than in Miami.

4:00 P.M.
+ 1:00 hora
5:00 P.M.

Son las cinco de la tarde en Caracas.

En los Estados Unidos

1. Es la una de la tarde en San Francisco.
2. Son las tres de la mañana en Denver.
3. Son las dos y media de la tarde en Chicago.
4. En Nueva York son las nueve y cuarto de la noche.

En la América Latina

¿Qué hora es en Bogotá?
¿Qué hora es en La Habana?
¿Qué hora es en la Ciudad de Panamá?
¿Qué hora es en la Ciudad de México?

2 La llamada

You're on a trip in Latin America and planning to call your friend back home. If you call from Caracas at 5:00 P.M. on Saturday, what time is it in your home town? Choose another Latin American city to visit and another time to call your friend. What time would it be then in your home town?   Answers will vary.

BOGOTÁ

CHICAGO

Son las 4:00 de la tarde aquí en Bogotá.

Son las 3:00 de la tarde en Chicago.

LAS MATEMÁTICAS

How the 24-hour system works:

3:00 8:30 12:00 19:30 23:00

Many countries around the world use schedules based on a 24-hour clock. This allows travelers to look quickly at schedules and know the difference between 9:00 A.M. and 9:00 P.M. For example, using a 24-hour clock for a train schedule, a morning train would leave at 9:00 and a night train would leave at 21:00.

3 Convertir a 24 horas

How would you write the following times using the 24-hour system? For P.M. hours, add 12:00 to the hour. For A.M. hours, write the same hour but without using the abbreviation "A.M."

MODELO   2:35 A.M.   **2:35**

1. 7:20 A.M.   3. 9:25 P.M.   5. 11:00 A.M.
2. 3:15 P.M.   4. 4:30 P.M.   6. 8:15 P.M.

1. 7:20
2. 15:15
3. 21:25
4. 16:30
5. 11:00
6. 20:15

```
  1:05 P.M.
+ 12:00
─────────
  13:05
```

4 Convertir de 24 horas

Rewrite these times using A.M. and P.M. For times before 12:00, add A.M. to the end. For times after 12:59, subtract 12:00 from the hour and add P.M. at the end of the result.

MODELO   2:35   **2:35 A.M.**

1. 23:40   3. 1:15   5. 20:39
2. 17:55   4. 15:25   6. 5:42

1. 11:40 P.M.
2. 5:55 P.M.
3. 1:15 A.M.
4. 3:25 P.M.
5. 8:39 P.M.
6. 5:42 A.M.

```
  13:05
− 12:00
─────────
  1:05 P.M.
```

5 Horario de aviones

Answer the following questions using the 12-hour system (A.M. and P.M.).

VUELO FLIGHT	SALIDAS DESTINO TO	HORA TIME
IB 346	MADRID	1250
AO 444	MADRID	1310
IB 834	BARCELONA	1405
AO 452	P.MALLORCA	1445
AAN106	P.MALLORCA	1450
IB 387	MELILLA	1500
IB 397	MELILLA	1615

1. What time does flight AO 444 to Madrid leave? 1:10 P.M.

2. If you got to the airport at 2:00 P.M., would you have enough time to catch the flight to Barcelona? Why or why not?   no; it departs at 2:05 P.M.

3. If you got out of school at 3:00 P.M., which flight to Melilla would you be able to catch?
the second flight, which leaves at 4:15 P.M.

ENLACES

ciento treinta y cinco **135**

CAPÍTULO 3

READING STRATEGY

Using background knowledge

MOTIVATING ACTIVITY

Discuss with students the basic reasons for having schedules and report cards. What information do they contain? What would schools be like without them?

☀ PREREADING

SUGGESTIONS

- You may wish to review the 24-hour clock, which is explained in the previous **Enlaces** on page 135.

- Ask students what information is listed on their report cards. (student name, classes, grades) What is the grading system that is most commonly used in the United States? What do the letters A, B, C, D, and F mean?

NATIVE SPEAKERS

If you have students who have studied in other countries, ask them to talk about the grading system in the countries where they lived. Was it a system of numbers or letters? What were the numbers or letters used and what did they mean?

 MULTICULTURAL LINK

Discuss with students ways to get schedules and report cards from other countries. Students can write to an education agency in Mexico (see page T58).

136

VAMOS A LEER

PA p. 37 Act. 20

📖 Estrategia
Using background knowledge

As soon as you know the topic of a reading, spend a couple of minutes just thinking about the topic. What do you already know about it? The reading should then be easier to understand, and you'll be better able to guess unknown words and make sense of difficult passages.

¡A comenzar!

A You'll probably be familiar with the topics of these items. Skim them briefly and then complete the following statement.

These items are

a. TV schedules and sports scores
b. report cards and TV schedules
c. sports scores and class schedules
d. class schedules and report cards

B Draw three columns on your paper. Title one <u>schedules</u>, the next <u>report cards</u>, and the third <u>neither</u>. Read the items below and decide if they would be found in report cards, in schedules, or in neither. Write the number of each item below in the correct column. Some items may belong under both <u>schedules</u> and <u>report cards</u>.

1. letter grades Answers on p. 101K
2. parents' names
3. class names

4. days of the week Answers on p. 101K
5. student's name
6. textbook names
7. numerical grades
8. best friend's name
9. class times

Now look at the report cards and schedule above and find the mentioned items.

Al grano

C Look at the last columns of each report card. Answers on p. 101K

1. The numerical grades are the achievement grades for the class. There are also letter grades. What do the letter grades on Juana's report card represent?
2. What is the highest grade each student got in science?
3. Who did better in physical education?
4. Who did better in Spanish?

D Contesta las siguientes preguntas.

1. ¿Cuántas clases tiene Gloria? ¿Óscar? ¿Juana?
2. ¿Te gustan las clases de Gloria? ¿Por qué?
3. ¿A qué hora empiezan *(begin)* las clases de Gloria?
   Answers on p. 101K

136 *ciento treinta y seis*   CAPÍTULO 3   Nuevas clases, nuevos amigos

ÓSCAR GONZÁLEZ LÓPEZ

(MÉXICO)

MATRÍCULA	SEPT.	OCT.	NOV.	ENE.	FEB.	MAR.
B0847842					9.2	8.4
ESPAÑOL	7.7	9.8	9.5	9.5	7.1	8.0
MATEMÁTICAS	8.8	8.2	9.0	6.4	10.0	10.0
LENG.A.A/ESPAÑOLA	8.5	6.5	7.5	9.0	8.8	7.7
C. NATURALES	7.2	7.4	7.6	8.1	9.7	9.4
C. SOCIALES	9.0	7.7	9.6	10.0	9.6	9.5
EDUC. FÍSICA	10.0	7.5	10.0	9.5	9.5	9.5
EDUC. ARTÍSTICA	10.0	10.0	10.0	10.0	9.5	9.5
EDUC. TECNOLÓGICA	10.0	10.0	10.0	10.0	10.0	10.0

ALUMNA: JUANA ACOSTA RUIZ

(ESPAÑA)

Segundo De B.U.P.	PRIMERA EVALUACIÓN			TERCERA EVALUACIÓN		
	Faltas de asistencia	conoci-mientos	Actitud	Faltas de asistencia	conoci-mientos	Actitud
Español		7	C		8	C
Francés		8	B	1	6	B
Geografía Humana		8	C		7	C
Matemáticas		5	C		5	C
Ciencias		9	B		6	C
Religión		7	C		7	B
Educ. Física y Deportes					6	C

El horario de Gloria

(México)

Hora	lunes	martes	miércoles	jueves	viernes
7:30–8:20	música	civismo	geografía	biología	historia
8:30–9:20	español	inglés	inglés	matemáticas	matemáticas
9:30–10:20	matemáticas	español	historia	educación física	civismo
10:30–11:20	historia	música	matemáticas	geografía	educación física
11:30–12:20	inglés	descanso	descanso	descanso	español
12:30–13:20	biología	matemáticas	español	español	biología
13:30–14:20					

READING

Have students work in groups of three. Ask them to scan the reading to find as many cognates as they can. Set a time limit of three minutes.

SLOWER PACE

Before they work with all the schedules, have students work with just one until they understand its parts and the vocabulary it uses.

POSTREADING

Have students review the start and finish times of the class schedules from this reading in groups of three. Have students talk about the advantages and disadvantages of the times the classes start and end. As a group, have them decide which schedule they would prefer. Then, have them present their choice to the class and explain why they like it best. Students may vote on which schedule is most appealing.

THINKING CRITICALLY

Have students design their own grading system. Would they use numbers, letters, or another system? How would they decide which work was excellent and which needed improvement?

TEACHER NOTE

For additional readings, see *Practice and Activity Book*, p. 37.

The **Repaso** reviews and integrates all four skills and culture in preparation for the Chapter Test.

SUGGESTIONS

1 As a prelistening warm-up, have students brainstorm questions about classes and schedules. Write the schedule-related vocabulary that they generate on the board. Ask volunteers to say a few sentences about their schedules.

• Have students make a checklist of the kinds of questions they might hear. As they hear the questions in the conversation, have them check them off.

• Ask students to role-play this dialogue to practice chapter vocabulary and functions. Limit the time to one or two minutes.

ADDITIONAL PRACTICE

Divide the class into pairs. Tell them that they will create a conversation for a classroom competition. One of each pair plays a student who has recently arrived from Mexico to study at your school. The new student is unfamiliar with U.S. school schedules, classes, and what should be done at what time. The partner answers the new student's questions. Partners present their conversations to the class. At the end of the competition, the class votes on which pair has the most spontaneous, interesting, or humorous conversation.

REPASO

CD-ROM
Disc 1

1 Listen as Miguel and Edgardo are talking on the phone about their plans for tomorrow.   Script and answers on p. 101F

Cass. 2A
CD 3
Tr. 17

A. First, match each of the sentences you hear with one of the drawings below.

a   b

c   d   e

B. Now listen to their conversation again. This time, write one of the times from the list next to each item number on a sheet of paper.

3 11:50   5 2:20   4 1:15

2 11:00   1 10:15

2 These are the classes that Martín and Gabriela have on Monday. Answer the following questions in Spanish.

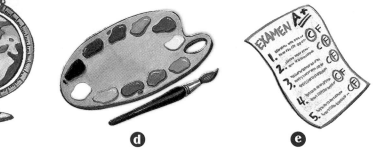

Hora	Martín	Gabriela
7:50 - 8:40	Francés	Ciencias sociales
8:40 - 9:30	Geografía	Computación
9:30 - 9:40	DESCANSO	DESCANSO
9:40 - 10:30	Arte	Inglés
10:30 - 11:20	Computación	Geografía
11:20 - 11:40	Inglés	Arte
11:40 - 12:30	ALMUERZO	ALMUERZO
12:30 - 13:20	Ciencias sociales	Español
13:20 - 13:30	DESCANSO	DESCANSO
13:30 - 14:20	Español	Educación física

1. ¿A qué hora es la clase de español de Gabriela? ¿Y la clase de español de Martín?

2. ¿Qué clase tiene Gabriela primero? ¿Y Martín?

3. ¿Qué clase tiene Gabriela después del almuerzo? ¿Y Martín?   Answers on page 101K

3 Answer the following questions according to what you've read in this chapter.

    1. Would you be pleased if you got a 16 on your report card in Peru? maybe

    2. And if you got a 9 on your report card in Mexico? yes

4 # Vamos a escribir

You and your friend want to join a pen pal club. You've offered to send in the required information for both of you. Write a paragraph with five sentences that tells what you like and don't like. Then do the same for your friend. Before writing, try organizing your ideas with a cluster diagram.

Estrategia

Cluster diagrams are a useful way to get organized. Draw a circle and label it **a mí me gusta.** Then draw 2 or 3 other circles around it, each connected to the circle labeled **a mí me gusta.** Label each with an activity you like. Repeat the process with **a mí no me gusta.** Now organize your ideas about your friend's likes and dislikes with circles that say **a (mi amigo/a) le gusta** and **a (mi amigo/a) no le gusta.** Answers will vary.

5 # S I T U A C I Ó N

Working with a partner, create a scene in which two friends who have known each other since elementary school meet while shopping in your town. One of the friends has been living in Cuernavaca for the past year. Find out what's new with each other by

    1. asking each other about classes (**¿Qué clases tienes este semestre?**) and schedules (**¿A qué hora es tu clase de...?**)

    2. asking each other what class he or she likes (**¿Cuál es tu clase favorita?**) and why (**¿Por qué?**)

End the conversation by having one friend say he or she is late and in a hurry. Answers will vary.

📁 **PORTFOLIO**

4 Written Mention to your students that this essay would be an appropriate entry for their Portfolios.

5 Oral You may suggest that students include the **Situación** interview in their Portfolio. For Portfolio information, see *Alternative Assessment Guide,* p. 14.

ADDITIONAL PRACTICE

Prepare color-coded cards. (verb = red, noun = blue, adjective = green) Prepare various forms of each part of speech. For example, **bonito, bonita, bonitos, lápiz, lápices,** etc. Arrange the cards to form complete sentences. Then replace a card and have students replace any other necessary cards. For example, create the sentence **Me gusta la fiesta.** Then replace the word **fiesta** with **fiestas.** Students must then replace **la** with **las** and **gusta** with **gustan.**

This page is intended to help students prepare independently for the Chapter Test. It is a brief checklist of the major points covered in the chapter. Students should be reminded that this is only a checklist and does not necessarily include everything that will appear on the Chapter Test.

Answers to Activity 1

Hoy tengo primero la clase de... Luego tengo la clase de... Después del almuerzo tengo la clase de... Mañana...

Answers to Activity 2

a. Son las diez.
b. Son las seis.
c. Son las ocho y media.
d. Son las tres y quarto.

Answers to Activity 3

Answers will vary. Possible answers:

1. —Sofía, ¿qué clases tienes y a qué hora?
   —Tengo educación física a las ocho y trece de la mañana y arte a las dos y diez de la tarde.
2. —Tengo la clase de francés a las doce menos veinte y la clase de geografía a las dos y veinticinco.
3. —Tengo la clase de ciencias a las nueve y siete y la clase de matemáticas a las tres y cuarto.
4. —Tengo la clase de español a las once menos veintidós y la computación a la una menos seis.

Answers to Activity 4

1. Tengo prisa.
2. Estoy atrasado/a.
3. Está atrasado/a.
4. ¡Date prisa!

A VER SI PUEDO...

▼ Can you talk about classes and sequencing events? p. 110

1 How would you tell a classmate what order you have your classes in today? And tomorrow? *Answers in side column*

▼ Can you tell time? p. 112

2 Write the time shown on each clock. *Answers in side column*

a

b

c

d

▼ Can you tell at what time something happens? p. 119

3 How would you ask each of these students what classes they have and at what time they meet? How would each student answer? *Answers in side column*

1. Sofía
   physical education (8:13)
   art (2:10)
2. César
   French (11:40)
   geography (2:25)
3. Simón
   science (9:07)
   mathematics (3:15)
4. Adela
   Spanish (10:38)
   computer science (12:54)

▼ Can you talk about being late or in a hurry? p. 122

4 How would you . . .? *Answers in side column*

1. say you're in a hurry
2. say that you're late
3. say that a friend is late
4. tell a friend to hurry up

▼ Can you describe people and things? p. 125

5 Look at the photos. Write a sentence describing each person or animal. *Answers on p. 101K*

Yolanda   Gabriela   Simón   Bruto

▼ Can you talk about things you like and explain why? p. 129

6
1. How would you say why you like or don't like your math class? (No) me gusta la clase de matemáticas porque es...
2. How would you ask a friend why he or she likes or doesn't like science? ¿Por qué (no) te gustan las ciencias?
3. How would you tell another person why your friend likes or doesn't like math? A mi amigo (no) le gusta la clase de matemáticas porque es...

VOCABULARIO

PRIMER PASO

Talking about classes and sequencing events

el almuerzo   *lunch*
el arte   *art*
las ciencias   *science*
las ciencias sociales   *social studies*
la computación   *computer science*
¿Cuándo?   *When?*
el descanso   *recess, break*
después   *after*
un día libre   *a day off*
la educación física   *physical education*
el francés   *French*
la geografía   *geography*
hoy   *today*
las, los   *the (pl.)*
luego   *then*
mañana   *tomorrow*
las matemáticas   *mathematics*
la materia   *subject*
por fin   *at last*
primero   *first*
¿Qué clases tienes?   *What classes do you have?*
el semestre   *semester*

Telling time

Es la una.   *It's one o'clock.*
menos cuarto   *quarter to (the hour)*
¿Qué hora es?   *What time is it?*
Son las...   *It's . . . o'clock*
tarde   *late*
¡Vamos!   *Let's go!*
y cuarto   *quarter past (the hour)*
y media   *half past (the hour)*

SEGUNDO PASO

Telling at what time something happens

ahora   *now*
¿A qué hora es...?   *At what time is . . . ?*
de   *of, from*
del   *of the, from the*
de la mañana   *in the morning (A.M.)*
de la noche   *in the evening (P.M.)*
de la tarde   *in the afternoon (P.M.)*
en punto   *on the dot*

Talking about being late or in a hurry

¡Date prisa!   *Hurry up!*
Está atrasado/a.   *He/She is late.*
Estoy atrasado/a.   *I'm late.*
Tengo prisa.   *I'm in a hurry.*

TERCER PASO

Describing people and things

aburrido/a   *boring*
alto/a   *tall*
antipático/a   *disagreeable*
bajo/a   *short (to describe people)*
bonito/a   *pretty*
bueno/a   *good*
cómico/a   *funny*
¿Cómo es...?   *What's . . . like?*
¿Cómo son...?   *What are . . . like?*

el (la) compañero/a   *friend, pal*
difícil   *difficult*
divertido/a   *fun, amusing*
Él/Ella es...   *He/She is . . .*
ellas, ellos   *they*
Ellos/Ellas son   *They are . . .*
estricto/a   *strict*
fácil   *easy*
feo/a   *ugly*
grande   *big*
guapo/a   *good-looking*
inteligente   *intelligent*
interesante   *interesting*
malo/a   *bad*
moreno/a   *dark-haired, dark-skinned*
No es aburrido/a.   *It's not boring.*
No te preocupes.   *Don't worry.*
nuevo/a   *new*
pequeño/a   *small*
el (la) profesor, -a   *teacher*
rubio/a   *blond*
simpático/a   *nice*
somos   *we are*

Talking about things you like and explaining why

el baile   *dance*
el concierto   *concert*
¿Cuál?   *Which?*
¿Cuál es tu clase favorita?   *Which is your favorite class?*
los deportes   *sports*
el examen   *exam (pl. los exámenes)*
favorito/a   *favorite*
la fiesta   *party*
le gusta(n)   *he/she likes*
me gustan   *I like*
¿no?   *isn't it?/right?*
la novela   *novel*
el partido de...   *game of . . . (sport)*
¿Por qué?   *Why?*
porque   *because*
te gustan   *you like*
¿verdad?   *don't you?/right?*
el videojuego   *videogame*

CHAPTER 3 ASSESSMENT

CHAPTER TEST
• *Testing Program,* pp. 43–48
• *Audio Program,* Assessment Items, Audiocassette 4A OR Audio CD 3 Trs. 21–22

SPEAKING TEST
• *Testing Program,* p. 113

TEST GENERATOR
Chapter 3

ALTERNATIVE ASSESSMENT
Performance Assessment
You might want to use the **Situación** on page 139 as a cumulative performance assessment activity.

Portfolio Assessment
ANNOTATED TEACHER'S EDITION
• **Written:** Activity 43, p. 132
• **Oral:** Activity 39, p. 130
ALTERNATIVE ASSESSMENT GUIDE, p. 14

MIDTERM EXAM
• *Testing Program,* pp. 115–120
• *Audio Program,* Assessment Items, Audiocassette 4A OR Audio CD 3 Trs. 23–24

¿Qué haces esta tarde?

CHAPTER OVERVIEW

De antemano pp. 144–147	¿Dónde está María Inés?			
	FUNCTIONS	**GRAMMAR**	**CULTURE**	**RE-ENTRY**
Primer paso pp. 148–157	• Talking about what you and others like to do, p. 149 • Talking about what you and others do during free time, p. 152	• **Gramática:** Present tense of regular **-ar** verbs, p. 150 • **Nota gramatical: con, conmigo, contigo,** p. 155 • **Nota gramatical:** Relative pronoun **que,** p. 157	• **Nota cultural:** Hispanic athletes, p. 154 • **Nota cultural:** Referring to or greeting friends, p. 156 • **Encuentro cultural: Un recorrido por la Plaza de las Armas,** pp. 158–159	• Present tense of **tener** • Present tense of **gustar**
Segundo paso pp. 160–167	• Telling where people and things are, p. 161	• **Nota gramatical:** The verb **estar,** p. 162 • **Gramática:** Subject pronouns, p. 166	• **Nota cultural: tú** and **usted,** p. 166 • **Panorama cultural: ¿Te gusta pasear con tus amigos?,** pp. 168–169	• Subject pronouns **yo, tú, él, ella** • Describing with **ser**
Tercer paso pp. 170–175	• Talking about where you and others go during free time, p. 171	• **Nota gramatical:** The verb **ir,** p. 172 • **Nota gramatical:** Days of the week, p. 174	• **Nota cultural:** Mail service, p. 170	• Telling time • Days of the week

Letra y sonido	**p. 175**	The letters **b** and **v**	**Dictado:** Textbook Audiocassette 2B / Audio CD 4 Tracks 13–17
Enlaces	**pp. 176–177**	**La música y los deportes**	
Vamos a leer	**pp. 178–179**	**Línea directa**	**Reading Strategy:** Scanning for information
Review	**pp. 180–183**	**Repaso,** pp. 180–181	**A ver si puedo...,** p. 182 **Vocabulario,** p. 183

Assessment

TESTING PROGRAM
• **Primer paso,** Quiz 4-1, pp. 55–56
• **Segundo paso,** Quiz 4-2, pp. 57–58
• **Tercer paso,** Quiz 4-3, pp. 59–60
• Assessment Items, Audiocassette 4B OR
• Audio CD 4 Tracks 19–21

• **Chapter Test,** pp. 61–68
• Assessment Items, Audiocassette 4B OR
• Audio CD 4 Tracks 22–23

Alternative Assessment
Portfolio Assessment
ANNOTATED TEACHER'S EDITION
• **Written: Repaso** p. 181, Activity 4
• **Oral:** p. 175, Activity 45
ALTERNATIVE ASSESSMENT GUIDE, p. 15

Adelante
LEVEL 1A

Pupil's Edition, pp. 142–183

Audio Program
- ◆ Textbook Audiocassette 2B
- ◆ Audio CD 4 Tracks 1–18

CD-ROM Teacher's Guide, pp. 14–17

Interactive CD-ROM Program
- ◆ Disc 1

Listening Activities
- ◆ Student Response Forms for Textbook Listening Activities, pp. 55–57
- ◆ Additional Listening Activities 4-1 to 4-6, pp. 14–16
- ◆ Scripts and Answers, pp. 35–37

Audio Program
- ◆ Additional Listening Audiocassette 5B OR
- ◆ Audio CD 4 Tracks 24–29

Testing Program
- ◆ **Paso** Quizzes and Chapter Test, pp. 55–66
- ◆ Score Sheet, Scripts and Answers, pp. 67–72

Audio Program
- ◆ Assessment Items Audiocassette 4B OR
- ◆ Audio CD 4 Tracks 19–23

Test Generator
- ◆ Chapter 4

Video Guide
- ◆ Teaching Suggestions, pp. 27–28
- ◆ Activity Masters, pp. 29–32

Video Program
- ◆ Videocassette 2

Teaching Transparencies
- ◆ Copying Masters 4-1 to 4-3 (Situations) and 4-A to 4-C (Vocabulary)
- ◆ Teaching Suggestions 4-1 to 4-3 and 4-A to 4-C

Teaching Transparencies
- ◆ Situations 4-1 to 4-3
- ◆ Vocabulary 4-A to 4-C

Activities for Communication
- ◆ Communicative Activities, pp. 19–24
- ◆ Situation Cards, pp. 76–77
- ◆ Realia and Teaching Suggestions, pp. 53–57

Lesson Planner
- ◆ Lesson Plan, pp. 19–23

Practice and Activity Book, pp. 39–50

Grammar and Vocabulary Workbook, pp. 27–36

¡Ven conmigo!
LEVEL 1

Videodisc Guide, pp. 40–49

Videodisc Program, Videodisc 2B

Native Speaker Activity Book, pp. 16–20

For a complete list of the media resources and their accompanying print matter Guides, see page 141B.

DE ANTEMANO pp. 144–147

Audio/Video

• Show or play *¿Dónde está María Inés?* See *Video Guide* pp. 26–27, 29 or *¡Ven conmigo! Level 1 Videodisc Guide* pp. 40, 42–43, 47 for synopsis, teaching suggestions, and activity masters.

PRIMER PASO pp. 148–157

Video

• Show the **paso** opener to model saying what people like to do and discussing what people do during free time. Have students role play the scene.

Audio

• Use Textbook Listening Activities 6 and 10 to practice saying what people like to do and what they often do during free time.
• Additional Listening Activities 4-1 and 4-2 practice expressing what people do during free time.

Transparencies

• Use Vocabulary Transparency 4-1 to introduce and model new vocabulary.

CD-ROM

• Activity 1 practices expressions for leisure time activities and responsibilities.
• Activity 2 practices regular present tense of -**ar** verbs.

ENCUENTRO CULTURAL pp. 158–159

Video

• Show the video after students have read Ofelia's speech bubbles. Have

students comment on which words they found easy to understand and more difficult to understand.

SEGUNDO PASO pp. 160–167

Video

• Show the **paso** opener and ask students to watch and listen for verbal and visual cues that model saying where people and things are.

Audio

• Use Textbook Activities 23 and 27 to practice saying where people and things are.
• Use Additional Listening Activities 4-3 and 4-4 to practice describing the locations of people and things.

Transparencies

• Situation Transparency 4-2 shows a downtown scene. Have students use it to practice locations.

CD-ROM

• Activity 3 practices telling where someone is.
• Activity 4 practices **estar** in the present tense.

PANORAMA CULTURAL pp. 168–169

Audio/Video

• Give students the topic of the **Panorama cultural.** Have them brainstorm the types of things they might hear and make a list as a class. Then play the interviews. Have them compare what they heard with what's on their list.

CD-ROM

• Have students do the **Panorama cultural** activity. Remind them that they can replay each interview as often as they need to.

TERCER PASO pp. 170–175

Video

• Show the **paso** opener to model telling where people go during leisure time. Have students read along. Then lead a discussion talking about where students go in their leisure time.

Audio

• Use Textbook Activity 37 to practice saying where people go during leisure time.
• Challenge students with Additional Listening Activities 4-5 and 4-6, which practice telling where people are going.

Transparencies

• Situation Transparency 4-3 practices telling where people go at various times. Use it after presenting the days of the week.

CD-ROM

• Activity 5 practices the verb **ir** in the present tense.
• After presenting the days of the week, have students do Activity 6.

REPASO pp. 180–181

Video

• Replay *¿Dónde está María Inés?* and ask students to point out exchanges in which the characters model the communicative functions targeted in this chapter.

CD-ROM

• Assign students the **En contexto,** in which students discuss plans for the weekend with a new friend.

Test Generator

• Use the Test Generator to make a short homework assignment to help students prepare for the Chapter Test.

¡Ven conmigo!
LEVEL 1

Videodisc Guide
◆ pp. 40–49

¿Qué haces esta tarde?

BARCODE DIRECTORY

CAPÍTULO
4

DE ANTEMANO

Barcodes A and B access **De antemano** and **A continuación** in their entirety. Subsequent barcodes show individual scenes. The barcode numbers correspond to the scene numbers as they appear in the **De antemano**.

¿Donde está María Inés? **A**
Search 1 , Play To 12010

Oye, María Inés... **5**
Search 6848, Play To 7993

Papi, él es... **1**
Search 450, Play To 3198

¿Está aquí María...? **6**
Search 7994, Play To 8541

Hola, Luis. **2**
Search 3211, Play To 5581

Bueno, ¿qué hacemos? **7**
Search 8542, Play To 11216

¡Tengo una muy...! **3**
Search 5582, Play To 5970

María Inés, no... **8**
Search 11236, Play To 12010

Ah, pero los... **4**
Search 5971, Play To 6824

¿Donde está María Inés?
(a continuación) **B**
Search 12010, Play To 26255

VIDEOCLIPS

This is an advertisement for a bank. You may want to preview it before showing it to students.

Banco popular

Search 29520, Play To 31280

PASO OPENERS

Each **paso** begins with a re-presentation of a scene from **De antemano** that models targeted functions, vocabulary, and grammar.

Papi, él es... **1** p. 148
Search 1925, Play To 2721

Oye, María Inés... **3** p. 170
Search 6848, Play To 7993

¿Está aquí María...? **2** p. 160
Search 7994, Play To 8541

PANORAMA CULTURAL

¿Te gusta pasear con tus amigos?
These barcodes access supplementary interviews that do not appear in the book. Not all barcodes are listed here. For a complete listing of supplemental interviews, see the *¡Ven conmigo! Level 1 Videodisc Guide*, p. 41.

Patricia, California **1**
Search 27227, Play To 27646

Jeimmy, Costa Rica **5**
Search 28604, Play To 28876

David, México **2**
Search 27647, Play To 27815

Leslie, Puerto Rico **6**
Search 28877, Play To 29086

Juan Pablo, España **3**
Search 27816, Play To 28305

Claudia, Texas **7**
Search 29087, Play To 29360

Jimena, Argentina **4**
Search 28306, Play To 28603

Kevin, Puerto Rico **8**
Search 29361, Play To 29502

¿Qué haces esta tarde?

TEXTBOOK LISTENING ACTIVITIES SCRIPTS

For Student Response Forms, see Listening Activities, pp. 55–57.

PRIMER PASO   pp. 148–157

6 Actividades   p. 150

1. Hola. Me llamo Tomás. Me gusta comprar muchas cosas. Por eso me gusta ir de compras.
2. ¿Qué tal? Me llamo Arturo. No me gustan las fiestas porque son muy aburridas.
3. Yo soy Bárbara. A mí me gusta hablar por teléfono... ¡día y noche!
4. Hola. Soy Patricia. No me gusta estudiar mucho, pero me gusta mirar la televisión.

Answers to Activity 6

1. A Tomás le gusta comprar cosas.
2. A Arturo no le gusta bailar en las fiestas.
3. A Bárbara le gusta hablar por teléfono.
4. A Patricia le gusta mirar la televisión.

10 El tiempo libre   p. 152

1. Hola, soy Carmen. Escucho música y miro la televisión en mi cuarto.
2. Me llamo Javier. Hablo por teléfono con Sofía, Manuel, Rebeca y Raúl...
3. Soy Armando. Ana y yo estudiamos en la biblioteca día y noche.
4. Me llamo Susana. Después de clases, practico el béisbol y el tenis.
5. Soy Pablo. En el tiempo libre, bailo y canto con mis amigos. Toco la guitarra también.

Answers to Activity 10

1. d   2. b   3. a   4. e   5. c

SEGUNDO PASO   pp. 160–167

23 ¿Dónde está?   p. 161

1. ¿El correo? Está en la Plaza de la Constitución.
2. Necesito encontrar mi mochila. No está en mi cuarto.
3. Hola. ¿Qué tal? Estoy atrasado. Todavía estoy en el trabajo.
4. ¡Mira, José! ¡Allí está la plaza!

Answers to Activity 23

1. d   2. c   3. b   4. a

27 ¿Quiénes son y dónde están?   p. 164

MODELO   Paco es bajo y moreno. Le gusta jugar con su perro.

1. Marisa y Ana Luisa son guapas y morenas. Tienen catorce años.
2. El señor Contreras es bajo y le gusta comprar ropa.
3. Eva es muy inteligente y le gusta estudiar matemáticas.
4. Isabel tiene seis años y le gustan los videos cómicos.
5. Mario y José son antipáticos. Siempre necesitan hablar con el director del colegio.
6. Anabel nada muy bien. Tiene treinta y cinco años y es muy bonita.
7. Guillermo es alto y rubio. Juega mucho al basquetbol con sus amigos.

Answers to Activity 27

1. f   2. g   3. e   4. c   5. h   6. b   7. d

TERCER PASO   pp. 170–175

37 **¿Cuál es la pregunta?**   p. 171

1. Julio va al centro comercial.
2. Voy a estudiar en la biblioteca.
3. La biblioteca está al lado del correo.
4. Primero voy a nadar en la piscina y después voy a la casa de Jorge.
5. Mi hermana Sandra va al restaurante italiano.
6. Esteban está en la tienda con su hermana.

Answers to Activity 37

1. b   **2.** a   **3.** c   **4.** a   **5.** b   **6.** c

38 **¿Adónde vamos?**   p. 172

1. — Y Pedro, ¿adónde va él?
   — Él va a la casa de Graciela.
2. — David y Luisa, entonces. ¿Adónde van ellos?
   — Ellos van al gimnasio.
3. — Y tú, Alicia, ¿adónde vas?
   — Voy a la piscina. Trabajo allí hoy.
4. — Y Carlos, ¿va al cine?
   — Sí, Carlos va al cine.
5. — Hola, Carlos.
   — Hola, Filiberto. ¿Adónde vas?
   — Voy al cine. ¡Contigo!

Answers to Activity 38

1. a la casa de Graciela
2. al gimnasio
3. al gimnasio
4. a la piscina
5. al cine
6. al cine

LETRA Y SONIDO   p. 175

For the scripts for Parts A and C, see page 175. The script for Part B is below.

B. Dictado

veinte, bolígrafo, librería, basura, el tiempo libre, jueves

REPASO   pp. 180–181

1 **p. 180**

MODELO   Hola, soy Carlos. El sábado vamos al parque para jugar al tenis. Vamos a las 10:00. ¿Quieres ir también?

1. Buenos días. Soy Carmen. Enrique y yo vamos a estudiar en la biblioteca hoy a las tres y media. ¿Quieres ir con nosotros?
2. Hola. Soy Gaby. ¿Cómo estás? Voy a la piscina mañana a las cuatro y media. ¿Quieres ir conmigo?
3. Buenos días. Soy Victoria. ¿Cómo estás? Sara y yo vamos al cine el domingo a las tres. A ti te gustan las películas, ¿no? Pues, ¡vamos!

Answers to Repaso Activity 1

1. c   **2.** a   **3.** b

CAPÍTULO 4

¿Qué haces esta tarde?

PROJECTS

UN MAPA DE MI CIUDAD

This activity, excellent for visual/spatial intelligence learners, provides students with the opportunity to use chapter vocabulary to show imaginary Spanish speakers visiting important places in town. Students will create a map and use it to present an oral guided tour.

Introduction

Talk to students about the importance of being able to use Spanish to explain where things are and to ask where things are when they travel. Ask students if they have ever been on a guided tour. What did the tour guide say? Which buildings, parks, and important places should be part of a guided tour of your town?

Materials students may need

- ◆ Poster board
- ◆ Blank overhead transparencies
- ◆ Markers
- ◆ Rulers
- ◆ Pens and pencils
- ◆ Toy vehicle (optional)

Sequence

1. Divide students into groups of four. Within each group assign the roles of Script-writer, Proofreader, Tour guide, and someone to point out the route on the map.

2. Groups will cooperatively draw a map of your town or the area around the school on poster board or an overhead transparency. The map will be used in the tour presentation and should include as many of the locations as possible from the **Vocabulario** on page 183.

3. Next, the Script-writer works with the other students to create a script in Spanish for the guided tour. The script should include what to say as they arrive at a location and a short description of each site (what it is near or next to; what it looks like; what they like to do there).

4. The Proofreader edits the script.

5. In front of the class, the Tour Guide narrates the trip. The person demonstrating the route on the map points to or

moves a toy vehicle to each location as the tour guide mentions it.

Grading the project

Suggested point distribution (total = 100 points):

Map appearance	**30**
Appropriate chapter vocabulary and detail	**30**
Spelling and grammar accuracy	**10**
Guided Tour	**30**

MI TIEMPO LIBRE

This project reinforces leisure activity vocabulary that students learn in this chapter. Students create posters that are visual representations of specific vocabulary.

Introduction

Discuss what leisure activities students take part in during the weekends, after school, and during vacations. Do they like to spend time with their friends, their families, or by themselves? What do they like to do in their free time? Play sports? Read? Watch TV? See friends? Students will make a collage of at least seven of their favorite activities by illustrating the activity and labeling the poster in Spanish. This project will consist of two parts: creating the poster and presenting it orally to the class.

Materials students may need

- ◆ Colored poster board
- ◆ Markers or colored pencils
- ◆ Pencils
- ◆ Rulers
- ◆ Scissors
- ◆ Cutouts from magazines
- ◆ Glue sticks

Sequence

1. Each student will draft a list of at least seven activities that he or she likes to do. The list should include activities

they do after school, during the weekend, and during vacations.

2 Students will look for pictures that illustrate the activities on their list or draw the activities on the poster themselves.

3 Students may arrange the illustrations or pictures in collage format or in order of preference. They should label illustrations and pictures in Spanish and title it **MI TIEMPO LIBRE**.

4 Students will share their leisure activities with the class by making oral presentations.

Grading the project

Suggested point distribution (total = 100 points):

Neatness **20**
Creativity and artistic design. **20**
Information and content **15**
Spelling and grammar accuracy. **15**
Oral presentation **30**

NUESTRA CIUDAD IDEAL

This activity taps into students' interpersonal and visual/spatial intelligence. It requires the planning, design, and hands-on construction of different locations within a city. Students work together to arrange the city buildings, park, and other places as a cooperative effort among all members of the class.

Introduction

Students decide what buildings or public spaces will make up their ideal city. Then they cooperatively construct models of buildings, and arrange the buildings and spaces according to their plan.

Materials students may need

◆ Shoe boxes or other larger cardboard boxes
◆ Construction paper
◆ Glue
◆ Colored markers
◆ Markers—fine tip and wide tip
◆ Magazines for decoration pictures
◆ Poster board

Sequence

1 Do the students like the city or town where they live? What do they like about it and what would they change? Brainstorm with them to get their ideas about what an ideal city would be. Would it have movie theaters? parks? libraries? shopping malls? schools?

2 Students choose a structure to build with a partner. (For example: a bank, a restaurant, a post office) They may construct building models using shoe boxes or larger cardboard boxes. Students label each building in Spanish. They may decorate the building with markers and magazine pictures.

3 Both partners will present their model to the class orally in Spanish.

4 Next, lead students through a city planning brainstorm. Have them think about the town in which they live. What is near the fire station? Where is the gas station? Where are the office buildings? Ask them more questions about their ideal city. Would their school be next to their house? the mall? a video arcade? a grocery store?

5 Using the ideas from the city planning brainstorm, the class will then decide how to organize the building models to design **Nuestra ciudad ideal**. As the class decides where to place the buildings, have one or two students draw the city plan on the board.

6 The ideal city can be placed on a table or in a corner of the room and can be on permanent display in the class.

Grading the project

Suggested point distribution (total = 100 points):

Model appearance, neatness **25**
Creativity, artistic design **25**
Information and content **20**
Oral presentation **20**
Partner cooperation **10**

FAMILY LINK

 Suggest that students practice their presentation with a family member or friend who may be able to suggest some things to say about why that object is important.

CAPÍTULO 4

¿Qué haces esta tarde?
GAMES

¿DÓNDE ESTÁ?

*This game reviews classroom vocabulary and practices the verb **estar**. It's especially good for students with spatial intelligence.*

Procedure

One student hides a pen, a book, or a notebook in the front of the room while the other students close their eyes. The rest of the class must ask the student questions in order to find the object. (**¿Está debajo de la mesa? ¿Está cerca del escritorio?**) The student who guesses correctly is the next person to hide an object.

CEREBRO

This game, played like Concentration®, helps students learn and review vocabulary by using the skills of concentration and recall.

Preparation

Have each student make three pairs of cards:

1 On one card students write a question from any **Así se dice** and on its mate they write an appropriate response.

2 On one card students write a verb (conjugated or infinitive) from the chapter, and on its mate they draw a stick figure that depicts the action.

3 Make cards using the vocabulary from the second and third shaded word boxes. On one card students write a verb from the second shaded word box from Activity 15 on page 155. On its mate they write an appropriate phrase from the third box. (Make sure that there is only one phrase from the third box that matches.)

Procedure

Divide the class into pairs or small groups. Have students place a combined set of their cards in a pattern on the desk, face down. Players take turns turning over two cards each. If the cards match, the player takes them. Play continues until all the cards have been matched. The player with the most matches wins. For a challenge, have students make additional sets of cards.

FAMILY LINK

Have students teach a relative or friend Spanish phrases using the **Cerebro** cards. Students are assigned to take home their own set of six **Cerebro** cards and teach someone the three Spanish phrases on them by playing the game. Have students report orally how their **estudiante** is doing.

BINGO®

This quick game of word Bingo® is an enjoyable way to reinforce familiar vocabulary from the chapter. It can be played in the last ten minutes of any class, when students have finished their work. It can be played with verbs or nouns in Spanish or from English to Spanish.

Preparation

1 Make a set of Bingo® cards to be used by students at any time, for any lesson. Using a piece of 8 1/2 × 11 paper, divide the sheet into quarters. Within each quarter, draw a tic-tac-toe grid. (two horizontal lines, two vertical lines)

2 Cut the quarters to be used as mini-sheets to play bingo.

3 Designate vocabulary to be used by students to play the game: **-ar** verbs, **ir, estar,** or locations in the city. Give the page references to students to access vocabulary. For this chapter, **Vocabulario** is on page 183.

4 The students write one Spanish word in each box.

5 Call out a word in Spanish. Students mark off the word they hear. The student who completes his card first wins and calls out "¡Bingo®!"

Alternatives

You can also write the words in Spanish, call the words in English, or write the words in English and call out the words in Spanish.

EL JUEGO DE CONJUGACIÓN

This game makes students think about the correlation between the personal pronoun and the personal ending of the conjugated verb. Students have fun while getting used to changing the ending of each verb, and it is excellent for body/kinesthetic and interpersonal intelligences.

Preparation

Make index cards with the following:

- 9 personal pronouns (**yo, tú, usted, él, ella, nosotros, ustedes, ellos, ellas**), each on a red (**rojo**) card.
- 5 personal endings (**o, as, a, amos, an**) on blue (**azul**) cards.
- 15 verb stems (**descans, dibuj, escuch, lav, mir, nad, sac, habl, pint, practic, prepar, trabaj, regres, bail, toc**) on green (**verde**) cards.
- 20 conjugated English verb forms *(I work, we draw, they speak, etc.)* on yellow (**amarillo**) cards.

Sequence

1 Divide the class into groups: **el grupo rojo**, pronouns; **el grupo azul**, personal endings, **el grupo verde**, stems.

2 Pass one card to each student. Cards remain in their group category.

3 Read the English from a yellow card. For example, *He works.* Students from **el grupo rojo** must find the pronoun **él**; students from **el grupo verde** must find the verb stem **trabaj**; and students in **el grupo azul** must find the ending -**a**, to cooperatively make the correct conjugation for the English translation.

CATEGORÍAS

The following game is patterned after the game Scattergories®. It is good for reinforcing vocabulary.

Preparation

1 Make a list of categories on transparencies to teach the game to the class. Number lists so students use a different list for each round. Make index cards with the letters of the alphabet on them.

2 Use categories of vocabulary already learned:

- **materias/clases**
- **deportes y pasatiempos**
- **en la ciudad**
- **instrumentos musicales**
- **palabras descriptivas**
- **colores**
- **números**
- **nombres**

3 Students prepare a sheet of paper with three numbered columns, one for each of the three rounds of play, numbered from one to the number of categories on the list. All students use the same list of categories.

Sequence

1 The object of the game is to quickly fill out a category list with items beginning with the same letter. Students score points if no other player matches their answers.

2 Display the transparency list of the categories. One student chooses a letter card from the stack of index cards. The student calls out the letter to be used in this round. A student sets the timer for one minute and the round begins.

3 All students quickly fill in the answer sheet with appropriate people, places, or things for each category that begins with the key letter. When the timer rings, students must immediately stop writing.

4 To score a round, students in turn read their answers aloud to the group. The students circle acceptable answers that **do not** match anyone else's. They continue until all categories have been scored. Then, score one point for each of the circled answers and record the score at the top of the first column of the answer sheet.

5 After three rounds, students total the scores on their answer sheets. The player with the highest score wins. This game may also be played with one small group competing against another in which each group produces a single list.

ANSWERS TO CHAPTER 4 ACTIVITIES

Listening activity answers appear on Scripts pages 141E–141F. Answers to all other activities appear on corresponding pupil pages.

PRIMER PASO   pp. 148–157

5
1. Sí, a Claudia le gusta cantar en el coro.
2. Sí, a Luis le gusta jugar al basquetbol.
3. Sí, a María Inés le gusta practicar el baile folklórico.
4. A mí me gusta...

12 Answers will vary. Possible answers:
1. En su tiempo libre, Marcus, Lee y Jeffrey nadan en la piscina.
2. Mi amiga Patricia escucha música popular.
3. Roberto pinta en el parque después de clases.
4. Después de clases, Lian habla por teléfono.
5. Franklin y Raquel lavan el carro del papá de Franklin.
6. Answers will vary.

SEGUNDO PASO   pp. 160–167

24
1. —¡Hola, Lupe! ¿Cómo estás?
   —Estoy bien. ¿Dónde estás?
   —Oye, estoy en el centro. Esta tarde quiero montar en bicicleta.
   —¡Qué bueno! Yo quiero ir también.
2. —Hola, Señora Montes. ¿Está Mariana en casa?
   —No, Alicia, no está.
   —¿Dónde está?
   —Está con Paco. Están en la biblioteca.
   —Gracias. ¡Hasta luego!

27
b. Ella está en la piscina.
c. Ella está en casa.
d. Ellos están en el gimnasio.
e. Ella está en la biblioteca.
f. Ellas están en el restaurante.
g. Él está en la tienda.
h. Ellos están en la escuela.

33
1. nosotros *or* nosotras
2. ellos *or* ellas
3. ella
4. yo
5. él
6. tú
7. usted
8. ustedes *or* vosotros/as
9. usted

ENLACES   pp. 176–177

4
1. Ariel Hernández
2. Cuba
3. 1:04.05
4. Cuba and Spain
5. 1.69 meters per second

A VER SI PUEDO...   p. 182

3
1. Caminamos en el parque.
2. Montamos en bicicleta.
3. Pasamos el rato con amigos.
4. Estudiamos en la biblioteca.
5. Escuchamos música.
6. Miramos la televisión.

4
1. Ella está en la biblioteca.
2. Ella está en el centro comercial.
3. Ellos están en el parque.
4. Ella está en el parque.
5. Estamos en la piscina.

5
1. El supermercado está al lado del parque.
2. La librería está lejos del colegio.
3. El gimnasio está cerca de la biblioteca.

6 Answers will vary. Possible answers:
1. Ella va a la librería.
2. Lupe va al gimnasio.
3. Ellos van al correo.

Chapter Section	Presentation	Homework Options
Primer paso	**Así se dice,** p. 149	*Pupil's Edition,* p. 149, #5
	Vocabulario, p. 149	*Practice and Activity Book,* pp. 38–40, #4 *Grammar and Vocabulary,* p. 27, #1–2 *CD-ROM,* Disc 1, Chapter 4, #1
	Gramática, p. 150	*Pupil's Edition,* p. 151, #8–9 *Grammar and Vocabulary,* pp. 28–29, #3–6 *CD-ROM,* Disc 1, Chapter 4, #2
	Así se dice, p. 152	*Pupil's Edition,* pp. 152–153, #11–12 *Practice and Activity Book,* p. 42, #5
	Vocabulario, p. 154	*Pupil's Edition,* p. 154, #14 *Grammar and Vocabulary,* p. 29, #7
	Nota gramatical, p. 157	*Grammar and Vocabulary,* p. 30, #9
Segundo paso	**Así se dice,** p. 161	*CD-ROM,* Disc 1, Chapter 4, #3
	Nota gramatical, p. 162	*Practice and Activity Book,* p. 43, #8 *Grammar and Vocabulary,* p. 31, #10–11
	Vocabulario, p. 163	*Grammar and Vocabulary,* p. 32, #12–13
	Gramática, p. 166	*Pupil's Edition,* p. 167, #34 *Grammar and Vocabulary,* p. 33, #14–16 *CD-ROM,* Disc 1, Chapter 4, #4
Tercer paso	**Así se dice,** p.171	*Pupil's Edition,* p. 172, #39
	Nota gramatical, p. 172	*Practice and Activity Book,* p. 46, #11–12 *Grammar and Vocabulary,* p. 34, #17–18 *CD-ROM,* Disc 1, Chapter 4, #5
	Vocabulario, p.174	*Grammar and Vocabulary,* p. 35, #19–20 *CD-ROM,* Disc 1, Chapter 4, #6
	Nota gramatical, p. 174	*Practice and Activity Book,* pp. 47–48, #13–16 *Grammar and Vocabulary,* p. 36, #21–23

pp. 28–29
Acts. 3–6

PRESENTATION
GRAMÁTICA

Have students work in pairs. They should point to themselves when they say **hablo** and then to their partner when they say **hablas**. Then, have them work in groups of four. One pair should point to themselves when they say **hablamos** and to the other pair when they say **hablan**. Model third-person forms by addressing the class and pointing to various students while saying **habla** or **hablan** as appropriate.

🗼 GAME

Write a regular **-ar** verb on the board. Have all students stand up. Call out a subject pronoun and toss a foam ball to a student. That student calls out the correct form of the verb, calls out another pronoun, tosses the ball to another student, and sits down. Continue until all students are seated. If a student is unsure of the correct form, he or she says **paso**, tosses the ball to a classmate, remains standing, and waits for another turn.

NATIVE SPEAKERS

Point out to speakers who use **vos** that **vos hablás** corresponds to **tú hablas**. Remind speakers who tend to drop the *s* at the ends of syllables to be sure to include the *s* when writing the **tú** form.

150

---

6 Actividades Script and answers on p. 141E

Cass. 2B
CD 4 Tr. 3

Based on what you hear, combine phrases to write a true statement about each person.

1. A Tomás
2. A Arturo
3. A Bárbara
4. A Patricia

no le gusta
le gusta

hablar por teléfono
bailar en las fiestas
comprar cosas
mirar la televisión

7 ¿A quién le gusta...?

Get together with a partner and take turns asking and answering the following questions. Fill in the blanks with words from the **Vocabulario** on page 149. Answers will vary.

Questions

1. ¿Qué te gusta hacer?

2. ¿A tu amigo/a le gusta _____?

3. ¿A quién le gusta _____?

Answers

a. A mí me gusta _____.
   También me gusta _____.
   Pero no me gusta mucho _____.

b. No, no le gusta _____.
   Pero le gusta _____.
   También le gusta _____.

c. A *(friend's name)* le gusta _____.
   También le gusta _____,
   pero no le gusta _____.

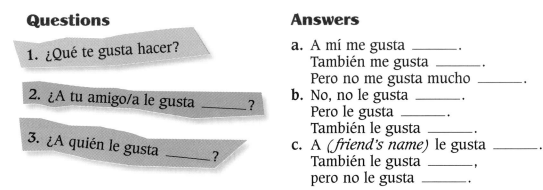

GRAMÁTICA   Present tense of regular -ar verbs

1. In Spanish and English, verbs change depending on the *subject* (the person doing the action). This is called *conjugating* the verb.

2. In Spanish, there are three main groups of verbs; their infinitives (the unchanged form of a verb) end in -**ar**, -**er**, or -**ir**. The first group of verbs in Spanish you'll learn to conjugate is the -**ar** verbs: habl**ar** *(to speak)*, trabaj**ar** *(to work)*, estudi**ar** *(to study)*.

3. To conjugate **hablar** or any other regular -**ar** verb, take the part of the verb called the *stem* (**habl-**) and add these endings:

(yo)	habl**o**	(nosotros) (nosotras)	habl**amos**
(tú)	habl**as**	(vosotros) (vosotras)	habl**áis**
(usted) (él) (ella)	habl**a**	(ustedes) (ellos) (ellas)	habl**an**

8 ¿Qué hacen?

Look at the drawings to see what different people are doing. Then match the letter for each drawing to the sentence that describes it.

1. Ellos cantan muy bien. i
2. El señor Cheng pinta muy bien. c
3. Le gusta bailar. d
4. ¡Tú hablas por teléfono mucho! g
5. La señora Bayamón escucha música. f
6. Tú estudias mucho, ¿no? a
7. Yo cuido a mi hermana todos los días. e
8. Tú y tu amigo sacan la basura. b
9. Cristina y yo nadamos en la piscina. h

9 Los sábados

Conjugate each of the following verbs in parentheses to say what you and others do on Saturdays.

1. Tú (cuidar) a tu hermano. cuidas
2. Él (escuchar) música rock. escucha
3. Ella (lavar) el carro. lava
4. Eva y yo (mirar) la televisión. miramos
5. María y Claudia (dibujar) mucho. dibujan
6. Nosotros (nadar) en la piscina. nadamos
7. Ustedes (sacar) la basura. sacan
8. Yo (descansar) en el parque. descanso

PRIMER PASO

ciento cincuenta y uno **151**

NATIVE SPEAKERS

Point out that **hacer** and **hablar** and all their forms begin with an *h.* Also point out that the forms of **hacer** are spelled with *c* and sometimes with *z* (**hizo**), but never with *s.* Have them add these to their spelling notebook.

KINESTHETIC/ VISUAL LEARNERS

8 Act out an activity and have students say what you're doing, using the **usted** form. Then have a volunteer stand up and act out an activity. Students say what the volunteer is doing using the **él** or **ella** form. Have pairs act out activities to practice plural forms.

AUDITORY LEARNERS

9 Read the completed sentences aloud to students and have them indicate who the subjects are.

PA
p. 42
Act. 5

ASÍ SE DICE — Talking about what you and others do during free time

To ask what a friend does after school, say:

Your friend might answer:

¿Qué haces después de clases?

¡Descanso!
I rest!

¿Tocas el piano?
Do you play the piano?

No, pero **toco la guitarra.**
No, but I play the guitar.

¿Baila María Inés **antes de regresar a casa?**
Does María Inés dance before returning home?

Sí, ella baila con su grupo de baile.

¿Practican deportes Luis y Carmen **en su tiempo libre?**
Do Luis and Carmen practice sports during their free time?

No, ellos no **practican** deportes.

PRESENTATION

ASÍ SE DICE
Role-play the first exchange with a volunteer. Then have students role-play the exchange with a partner. Next have them role-play the exchange again but this time replacing **descanso** with the **yo** form of a verb of their choice. Have them report what their partner does to another classmate or to the class.

ADDITIONAL PRACTICE
10 Have students write sentences about what each student probably does after school.

SLOWER PACE
11 Write the correct answers to these items on the board and have students match them to the correct sentences.

**Cass. 2B
CD 4 Tr. 4**

10 El tiempo libre   Script and answers on p. 141E

Listen as the following people tell you what they do during their free time. Match each person with the correct activity.

1. Carmen
2. Javier
3. Armando y Ana
4. Susana
5. Pablo

a. estudiar en la biblioteca
b. hablar con amigos
c. bailar con sus amigos
d. escuchar música
e. practicar deportes

11 Después de clases

Read what each of the following people likes. Then write a sentence telling what he or she probably does after school.

MODELO   A Reynaldo le gustan los quehaceres *(chores)*.
Reynaldo saca la basura.   Answers will vary. Possible answers:

1. A Ema le gustan los días bonitos en el parque. Ema descansa en el parque.
2. A Luisa le gusta la clase de arte. A Ramón le gusta el arte también. Luisa y Ramón dibujan.
3. A Tyrone le gusta mucho la música rock. A Marcela le gusta la música también. Tyrone y Marcela escuchan música.
4. A Pablo le gustan muchos programas de televisión. Pablo mira la televisión.
5. A Joaquín le gusta mucho la natación. Joaquín nada en la piscina.

152   *ciento cincuenta y dos*   CAPÍTULO 4   ¿Qué haces esta tarde?

152

12 Hacemos un poco de todo

Your pen pal in Cuernavaca wants to know what everyone does in their free time. Write sentences based on the photos. Write one extra sentence saying what you like to do in your free time. Answers on p. 141K

1. Marcus, Lee y Jeffrey

2. Patricia

3. Roberto

4. Lian

5. Franklin y Raquel

13 ¡Te toca a ti!

With a partner, take turns asking and answering questions using the words below. Be sure to ask each other at least four questions. Also, use words that describe when or how things are done. Answers will vary.

MODELO —¿Dibujas bien?
—Sí, dibujo muy bien.

practicar deportes

hablar español

bien

nadar

tocar el piano

cantar

todos los días

mal

con tu amigo/a

dibujar

bailar

en mi tiempo libre

pintar

regular

CULTURE NOTE
Addresses and postal codes in Mexico are different from those in the United States. For example:

Juan García
Ap. postal 20673
CP 01001 México, D.F.
México

Ap. stands for **apartado** and is the equivalent of a post office box. **CP** stands for **código postal** and is the equivalent of zip code. **D.F.** stands for **Distrito Federal** and is the designation for Mexico's capital very much like *District of Columbia (D.C.)* designates the United States' capital.

AUDITORY LEARNERS
Cut pictures from magazines or draw new vocabulary items. Then randomly number them. As you say the Spanish word for a picture, students say the number in Spanish. Once they are familiar with the words, the students can say the Spanish words for each picture as you cue them with the number.

ADDITIONAL PRACTICE
12 Have students work in pairs and ask each other ¿**Qué hacen tus amigos después de las clases?**

13 Have students ask questions using the **ustedes** form of the verb to practice plurals.

PA
p. 42
Acts. 6–7

GV
p. 29
Act. 7

4-B

VOCABULARIO

CD-ROM
Disc 1

pasar el rato con amigos   caminar con el perro   montar en bicicleta

trabajar en un restaurante   tomar un refresco   tomar un helado   preparar la cena

PRESENTATION

VOCABULARIO

After they look at the pictures, ask students to raise their hands to answer the following questions about their own activities: **¿A quién le gusta montar en bicicleta? ¿A quién no le gusta preparar la cena? ¿A quién le gusta caminar con el perro? ¿Quiénes de ustedes no toman el refresco _____? ¿Ustedes pasan el rato con amigos?**

KINESTHETIC LEARNERS
Have students play charades to familiarize themselves with the new vocabulary.

SUGGESTION
14 Have students write about four activities they usually do with their friends using the vocabulary on page 149 and on this page.

14 ¿Dónde?

Read the sentences below. Then match them with the places where the activities might take place. You may use each place more than once.

a. en una fiesta
b. en el parque
c. en casa

1. Camino con el perro con mi amiga. b
2. Preparas la cena con tus padres. c
3. Montamos en bicicleta los sábados. b
4. Paso el rato con amigos los viernes. a, b, c
5. Miramos la televisión con mamá y papá. c
6. Bailamos a la música rock. a, c

Nota cultural

Soccer, bike riding, tennis, and baseball are especially popular in Spanish-speaking countries. In the United States, athletes like tennis star Mary Joe Fernández and baseball great Fernando Valenzuela have thrilled sports fans with their skills and spirit. Can you name any other outstanding Spanish-speaking athletes?

154   *ciento cincuenta y cuatro*   CAPÍTULO 4   ¿Qué haces esta tarde?

154

15 Combina las frases

Combine words and phrases from each of the boxes to write five original sentences. Remember to conjugate the verbs! Answers will vary.

yo tú ella él nosotros ellos ustedes ellas	trabajar montar caminar con el perro tomar pasar el rato preparar practicar escuchar tocar	la cena el piano un refresco música deportes un helado en bicicleta	con amigos en una fiesta en el parque en un restaurante en la piscina

16 ¿Qué hacen tus amigos?

Look at the photos on page 154. Write a complete sentence for each photo about what everyone is doing. Use words like **él, ella, ellos,** etc.

MODELO **Ellos pasan el rato con amigos.** Answers will vary.

NOTA GRAMATICAL

p. 30
Act. 8

To talk about doing things with someone else, **con** is used with a pronoun like **él** or **ella**. The expressions *with me* and *with you* have special forms.

¿Quién estudia **contigo?**
Who studies with you?

Mi amigo Miguel estudia **conmigo.**
My friend Miguel studies with me.

17 ¡Conmigo!

Ask a partner to say who (**Quién**) does the following activities with him or her. Then switch roles and answer the questions. Notice that **Quién** always takes the **él/ella** form of the verb.

MODELO practicar deportes   Answers will vary.
—¿Quién practica los deportes contigo?
—Juan practica los deportes conmigo.

1. montar en bicicleta
2. dibujar
3. estudiar
4. mirar la televisión
5. escuchar música
6. caminar con el perro
7. tomar un helado
8. practicar el basquetbol
9. tocar la guitarra

KINESTHETIC LEARNERS

15 Write subject pronouns, conjugated verb forms, direct objects, and prepositional phrases on index cards and pass them out among students. Students then have to get together with other students to make a complete sentence. Once they have formed their group, a representative will read the sentence aloud. You will need to use some verbs and subjects more than once when preparing cards.

PRESENTATION

NOTA GRAMATICAL
Teach students that **solo/a** means alone. Then ask them yes-or-no questions such as ¿**Estudias? ¿Nadas? ¿Escuchas música? ¿Montas en bicicleta?** If they say yes, ask them if they do these things alone. (¿**solo/a?**) If they say that they don't do them alone, ask them ¿**Con quién?**

LANGUAGE NOTE

Teach students this riddle: What's a funny way to say in Spanish "a dog with a gorilla on the beach"? (**un can con King Kong en Cancún**) The word **can** is an alternate word for **perro.**

18 Have students use days of the week (from **Capítulo preliminar**) in their answers.

🌐 CULTURE NOTE
Explain to students that in Mexico and other Spanish-speaking countries, people often take a long lunch at midday. That means that schoolchildren often have at least an hour off for lunch. This gives families time to have their main meal together. In areas with hot weather, this break may include a **siesta**. This custom of the **siesta** allows people to stay out of the sun during the hottest part of the day.

ADDITIONAL PRACTICE
19 Have students role-play the conversation as if they were conducting a television interview. If possible, have them record the interview on audio- or videotape. Suggest that students include the recording in their porfolios.

18 ¿Con quién?

Write a short note to Claudia describing three of your friends. Mention three activities they do with you or others. End your note by asking Claudia who studies with her. Look at the example below for help.   Answers will vary.

> *Hola Claudia,*
> *Mi amigo David es muy inteligente. Estudia conmigo en la biblioteca. También vamos al c*

▶ Nota cultural

In Spain and Latin America, there are many different ways of referring to or greeting friends. Friends often call each other **'mano/a** (short for **hermano/a**) or **compañero/a**. In Peru, friends sometimes say **¡Hola, pata!** Some Mexican expressions for friends include **chamaco/a, chavo/a,** or **cuate.** Throughout Latin America, men often call each other **compadre.**

19 ¿Qué haces después de clases?

Work in pairs. Find out what your partner does in his or her free time with friends. Ask two questions using the expressions **después de clases** and **en el tiempo libre.** Report your partner's answer for each question in writing. Switch roles and answer your partner's questions.   Answers will vary.

MODELO   —¿Qué haces con tus amigos después de clases?
—Después de clases tomo un refresco con mi amiga Carolina.
(You write:) Toma un refresco con su amiga Carolina.

NOTA GRAMATICAL

p. 30
Act. 9

Que is a very common word in Spanish. It can refer to either people or things and can mean *that, which,* or *who.*

Tengo una amiga **que** canta bien.

La música **que** me gusta escuchar es rock en español.

20 ¿Quién es?

Match the description of the person in the first column to his or her name from the second column.

a. el/la profesor/a de matemáticas

1. Es una persona que canta bien. b
2. Es una persona que trabaja en la televisión. d
3. Son personas que practican deportes en Denver, Colorado. e
4. Soy una persona que estudia español. c
5. Es una persona que trabaja en tu colegio. a

b. Gloria Estefan

c. yo

d. Daisy Fuentes

e. los "Broncos"

21 Preferencias

With a partner, create questions from the phrases below. Then take turns asking and answering these questions. Be sure to use **que** in your answer. Answers will vary.

MODELO   clase / te gusta más
— ¿Cuál es la clase que te gusta más?
— La clase que me gusta más es el español.

1. música / te gusta escuchar
2. programa de televisión / te gusta mirar
3. cosa / necesitas comprar
4. deporte / te gusta practicar

El deporte que me gusta practicar es el béisbol.

PRESENTATION

NOTA GRAMATICAL

Write the following sentences on the board:
Tengo un amigo.
Mi amigo canta muy bien.

Point out that if they mean the same person when they say **amigo,** they can put the two sentences together with **que: Tengo un amigo que canta muy bien.**

Have them put the following pairs of sentences together:

1. **Tengo una clase; la clase me gusta.**
2. **Tengo un amigo; mi amigo es simpático.**
3. **Quiero el libro; el libro es interesante.**

☼ CLOSE

Use Teaching Transparency 4-1 or 4-A to review activities and verb forms with the class.

☼ ASSESS

QUIZ 4-1
Testing Program, pp. 55–56
Audio Program,
Audiocassette 4B OR
Audio CD 4 Track 19

PERFORMANCE ASSESSMENT

Have students describe their preferences for free-time activities and those of the ideal "roommate" at summer camp. This could be done in writing or orally on audiocassette.

VIDEO INTEGRATION

Adelante LEVEL 1A
Video Program,
Videocassette 2, 15:55–18:46

MOTIVATING ACTIVITY
Ask students where they go to get together with friends. Where would they go to mail a letter? Where would they go to buy clothes?

PRESENTATION
The project **Un mapa de mi ciudad** on page 141G would be a good introduction to the topic of this **Encuentro cultural.** The project **Nuestra ciudad ideal** on page 141H would be a good culminating activity to use after presenting this **Encuentro cultural.**

ENCUENTRO CULTURAL

Un recorrido por la Plaza de las Armas

Ofelia es de Cuernavaca, México. A ella le gusta ir a la Plaza de las Armas con sus amigas para pasear y ver a la gente. ¿Adónde te gusta ir con tu familia o con tus amigos?

Ésta es la Plaza de las Armas. Es bonita, ¿verdad? Las oficinas del gobierno están en ese edificio. Mi tío trabaja allí. Al lado del Palacio del Gobierno está el correo. Cerca del correo hay una zapatería.

1 ¿Qué dijo?
Ofelia describes the **plaza** in different ways. Read what she says and see if it sounds like a place in your neighborhood.

Mi colegio no está muy lejos de aquí. Mucha gente viene a la plaza para pasear, leer, hacer compras, tocar música, jugar y pasar el rato entre amigos.

▶ "Las **oficinas del gobierno** están en ese edificio." ··········▶

▶ "Cerca del correo hay una zapatería." ··········▶

▶ "Mucha gente viene a la plaza para **pasear, leer, hacer compras, tocar música, jugar** y pasar el rato entre amigos." ··········▶

1. Ofelia's uncle probably works:
   a. in an office
   b. in a classroom
   c. on a farm

2. In Cuernavaca, there is a shoe store near the post office. Can you walk from the post office to a shoe store where you live?
   Answers will vary.

3. Name three things people like to do when they come to the Plaza de las Armas.
   Answers will vary. Possible answers: read, go shopping, spend time with friends

2 ¡Piénsalo!

Use Ofelia's Web page to answer the following questions. <small>Answers in side column</small>

1. Ofelia says the name of her city comes from an ancient Mexican language, not Spanish. Can you name five U.S. cities or states whose names do not come from English?

2. According to Ofelia's Web page, where in the Plaza de las Armas would you go if you wanted to see fine art?

3. If you could send Ofelia an e-mail message, what two things would you ask about her city?

¡Bienvenidos a la página web de Ofelia!

¡Hola! Me llamo Ofelia y vivo en Cuernavaca. ¡Me encanta mi ciudad!

Cuernavaca viene de la palabra náhuatl Cuauhnáhuac, que quiere decir "cerca de la arboleda". Náhuatl es el idioma de los aztecas. Cuernavaca es una ciudad muy bonita.

El **Palacio Cortés** fue construido en el siglo dieciséis. Hoy en día se llama el Museo Cuauhnáhuac. Tiene pinturas de Diego Rivera y Frida Kahlo.

En el **zócalo**, puedes comprar de todo: libros, carteles, discos compactos, plantas. Mi favorito es un raspado de fresa.

Regresar

Avanzar

Página inicial

"Dale un click en estas fotos si quieres ver más imágenes de **Cuernavaca**".

3 ¿Y tú?

What would you say to Ofelia if you were describing what you do in your free time? <small>Answers will vary.</small>

1. En mi tiempo libre, a mí me gusta ═══.

2. Un lugar de mi ciudad adonde va la gente a pasear, comer y hacer compras es ═══.

3. Un lugar de mi barrio que me gusta es ═══. Me gusta porque ═══.

ENCUENTRO CULTURAL

ciento cincuenta y nueve **159**

CHALLENGE

2 Have students work in groups to research the history of the city or town they live in. Assign each group one of the following questions:

1. What is the origin of the town's name? What language does it come from?

2. When was the town founded?

3. How many people lived in the town 50 years ago?

4. How many people live here now?

NATIVE SPEAKERS

Have native speakers scan this reading for one word with that begins with *h,* one that begins with *j,* and two words that begin with *v.* They should add those words to their spelling notebooks. (**hacer, jugar, vamos, viene**)

Answers to Activity 2

1. Answers will vary. Possible answers: San Diego, Massachusetts, Baton Rouge, Colorado, Minnesota

2. to the Museo Cuauhnáhuac

3. Answers will vary.

VIDEO INTEGRATION

Adelante LEVEL 1A
Video Program,
Videocassette 2, 5:45–6:03 OR
¡Ven conmigo! LEVEL 1
Videodisc Program,
Videodisc 2B

Search 7994, Play To 8541

JUMP START!

On a transparency or the board, write a familiar Spanish word such as **LIBRO**. Ask students to use each letter in **LIBRO** to write a Spanish word. In this case, they should end up with five words (**L**uego, estud**I**a, **B**icicleta, ma**R**tes, est**O**).

SUGGESTION

22 Have students use these questions as advance organizers before they watch the video.

LANGUAGE NOTE

Diminutive forms are more common in some Spanish-speaking countries than in others. In Mexico the diminutive form of **ahora** (**ahorita**) is very common and can mean *right now, very recently,* or *very soon.* Ask native speakers if they can think of any other words that end in **-ito/a.**

SEGUNDO PASO

Telling where people and things are

22 ¿Qué pasa?

Use the photo above to answer the following questions.

1. Who is Claudia looking for?
2. What words does she use to ask if María Inés is there?
3. What words does Claudia use to ask where the post office is?
4. Where is the post office?

1. María Inés.
2. ¿Está aquí María Inés Hernández?
3. ¿Dónde está?
4. En la Plaza de la Constitución.

ASÍ SE DICE Telling where people and things are

p.43
Act. 8

To find out where someone or something is, ask:

¿Dónde estás?
Where are you?

CD-ROM
Disc 1

¿No está en la escuela de baile?
Isn't she at dance school?

Your friend might answer:

Estoy en el centro. Necesito encontrar a María Inés.
I'm downtown. I need to find María Inés.

No, no está aquí.
No, she's not here.

Está en el trabajo. *She's at work.*

---

23 ¿Dónde está? Script and answers on p. 141E

Listen to these people talk about where things are. Match each statement you hear with the correct drawing.
Cass. 2B CD 4 Tr. 5

a

b

c

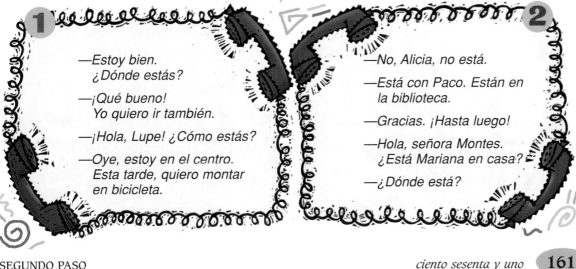
d

24 El teléfono Answers on p. 141K

Put each of the following telephone conversations in order.

1

—*Estoy bien.*
¿Dónde estás?

—*¡Qué bueno!*
Yo quiero ir también.

—*¡Hola, Lupe! ¿Cómo estás?*

—*Oye, estoy en el centro.*
Esta tarde, quiero montar
en bicicleta.

2

—*No, Alicia, no está.*

—*Está con Paco. Están en*
la biblioteca.

—*Gracias. ¡Hasta luego!*

—*Hola, señora Montes.*
¿Está Mariana en casa?

—*¿Dónde está?*

☀ MOTIVATE

Ask students when it is necessary to know where something or someone is. (when you're meeting someone or giving directions) What expressions are needed to ask and to say where something is?

☀ TEACH

PRESENTATION
ASÍ SE DICE

Write each of the following places on two different slips of paper: **la clase de arte, la clase de español, la clase de computación, la clase de inglés, la clase de matemáticas, la clase de ciencias sociales, el cuarto, el centro, cl trabajo, Madrid, Cuernavaca, el centro comercial, la cafetería, la pizzería, casa.** You may need more if you have more than 30 students. Shuffle the slips of paper and pass them out to students. The word on the paper represents where they are right now. Without showing each other their papers, have them find the other person who is in the same place by asking **¿Dónde estás? Estoy en...** Follow up by asking them where they and their partners and classmates are.

NOTA GRAMATICAL

The verb **estar** *(to be)* is used to talk about where people and things are. Here are the present tense forms of the verb.

(yo)	est**oy**	(nosotros) (nosotras)	est**amos**
(tú)	est**ás**	(vosotros) (vosotras)	est**áis**
(usted) (él) (ella)	est**á**	(ustedes) (ellos) (ellas)	est**án**

PA p.43 Act. 8

GV p. 31 Acts. 10–11

25 Vamos a Taxco

This is the first time Luis has been to Taxco, so María Inés is describing the city to him as she shows him around. Use **estar** to complete her sentences.

Luis, es la primera vez que tú ___1___ en Taxco, ¿no? Bueno, allá ___2___ el parque, y allá ___3___ la biblioteca. El museo ___4___ en la Plaza Borda. Hay muchos buenos hoteles en esta ciudad. Muchos ___5___ en la calle Hidalgo. Dos tiendas muy buenas ___6___ en la Plazuela de San Juan.

Answers in side column

26 ¿Quiénes o qué?

Work with a partner. Take turns asking each other who is in each of the following places. Answer by naming three people or things that are in each of the following places right now. Answers will vary.

MODELO ¿Quiénes están en la clase de matemáticas?
—Jimena y Esteban están en la clase de matemáticas.
¿Qué está en la clase de matemáticas?
—La calculadora está en la clase de matemáticas.
—La profesora está en la clase de matemáticas.

1. en la clase de español
2. en tu cuarto
3. en tu casa
4. en México

Hotel Agua Escondida

UNICO EN EL ZOCALO DE TAXCO

- Restaurant "LA HACIENDA"
  Comida nacional e internacional con sabor casero. Menús especiales
- Estacionamiento cubierto
- Alberca
- Salones para convenciones y banquetes
- Tres amplias terrazas panorámicas

GUILLERMO SPRATLING No. 4

VOCABULARIO

GV

p. 32
Acts.
12–13

4-2

al lado de   *next to;*
   to one side of, beside
allá   *there*
aquí   *here*

cerca de   *near*
debajo de   *under; beneath*
encima de   *on top of*
lejos de   *far from*

PRESENTATION

VOCABULARIO

Use local places to present the new vocabulary. (**El cine "Expo" está en la calle Guadalupe. Clase, ¿dónde están otros cines?**) Students respond with the names of other theaters. Check comprehension by having students correct false statements. (**—El cine "Expo" está en la avenida Lincoln. —No, profesora, está en la calle Guadalupe.**) Have students practice with a partner: one gives a new vocabulary word and the other responds with the proper name of a local place.

VISUAL/AUDITORY LEARNERS

Have students look at the city scene in the **Vocabulario.** Make statements about the town and ask students to tell you if they are **cierto** or **falso.** Have students correct false statements. For example,

1. **El supermercado está cerca del parque. (cierto)**
2. **El cine está lejos del supermercado. (falso)**
3. **La piscina está encima del gimnasio. (cierto)**
4. **La tienda está lejos del gimnasio. (falso)**

163

AUDITORY/VISUAL LEARNERS
27 Read the following sentences and have students match each statement with the correct picture.

1. Carlos y Marcos no están en la clase. Están en la oficina del director. (h)
2. Mario y Fernando están en el gimnasio. (d)
3. Mariana está en el gimnasio también. Está en la piscina. (b)
4. Federico y su perro Bandido están en el parque. (a)
5. María y Claudia están en el restaurante. (f)
6. El señor Pérez está en la tienda de ropa. (g)
7. Elena está en la biblioteca. (e)

ADDITIONAL PRACTICE
28 Have students bring in drawings or photos of their room or an imaginary one. Have them identify the things in it and where they are in relation to each other.

27 ¿Quiénes son y dónde están? Script and answers on p. 141E

Cass. 2B
CD 4 Tr. 6

A Listen as Luis Miguel describes his friends and family to you. Match each drawing with the description you hear.

MODELO Paco es bajo y moreno. Le gusta jugar con su perro. **(a)**

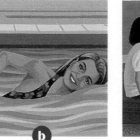

B Now look at the drawings again. Write a sentence saying where each person is. Answers on p. 141K

MODELO **a.** Él está en el parque.

28 En mi cuarto

Look at the drawing. Then match the items with their locations below.

1. El lápiz e
2. El reloj a
3. Los zapatos b
4. El cuaderno f
5. El papel c
6. Los bolígrafos d

a. está lejos de la cama.
b. están debajo de la mesa.
c. está cerca de los zapatos.
d. están encima del cuaderno.
e. está al lado del libro.
f. está debajo del bolígrafo.

29 Necesito un...

You and your friends are visiting a new town. Help your friends decide where to go to do a variety of activities. Write a complete sentence that tells where each friend should go. Come up with your own suggestion of what you want to do and where you need to go for the last item. Answers will vary. Possible answers in side column

MODELO Blanca y Ángel quieren estudiar.
          Necesitan ir a la biblioteca.

1. Yo quiero comprar ropa.
2. Melissa y Ana quieren caminar con el perro.
3. Deon necesita comprar estampillas *(stamps)*.
4. Paula y David quieren nadar.
5. Josh quiere comprar una pizza.
6. Tú quieres ¿?

30 ¿Dónde está?

Now help your friends find their way around the new town by giving them directions. First look at the map on page 163. Match the location in the first column with the directions in the second column.

MODELO la biblioteca
          Está al lado del correo.

1. el parque d
2. la tienda e
3. el cine f
4. el correo a
5. el restaurante b
6. la piscina c

a. Está cerca del cine, al lado de la biblioteca y lejos del gimnasio.
b. Está al lado de la biblioteca, cerca de la tienda y lejos del parque.
c. Está encima del gimnasio.
d. Está cerca del supermercado, el cine y el gimnasio.
e. Está al lado del gimnasio y debajo de la piscina.
f. Está al lado del supermercado y cerca del parque.

31 ¿Dónde están tus cosas?

Get together with two other classmates. Using the words shown here and other words you know, take turns describing where four things are in your own room. While one person describes, the other two draw what they hear on a sheet of paper. Then compare the drawings and make corrections: **No, el reloj no está allí. Está encima de la mesa.** Answers will vary.

el escritorio   el reloj
la cama   el cuaderno
la mochila   la radio

TPR Have students take out the following items: **un lápiz, un bolígrafo, papel, un libro, un diccionario, una goma de borrar.** Teach the command **¡Pongan!** and practice the prepositions from the **Vocabulario** on page 163 by having students follow your instructions. **Pongan el lápiz al lado del bolígrafo. Pongan el papel lejos del lápiz,** etc. Have them follow up by using the question **¿Dónde está?** and these vocabulary words.

VISUAL LEARNERS
29 Display Teaching Transparency 4-C. Instead of having students speak or write a response, have volunteers point to the place where each person needs to go.

GAME
31 Have students play **¿Dónde está?** from page 141I to practice the prepositions from **Vocabulario** page 163.

Answers to Activity 29
1. Necesita ir a la tienda.
2. Necesitan ir al parque.
3. Necesita ir al correo.
4. Necesitan ir a la piscina.
5. Necesitan ir al restaurante.
6. Answers will vary.

PA
p. 45
Act. 10

GV
p. 33
Acts. 14–16

GRAMÁTICA   Subject pronouns

In Spanish, you don't need to use subject pronouns as often as you do in English. That's because the verb ending usually shows the subject of the verb. But the pronoun may be used to clarify or emphasize the subject.

yo	compr**o**	nosotros nosotras	compr**amos**
tú	compr**as**	vosotros vosotras	compr**áis**
usted		ustedes	
él ella	compr**a**	ellos ellas	compr**an**

1. In general, **tú** is used to speak to people with whom you're on a first-name basis. Use **usted** with adults and people in authority.

2. In Spain, **vosotros/as** is the plural of **tú**, while **ustedes** is the plural of **usted**. In Latin America, **ustedes** is the plural of both **tú** and **usted**.

   SPAIN   Vosotros sois de San José, ¿verdad?
   LATIN AMERICA   Ustedes son de San José, ¿verdad?

3. The masculine forms (**nosotros** and **vosotros**) are used to refer to groups of males or groups including both males and females. The feminine forms **nosotras** and **vosotras** refer to groups that include only females.

   —José y María, ¿de dónde sois vosotros?
   —Nosotros somos de Madrid.

PRESENTATION
GRAMÁTICA
Use gestures to demonstrate each pronoun. Then break students into groups of three or four and have them demonstrate each pronoun as you say it. Explain that there are six different endings for regular **-ar** verbs, and each corresponds to a subject pronoun. Give students several sentences without subject pronouns and have them identify the subject.

LANGUAGE NOTE
The second-person singular pronoun **vos** is common throughout Latin America. It is especially common in Argentina, Uruguay, and most of Central America. The second person plural pronoun **vosotros** is only heard in Spain. The **vos** form of the verb in the present tense is the same as the **vosotros** except without the **i: vos hablás.**

CULTURE NOTE
The use of **tú, vos, usted(es),** and **vosotros** varies from country to country. In some places, **tú** is more common than **usted**. In others **tú** is considered rude and **vos** is preferred. Yet in other countries, **vos** is insulting and **tú** or **usted** is preferred. In Spain, **tú** and **vosotros** are used almost exclusively. Emphasize that it's best to start out with **usted**.

32 ¿Quién es?
What subject pronoun would you use to replace the names below?
MODELO   Pedro→él

1. Natalia y Hugo ellos
2. tú y Felicia ustedes
3. el señor Ling él
4. Robert y yo nosotros
5. la señora Ryan ella
6. Julia y Tamara ellas

▶ Nota cultural

The use of **tú** and **usted** varies from country to country. Children in some areas are likely to address a parent as **usted,** while children in other areas use **tú.** If you're in a Spanish-speaking area, listen to others and try to use **tú** and **usted** as they do. When in doubt, use **usted** and wait for the other person to invite you to be less formal. How would you address your principal in Spanish?

166   *ciento sesenta y seis*   CAPÍTULO 4   ¿Qué haces esta tarde?

166

33 Yo, tú, ella... Answers on p. 141K

Which pronoun would you use if you were talking *about* . . .?

1. you and your friends
2. your next-door neighbors
3. a teacher who is a woman
4. yourself
5. your grandfather

Which pronoun would you use if you were talking *to* . . .?

6. your little brother
7. your doctor
8. your three cousins
9. your principal

ella
Yo tú
ellos

34 ¡Zapatos nuevos!

Complete the conversation by filling in the subject pronouns that are missing.

—___1___ necesito comprar unos zapatos en una tienda en el centro comercial. Yo

—¿Ah, sí? ___2___ quiero zapatos nuevos también. Yo

—¿___3___ quieres ir a la tienda esta tarde? Mi familia tiene Tú
que comprar muchas cosas. ___4___ vamos a las tres. Nosotros/Nosotras

—¡Sí! ___5___ quiero ir. ¿Quiere ir Marta también? Yo

—No, ___6___ está en el gimnasio. Bueno, hasta luego. ella

—¡Adiós!

35 Buenos días

During the course of the day, Octavio greets several people and asks how they are. Write both Octavio's greetings and the people's responses. Include the subject pronouns in your sentences.

Answers will vary.

1

2

3

4

VIDEO INTEGRATION

Adelante LEVEL 1A
Video Program,
Videocassette 2, 18:47–21:31

TEACHER NOTES

• Remind students that cultural information may be included in the Quizzes and the Chapter Test.

• The language of the people interviewed represents informal, unrehearsed speech. Occasionally, text has been edited for clarity.

MOTIVATING ACTIVITIES

• Ask students to discuss what they and their friends do together. Where do they go to see and be seen by others?

• Using the new vocabulary from Chapter 4, have students make a list of places in a town. Write their suggestions on the board or on a transparency.

Panorama cultural

CD-ROM Disc 1

Cass. 2B
CD 4 Trs. 7–10

¿Te gusta pasear con tus amigos?

The **paseo** is a tradition in Spanish-speaking countries; people stroll around the **plaza** or along the streets of a town in the evening to socialize, and to see and be seen by others. In this chapter, we asked some teens about the **paseo**.

N

After school, Alejandra and her friends get together. Where does she say they like to go?

Sevilla, where Álvaro lives, has many parks and outdoor cafés. They're perfect for hanging out with friends.

● Alejandra
San Antonio, Texas
CD 4 Tr. 8

Sí, me encanta pasear. A mí me gusta ir al cine, al parque. Nos juntamos y hablamos mucho de lo que pasó en la escuela.

● Álvaro
Sevilla, España
CD 4 Tr. 9

Sí, me encanta pasear. Voy al parque de María Luisa porque es muy divertido. Todo el mundo va a pasear.

Fernando likes to do active things, such as rent a rowboat in Chapultepec Park.

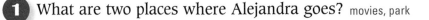

● **Fernando** CD 4 Tr. 10
*Ciudad de México,
México*

Sí. Mi papá, mi hermano y mi mamá y yo vamos a remar *(row)* a Chapultepec; [hacemos] cosas muy divertidas.

1 What are two places where Alejandra goes? movies, park

2 When Alejandra goes walking with her friends, what do they talk about? what happened in school

3 Why does Álvaro go walking in the park? because it's fun

4 What's the name of the park where Álvaro goes? María Luisa

5 What activity does Fernando mention? rowing

6 How can you tell that Fernando likes to go out with his family? he says they do "cosas divertidas"

Para pensar y hablar... Answers will vary.
A. What activities do you do together with your family? Do you ever go somewhere to watch people and talk with friends?
B. Name one place where all the interviewees go to socialize. Who do they go there with? Do you think it's a good idea for people from a neighborhood to get together and socialize on a regular basis? Why or why not?

169

PRESENTATION
Remind students of the reading strategies they have learned: recognizing cognates, scanning titles, and using previous knowledge. Have them go through the interviewees' answers to find five cognates. They may not know what **juntamos** means, but encourage them to identify the **nosotros** form. Have them use context and background knowledge to guess the meaning of the word **juntamos**. Compare **me encanta** (which both Alejandra and Álvaro use) and **me gusta** to show students their shared verb structure. Then show students the video so they may hear the language in context.

 **CULTURE NOTE**
Although the **paseo** is no longer a tradition in very large Latin American cities, urban families may still take strolls in their **barrio.** Urban neighborhoods in Latin American countries often have the feel of small towns, with family-owned shops and small cafés and restaurants. This is also true in urban Spanish-speaking neighborhoods of the United States, such as those in New York.

Talking about where you and others go during free time

VIDEO INTEGRATION

Adelante LEVEL 1A

Video Program,
Videocassette 2, 5:07–5:45 OR

¡Ven conmigo! LEVEL 1

Videodisc Program,
Videodisc 2B

Search 6848, Play To 7993

JUMP START!

On the board write two columns of phrases. Students will match the phrases correctly to form sentences. (Column one: **El libro está, Claudia y Luis están, Nosotros estamos, Los lápices no están;** Column two: **en el gimnasio, encima del escritorio, en la escuela, debajo de la mesa)**

SUGGESTION

36 Have students read these questions as a previewing activity.

Oye, María Inés... voy al centro. ¿Me acompañas?

Gracias, Juan, pero no. Necesito ir al correo. ¡Adiós!

36 Juan y María Inés

Match each question with the correct answer.

1. ¿Adónde va Juan? c
2. ¿Adónde necesita ir María Inés? a
3. ¿Quiere ir María Inés con Juan? b

a. Necesita ir al correo.
b. No quiere ir con Juan.
c. Va al centro.

Nota cultural

In most Spanish-speaking cities, people don't receive mail delivery at their homes. In most cases, people have a mail box at a central post office where they go to pick up their mail. The address on these letters identifies an **apartado** or **casilla** (post office box) with a number, instead of a street address. Because it's not convenient to travel to the central post office every day, there are many couriers who deliver mail and packages. These couriers often travel on mopeds, and make deliveries to offices and homes. How does your family get its mail?

ASÍ SE DICE

Talking about where you and others go during free time

To ask where someone goes, say:

¿Adónde vas?
Where do you go?

¿Adónde va María Inés?
Where does María Inés go?

Your friend might answer:

Voy a la biblioteca **para estudiar**.
I go to the library in order to study.

María Inés va a la piscina. Luego va al cine **para ver una película**.
María Inés goes to the pool. Later, she goes to the theater to see a movie.

37 ¿Cuál es la pregunta? Script and answers on p. 141F

Cass. 2B
CD 4 Tr. 11

Listen to the following people as they answer questions about where they and others go during free time. Then choose the question that each one answered. You may use each question more than once.

a. ¿Adónde vas?

b. ¿Adónde va?

c. ¿Dónde está?

¿Oye, adónde vas?

Voy a la clase de música y después voy al parque.

TERCER PASO

ciento setenta y uno **171**

MOTIVATE

Ask students to make a list of the places where they go during the week. Have them share their list with a class-mate. Where do they both go? Explain that they will learn how to express in Spanish that they go to these places.

TEACH

PRESENTATION
ASÍ SE DICE
Role-play the first exchange in **Así se dice** with a volunteer or use stick figures with speech bubbles on the board. Then have students role-play the same exchange in groups of two. Once they are comfortable with the exchange, have them replace **la biblioteca** with a destination of their choice from page 163. Then have them replace **estudiar** with a verb of their choice. Ask for volunteers to report their partner's destination using the second exchange in **Así se dice** as a model.

LANGUAGE NOTE
Point out that the present tense of **ir** is also used to ask where someone is going right now: **¿Adónde vas?** *Where are you going?*

PRESENTATION

NOTA GRAMATICAL

Have all students stand up. Call out a subject pronoun and toss a foam ball to a student. That student calls out the correct form of the verb **ir**, calls out another pronoun, tosses the ball to another student, and sits down. Continue until all students are seated. If a student is unsure of the correct form, he or she says **paso**, tosses the ball to a classmate, remains standing, and waits for another turn.

KINESTHETIC LEARNERS

39 Have students role-play this conversation in groups of four.

Answers to Activity 39

1. va
2. voy
3. vas
4. voy
5. vas
6. voy
7. van
8. vamos

NOTA GRAMATICAL

Ir *(to go)* is an irregular verb; the conjugation follows its own pattern. To ask where someone is going, use the question word **¿adónde?** *(where to?)*.

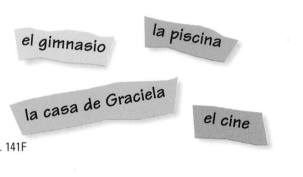

(yo)	**voy**	(nosotros) (nosotras)	**vamos**
(tú)	**vas**	(vosotros) (vosotras)	**vais**
(usted) (él) (ella)	**va**	(ustedes) (ellos) (ellas)	**van**

CD-ROM
Disc 1

PA
p. 46
Acts. 11–12

GV
p. 34
Acts. 17–18

38 ¿Adónde vamos?

Cass. 2B
CD 4 Tr. 12

Listen as Filiberto asks his friends where they're going this afternoon after school. On a sheet of paper, write where each person is going. Use the phrases from the word box. Script and answers on p. 141F

 el gimnasio   la piscina   la casa de Graciela   el cine

1. Pedro
2. David
3. Luisa
4. Alicia
5. Carlos
6. Filiberto

39 En Taxco   Answers in side column

Claudia and her friends are visiting Taxco and everyone is going to a different place. Fill in the blanks with the correct form of the verb **ir.**

ROSA   Claudia ___1___ a la casa de su tío y yo ___2___ con ella. Luis, ¿adónde ___3___ tú?

LUIS   Yo ___4___ al parque. Oye, María Inés, ¿adónde ___5___ tú?

MARÍA INÉS   Yo ___6___ al centro.

LUIS   ¿A qué hora ___7___ ustedes a la casa del tío?

CLAUDIA   ¡Nosotras ___8___ a la casa de mi tío a las nueve!

40 Los planes de todos

You need to keep track of what everyone is doing today. Write five sentences using the information below. Combine words from each column. Be sure your sentences make sense! Answers will vary.

Felipe y yo Inocencia Mis amigos Tú Yo	va van voy vas vamos	al centro al supermercado al parque a la tienda a la casa	para jugar al voleibol para pasar el rato con amigos para comprar fruta para comprar ropa para tomar un refresco

41 Cosas que hacer

You're trying to think of something to do this weekend. Look at the entertainment guide and say where you or your friends have decided to go. Base your answers on the newspaper clipping below.

MODELO   Te gusta nadar.
               Voy a las piscinas
               Municipales Aluche.

Answers will vary. Possible answers:

1. Te gusta jugar al tenis. Voy al Club de Tenis Las Lomas.
2. A tu amigo/a le gusta nadar. Mi amigo/a va a las piscinas Municipales Aluche.
3. Quieres hacer ejercicios aeróbicos *(aerobics)*. Voy al Gimnasio García.
4. Quieres ver una película. Voy a Cines Lumiere.

CINE
CINES LUMIERE.
Pasaje Martín de los Heros o
Princesa, 5. Tel. 542 11 72.
Acceso directo desde el parking.
Precio por sesión, 500 ptas. y
otra película sin determinar.
Confirmar cambios de horarios y
película en taquilla.

GIMNASIOS
GIMNASIO GARCÍA.
Andrés Bello, 21-23. Teléfono.
312 86 01. Karate (club campeón
de España), clases de aeróbicos,
gimnasia, jazz, voleibol, basquetbol y baile. Máquinas Polaris.

PISCINAS
MUNICIPALES ALUCHE
(Latina). A. General Fanjul, 14
(metro Aluche, autobuses 17, 34 y
39). Tel. 706 28 68.

TENIS
CLUB DE TENIS LAS LOMAS.
Avenida de Las Lomas. Tel. 633
04 63. Escuela de tenis. Todos
los niveles. Todos los días de la
semana.

42 Destinos

Write six sentences naming places where you, your friends, and your parents (**mis padres**) go in your free time. Answers will vary.

MODELO   Voy al parque para montar en bicicleta.

AUDITORY LEARNERS
40 Create random sentences using the elements in these boxes, some that make sense and some that don't. Read them aloud and have students indicate whether they are **lógico** (thumbs up) or **ilógico** (thumbs down).

RE-ENTRY
41 Have students recycle question formation as well as previously-learned vocabulary in an oral variation. (**¿Vas a la piscina? Sí, voy a la piscina. ¿A qué hora vas? Voy a las cuatro.**)

GV
p. 35
Acts.
19–20

4-C

VOCABULARIO

Los días de la semana

Monday					el fin de semana	
OCTUBRE						
lunes	martes	miércoles	jueves	viernes	sábado	domingo
1	2	3	4	5	6
7	8	9	10	11	12	13

43 Los días

A With a partner, take turns saying the days of the week in Spanish. For each day, your partner will say the name of that day in English.   Answers will vary.

B Next, say a day of the week in Spanish, and your partner will name the following day in Spanish.   Answers will vary.

PA
pp. 47–48
Acts. 13–16

GV
p. 36
Acts. 21–23

4-3

NOTA GRAMATICAL

1. Always use **el** before a day of the week except when stating what day it is. **Hoy es martes.**
2. To say *on Monday, on Tuesday,* etc., use **el lunes, el martes**.
3. To say *on Mondays, on Tuesdays, the weekends,* etc., use **los lunes, los martes, los fines de semana**.
4. To make **sábado** and **domingo** plural, add **-s**: **los sábados, los domingos.**
5. Days of the week are not capitalized in Spanish.

Los sábados por la mañana ellos trabajan en el jardín (*garden*).

44 ¡Una encuesta!

Take a survey of three classmates to find out where they go on the weekend. Write the name of each person and at least two places where he or she goes. Be prepared to present the class with the results of your survey.   Answers will vary.

MODELO   —Kevin, ¿adónde vas los fines de semana?
        —Voy al parque y al cine.
        Kevin va al parque y al cine.

174   *ciento setenta y cuatro*   CAPÍTULO 4   ¿Qué haces esta tarde?

174

PRESENTATION

VOCABULARIO

Teach the phrases **Ayer fue** _____, **Hoy es** _____, and **Mañana será** _____. Display Teaching Transparency 4-3 (or 4C). Ask the question **¿Qué día es hoy?** Point to a day and model the answer. Then ask **¿Qué día fue ayer?** Have a volunteer give the answer. Then ask **¿Qué día será mañana?**

NOTA GRAMATICAL

Have all students stand up. Call out a day of the week and toss a foam ball to a student. That student calls out the next day in the sequence, tosses the ball to another student, and sits down. Continue until all students are seated. If a student is unsure of the next day, he or she says **paso**, tosses the ball to a classmate, remains standing, and waits for another turn.

VISUAL LEARNERS

Ask students to develop a Spanish calendar for the current month, putting the days of the week and the dates in their proper places. Remind them that the days of the week are not capitalized. Have them fill in one week of the calendar with a sentence for each day, telling what they or someone they know usually does on that day.

45 Si son las ocho, ¿dónde estás?

Compare schedules with a partner. Ask each other where you are at the following times during the week. Answers will vary.

MODELO ¿Dónde estás los lunes a las ocho de la mañana?
—Estoy en la clase de inglés.

1. los viernes a las cuatro de la tarde
2. los sábados a las diez y media de la mañana
3. los martes a la una de la tarde
4. los jueves a las once de la mañana
5. los lunes por la mañana
6. los miércoles por la noche

46 En mi cuaderno

Write a short description of a typical week in your life. Start by making a calendar for the week and include at least one activity for each day. Then write a paragraph describing your week. Answers will vary.

miércoles	jueves	viernes
ir a la casa de María, hacer la tarea		jugar al fútbol

LETRA Y SONIDO

Script on p. 141F

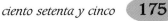

Cass. 2B
CD 4
Trs. 13–17

A. The letters **b** and **v** in Spanish represent the same sound. That single sound has two possible variations.

1. At the beginning of a phrase, or after an **m** or an **n**, these letters sound like the *b* in the English word *bean*.

   biblioteca   basquetbol   bailar   invierno   viernes

2. Between vowels and after other consonants, their pronunciation is softened, with the lower lip slightly forward and not resting against the upper teeth.

   lobo   lo bueno   uva   Cuba

3. Note that the **b** and **v** in the following pairs of words and phrases have exactly the same pronunciation.

   tubo/tuvo   los huevos/los suebos   a ver/haber   botar/votar

B. Dictado
Pablo hasn't learned to spell words that use **b** and **v** yet. As he says the words he's not sure of, write what you hear.

C. Trabalenguas
El lobo sabe bailar bien el vals bajo el árbol.

CULTURE NOTE
In many Spanish-speaking countries, calendars often begin with **el lunes** (Monday), not **el domingo** (Sunday).

PORTFOLIO
45 **Oral** You may wish to suggest this activity to your students as an appropriate oral Portfolio entry. For Portfolio suggestions, see *Alternative Assessment Guide,* p. 15.

SUGGESTION
45 If two people they interviewed said they go to the same place on the weekend, have students use the plural form.

CLOSE
Use Teaching Transparency 4-3 to review material in this **paso**.

ASSESS
QUIZ 4-3
Testing Program, pp. 59–60
Audio Program,
Audiocassette 4B OR
Audio CD 4 Track 21

PERFORMANCE ASSESSMENT
In pairs, have students role-play the following situation: You are going to spend the weekend with a friend in a neighboring town. Call a relative and let him or her know your plans. Your relative asks where you and your friend are going and what times you expect to be at each location. Plan at least four activities for the weekend.

175

LA MÚSICA

1 Los instrumentos

People in Spanish-speaking countries
play many different musical instruments.
Some of these instruments are described
below. Look at the photographs as you
read the descriptions.

1. La **flauta** azteca es un instrumento muy
bonito. Es parecida al *(it looks like)* clarinete.

2. El **charango** es popular en los Andes.
Es parecido a la guitarra.

3. El **güiro** es un instrumento percusivo
(percussion instrument). ¡Pero es
muy diferente al tambor *(drum)*!

4. En muchos países el **arco** se usa
(is used) para tocar el violín. En
Centroamérica el **arco** es un instrumento musical.

el charango

la flauta

el güiro

el arco

2 ¿De qué se hace?

People have always made musical
instruments from materials that
are readily available. For example,
people have made pottery flutes
from clay and percussion instruments from gourds. If you had
to make your own musical
instrument from materials you
have around your classroom,
what materials would you use?
What instrument would you
make? Share your answers
with a partner. Answers will vary.

**Estos músicos en la región de Asturias,
España, tocan las gaitas *(bagpipes).***

176   *ciento setenta y seis*   CAPÍTULO 4   ¿Qué haces esta tarde?

176

LAS MATEMÁTICAS/LAS CIENCIAS SOCIALES

3 Los deportes

Pablo Lara

SECCIÓN R Deportes
EL TIEMPO • Sábado

Cuba Logra El Oro En Béisbol

Triunfan los cubanos.

Los Niños

Claudia Poll

EL TIEMPO • Sábado

Deportes Individuales 1996

Evento	
Atletismo varonil 1500 metros	Fermín Cacho, España plata
Ciclismo varonil 1-kilómetro prueba contra reloj	Miguel Induráin, España oro: 1:04.05
Natación femenil 200 metros libre	Claudia Poll, Costa Rica oro: 1:58.16
Levantamiento de pesas varonil Categoría: 167.5 libras	Pabla Lara, Cuba oro: 809 lbs
Boxeo varonil, Categoría mediano (165 libras)	Ariel Hernández, Cuba oro
Judo femenil, Categoría liviano (123 libras)	Driulis González, Cuba oro

---

el atletismo   *track and field*
categoría mediano   *middleweight*
categoría liviano   *lightweight*
la cima   *summit*
femenil   *women's*
el levantamiento de pesas   *weightlifting*

el oro   *gold*
la plata   *silver*
prueba contra reloj   *time trial; race against the clock*
varonil   *men's*

---

4 Héroes olímpicos históricos   Answers on p. 141K

1. Who won a gold medal in middleweight boxing in the 1996 Olympics?

2. Where is Driulis González, Lightweight Class champion in Women's Judo, from?

3. What was the winning time for time-trial cycling in 1996?

4. According to this list of medal-winners, which two Spanish-speaking countries won the most medals in 1996?

5. How many meters per second did Claudia Poll travel in the 200-meter freestyle race? (Hint: Convert the time from minutes to seconds. Divide the number of meters by the total number of seconds to find out the number of meters per second.)

ENLACES

ciento setenta y siete   **177**

MOTIVATING ACTIVITY
Ask students if they have seen the Olympic Games on television. What countries participated? What were the most interesting sports to watch? Ask students which athletes they admire and why. What is the purpose of the Olympic Games?

PRESENTATION
In pairs, have students use the new vocabulary from this page to ask each other about their likes and dislikes. For example, **¿Te gusta el judo?** or **¿Te gusta el ciclismo?** Tell students to be ready to report on their partner's likes and dislikes, for example, **A María le gusta el ciclismo.**

HISTORY LINK
The Cuban baseball team won the gold medal in the 1996 Olympic games in Atlanta. They won 13-9 against the team from Japan. Cuba, Spain, Argentina, Costa Rica, Ecuador, Mexico, and Puerto Rico were the Spanish-speaking countries that won Olympic medals that year. They won medals in a variety of sports such as tennis, cycling, swimming, water polo, boxing, soccer, track and field, judo, and basketball.

READING STRATEGY

Scanning for specific information

SUGGESTION

Ask students to think of times when they scan for information, such as looking up a name in the phone directory.

☀ PREREADING

MOTIVATING ACTIVITY

Ⓐ and Ⓑ Ask students to think about what they like in a friend or pen pal. Do they like people with whom they share similar interests and hobbies, or do they prefer to spend time with people who are different from them?

☀ READING

SUGGESTION

Ⓒ Have students scan the pen pal ads for obvious cognates (**música rock, teléfono**) and make a list of the ones they find. Then ask them to scan again for words or cognates that are not so easy (**turista, estudiar**). See if they can guess or derive their meanings.

Estrategia

Scanning for specific information means looking for one thing at a time, without worrying about the other information in the reading. For example, you scan when looking up the spelling of a word in a dictionary or looking through the TV listing to see what time a certain show comes on.

¡A comenzar!

The ads on these pages are for pen pals. They come from *Tú,* a magazine for Spanish-speaking teens. Before doing any scanning, gather some general information.

¿Te acuerdas?

Use your background knowledge before you read in depth.

Ⓐ If you were writing an ad for a pen pal, what would you tell about yourself? The items below are examples of what you might want to write about. Answers will vary.

- your name
- your best friend's name
- your address
- the name of your school
- your age
- what you look like
- what your parents do
- your hobbies

Ⓑ Now look briefly at the ads. Of the eight possibilities listed above, which four are included in the ads? name, address, age, hobbies

Al grano

Now that you have a general overview of the pen pal ads, you can scan for more details.

Ⓒ Imagine that you're setting up a letter exchange for your Spanish class. Your classmates have listed the kinds of things they're looking for in a pen pal. Which pen pal would be best for each classmate?

1. someone from Venezuela Wilmer
2. someone who's 11 years old Juan
3. a boy from Panama Esteban
4. a 13-year-old girl Susana
5. someone from the United States Gerardo
6. someone who lives in the city of Buenos Aires Julia
7. a 13-year-old boy Wilmer

Ⓓ Now it's time to choose a pen pal for yourself. You're hoping to develop a long-term friendship with someone who shares your own interests and hobbies. Who will you choose if you . . .?

1. like to dance Gerardo or Susana
2. like to play sports Esteban or Julia
3. like to listen to music
   Wilmer, Juan, Gerardo, or Julia

Who won't you choose if you . . .?

4. don't like to study Wilmer
5. don't like video games Esteban
6. don't like to swim Julia

178 *ciento setenta y ocho* CAPÍTULO 4 ¿Qué haces esta tarde?

178

LÍNEA DIRECTA

Nombre: Wilmer Ramírez
Edad: 13 años
Dirección: Urb. Las Batallas, Calle La Puerta #2, San Félix, Edo. Bolívar, VENEZUELA.
Pasatiempos: Leer tiras cómicas, escuchar música y estudiar.

▲▲▲▲▲▲▲▲▲▲▲▲▲▲▲▲▲▲▲▲▲▲

Nombre: Susana Tam
Edad: 13 años
Dirección: 4ta. Ave., N #41-07, La Flora, Cali, COLOMBIA.
Pasatiempos: Ir al cine, a fiestas, a bailar y hablar por teléfono. Pueden escribirme en inglés.

▲▲▲▲▲▲▲▲▲▲▲▲▲▲▲▲▲▲▲▲▲▲

Nombre: Juan Dos Santos
Edad: 11 años
Dirección: 55 mts sur, Bomba Gasotica, Pérez Zeledón, COSTA RICA.
Pasatiempos: Escuchar música rock, hablar con los turistas.

▲▲▲▲▲▲▲▲▲▲▲▲▲▲▲▲▲▲

Nombre: Gerardo Vargas
Edad: 14 años
Dirección: P.O. Box 2002, Borrego Springs, California 92004, ESTADOS UNIDOS.
Pasatiempos: Leer, bailar y escuchar música rock en español. Mantener correspondencia con chicas de otros países.

▲▲▲▲▲▲▲▲▲▲▲▲▲▲▲▲▲▲▲▲▲

Nombre: Esteban Hernández
Edad: 15 años
Dirección: Apartado 8-3009, El Dorado, PANAMÁ
Pasatiempos: Ir al cine, practicar deportes, jugar a los videojuegos.

▲▲▲▲▲▲▲▲▲▲▲▲▲▲▲▲▲▲

Nombre: Julia Ileana Oliveras
Edad: 15 años
Dirección: Yapeyú 9550 (1210) Cap. Fed. Buenos Aires, ARGENTINA
Pasatiempos: Escuchar la radio, leer, nadar y jugar al tenis. Pueden escribirme también en inglés y en alemán.

▲▲▲▲▲▲▲▲▲▲▲▲▲▲▲▲▲▲▲▲

THINKING CRITICALLY
Ask students why they see so many cognates in Spanish. (English uses many words of French origin and both Spanish and French come from Latin. Also, modern Spanish adopts many Anglicisms because of the universality of English in the fashion, travel, and business worlds.) Encourage students with this fact: Spanish may be easier to learn than they think!

NATIVE SPEAKERS
Have native speakers find five words that contain *b* and five that contain *v* to include in their spelling notebook.

TEACHER NOTE
For additional readings, see *Practice and Activity Book,* p. 49, and *Native Speaker Activity Book,* pp. 16–19.

☀ POSTREADING

SUGGESTION
Ⓓ Have students copy their pen pal ads without putting their names or street addresses on them and turn them in. Randomly number the anonymous ads. Tape the ads around the room. Have students walk around and find the ad of someone they'd like to get to know. They should copy the number of the ad they like and that of their own ad and sit down. Then call out the numbers of the ads and ask whose they are. Students may be surprised at the people they've picked.

The **Repaso** reviews and integrates all four skills and culture in preparation for the Chapter Test.

SUGGESTION

2 Have students write questions about the contents of the letter. With a partner, have them write five questions that Isabel's mother could have asked her about the letter. Each pair then role-plays the conversation between the mother and Isabel. They may wish to include the expression **Silvia dice** _____ or simply **Dice** _____.

REPASO

CD-ROM
Disc 2

1 Listen to these messages left on Pedro's answering machine. Match the person in Column A with the activity he or she mentions in Column B. Script and answers on p. 141F

Cass. 2B
CD 4
Tr. 18

MODELO   Carlos—ir al parque

1. Carmen
2. Gaby
3. Victoria

a. ir a la piscina
b. ir al cine
c. ir a la biblioteca

2 Complete Silvia's letter to her friend Isabel using the verbs in the word box. Use each verb only once.

6 practican   1 estoy   3 vamos   7 camino

2 gusta   5 trabajan   4 voy

> Querida Isabel,
> Aquí __1__ yo en St. Louis. Me __2__ mucho mi colegio. Mis amigos son muy simpáticos. Nosotros __3__ al partido de fútbol los viernes, y yo __4__ al centro comercial los sábados. Mis hermanos Teresa y Andrés __5__ en el cine porque necesitan dinero, pero __6__ deportes todas las tardes a las cuatro. Después de clases yo __7__ con el perro.
> Bueno, voy a estudiar. Tengo un examen mañana..
> ¡Hasta luego!
>
> Un abrazo,
> Silvia

3 Based on what you have learned in this chapter, choose two reasons why the **paseo** is popular in Latin America.
  (a.) People have an opportunity to get together with friends.
  b. Everyone thinks the food is great.
  c. The weather is better in Latin America.
  (d.) Families can spend time together.

4 Vamos a escribir

Write a paragraph explaining where different places in your school are located. Use words like **al lado de**, **cerca de**, and **lejos de.** Answers will vary.

Estrategia

Using drawings can help you write. Try drawing a map of your school and its surroundings to help you organize your thoughts. Then choose the best words to describe where things are on your map.

la cafetería   el auditorio   la oficina del director

la sala de clase   la biblioteca

el gimnasio   la sala de clase   la sala de clase

5 SITUACIÓN

Work with a classmate to create this conversation in Spanish. One of you will be **Student A** and the other will be **Student B.** Answers will vary.

Student A: Ask your friend if he or she studies in the library on weekends.

Student B: Answer that you study in the library on Saturdays. Ask your friend if he or she goes to the park on weekends.

Student A: Answer that you go to the park on Sundays. Tell your friend two different activities you do there. Ask your friend if he or she goes to the park on weekends.

Student B: Answer that you go to the park on Sundays, too. Tell your friend two different activities you do there.

PORTFOLIO

4 Written Your students may want to consider this activity as a potential Portfolio item. For Portfolio suggestions, see *Alternative Assessment Guide,* pp. 9 and 15.

CHALLENGE

5 Have students do the dialogue in the **Situacíon** using their own information, and not the cues provided.

CAPÍTULO 4

This page is intended to prepare students for the Chapter Test. It is a brief checklist of the major points covered in the chapter. The students should be reminded that it is a checklist only and does not necessarily reflect everything that will appear on the Chapter Test.

ADDITIONAL PRACTICE

1 To review **gustar**, have students role-play a disagreement about where they should go on a day off.

🏰 GAME

Clave Divide the class into two teams. On a dry-erase board, chalkboard, or flipchart paper, write various Spanish phrases, verbs, and nouns. Give a verbal clue describing one of the items listed. **(los días sábado y domingo)** A representative from each team points to the words described. **(el fin de semana)** The first to correctly identify it circles the item with that team's colored marker. The team with the most words circled at the end wins.

Answers to Activity 1

1. Le gusta nadar.
2. Le gusta comprar.
3. Le gusta bailar.
4. Te gusta caminar.
5. Me gusta estudiar.

Answers to Activity 2

1. Toco la guitarra.
2. Preparo la cena.
3. Lavo el carro.
4. Miro la televisión.

A VER SI PUEDO...

▼ **Can you talk about what you and others like to do?**
p. 149

▼ **Can you talk about what you and others do during free time?**
p. 152

▼ **Can you tell where people and things are?**
p. 161

▼ **Can you talk about where you and others go during free time?**
p. 171

1 How would you tell what these people like to do at the place given? Answers will vary. Possible answers in side column

MODELO el señor López—la oficina
Le gusta trabajar.

1. Cecilia—la piscina
2. Gustavo—el centro comercial
3. Berta—la fiesta
4. tú—el parque
5. Yo—la biblioteca

2 How would you tell someone that you . . .? Answers in side column

1. play the guitar
2. make dinner
3. wash the car
4. watch television

3 How would you say that you and someone else. . .? Answers will vary. Possible answers on p. 141K

1. walk in the park
2. ride bicycles
3. spend time with friends
4. study in the library
5. listen to music
6. watch television

4 Can you tell where the following people are? Answers will vary. Possible answers on p. 141K

1. Rosa estudia.
2. Claudia compra un regalo.
3. Geraldo y Fernando caminan con el perro.
4. Sofía monta en bicicleta.
5. Tú y tus amigos nadan.

5 How would you tell a visitor who needs directions that . . .? Answers on p. 141K

1. the supermarket is next to the park
2. the bookstore is far from the school
3. the gym is near the library

6 Write a sentence telling where each person is going. Answers on p. 141K

MODELO Mr. Súarez is really thirsty.
Va al restaurante para tomar un refresco.

1. Mariana wants to buy some books and magazines.
2. Lupe wants to lift weights.
3. Carlos and Adriana need to buy stamps.

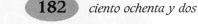
182 *ciento ochenta y dos*   CAPÍTULO 4   ¿Qué haces esta tarde?

182

VOCABULARIO

PRIMER PASO

Talking about what you and others like to do

A mí me gusta + inf.
I (emphatic) like to . . .
¿A quién le gusta...? *Who likes to . . .?*
¿A ti qué te gusta hacer?
What do you (emphatic) like to do?

bailar *to dance*
cantar *to sing*
cuidar a tu hermano/a *to take care of your brother/sister*
descansar en el parque *to rest in the park*
dibujar *to draw*
escuchar música *to listen to music*
estudiar *to study*
hablar por teléfono *to talk on the phone*
lavar el carro *to wash the car*
lavar la ropa *to wash the clothes*
me gusta(n) *I like*
mirar la televisión *to watch TV*
nadar *to swim*
pintar *to paint*
la piscina *swimming pool*
por eso *that's why, for that reason*
¿Quién? *Who?*
sacar la basura *to take out the trash*

Talking about what you and others do during free time

antes de *before*
caminar con el perro *to walk the dog*

la cena *dinner*
con *with*
conmigo *with me*
contigo *with you*
descansar *to rest*
después de *after*
la guitarra *guitar*
el helado *ice cream*
montar en bicicleta *to ride a bike*
pasar el rato con amigos *to spend time with friends*
el piano *piano*
practicar *to practice*
preparar *to prepare*
que *that, which, who*
¿Qué haces después de clases? *What do you do after school?*
el refresco *soft drink*
regresar *to return, go back, come back*
restaurante *restaurant*
(en) el tiempo libre *(during) free time*
tocar *to play an instrument*
tomar *to drink, to take*
trabajar *to work*

SEGUNDO PASO

Telling where people and things are

al lado de *next to, to one side of, beside*
allá *there*
aquí *here*
la biblioteca *library*
la casa *house, home*
el centro *downtown*
cerca de *near*
el cine *movie theater*
el correo *post office*

debajo de *under, beneath*
¿Dónde? *Where?*
encima de *on top of*
estar *to be*

el gimnasio *gym*
lejos de *far from*
nosotros/nosotras *we*
el parque *park*
el paseo *walk, stroll*
el supermercado *supermarket*
la tienda *store*
el trabajo *work, job*
usted *you (formal)*
ustedes *you (plural, formal)*
vosotros/vosotras *you (plural, informal)*

TERCER PASO

Talking about where you and others go during free time

¿Adónde? *Where (to)?*
¿Adónde vas? *Where are you going?*
al *to the*
el día *day*
el domingo *Sunday*
el fin de semana *weekend*
el jueves *Thursday*
el lunes *Monday*
el martes *Tuesday*
el miércoles *Wednesday*
para + infinitive *(in order) to*
la película *movie*
el sábado *Saturday*
la semana *week*
ver *to see*
el viernes *Friday*

¡Ven conmigo a la Florida!
LOCATION OPENER CHAPTERS 5, 6

PRINT	MEDIA

Adelante LEVEL 1A

CD-ROM Teacher's Guide
◆ Location 3, p. 18

Video Guide
◆ Activity Masters and Suggestions, pp. 33–34

Interactive CD-ROM Program
◆ Disc 2

Video Program
◆ Videocassette 2

¡Ven conmigo! LEVEL 1

Videodisc Guide
◆ Activity Masters and Suggestions, pp. 50–52

Videodisc Program
◆ Videodisc 3A

Little Havana, or **la Pequeña Habana,** stretches along several blocks of **Calle Ocho** through downtown Miami. In mid-March, **Calle Ocho** fills with people celebrating Cuban culture and heritage. This festival features music, dancing, food, and special activities for children. The *Guinness Book of World Records* states that in the 1988 **Calle Ocho** Festival, 119,986 people formed the longest conga dance line ever.

Little Havana
Search Frame 2795

The quickest way to get around Miami is on the Metrorail, a train that glides on a 21-mile track connecting downtown Miami with several suburbs. The **Metromover**, a monorail, makes two loops in downtown Miami, and has 4.4 miles of track with 12 stations at major business and shopping centers.

The Metromover
Search Frame 1219

Art Deco was a decorative and architectural style of the period between 1925 and 1940, characterized by bold colors and the use of industrial materials. Miami's Art Deco architects developed a unique style called **Tropical Deco** which included the use of tropical colors and etched-glass panels featuring mermaids, sea horses, flamingos, pelicans, and palm trees.

Tropical Deco
Search Frame 2973

The **Everglades** extend from Lake Okeechobee to Florida Bay and include land covered by shallow water and saw grass in the northern part, and saltwater marshes and mangrove swamps in the southern region. Alligators, deer, fish, panthers, pelicans, and snakes inhabit the Everglades. The Seminole Indians have reservations in the Everglades. Many residents of the Everglades offer airboat tours of the area.

Everglades
Search Frame 2086

Alligators were once common along the Gulf of Mexico and the Atlantic coast from Florida to North Carolina. So many were hunted for their hides that they nearly became extinct. In 1967, the U.S. Fish and Wildlife Service classified them as an endangered species. By 1977, the population had increased so much that they were reclassified from endangered to threatened; however, alligator hunting is still tightly restricted.

Alligators
Search Frame 2029

The following Web sites contain additional information on Florida. Since addresses and content change frequently, you might want to preview them before attempting to access them in class.

Miami City (links to museums, restaurants, and sports, cultural, and business sites) http://www.miamicity.com/miami/

Historic Places atlas (Florida State University site) http://cartlab-www.freac.fsu.edu/historicplaces/atlas.html

Everglades National Park (National Park Service site) http://ice.ucdavis.edu/us_national_park_service/everglades_national_park/

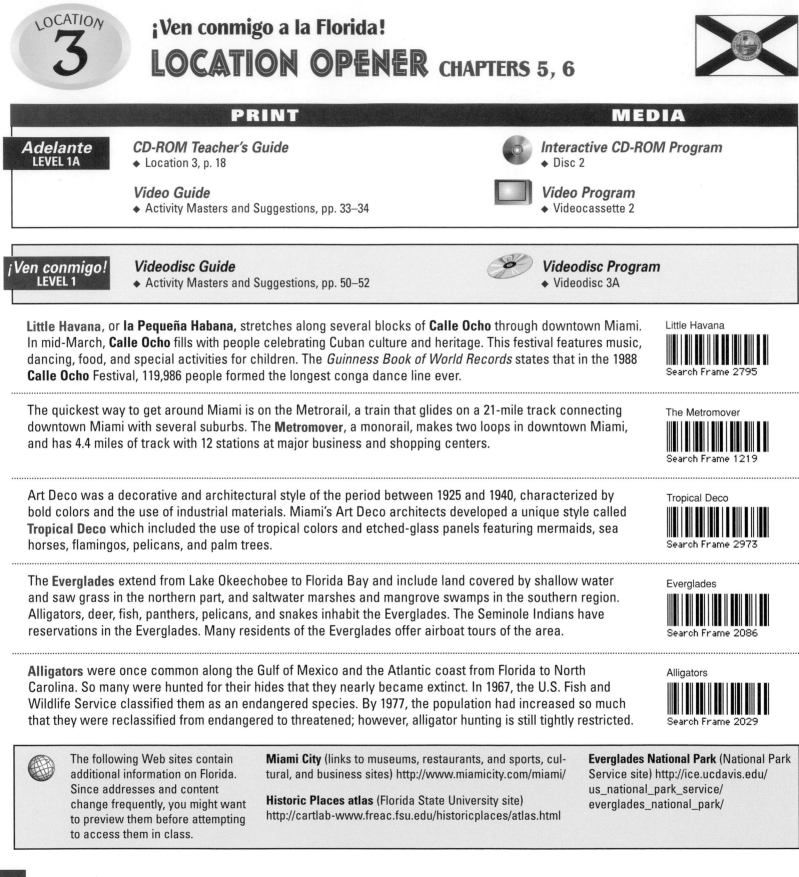

PROJECTS

UNA VISITA A LA FLORIDA

This activity will familiarize students with the geography of the southern United States, primarily Florida. It will emphasize Spanish speakers' linguistic, social, and cultural contributions to this state.

Introduction

Ask students if they are familiar with Spanish-speaking influence in this part of the South. Show students a detailed map of Florida and ask them to pick out names of cities that look or sound Spanish in origin. Ask them why they think so many people in the Miami area speak Spanish as their native language. Ask them if they know of sports, foods, music, art, or leisure activities that are of Hispanic origin. Have students imagine that they are planning a family vacation to Florida. Popular tourist destinations include Orlando, Miami, and Saint Augustine. Have students learn about these and other places by writing to the Chamber of Commerce of a given city or by checking on the Internet. From the information gathered, students will prepare a bulletin board to be used as a reference for Chapters 5 and 6.

Materials students may need

- ◆ Brochures on Florida
- ◆ Large sheets of construction paper
- ◆ Large- and medium-point felt-tipped markers
- ◆ Strips of posterboard
- ◆ Thumbtacks
- ◆ Pictures of Florida
- ◆ Map of Florida

Sequence

1. Divide students into groups. Within each group, assign the roles of Researcher, Cartographer, and Reporter.

2. Groups gather information about a specific city in Florida. The Researcher writes to the Chamber of Commerce for information. The group members decide which information to illustrate or cut out to put on the class bulletin board. The Researcher can also use the Internet or library resources for material.

3. Topics that student groups should consider include Hispanic influence on this city, activities, food, climate, attractions, weather, map of the city, sports, and airport connections with other cities in the U.S.

4. The Cartographer from each group begins preparing the bulletin board for the class. The Cartographer draws a large map of Florida and identifies the researched cities on the map.

5. The Cartographer in the group makes labels in Spanish to emphasize the categories of interest for each city. He or she puts the labels on the bulletin board, along with the visuals.

6. Before the Cartographers have prepared the bulletin board of the map of Florida, be sure to emphasize the proximity to Cuba. Have them include the island of Cuba as a part of the map.

7. The Reporter for each group presents the findings of his or her group to the class. Reporters can imagine that they are doing an on-the-spot live interview for a TV network station to promote their city.

Grading the project

Suggested point distribution (total = 100 points):

Research information 30
Map 30
Oral presentation 30
Group effort 10

¡Ven conmigo a la Florida!
LOCATION OPENER CHAPTERS 5, 6 (cont.)

⬤ Using the Map

You may want to have students refer to the maps on pages xxi and xxiii.

- Ask students to identify the two states that border Florida. (Alabama and Georgia)
- Have students measure the distance between Miami and **La Habana** (approximately 200 miles). What significance might this short distance have? (The culture in Miami has a lot of Cuban influence.)
- Tourism is crucial to Florida's economy. Ask students to locate some of the tourist spots on the map and to discuss their attractions.

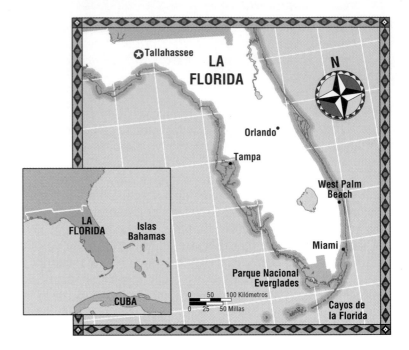

History/Geography Links

- Explain to students that Havana is the capital of Cuba.
- Florida and the states bordering Mexico bear the unmistakable stamp of Spanish influence. Ask students which areas in the United States reveal a strong French heritage. (Louisiana, Northern New England)
- Ask students if they can think of a Caribbean island that was colonized by both the French and the Spanish. (Hispaniola—divided between Haiti, a former French colony, and the Dominican Republic, a former Spanish colony) Have them locate it on the map on page xxi.

Culture Notes

• Southern Florida has a diverse population with an overall Hispanic flavor. Many of the state's Hispanic residents are of Cuban heritage and came to the United States to escape the communist policies of Fidel Castro after 1959. Cubans and Cuban Americans have often overcome difficult circumstances to excel in politics, business, sports, art, and entertainment. (mayor of Miami Xavier Suárez; baseball player Tony Oliva; actor Andy Garcia; salsa musician Celia Cruz, and pop singer Gloria Estefan)

• Thanks to its Cuban influence, southern Florida is virtually bilingual. Spanish is heard everywhere: in schools and shops, on the streets, and over the airwaves. Spanish-language radio, television, and newspapers are popular and profitable. Florida's bilingualism is doubtless a strong attraction for Spanish-speaking tourists and businesspeople from around the world.

• The beaches of Miami are famous for their size and beauty. On weekends, it is common to see families and groups of people at the beach having cookouts, listening to music, and, of course, swimming in the ocean.

Art Link

Explain that Art Deco was a popular architectural style between 1925 and 1940 that used geometric designs, bold colors, chrome, plastic, and other industrial materials. It was used mostly in architecture, furniture, jewelry, pottery, and textiles. Ask students if they can name any famous buildings that have Art Deco style. (the Empire State Building and Radio City Music Hall in New York City) Ask students to research and report on Hispanic influence on architecture in the southwestern United States.

ANSWERS TO CHAPTER 5 ACTIVITIES

Listening activity answers appear on Scripts pages 187E–187F. Answers to all other activities appear on corresponding pupil pages.

PRIMER PASO   pp. 194–199

12 1. ¿Quién habla por teléfono? Zoraida habla por teléfono.
2. ¿Quiénes preparan la cena? La señora Vivanco y Anita preparan la cena.
3. ¿Quiénes caminan por el parque? La señora Chávez y Luis caminan por el parque.
4. ¿Quiénes compran ropa? Sarah y tú compran ropa.
5. ¿Quién practica al fútbol? Jaime practica al fútbol.
6. ¿Quién toca el piano? Alejandra toca el piano.
7. ¿Quiénes montan en bicicleta? Patty y yo montamos en bicicleta.

SEGUNDO PASO   pp. 202–211

17 1. leer / escribir / recibir
2. comer / recibir
3. leer / recibir
4. beber
5. asistir a
6. comer

20 1. ¿A ellas les gusta practicar deportes?
2. ¿A ellos les gusta escuchar música clasica?
3. ¿A ellos les gusta bailar?
4. ¿A ellos les gusta comer la comida china?
5. ¿A ella le gusta beber el jugo de frutas?
6. ¿A ustedes les gusta escuchar la música pop?

23 Answers will vary. Possible answers:
1. Ustedes corren juntos por el parque los sábados.
2. Tú y tu familia comen juntos todos los días.
3. Nosotros leemos juntos las tiras cómicas del periódico de vez en cuando.
4. La señora Pérez escribe tarjetas postales cada tres días durante las vacaciones.
5. Ellas asisten a una clase de ejercicios aeróbicos todos los martes por la tarde.
6. Elisa lee novelas a menudo.

TERCER PASO   pp. 212–219

38 1. true
2. false. Elsa swims in a pool every day.
3. true
4. false. Elsa runs in the morning when it's cooler.

VAMOS A LEER   pp. 222–223

C 1. **rápidamente**   *rapidly*
2. **divertido**   *fun*
3. **cubierta**   *covered*
4. **diversión**   *fun*
5. **lecciones**   *lessons*
6. **barcos**   *boats*

REPASO   pp. 224–225

2 Answers will vary. Possible answers:

En Asunción hace fresco y hace sol. Vamos a caminar en el parque.

En Bogotá está lloviendo a cántaros. Voy a leer una novela en casa.

En Buenos Aires hace mucho viento. Vamos a volar una cometa.

En La Paz hace mucho frío. Voy a mirar la televisión.

4 1. el veinticuatro de junio
2. el treinta de marzo
3. el doce de septiembre
4. el primero de febrero
5. el dieciocho de noviembre
6. el ocho de agosto

A VER SI PUEDO...   p. 226

3 Answers will vary. Possible answers:

Típicamente preparamos el desayuno los sábados. Los domingos, voy a la casa de mi amiga. Después leo una novela. Durante la semana, voy al colegio. Por la tarde, hago la tarea y miro la televisión.

5 1. Está lloviendo y hace frío.
2. Hace frío y hace mucho viento.
3. Está nevando. / Nieva mucho hoy.
4. Hace calor y mucho sol.
5. Está nublado.
6. Hace fresco.

HOMEWORK SUGGESTIONS

CAPÍTULO 5

Chapter Section	Presentation	Homework Options
Primer paso	**Así se dice,** p. 195	*Pupil's Edition,* p. 195, #6 *Practice and Activity Book,* p. 52, #2; p. 54, #7 *CD-ROM,* Disc 2, Chapter 5, #1
	Gramática, p. 196	*Pupil's Edition,* pp. 196–197, #7–8, 10 *Grammar and Vocabulary,* pp. 37–38, #1–3 *CD-ROM,* Disc 2, Chapter 5, #2
	Nota gramatical, p. 198	*Pupil's Edition,* p. 198, #11 *Grammar and Vocabulary,* p. 38, #4
Segundo paso	**Así se dice,** p. 203	*Practice and Activity Book,* pp. 55–56, #8–10 *Grammar and Vocabulary,* p. 39, #5
	Vocabulario, p. 204	*Pupil's Edition,* p. 205, #18 *Grammar and Vocabulary,* p. 39, #6 *CD-ROM,* Disc 2, Chapter 5, #3
	Nota gramatical, p. 206	*Pupil's Edition,* p. 206, #20 *Grammar and Vocabulary,* p. 40, #7
	Gramática, p. 207	*Grammar and Vocabulary,* pp. 40–41, #8–10 *Practice and Activity Book,* p. 56, #11 *CD-ROM,* Disc 2, Chapter 5, #4
	Así se dice, p. 209	*Pupil's Edition,* p. 211, #29 *Practice and Activity Book,* p. 57, #12
Tercer paso	**Así se dice/Nota gramatical,** p. 213	*Pupil's Edition,* p. 213, #32 *Grammar and Vocabulary,* pp. 42–43, #12–14
	Vocabulario, p.214	*Pupil's Edition,* p. 214, #33 *Grammar and Vocabulary,* p. 42, #11 *Practice and Activity Book,* pp. 58–59, #13–15 *CD-ROM,* Disc 2, Chapter 5, #6
	Así se dice/ Vocabulario, p. 216	*Pupil's Edition,* pp. 217–218, #37–38 *Grammar and Vocabulary,* p. 44, #15–16 *Practice and Activity Book,* pp. 59–60, #16–18 *CD-ROM,* Disc 2, Chapter 5, #5

El ritmo de la vida

MOTIVATING ACTIVITY
Have students list what they typically do with friends and family during an average week. Ask them to share what they have to do, what they choose to do, and how often they do it.

BACKGROUND
The southern part of Florida depends on rain for fresh water. It receives a drenching 40 to 65 inches a year, largely from May to October. You may wish to ask students how this compares with the amount typically received in the area where you live. (They could get this information from a weather forecaster.)

PHOTO FLASH!
(1) This is a photo of Armando and Raquel, two video characters from Chapters 5 and 6.

SCIENCE LINK
Have students research the damaging effects of draining fresh water from the Everglades. (Draining fresh water allows saline sea water to flow into the Everglades and destroy the plant and animal life there.)

CAPÍTULO 5

5
El ritmo de la vida

(1) **Armando y Raquel dibujan en el parque en el verano.**

In a typical week, Spanish-speaking teens go to school and spend time with friends and family. In many ways, they're probably a lot like you. For example, they worry about the weather when planning weekends or vacations!

In this chapter you will learn

- to discuss how often you do things
- to talk about what you and your friends like to do together; to talk about what you do during a typical week
- to give today's date; to talk about the weather

And you will

- listen to people talk about how they spend their time at different seasons of the year
- read a weather map in Spanish
- write a diary entry about your weekly routine
- find out about the typical routines of several Spanish-speaking people

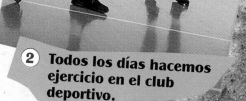

② **Todos los días hacemos ejercicio en el club deportivo.**

③ **¡Está lloviendo a cántaros!**

ciento ochenta y nueve **189**

FOCUSING ON OUTCOMES

- Have students look at the chapter outcomes and match them with the three photos. (Photo 1: talking about what you and your friends do together; Photo 2: discussing how often you do things; Photo 3: talking about the weather)
- Ask students to talk about their plans for this week and how often they plan to do certain events.
- Bring in the weather map and the forecast from a local newspaper to provide students with some first-hand information about what the weather will be in their area. Students can identify the expressions they will need to know in order to discuss the forecast in Spanish.
- Tell students that they will learn how to talk about these subjects in Spanish in this chapter.

SUGGESTION

③ You may want to teach your students **el impermeable** to discuss this photo.

LANGUAGE NOTE

A **cántaro** is a large, narrow-mouthed pitcher. Therefore the expression **está lloviendo a cántaros** is the equivalent of the English expression "it's raining cats and dogs," or "it's pouring."

VIDEO INTEGRATION

Adelante LEVEL 1A

Video Program,
Videocassette 2, 24:45–28:51 OR

¡Ven conmigo! LEVEL 1

Videodisc Program,
Videodisc 3A

Search 3650, Play To 11075

TEACHER NOTE

The **fotonovela** is an abridged version of the video episode.

VIDEO SYNOPSIS

In this episode, students in Miami prepare a news-broadcast program for their high school. They present a national weather forecast, interviews with students and a teacher about their free-time activities, and an interview with a new student. At the end of the episode, a problem with the camera interrupts the broadcast.

MOTIVATING ACTIVITY

Have students imagine that a reporter has stopped them on the street to interview them about their free-time activities. Have students make a list: What questions might the reporter ask? How might they answer?

DE ANTEMANO

¿Cómo es el ritmo de tu vida?

Cass. 3A
CD 5 Trs. 1–2

Look at the pictures in the **fotonovela.** Can you tell what Patricia, José Luis, and Raquel are doing? Where are they? Does something go wrong? How can you tell?

p. 51
Act. 1

Patricia **José Luis**

Raquel

RAQUEL ¡Hola! Raquel Villanueva a sus órdenes. Todos estamos aquí, en el colegio, durante las horas de clase. ¿Pero qué hacemos cuando no estamos aquí? Ramón... ¿qué haces por la tarde?

RAMÓN Bueno... los martes y los jueves, trabajo en el restaurante de mis padres. Y cuando no trabajo, hago la tarea o paso el rato con mis amigos.

PRESENTATION

Have students break into pairs before they read the **fotonovela** to discuss in detail the visual clues in the photos that help them predict what's going on. Then play the audio recording or read aloud the different characters' parts, having students repeat each character's lines after you as they read along in the book. Then have the students practice with each other, taking turns reading the parts of different characters in the story. Finally, play the video. Have students see if the predictions they made based on the visual cues in the photos were accurate.

RAQUEL ¿Qué tal, Anita y Josué? Dime, Anita... ¿qué haces típicamente los domingos?

ANITA Eh... todos los domingos, descanso y leo el periódico. Y Josué y yo siempre corremos juntos por la tarde.

RAQUEL Ah, ¿sí? ¿Y corren mucho?

JOSUÉ Sí, mucho. Nos gusta correr. ¡Pero en el verano no, porque hace demasiado calor!

LANGUAGE NOTES

- Ramón's pronunciation of **mis amigos** is an example of aspiration, pronouncing the final **-s** of a syllable as an **-h** or not pronouncing it at all. It is very common in many Spanish dialects.

- The expression **a sus órdenes** is a traditional way of saying *at your service*.

- Professor Williams speaks Spanish with an American-English accent.

RAQUEL Buenos días, profesor Williams. ¿Qué hace usted por la noche cuando está en casa?

PROFESOR WILLIAMS Bueno, Raquel...primero la señora Williams y yo preparamos la cena. Después, a veces escucho música o escribo cartas.

THINKING CRITICALLY

On a current weather map from a newspaper or from The Weather Channel Homepage (http://www.weather.com/twc/homepage.twc), ask students to locate a report on Miami. Is the weather in Miami today the same as it is in the **fotonovela**? You might have students also compare the weather in the additional locations mentioned in the **fotonovela** with the current weather in those places.

VIDEO INTEGRATION

Adelante LEVEL 1A
Video Program,
Videocassette 2, 28:52–33:24 OR
¡Ven conmigo! LEVEL 1
Videodisc Program,
Videodisc 3A

Search 11075, Play To 19250

VIDEO SYNOPSIS

In **A continuación,** the students resolve the camera problem that interrupted the show and clean up all the scattered papers as best they can. The next day Raquel and her friends show Armando the Vizcaya Gardens.

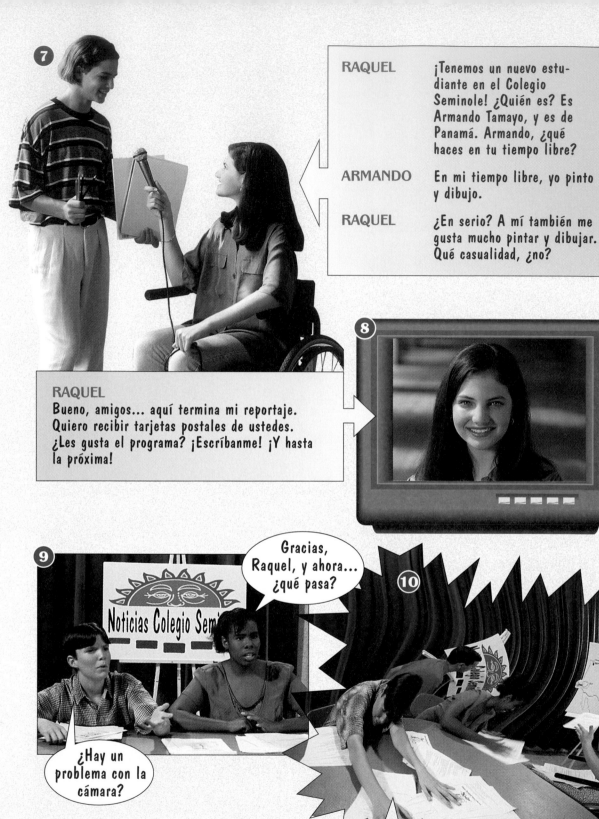

7

RAQUEL	¡Tenemos un nuevo estudiante en el Colegio Seminole! ¿Quién es? Es Armando Tamayo, y es de Panamá. Armando, ¿qué haces en tu tiempo libre?
ARMANDO	En mi tiempo libre, yo pinto y dibujo.
RAQUEL	¿En serio? A mí también me gusta mucho pintar y dibujar. Qué casualidad, ¿no?

RAQUEL
Bueno, amigos... aquí termina mi reportaje. Quiero recibir tarjetas postales de ustedes. ¿Les gusta el programa? ¡Escríbanme! ¡Y hasta la próxima!

8

9 Noticias Colegio Sem...

Gracias, Raquel, y ahora... ¿qué pasa?

10

¿Hay un problema con la cámara?

1 ¿Comprendes?

Answer the questions below. If you're not sure about what's happening in the **fotonovela**, make an educated guess!

1. What are the teenagers in the story doing? Filming a TV show.
2. What kind of report does José Luis give? A weather report.
3. What does Raquel do in her special report? She interviews people about free-time activities.
4. How do you think the crew will deal with the accident at the end of the broadcast? Answers will vary.

These activities check for global comprehension only. Students should not yet be expected to produce language modeled in **De antemano.**

2 ¿Cuál es la verdad?

For each pair of sentences below, choose the letter of the sentence that is true.

1. a. Patricia y José Luis están en Nueva York.
   (b.) Patricia y José Luis están en Miami.
2. (a.) Hace un poco de frío en Nueva York.
   b. Está lloviendo en Nueva York.
3. a. En su tiempo libre, Armando juega al voleibol.
   (b.) Armando pinta y dibuja en su tiempo libre.
4. (a.) Josué y Anita corren por la tarde.
   b. Josué y Anita trabajan en un restaurante.

3 ¿Cómo se dice?

Use the **fotonovela** to help you match a sentence in English with its corresponding sentence in Spanish.

1. to say the weather is nice c
2. to ask a friend what he or she usually does on Sundays d
3. to tell someone you write letters a
4. to tell someone you listen to music e
5. to say you spend time with your friends b

a. Escribo cartas.
b. Paso el rato con mis amigos.
c. Hace buen tiempo.
d. ¿Qué haces típicamente los domingos?
e. Escucho música.

VIDEO INTEGRATION

Adelante LEVEL 1A
Video Program,
Videocassette 2, 27:37–27:58 OR
¡Ven conmigo! LEVEL 1
Videodisc Program,
Videodisc 3A

Search 8856, Play To 9505

JUMP START!

To review material from Chapter 4, ask students to write five things they do in their free time. Next to each activity have them write how often they do it. (**Juego al baloncesto con mis amigos. Always.**)

 CULTURE NOTE
In small towns in many Latin American countries, communities pool their resources to build homes for one another. They also work together to improve the community by planting trees and flowers in central **plazas**. Lead a discussion about what the class could do together to benefit the school or the community.

LANGUAGE NOTE

In Mexico, kites are called **los papalotes**.

PRIMER PASO

Discussing how often you do things

RAQUEL	Buenos días, profesor Williams. ¿Qué hace usted por la noche cuando está en casa?
PROFESOR WILLIAMS	Bueno, Raquel... primero la señora Williams y yo preparamos la cena. Después, a veces escucho música o escribo cartas.

🌐 Nota cultural

In Spanish-speaking countries, young people and adults enjoy doing a variety of activities in their free time. Dominoes is a popular game throughout Latin America; it's common to see the game being played on the side of the street or in a **plaza** in small towns. **Plazas** are a great place to roller skate, or for a village to hold a dance. As in the United States, many activities depend on the weather. In windy weather, children often go out to fly kites (**volar cometas**). During hot weather, they swim. Is there a place in your neighborhood where people go to have fun? What activities are popular?

4 El profesor Williams

Write what Mr. Williams says he does when he gets home in the evenings.

preparamos la cena, escucho música, escribo cartas

CD-ROM
Disc 2

ASÍ SE DICE   Discussing how often you do things

PA
p. 52
Act. 2,
p. 54
Act. 7

To find out how often a friend does things, ask:

¿Con qué frecuencia desayunas?
How often do you eat breakfast?

¿Siempre organizas tu cuarto?
Do you always organize your room?

¿Y qué haces **durante la semana?**
And what do you do during the week?

¿Todavía tocas la guitarra?
Do you still play the guitar?

Your friend might respond:

Desayuno todos los días.
I eat breakfast every day.

Nunca organizo mi cuarto.
I never organize my room.

A veces cuido a mi hermano.
Sometimes I take care of my brother.

Muchas veces ayudo en casa.
Often I help at home.

Sí, pero **sólo cuando** no tengo tarea.
Yes, but only when I don't have homework.

Cass. 3A
CD 5 Tr. 3

5 El cine Script and answers on p. 187E

Listen as Teresa, Maité, and Carlos talk about what they do in their free time. Match each person with how often he or she participates in the activity.

1. Teresa practica el piano
2. Maité va al centro comercial
3. Carlos va al cine

a. todos los viernes.
b. muchas veces los sábados.
c. todos los sábados y miércoles.

6 ¿Qué haces tú durante la semana?

Write four sentences. Choose phrases from each word box to say what you do, and when, how often, and where you do each activity.

Answers will vary.

A veces
Todos los días
Los sábados (domingos,...)
Muchas veces
Todos los...
Nunca

desayuno
estudio matemáticas
practico la natación (el fútbol,...)
preparo la cena
voy al cine
compro...

en el centro comercial
en casa
en el colegio
en el parque
en la piscina
en ¿ ?

☀ MOTIVATE

Ask students how often they and their friends and family do different things such as have a cookout, or go to the beach or lake. Remind them that their answers may be fictional.

☀ TEACH

PRESENTATION
ASÍ SE DICE

Write the days of the week in Spanish on the board or on a transparency. Beneath each one list a few activities you do each day of the week. Write the new adverbs of frequency next to your weekly schedule. Describe to the class how often you do these different activities. Use only -**ar** verbs. Then have the students write sentences describing how often you do them. (**Usted siempre monta en bicicleta los sábados.**) Model the expressions by asking several questions and have students answer them. Then, have students ask and answer the questions in **Así se dice** with a partner.

SUGGESTION

5 Have students read these phrases as advance organizers.

SUGGESTIONS

Tira cómica First, ask your students to scan the comic for cognates and familiar words. What do they think is happening?

7 Have students write six statements of their own using **siempre, nunca, nada,** and **nadie.** Each writes three true statements and three false statements about what they like to do. Then, in pairs, one reads his or her statements and the other guesses whether they are **cierto** or **falso.** After guessing all six, the partners switch roles.

RE-ENTRY

Write these words on the board or on a transparency: **Siempre, Muchas veces, A veces, Nunca.** Ask students to use Chapter 4 vocabulary to write as many activities as they can under each heading. Then discuss what students always, often, sometimes, and never like to do.

CD-ROM Disc 2

PA
pp. 52–53
Acts. 3–5

GV
pp. 37–38
Acts. 1–3

GRAMÁTICA   Negation

In Chapter 2 you learned to make sentences negative by putting **no** before the verb. To say *never* or *not ever,* put **nunca** before the verb.

> **Nunca** tomo el autobús.   *I never take the bus.*

In Spanish, you'll often use **no** and **nunca** or **no** and **nada** together in the same sentence. In that case, be sure to put **no** in front of the verb, and **nunca** or **nada** after the verb.

> **No** tomo el autobús **nunca.**   *I never take the bus.*
> Los sábados **no** hago **nada.**   *On Saturdays I don't do anything.*

Another negative word is **nadie** *(no one).* It's always used with the **él** or **ella** form of the verb.

> **No** toca la guitarra **nadie.** }   *Nobody plays the guitar.*
> **Nadie** toca la guitarra.

7 ¿Cierto o falso? 🏠

Read the following sentences and respond **cierto** if the sentence is true or **falso** if it's false. Change the false sentences to make them true.   Answers will vary.

MODELO   Nadie habla inglés. (falso)
Nosotros hablamos inglés todos los días.

1. Nadie estudia español.
2. Nunca escuchamos música en las fiestas.
3. Siempre preparamos la cena en la clase de matemáticas.
4. Los profesores no bailan nunca.
5. Siempre hago mi tarea.
6. Nadie en esta clase tiene ropa amarilla.

Nunca practico la guitarra.

¡No es cierto! Practicas todas las tardes, ¿verdad?

8 Mi semana

What do you do during a typical week? Write six sentences using activities from the word box. Be sure to explain how often you do each activity. Answers will vary.

MODELO —Practico el basquetbol todos los días.

> tocar un instrumento
> ir al colegio
> escuchar música rock
> desayunar
> practicar un deporte
> pintar   ir al centro comercial
> cuidar a tu hermano/a

9 Una encuesta

Interview three classmates to find out how often they do the activities listed below. Your classmates will answer by using phrases from both columns. Answers will vary.

MODELO —¿Con qué frecuencia miras la televisión?
—Miro la televisión sólo cuando tengo tiempo.

Actividad	Frecuencia
practicar la natación	a veces
practicar el fútbol	sólo cuando tengo tiempo
ir al centro comercial	los lunes, los martes,...
patinar	los fines de semana
escuchar música	todos los días
hablar por teléfono	nunca

10 ¿Quién?

Look at the photographs. Then, for each activity below, write a sentence about who is doing it, or say if no one is doing the activity. Answers in side column

1. desayunar
2. estudiar
3. practicar el piano
4. hablar
5. escuchar
6. hablar por teléfono
7. practicar el béisbol
8. mirar la televisión
9. montar en bicicleta

Miguel

Graciela y Ana

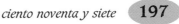

el señor Guzmán
y Adolfo

THINKING CRITICALLY

8 Ask students to imagine a list left by a parent or guardian asking the student to do three things immediately. Ask students to create such a note, using the activities from the word box. They can begin the list with **Necesitas...**

MATH LINK

9 After groups have completed their surveys, ask them to compile the results. Then ask each group to graph the results. Display the graphs labeled in Spanish for the entire class.

VISUAL LEARNERS

9 If you have access to a video camera, have students videotape one another interviewing classmates, or do the videotaping yourself. A good time to do this would be during a class **fiesta** or during group work.

Answers to Activity 10

1. Nadie desayuna./No desayuna nadie.
2. Graciela y Ana estudian.
3. Nadie practica el piano./No practica el piano nadie.
4. El señor Guzmán habla con Adolfo.
5. Adolfo escucha al señor Guzmán.
6. Nadie habla por teléfono./No habla por teléfono nadie.
7. Miguel practica el béisbol.
8. Nadie mira la televisión./No mira la televisión nadie.
9. Nadie monta en bicicleta. /No monta en bicicleta nadie.

¿Quiénes miran la televisión?
Roberto y Laura.

PA p. 54 Act. 6

GV p. 38 Act 4

NOTA GRAMATICAL

You've already learned the question word **¿quién?** *(who?).* **¿Quién?** is used to ask about one person. When asking about more than one person, use **¿quiénes?** Compare the two sentences below.

¿Quién es el chico rubio?
Who is the blond boy?

¿Quiénes son las chicas altas?
Who are the tall girls?

11 ¿Quiénes son?

Complete Sandra and Melisa's conversation during lunch in the cafeteria. Fill in the blanks with **quién** or **quiénes.**

SANDRA ¿___1___ es el chico con la ropa negra? Quién

MELISA Se llama Daniel. Es un estudiante nuevo.

SANDRA ¿Y ___2___ son las chicas que están cerca de la puerta? quiénes

MELISA Se llaman Sonia y Eva. Están en mi clase de ciencias. Oye, ¿ ___3___ van al cine hoy? quiénes

SANDRA María y yo. ¿Quieres ir?

MELISA Sí, claro. ¿Qué película van a ver?

SANDRA La nueva película de aventuras.

MELISA ¿___4___ es la estrella *(star)*? Quién

SANDRA Lupita Cárdenas. ¡Es excelente!

SUGERENCIA

At first, it's often hard to write in a foreign language. Remember that learning to write is like learning other skills in Spanish. Take it slowly, and go in small steps. Begin by writing short messages. For example, you can write brief reminders to yourself about what you need to do, or try writing out your weekly schedule in Spanish. Start now by making a list of three or four activities you usually do during a particular day—for example, on Mondays.

hoy
estudiar para el examen de ciencias
hablar por teléfono con Susana
practicar la guitarra
escuchar el disco compacto de José Miquel
montar en bicicleta con Raúl
sacar la basura

12 ¿Quién hace eso?

With a partner, take turns asking and answering questions about the people and activities shown in the drawings. Answers on p. 187K

MODELO   ¿Quiénes nadan en la piscina?
Julia y Silvia nadan en la piscina.

1. hablar / teléfono
2. preparar / la cena
3. caminar / por el parque
4. comprar / ropa

5. practicar / el fútbol
6. tocar / el piano
7. montar / bicicleta

Alejandra

Jaime

la señora Vivanco y Anita

Zoraida

tú y Sarah

Patty y yo

la señora Chávez
y Luis

13 ¿Tienes buena memoria?

Work in groups of four. On three slips of paper write the categories **siempre, a veces,** and **nunca.** Under each category write two activities. Next, shuffle the papers. Each person draws three slips and asks who does the activity that is written. Everyone tries to guess who wrote the activities on each slip.

MODELO   ¿Quién toca el piano siempre?

☀ CLOSE

On a small piece of paper, write activities and expressions of frequency. Make enough to give one to each student. List some activities only once and others on several pieces of paper with different adverbs of frequency. If you use **mirar la televisión,** ask **¿Quién no mira la televisión nunca?** Students with this activity and **nunca** raise their hands. Then have a student ask another question. (**¿Quién siempre escucha música?**)

☀ ASSESS

QUIZ 5-1
Testing Program, pp. 73–74
Audio Program,
 Audiocassette 4B OR
Audio CD 5 Track 17

PERFORMANCE ASSESSMENT

Ask students to write a letter in Spanish to a friend who is spending the year in Mexico. Ask them to include information about what three of their friends are doing this year including the day of the week or how often the friend does the activity. You may teach students the Spanish style of using numbers for the date. (25/01/03 = January 25, 2003). The letter might begin with **Querido/a** _____ and end with **Un saludo de** _____.

VIDEO INTEGRATION

Adelante LEVEL 1A
Video Program,
Videocassette 2, 33:25–35:42

TEACHER NOTES

- See *Video Guide* for activities related to the **Panorama cultural**.
- Remind students that cultural information may be included in the Quizzes and Chapter Test.
- The language of the people interviewed represents informal, unrehearsed speech. Occasionally, text has been edited for clarity.

MOTIVATING ACTIVITY

Ask students what they imagine the daily routines of teenagers in Spain and Latin America to be like. Do they think they are the same or different from their own? Why?

LANGUAGE NOTE

Point out that it's possible to use infinitives to list activities as Juan Fernando does.

Panorama cultural

CD-ROM
Disc 2

Cass. 3A
CD 5 Trs. 4–7

¿Cómo es una semana típica?

In this chapter, we asked some students what they usually do during the week and on weekends.

Verónica trabaja todos los fines de semana en casa. ¿Qué haces tú para ayudar en casa?

● **Verónica**
San Antonio, Texas
CD 5 Tr. 5

[Yo] hago mi tarea, estudio, como con mi familia, duermo... Cada sábado, tengo que organizar mi cuarto, entonces limpio la cocina.

Juan Fernando hace algunas actividades durante la semana y otras durante el fin de semana. ¿Qué haces tú los fines de semana?

● **Juan Fernando**
Quito, Ecuador
CD 5 Tr. 6

De lunes a viernes... ir al colegio, hacer las tareas y descansar un poco. Los sábados y domingos practico deportes.

Después de sus clases en el colegio, Bárbara toma una clase más. ¿Qué haces tú por la tarde?

● **Bárbara**
Sevilla, España
CD 5 Tr. 7

Pues, regreso a casa, almuerzo, después descanso un tiempo, estudio un par de horas, y seguidamente voy a danza clásica.

1 ¿Con quién come Verónica? Come con su familia.

2 ¿Cómo ayuda Verónica en casa los sábados? Limpia su cuarto y limpia la cocina.

3 ¿Qué hace Juan Fernando los fines de semana? Practica los deportes.

4 ¿Qué hace Juan Fernando después del colegio? Descansa y hace las tareas.

5 ¿Adónde va Bárbara a comer durante la semana? Va a comer en casa.

6 ¿Qué hace Bárbara después del almuerzo? Estudia y va a la clase de danza.

Para pensar y hablar... Answers will vary.
A. Look at all three interviews again. See if you can find three things they **all** do that you also do during the week or on the weekend. What are they?
B. Two of the interviewees mention relaxing during the week. Is your weekly schedule busy? Do you have time to relax? Why or why not?

VIDEO INTEGRATION

Adelante LEVEL 1A
Video Program,
Videocassette 2, 27:12–27:36 OR
¡Ven conmigo! LEVEL 1
Videodisc Program,
Videodisc 3A

Search 8106, Play To 8855

JUMP START!

Before class, write several phrases from Chapter 4 on the board or on a transparency. Put blanks in for some of the letters. Have students complete them. (m _ _ ta _ _n _i _ _ cl_t_ = montar en bicicleta)

MOTIVATING ACTIVITY

Write the following questions on the board: **¿Quiénes hacen ejercicio? ¿Quiénes van a la biblioteca? ¿Quiénes van al centro comercial los sábados?** Students need to copy them down then write their answers.

CHALLENGE

Write some well-known Spanish sayings without the English equivalents on the board before class. **Lo bueno, si breve, dos veces bueno.** *Keep it short and sweet.* **Querer es poder.** *Where there's a will, there's a way.* **Más ven cuatro ojos que dos.** *Two heads are better than one.* Ask if students can figure out what some of the words mean and if they can think of the English equivalents.

SEGUNDO PASO

Talking about what you and your friends like to do together; talking about what you do during a typical week

RAQUEL	¿Qué tal, Anita y Josué? Dime, Anita... ¿qué haces típicamente los domingos?
ANITA	Eh... todos los domingos, descanso y leo el periódico. Y Josué y yo siempre corremos juntos por la tarde.
RAQUEL	Ah, ¿sí? ¿Y corren mucho?
JOSUÉ	Sí, mucho. Nos gusta correr. ¡Pero en el verano no, porque hace demasiado calor!

14 ¿Qué hacen?

Complete each sentence with one of the words below, according to what Anita, Raquel, and Josué say. Two words will not be used.

1. Los domingos Anita ———. descansa
2. Anita y Josué siempre ——— por la tarde. corren
3. Anita dice *(says):* "Josué y yo siempre corremos ——— por la tarde". juntos
4. ¿Qué haces ——— los domingos? típicamente

típicamente   juntos   verano   calor   corren   descansa

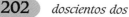

ASÍ SE DICE

Talking about what you and your friends like to do together

So far, you've been using **gustar** with the pronouns **me**, **te**, and **le** to talk about what just one person likes and dislikes.

To find out what a group of your friends likes to do, ask:

Your friends might answer:

¿Qué **les gusta** hacer, chicos?
What do you guys like to do?

Nos gusta hacer ejercicio o correr por la playa.
We like to exercise or run on the beach.

¿**Les gusta acampar y pescar?**
Do you like to camp and fish?

Sí, **especialmente** durante **las vacaciones.**
Yes, especially on vacation.

Y a los señores Bello, ¿**les gusta esquiar?**
And Mr. and Mrs. Bello, do they like to ski?

No sé, pero les gusta **bucear juntos.**
I don't know, but they like to scuba dive together.

PA
pp. 55–56
Acts. 8–10

GV
p. 39
Act. 5

5-2

15 Mejores amigos
Script and answers on p. 187E

Cass. 3A
CD 5 Tr. 8

Gloria is interviewing Carlos and Eddie on the radio about sports. Listen to their interview. Then match the people that like each sport with the photo of that sport.

1. Carlos
2. Eddie
3. Carlos y Eddie
4. Nadie

a   b   c   d

MOTIVATE

Tell students to imagine they have just met a group of teenagers from Chile who speak no English. Have students jot down in English what types of questions they might want to ask the visitors. What would they want to be able to say to them in Spanish?

TEACH

PRESENTATION
ASÍ SE DICE
Ask individual volunteers **¿Qué te gusta hacer?** Then begin asking groups of students or the entire class **¿Qué les gusta hacer?** Elicit responses from them by acting out swimming, dancing, etc. Point to everyone and yourself and say **Nos gusta (nadar, bailar, etc.).**

SUGGESTION
Have students do a find-your-twin activity. Pass out two sets of cards with the verbs from **Así se dice.** Students must go around the room asking and responding to the question **¿Qué te gusta hacer?** until they find the student with the identical verb. Then ask each pair **¿Qué les gusta hacer?**

16 Elena y su abuelo

Elena is telling Manuel about her vacation with her grandparents. Look at this drawing and fill in the blanks to complete the conversation. Use the words in the word box.

ELENA Cuando estoy con mis abuelos, ___1___ gusta acampar.

MANUEL ¿Dónde acampas?

ELENA Cerca del río *(river)*. A mi abuelo y a mí nos gusta ___2___. Pero mi abuela ___3___ pesca.

MANUEL Pues, ¿tú y tu abuelo pescan ___4___?

ELENA Sí, mis vacaciones con ellos ___5___ son buenas.

Answers in side column

word box: nos   juntos   pescar   siempre   nunca

GV
p. 39
Act. 6

5-A

VOCABULARIO

asistir a una clase de ejercicios aeróbicos

beber agua o jugo

comer un sándwich o una hamburguesa con papas fritas

leer las tiras cómicas en el periódico

escribir tarjetas postales

recibir cartas

17 Pienso en...

Write a verb that corresponds to each item. Some phrases may have more than one possible answer. Be prepared to explain your choices. Answers on p. 187K

MODELO la tarea de inglés—escribir

1. una carta a...
2. una pizza
3. una revista
4. un jugo de frutas
5. un concierto de música rock
6. una ensalada

18 ¿Qué les gusta hacer?

Tell what you and your friends like to do at each of these times and places. For each answer, choose at least one item from the **Vocabulario** on page 204. Answers will vary.

MODELO después de correr
Después de correr, nos gusta descansar y beber jugo.

1. en el tiempo libre
2. el sábado por la tarde
3. después de la clase de ejercicios aeróbicos
4. después de escribir cartas
5. en el gimnasio después de las clases

19 Preferencias

Work in pairs. Using the cues, ask a series of questions to find out which activities your partner likes to do and how often (**con qué frecuencia**). Switch roles after three questions. Be prepared to tell the class what you learned. For activities you both like to do, use **nos gusta.** Answers will vary.

MODELO correr: playa / parque
—¿Te gusta correr por la playa o por el parque?
—Bueno, me gusta correr por el parque pero no me gusta correr por la playa.
—¿Y con qué frecuencia? ¿Todos los días?
—No, sólo a veces.

1. escribir: cartas / tarjetas postales
2. recibir: notas de amigos / cartas de tu abuela
3. comer: ensalada / un sándwich
4. leer: revistas / periódico
5. asistir: a clases / a un concierto de...
6. beber: jugo / agua

¿Te gusta correr por la playa?

doscientos cinco 205

ADDITIONAL PRACTICE
Have volunteers call out infinitives from **Vocabulario** on page 204. The class responds with the corresponding noun. For example, the volunteer says **leer,** and the class says **el periódico.**

ADDITIONAL PRACTICE
18 Have students work in pairs to find three things that they both like to do. Then have the pairs interview each other by asking each other what they like to do. Have the pairs practice these plural forms for about three minutes.

SUGGESTIONS
19 Divide the class into teams..Use a big clock or draw one on the board. Ask a student what he or she likes to do at the indicated time. The student pantomimes the action, as students from the same team guess what activity is being acted out. The team earns a point if they guess correctly. For example: **Le gusta hablar por teléfono a las nueve.**

19 Encourage students to add personalized information to their answers. For example, **Me gusta leer revistas de deportes.**

CHALLENGE
Ask students to create a **tira cómica** that incorporates vocabulary from this chapter.

206

PRESENTATION

NOTA GRAMATICAL

Model ¿**Qué les gusta hacer?**
and have the class repeat
after you. Assign one group
of students to pretend to be
Chilean visitors. Have the
other group make up ques-
tions for them using those in
the **Nota gramatical** as
examples. Model answers
to the questions. Then have
the group ask the Chilean
visitors ¿**A ustedes les gusta
nadar?** Each visitor gives a
thumbs up or thumbs down
to vote on what the group's
answer will be. If the majority
vote yes, they say in unison,
Sí, nos gusta nadar, and if
not, **No, no nos gusta nadar.**

ADDITIONAL PRACTICE

20 In pairs, have students
write similar questions for
various members of their class.
They should circulate around
the room asking their classmates questions. Then have
students explain what their
fiesta ideal is like.

GV
p. 40
Act. 7

NOTA GRAMATICAL

Look at the examples in the **Así se dice** box on page 203. Notice that the same pronoun, **les,** can be used to mean both *to them* and *to you* (plural). The phrases **a ustedes** and **a ellos** or **a ellas** are some-times added for clarification or emphasis.

Look at the literal translations of these questions.

> ¿**A ustedes les gusta nadar?**
> *Is swimming pleasing to you?*

> ¿**A ellos les gusta preparar la cena juntos?**
> *Is preparing dinner together pleasing to them?*

What would the nonliteral English translations be?[1]

¿A ustedes les gusta el videojuego nuevo?

A los amigos de Maritza les gusta pasar el rato juntos.

20 Necesitas preguntarle a...

You're in charge of planning a party at your local recreation center. Your neighbor señora Sánchez knows everybody better than you. Write how you would ask her if the following people would like some of the refreshments and activities you had in mind. Answers on page 187K

MODELO A Cristina y a Rodrigo — videojuegos
¿A ellos les gusta practicar los videojuegos?

1. A Norma y a Susana — deportes
2. A los señores Silva *(Mr. and Mrs. Silva)* — música clásica
3. A Beto y a Carlos
   — bailar en las fiestas
4. A Adriana y a Paco
   — la comida china
5. A la señora Bello
   — el jugo de frutas
6. A ustedes — la música pop

---

[1] *Do you like to swim? Do they like to fix dinner together?*

GRAMÁTICA -er and -ir verbs

p. 56
Act. 11

pp. 40–41
Acts.
8–10

1. In Chapter 4 you learned how to conjugate -ar verbs, such as **hablar**. Now look at the conjugation of **comer** to see how -er verbs work.

(yo)	com**o**	(nosotros)(nosotras)	com**emos**
(tú)	com**es**	(vosotros)(vosotras)	com**éis**
(usted)(él)(ella)	com**e**	(ustedes)(ellos)(ellas)	com**en**

2. Escribir is a regular -ir verb.

escrib**o**	escrib**imos**
escrib**es**	escrib**ís**
escrib**e**	escrib**en**

3. You already know the verb **ver**. It is regular except in the (**yo**) form.

v**eo**	v**emos**
v**es**	v**eis**
v**e**	v**en**

21 De vacaciones en Miami

Match the following people with what they do when they go to Miami.

1. Carolina d   a. como mucha comida cubana *(Cuban)*.
2. Yo a   b. corremos por la playa.
3. Esteban y yo b   c. escriben tarjetas postales a mis abuelos.
4. Mamá y papá c   d. lee libros románticos.

22 ¿Qué hacen?

Tell your partner what the following people do during their free time. Use the correct form of the verbs in the word box.   Answers will vary.

1. Tu mejor amigo/a y tú
2. Tus padres
3. Una estrella de cine *(choose a movie star's name)*
4. Tu profesor/a
5. Tú

comer   leer

asistir a   correr

recibir   escribir

PRESENTATION
GRAMÁTICA

To practice these verb forms begin by asking a student **¿Qué comes?** The student answers **Como un sándwich.** Then ask another student **¿Qué come él?** and that student responds **Come un sándwich.** To practice plural forms, ask two students **Juan y Gloria, ¿qué comen ustedes?** Juan and Gloria answer together **Comemos un sándwich.** Ask **¿Qué comen ellos?** Students answer **Comen un sándwich.** Repeat the pattern with **escribir**, then have students ask and answer each other to use all of the forms.

THINKING CRITICALLY

Ask students which two endings are not identical for both types of verbs.

VISUAL/KINESTHETIC LEARNERS

22 Conjugate six verbs for each pronoun and write the verbs and pronouns on notecards. Distribute the notecards to the students and then read a sentence in English. Students with the cards **tú** and **lees** move to the front of the room as the class checks their answer. Practice this several times with all the cards.

23 ¡Todos juntos!

 For each photo, write a sentence describing what the people are doing and how often they do this activity. Use the phrases in the **Vocabulario extra** box below.   Answers on p. 187K

1. ustedes

2. tú y tu familia

3. nosotros

4. la señora Pérez

5. ellas

6. Elisa

VOCABULARIO EXTRA

de vez en cuando   *once in a while*

todo el tiempo   *all the time*

a menudo   *often*

pocas veces   *not very often*

cada (dos, tres...) dias   *every (two, three . . .) days*

tres veces por semana   *three times a week*

Nota cultural

Spending time with a group of friends is an important part of life for young teens in the Spanish-speaking world. It's more common to meet friends in public than at one's house. People often get together in parks and cafés. The streets of many Spanish-speaking towns are usually lively, and often crowded, both day and night. Where do you spend time with your friends?

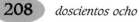

ASÍ SE DICE Talking about what you do during a typical week

PA
p. 57
Act. 12

5-1

To find out what your friends typically do during the week, ask:

Some responses might be:

¿Qué haces **típicamente** durante el día?

Asisto a clases, trabajo y paso el rato con amigos.

¿Qué hace Josué **por la mañana?**
What does Josué do in the morning?

Corre **dos millas** por la playa.
He runs two miles on the beach.

¿Hacen ustedes ejercicio juntos?

Sí, pero sólo **por la tarde.**
Yes, but only in the afternoon.

¿Y qué hacen Raquel y Anita **por la noche?**
And what do Raquel and Anita do at night?

A veces van a un restaurante.

24 Un día típico Script and answers on p. 187E

Cass. 3A
CD 5 Tr. 9

Listen as Miguel's mother describes a typical day in his life. Look at each drawing and answer **cierto** if it shows what she says. If the drawing doesn't represent what she says, answer **falso**.

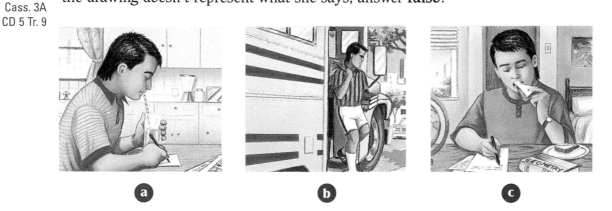

a   b   c

25 Por la mañana...

Raquel is a newscaster for her school's radio show. While preparing for a broadcast about what she does on a typical day, Raquel got her script notes all mixed up. Help put what she says in the correct order. Write the letters in order on your paper. d, b, c, a

a. A veces comemos en un restaurante por la noche.
b. Típicamente, asisto a mis clases por la mañana.
c. Leo cartas de mis amigas por la tarde.
d. Antes de ir al colegio, bebo mucho jugo con mi desayuno.

SUGGESTIONS

26 Remind students that **tú** questions and **yo** answers should be included. Practice of these forms will help them prepare for Activity 28 as well.

27 Have students exchange postcards with a partner and write a note answering their partner's card.

NATIVE SPEAKERS

Some native speakers from the Southwestern United States say **nadien** for **nadie**. Explain that **nadien** is an archaism, in this case a word from an older form of Spanish that has been replaced by **nadie** in standard speech. This is an example of what happens when language speakers are isolated over a long period of time from the changes that occur in the standard form of the language.

26 ¿Quién lo hace?

Work in small groups. Try to identify at least one person in your partners' circle of friends who does each of the activities listed. Then find out how often each person does the activity. Take notes, and try to find activities that your friends have in common. If nobody does the activity, use **nadie** in your answer.

MODELO —Juana, ¿quién lee revistas? *Answers will vary.*
—Nadie, pero Juan lee el periódico todos los días porque le gustan los deportes.

leer: revistas, las tiras cómicas, el periódico, novelas

escribir: poemas, cartas, tarjetas postales

comer: ensaladas, fruta, hamburguesas

correr: en el parque, después de clases, cinco millas

VOCABULARIO EXTRA

los poemas *poems*
los cuentos de aventuras *adventure stories*
la ciencia ficción *science fiction*
el misterio *mystery*

27 La tarjeta

Pretend that you're writing a postcard to a close friend who is on vacation. Write at least three sentences about activities that you're doing.

¡Anímate a escribir!

Una tarjeta postal

No escribes de maravilla, vale. Pero muchos de tus *compas* se han ido de vacaciones y una tarjeta postal les demostrará que te acuerdas de ellos.

Enviar noticias de vez en cuando.

Un diario

Una poesía

28 ¿Cómo pasas tú los días?

Interview a partner to find out how he or she spends a typical weekday. Ask about morning, afternoon, and evening activities. Switch roles and answer your partner's questions about a typical weekend morning, afternoon, or evening. Be prepared to tell the class two of your partner's activities.

MODELO —¿Qué haces los lunes por la mañana?
—Los lunes asisto al colegio y hablo con mis amigos.
—Mirla asiste al colegio los lunes y habla con sus amigos.

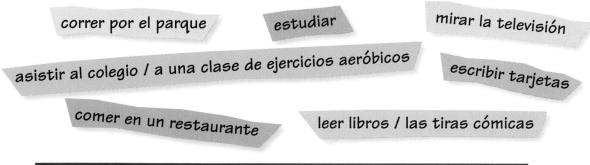

correr por el parque

estudiar

mirar la televisión

asistir al colegio / a una clase de ejercicios aeróbicos

escribir tarjetas

comer en un restaurante

leer libros / las tiras cómicas

Hablo con mis amigos todos los sábados.

29 Los sábados [H]

With whom do you usually spend Saturdays? Write a paragraph about things you typically do on Saturday. Be sure to tell what time of day it is when you do each activity, and who does each activity with you. Use the expressions in the word box to help you write.

siempre
especialmente
típicamente
primero
nunca
por fin
a veces

luego
después
vamos a
nos gusta

SUGGESTION
28 To practice negation, vary Activity 28 so that students explain what they don't do on weekdays and weekends. **(En el colegio no miro la televisión, no escucho música... Los fines de semana nunca tengo clases...)**

☀ CLOSE

Ask students to form groups. Give each group a list of several activities. Have students divide the activities into three categories—**por la mañana, por la tarde,** and **por la noche**—according to the time of day that they do each. Ask a spokesperson for each group to report when the activities are done.

☀ ASSESS

QUIZ 5-2
Testing Program, pp. 75–76
Audio Program,
Audiocassette 4B OR
Audio CD 5 Track 18

PERFORMANCE ASSESSMENT
Ask each student to make a daily planner for the coming weekend. Ask them to list the day of the week and use **por la mañana, por la tarde,** or **por la noche** with any activity they plan for that day.

VIDEO INTEGRATION

Adelante LEVEL 1A
Video Program,
Videocassette 2, 25:41–26:30 OR
¡Ven conmigo! LEVEL 1
Videodisc Program,
Videodisc 3A

Search 5365, Play To 6849

JUMP START!

On the board or a transparency, write several simple addition and subtraction problems using numbers in written form from **uno** to **treinta y uno.** Have students solve the problems and write the answers in Spanish.

VISUAL LEARNERS

30 Have students cover José Luis's speech bubble and answer the questions by looking at the weather map.

☀ MOTIVATE

Ask students to list five dates that are important to them and to explain why.

TERCER PASO

Giving today's date; talking about the weather

Pero primero, ¿qué tiempo hace? Aquí en Miami, hace buen tiempo. Hace mucho sol. En Nueva York, hace un poco de frío... Y en Texas, está lloviendo... ¡a cántaros!

Nota cultural

In many parts of the tropics, weather reports are uncommon. There is little variety in weather from day to day. Because there is little change in temperature over the course of the year, people don't rely on a forecast to figure out what to wear. However, during hurricane season in the Caribbean, people pay close attention to warnings. Do you listen to weather forecasts regularly? Do you adjust what you plan to wear or do based on the forecast?

30 ¿Qué tiempo hace?

Fill in the blanks to complete what José Luis says about the weather.

1. En Texas, está ———— a cántaros.
2. En Miami, hace mucho ————.
3. En Nueva York, hace un poco de

————.

1. lloviendo
2. sol
3. frío

ASÍ SE DICE Giving today's date

p. 58
Act. 14

To find out today's date, ask:

¿Cuál es la fecha?
¿Qué fecha es hoy?

To give today's date, say:

Hoy es el primero de diciembre.
Today is the first of December.

Es el quince de enero.
It's the fifteenth of January.

To tell on what date something happens, say:

El cuatro de este mes hay un examen.
On the fourth of this month there's a test.

NOTA GRAMATICAL

The formula for giving today's date is **el** + *number* + **de** + *month:* **el quince de junio.** The first day of the month is called **el primero.** Note that in Spanish no preposition is needed in expressions like *on the fifth.*

La fiesta es el cinco.
The party is on the fifth.

pp. 42–43
Acts. 12–14

31 ¿Qué fecha es hoy? Script and answers on p. 187F

Listen and match the date you hear with the correct drawing.

Cass. 3A
CD 5 Tr. 10

32 Las fechas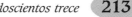

Complete each sentence with the correct date. Answers will vary.

1. La Navidad *(Christmas)* es...
2. Mi cumpleaños es...
3. El Día de los Enamorados *(Valentine's Day)* es...
4. El cumpleaños de mi mamá es...
5. El primer día del año *(year)* es...
6. El Día de la Independencia *(Independence Day)* es...
7. El cumpleaños de mi mejor *(best)* amigo/a es...

PA
pp. 58–59
Acts. 13, 15

GV
p. 42
Act. 11

5-B

VOCABULARIO

CD-ROM
Disc 2

PRESENTATION

VOCABULARIO

Use Transparency 5-B or pictures from magazines to represent the four seasons as you ask what season it is. Have students read the **Nota cultural** on page 215. Then write four sentences on the board or a transparency. (**Los meses de verano son...**, and so on for each season) Ask students to complete each statement for the Northern then for the Southern Hemisphere.

ADDITIONAL PRACTICE

Have students write their birthdate in Spanish on one side of a card and their name on the other. Collect the cards and have a volunteer shuffle and pass them out. Call on students to ask the first question using the date on their paper: **¿Quién cumple años el... de...?** The student recognizing his or her birthday answers **Yo cumplo años el... de...** If no one answers, the student asks individual students until he or she finds the right person.

la primavera
- marzo
- abril
- mayo

el verano
- junio
- julio
- agosto

el otoño
- septiembre
- octubre
- noviembre

el invierno
- diciembre
- enero
- febrero

◆ El otoño es una estación.
◆ Hay cuatro estaciones en un año.

◆ Octubre es un mes.
◆ Hay doce meses en un año.

33 Actividades

What do you usually do during various seasons of the year? Write a sentence for each season by combining words and phrases from each column. Answers will vary.

MODELO En el verano voy a la playa.

En el invierno
En la primavera
En el verano
En el otoño

hacer ejercicio
comer
nadar
montar en bicicleta
bucear
estudiar
beber agua
leer

en el colegio
en el gimnasio
en el parque
en la cafetería
en la playa
en la biblioteca
en el centro comercial

34 ¿Cuál es la fecha?

Make a list of five dates, including at least one from each season. Then read them to your partner one at a time. Your partner will tell you what season each is in, and at least one activity he or she associates with that time of year.

MODELO —Es el treinta de abril.
—Es la primavera y juego al béisbol.

Es el 3 de enero. La familia Sánchez juega en la playa en Puerto Rico.

Es el 27 de julio. Mi amigo Daniel esquía en las montañas de Chile.

Nota cultural

The seasons in the southern part of South America are opposite to the seasons north of the equator. In the south, summer begins in December and winter begins in June. The tropical region of South America, which is on or near the equator, has only two seasons: rainy and dry. In the equatorial lowlands the temperature stays warm all year round. However, in the mountains near the equator (such as the Andes), it is generally cool and often gets quite cold. The temperature is determined by altitude rather than by latitude. Look at the dates on the photos. What is the weather like on those dates where you live?

35 Las estaciones

Pretend that you live in the following places. Write what season it is. You may want to look at the maps on pages xviii–xx.

MODELO Es el 12 de noviembre. Estoy en Sacramento, California. **Es el otoño.**

1. Es el 7 de julio. Estoy en Buenos Aires, Argentina. Es el invierno.
2. Es el 8 de agosto. Estoy en Chicago, Illinois. Es el verano.
3. Es el 23 de diciembre. Estoy en Asunción, Paraguay. Es el verano.
4. Es el 2 de mayo. Estoy in Portland, Oregón. Es la primavera.
5. Es el 22 de septiembre. Estoy en Montevideo, Uruguay. Es la primavera.
6. Es el 30 de octubre en Albuquerque, Nuevo México. Es el otoño.

ADDITIONAL PRACTICE
34 Have students look at the maps at the beginning of the book and then write similar sentences. Their partner writes what season it is.

SUGGESTION
35 Tell students that in Argentina and Chile fall begins March 20 or 21; winter begins June 21 or 22; spring begins September 22 or 23; summer begins December 22 or 23.

THINKING CRITICALLY
Explain latitude and longitude to students. (latitude lines run side to side and longitude run up and down) Ask if altitude or latitude has more effect on the weather in Latin America. (altitude, especially in the Andes and other high mountains)

GEOGRAPHY LINK
35 Using the dates from this activity, have students write a short report about the weather in Cuzco, Peru; in Guadalajara, Mexico; or in San Juan, Puerto Rico.

SCIENCE LINK
Ask students to explain why the seasons occur at opposite times of the year in the Southern and Northern Hemispheres. (Due to tilt of the earth's axis, sunlight is more direct in the Southern Hemisphere in December and more direct in the Northern Hemisphere in June.)

5-3

ASÍ SE DICE   Talking about the weather

To find out what the weather is like, ask:

To answer, say:

¿Qué tiempo hace?

Hace buen tiempo.
Hace muy mal tiempo hoy.

PA
pp. 59–60
Acts.
16–18

GV
p. 44
Acts.
15–16

5-C

VOCABULARIO

CD-ROM
Disc 2

Hace frío.

Hace sol.

Hace fresco.

Está nevando. / Nieva.

Está lloviendo. / Llueve.

Hace viento.

Hace calor.

Está nublado.

36 ¿Qué tiempo hace?

Get together with a partner. Take turns asking and answering what the weather is usually like where you live during the following months and seasons. Answers will vary.

MODELO   —¿Qué tiempo hace en diciembre?
—Hace mucho frío y nieva.

1. julio
2. la primavera
3. octubre
4. marzo
5. el verano
6. febrero
7. agosto
8. el otoño

37 El pronóstico del tiempo

Look at the weather map and match the weather to the corresponding city. Each city can match with more than one kind of weather.

Hace (mucho) frío.　　　Hace (mucho) calor.

−10s −0s　0s　10s　20s　30s　40s　50s　60s　70s　80s　90s　100s 110s

Está nevando. / Nieva.

Portland

Great Falls

Fargo

Está lloviendo.
Llueve.

Milwaukee

Chicago

Nueva York

Sacramento

Denver

Hace (mucho) viento.

Los Angeles

Yuma

Hace sol.

Shreveport

Montgomery

San Antonio

Miami

1. En Miami...　a, c, d, h
2. En Nueva York...　i
3. En Fargo...　g
4. En Sacramento...　a, c, d, h
5. En Shreveport...　a, c
6. En Chicago...　e

a. hace sol y hace buen tiempo.
b. está lloviendo.
c. hace buen tiempo.
d. hace calor y hace sol.
e. hace viento.
f. hace mucho frío.
g. hace frío y está nevando.
h. hace calor.
i. hace fresco.

VOCABULARIO EXTRA

¡Hace un frío tremendo!
It's incredibly cold!

¡Hace un calor espantoso!
It's terribly hot!

Está lloviendo a cántaros.
It's raining cats and dogs.

Hace un tiempo precioso.
It's a beautiful day.

38 Cuando hace calor... 🏠

Elsa lives in Santiago de Chile. Read a part of the letter she wrote to her pen pal in Albany, New York. Then say if the sentences about the letter are true or false. Correct the false statements.
Answers on p. 187K

Hola Ricardo,

Hace mucho calor este verano. Voy con mi amiga Sonia a la piscina todos los días. A veces los fines de semana voy con mi familia a la playa. Nos gusta acampar. Cuando acampamos en la playa corro por la mañana antes de desayunar. A esa hora no hace mucho calor.

Y tú, ¿cómo estás? Vemos en la televisión que hace muy mal tiempo donde tú vives. ¿Está nevando mucho? ¿Te gusta esquiar?

1. It's summer in Santiago.
2. Ricardo probably will go swimming in a lake after school today.
3. Elsa likes to camp on the beach.
4. Elsa likes to run when it's hot.

39 ¿Qué haces cuando...?

Find out what your partner does in the following kinds of weather. Be prepared to report your findings to the class. Answers will vary.

MODELO —¿Qué haces cuando hace calor?
—Cuando hace calor descanso en el parque y bebo muchos refrescos.

40 En mi cuaderno

Write two paragraphs describing your favorite season and explain why you like it. First, tell what the months are in that season and describe the weather. In the second paragraph, write about the activities that you and your friends like to do, and any special places where you go at that time. Answers will vary.

En el verano, a Mireli y a sus hermanos les gusta jugar a las cartas en la playa.

LETRA Y SONIDO

Script on p. 187F

Cass. 3A
CD 5
Trs. 11–15

A. One purpose of accent marks is to show which syllable to stress.

1. Words ending in a vowel, **n,** or **s** are stressed on the next to the last syllable.

examen	hablan	discos	toma	quiero

2. Words ending in any consonant besides **n** or **s** are stressed on the last syllable.

animal	feliz	Madrid	hablar

3. Exceptions to rules 1 and 2 get an accent mark over the syllable to be stressed.

semáforo	lápices	rápido	lámpara	música	Víctor	suéter

4. All question words have an accent mark.

¿qué?	¿cuándo?	¿quién?	¿cómo?	¿cuánto?	¿dónde?

B. Some words have an accent mark to tell them apart from a similar word.

mi *my*	mí *me*	tu *your*	tú *you*	si *if*	sí *yes*

C. Dictado

Listen and read the phone conversation, and rewrite the words that need accent marks.

Voy al almacen hoy porque necesito una camara nueva. Pero, ¿donde esta mi sueter? ¿Y el cinturon para mi falda? Ah, aqui estan. ¿Tu quieres ir conmigo?

D. Trabalenguas

Tin marín dedós pingüé, cúcara, mácara, tútere fue

EN MI CUADERNO

40 For an additional journal entry suggestion, see *Practice and Activity Book,* page 79.

PORTFOLIO

40 **Written** This is an appropriate portfolio entry. For portfolio suggestions, see *Alternative Assessment Guide,* p. 16.

KINESTHETIC LEARNERS

Letra y sonido Have students gesture where the accent falls as they say the words.

☀ CLOSE

Read statements and ask students to illustrate each. **Es el invierno, hace frío y nieva mucho. Hace sol y mi amigo y yo nadamos.**

☀ ASSESS

QUIZ 5-3
Testing Program, pp. 77–78
Audio Program,
Audiocassette 4B OR
Audio CD 5 Track 19

PERFORMANCE ASSESSMENT

Ask pairs of students to role-play the following: One is a cousin from Argentina visiting the United States. The Argentinean asks about the weather and what they usually do in order to know what to bring. The cousin from the U.S. asks when the cousin plans to come in order to describe the weather.

LAS CIENCIAS SOCIALES

Los calendarios   Most of the days of the week in Spanish come from Latin. Look at the chart to see the roots of the Spanish words. Then answer the questions that follow.

lunes	martes	miércoles	jueves	viernes	sábado	domingo
Latin: *lunae*	Latin: *Martis*	Latin: *Mercurii*	Latin: *Jovis*	Latin: *Veneris*	Hebrew: *shabbat*	Latin: *dominus*
moon	Mars: Roman god of war	Mercury: Roman messenger of the gods	Jupiter: Roman king of the gods	Venus: Roman goddess of love	sabbath	Lord's day

1 Los planetas
¿Qué planeta corresponde a cada día de la semana?

1. viernes b   **3.** jueves a   **a.** Júpiter   **c.** Mercurio

2. miércoles c   **4.** martes d   **b.** Venus   **d.** Marte

2 El calendario azteca

The Aztec Sun Calendar, the **xihuital** (shee-wee-TAL) or "count of the years," is similar to ours. Both are 365 days long, the number of days it takes the earth to orbit the sun. The **xihuital,** however, has 18 months of 20 days each, with extra "unlucky days" at the end of the year.

1. Can you find the ring on the Sun Calendar that represents the twenty days?

2. Since 18 months of 20 days each do not add up to 365 days, what is the number of "unlucky days" at the end of the year?

1. The ring is the next circle out from the center face.
2. 5 days

LAS CIENCIAS

El huracán Hurricanes are violent tropical thunderstorms with extremely heavy rains and high wind speeds of up to 186 mph. Hurricanes usually occur in the Atlantic Ocean, the Gulf of Mexico, and the Caribbean Sea between June 1 and November 30. During the worst hurricanes, streets become rivers, whole cities lose their electricity, and people must sometimes leave their homes and go to higher ground. The word *hurricane* comes from *hurakán,* the storm god of the Caribbean Taino Indians.

Floods from Hurricane Gert in Tampico, Mexico

▷ 3 ¿Dónde están los huracanes?

Use the information in the table to track Hurricane Dolly on graph paper. Draw a line connecting the points of the hurricane's path. Put a dot on the map where the latitudes and longitudes listed cross on your graph. Find out which country it hit. See the example of Hurricane Hortense drawn on the chart. Dolly struck Mexico.

Day	Latitude	Longitude
1	19° N	88° W
2	19.5° N	90° W
3	21° N	95° W
4	22° N	99° W

Hurricane Dolly

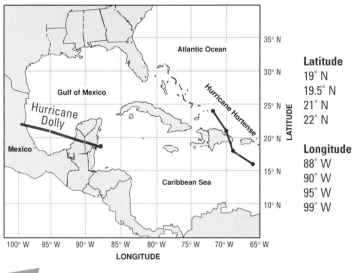

Latitude
19° N
19.5° N
21° N
22° N

Longitude
88° W
90° W
95° W
99° W

▷ 4 ¿Cómo se llama?

Each tropical storm of the season is given a name. The names are chosen ahead of time, and they alternate between female and male names in alphabetical order. For example, the first storm would be Alex, the next Brenda, and so on. Write Spanish names for the first ten tropical storms of the season. Would a hurricane named Rosa be early or late in the hurricane season? Answers will vary.
Rosa would be late in the season.

LANGUAGE NOTE
Hurricanes are known by different terms in different parts of the world. In the Pacific Ocean this kind of tropical storm is called a *typhoon.* Around the Indian Ocean, they are called *cyclones.* Australians call them *willy-willies.* Have students look at the world maps on pages xviii–xix with partners to locate those regions of the world.

✄ HURACÁN EN UNA BOTELLA
Materials you may need
- Two empty 2–3 liter plastic soft drink bottles with their lids
- Glue
- Hammer and nail
- Water

Sequence
1. Glue the lids of two 2–3 liter plastic soft drink bottles together top to top. Make a hole through the center of the lids with a hammer and nail.
2. Fill one bottle three-quarters full with water and screw the connected lids on tightly. Screw the empty bottle to the bottle full of water.
3. Turn the connected bottles upside down. Swirl the bottles in a circle. Then place the connected bottles, empty one down, on a steady, flat surface and watch the vortex form as the water goes into the other bottle.

ENLACES

doscientos veintiuno **221**

VAMOS A LEER

P A
p. 61
Act. 19

Estrategia
Using context
As you know, it's easy to understand pictures, cognates, and words you've already studied. You can understand many other words, too, based on how they're used in the sentence or paragraph. When you come to an unknown word, try to guess its meaning based on context (the other words around it).

¡A comenzar!
A Before you do any in-depth reading, first remember to get the general idea and to recall your background knowledge of the topic. It should be easy to tell what these readings are about based on the pictures.

¿Te acuerdas?

Look at pictures and titles first.
What is the reading on page 223 about?
a. a sporting goods store
b. racing
c. water sports
d. the environment

Al grano
B Imagine that your family will be vacationing in Miami this summer. Each of you wants to try out a different sport. Read the passages and decide which sport would be best for each member of your family.

1. your father, who loves high speeds el motoesquí
2. your mother, who likes the most popular of all water sports la natación
3. your sister, who likes small, one- or two-person boats el kayak
4. your brother, who wants to take lessons to learn something new el windsurf

C Your parents are trying to read the descriptions of these sports, but they don't know Spanish as well as you do. They underlined the words they didn't know so that you could help them. Use your knowledge of context to help them guess the meanings of these words. Answers on p. 187K

D Tus padres dicen *(say)* que tienes el día libre para participar en tu deporte acuático favorito. ¿Cuál de estos cuatro deportes prefieres? ¿Por qué? Answers will vary.

DEPORTES EN EL AGUA

EL MOTOESQUÍ corre muy rápidamente. Es fácil usar esta máquina. Se puede usar en el océano, el río o el lago. Es muy divertido usarlo en las olas.

LA NATACIÓN es un deporte favorito durante el verano. Es posible nadar en el océano, en un lago o en la piscina. Se puede nadar en una piscina cubierta durante el invierno, el otoño y la primavera. Algunas personas usan la natación como diversión y otros la usan como ejercicio.

Si no tienes experiencia con el **WINDSURF** es muy importante tomar lecciones de un instructor. Tu primera experiencia debe ser en el verano porque el viento es ideal. En la primavera hace demasiado viento para las personas que no tienen experiencia en el deporte.

En la primavera y en el verano, hay muchos **KAYAKS** en el agua. Son barcos pequeños para una o dos personas. Generalmente se operan en los ríos, pero también hay kayaks de océano.

☀ READING

SUGGESTION

C Tell students to focus on the main idea of each sentence as they read through the first time. The second time through, have them look up words in the Spanish-English glossary in their book and write a list of words they don't know. Then have them write one sentence to summarize each paragraph.

☀ POSTREADING

ADDITIONAL PRACTICE

D As a follow-up activity, put students in groups of two or three, give them a picture of a different sport from those listed here, and have them write a brief description.

AUDITORY LEARNERS

Write the names of the sports illustrated in the photos on a transparency or on the board. Have students close their books. Then read a portion of the description of each photo from the text and ask students to identify the sport you are describing.

CAPÍTULO 5   CAPÍTULO 5   CAPÍTULO 5   CAPÍTULO 5   CAPÍTULO 5   CAPÍTULO 5   CAPÍTULO 5   CAPÍTULO 5   CAPÍTULO 5

The **Repaso** reviews and integrates all four skills and culture in preparation for the Chapter Test.

2 Ask students to read or listen to the local weather forecast and to prepare their own brief **pronóstico del tiempo** for your city or town for the following day. It could be done as an audio or video recording or as a newspaper article. (You may wish to bring in a newspaper in case some students do not have access to a forecast.)

ADDITIONAL PRACTICE

2 After students have done Activity 2, ask them whether one could normally expect to do a given activity on a given date, in a given city or country. (—¿**Nadan en Buenos Aires en julio? —No, porque hace frío.**)

REPASO

CD-ROM Disc 2

1

Cass. 3A
CD 5
Tr. 16

For each weather report you hear, determine which of the photos is being described.
Script and answers on p. 187F

a

b

c

d

2 Look at the weather map. Then, complete a sentence by matching each city with a phrase. Use the information on the map, and the phrases in the boxes.
Answers on p. 187K

En Asunción
En Bogotá
En Buenos Aires
En La Paz

está lloviendo a cántaros
hace mucho frío
hace mucho viento
hace fresco y hace sol

Voy a mirar la televisión.
Vamos a volar una cometa (fly a kite).
Vamos a caminar en el parque.
Voy a leer una novela en casa.

Caracas
Bogotá
Quito
Lima
La Paz
Santiago
Montevideo
Asunción
Buenos Aires

Caracas 35°C/95°F
Bogotá 20°C/68°F
Quito 23°C/74°F
Lima 19°C/66°F
La Paz 2°C/35°F
Asunción 17°C/63°F
Santiago 12°C/53°F
Buenos Aires 16°C/61°F
Montevideo 10°C/50°F

3 Vamos a escribir

Write a paragraph about what you would typically do on a Monday in January and another paragraph about what you would do on a Saturday in May. Write what season it is, what the weather is usually like, and what activities you are likely to do. Start by making an outline.

Estrategia

Outlining is a way for you to organize what you want to write about before you write it. Put your ideas in related groups. In this case it could be the month, the weather, and the activities you do.

> I. Un lunes en enero
>   A. El tiempo
>   B. Mis actividades
>
> II. Un sábado en mayo

4 Write the following dates as they would be written in Spanish. Write the numbers as words. Answers on p. 187K

1. June 24
2. March 30
3. September 12
4. February 1
5. November 18
6. August 8

5 Where do young people in Spanish-speaking countries more commonly spend time together?

a. at a friend's house   **(b.)** in the **plaza**   c. at the mall

6 SITUACIÓN

Imagine that you're the host of your own late night talk show. With a partner, choose a famous person and role-play the interview. Be sure to ask what your guest does during certain times of the year, what he or she likes to do on vacation, where he or she likes to go, and why.

    MODELO   —Típicamente, ¿qué haces durante el invierno?
                 —Me gusta esquiar con mis amigos.
                 —Y a ti y tu familia, ¿les gusta ir de vacaciones juntos?
                 —Siempre...

ADDITIONAL PRACTICE

3 After students have completed this activity on their own, have them work in pairs to create a dialogue. In the conversation, they will talk about five activities they typically do each week. At the end, they decide to get together the evening or weekend day when they are free.

PORTFOLIO

3 Written You may wish to suggest this activity as an appropriate entry for your students' Portfolio. For Portfolio suggestions, see *Alternative Assessment Guide,* pages 9 and 16.

SUGGESTION

6 You might like to videotape the interview, in which one student assumes the role of a late night talk show host and the other pretends to be a famous person. Then partners can switch roles.

PORTFOLIO

6 Oral You might suggest that students include the **Situación** interview in their portfolio. For portfolio information, see *Alternative Assessment Guide,* pages 9 and 16.

A VER SI PUEDO...

This page is intended to help students prepare for the Chapter Test. It is a brief checklist of the major points covered in the chapter. The students should be reminded that it is only a checklist and does not necessarily include everything that will appear on the Chapter Test. Remind students also that cultural information is included on the Chapter Test.

Answers to Question 1

1. Nunca nado.
2. Siempre desayuno.
3. A veces hablo con Luisa los fines de semana.
4. A veces voy al cine los viernes.

Answers to Question 2

Answers will vary. Possible answers:

1. ¿A ustedes les gusta correr juntas en el parque?
2. ¿A ustedes les gusta bucear juntos?
3. ¿Te gusta leer novelas?
4. ¿Les gusta esquiar juntas?
5. ¿Te gusta hacer ejercicio en el gimnasio?
6. ¿Te gusta escribir cartas?

Answers to Question 4

1. el cinco de marzo
2. el catorce de septiembre
3. el veintisiete de enero

▼ **Can you discuss how often you do things?** p. 195

▼ **Can you talk about what you and your friends like to do together?** p. 203

▼ **Can you talk about what you do during a typical week?** p. 209

▼ **Can you give today's date?** p. 213

▼ **Can you talk about the weather?** p. 216

1 How would José Luis say that . . .? Answers in side column

1. he never swims
2. he always eats breakfast
3. he sometimes talks to Luisa on weekends
4. he sometimes goes to the movies on Fridays

2 How would you ask these people if they like to do the activities mentioned? How would they answer you?

1. Cristina and Marta / run in the park Answers in side column
2. Geraldo and Esteban / scuba dive
3. Pablo / read novels
4. Linda and Laura / ski
5. Daniel / exercise in the gym
6. Isabel / write letters

3 How would you tell a classmate about five activities you typically do each week?
Answers on p. 187K

4 How would you tell a classmate the date of the following things?
Answers in side column

1. the Spanish test—March 5
2. the football game—September 14
3. the birthday party—January 27

5 How would you describe the weather if it were . . .?

1. rainy and cold
2. cold and windy
3. snowy
4. hot and sunny Answers on p. 187K
5. a cloudy day
6. cool

6 What would be a typical weather description in your hometown during the following times of year? Answers will vary.

1. el otoño
2. el invierno
3. la primavera
4. el verano

VOCABULARIO

PRIMER PASO

Discussing how often you do things

a veces *sometimes*
ayudar en casa *to help at home*
la chica *girl*
el chico *boy*
¿con qué frecuencia? *how often?*
desayunar *to eat breakfast*
durante *during*
muchas veces *often*
nada *nothing*
nadie *nobody*
nunca *never*
¿Quiénes? *Who? (plural)*
la semana *week*
siempre *always*
sólo cuando *only when*
todavía *still, yet*
todos los días *every day*
tomar el autobús *to take the bus*

SEGUNDO PASO

Talking about what you and your friends like to do together

a ellos/as *to them*
a ustedes *to you (plural)*
acampar *to camp*
el agua (f.) *water*
asistir a *to attend*
beber *to drink*
bucear *to scuba dive*
la carta *letter*
una clase de ejercicios aeróbicos *aerobics class*
comer *to eat*
correr *to run*
escribir *to write*

especialmente *especially*
esquiar *to ski*
hacer ejercicio *to exercise*
la hamburguesa *hamburger*
el jugo *juice*
juntos/as *together*
leer *to read*
Les gusta + infinitive *They/you (pl.) like to . . .*
Nos gusta + infinitive *We like to . . .*
las papas fritas *french fries*
el periódico *newspaper*
pescar *to fish*
por la playa *along the beach*
recibir *to receive*
el sándwich *sandwich*
las tarjetas postales *postcards*
las tiras cómicas *comics*
las vacaciones *vacation*

Talking about what you do during a typical week

la milla *mile*
por la mañana *in the morning*
por la noche *at night (in the evening)*
por la tarde *in the afternoon*
típicamente *typically*

TERCER PASO

Giving today's date

abril *April*
agosto *August*
el año *year*
¿Cuál es la fecha? *What is today's date?*
diciembre *December*
El... de este mes hay... *On the (date) of this month, there is / are . . .*
enero *January*

Es el... de... *It's the (date) of (month).*
las estaciones *seasons*
febrero *February*
Hoy es el... de... *Today is the (date) of (month).*
el invierno *winter*
julio *July*
junio *June*
marzo *March*
mayo *May*
el mes *month*

noviembre *November*
octubre *October*
el otoño *fall*
la primavera *spring*
el primero *the first (of the month)*
¿Qué fecha es hoy? *What's today's date?*
septiembre *September*
el verano *summer*

Talking about the weather

Está lloviendo. *It's raining.*
Está nevando. *It's snowing.*
Está nublado. *It's cloudy.*
Hace buen tiempo. *The weather is nice.*
Hace calor. *It's hot.*
Hace fresco. *It's cool.*
Hace (mucho) frío. *It's (very) cold.*
Hace mal tiempo. *The weather is bad.*
Hace sol. *It's sunny.*
Hace (mucho) viento. *It's (very) windy.*
Llueve. *It's raining.*
Nieva. *It's snowing.*
¿Qué tiempo hace? *What's the weather like?*

SUGGESTION

See Games pages 187I–187J for games to review this chapter's material.

CHAPTER 5 ASSESSMENT

CHAPTER TEST
• *Testing Program,* pp. 79–84
• *Audio Program,* Assessment Items, Audiocassette 4B OR Audio CD 5 Trs. 20–21

SPEAKING TEST
• *Testing Program,* p. 114

TEST GENERATOR
Chapter 5

ALTERNATIVE ASSESSMENT
Performance Assessment
You might want to use the **Situación** on page 225 as a cumulative performance assessment activity.

Portfolio Assessment
ANNOTATED TEACHER'S EDITION
• **Written: Repaso** Activity 3, p. 225
• **Oral:** Activity 39, p. 218
ALTERNATIVE ASSESSMENT GUIDE, p. 16

227

CAPÍTULO
6

Entre familia

CHAPTER OVERVIEW

De antemano pp. 230–233	*¿Cómo es tu familia?*			
	FUNCTIONS	**GRAMMAR**	**CULTURE**	**RE-ENTRY**
Primer paso pp. 234–241	• Describing a family, p. 236	• **Gramática:** Possessive adjectives, p. 237	• **Nota cultural:** El compadrazgo, p. 239 • **Encuentro cultural:** La importancia de la familia hispana, pp. 242–243	• **hay** • Possessive adjectives • Demonstrative adjectives • Use of **de**
Segundo paso pp. 244–251	• Describing people, p. 245 • Discussing things a family does together, p. 248	• **Gramática:** The verbs **hacer** and **salir**, p. 249 • **Nota gramatical:** The personal **a**, p. 250	• **Nota cultural:** Diminutive names, p. 247	• Colors • Descriptions of people • Pastimes/hobbies • **¿Con qué frecuencia?** • Adjective agreement
Tercer paso pp. 254–259	• Discussing problems and giving advice, p. 255	• **Así se dice:** Present tense of **decir: dice**, p. 255 • **Nota gramatical:** The verb **deber**, p. 255 • **Nota gramatical:** The verb **poner**, p. 257	• **Panorama cultural:** ¿Cuántas personas hay en tu familia?, pp. 260–261	• Forming questions with **¿cómo?** and **¿cuántos?**

Letra y sonido	**p. 259**	The Spanish *r*	**Dictado:** Textbook Audiocassette 3B/ Audio CD 6
Enlaces	**pp. 252–253**	**La familia**	
Vamos a leer	**pp. 262–263**	**Diversiones en la Pequeña Habana**	**Reading Strategy:** Organization
Review	**pp. 264–267**	**Repaso,** pp. 264–265	**A ver si puedo...,** p. 266 **Vocabulario,** p. 267

Assessment

TESTING PROGRAM
- **Primer paso**, Quiz 6-1, pp. 91–92
- **Segundo paso**, Quiz 6-2, pp. 93–94
- **Tercer paso**, Quiz 6-3, pp. 95–96
- Assessment Items, Audiocassette 4B OR Audio CD 6 Tracks 19–21

- **Chapter Test**, pp. 97–102
- Assessment Items, Audiocassette 4B OR
- Audio CD 6 Tracks 22–23

- **Final Exam,** pp. 125–132
- *Audio Program,* Assessment Items: Audiocassette 4B OR Audio CD 6 Tracks 24–26

Alternative Assessment
Portfolio Assessment
ANNOTATED TEACHER'S EDITION
- **Written: Repaso** Activity 5, p. 265
- **Oral: Repaso** Activity 4, p. 265
ALTERNATIVE ASSESSMENT GUIDE, p.17

Adelante
LEVEL 1A

Pupil's Edition, pp. 228–267

Audio Program
- Textbook Audiocassette 3B
- Audio CD 6 Tracks 1–18

CD-ROM Teacher's Guide, pp. 23–26

Interactive CD-ROM Program
- Disc 2

Listening Activities
- Student Response Forms for Textbook Listening Activities, pp. 61–63
- Additional Listening Activities 6-1 to 6-6, pp. 22–24
- Scripts and Answers, pp. 41–43

Audio Program
- Additional Listening Audiocassette 5B OR
- Audio CD 6 Tracks 27–33

Testing Program
- **Paso** Quizzes and Chapter Test, pp. 91–102
- Score Sheet, Scripts and Answers, pp. 103–108, 126–138
- Final Exam, pp. 125–132

Audio Program
- Assessment Items Audiocassette 4B OR
- Audio CD 6 Tracks 19–26

Test Generator
- Chapter 6

Video Guide
- Teaching Suggestions, pp. 42–43
- Activity Masters, pp. 44–47

Video Program
- Videocassette 2

Teaching Transparencies
- Copying Masters 6-1 to 6-3 (Situations) and 6-A to 6-C (Vocabulary)
- Teaching Suggestions 6-1 to 6-3 and 6-A to 6-C

Teaching Transparencies
- Situations 6-1 to 6-3
- Vocabulary 6-A to 6-C

Activities for Communication
- Communicative Activities, pp. 31–36
- Situation Cards, pp. 80–81
- Realia and Teaching Suggestions, pp. 63–67

Lesson Planner
- Lesson Plan, pp. 29–33

Practice and Activity Book, pp. 63–74

Grammar and Vocabulary Workbook, pp. 45–52

¡Ven conmigo!
LEVEL 1

Videodisc Guide, pp. 63–72

Videodisc Program, Videodisc 3B

Native Speaker Activity Book, pp. 26–30

TECHNOLOGY APPLICATIONS IN THE CLASSROOM

For a complete list of the media resources and their accompanying print matter guides, see page 227B.

DE ANTEMANO pp. 230–233

Audio/Video

• Show or play *¿Cómo es tu familia?* See *Video Guide* pp. 41–44 or *Level 1 Videodisc Guide* pp. 63, 65–66, 70.

PRIMER PASO pp. 234–241

Video

• Show the **paso** opener to model describing a family. Have students read along.

Audio

• Use Textbook Listening Activity 5 to practice describing a family.
• Additional Listening Activities 6-1 and 6-2 practice describing families.

Transparencies

• Use Situation Transparency 6-1 to present and practice activities using the teaching suggestions.

CD-ROM

• Activity 1 practices expressions for family members.
• Activity 2 practices plural possessive adjectives.

ENCUENTRO CULTURAL pp. 242–243

Video

• Show the video after students read Valeria's speech bubble.

SEGUNDO PASO pp. 244–251

Video

• Show the **paso** opener to model describing people and discussing things a family does together.

Audio

• Use Textbook Activities 17, 19, and 25 to practice describing people.
• Additional Listening Activities 6-3 and 6-4 practice describing people and discussing things a family does together.

Transparencies

• Situation Transparency 6-2 contains drawings of several people. Students can use the transparency to practice descriptions.

CD-ROM

• Activity 3 practices **hacer** in the present tense.
• Activity 4 practices expressions for describing people.

TERCER PASO pp. 254–259

Video

• Show the **paso** opener to model expressions for discussing problems and giving advice. Have students read along.

Audio

• Use Textbook Activities 33 and 35 to practice expressions for household chores.
• Additional Listening Activities 6-5 and 6-6 practice discussing household chores and responsibilities. Use the activities as a challenge for students.

Transparencies

• Situation Transparency 6-3 contains a drawing of a disorganized house. Use it to practice discussing chores.

CD-ROM

• Activity 5 practices words and expressions for household chores.
• After presenting the verbs **deber** and **poner,** have students do Activity 6.

PANORAMA CULTURAL pp. 260–261

Audio/Video

• Show or play the interviews for students. See *Video Guide* pp. 43–47.

CD-ROM

• Have students do the **Panorama cultural** activity for Chapter 6.

REPASO pp. 264–265

Video

• Replay *¿Cómo es tu familia?* and ask students to point out exchanges in which the characters perform communicative functions from this chapter.

CD-ROM

• Have students do the **En contexto** to help write an article about a new student with a friend.

Test Generator

• Use the Test Generator to make a short practice test to help students prepare for the regular chapter test.

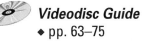
DE ANTEMANO

Barcodes A and B access **De antemano** and **A continuación** in their entirety. Subsequent barcodes show individual scenes. The barcode numbers correspond to the scene numbers as they appear in **De antemano**.

¿Cómo es tu familia? **A**
Search 1, Play To 7465

A ver, Raquel... **1**
Search 450, Play To 3255

¿Y cómo son...? **2**
Search 3256, Play To 3824

Éstos son mis padres... **3**
Search 3825, Play To 4712

Éstos son mis hermanos... **4**
Search 4713, Play To 5080

Nosotros hacemos muchas... **5**
Search 5081, Play To 5978

Aquí estamos en... **6**
Search 5979, Play To 6409

Comemos de todo... **7**
Search 6410, Play To 6954

Aquí hay una foto... **8**
Search 6955, Play To 7240

¡Ay, no! ¿Dónde...? **9**
Search 7241, Play To 7465

¿Cómo es tu familia? (a continuación) **B**
Search 7465, Play To 18965

VIDEOCLIPS

This clip is about families. You may want to preview it before showing it to students.

Estar en familia

Search 24925, Play To 25985

PASO OPENERS

Each **paso** begins with a re-presentation of a scene from the dramatic episode that models targeted functions, vocabulary, and grammar.

A ver, Raquel... **1** p. 234

Search 2500, Play To 3255

¡Ay, no! ¿Dónde...? **3** p. 254

Search 7241, Play To 7465

Éstos son mis padres... **2** p. 244
Search 3825, Play To 4712

PANORAMA CULTURAL

¿Cuántas personas hay en tu familia?
These barcodes access supplementary interviews that do not appear in the textbook. Not all barcodes are listed here. For a complete listing of supplemental interviews, see the ***¡Ven conmigo!*** Level 1 *Videodisc Guide*, p. 64.

First four interviews **1**
Search 19655, Play To 23230

All interviews **2**
Search 19655, Play To 24950

Arantxa, España **3**
Search 20352, Play To 20720

Pablo, Ecuador **4**
Search 20721, Play To 21228

Brenda, Texas **5**

Search 21229, Play To 23234

Éric, Puerto Rico **6**
Search 23235, Play To 23471

Diego, Argentina **7**
Search 23472, Play To 23874

Angie, Ecuador **8**

Search 23875, Play To 24513

Paola, Argentina **9**

Search 24514, Play To 24950

TEXTBOOK LISTENING ACTIVITIES SCRIPTS

For Student Response Forms, see Listening Activities pp. 62–64

PRIMER PASO pp. 234–241

5 ¿Quién es quién? p. 235

1. Es una familia bastante grande. Hay nueve personas en total.
2. La familia es muy simpática. Tiene un perro muy travieso.
3. Hay dos personas en la familia. Tienen dos gatos y un perro también.
4. Hay cuatro en la familia. El padrastro es muy simpático.
5. Los chicos son muy buenos. El gato también.

Answers to Activity 5

1. b
2. d
3. ninguna foto
4. c
5. a

SEGUNDO PASO pp. 244–251

17 ¿Ciencia o ficción? p. 245

1. Alma tiene veintidós años y tiene el pelo blanco.
2. Guillermo es pelirrojo. Tiene los ojos negros.
3. Olivia tiene el pelo rubio y tiene ojos azules.
4. Adolfo tiene ochenta y cinco años. Tiene el pelo negro.
5. Liliana tiene los ojos blancos y el pelo verde.
6. Anselmo tiene pelo rubio y ojos de color café.

Answers to Activity 17

1. improbable
2. improbable
3. probable
4. improbable
5. improbable
6. probable

19 ¿Cómo son tus amigos? p. 246

1. Es pelirrojo, tiene ojos azules y es muy alto.
2. Es muy simpática y guapa. Tiene pelo negro y ojos de color café.
3. Ella es baja, tiene pelo rubio y ojos verdes. Él es alto y tiene ojos verdes también.
4. Es una persona muy especial. Es muy cariñosa conmigo. Tiene cincuenta años, pero se ve joven.
5. Son muy cómicos cuando están juntos. Uno de ellos es delgado y el otro es un poco gordo. Son muy traviesos.

Answers to Activity 19

1. David
2. Rebeca
3. Conchita y Gabriel
4. Maki
5. Simón y Quique

25 Con la familia p. 249

1. Durante el verano mi familia y yo hacemos un viaje. Casi siempre visitamos a nuestros primos. Ellos viven en Colorado.
2. Salgo con frecuencia con mis amigos. A veces vamos a la playa.
3. Soy muy atlética. Hago ejercicio por la mañana con mis amigos. A veces los sábados corro con ellos en el parque.
4. Mi familia y yo salimos a comer juntos todos los viernes. Nos gusta hablar sobre nuestras actividades, las clases y el trabajo.

Answers to Activity 25

1. b
2. d
3. c
4. a

33 Los problemas de Mónica   p. 255

Mi tía es divorciada y vive con nosotros. Ella dice que mi mamá trabaja demasiado. Mi mamá sale de la casa a las siete de la mañana y regresa a las nueve de la noche. Debe descansar más, ¿verdad? Mi hermana es muy inteligente. Estudia ciencias y siempre está en la biblioteca con sus libros. Debe salir con amigos a veces. ¿Y yo? Pues, soy bastante perezosa. Toco la guitarra pero toco muy mal. Claro, debo practicar más.

Answers to Activity 33

1. c
2. a
3. b
4. not pictured

35 El sábado   p. 257

MAMÁ   Buenos días, mis hijos queridos.

BERNARDO   Buenos días, mamá. Queremos ir a patinar en línea esta mañana.

MAMÁ   Hoy es sábado y primero necesitan hacer los quehaceres de la casa.

LUISA   Después de desayunar, voy a hacer mi cama.

MAMÁ   ¡Excelente! Esta semana, le toca a Daniel limpiar la cocina. Bernardo debe pasar la aspiradora cn la sala y Luisa dcbc cortar cl césped.

BERNARDO   Voy a cuidar al gato. Se ve que quiere su desayuno también.

Answers to Activity 35

1. no
2. sí
3. sí
4. no
5. sí
6. sí

For the scripts for Parts A and C, see page 259. The script for Part B is below.

B. Dictado

Rafael Ramírez es rubio y tiene ojos verdes. Él corre muy rápido en sus zapatos rojos de rayas.

1 p. 264

Roberto, ésta es mi familia. Ésta es mi madre. Lee muchas novelas y lee el periódico todos los días. Y éste es mi padre. Es artista y trabaja en un museo. Debe trabajar menos. Ésta es mi hermana. Ella es muy lista pero debe estudiar más. Éste es mi tío Miguel. A él le gusta tocar la guitarra día y noche. Éste es nuestro perro. Es un poco gordo porque come demasiado. Y finalmente éste soy yo. Yo soy muy responsable y siempre limpio mi cuarto.

Answers to Repaso Activity 1

1. el perro
2. el padre
3. la madre
4. Marcos
5. el tío Miguel
6. la hermana

6

Entre familia
PROJECTS

EL ÁLBUM DE MI FAMILIA

This project invites students to illustrate their families in book or collage form.

Introduction

Ask your students how they define family. Who are the people in a family? Uncles? Neighbors? Grandmothers? Guardians? Friends?

Grading the project

Suggested point distribution (total = 100 points):

Neatness **20**

Creativity **20**

Correct grammar **20**

Imaginative descriptions **20**

Oral presentation **20**

Materials students may need

- ◆ White 8 1/2 × 11 paper
- ◆ Colored markers
- ◆ Glue sticks
- ◆ Photos of family members
- ◆ Magazines

Sequence

1. Have students use the vocabulary from Chapter 6 to list nuclear or extended family. Students may consider pets as part of their families as well. Allow students to make up an imaginary family for this activity.

2. Have students draw portraits, use magazine pictures, or bring in photographs of the members of their families for the album.

3. Have students label the pictures or photos and write a brief descriptive sentence in Spanish about each family member using vocabulary from this chapter and Chapter 3. For example, **Mi madre es creativa y simpática.** Students should use two adjectives for each person.

4. The cover of the album should have a title, a dedication, and a by-line.

5. When students have completed the project, assign them to groups of four. Have students show their albums to each other and give an oral presentation in Spanish.

EL ÁRBOL GENEALÓGICO

With this hands-on project, students make a mobile that reinforces vocabulary about the family from this chapter. Students prepare a visual representation of their family members and share the information about them orally with classmates.

Introduction

Students make mobiles that illustrate the main characteristics of their family members, including pets. Lead a brainstorming session about what family means to the students. What members make up a family for them? How would they describe their family members to a new friend? Do they include pets as part of their definition of a family?

Materials students may need

- ◆ Clothes hangers
- ◆ Colored paper
- ◆ Glue sticks
- ◆ Scissors
- ◆ Markers
- ◆ String or yarn
- ◆ Single-hole punch

Sequence

1. Have each student make a list in Spanish of five family members to describe. They write a descriptive sentence about each person. For example: **Mi padre es bajo y atlético.**

2. Have students cut out five shapes from the colored paper large enough to glue the pictures, photos, or drawings to. They then punch a hole in the top. Afterwards, they select photos of their family members, use cutouts from magazines, or draw them and glue them to the paper. They can write the person's name and a short description over or under the picture.

3. Have students punch holes at the top of their colored-paper shapes and use yarn or string to tie them to a coat hanger. They can use different lengths of string for variety.

4. When the mobile is complete, students present it to the class by describing their family members.

5. Mobiles can be displayed from the ceiling in the classroom to reinforce this chapter's vocabulary.

Grading the project

Suggested point distribution (total = 100 points):

Overall appearance, neatness	20
Creativity	20
Information and content	20
Spelling, gender agreement	20
Oral presentation	20

LOS JUEGOS DE MESA

In this challenging activity students use listening, speaking, reading, and writing to create their own board game. This will be a group project involving cooperative learning, delegating tasks, and creative organization of ideas.

Introduction

Ask students to think of all the board games they have played. Ask which are their favorites and why. Bring in various games in Spanish to show the class if you have them, or ask your students to bring some.

Materials students may need

- ◆ Poster board or cardboard
- ◆ Toy cars, play figures, or other game pieces
- ◆ Markers
- ◆ Index cards
- ◆ Old magazines

Sequence

1. Have students work in groups of four. Each group selects a game to imitate or creates a new one.

2. Give students time to brainstorm. Suggest that they check the rules of board games they are familiar with.

3. Students may use the format of a game you have already played in class, but they must design a gameboard to go with it. Encourage them to be creative, but mention the possibility of using a favorite classic board game as a model. Some examples are Monopoly®, Go to the Head of the Class®, Clue®, and Payday®.

4. Set a date for a game proposal to be peer-reviewed by another group. This proposal should include basic rules and how they propose to create the game.

5. Have a game day when groups play their game, then exchange with other groups.

Grading the project

Suggested point distribution (total = 100 points):

Vocabulary use	20
Appearance	20
Creativity	20
Grammar usage	20
Rules easy to understand	20

CAPÍTULO 6

Entre familia
GAMES ♜

¡DIBÚJALO!

In this game students review chapter vocabulary by drawing pictures of the vocabulary words and naming them in Spanish. It is a very effective review method for visual learners.

Materials you may need
- ◆ Markers
- ◆ Index cards

Preparation
Make index cards for family vocabulary and adjectives. For example: **madre, hijo, cómico, guapo.**

Procedure
1. Divide the class into two teams. Remind students that drawing a family tree can be useful to show family relationships.
2. Have a student from Team A come forward to pick a vocabulary card and begin drawing for his or her team to guess. Members of Team A call out the possible word in Spanish. If they guess it within the two-minute time limit, they win a point.
3. Repeat steps one and two for Team B. Be sure each team member has a chance to draw. The team with the higher score wins.
4. For a challenge, give students a noun and an adjective to draw simultaneously. For example: **madre** and **alta.**

¿ERES MI HERMANO?

*This game reinforces new vocabulary related to the family and descriptive adjectives. It can be played any time after the **Primer paso.***

Preparation
1. Draw a large family tree on the board or use the family tree in Teaching Transparency 6-A.
2. Include additional words such as **divorciado/a** *divorced* and **adoptado/a** *adopted.*

Procedure
1. Divide the class into two teams. One player from each team chooses a person on the tree that he or she will be. The Team A player announces aloud the person he or she is going to be. The Team B player tells only you.
2. The Team A player asks the Team B player five questions to find out his or her identity, but never uses any names on the tree. (**¿Eres viejo o joven? ¿Tienes hijos? ¿Cuántos hermanos tienes? ¿Eres mi madre?**)
3. If the Team A player guesses the Team B player's identity, Team A gets one point. If not, Team B gets one point. The next round, the teams reverse roles.

CHALLENGE

After the **Segundo paso,** write descriptions of some of the people on the tree you made for **¿Eres mi hermano?** Have a student from each group come to the front. Describe a person on the tree using a string of relationships, never mentioning the name of the person. Start out with simple sentences and gradually make your sentences more complicated. **Este hombre es bajo...** One of the two students will respond **Es el abuelo de Jaime.** The player who identifies the person first gets one point and both players return to their seats. Then call up two more players and describe another person.

UNA PALABRA MÁS

The object of this game is for students to build logically on words to make complete sentences. The sentences can be odd or funny, but they should be grammatically correct.

Procedure
1. Divide the class into two or more teams. Write one word on the board to begin a sentence, for example, **Mi.** Have a student from another team write a word to continue the sentence, for example, **hermano.** The next team's player should write another word, for example, **tiene.**
2. Play continues until the sentence is long. Students may add words either before or after previous ones. For example, a later student could write **inteligente** between **hermano** and **tiene.** Each time a student adds a word correctly, his or her team gets a point.

¡NO HAY SUJETO!

*The object of this game is for students to identify the grammatical subject of a sentence from context. It may be used at any time to review the vocabulary of the **paso** you are working on.*

Preparation

1 Cut out a small slip of paper for each student.

2 Write a Spanish sentence on each slip, leaving out the subject in each and using the vocabulary of the **paso** you are working on. For the **Primer paso,** you might write sentences such as **Mi _____ es el hijo de mis abuelos.** Place all the slips in a hat.

Procedure

1 Divide the class into two teams. Have a player from Team A draw a slip, read it aloud, and supply the missing subject. For this example, the Team A player could say **Mi padre es el hijo de mis abuelos.**

2 Follow the same procedure with Team B. Have teams alternate turns until each student has had a chance to make a complete sentence. Teams score one point for each sentence they make with a correct subject. The winner is the team with the highest score.

EL RITMO

Use this game to review a variety of vocabulary and vocabulary categories.

Preparation

1 Write categories on the board, for example, **la familia, las descripciones, los quehaceres.**

2 Demonstrate the following four-beat rhythm. On beat 1, slap your hands on your thighs. On beat 2, clap your hands. On beat 3, snap with the fingers of your left hand. On beat 4, snap with the fingers of your right hand.

3 Have students copy the four-beat rhythm.

Procedure

1 One person begins by calling out a category, such as **la familia,** on beats three and four.

2 The next student adds an appropriate vocabulary item such as **el hijo** on the subsequent count of three and four. The next student adds **el tío,** and so on.

3 If the rhythm breaks down, stop and start again with a new category.

LA GEOGRAFÍA

This game may be used to review basic geography, forming questions (Chapter 1), telling where things are (Chapter 4), and pronunciation. It also calls upon higher-order thinking skills.

Preparation

Tell students to pretend they are in training to become experts in world geography to assist a team of Spanish-speaking scientists on a trip around the world.

Procedure

1 Write questions like the following on the board: **¿Qué país está al sur de España? ¿Cuántos océanos hay en el mundo? ¿Dónde está la Argentina? ¿Cuántos países hay en Sudamérica?**

2 Divide students into groups and choose a leader for each. The leader begins the game by asking a question that can be answered by looking at the map. (one from the board or one of his or her own design)

3 The other students in the group try to answer the question. Allow students to look at the maps on pages xvii–xxiii if they need to, but insist they try to answer without looking at the book first. The first student to answer correctly becomes the leader.

Entre familia
ANSWERS TO CHAPTER 6 ACTIVITIES

Listening Activity answers appear or Scripts pages 227E–227F. Answers to all other activities appear on corresponding pupil pages.

DE ANTEMANO   pp. 230–233

3
1. ¿Cómo es tu familia?
2. Éstos son mis padres.
3. ¿Y cuántos viven aquí?
4. Nosotros hacemos cosas juntos los domingos.
5. Alguna vez debes probar la barbacoa que prepara mi mamá.

PRIMER PASO   pp. 234–241

8
1. nuestra
2. su
3. tus
4. su
5. mi
6. nuestra
7. nuestros

9 Answers will vary. Possible answers:
1. Sí, es nuestro primo.
2. Sí, es nuestra abuela *or* Sí, es su madre.
3. No, no son mis tíos.
4. Sí, son sus hijas.
5. Sí, es nuestro tío *or* Sí, es su esposo.
6. Sí, nuestros amigos son mucho más altos que mis hermanos.

ENCUENTRO CULTURAL   pp. 242–243

2
1. Answers will vary. Possible answer: 3
2. Answers will vary. Possible answers: grandfather, granddaughter, mother, son, aunt, niece
3. preparing the cornhusks, fill the cornhusks, rolling up and folding the tamales

SEGUNDO PASO   pp. 244–251

24
1. hacen
2. salimos
3. cenamos
4. comida
5. algo
6. hacemos
7. viaje

ENLACES   pp. 252–253

1
1. Cabrera: 3; Miró: 3
2. Cabrera: father, mother and daughter; Miró: father, mother, and child
3. Answers will vary.

3
1. Se llaman Xavier y Leticia.
2. Los abuelos paternos se llaman Gustavo Lomas Mendoza y Estela Muñoz de Lomas.
3. Se llama Ana Díaz de Lomas.

4
1. Antonio Lomas Muñoz
2. Pablo Lomas Díaz

TERCER PASO   pp. 254–259

37 Answers will vary. Possible answers:
a. Pablo no debe poner la mesa en la cama. Debe poner la mesa en la cocina.
b. Diana y Lola no deben trabajar en la sala. Deben trabajar en el jardín.
c. Federico no debe pasar la aspiradora en el jardín. Debe pasar la aspiradora en la sala.
d. Miguelito no debe poner la basura en el armario. Debe sacar la basura.
e. Frida no debe cuidar la planta. Debe cuidar al perro.

38 Answers will vary. Possible answers:
1. Mi hermana y yo debemos cuidar al gato y al perro.
2. Mis abuelos deben trabajar en el jardín.
3. Mi primo debe cuidar a mis hermanos.
4. Mi hermano debe preparar la cena.
5. Debo cortar el césped.
6. Debemos planchar la ropa.

A VER SI PUEDO...   p. 266

4 Answers will vary. Possible answers:
1. Casi siempre cenamos juntos.
2. A veces los sábados visitamos a mi tía Elena.
3. Todos los domingos en el verano salimos juntos a pescar.

5 Answers will vary. Possible answers:
1. Debe limpiar su cuarto.
2. Debe trabajar menos.
3. Debemos preparar la cena.

Chapter Section	Presentation	Homework Options
Primer paso	**Vocabulario,** p. 235	*Grammar and Vocabulary,* p. 45, #1–2 *Practice and Activity Book,* p. 63, #3–4 *CD-ROM,* Disc 2, Chapter 6, #1
	Así se dice, p. 236	*Pupil's Edition,* p. 236, #6 *Practice and Activity Book,* p. 65, #5
	Gramática, p. 237	*Pupil's Edition,* p. 237, #8 *Grammar and Vocabulary,* p. 46, #3–4 *CD-ROM,* Disc 2, Chapter 6, #2
Segundo paso	**Así se dice,** p. 245	*Practice and Activity Book,* p. 67, #9 *CD-ROM,* Disc 2, Chapter 6, #4
	Vocabulario, p. 245	*Pupil's Edition,* pp. 247–248, #21–22 *Grammar and Vocabulary,* p. 47, #5–6 *Practice and Activity Book,* p. 67, #10
	Así se dice, p. 248	*Pupil's Edition,* p. 248, #24 *Practice and Activity Book,* p. 69, #13
	Gramática, p. 249	*Grammar and Vocabulary,* p. 48, #8 *CD-ROM,* Disc 2, Chapter 6, #3
	Nota gramatical, p. 250	*Pupil's Edition,* p. 250, #28
Tercer paso	**Así se dice,** p. 255	*Pupil's Edition,* p. 255, #32 *Practice and Activity Book,* pp. 70–71, #14–15
	Nota gramatical, p. 255	*Grammar and Vocabulary,* p. 50, #11–12
	Vocabulario, p. 256	*Grammar and Vocabulary,* p. 51, #13–15 *Practice and Activity Book,* pp. 71–72, #16–17 *CD-ROM,* Disc 2, Chapter 6, #5
	Nota gramatical, p. 257	*Pupil's Edition,* p. 257, #36 *Grammar and Vocabulary,* p. 52, #16–17 *CD-ROM,* Disc 2, Chapter 6, #6

Entre familia

MOTIVATING ACTIVITY
Ask students to discuss what they do with their families. (weddings, birthdays, baseball games, etc.) Do members of their families advise each other? Who gives whom advice? Do they mostly solve problems alone, or do they seek help from friends and family?

LANGUAGE NOTE
① **Jesús** is often used as a first name in Spanish. Some common nicknames for **Jesús** in Spanish-speaking countries are **Chucho** and **Chuy.**

RE-ENTRY
① Use this photo to review numbers, **tener,** and **llamarse,** asking several students to tell the class how many cousins they have and what their names are. (**Tengo tres primos. Se llaman Susan, Bill y Joe.**)

228

CAPÍTULO

6
Entre familia

① Éstos son mis primos, Jesús, Luisa y Esteban.

228 *doscientos veintiocho*

Many teenagers in the Spanish-speaking world live in large, close-knit families. Child care, parties, music, and meals are some of the many activities shared by all. How would you describe your family?

In this chapter you will learn

- to describe a family
- to describe people; to discuss things a family does together
- to discuss problems and give advice

And you will

- listen to some descriptions of different Spanish-speaking families
- read about some things to do in Miami
- write a description of a family and fill out a questionnaire
- find out what Spanish-speaking teenagers and their families do together
- find out about why one teenager considers her family very important

(2) Tiene pelo negro y ojos de color café.

(3) Si tienes problemas, debes hablar conmigo.

229

FOCUSING ON OUTCOMES
Refer students to the photos and have them match the outcomes with photos. (Photo 1: describing your family; Photo 2: describing people; Photo 3: discussing problems and giving advice) Then have students look at these photos and describe the people. Ask volunteers to describe their family members.

THINKING CRITICALLY
(2) Ask students if they can guess what color **ojos de color café** are. They can indicate some students in the class who have brown eyes using the correct form of the verb **tener**. (**María tiene ojos de color café.**)

CULTURE NOTE
In Spanish-speaking countries, **la familia** often includes aunts, uncles, cousins, grandparents, and godparents. The extended family in the United States often includes members who are not biological relatives: stepparents, stepsiblings, stepgrandchildren, for example. In the United States, three or more generations do not live in the same house as often as they do in Spanish-speaking countries.

VIDEO INTEGRATION

Adelante LEVEL 1A

Video Program,
Videocassette 2, 36:56–41:06 OR
¡Ven conmigo! LEVEL 1

Videodisc Program,
Videodisc 3B

Search 1 , Play To 7465

TEACHER NOTE
The **fotonovela** is an abridged version of the video episode.

VIDEO SYNOPSIS
Armando is visiting Raquel's house and she is describing her family to him. As they look at a photo album, he asks her questions about her family members and she tells him about them and their interests. At the end of the scene, she is describing her dog when they are interrupted by a loud crash.

MOTIVATING ACTIVITY
Ask students if they keep a photo album of their friends and families. Ask them to bring in their photo albums and write captions for photos in Spanish. See **El álbum de mi familia** on page 227G.

DE ANTEMANO

Cass. 3B
CD 6 Trs. 1–2

¿Cómo es tu familia?

Look at the photos below. What is going on? Who is Raquel talking about with Armando? Does something surprising happen at the end? What could have happened?

p. 63
Acts. 1–2

Raquel

Armando

Pepe

Éstos son mis padres.
Ellos son de Cuba. Les gusta
mucho trabajar en el jardín.
Mi mamá es muy buena cocinera.
Alguna vez debes probar
la barbacoa que ella prepara.
¡Es fenomenal!

Éstos son mis
hermanos mayores.
Y ella es
mi hermana menor.

Nosotros hacemos muchas cosas juntos,
especialmente los domingos. Primero,
vamos a la iglesia. Después, comemos
juntos y salimos a alguna parte. En
esta foto, salimos al parque.

SUGGESTION
Ask students some previewing questions: **¿Cómo se llaman los chicos? ¿Cuántas personas hay en la familia de Raquel? ¿De dónde son los papás de Raquel? ¿Qué deporte practican los hermanos de Raquel?**

PRESENTATION
Have students look at the **fotonovela.** What do they think is going on in the story? What visual cues help them make intelligent guesses? Next, play the video. Have students work with a partner to see if they agree about what is happening. Discuss the plot with the whole class, then have them repeat the lines after you or the audio recording. If time permits, ask volunteers to read the lines aloud.

ADDITIONAL PRACTICE
After you have presented the **fotonovela,** have students review the learner outcomes listed on page 229. Ask them to identify the phrases in the **fotonovela** that describe family and other people. Discussing problems and giving advice are functions modeled in the continuation of the **fotonovela** in the *Video Program* and *¡Ven conmigo!* Level 1 *Videodisc Program.*

VIDEO INTEGRATION

Adelante LEVEL 1A
Video Program,
Videocassette 2, 38:20–38:46 OR
¡Ven conmigo! LEVEL 1
Videodisc Program,
Videodisc 3B

Search 2500, Play To 3255

JUMP START!
On the board or on a transparency, write the expressions **Nos gusta... juntos** and **No nos gusta... juntos.** Have students write five sentences listing what their families like or don't like to do together.

AUDITORY LEARNERS
4 Have students write their answers on a separate sheet of paper as they listen to the audio portion of this scene.

LANGUAGE NOTES
• The word **bastante** means *enough* but very often implies *quite* or *plenty.* When Raquel says her family is **bastante grande,** she means *quite* or *very big.*

• Point out that **ser** is often used to indicate the number of people in a group:
  —**¿Cuántos son?** *How many of you are there?*
  —**Somos ocho.** *There are eight of us.*

234

PRIMER PASO

Describing a family

> A ver, Raquel, ¿cómo es tu familia?

> Bueno, es bastante grande... tengo tres hermanos, una hermana... y muchísimos primos...

> ¿Y cuántos viven aquí?

> Somos ocho en casa: mis padres, todos mis hermanos menos uno, una abuela y una tía.

4 ¿Cómo es la familia de Raquel?
Complete this paragraph about Raquel's family with the words below.

La familia de Raquel es bastante ___1___. Son ___2___ en su casa. Ella tiene tres hermanos y una ___3___. Su abuela y una ___4___ viven con ellos. Un ___5___ ya no vive en casa.

3 **hermana**   2 **ocho**   4 **tía**

5 **hermano**   1 **grande**

CD-ROM
Disc 2

PA
p. 64
Acts. 3–4

GV
p. 45
Acts. 1–2

6-A

CAPÍTULO 6

a

Ésta es la **familia** de Miguel: su **madre**, su **media hermana** *(half sister)* y su **gato**.

b

La familia Pérez es grande. Aquí están el **padre** y su **esposa** *(wife)*, los dos **hijos** y una **hija** *(daughter)*, la **abuela** *(grandmother)* y el **tío** *(uncle)* de los chicos. La **tía** *(aunt)* Catalina y el **abuelo** no están en la foto.

c

En mi casa hay cuatro personas: mi **medio hermano**, mi madre y yo, y el **esposo** *(husband)* de mamá, Rolando. Es mi **padrastro** *(stepfather)*.

d

Soy María. Aquí están mis **padres** (mi **padre** y mi **madre**) y mi **perro** Chuleta.

los abuelos	*grandparents*	los hermanos	*brothers and sisters*
la hermanastra	*stepsister*	los hijos	*children*
el hermanastro	*stepbrother*	la madrastra	*stepmother*

Cass. 3B
CD 6 Tr. 3

5 **¿Quién es quién?** Script and answers on p. 227E

Imagine that you're on the phone with the photographer who took the family portraits above. First, study the photos to see how many people are in each family and what they're like. Then, as the photographer describes members of each family, find the photo that matches. If no photo matches, answer **ninguna foto**.

ASÍ SE DICE   Describing a family

To find out about a friend's family, ask:

> **¿Cuántas personas hay en tu familia?**

Your friend might answer:

> **Hay** cinco personas **en mi familia.** Mi abuela **vive** con nosotros también.
> *My grandmother lives with us too.*
>
> **Somos** cinco.
>
> También **tenemos** un perro.
> *We also have a dog.*

> **¿Cómo es tu familia?**

> Nuestra familia es muy grande. Tenemos muchos **primos.**
> *We have lots of cousins.*
>
> **Somos** muy **unidos.**
> *We're very close-knit.*

6 ¿Cómo es tu familia?

Look at the sentences below. Find which family tree each sentence best describes. For each description, write the name of the family.

MODELO Mi hermano se llama Andrés. (Andrade)

1. Somos ocho en casa. Andrade
2. Somos seis personas en mi familia: mis padres, mi tía, mis dos hermanos y yo. Canales
3. Somos tres hermanas, dos hermanos, mis padres y mi abuelo. Andrade
4. Mi hermana menor tiene tres años y es rubia. Andrade
5. La hermana de mi papá vive con nosotros. Canales

la familia Andrade

abuelo

papá = mamá

Leticia   Andrés   Rosa

Felipe   Esperanza

la familia Canales

tía Rosa   papá = mamá

Alberto   Rodolfo   Zenaida

7 Retrato de familia

Work in pairs. Pretend that you're a member of the Andrade or Canales family in Activity 6. Tell about yourself and the other members of your family. Your partner will pretend to be a member of the other family. Then switch roles.

MODELO   Me llamo Leticia y tengo dos hermanos...

GRAMÁTICA   Possessive adjectives

You've been using **mi(s)**, **tu(s)**, and **su(s)**, which are *possessive adjectives.* Here are some others:

nuestro(s)	*our*
nuestra(s)	
vuestro(s)	*your (when "you" is plural)*
vuestra(s)	
su(s)	*your (when "you" is plural)*
su(s)	*their*

Y aquí está Verónica con sus abuelos.

1. Note that **nuestro** and **vuestro** have a feminine form:

   Nuestra familia es pequeña.

2. Like **mi, tu,** and **su,** these forms add an -**s** when they modify a plural noun: **sus primos, nuestros gatos.**

PA
pp. 65–66
Acts. 6–7

GV
pp. 46
Acts. 3–4

8 En nuestra familia...

Liang and Tranh are looking at pictures of Liang's family. Complete their conversation using the correct possessive adjective.

TRANH   ¿Quiénes están contigo en esta foto?

LIANG   Aquí está (1. <u>nuestra</u>/nuestro) abuela conmigo y con mis primos.

TRANH   ¿Y quién es este señor?

LIANG   ¿Con mi tía? Es (2. <u>su</u>/sus) esposo. Es el padrastro de mis primos.

TRANH   Es bastante grande la familia de (3. tu/<u>tus</u>) primos, ¿verdad?

LIANG   Sí, (4. <u>su</u>/sus) familia es grande. Hay siete personas. En (5. <u>mi</u>/mis) familia somos cuatro.

TRANH   En (6. <u>nuestra</u>/nuestras) casa somos cuatro también. Pero si contamos *(count)* (7. nuestro/<u>nuestros</u>) perros, ¡somos siete!

9 Una reunión familiar

 Your partner doesn't know your family well. Answer his or her questions using the correct possessive adjectives. Use the hints in parentheses to help you answer. Then switch roles.

MODELO —¿Quién es ella? ¿Es su tía? (sí)
—Sí, es nuestra tía. Se llama Melinda. Answers on p. 227K

1. ¿El chico alto es el primo de ustedes? (sí)
2. ¿Es ella la madre de Melinda? (sí)
3. ¿Los señores son tus tíos? (no)
4. ¿Quiénes son ellas? ¿Son las hijas de tía Melinda? (sí)
5. Es el esposo de tía Melinda, ¿no? (sí)
6. Y nuestros amigos, ¿son más altos que tus hermanos? (sí)

Ésta es nuestra tía Melinda.

10 La familia de Cristina

Cristina is describing her family to you. Use the word box to help you complete the sentences. Remember to use the correct form of the adjective! Answers in side column

guapo/a
bonito/a
alto/a
bajo/a
simpático/a
cómico/a
inteligente
rubio/a

Mi tío Martín es muy ___1___. Aquí está mi prima Mayra. Es ___2___ y ___3___. A mi abuelita le gusta leer. Es ___4___ y ___5___ y tiene canas. Mi hermano Jacobo es ___6___, ¿verdad?

11 ¿Quién en tu familia es...?

Work in pairs. Pretend that your partner is a member of the family pictured on page 238. Ask your partner three questions using **¿Quién en tu familia es...?** and adjectives like those in the box on page 238. Then switch roles.

MODELO   ¿Quién en tu familia es cómico?
Mi hermano Jacobo es cómico.

12 Una entrevista

A Work in a group. Create a questionnaire with four or five questions about someone's family. Include questions about what people look like, what they're like, what their house is like, and if they have a dog or a cat. Take turns interviewing each other.

B Then make a list of what is similar about all the families. Be prepared to share your list with the rest of the class. Keep your questionnaire for use in Activity 14.

1. ¿Cuántos son en tu familia?

2. ¿Tienes un perro o un gato?

3. ¿Quién es la persona más alta en tu familia?

Nota cultural

When a man and a woman serve as **padrino** (godfather) and **madrina** (godmother) at a baby's baptism, it's understood that they'll have a special lifelong relationship with their godchild. The godparents give their **ahijados** (godchildren) love, advice, and even help with education and careers. **El compadrazgo** is the relationship between the child's parents and godparents. The father and the godfather call each other **compadre** and the mother and the godmother call each other **comadre. Compadres** and **comadres** often consider each other family. Is there someone that you think of as a relative but who isn't related to you?

CULTURE NOTE
Many Spanish-speaking families ask close friends to be the godparents of their children; however, they also frequently choose family members. The godfather (**el padrino**) is often an uncle or an older cousin whereas the godmother (**la madrina**) may be an aunt or an older cousin. Not only is there a special relationship between the child and their godparents but also between the parents and godparents.

PHOTO FLASH!
This is a photo of a baptism on Olvera Street in Los Angeles, California. Olvera Street is the oldest street in Los Angeles and the site of the oldest house. It is near the **Pueblo de los Ángeles,** where the city began in 1781. In 1930, it was restored as a Mexican-style marketplace for pedestrians only.

COOPERATIVE LEARNING

13 Have students work in groups of four to create a questionnaire. Each group member prepares two questions about a different family in the photos on page 235. (**¿Cuántos hermanos tiene Miguel? ¿Hay una hija en la familia Pérez?**) One person proofreads the questions and another puts them together as a questionnaire. Groups exchange questionnaires, answer their classmates' questions, and return them. The two remaining group members check the answers.

FAMILY LINK

Have students create a questionnaire about what their family likes to do together and have a family member answer it. Tell students that they may make up answers about an imaginary family. Have students write a short report of their findings in Spanish.

Answers to Activity 13

Answers will vary. Possible answers:
1. Ésta es una familia nuclear.
2. En la familia hay tres hijos.
3. Viven en un apartamento.
4. Probablemente tienen cinco personas en la familia.
5. Les gusta ir al cine.
6. Sus hermanos tienen dieciséis y doce años.

240

---

13 Cuestionario sobre la familia

Based on what you see in the questionnaire below, work with your partner to describe the family. Answers in side column

1. Ésta es una familia...
2. En la familia hay...
3. Viven *(They live)* en...
4. Probablemente tienen...
5. Les gusta...
6. Sus hermanos tienen...

Información Personal

1 *Datos personales*

a. **Nombre completo:**
   Apellido   Young
   Nombre(s)   Kelly
b. **Edad:**   14   años
c. **Domicilio:**
   una casa ☐
   un apartamento ☒

2 *Vivo*

a. con unos parientes ☐
b. con una familia extensa ☐
c. en una familia nuclear ☒

3 *Datos familiares*

a. **¿Tienes hermanos?**   sí
   ¿Cuántos?   2
b. **¿Cuántos años tiene cada uno?**
   Mi hermano mayor Mike tiene 16 años
   Mi hermana menor Lynn tiene 12 años

4 *Actividades*

a. **pescar**
b. **visitar a los parientes**
c. **ir al cine**   todos los viernes
d. **limpiar la casa**
e. **acampar**   a veces durante el verano
f. **ir de vacaciones**

14 ¿Cómo es tu familia?

A Work with a partner. Each of you should think of a fictional family (from a book, movie, or TV show). Choose which member of the family you'll be.

B Interview each other using the questionnaire you wrote in Activity 12. Fill in the blanks as you go. After your partner interviews you, compare answers to see what your families have in common. Be prepared to share your findings with the rest of the class.

15 Mi mascota

Could your pet be the next Pet of the Week? Write a description of your real or imaginary pet to be featured in **La mascota de la semana.** You should write at least four sentences. Be sure to mention your pet's name, color, age, and at least one interesting thing your pet does.

La mascota de la semana

Ésta es mi perrita. Se llama Reina y tiene ocho meses. Mi perrita es muy mimosa. Ella es muy juguetona pero a veces me muerde. También muerde mis zapatos. Voy al parque con ella todos los días. Le gusta mucho correr conmigo.

Evelina Pérez
(Maracaibo)

VOCABULARIO EXTRA

el caballo	*horse*
el conejo	*rabbit*
juguetón, juguetona	*playful*
la mascota	*pet*
mimoso/a	*affectionate*
muerde	*bites*
el pájaro	*bird*
el pez de colores	*goldfish*

☀ CLOSE

Divide the class into groups of three or four. Each group comes up with eight to ten questions about the families on page 235 and then answers them. Students peer-edit each other's work and then read the questions and answers aloud. Groups take turns asking each other questions.

☀ ASSESS

QUIZ 6-1
Testing Program, pp. 91–92
Audio Program,
Audiocassette 4B OR
Audio CD 6 Track 19

PERFORMANCE ASSESSMENT
Ask students to develop a conversation with a partner to present to the class. They pretend to be new acquaintances and ask each other about their families. They demonstrate interest in each other's family with their questions. Answers should include descriptions of the family members. Remind students that their answers may be about an imaginary family. For additional Performance Assessment ideas, see Situation Cards 6-1.

VIDEO INTEGRATION

VIDEO INTEGRATION

Adelante LEVEL 1A
Video Program,
Videocassette 2, 47:53–50:30

MOTIVATING ACTIVITY
Ask students to think about how often they see members of their extended families. Ask them how often they write or speak to their relatives on the phone. Are they close?

PRESENTATION
Show the video or read Valeria's speech bubble and then have students answer the questions in **¿Qué dijo?** Afterwards, have students describe their own (or an imaginary) family by reading through Valeria's speech bubble and replacing her information with theirs.

 CULTURE NOTE
Point out that **tamales** are made from corn meal. The corn meal is ground into a paste (**masa**), spread onto corn husks, and filled with meat or other fillings. The husks are then rolled and steamed. **Tamales** are a favorite food especially on holidays or other special occasions.

ENCUENTRO CULTURAL

La importancia de la familia hispana

Valeria lives in San Antonio, Texas, although she has relatives all over the world. She keeps in touch with her relatives with letters and video-tapes. And when she's with loved ones in San Antonio, she spends as much time with them as she can.

¡Hola! Me llamo Valeria. Para mí, la familia es muy importante. Ésta es mi abuela. También vive en San Antonio. Es muy cariñosa. Siempre cuenta historias de su pasado. Y ésta es mi hermana... Cuando hay una fiesta, ellas siempre preparan tamales juntas.

1 ¿Qué dijo?
Valeria describes how she feels about her family and what they do together.

"...Para mí, la familia **es muy importante**."

"...siempre **cuenta historias** de su pasado."

"Cuando hay una fiesta, ellas siempre **preparan tamales juntas**."

1. How does Valeria feel about her family? Her family is very important.
2. What does Valeria's grandmother always do? tells stories
3. For special occasions, what traditional dish does Valeria's family prepare? tamales

2 ¡Piénsalo! Answers on p. 227K

1. How many generations do you see in the painting?

2. What family relationships do you think are portrayed?

3. There are three main activities going on in this painting of a **tamalada**, or **tamal**-making party. In what order would the following steps be done?
   a. rolling up and folding the **tamales**
   b. filling the cornhusks
   c. preparing the cornhusks

Carmen Lomas Garza, **Tamalada,** 1987, Gouache on paper. 20 ″ × 27 ″.

3 ¿Y tú?

How would you describe your family?   Answers will vary.

1. ¿Hay una persona en tu familia que es importante para ti? ¿Quién es?

2. ¿Por qué es especial esa persona?

3. ¿Qué te gusta hacer con tu familia? ¿Tienen ustedes algunas tradiciones especiales? Explica.

BACKGROUND
Carmen Lomas Garza, born in Kingsville, Texas, later moved to San Francisco, California. Her art typically depicts recollections of family and friends from her childhood in South Texas. She often illustrates everyday activities or special family traditions such as the **Tamalada** shown here.

SUGGESTION
Have students look at the **Tamalada** and describe the family. Allow students to be creative in their answers.

ART LINK
Have students choose a family event and paint a mat drawing similar to the **Tamalada.** Students can present their work to the class by introducing and describing their family as well as the traditional family event they have depicted. Students will learn more expressions for describing family members in the **Segundo paso.**

VIDEO INTEGRATION

Adelante LEVEL 1A
Video Program,
Videocassette 2, 39:06–39:34 OR
¡Ven conmigo! LEVEL 1
Videodisc Program,
Videodisc 3B

Search 3825, Play To 4712

JUMP START!

Tell students there will be a family reunion with these people present: **madre, padre, hermanos, abuelos, tíos.** Have them write four sentences, each one describing a different family member with at least two adjectives.

SUGGESTION

16 Have students read these questions as advance organizers before showing the video.

SEGUNDO PASO

Describing people; discussing things a family does together

> Éstos son mis padres.
> Ellos son de Cuba. Les gusta
> mucho trabajar en el jardín.
> Mi mamá es muy buena cocinera.
> Alguna vez debes probar
> la barbacoa que ella prepara.
> ¡Es fenomenal!

16 El álbum de Raquel

Use the information that Raquel gives about her family to answer the following questions.

1. ¿Quiénes están en la foto? Los padres de Raquel.
2. ¿De dónde son ellos? Son de Cuba.
3. ¿Quién cocina *(cooks)* bien? La mamá de Raquel.
4. ¿Qué les gusta hacer a estas personas? Les gusta trabajar en el jardín.

ASÍ SE DICE
Describing people

PA
p. 67
Act. 9

To ask for a description of someone, say:

Some responses might be:

**CD-ROM
Disc 2**

¿**Cómo es** tu abuelo?

Él es alto y cariñoso.

¿**De qué color son** sus ojos?

Tiene los ojos verdes.
He has green eyes.

¿**De qué color es** su pelo?

Tiene canas.
He has gray hair.

17 ¿Ciencia o ficción?   Script and answers on p. 227E

Listen to the following descriptions of some fictional characters. Use **probable** or **improbable** to tell what you think of their appearances.

Cass. 3B
CD 6 Tr. 4

VOCABULARIO

La profesora Fajardo es muy lista. Es pelirroja *(redheaded)*, delgada *(thin)* y tiene los ojos azules.

Los hijos de Julio son traviesos *(mischievous).* Pepe es mayor *(older)* y Pedro es menor *(younger).* Julio y sus hijos tienen pelo negro y los ojos de color café.

PA
p. 67
Act. 10

GV
pp. 47–48
Acts. 5–7

6-B

Los abuelos son muy cariñosos. La abuela es guapa y un poco gorda *(a little overweight).* El abuelo es viejo *(old).* Tiene canas pero se ve joven *(he looks young).*

 doscientos cuarenta y cinco **245**

MOTIVATE

Ask students if they can think of occasions on which it is important to be able to describe someone's appearance. (to point out people in a crowd, to describe a new classmate)

TEACH

PRESENTATION
ASÍ SE DICE

Post pictures from magazines or display Teaching Transparency 6-1. Use phrases from **Así se dice** to describe each person. Point out the use of the definite articles **el, la, los,** and **las** for parts of the body. Model pronunciation and ask students to identify classmates or celebrities who have eyes or hair of a certain color. (¿**Quién tiene los ojos azules? ¿Quién tiene el pelo negro?**)

VOCABULARIO

Have students repeat the captions after you. Then have students describe themselves to a partner. Remind them to make the adjective endings agree.

CHALLENGE

17 Ask students to make the improbable statements into probable ones.

18 **¿Cómo somos?**

With a partner, take turns asking and answering these questions.

MODELO   ¿De qué color son tus ojos?
Tengo los ojos azules.

1. ¿De qué color son tus ojos?
2. ¿De qué color es tu pelo?
3. ¿De qué color son los ojos de *(name)*?
4. ¿De qué color es el pelo de *(name)*?

VOCABULARIO EXTRA

pelo castaño	*brown hair*
pelo rizado	*curly hair*
pelo liso	*straight hair*
pelo largo	*long hair*
pelo corto	*short hair*

19 **¿Cómo son tus amigos?**

Cass. 3B
CD 6 Tr. 5

Listen as Rogelio describes some people and his pets to his Aunt Maki. For each item, write the name of the character or characters he is describing.   Script and answers on p. 227E

Rebeca

Simón y Quique

Conchita y Gabriel

David

Maki

20 **Los amigos de Rogelio**

Choose one of Rogelio's friends from the drawings in Activity 19. Write three sentences describing him or her. Include hair and eye color, and say how old he or she is. You can also use words from the **Vocabulario** on page 245. Then write a description of another of Rogelio's friends.

21 Así son

María is telling you about her friends and neighbors. Complete her descriptions using the words below. Make sure to use the right form of the word!

1. Eduardo tiene catorce años. Su hermana tiene trece años. Su hermana es ———. menor
2. Amparo es una chica muy ———. Mide seis pies *(she's six feet tall)*. alta
3. Carlos es ———. Tiene seis años. joven
4. Carlos tiene quince años. Luisa tiene veinte. Luisa es ———. mayor
5. La señora Medina es muy ——— con los niños. cariñosa
6. Daniel es muy ———. Trabaja como modelo *(model)*. atractivo
7. El señor Villa tiene ochenta y cinco años. Él es ———. viejo

cariñoso/a   menor   joven   viejo/a

atractivo/a   mayor   alto/a

Nota cultural   PA   p. 74 Act. 21

Spanish speakers often use special names when they're talking to someone they like a lot. You might use **Juanito** for your friend Juan, or **Rosita** for your friend Rosa. You could call your grandmother **abuelita** and your parents **mami** and **papi**. Other words adults often use to refer to people they care about are **mi cielo** or **mi vida** *(darling or dear).* **Mi hijo/a** doesn't necessarily refer to an actual son or daughter, but to a young person the speaker is very fond of. What affectionate names have you heard people use in English?

Estoy lista, papi.

Toma la pelota, mi vida.

El papá de Cristina es muy cariñoso.

22 Adivina, adivinador

Work in a group of three or more. First choose a movie or TV show the whole group has seen. Take turns describing characters from the movie or show. Your partners must guess who you're describing.

SUGGESTION

22 Have students peer-edit each other's descriptions. Take them up and read them aloud. Have students guess as a class.

LANGUAGE NOTE

Point out that when **joven** becomes plural, it has an accent mark over the *o*. (**jóvenes**)

CULTURE NOTES

Many native speakers use the diminutive forms **abuelita** and **abuelito** when referring to their grandparents. They are similar to the English words *grandma* and *grandpa*.

The diminutive forms **hijito** and **hijita** are not only common for one's own children but for any young person thought of fondly.

ENGLISH LINK

Point out that English can in some instances form diminutives by adding *-y* or *-ette* to words. (*doggy, kitty, kitchenette*) Ask students if they can think of any other examples.

ART LINK

23 Have students draw a picture of themselves to go with the descriptions they write. You might want to post students' work throughout the class.

PRESENTATION

ASÍ SE DICE

On pairs of cards write infinitive verb phrases of things people do on weekends. (**salir, ir al parque, nadar, hacer un viaje**, etc.) Pass the cards out among students and have them "find their twin" by asking the question **¿Qué haces los fines de semana?** Once they have found their twin, ask each newly-formed pair **¿Qué hacen ustedes los fines de semana?** Use gestures to make sure it's clear to students that their answers should be in the **nosotros** form. Follow up with Activity 24 and Additional Listening Activity 6-3. Or, display Transparency 6-2 and have students describe what the families do together.

---

23 El anuario

Imagine that you're a member of the Spanish club. You've decided to have a page in your school yearbook with descriptions of all the club members. First, write a description of yourself using at least five sentences. Include what you look like and how old you are. Describe your personality. You can also use vocabulary from pages 245 and 246. Then write three sentences describing the club's sponsor.

VOCABULARIO EXTRA

egoísta   *selfish*

perezoso/a   *lazy*

trabajador/a   *hard-working*

What do you think these words mean?

agresivo/a	desorganizado/a
artístico/a	generoso/a
atlético/a	responsable
creativo/a	independiente
	tímido/a

PA
p. 69
Act. 13

6-2

ASÍ SE DICE   Discussing things a family does together

To find out what a family does together, ask:

> **¿Qué hacen ustedes** los fines de semana? *What do you do on weekends?*

Some responses might be:

> **Salimos** juntos y **visitamos a** nuestros abuelos. **Casi siempre cenamos** con ellos los domingos. *We go out together and visit our grandparents. We almost always eat dinner with them on Sundays.*

> ¿Hacen ustedes **algo** durante el verano? *Do you do something in the summer?*

> Sí. Siempre **hacemos un viaje.** *Yes. We always take a trip.*

---

24 Lupe y Víctor

Lupe is curious about her friend Víctor's family. Complete their conversation with the words from the word box.

LUPE   ¿Qué ___1___ ustedes los fines de semana?

VÍCTOR   Los fines de semana ___2___ juntos a pasear en la plaza. A veces, si tenemos dinero, ___3___ en un restaurante. Mi restaurante favorito sirve *(serves)* ___4___ mexicana. Casi siempre visitamos a mis tíos Elena y Juan los sábados por la tarde.

LUPE   ¿Y hacen ustedes ___5___ durante el verano?

VÍCTOR   Siempre ___6___ algo. A veces hacemos un ___7___ a las montañas o a la playa. Answers on p. 227K

cenamos
hacen
comida
salimos
hacemos
viaje
algo

GRAMÁTICA
The verbs hacer and salir

Hacer *(to do, make)* and **salir** *(to go out)* are regular verbs in the present tense except in the **yo** form, which has an irregular **-go** ending.

(yo)	hag**o**	(nosotros) (nosotras)	hac**emos**
(tú)	hac**es**	(vosotros) (vosotras)	hac**éis**
(usted) (él) (ella)	hac**e**	(ustedes) (ellos) (ellas)	hac**en**
	sal**go**		sal**imos**
	sal**es**		sal**ís**
	sal**e**		sal**en**

GV
pp. 48–49
Acts. 8–9

GV pp. 48–49 Acts. 8–9

25 Con la familia
Script and answers on p. 227E

Listen as four friends discuss what they do with their families and friends. Match the description you hear with the correct photo.

Cass. 3B
CD 6 Tr. 6

PRESENTATION

GRAMÁTICA

Teach students the following rhyme:
**Salir y hacer
como tú puedes ver
en la forma de yo
terminan en -go.
En las otras personas
no hay que olvidar
que la conjugación
es muy regular.**

SUGGESTION

25 As a prelistening activity, have students list phrases or expressions they're likely to hear according to the pictures. As they listen, have them check the phrases off.

LANGUAGE NOTE

The verbs **ir** and **salir** are often followed by **a** plus a destination. Often, when an infinitive comes between the conjugated verb and the destination, the preposition **a** does not change if the speaker wants to stress motion toward that destination. (**Salimos a jugar al parque. Voy a estudiar a la biblioteca.**)

26 El verano

Look at the cartoon and answer the questions based on what you see and read.   Answers in side column

1. ¿Dónde están los chicos?
2. ¿Qué hacen?
3. ¿Dónde están los tiburones *(sharks)*? (Hint: **Mar** means sea.)

27 ¿Qué haces cuando sales?   Answers will vary.

Contesta estas preguntas personales. Escribe oraciones completas.

MODELO   Casi siempre salgo al parque los fines de semana.

1. ¿Sales los fines de semana?
2. ¿Qué te gusta hacer cuando sales?
3. ¿Con quién o con quiénes sales?
4. ¿Qué te gusta hacer cuando sales con tu familia?
5. Si no sales, ¿qué haces?

GV   NOTA GRAMATICAL

p. 49
Act. 10

After most verbs, a "personal **a**" is used with nouns referring to people and pets. When referring to a place or thing, no "a" is used.

Visito **a** mis tíos en Guatemala todos los veranos. Cuando estoy con ellos, siempre visitamos las ruinas mayas.

28 Visitas

Complete the sentences that need the "personal **a**." If the sentence doesn't need it, write "no personal **a**" on your paper.

1. Visitamos ══ nuestros primos tres veces por mes. a
2. Mario va a ver ══ la Exhibición de Arte con su hermana. no personal **a**
3. Llamo ══ mis abuelos todos los domingos. a
4. Voy a visitar ══ mis amigos en Colorado este verano. a
5. Paula quiere conocer ══ unos nuevos amigos este año. a
6. Miro ══ la televisión con mi familia por la noche. no personal **a**

29 ¿Con qué frecuencia?

Use the following questions to interview a partner about his or her family, or about an imaginary family. Switch roles and be prepared to report your findings to the class.

1. ¿Dónde vives? ¿Quiénes viven contigo?
2. ¿Sales con tu familia los fines de semana? ¿Adónde van ustedes y qué hacen?
3. ¿Con quién vas al centro comercial? ¿Cómo se llama el centro comercial?
4. ¿Con qué frecuencia visitas a (tus abuelos, tus primos...)?
5. ¿A tu familia le gusta pescar, acampar, bucear o hacer esquí acuático? ¿Qué les gusta hacer?

30 Los hermanos

Together with a partner, read the descriptions of **la hermana mayor, la "chica sándwich"** (middle child), and **el hermano menor.** Imagine that you're one of the three pictured and describe yourself to your partner. See if your partner can guess if you're the oldest, the youngest, or the middle child in the family.

TRES HERMANOS, TRES PERSONALIDADES

Retrato de "la mayor". Madura, responsable, trabajadora y organizada.

Retrato de "la chica sándwich". Es completamente diferente de sus hermanos.

Retrato de "el baby de la familia". Es simpático, alegre y divertido, pero nada responsable.

ADDITIONAL PRACTICE
29 Teach the words for street (**la calle**), avenue (**la avenida**), and boulevard (**el paseo**) so that students will be able to give their addresses when asked **¿Dónde vives?** Teach them to say the street name first and then the number.

✸ CLOSE

Use Teaching Transparency 6-2 to review descriptive adjectives and terms presented in the **paso**. Ask students questions and elicit appropriate answers with these terms.

✸ ASSESS

QUIZ 6-2
Testing Program, pp. 93–94
Audio Program,
 Audiocassette 4B OR Audio CD 6 Track 20

PERFORMANCE ASSESSMENT
Ask each student to develop a set of interview questions to find out about someone's family and what they like to do. You might set up your classroom like a TV talk show. Ask students to serve as host or hostess and interview someone in the class using their list of questions. Students should be sure to use questions and expressions from **Así se dice** on pages 245 and 248. For additional Performance Assessment ideas, see Situation Cards 6-2.

Énlaces

EL ARTE

La familia The word "family" has different meanings for different people. **La familia extendida** (extended family) includes relatives such as grandparents, aunts and uncles, and cousins. When Spanish speakers talk about **mi familia**, they often include their extended family.

Look at the two portraits of families, one by Miguel Cabrera and the other by Joan Miró. Miguel Cabrera lived in Mexico in the 1700s. He is famous for his paintings of families. Joan Miró, born near Barcelona, Spain, in 1893, is famous for his playful drawings and paintings.

Answers on p. 227K

1 La familia y el arte

Work with a partner to answer these questions about the family portraits.

1. How many people are in each family?

2. Identify the family members.

3. Which portrait do you like the most and why?

2 Un dibujo

Draw a picture of your idea of family. Show your drawing to a classmate and explain it. How does your drawing compare to your classmate's?

Miguel Cabrera, *De Español y d'India, Mestisa,* 1763, 132 × 101 cm. México, Colección Particular

Joan Miró, *La Familia,* 1924, Chalk on glass paper. 29 1/2" × 41", The Museum of Modern Art, New York

LA HISTORIA

Un árbol genealógico   Have you ever seen your own family tree? How many relatives can you think of in your family? Where do they go on your tree? Family trees can be drawn in many different ways. Gabriela's family tree goes from the top (the past) down the page to the present. Complete the family tree by figuring out the missing relatives. Copy the tree on your own paper to complete it.

La familia de Gabriela

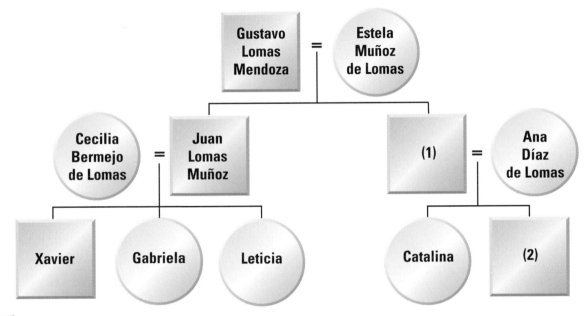

3 ¿Cómo se llaman?   Answers on p. 227K

1. ¿Cómo se llaman los hermanos de Gabriela?
2. ¿Cómo se llaman sus abuelos paternos (los padres de su padre)?
3. ¿Cómo se llama la tía de Gabriela?

4 La familia de Gabriela   Answers on p. 227K

1. El hermano de Juan es Antonio. Escribe su nombre completo en tu copia del árbol genealógico.
2. El primo de Gabriela es Pablo. Escribe su nombre completo en tu copia del árbol genealógico.

5 ¡Te toca a ti!

Work with a partner to draw your own real family trees or imaginary ones. Come up with your own symbols for events like marriage, divorce, death, and other events that affect your family. Compare your trees with those of other classmates.

ENLACES

doscientos cincuenta y tres 253

ADDITIONAL PRACTICE

3 After finishing this activity, students answer the questions in Spanish as if they were taking a survey, substituting their names for Gabriela's name. For the second question, students may choose to write about **los abuelos maternos de** _____ **(los padres de su madre)** and for the third question they may talk about **el tío** if they wish.

TEACHER NOTE

5 Allow students to talk about and draw an imaginary family if they feel uncomfortable talking about and drawing their own family.

SLOWER PACE

5 Ask volunteers how many brothers and sisters they have. Have them write the real or imaginary names of their brothers and sisters. Then lead a brainstorming session in which students suggest symbols for marriage, divorce, death, and other events. Finally, draw your family tree (or an imaginary one) as a further example. Then have students work in pairs to make their own family trees.

CHALLENGE

5 Have students present their family trees to the class in Spanish.

VIDEO INTEGRATION

Adelante LEVEL 1A

Video Program,
Videocassette 2, 40:59–41:06 OR

¡Ven conmigo! LEVEL 1

Videodisc Program,
Videodisc 3B

Search 7241, Play To 7465

JUMP START!

On the board or on a transparency write the following scrambled expressions:
1. **ecahr nu jeavi**, 2. **tarivis a ols obeausl**, and 3. **rlias raap reocm.** Ask students to unscramble them to find three things they might do with their families. (1. **hacer un viaje**, 2. **visitar a los abuelos**, 3. **salir para comer**)

SUGGESTION

31 Show the video without sound and ask students to try to remember what's happening in the story at this point.

※ MOTIVATE

Ask students to think of advice they might give to their family and friends. Ask them to share some of those things they already know how to say in Spanish.

254

TERCER PASO

Discussing problems and giving advice

31 Pepe, el travieso

Answer these questions based on what you see in the photo.

1. What do you think happened in the photo? Pepe, the dog, broke something.
2. What does Raquel say to show she's surprised and upset? ¡Ay, no! ¿Dónde está Pepe?
3. What problem does she possibly have now? She might need to clean up the mess that the dog made.

ASÍ SE DICE   Discussing problems and giving advice

PA
pp. 70–71
Acts. 14–15

To discuss a problem, say:

> **Tengo un problema.** El profesor **dice que** hablo **demasiado** en clase, **pero no es cierto. ¿Qué debo hacer?**
> *I have a problem. The teacher says that I talk too much in class, but it's not true. What should I do?*

Your friend might answer:

> **Debes** hablar **menos** en clase y escuchar más.
> *You should talk less in class and listen more.*

NOTA GRAMATICAL

CD-ROM
Disc 2

The verb **deber** *(should, ought to)* is a regular -er verb.

(yo)	deb**o**	(nosotros) (nosotras)	deb**emos**	
(tú)	deb**es**	(vosotros) (vosotras)	deb**éis**	
(usted)		(ustedes)		
(él) (ella)	deb**e**	(ellos) (ellas)	deb**en**	

GV
p. 50
Acts. 11–12

32 El consejo

You love to give advice, even to yourself! Complete each sentence with the correct form of **deber**.

1. Mi hermano ═══ hacer su tarea. debe
2. Yo ═══ organizar mis cosas para el colegio. debo
3. Rita y Naomi ═══ escuchar a la profesora. deben
4. Tú y yo ═══ comer el desayuno antes de ir al colegio. debemos
5. Tú ═══ practicar para la clase de piano. debes
6. Efraín y Saúl ═══ cuidar a su hermana menor todos los miércoles por la tarde. deben

33 Los problemas de Mónica   Script and answers on p. 227F

Cass. 3B
CD 6 Tr. 7

Listen as Mónica describes her family. Then match a photo below to each description you hear. One of her relatives isn't pictured. Who is it?

1. Mónica
2. su mamá
3. su hermana
4. su tía

a   b   c

☀ TEACH

PRESENTATION

ASÍ SE DICE
Read the problem and question from column 1 and have a student reply with the advice in column 2. Repeat this two or three times. Then ask students to practice the new expressions in pairs, using a new problem and new advice.

NOTA GRAMATICAL
Explain **deber** in Spanish as follows: **El verbo *deber* es un verbo regular que termina en -er. Se usa con el infinitivo: Debemos hablar español en clase.** Have students list five things they should and shouldn't do to do well in school. They work in pairs to compare lists. Ask one student **¿Qué debes hacer para ser buen estudiante?** He or she should reply **(No) debo _____.** Then ask **¿Qué deben hacer ustedes?** to the other partner. He or she should answer with **Nosotros (no) debemos _____.**

SUGGESTION
33 As a prelistening activity, ask students what problems they see in the photos.

PRESENTATION

VOCABULARIO

Model the vocabulary by telling the class which member of your family does or doesn't need to do each of the chores listed. Then ask students what they have to do at home. (**¿Quién debe cortar el césped?**)

TPR Bring in as many objects from **Vocabulario** as possible (a plant, a stuffed animal, a vacuum cleaner, a pillow, a sheet, a sponge, a plate, silverware, an iron). Tell various students what chores they should do and have them respond by picking up the appropriate object and mime the activity.

LANGUAGE NOTES

• The word for *grass* varies from one Spanish-speaking country to another. In Spain the word is **el césped.** In many parts of South America **la grama** is common. In Mexico, the word is **el zacate.** The words **hierba** (also **yerba**) and **pasto** are also common.

• A common expression for *to feed the cat* is **dar de comer al gato.**

---

34 ¿Qué deben hacer?

Think about what you heard Mónica say about her family's problems in Activity 33. Match the columns to identify each person's problems. Then suggest a solution from the phrases below.

Persona

1. La mamá de Mónica
2. La hermana de Mónica
3. Mónica

Problema

a. estudia todo el tiempo
b. toca la guitarra muy mal
c. trabaja demasiado

3, b Debe practicar más.

1, c Debe descansar más.

2, a Debe salir con amigos a veces.

PA p. 72 Act. 17

VOCABULARIO

GV p. 51 Acts. 13–15

6-C

Los quehaceres domésticos   *Household chores*

cortar el césped   trabajar en el jardín   hacer la cama   limpiar la cocina

pasar la aspiradora en la sala   poner la mesa   cuidar al gato   planchar

35 El sábado
Script and answers on p. 227F

Cass. 3B
CD 6 Tr. 8

Today is Saturday and Luisa and her family have made some plans. First, read the list of activities below. Then, listen as they tell about their plans. Answer **sí** for every activity Luisa is going to do, and answer **no** for each activity she isn't going to do.

1. cuidar al gato
2. patinar en línea
3. hacer la cama
4. limpiar la cocina
5. cortar el césped
6. desayunar

CD-ROM
Disc 2

NOTA GRAMATICAL

GV

p. 52
Acts.
16–17

On page 249, you learned the verbs **hacer** and **salir**. The verb **poner** also has **–go** in the **yo** form. **Poner** means *to put, to place,* or *to set (a table).*

(yo)	pon**go**	(nosotros) (nosotras)	pon**emos**
(tú)	pon**es**	(vosotros) (vosotras)	pon**éis**
(usted) (él) (ella)	pon**e**	(ustedes) (ellos) (ellas)	pon**en**

Pongo la mesa todos los días. Mi hermanita nunca la **pone**.

36 ¿Dónde lo pongo? H

A friend is staying with you for a few weeks and wants to know where you put all the stuff at your house. Complete the sentences with the correct form of **poner**. Answers in side column

1. Yo ===== mis libros en el escritorio en mi cuarto.
2. Papá ===== las zapatillas debajo de la cama.
3. Mi hermana y yo siempre ===== la ropa en el armario.
4. Martín y Daniel ===== sus libros en el estante.
5. Lola ===== el gato en el patio.
6. ===== mis lápices y cuadernos en mi mochila.

37 ¿Qué pasa aquí?
Answers on p. 227K

Get together with a partner. For each drawing, write two sentences. In the first sentence tell what the person should not be doing. In the second sentence tell what the person should be doing. Compare your sentences with your partner's.

MODELO   Pablo no debe poner la mesa en su cama.
Debe poner la mesa en la cocina.

  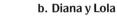

a. Pablo   b. Diana y Lola   c. Federico   d. Miguelito   e. Frida

TERCER PASO

doscientos cincuenta y siete **257**

PRESENTATION

NOTA GRAMATICAL
Write the paradigms of **hacer** and **salir** side by side in vertical columns on the board. In a third column, add the forms of **poner** as you use them in sentences. **(En mi casa, nunca pongo la mesa. ¿Pones la mesa en tu casa?)** Model pronunciation and then elicit sentences with forms of **poner** from students.

AUDITORY LEARNERS
37 Do this as a listening activity with the following script. Have students match each photo with the correct sentence. Emphasize the italicized words.
1. No debe pasar aspiradora *en el césped*. (c)
2. No debe poner la mesa *en la cama*. (a)
3. Deben trabajar *en el jardín*. (b)
4. Debe *sacar* la basura. (d)
5. Debe cuidar *al gato*. (e)

Answers to Activity 36
1. pongo
2. pone
3. ponemos
4. ponen
5. pone
6. Pongo

ADDITIONAL PRACTICE

38 Have students assign chores to people in their house, according to what members of their family like to do. (**Mi hermano debe lavar los platos porque come mucho.**)

🏰 GAME

Tell students you are **el sabio** or **la sabia** *(the wise one)*. Offer to help them with an imaginary problem they have. Provide them with a suitable answer. After you have modeled this several times, have a student take your place as **el sabio** or **la sabia**.

CHALLENGE

39 Have students write their own letters to an advice columnist about a simple problem, real or imaginary. Students exchange letters and write responses offering each other advice.

38 ¡Todo bajo control!

You're assigning everyone a chore using phrases from the **Vocabulario** on page 256. Try to assign each person the chore he or she likes. Some people may have more than one job. Answers on p. 227K

MODELO A mí me gusta tener el cuarto organizado.
Debo limpiar mi cuarto.

1. A ti y a tu hermana menor les gustan los animales.
2. A tus abuelitos les gustan las plantas.
3. A tu primo le gusta pasar el rato con tus hermanos menores.
4. A tu hermano mayor le gusta la comida.
5. A ti te gusta estar afuera *(outside)* y te gustan las máquinas *(machines)*.
6. A Ana y a ti les gusta tener la ropa bonita.

39 Querida Amalia

A Read this letter that was written to a newspaper advice columnist.

> Querida Amalia,
> Nosotros vivimos en una casa muy bonita, pero nunca se ve bien porque mis hermanitos no limpian la casa. Yo no tengo mucho tiempo libre. El problema es que mis padres dicen que yo nunca ayudo en casa. ¿Qué debo hacer?
> Un cordial saludo de,
> Una chica trabajadora

B Now help complete the letter with Amalia's advice. Use the words below. Each word will be used only once.

2 quehaceres
3 limpia
4 cocina
1 ayudar
5 trabajan
6 bonita

Querida Chica trabajadora,
¡Qué bueno que quieres ___1___!
Pregúntale a tu mamá por qué no divide los ___2___. Cada semana alguien ___3___ la sala, y todos los días otra persona limpia la ___4___ después de cenar. De esa forma ustedes ___5___ un poco, y tienen una casa limpia y ___6___.
Atentamente,
Amalia

40 Una encuesta

Take a survey of five classmates. Ask them what chores they do around the house. Using **dice que...**, write five sentences reporting what your classmates say. Be prepared to share your survey with the class.

41 En mi cuaderno

Write a description of two friends or family members from a book, movie, or TV series. Include their ages, where they live, and what they're like. Next, describe any problems they may have, such as household chores they don't like doing, or problems they have at home or at school. Finally, give them some advice about what to do. Write at least ten sentences in your journal.

Leonardo dice que lava los platos todos los días.

Script on p. 227F

LETRA Y SONIDO

Cass. 3B
CD 6
Trs. 9–13

A. The **r** in Spanish does not sound like the *r* in English. English does have a sound that is similar, however. It's the sound made by quickly touching the tip of the tongue to the ridge behind the upper teeth, as in bu*tt*er, ba*tt*er, la*dd*er.

1. The **r** is pronounced this way between vowels.

| cariñoso | cara | moreno | favorito | pero |

2. At the beginning of a word or after an **n** or **l**, the single **r** has a trilled or rolled sound. It is also usually trilled at the end of a word.

| rojo | rubio | enrojecer | Enrique | alrededor |

3. The double **r** in Spanish always has a trilled or rolled sound.

| pelirrojo | perro | carro | correo |

B. Dictado
Listen to a TV ad that features a famous athlete, Rafael Ramírez. Write what you hear.

C. Trabalenguas
La rata roe la ropa del rey de Roma.

CAPÍTULO 6

📖 EN MI CUADERNO
41 For an additional journal entry suggestion, see *Practice and Activity Book,* p. 80.

AUDITORY LEARNERS
Before practicing the **trabalenguas,** have students practice the sound used to imitate a motor boat or the revving of an engine to convince them that they can do it.

NATIVE SPEAKERS
Some speakers from Puerto Rico and other parts of the Caribbean may pronounce the trilled *r* like the *j* in Spanish and the single *r* at the end of a syllable as an *l.* They should check the spelling of words with these sounds.

☀ CLOSE

Write common problems on slips of paper. (**Tengo mucha tarea.**) Place the slips in a bag. Have each student draw a slip of paper and write helpful advice.

☀ ASSESS

QUIZ 6-3
Testing Program, pp. 95–96
Audio Program,
Audiocassette 4B OR
Audio CD 6 Track 21

PERFORMANCE ASSESSMENT
Ask students to list five chores their younger brother or sister should do on Saturday.

VIDEO INTEGRATION

Adelante LEVEL 1A
Video Program,
Videocassette 2, 50:33–52:08

TEACHER NOTES

• See *Video Guide* for activities related to the **Panorama cultural.**

• Remind students that cultural information may be included in the Quizzes and Chapter Test.

• The language of the people interviewed represents informal, unrehearsed speech. Occasionally, text has been edited for clarity.

MOTIVATING ACTIVITY

Ask students to think about the number of people in their family. Ask them if they have an opinion on how big a family should be. Ask students what sorts of things they enjoy doing with their families. Would they like to spend more or less time with them? Why? Would they like to spend more time with their grandparents if they could? Why or why not?

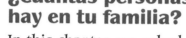

Panorama cultural

CD-ROM Disc 2

Cass. 3B
CD 6 Trs. 14–17

¿Cuántas personas hay en tu familia?

In this chapter, we asked some people about their families and what they do to help around the house.

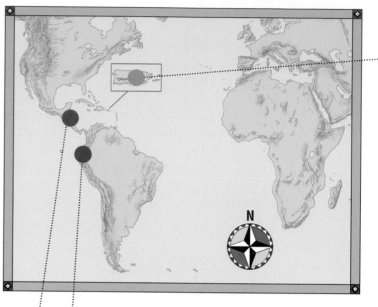

N

Hay cuatro personas en la familia de Melisa. ¿Cuántos son en tu familia?

Pablo trabaja bastante en casa. ¿Y tú? ¿Qué haces en casa? ¿Tienes hermanos que ayudan?

● **Melisa**
Santo Domingo de Heredia, Costa Rica
CD 6 Tr. 15

Somos cuatro. Mi mamá, mi papá, mi hermano y yo. [Mi hermano y yo] peleamos mucho a veces.

● **Pablo**
Quito, Ecuador
CD 6 Tr. 16

En mi familia hay cinco personas. Yo lavo los platos, eh... limpio la cocina, arreglo mi cuarto y limpio mi baño.

En la familia de Éric hay siete personas.
¡Claro que hay mucho que hacer en casa!

 Éric CD 6 Tr. 17
Ponce,
Puerto Rico

Somos siete:
mis dos hermanas y tres
hermanos. Tengo un hermano
menor. Algunas veces tengo
que cuidarlo.

PRESENTATION
After showing the video,
have students assume the
identity of one of the interviewees. Ask the question
¿Cuántos son en tu familia?
Have students answer
based on their new identity.
Encourage students to
answer without looking at
their books. Stress that the
fluency of the exchange is
more important than providing the exact information.

1 ¿Cuántos hermanos tiene Melisa? un hermano

2 ¿Se llevan bien Melisa y su hermano? ¿Cómo lo
sabes? *(How do you know?)* No. Pelean muchas veces.

3 ¿Cuántos son en la familia de Pablo? cinco

4 ¿Cuáles son tres de los quehaceres que hace Pablo?
Possible answers: Lava los platos, limpia el baño y limpia su cuarto.

5 ¿Cuántos hermanos mayores tiene Éric? dos hermanos

6 ¿Cómo ayuda Éric en casa? Cuida a su hermano menor.

THINKING CRITICALLY
Have students deduce the
meaning of **peleamos.** *(we
fight)* They should first be able
to identify it as a verb, then as
a verb in the **nosotros** form.

Para pensar y hablar...

A. Of the three interviewees, whose family is most like your
own? Name two ways in which that interviewee's family is
like yours.

B. Pablo mentions several chores he does at home. With a
partner, talk about how you help out at home. Use Spanish
to describe the chores you do. Use the vocabulary on
page 256.

261

VAMOS A LEER

Estrategia

Organization Before beginning to read, use the pictures, title, and subtitles to get a feeling for how the passage is organized. Knowing how the passage is organized will help you figure out what it's about. It can also help you quickly find a specific piece of information.

¡A comenzar!

A This reading is from the **Guía oficial de la Pequeña Habana**, a guide for tourists in Miami. Skim it to find out which of these items is not among the four suggestions.

- buying fruit
- watching a cultural dance
- ⊙ visiting museums
- playing dominoes
- eating Chinese-Cuban food

Al grano

B You've already studied two important ways to guess the meanings of words: using cognates and using context. Now you can combine these two skills to read more effectively.

Cognates. See if an unknown word looks like an English word. Does the English meaning make sense in context?

Context. Look at all the words before and after the word you don't know. Understanding the rest of the sentence will help you guess what the unknown word means.

C Your family needs help reading the guide. Listed here are the words they're having trouble with. The first two words in each item are cognates. You can guess the third word through context. Go back and be sure your guess makes sense with the rest of the sentence.

1. Your brother might like to try a game of dominoes. Help him with these words:
   cognates: **espectáculo, interrumpe**
   context: **cafetín** (a. caffeine b. game ⓒ café)
2. Help your mother with these words about the Chinese-Cuban restaurant:
   cognates: **tradiciones, numerosos**
   context: **probar** (a. break b. prepare ⓒ taste)
3. Your sister is trying to decide if she wants to watch a flamenco performance.
   cognates: **fabulosos, movimientos**
   context: **cuerpo** (a. handsome ⓑ body c. carpet)
4. You have decided to buy some fruit. Decide what these words mean:
   cognates: **variedades, coco**
   context: **paradores** (ⓐ roadside stands b. walls c. parades)

D Write a list in Spanish of four interesting things you can do where you live. Then discuss these activities with a partner.

La Pequeña Habana

VER UN BAILE FLAMENCO

El flamenco es una danza expresiva y emocionante. Es una celebración de la forma del cuerpo humano. Tradicional en España, el flamenco es un espectáculo que se presenta diariamente en fabulosos restaurantes de la Pequeña Habana, como el Málaga.

IR A UN RESTAURANTE CHINO-CUBANO Y PROBAR SUS PLATOS

Durante los años de 1800 a 1900, muchos chinos llegaron a Cuba como esclavos y combinaron su cultura con la cultura cubana. Todavía se mantienen las tradiciones de la cocina china en los numerosos restaurantes aquí en la Pequeña Habana.

JUGAR DOMINÓ EN EL PARQUE DEL DOMINÓ

Éste es un espectáculo que no tiene igual en todos los Estados Unidos. Los hombres se reúnen alrededor de las mesas de dominó para jugar. Aquí los hombres (no hay mujeres) juegan casi sin hablar. Sólo se interrumpe el juego para ir al cafetín de al lado y comprarse un fuerte café cubano.

COMPRAR DIFERENTES VARIEDADES DE FRUTAS

Abundan mangos, papayas, mameyes, cocos, plátanos, bananas, naranjas y toronjas en diferentes tiendas y paradores.

☀ READING

B and **C** Have students do Activity B as individual work. If needed, this may be assigned as homework. Emphasize the importance of testing a word in context, even if the word is a cognate. For example, many students may want to guess that **política** means *political,* but an adjective does not fit in the context. Other words you may want your students to guess: **espectáculo, esclavos, diariamente.**

☀ POSTREADING

D If this task is challenging to some students, assign pairs so that one of each pair is able to help the other.

GROUP WORK

Have students construct a bulletin board about interesting things to do in your community. Decide on five locations. Then assign each one to a group. Each group prepares the Spanish description of a location and brings in photographs.

COMMUNITY LINK

Ask students to interview a local grocer to find out which fruits are grown in their area and which are imported.

CAPÍTULO 6 · CAPÍTULO 6 · CAPÍTULO 6 · CAPÍTULO 6 · CAPÍTULO 6 · CAPÍTULO 6 · CAPÍTULO 6 · CAPÍTULO 6

The **Repaso** reviews and integrates all four skills and culture in preparation for the Chapter Test.

ADDITIONAL PRACTICE

Have students clip comic strips from the newspaper and cover the speech bubbles. Exchanging comics, students can then use Spanish to describe a problem and tell what should be done.

Answers to Activity 3

Answers will vary. Possible answers:

A **padrino** is a godfather and a **madrina** is a godmother.

Godparents provide love, support, and advice for their godchild.

Godparents are usually very close with the parents of their godchild and are often considered part of the family.

REPASO

1

Cass. 3B
CD 6
Tr. 18

First read the statements about Marcos and his family. Then listen as Marcos describes his family. Match a family member with each numbered item.   Script and answers on p. 227F

1. Es un poco gordo.
2. Debe trabajar menos.
3. Ella es inteligente.
4. Tiene un cuarto organizado.
5. Es músico (a musician).
6. Debe estudiar más.

2

Complete the following letter with words from the box. Make sure to use the correct form of the verbs.

viaje	vivir	primo/a
tener	delgado/a	
ayudar	gato/a	
hermanos/as		alto/a

1. prima
2. alta
3. hermanos
4. delgado
5. gato
6. vive
7. ayudamos
8. Tengo
9. viaje

¡Hola!

Me llamo Carolina. Soy tu __1__ . Tengo doce años. Soy morena y tengo los ojos de color café. Soy __2__ y un poco gorda. Tengo dos __3__ , Guillermo y Paco. Paco tiene catorce años y es muy __4__ . Guillermo tiene cinco años y es travieso pero cariñoso. Tenemos un __5__ . Se llama Nacho.
Mi familia __6__ en una casa grande. Todos __7__ a limpiar la casa. __8__ un cuarto muy bonito. ¿Y tú? ¿Cómo es tu casa? ¿Y tu familia? Siempre hacemos un __9__ durante el verano. ¡Algún día te visitamos!

Saludos,

Carolina

3

Work with a partner. What are a **padrino** and **madrina**? Explain two things about this relationship.   Answers in side column

4 Your drama class is going to write a one-act comedy about a large family. Your task is to describe the cast of characters. Tell how many there are, where they live, their names, ages, and what each one looks like. Also say what each is like or what things each one likes.

MODELO El abuelo se llama Pablo. Tiene setenta y ocho años. Tiene canas y tiene los ojos de color café. Es muy inteligente. A él le gusta…

5 Vamos a escribir

Answer your pen pal Carolina's letter. Write at least two paragraphs. In the first paragraph, describe your family and yourself. In the second paragraph, tell Carolina what you do with your family. You may write a third paragraph with anything else you want to say. Use an appropriate closing.

Estrategia

Writing a letter When writing a personal letter, always start with the date and then the salutation or greeting. Some salutations you might use include **Hola…**, **Querido/a….** Remember to indent the first line of each paragraph. Finally, write a closing such as **Saludos,** *(Greetings)*, **Abrazos,** *(Hugs)*, **Recuerdos,** *(Regards)*, followed by a comma. Write your name directly under the closing.

> 3 de julio de ____
> Querida ____,
> _____
> _____
> _____
>   Saludos,

6 SITUACIÓN

It's summer, and your pen pal Carolina has come from Miami to visit for a week. Introduce her to your family. Be sure to tell what activities your family does together. Ask Carolina about her family.

PORTFOLIO

4 Oral You might have students work in groups to create a dialogue for their one-act comedy. They might then perform their work for the class and record it for their oral Portfolio. For Portfolio information, see *Alternative Assessment Guide,* p. 17.

5 Written Your students may wish to enclose their letter to Carolina as an addition to their Portfolio. For Portfolio suggestions, see *Assessment Guide,* p. 17.

This page is intended to help students prepare for the Chapter Test. It is designed for the students to work on their own initiative and consists of a brief checklist of the major points covered in the chapter. The students should be reminded that it is only a checklist and does not necessarily include everything that will appear on the Chapter Test.

Answers to Question 3

Answers will vary. Possible answers:

a. Su abuelo tiene canas. Es viejo y delgado y es muy cariñoso.

b. Su mamá tiene pelo negro y trabaja en el jardín.

c. Toño tiene pelo negro y ojos de color café. Es cómico.

d. Óscar es moreno. Tiene pelo negro y es travieso.

A VER SI PUEDO...

▼ Can you describe a family? p. 236

1 Can you tell Ramiro, a new student at your school. . .?   Answers will vary.

1. how many people there are in your family
2. how many brothers and sisters you have
3. what the names of your family members are
4. what they like to do in their free time

2 Can you complete each sentence with the correct family member?

1. La mamá de mi papá es mi ___abuela___.
2. El hijo de mi tía es mi ___primo___.
3. La hija de mis padres es mi ___hermana___.
4. El hermano de mi mamá es mi ___tío___.

▼ Can you describe people? p. 245

3 Describe these members of Florencia's family.   Answers in side column

a. su abuelo

b. su mamá

c. su hermano, Toño

d. su hermano, Óscar

▼ Can you discuss things a family does together? p. 248

4 Can you tell someone . . .?   Answers on p. 227K

1. how often your family has dinner together
2. who your family visits and how often you visit
3. where your family goes on outings

▼ Can you discuss problems and give advice?   p. 255

5 Paula and her family need help solving these problems. What should each person do?   Answers on p. 227K

1. Her sister is disorganized and can't find any of her things.
2. Paula's brother works all the time and he's very tired.
3. It's six o'clock in the evening and everyone's hungry.

VOCABULARIO

PRIMER PASO

Describing a family

la abuela *grandmother*
el abuelo *grandfather*
los abuelos *grandparents*
¿Cómo es tu familia? *What is your family like?*
¿Cuántas personas hay en tu familia? *How many people are there in your family?*
la esposa *wife*
el esposo *husband*
éstas *these (feminine)*
éstos *these (masc., masc. and fem.)*
la familia *family*
el gato *cat*
la hermana *sister*
la hermanastra *stepsister*
el hermanastro *stepbrother*
el hermano *brother*
los hermanos *brothers, brothers and sisters*
la hija *daughter*
el hijo *son*
los hijos *children*
la madrastra *stepmother*
la madre/mamá *mother/mom*
la media hermana *half sister*
el medio hermano *half brother*
mi/mis *my*
nuestro/a *our*
el padrastro *stepfather*
el padre/papá *father/dad*
los padres *parents*
la prima *female cousin*
el primo *male cousin*
los primos *cousins*
ser unido *to be close-knit*
Somos cinco. *There are five of us.*
su/sus *his, her, their, your (formal)*
la tía *aunt*
el tío *uncle*
tu/tus *your (familiar)*
unido/a *close-knit*
vivir *to live*
vuestro/a *your (pl., Spain)*

SEGUNDO PASO

Describing people

azul *blue*
cariñoso/a *affectionate*
de color café *brown*
¿De qué color es/son...? *What color is/are . . . ?*
delgado/a *thin*
listo/a *clever, smart (with ser)*
mayor *older*
menor *younger*
negro/a *black*
los ojos *eyes*
pelirrojo/a *redheaded*
el pelo *hair*
un poco gordo/a *a little overweight*
Se ve joven. *He/She looks young.*
Tiene canas. *He/She has gray hair.*
Tiene los ojos verdes/azules. *He/She has green/blue eyes.*
travieso/a *mischievous*
verde *green*
viejo/a *old*

Discussing things a family does together

algo *something*
casi siempre *almost always*
cenar *to eat dinner*
hacer un viaje *to take a trip*

¿Qué hacen ustedes los fines de semana? *What do you do on weekends?*
salir *to go out, to leave*
visitar *to visit*

TERCER PASO

Discussing problems and giving advice

cortar el césped *to cut the grass*
cuidar al gato *to take care of the cat*
deber *should, ought to*
Debes... *You should . . .*
demasiado *too much*
dice que *he/she says that*
hacer la cama *to make the bed*
limpiar la cocina *to clean the kitchen*
menos *less*
No es cierto. *It's not true.*
pasar la aspiradora *to vacuum*
planchar *to iron*
poner la mesa *to set the table*
un problema *a problem*
¿Qué debo hacer? *What should I do?*
los quehaceres domésticos *household chores*
la sala *living room*
trabajar en el jardín *to work in the garden*

🏰 **GAME**
El ritmo See pages 227I–227J for this game and others to review vocabulary.

CHAPTER 6 ASSESSMENT

CHAPTER TEST
• *Testing Program,* pp. 97–104
• *Audio Program,*
Assessment Items,
 Audiocassette 4B OR
Audio CD 6 Trs. 22–23

SPEAKING TEST
• *Testing Program,* p. 114

TEST GENERATOR
Chapter 6

ALTERNATIVE ASSESSMENT
Performance Assessment
You might want to use the **Situación** on page 265 as a cumulative performance assessment activity.

📁 **Portfolio Assessment**
ANNOTATED TEACHER'S EDITION
• **Written: Repaso** Activity 5, p. 265
• **Oral: Repaso** Activity 4, p. 265
ALTERNATIVE ASSESSMENT GUIDE, p. 17

FINAL EXAM
• *Testing Program,* pp. 125–136
• *Audio Program,*
Assessment Items,
Audiocassette 4B OR
Audio CD 6 Trs. 24–26

SUMMARY OF FUNCTIONS

Functions are probably best defined as the ways in which you use a language for particular purposes. When you find yourself in specific situations, such as in a restaurant, in a grocery store, or at a school, you'll want to communicate with those around you. In order to do that, you have to "function" in Spanish: you place an order, buy something, or talk about your class schedule.

Such language functions form the core of this book. They're easily identified by the boxes in each chapter labeled **Así se dice.** The functional phrases in these boxes are the building blocks you need to become a speaker of Spanish. All the other features in the chapter—the grammar, the vocabulary, even the culture notes—are there to support the functions you're learning.

Here is a list of the functions presented in this book and the Spanish expressions you'll need in order to communicate in a wide range of situations. Following each function is the chapter and page number where it was introduced.

SOCIALIZING

Saying hello   Ch. 1, p. 27

Buenos días.	Buenas noches.
Buenas tardes.	Hola.

Saying goodbye   Ch. 1, p. 27

Adiós.	Hasta luego.
Bueno, tengo clase.	Hasta mañana.
Chao.	Tengo que irme.

Introducing people and responding to an introduction   Ch. 1, p. 29

Me llamo...	Se llama...
Soy...	¡Mucho gusto!
¿Cómo te llamas?	Encantado/a.
Éste es mi amigo...	Igualmente.
Ésta es mi amiga...	

Asking how someone is and saying how you are   Ch. 1, p. 31

¿Cómo estás?	Estupendo/a.
¿Y tú?	Excelente.
¿Qué tal?	Regular.
Estoy (bastante) bien, gracias.	Más o menos.
	(Muy) mal.
Yo también.	¡Horrible!

EXCHANGING INFORMATION

Asking and saying how old someone is   Ch. 1, p. 35

¿Cuántos años tienes?	¿Cuántos años tiene?
Tengo ... años.	Tiene ... años.

Asking where someone is from and saying where you're from   Ch. 1, p. 38

¿De dónde eres?	¿De dónde es...?
Soy de...	Es de...

Talking about what you want and need   Ch. 2, p. 66

¿Qué quieres?	Necesito...
Quiero...	¿Qué necesita?
Quiere...	Ya tengo...
¿Qué necesitas?	Necesita...
¿Necesitas...?	

Saying what's in your room   Ch. 2, p. 76

¿Qué hay en tu cuarto?	Hay ... en su cuarto.
(No) tengo ... en mi cuarto.	¿Tienes...?
¿Qué hay en el cuarto de...?	¿Qué tiene ... en su cuarto?
	Tiene ... en su cuarto.

Talking about what you need and want to do   Ch. 2, p. 85

¿Qué necesitas hacer?	Quiero hacer...
Necesito...	No sé, pero no quiero...
¿Qué necesita hacer...?	
Necesita...	¿Qué quiere hacer...?
¿Qué quieres hacer?	Quiere...

Talking about classes and sequencing events   Ch. 3, p. 110

¿Qué clases tienes este semestre?	Primero tengo..., después... y luego...
Tengo...	¿Y cuándo tienes un día libre?
¿Qué clases tienes hoy?	Mañana por fin...

Telling time   Ch. 3, p. 112

¿Qué hora es?	Son las ... y cuarto.
Es la una.	Son las ... y media.
Es la una y cuarto.	¿Ya son las...?
Es la una y media.	Es tarde.
Son las...	

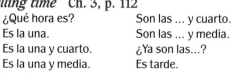

Telling at what time something happens
Ch. 3, p.119

¿A qué hora es...?	¡Es ahora!
(Es) a las ... de la tarde.	En punto.

Talking about being late or in a hurry
Ch. 3, p. 122

Estoy atrasado/a.	Tengo prisa.
Está atrasado/a.	¡Date prisa!

Describing people and things   Ch. 3, p. 125

¿Cómo es...?	¿Cómo son...?
Es...	Son...
No es...	No son...

Talking about what you and others do during free time   Ch. 4, p. 152

¿Qué haces después de clases?	¡Descanso! En el tiempo libre
Antes de regresar a casa...	practico la guitarra...

Telling where people and things are
Ch. 4, p. 161

¿Dónde estás?	No, no está aquí.
Estoy en...	Está en...
¿No está en...?	

Talking about where you and others go during free time   Ch. 4, p. 171

¿Adónde vas?	Va a...
Voy a...	Va al...
¿Adónde va...?	Va a la...

Discussing how often you do things
Ch. 5, p. 195

¿Con qué frecuencia...?	Durante la semana
Todos los días	A veces
Siempre	Muchas veces
Nunca	Sólo cuando...
¿Todavía...?	

Talking about what you do during a typical week   Ch. 5, p. 209

¿Qué haces típicamente durante el día?
¿Qué hace ... por la mañana?
¿Qué hacen ... por la tarde?
¿Qué hacen ... por la noche?

Giving today's date   Ch. 5, p. 213

¿Cuál es la fecha?	Hoy es el primero de...
¿Qué fecha es hoy?	Hoy es el ... de...
El cuatro de este mes hay...	

Talking about the weather   Ch. 5, p. 216

¿Qué tiempo hace?
Hace buen tiempo.
Hace muy mal tiempo hoy.

Describing a family   Ch. 6, p. 236

¿Cuántas personas hay en tu familia?	Somos cinco. Somos muy unidos.
¿Cómo es tu familia?	Tenemos...
Hay ... en mi familia.	

Describing people   Ch. 6, p. 245

¿Cómo es...?	¿De qué color es...?
Tiene...	¿De qué color son...?

Discussing things a family does together
Ch. 6, p. 248

¿Qué hacen ustedes los fines de semana?	Salimos ... y visitamos a...
¿Hacen ustedes algo durante el verano?	Hacemos un viaje juntos.

EXPRESSING ATTITUDES AND OPINIONS

Talking about what you like and don't like
Ch. 1, p. 43

¿Qué te gusta?	Me gusta (más)...
¿Te gusta...?	No me gusta...

Talking about things you like and explaining why   Ch. 3, p. 129

¿Te gustan...?	Sí, a ella le gustan
Sí, me gustan.	mucho.
¿Cuál es...?	¿Por qué?
¿A ella le gustan...?	Porque...

Talking about what you and others like to do   Ch. 4, p. 149

¿Qué te gusta hacer?	¿A quién le gusta...?
Me gusta...	A mí me gusta...
¿A él le gusta...?	Por eso, me gustan...
No, no le gusta...	
pero le gusta...	

Talking about what you and your friends like to do together   Ch. 5, p. 203

¿Qué les gusta hacer?	Especialmente durante
¿Les gusta ... juntos?	las vacaciones.
Nos gusta...	

Discussing problems and giving advice
Ch. 6, p. 255

¿Qué debo hacer?	Dicen que... demasiado
Tengo un problema.	pero no es cierto.
Debes ... más/menos.	

The **Grammar and Vocabulary Workbook** re-presents all major grammar points and offers additional focused practice with the structures, words, and phrases targeted in each **Paso**.

GRAMMAR SUMMARY

NOUNS AND ARTICLES

GENDER OF NOUNS

In Spanish, nouns (words that name a person, place, or thing) are grouped into two classes or genders: masculine and feminine. All nouns, both persons and objects, fall into one of these groups. Most nouns that end in -**o** are masculine, and most nouns that end in -**a**, -**ción**, -**tad**, and -**dad** are feminine.

MASCULINE NOUNS	FEMININE NOUNS
libro	casa
chico	universidad
cuaderno	situación
bolígrafo	mesa
vestido	libertad

FORMATION OF PLURAL NOUNS

Add -**s** to nouns that end in a vowel.		Add -**es** to nouns that end in a consonant.		With nouns that end in -**z**, the -**z** changes to -**c**.	
SINGULAR	PLURAL	SINGULAR	PLURAL	SINGULAR	PLURAL
libro	libro**s**	profesor	profesor**es**	vez	ve**ces**
casa	casa**s**	papel	papel**es**	lápiz	lápi**ces**

DEFINITE ARTICLES

There are words that signal the class of the noun. One of these is the definite article. In English there is one definite article: *the.* In Spanish, there are four: **el, la, los, las.**

SUMMARY OF DEFINITE ARTICLES

	MASCULINE	FEMININE
Singular	**el** chico	**la** chica
Plural	**los** chicos	**las** chicas

CONTRACTIONS

a	+	el	→	**al**
de	+	el	→	**del**

INDEFINITE ARTICLES

Another group of words that are used with nouns is the *indefinite article:* **un, una,** *(a* or *an)* and **unos, unas** *(some* or *a few).*

SUMMARY OF INDEFINITE ARTICLES

	MASCULINE	FEMININE
Singular	**un** chico	**una** chica
Plural	**unos** chicos	**unas** chicas

SUBJECT PRONOUNS	DIRECT OBJECT PRONOUNS	INDIRECT OBJECT PRONOUNS	OBJECTS OF PREPOSITIONS
yo	me	me	mí (conmigo)
tú	te	te	ti (contigo)
él, ella, usted	lo, la	le	él, ella, usted
nosotros, nosotras	nos	nos	nosotros, nosotras
vosotros, vosotras	os	os	vosotros, vosotras
ellos, ellas, ustedes	los, las	les	ellos, ellas, ustedes

ADJECTIVES

Adjectives are words that describe nouns. The adjective must agree in gender (masculine or feminine) and number (singular or plural) with the noun it modifies. Adjectives that end in -e or a consonant only agree in number.

		MASCULINE	FEMININE
Adjectives that end in -o	Singular	chico alto	chica alta
	Plural	chicos altos	chicas altas
Adjectives that end in -e	Singular	chico inteligente	chica inteligente
	Plural	chicos inteligentes	chicas inteligentes
Adjectives that end in a consonant	Singular	examen difícil	clase difícil
	Plural	exámenes difíciles	clases difíciles

DEMONSTRATIVE ADJECTIVES

	MASCULINE	FEMININE
Singular	**este** chico	**esta** chica
Plural	**estos** chicos	**estas** chicas

	MASCULINE	FEMININE
Singular	**ese** chico	**esa** chica
Plural	**esos** chicos	**esas** chicas

When demonstratives are used as pronouns, they match the gender and number of the noun they replace and are written with an accent mark.

POSSESSIVE ADJECTIVES

These words also modify nouns and tell you *whose* object or person is being referred to (*my* car, *his* book, *her* mother).

SINGULAR		PLURAL	
MASCULINE	FEMININE	MASCULINE	FEMININE
mi libro	**mi** casa	**mis** libros	**mis** casas
tu libro	**tu** casa	**tus** libros	**tus** casas
su libro	**su** casa	**sus** libros	**sus** casas
nuestro libro	**nuestra** casa	**nuestros** libros	**nuestras** casas
vuestro libro	**vuestra** casa	**vuestros** libros	**vuestras** casas

AFFIRMATIVE AND NEGATIVE EXPRESSIONS

AFFIRMATIVE	NEGATIVE
algo	nada
alguien	nadie
alguno (algún), -a	ninguno (ningún), -a
o ... o	ni ... ni
siempre	nunca

INTERROGATIVE WORDS

¿Adónde? ¿Cómo? ¿Cuál(es)? ¿Cuándo?	¿Cuánto(a)? ¿Cuántos(as)? ¿De dónde? ¿Dónde?	¿Por qué? ¿Qué? ¿Quién(es)?

COMPARATIVES

Comparatives are used to compare people or things. With comparisons of inequality, the same structure is used with adjectives, adverbs or nouns. With comparisons of equality, **tan** is used with adjectives and adverbs, and **tanto/a/os/as** with nouns.

COMPARATIVE OF INEQUALITY

$$\left.\begin{array}{c} \text{más} \\ \text{menos} \end{array}\right\} + \left\{\begin{array}{c} \text{adjective} \\ \text{adverb} \\ \text{noun} \end{array}\right\} \qquad \left.\begin{array}{c} \text{más} \\ \text{menos} \end{array}\right\} + \textbf{de} + \text{number}$$

COMPARATIVE OF EQUALITY

tan + adjective or adverb + **como**
tanto/a/os/as + noun + **como**

VERBS

REGULAR VERBS

In Spanish we use a formula to conjugate regular verbs. The endings change for each person, but the stem of the verb remains the same.

PRESENT TENSE OF REGULAR VERBS

INFINITIVE	PRESENT			
hablar	(yo)	habl**o**	(nosotros/as)	habl**amos**
	(tú)	habl**as**	(vosotros/as)	habl**áis**
	(él/ella/usted)	habl**a**	(ellos/ellas/ustedes)	habl**an**
comer	(yo)	com**o**	(nosotros/as)	com**emos**
	(tú)	com**es**	(vosotros/as)	com**éis**
	(él/ella/usted)	com**e**	(ellos/ellas/ustedes)	com**en**
escribir	(yo)	escrib**o**	(nosotros/as)	escrib**imos**
	(tú)	escrib**es**	(vosotros/as)	escrib**ís**
	(él/ella/usted)	escrib**e**	(ellos/ellas/ustedes)	escrib**en**

VERBS WITH IRREGULAR YO FORMS

hacer		poner		saber		salir		traer	
hago	hacemos	**pongo**	ponemos	**sé**	sabemos	**salgo**	salimos	**traigo**	traemos
haces	hacéis	pones	ponéis	sabes	sabéis	sales	salís	traes	traéis
hace	hacen	pone	ponen	sabe	saben	sale	salen	trae	traen

VERBS WITH IRREGULAR FORMS

ser		estar		ir	
soy	somos	estoy	estamos	voy	vamos
eres	sois	estás	estáis	vas	vais
es	son	está	están	va	van

PRESENT PROGRESSIVE

The present progressive in English is formed by using the verb *to be* plus the *-ing* form of another verb. In Spanish, the present progressive is formed by using the verb **estar** plus the -**ndo** form of another verb.

-**ar** verbs	-**er** and -**ir** verbs	For -**er** and -**ir** verbs with a stem that ends in a vowel, the -**iendo** changes to -**yendo**:
hablar → estoy habl**ando** trabajar → trabaj**ando**	comer → com**iendo** escribir → escrib**iendo**	leer → le**yendo**

STEM-CHANGING VERBS

In Spanish, some verbs have an irregular stem in the present tense. The final vowel of the stem changes from **e** → **ie** and **o** → **ue** in all forms except **nosotros** and **vosotros.**

e → ie		o → ue		u → ue	
preferir		**poder**		**jugar**	
pref**ie**ro	preferimos	p**ue**do	podemos	j**ue**go	jugamos
pref**ie**res	preferís	p**ue**des	podéis	j**ue**gas	jugáis
pref**ie**re	pref**ie**ren	p**ue**de	p**ue**den	j**ue**ga	j**ue**gan

The following is a list of some **e** → **ie** stem-changing verbs:	The following is a list of some **o** → **ue** stem-changing verbs:
empezar **pensar** **querer** **preferir**	**almorzar** **doler** **encontrar** **poder**

THE VERBS GUSTAR AND ENCANTAR

To express likes and dislikes, the verb **gustar** is used in Spanish. The verb **encantar** is used to talk about things you really like or love. The verb endings for **gustar** and **encantar** always agree with what is liked or loved. The indirect object pronouns always precede the verb forms.

gustar		encantar	
If one thing is liked:	If more than one thing is liked:	If one thing is really liked:	If more than one thing is really liked:
me te le } gusta nos les	me te le } gustan nos les	me te le } encanta nos les	me te le } encantan nos les

PRETERITE OF REGULAR VERBS

INFINITIVE	PRETERITE OF REGULAR VERBS			
hablar	(yo) hablé	(nosotros/as) hablamos	(tú) hablaste	(vosotros/as) hablasteis
	(él/ella) habló	(ellos/ellas) hablaron		
comer	(yo) comí	(nosotros/as) comimos	(tú) comiste	(vosotros/as) comisteis
	(él/ella) comió	(ellos/ellas) comieron		
escribir	(yo) escribí	(nosotros/as) escribimos	(tú) escribiste	(vosotros/as) escribisteis
	(él/ella) escribió	(ellos/ellas) escribieron		

PRETERITE OF HACER, IR, SER, AND VER

hacer	ir	ser	ver
hice	fui	fui	vi
hiciste	fuiste	fuiste	viste
hizo	fue	fue	vio
hicimos	fuimos	fuimos	vimos
hicisteis	fuisteis	fuisteis	visteis
hicieron	fueron	fueron	vieron

274

ADDITIONAL VOCABULARY

Use this additional vocabulary to personalize activities. If you can't find a word you need here, try the Spanish-English and English-Spanish vocabulary sections beginning on page 277.

ANIMALES

el caballo *horse*
el canguro *kangaroo*
la cebra *zebra*
el conejillo de Indias
    hamster
el delfín *dolphin*
el elefante *elephant*
la foca *seal*
el gorila *gorilla*
la jirafa *giraffe*
el león *lion*
el mono *monkey*
el oso *bear*
el pájaro *bird*
el pingüino *penguin*
el ratón *mouse*
la serpiente *snake*
el tigre *tiger*

COMIDA *(FOOD)*

el aguacate *avocado*
el bróculi *broccoli*
la carne asada *roast beef*
la cereza *cherry*
la chuleta de cerdo *pork chop*
el champiñón *mushroom*
las espinacas *spinach*
los fideos *noodles*
los mariscos *shellfish*
la mayonesa *mayonnaise*
el melón *cantaloupe*
la mostaza *mustard*
la pimienta *pepper*
la sal *salt*
el yogur *yogurt*

COMPRAS *(SHOPPING)*

el álbum *album*
los aretes *earrings*
la billetera *wallet*
el collar *necklace*
las flores *flowers*

el juego de mesa *(board) game*
las llaves *keys*
el regalo *present, gift*

DEPORTES

las artes marciales *martial arts*
el atletismo *track and field*
el boxeo *boxing*
el ciclismo *cycling*
la gimnasia *gymnastics*
el levantamiento de pesas *weightlifting*
patinar sobre hielo *ice skating*

DIRECCIONES *(GIVING DIRECTIONS)*

a la derecha de *to the right of*
a la izquierda de *to the left of*
en frente de *in front of*
Dobla a la derecha. *Turn right.*
Sigue derecho. *Go straight.*

EN LA CASA

la alcoba *(bed)room*
la alfombra *rug; carpet*
el balcón *balcony*
las cortinas *curtains*
el cuarto de baño
    bathroom
el despertador *alarm clock*
las escaleras *stairs*
el espejo *mirror*
el garaje *garage*
la lavadora *washing machine*
los muebles *furniture*
el patio *patio*
el refrigerador *refrigerator*
la secadora *(clothes) dryer*
el sillón *easy chair*
el sofá *couch*
el timbre *doorbell*

EN LA CIUDAD *(IN THE CITY)*

el aeropuerto *airport*
la autopista *highway, freeway*

la avenida *avenue*
la calle *street*
el banco *bank*
la barbería *barber shop*
el cuartel *police station*
la esquina *corner*
la farmacia *pharmacy*
el hospital *hospital*
la iglesia *church*
la mezquita *mosque*
la parada de autobuses
    bus stop
el pueblo *town*
el puente *bridge*
el rascacielos *skyscraper*
el salón de belleza *beauty salon*
el semáforo *traffic light*
el templo *temple*

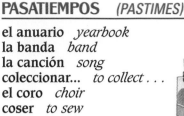

MÚSICA

el bajo *bass*
la batería *drum set*
el clarinete *clarinet*
la guitarra eléctrica
    electric guitar
el oboe *oboe*
el saxofón *saxophone*
el sintetizador *synthesizer*
el tambor *drum*
el trombón *trombone*
la trompeta *trumpet*
la tuba *tuba*
la viola *viola*

NÚMEROS ORDINALES

primero/a *first*
segundo/a *second*
tercero/a *third*
cuarto/a *fourth*
quinto/a *fifth*
sexto/a *sixth*
séptimo/a *seventh*
octavo/a *eighth*
noveno/a *ninth*
décimo/a *tenth*

PALABRAS DESCRIPTIVAS

amistoso/a *friendly*
bien educado/a *polite*

llevar anteojos *to wear glasses*
las pecas *freckles*
el pelo liso *straight hair*
el pelo rizado *curly hair*
ser calvo/a *to be bald*
tener barba *to have a beard*
tener bigote *to have a moustache*

PASATIEMPOS (PASTIMES)

el anuario *yearbook*
la banda *band*
la canción *song*
coleccionar... *to collect . . .*
el coro *choir*
coser *to sew*
el drama *drama*
la fotografía *photography*
jugar a las cartas *to play cards*
jugar a las damas *to play checkers*
jugar al ajedrez *to play chess*
la orquesta *orchestra*

PROFESIONES

la abogada, el abogado *lawyer*
la agricultora, el agricultor *farmer*
la bombera, el bombero *firefighter*
la carpintera, el carpintero *carpenter*
la cartera, el cartero *mail carrier*
la enfermera, el enfermero *nurse*
el hombre de negocios *businessman*
la mujer de negocios *businesswoman*
la plomera, el plomero *plumber*
el policía *police officer*
la policía *police officer (fem.)*
la secretaria, el secretario *secretary*
la trabajadora, el trabajador *worker*

ROPA (CLOTHING)

los bluejeans *bluejeans*
las botas *boots*
la camisa *shirt*
la camiseta *T-shirt*
la chaqueta *jacket*
la falda *skirt*
los pantalones *pants*
las sandalias *sandals*
el suéter *sweater*
el traje de baño *bathing suit*
el vestido *dress*

SPANISH-ENGLISH VOCABULARY

This vocabulary includes almost all words in the textbook, both active (for production) and passive (for recognition only). Active words and phrases are practiced in the chapter and are listed on the **Vocabulario** page at the end of each chapter. You are expected to know and be able to use active vocabulary. An entry in **boldface** type indicates that the word or phrase is active. All other words are for recognition only. These are found in **De antemano**, in the **Pasos**, in realia (authentic Spanish-language documents), in **Enlaces, Panorama cultural, Encuentro cultural,** and **Vamos a leer,** and in the **Location Openers** (travelogue sections). Many words have more than one definition; the definitions given here correspond to the way the words are used in the book. Other meanings can be looked up in a standard dictionary.

Nouns are listed with definite article and plural form, when applicable. The numbers after each entry refer to the chapter where the word or phrase first appears or where it becomes an active vocabulary word. Vocabulary from the preliminary chapter is followed by the letter "P".

Although the **Real Academia** has deleted the letters **ch** and **ll** from the alphabet, many dictionaries still have separate entries for these letters. This end-of-book vocabulary follows the new rules, with **ch** and **ll** in the same sequence as in English.

Stem changes are indicated in parentheses after the verb: **poder (ue).**

A

a *to,* 4; *at,* 3
a comenzar *let's begin,* 1
a ellas *to them,* 5
a ellos *to them,* 5
a menudo *often,* 5
A mí me gusta + infinitive *I* (emphatic) *like to . . . ,* 4
¿A qué hora es ...? *At what time is . . .?,* 3
¿A quién le gusta...? *Who likes (to) . . .?,* 4
¿A ti qué te gusta hacer? *What do you* (emphatic) *like to do?,* 4
a todo color *in full color,* 2
a ustedes *to you,* 5
a veces *sometimes,* 5
a ver si puedo *let's see if I can,* 1
el abrazo *hug,* 1
abril (m.) *April,* 5
la abuela *grandmother,* 6
el abuelo *grandfather,* 6
los abuelos *grandparents,* 6
abundar *to abound,* 6
aburrido/a *boring,* 3; **No es aburrido/a.** *It's not boring.,* 3
acabemos *let's finish,* 5
acampar *to camp,* 5
el acceso *access,* 4
el acento *accent mark,* P
acompañar *to accompany,* 4
la actitud *attitude,* 3

la actividad *activity,* 4
el actor *actor* (male); mi actor favorito es *my favorite actor is,* P
la actriz *actress;* mi actriz favorita es *my favorite actress is,* P
acuático/a *aquatic, water* (adj.)
adelante *let's get started,* P
adiós *goodbye,* 1
adivinar *to guess,* 6; ¡Adivina, adivinador! *Guess!,* 6
¿adónde? *where (to)?,* 4; **¿Adónde vas?** *Where are you going?,* 4
aeróbico/a *aerobic,* 5; **una clase de ejercicios aeróbicos** *aerobics class,* 5
agitar *to agitate, to stir up,* 3
agosto (m.) *August,* 5
agotar *to use up; to exhaust,* 3
agresivo/a *aggressive,* 6
la agricultura *agriculture,* 3
el agua (f.) *water,* 5
el águila *eagle,* P
la ahijada *godchild,* 6
el ahijado *godchild,* 6
ahora *now,* 1
el ajedrez *chess,* 5
el ají *chile pepper,* 3
al (a + el) *to the,* 4; al contrario *on the contrary,* 3; al grano *to the point,* 1; **al lado de** *next to, to one side*

of, beside, 4; el cafetín de al lado *the coffee shop around the corner,* 6
la alberca *swimming pool,* 4
el álbum *album,* 6
alegre *happy,* 6
el alfabeto *alphabet,* P
algo *something,* 6
alguno/a (masc. sing. algún) *some, any;* alguna parte *someplace;* alguna vez *sometime,* 6
allá *there,* 4
allí *there,* 4
el almacén *department store,* 5
el almuerzo *lunch,* 3
alquilar *to rent,* 5
alrededor de *around,* 6
alta mar: en alta mar *on the high seas,* 6
alto/a *tall,* 3
la alumna *student* (female), 3
el alumno *student* (male), 3
amarillo *yellow,* P
americano/a *American,* 1
la amiga *friend* (female), 1, 4; **Ésta es mi amiga.** *This is my* (female) *friend.,* 1
el amigo *friend* (male), 1, 4; amigo/a por correspondencia *pen pal,* P; **Éste es mi amigo.** *This is my* (male) *friend.,* 1; **nuevos amigos** *new friends,* 2; **pasar el rato con amigos** *to spend time with friends,* 4

la amistad *friendship*, 1
amplio/a *large*, 4
anaranjado/a *orange*, P
¡Ándale! *Hurry up!*, 3
los anfibios *amphibians*, 2
el ángulo *angle*, 3
el animal *animal*, 2
antes de *before*, 4
antipático/a *disagreeable*, 3
el año *year*, 5; **¿Cuántos años tiene?** *How old is (he/she)?*, 1; **¿Cuántos años tienes?** *How old are you* (familiar)?, 1; **Tengo ... años.** *I'm . . . years old.*, 1; **Tiene ... años.** *He/she is . . . years old.*, 1
el apartado postal *post office box*, 4
el apellido *last name*, 1
aquí *here*, 4
el árbol *tree*, 4; el árbol genealógico *family tree*, 6
la arboleda *grove (of trees)*, 4
el arco *bow*; Andean stringed musical instrument, 4
el armario *closet*, 2
la arquitecta *architect*, 3
el arquitecto *architect*, 3
arreglar *to arrange, to pick up (one's room)*, 6
el arroz *rice*, 6
el arte *art*, 3 (pl. las artes)
artístico/a *artistic*, 6
las arvejas *peas*, 1
asado/a *roasted*, 6
así *in this way, so, thus*, 6; así se dice *here's how you say it*, 1
la asistencia *attendance*, 3
asistir a *to attend*, 5
la aspiradora *vacuum cleaner*; **pasar la aspiradora** *to vacuum*, 6
atlético/a *athletic*, 6
el atletismo *track and field*, 4
atractivo/a *attractive*, 2
atrasado/a *late*; **Está atrasado/a.** *He/She is late.*, 3; **Estoy atrasado/a.** *I'm late.*, 3
el auditorio *auditorium*, 4
el autobús *bus*, 5; **tomar el autobús** *to take the bus*, 5
la avenida *avenue*, 4
las aventuras *adventures*, 1
las aves *birds*, 2
el avión *airplane* (pl. los aviones), 4
ayudar *to help*; **ayudar en casa** *to help at home*, 5
azul *blue*, 6

bailar *to dance*, 4
el baile *dance*, 3
bajo/a *short*, 3; *under*, 4
el baloncesto *basketball*, 1
el banco *bank*, 2
los banquetes *banquets*, 4
bañarse *to take a bath*, 5
las barajas *card games; decks of cards*, 3
la barbacoa *barbecue*, 6
el barco *boat, ship*, 5
el basquetbol *basketball*, 1
bastante *quite; pretty* (adv.), 1; **Estoy (bastante) bien, gracias.** *I'm (pretty) well, thanks.*, 1
la basura *garbage, trash*; **sacar la basura** *to take out the trash*, 4
el bautizo *baptism*, 1
beber *to drink*, 5
el béisbol *baseball*, 1
el beso *kiss*, 2
la biblioteca *library*, 4
la bicicleta *bicycle*; **montar en bicicleta** *to ride a bike*, 4; pasear en bicicleta *to ride a bicycle*, 3
bien *good; well*, 1; Está bien. *All right.*, 2; **Estoy (bastante) bien, gracias.** *I'm (pretty) well, thanks.*, 1
bienvenido/a *welcome*, P
la biología *biology*, 3
blanco/a *white*, P
el bolígrafo *ballpoint pen*, 2
el bolívar *unit of currency in Venezuela*, 2
bonito/a *pretty*, 3
borrar *to erase*; **goma de borrar** *eraser*, 2
botar *to throw (out)*, 4
el boxeo *boxing*, 4
Bs. abbreviation for *bolívares*, unit of Venezuelan currrency, 2
bucear *to scuba dive*, 5
Bueno... *Well . . .*, 1; **Bueno, tengo clase.** *Well, I have class (now).*, 1
bueno/a *good*, 3; **Buenos días.** *Good morning.*, 1; **Buenas noches.** *Good night.*, 1; **Buenas tardes.** *Good afternoon.*, 1
el burro *donkey*, P
buscar *to look for*, 5; busco *I'm looking for*, P

el caballo *horse*, 6
cada *each*, 2
el café *coffee*; **de color café** *brown*, 6
el cafecito *little cup of coffee*, 5
la cafetería *cafeteria*, 1
el cafetín *coffee shop*, 6
el caimán *alligator* (pl. los caimanes), 5
la caja *box*, 3
la calculadora *calculator*, 2; la calculadora gráfica *graphing calculator*, 2
el calendario *calendar*, P
la calificación *grade*, 3
el calor *heat*; **Hace calor.** *It's hot.*, 5; Hace un calor espantoso. *It's frightfully hot.*, 5
la cama *bed*, 2; **hacer la cama** *to make the bed*, 6
la cámara *camera*, 1
el cambio *change*, 4
caminar *to walk*; **caminar con el perro** *to walk the dog*, 4
la campana *bell*, 3
el campeón *champion* (f. la campeona), 4
las canas *gray hair*, 6; **Tiene canas.** *He/She has gray hair.*, 6
cantar *to sing*, 4
el cántaro *pitcher*; llover a cántaros *to rain cats and dogs*, 5
la capital *capital city*, 3
el capítulo *chapter*, 1
la cara *face*, 6
el Caribe *Caribbean Sea*, 1
el cariño *affection*, 2
cariñoso/a *affectionate*, 6
la carne; *meat*; la carne asada *roast beef*, 1
la carpeta *folder*, 2
el carro *car*; **lavar el carro** *to wash the car*, 4
la carta *letter*, 5; la carta de amor *love letter*, 5
el cartel *poster*, 2
la casa *house, home*, 4
casero/a *home-made*, 4
casi *almost*, 6; **casi siempre** *almost always*, 6
la casilla *post office box*, 4
caso: en caso de *in case of*, 1
castaño/a *brown, chestnut-colored*, 6
las castañuelas *castanets*, P
el castellano *Spanish language*, 2

el castillo *castle*, 1
la cátedra bolivariana *teachings about Bolívar*, 3
la categoría *category*, 1; categoría liviano *lightweight* (adj.), 4; categoría mediano *middleweight* (adj.), 4
catorce *fourteen*, 1
la cena *dinner*, 4; preparar la cena *to prepare dinner*, 4
cenar *to eat dinner*, 6
el centro *downtown*, 4
Centroamérica *Central America*, 1
el centro comercial *shopping mall*, 2
cerca de *near*, 4
el cerdo *pig*, 2
cero *zero*, 1
el césped *grass*, 6; cortar el césped *to cut the grass*, 6
el chaleco *vest*, P
la chamaca *girl*, 4
el chamaco *guy*, 4
Chao. *'Bye.*, 1
el charango *Andean stringed musical instrument*, 4
la charla *chat*, 1
la charrería *rodeo-like exhibition of horseback riding skills*, 3
la chava *girl*, 4
el chavo *guy*, 4
la chica *girl*, 5
el chico *boy*, 5
chino/a *Chinese*, 6
el chocolate *chocolate*, 1
el ciclismo *cycling*, P
cien, ciento *one hundred*, 2
las ciencias *science*, 3; ciencia ficción *science fiction*, 5; ciencias naturales *natural sciences*, 3; ciencias sociales *social studies*, 3
cierto *true*, 6; No es cierto. *It isn't true.*, 6
la cima *summit, top*, 4
cinco *five*, 1
cincuenta *fifty*, 2
el cine *movie theater*, 4
el cinturón *belt*, 5
la ciudad *city*, 4
el civismo *civics*, 3
el clarinete *clarinet*, 4
claro/a *light color*, P
la clase *class, classroom*, 1; Bueno, tengo clase. *Well, I have class* (now)., 1; la clase de baile *dance class*, 5; la clase de inglés *English class*, 1; una clase de ejercicios aeróbicos *aerobics class*, 5; ¿Qué

clases tienes? *What classes do you have?*, 3; ¿Qué haces después de clases? *What do you do after school?*, 4
clásico/a *classical*, 1
el club campeón *champion (first-rank) club*, 4; club deportivo *sports club, gym*, 5
la cocina *kitchen*, 6; limpiar la cocina *to clean the kitchen*, 6
la cocinera *cook* (female), 6
el cocinero *cook* (male), 6
el coco *coconut*, 6
el cognado *cognate*, 1
el colegio *high school*, 2
la coliflor *cauliflower*, 1
el color *color*, 6; a todo color *in full color*, 2; de color café brown, 6; ¿De qué color es/son...? *What color is/are . . .?*, 6; lápiz de color *colored pencil*, 2
la comadre *term used to express the relationship between mother and godmother*, 6
la comedia *comedy*, 3
comer *to eat*, 5
comercial: centro comercial *shopping mall*, 2
la cometa *kite*, 5
cómico/a *comical, funny*, 3
la comida *food; meal* (Mex.); *lunch;* la comida mexicana/ italiana/ china *Mexican/ Italian/Chinese food*, 1
el comienzo *beginning*, 1
como *like; as*
¿Cómo? *How?*, 1; ¿Cómo es...? *What's . . . like?*, 3; ¿Cómo es tu familia? *What's your family like?*, 6; ¿Cómo estás? *How are you* (familiar)?, 1; ¿Cómo se escribe? *How do you write (spell) it?*, P; ¿Cómo son? *What are . . . like?*, 3; ¿Cómo te llamas? *What's your name?*, 1
el compadrazgo *relationship between parents and godparents of a child*, 6
el compadre *friend* (male), 4; *term used to express the relationship between father and godfather*, 6
la compañera *friend, pal, companion* (female), 3
el compañero *friend, pal, companion* (male), 3; compañero/a de clase *classmate*, 3

la comparación *comparison*, 2
la competencia *competition*, 3
completamente *completely*, 6
la compra *purchase;* las compras *shopping*, 2
comprar *to buy*, 2; comprarse *to buy (for) oneself*, 6
comprender *to understand*, 1
compuesto/a *composed*, 2
la computación *computer science*, 3
la computadora *computer*, 2
común *common* (pl. comunes), P
con base en *based on*, 6
con *with*, 4; con frecuencia *often;* conmigo *with me*, 4; contigo *with you*, 4; ¿con qué frecuencia? *How often?*, 5
el concierto *concert*, 3
el concurso *game; competition, contest*, 3
el conejo *rabbit*, 6
confirmar *to confirm*, 4
el conflicto *conflict*, 6
conmigo *with me*, 4
conocer a *to get to know (someone)*, 2; conocer *to be familiar or acquainted with*
los conocimientos *information; knowledge*, 2
el consejo *advice*, 6
la constitución *constitution*, 4
la construcción *construction*, 1
construido/a *built*, 4
contestar *to answer*, 1
contigo *with you*, 4
convertir *to convert*, 3
la cordillera *mountain range*, 1
el córdoba *unit of currency in Nicaragua*, 2
el coro *choir*, 3
corregir *to correct*, 3
el correo *post office*, 4
correr *to run*, 5
la correspondencia *mail*, 1
cortar *to cut*, 6; cortar el césped *to cut the grass*, 6
la cortesía *courtesy*, 1
corto/a *short* (to describe things), 6; pelo corto *short hair*, 6
la cosa *thing*, 2
creativo/a *creative*, 6
la cruz *cross* (pl. las cruces), 2
el cuaderno *notebook*, 2; en mi cuaderno *in my journal*, 1; cuaderno de rayas *lined notebook*, 2; cuaderno de cuadros *graph paper notebook*, 6

cual, cuales *which* (relative pronoun)
¿**cuál**? *which?*, 3; ¿**Cuál es la fecha**? *What is today's date?*, 5; ¿**Cuál es tu clase favorita**? *Which is your favorite class?*, 3
cuando *when?*, 4; **sólo cuando** *only when*, 4
¿**cuándo**? *when?*, 3
¿**cuánto/a**? *how much?*, 2; ¿**cuántos/ as**? *how many?*, 2; ¿**Cuántas personas hay en tu familia**? *How many people are there in your family?*, 6; ¿**Cuántos años tiene**? *How old is (he/she)?*, 1; ¿**Cuántos años tienes**? *How old are you?*, 1; ¿Cuántos son en tu familia? *How many (people) are in your family?*, 6
cuarenta *forty*, 2
cuarto *quarter, fourth*; **menos cuarto** *quarter to (the hour)*, 3; **y cuarto** *quarter past (the hour)*, 3
el cuarto *room*, 2
el cuate *friend*, 4
cuatro *four*, 1
cubano/a *Cuban*, 6
cubierto/a *covered*, 4
cuenta *he/she tells*, 6; cuéntame *tell me*, 1
el cuento *story*, 3; los cuentos de aventuras *adventure stories*, 5
el cuerpo *body*, 6
la cuestión *question*, 1
el cuestionario *questionnaire*, 6
cuidar *to take care of*; **cuidar al gato** *to take care of the cat*, 6; **cuidar a tu hermano/a** *to take care of your brother/sister*, 4
el cumpleaños *birthday*, 3
curioso/a *curious, strange*, 6

da *he/she gives*, 2; dale un click a... *click on . . .*, 4
los dados *dice*, 2
la danza *dance*, 3
¡**Date prisa!** *Hurry up!*, 3
los datos *facts, data*, P; datos personales *personal information*, 6
de antemano *beforehand*, 1
de *from*, 1; *of*, 2; el cafetín de al lado *the coffee shop around the corner*, 6; de

antemano *beforehand;*
de color café *brown*, 6; ¿**De dónde eres**? *Where are you* (familiar) *from?*, 1; ¿**De dónde es**? *Where is she/he from?*, 1; **de la mañana** *in the morning* (A.M.), 3; **de la noche** *in the evening* (P.M.), 3; **de la tarde** *in the afternoon* (P.M.), 3; ¿**De qué color es/son**? *What color is/are?*, 6; ¿De qué se hace? *What is it made of?*, 4; de todo *all kinds of things*, 4; de vacaciones *on vacation*, 5; de vez en cuando *once in a while*, 5; de visita *visiting*, 3; de vuelta *returning*, 2; **del (de + el)** *of the, from the*, 3
debajo de *under, beneath*, 4
el debate *debate*, 1
deber *should, ought to*, 6; **Debes...** *You should . . .*, 6; **Qué debo hacer?** *What should I do?*, 6
decir *to say*, P; para decir *for speaking*, P
el dedo *finger; digit*, 2
del (de + el) *of the, from the*, 3
delgado/a *thin*, 6
demasiado *too much*, 6
los **deportes** *sports*, 1
el derecho *right*, 1
el desastre *disaster*, 2
desayunar *to eat breakfast*, 5
descansar *to rest*, 4; **descansar en el parque** *to rest in the park*, 4
el descanso *recess, break*, 3
la descripción *description*, 3
el descubrimiento *discovery*, 2
desde *since*, 3
desorganizado/a *disorganized*, 6
la despedida *farewell, goodbye, leave-taking*, 1
después *after*, 3; **después de** *after*, 4; ¿**Qué haces después de clases**? *What do you do after school?*, 4
el destino *destination*, 3
determinar: sin determinar *undetermined*, 4
el día *day*, 4; **Buenos días.** *Good morning.*; día de santo *saint's day*, 1; cada ... días *every . . . days*, 5; día escolar *school day*, 3; **día libre** *day off*, 3; los días de semana *weekdays*, 4; los días de la semana *the days of*

the week, 5; **todos los días** *every day*, 5
diariamente *daily*, 6
dibujar *to draw*, 4
el dibujo *drawing*; dibujos animados *animated cartoons*, 2
el diccionario *dictionary*, 2
dice *he/she says*, 1
dice que *he/she says that*, 6
diciembre (m.) *December*, 5
el dictado *dictation*, 1
diecinueve *nineteen*, 1
dieciocho *eighteen*, 1
dieciséis *sixteen*, 1
diecisiete *seventeen*, 1
diez *ten*, 1
difícil *difficult*, 3
dijo *he/she said*, 2
el dineral *large sum of money*, 2
el dinero *money*, 2
el dinosaurio *dinosaur*, 2
la dirección *address*, 4
directo/a *direct*, 4
el director *principal (of a school)* (male), 3
la directora *principal (of a school)* (female), 3
el disco compacto *CD*, 2
el disgusto *distaste*, 1
la diversión *entertainment*, 5
divertido/a *fun, amusing*, 3
divorciado/a *divorced*, 6
doblado/a *dubbed* (film), 2
doce *twelve*, 1
el doctor *doctor* (male), 3
la doctora *doctor* (female), 3
documental *documentary*, 2
el dólar *dollar*, 2
doméstico/a *household*; **los quehaceres domésticos** *household chores*, 6
el domicilio *residence*, 1
el domingo *Sunday*, 4
el dominó *dominoes*, 6
don *(title of respect for men)*, 1
donde *where*; ¿**Adónde**? *Where (to)?*, 4; ¿**De dónde eres**? *Where are you* (familiar) *from?*, 1; ¿**De dónde es**? *Where is he/she from?*, 1; ¿**Dónde**? *Where?*, 4; ¿Dónde te gustaría estudiar? *Where would you* (familiar) *like to study?*, 3
dos *two*, 1
la duración *length, duration*, 2
durante *during*, 5

la ecología *ecology*, 1
la edad *age*, 1

la edición *edition*, 5
el edificio *building*, 4
la educación *education*, 3;
la educacion artística
art education, 3; **la educación física** *physical
education*, 3; la educación
tecnológica *shop* (school
subject), 3
educar *to educate*, 2
egoísta (m/f) *selfish*, 6
el ejercicio *exercise*, 5; **una
clase de ejercicios aeróbi-
cos** *aerobics class*, 5;
hacer ejercicio *to exercise*,
5; hacer ejercicios aeróbicos
to do aerobics, 5
el *the* (sing.), 1; **Es el...
de...** *It's the (date) of
(month).*, 5
El... de este mes hay... *On
the (date) of this month,
there is/are . . .* , 5
él *he*, 2; **Él es...** *He is . . .*, 3
ella *she*, 2; **Ella es...** *She
is . . .*, 3
ellas *they*, 3; **a ellas** *to
them*, 5
ellos *they*, 3; **a ellos** *to
them*, 5
Ellos/Ellas son... *They
are . . .*, 3
emocionante *thrilling*, 6
empezar *to begin*; empiezan
they begin, 3
en *in, on*, 3; *at*, 4; en alta
mar *on the high seas*, 6;
en punto *on the dot*, 3
Encantado/a. *Delighted to
meet you.*, 1
la enciclopedia *encyclopedia*, 2
encima de *on top of*, 4
encontrar (ue) *to find*, 2
el encuentro *encounter,
meeting*, 2
la encuesta *survey*, 1
enero (m.) *January*, 5
los enlaces *links, connections,
ties*, 1
enrojecer *to turn red; to
blush*, 6
la ensalada *salad*, 1
entonces *then*, 3
entrar *to go in, to enter*, 3
entre *among*, 6; entre clases
between classes, 1
la entrevista *interview*, 1
¡Epa, 'mano! *What's up,
brother?*, 1
eres *you* (familiar) *are*, 1
es *he/she/it is*, 1; **es de...**
he/she/it is from . . ., 1;

Es el ... de ... *It's the
(date) of (month).*, 5; **Es la
una.** *It's one o'clock.*, 3
el esclavo *slave* (f. la esclava), 6
escolar *school* (adj.), 3; día
escolar *school day*, 3
escondido/a *hidden*, 4
escribamos *let's write*, 3
escribir *to write*, 5
el escritorio *desk*, 2
escuchar *to listen*, 4;
escuchar la radio *listen
to the radio*, 4; **escuchar
música** *to listen to music*,
4; para escuchar *for
listening*, P
la escuela *school*, 3
eso *that* (pron.), 5; **por eso**
that's why, for that reason, 4
los espaguetis *spaghetti*, 1
espantoso/a *terrible*, 5;
Hace un calor espantoso.
It's terribly hot., 5
España (f.) *Spain*, 1
el español *Spanish (language)*, 1
especial *special*, 3
especialmente *especially*, 5
el espectáculo *show; spectacle*, 6
la esposa *wife*, 6
el esposo *husband*, 6
esquiar *to ski*, 5
esta *this* (adj.), 1; **estas**
these (adj.), 6
ésta *this* (pron.); **Ésta es mi
amiga.** *This is my friend
(female).*, 1
el estacionamiento *parking*, 4
las estaciones *seasons*, 5
la estadística *statistic*, 2
el estado *state*, 4
estamos *we are*, P
las estampillas *stamps*, 4
el estante *bookcase*, 2
estar *to be*, 4; **¿Cómo estás?**
How are you?, 1; **Está
atrasado/a.** *He/She is
late.*, 3; Está bien. *It's all
right;* **Está lloviendo.** *It's
raining.*, 5; Está lloviendo a
cántaros *It's raining cats
and dogs*, 5; **Está nevando.**
It's snowing., 5; **Está
nublado.** *It's cloudy.*, 5;
Estoy atrasado/a. *I'm
late.*, 3; **Estoy (bastante)
bien, gracias.** *I'm (pretty)
well, thanks.*, 1
éstas *these* (pron.), 6
este *this* (adj.), 1; **El ... de
este mes hay...** *On the
(date) of this month, there
is/are . . .* , 5

el este *east*, 1
éste *this* (pron.); **Éste es mi
amigo.** *This is my friend
(male).*, 1
el estéreo *stereo*, 2
el estilo *style*, 1; el estilo personal *personal style*, 1
estos *these* (adj.), 6
éstos *these* (pron.), 6
estoy *I am*, 1; **Estoy
atrasado/a.** *I'm late.*, 3;
**Estoy (bastante) bien,
gracias.** *I'm (pretty) well,
thanks.*, 1
la estrategia *strategy*, 1
la estrella *star*, 1
estricto/a *strict*, 3
el estudiante *student* (male), 3
la estudiante *student* (female), 3
estudiar *to study*, 4
Estupendo/a.
Great./Marvelous., 1
la etiqueta *etiquette*, 1
Europa *Europe*, 1
la evaluación *grade; grading
period*, 3
el examen *exam* (pl. **los
exámenes**), 3
Excelente. *Great./Excellent.*, 1
la experiencia *experience*, 5

F

fabuloso/a *fabulous*, 6
fácil *easy*, 3
la falda *skirt*, 5
falso/a *false*, 1
la falta de asistencia *absence
(from class)*, 3
la familia *family*, 6; familia
extendida *extended family*,
6; familia extensa *extended
family*, 6; familia nuclear
*nuclear family, immediate
family*, 6
familiar *family* (adj.), 6
favorito/a *favorite*, 3; **¿Cuál
es tu clase favorita?**
*Which is your favorite
class?*, 3
febrero (m.) *February*, 5
la fecha *date*, 1
la fecha *date*, 5; **¿Cuál es la
fecha?** *What is today's
date?*, 5; **¿Qué fecha es
hoy?** *What's today's
date?*, 5
feliz *happy*, 5
femenil *women's* (adj.), 4
fenomenal *phenomenal*, 6
feo/a *ugly*, 3
la fiesta *party*, 3

filmado/a *filmed*, 2
la filosofía *philosophy*, 2
el fin *end*, 4; **el fin de semana**
weekend, 4
la firma *signature*, 1
la física *physics*, 3
flamenco *flamenco* (music,
singing, dancing), 6
la flauta *flute*, 4
la forma *shape*, 6
la foto *photo*, 6
la fotonovela *illustrated story*, 1
el francés *French*, 3
la frase *sentence, phrase*, P
la frecuencia *frequency*, 5;
¿con qué frecuencia? *how
often?*, 5
la fresa *strawberry*, 4
fresco/a: Hace fresco. *It's
cool (weather).*, 5
los frijoles *beans*, 6
frío *cold*, 5; **Hace frío.** *It's
cold.*, 5; Hace un frío
tremendo. *It's incredibly
cold.*, 5
la fruta *fruit*, 1
la frutería *fruit store*, 2
fue *was*, 4; fue construido/a
was built, 4
fuerte *strong*, 6
fundado/a *founded*, 2
el fútbol *soccer*, 1; **el fútbol
norteamericano** *football*, 1
el futuro *future*, 2

la gaita *bagpipes*, 4
gallego/a *Galician*, 3
ganar *to win*, 3
ganas: tener ganas (de) *to
feel like doing something*, 3
el gato *cat*, 6; **cuidar al gato**
to take care of the cat, 6
general *general;* por lo
general *in general*, 4
generoso/a *generous*, 6
¡Genial! *Great!*, 2
la gente *people*, 3
la geografía *geography*, 3
el gimnasio *gym*, 4
el gobierno *government*, 6
la goma de borrar *eraser*, 2
gordo/a *fat, overweight*, 6;
un poco gordo/a *a little
overweight*, 6
Gracias. *Thanks.*, 1; **Estoy
(bastante) bien, gracias.**
I'm (pretty) well, thanks., 1
la gráfica *graphic*, 2
la gramática *grammar*, 1
grande *big*, 3

gris *gray*, P
el grupo *group*, 1
guapo/a *good-looking*, 3
la guerra *war*, 3
la guía *guide*, 2
el güiro *Andean percussive
musical instrument*, 4
la guitarra *guitar*, 4
gustar *to like
someone/something;* **A mí
me gusta** + infinitive
I (emphatic) *like to . . .* , 4;
¿A quién le gusta...? *Who
likes . . .?*, 4; **le gustan**
he/she likes, 3; **les gusta**
they like, 5; **Me gusta...**
I like . . . , 1; **Me gusta
más...** *I prefer . . .* , 1; **me
gustan** *I like*, 3; **No me
gusta...** *I don't like . . .* , 1;
nos gusta *we like*, 5; **Nos
gustan...** *We like . . .* , 5;
¿Qué te gusta? *What do
you* (familiar) *like?*, 1; **¿Qué
te gusta hacer?** *What do
you* (familiar) *like to do?*, 4;
Sí, me gusta. *Yes, I like it.*,
1; **¿Te gusta...?** *Do you*
(familiar) *like . . .?*, 1; **Te
gustan...** *You* (familiar)
like . . . , 3
gusto: Mucho gusto. *Nice to
meet you.*, 1; gustos personales *personal likes*, 1

haber *to have* (auxiliary
verb), 4
hablando *speaking*, 2
hablar *to speak, to talk;*
hablar por teléfono *to talk
on the phone*, 4
hacer *to do, to make*, 2;
Hace buen tiempo.
The weather is nice., 5;
Hace calor. *It's hot.*, 5;
Hace fresco. *It's cool.*, 5;
Hace frío. *It's cold.*, 5;
Hace mal tiempo. *The
weather is bad.*, 5; **Hace
(mucho) frío.** *It's (very)
cold.*, 5; **Hace sol.** *It's
sunny.*, 5; Hace un calor
espantoso. *It's terribly
hot.*, 5; Hace un frío
tremendo. *It's incredibly
cold.*, 5; Hace un tiempo precioso. *It's a beautiful day.*,
5; **Hace viento.** *It's
windy.*, 5; **hacer ejercicio**
to exercise, 5; **hacer la cama**

to make the bed, 6; **hacer
un viaje** *to take a trip*, 6;
haga *do* (command), 3;
¿Qué debo hacer? *What
should I do?*, 6; ¿Qué hacemos? *What shall we do?*,
4; ¿Qué hacen ustedes los
fines de semana? *What
do you do on weekends?*, 6;
¿Qué tiempo hace?
What's the weather like?, 5
el hado *destiny, fate*, 2
haga *do* (command), 3
la hamburguesa *hamburger*, 5
haría *he/she would
do/make*, P
hasta *until;* Hasta luego.
See you later., 1; Hasta
mañana. *See you
tomorrow.*, 1
hay *there is, there are*, 2
el helado *ice cream*, 4; **tomar
un helado** *to eat ice
cream*, 4
el helicóptero *helicopter*, P
la herencia *heritage*, P
la hermana *sister*, 6; **la media
hermana** *half sister*, 6
la hermanastra *stepsister*, 6
el hermanastro *stepbrother*, 6
el hermano *brother*, 6;
el medio hermano
half brother, 6
los hermanos *brothers, brothers
and sisters*, 6
el héroe *hero*, 3
la hija *daughter*, 6
el hijo *son*, 6
los hijos *children*, 6
hispano/a *Hispanic*, P
hispanohablante *Spanish
speaking*, P
la historia *history*, 3
¡Hola! *Hello!*, 1
el hombre *man*, 6
la hora *hour, time;* **¿A qué
hora es...?** *At what time
is . . .?*, 3; es hora de... *it's
time to . . .* , 5; hora latina
Latin time, 3; hora local
local time, 3; **¿Qué hora es?**
What time is it?, 3
el horario escolar *school
schedule*, 3
Horrible. *Horrible.*, 1; ¡Qué
horrible! *How terrible!*, 2
el hospital *hospital*, 3
hoy *today*, 3; ¿Cuál es la
fecha hoy? *What is
today's date?*, 5; **Hoy es
el... de...** *Today is the
(date) of (month).*, 5;

¿Qué fecha es hoy? *What's today's date?*, 5
el huevo *egg*, 4
el humor *humor*, 1
el huracán *hurricane*, 5

el idioma *language*, 4
la iglesia *church*, 6
igual *equal*, 6
Igualmente. *Same here.*, 1
ilustrada *illustrated*, 2
la imagen *image* (pl. las imágenes), 4
¡Increíble! *Incredible!*, 2
independiente *independent*, 6
la industria extractiva *mining industry*, 3
infantil *for children*, 3
la ingeniera *engineer* (female), 3
el ingeniero *engineer* (male), 3
el inglés *English (language)*, 1; **la clase de inglés** *English class*, 1
ingresar *to enter*, 1
la instalación *installation, facility*, 1
el instituto *institute*, 3
el instrumento (musical) *instrument*, 4; **tocar un instrumento** *to play a musical instrument*, 4
inteligente *intelligent*, 3
interesante *interesting*, 3
interrumpirse *to be interrupted*, 6; interrumpe *interrupts*, 6
intocable *untouchable*, 3
la intriga *intrigue*, 3
el invierno *winter*, 5
ir *to go*, 2; **ir al centro comercial** *to go to the mall*, 2; ir de compras *to go shopping*, 4
la isla *island*, 2
italiano/a *Italian*, 1; **la comida italiana** *Italian food*, 1

el jabón *soap*, P
el jardín *garden*, 6; **trabajar en el jardín** *to work in the garden*, 6
el jazz *jazz*, 1
el jefe *boss*, 3
joven *young*, 6; **Se ve joven.** *He/She looks young.*, 6
el juego *game*; juego de ingenio *guessing game*, 1; **el video-juego** *videogame*, 3
el jueves *Thursday*, 4
jugar (ue) *to play*, 4; jugar al tenis *to play tennis*, 4
el jugo *juice*, 5
juguetón *playful* (f. jugue-tona), 6
julio (m.) *July*, 5
junio (m.) *June*, 5
juntamos: nos juntamos *we get together*, 4
juntos/as *together*, 5
la juventud *youth*, 3

el kilómetro *kilometer*, P

la *the* (sing.), 1
el lado *side*; **al lado de** *next to*, 4; el cafetín de al lado *the coffee shop around the corner*, 6
el lago *lake*, 5
la lámpara *lamp*, 2
la lancha *launch, boat*, 5
el lápiz *pencil*, 2; lápiz de color *colored pencil*, 2
largo/a *long*, 5
las *the* (pl.), 3
el latín *Latin (language)*, 3
lavar *to wash*; **lavar el carro** *to wash the car*, 4; **lavar la ropa** *to wash the clothes*, 4
las lecciones *lessons*, 5; tomar lecciones *to take lessons*, 5
leer *to read*, 5
lejos *far*; **lejos de** *far from*, 4
el lempira *unit of currency in Honduras*, 2
Les gusta + infinitive *They/You (plural) like to . . .*, 5
la letra *(alphabet) letter*, 1
el levantamiento de pesas *weightlifting*, 4
el libertador *liberator*, P
libre *free*, 3; **día libre** *free day*, 3; **tiempo libre** *free time*, 4
la librería *bookstore*, 2
el libro *book*, 2
la licenciada *woman with academic degree comparable to Bachelor of Arts*, 3
el licenciado *man with academic degree comparable to Bachelor of Arts*, 3

limpiar *to clean*, 6; **limpiar la cocina** *to clean the kitchen*, 6
la línea *line*, 4
el lío *mess*; ¡Qué lío! *What a mess!*, 3
liso/a *straight*; pelo liso *straight hair*, 6
la lista *list*, 2
listo/a *clever, smart* (with **ser**), 6; *ready* (with **estar**), 2
la literatura *literature*, 3
la llamada *telephone call*, 3
llamarse *to be named*; **¿Cómo te llamas?** *What's your (familiar) name?*, 1; **Me llamo...** *My name is . . .*, 1; **Se llama...** *His/Her name is . . .*, 1
la llanta *tire*, P
llegué *I arrived*, 3
llover (ue) *to rain*; 5; **Está lloviendo.** *It's raining.*, 5; Está lloviendo a cántaros. *It's raining cats and dogs.*, 5; Llueve. *It's raining.*, 5
lo más rápido posible *as quickly as possible*, 5; lo que pasó *what happened*, 4; lo bueno *what's good; the good thing*, 5
el lobo *wolf*, 4
lograr *to achieve*, 4
los *the* (pl.), 3
¿los conoces? *do you know them?*, P
las luces *lights*, 2
la lucha libre *wrestling*, 1
luego *then, later*, 3; **Hasta luego.** *See you later.*, 1
el lunes *Monday*, 4
la lupa *magnifying glass*, 2
la luz *light*, 2

la madrastra *stepmother*, 6
la madre *mother*, 6
la madrileña *resident of Madrid* (female), 1
el madrileño *resident of Madrid* (male), 1
la madrina *godmother*, 6
maduro/a *mature*, 6
los maduros *ripe plantains*, 6
la maestra *teacher* (female), 3
el maestro *teacher* (male), 3
mal *poorly; bad*, 1; No está mal. *It's not bad.*, 2
malo/a *bad*, 3; **Hace mal tiempo.** *The weather is bad.*, 5

la mamá *mom,* 6
el mamey *mamey (fruit),* 6
el mamífero *mammal,* 2
el mango *mango (fruit),* 3
'mano *friend* (short for 'hermano'), 4
mantener (ie) *to maintain,* 6; mantener correspondencia *to write letters back and forth,* 4
mantuvieron *they maintained,* 6
la mañana *morning,* 3; **de la mañana** *in the morning* (A.M.), 3; **por la mañana** *in the morning,* 5
mañana *tomorrow,* 3; **Hasta mañana.** *See you tomorrow.,* 1;
el mapa *map,* 1
la máquina del tiempo *time machine,* 2
el mar *sea,* 6; el Mar Mediterráneo *Mediterranean Sea,* 1
el marcador *marker,* 2
marrón *brown,* P
el martes *Tuesday,* 4
marzo (m.) *March,* 5
más *more,* 1; **Más o menos.** *So-so.,* 1; **Me gusta más...** *I prefer . . .,* 1
la máscara *mask,* P
la mascota *pet,* 6
las matemáticas *mathematics,* 3
la materia *subject,* 3
la matrícula *enrollment,* 3
mayo (m.) *May,* 5
mayor *older,* 6
me *(to, for) me,* 1; me acuesto *I go to bed,* 3; **Me gusta...** *I like . . .,* 1; **Me gusta más...** *I prefer . . .,* 1; **me gustan...** *I like . . .,* 3; **Me llamo...** *My name is . . .,* 1; me meto, *I go in,* 6; me pongo *Me pongo a estudiar.: I start studying.,* 3; me quedo con *I stay with,* 6
medio/a *half;* **media hermana** *half sister,* 6; **medio hermano** *half brother,* 6; **y media** *half past (the hour),* 3
el mediodía *noon, midday,* 3
mejor *best; better,* 5
menor *younger,* 6
menos *less,* 6; **Más o menos.** *So-so.,* 1; **menos cuarto** *quarter to (the hour),* 3
menudo/a *minute, small;* a menudo *often,* 5

el mercado *market,* 3
el mes *month,* 5; **El ... de este mes hay ...** *On the (date) of this month, there is/are . . . ,* 5
la mesa *table,* 2; **poner la mesa** *to set the table,* 6
mestizo/a *of mixed Indian and European descent,* 6
meter *to put in,* 6; me meto *I go in,* 6
mi *my,* 2; **mis** *my,* 6
mí *me (emphatic);* **A mí me gusta** + infinitive *I (emphatic) like to . . .,* 4
el microscopio *microscope,* 2
el miedo *fear,* 6
el miércoles *Wednesday,* 4
la milla *mile,* 5; las millas por hora *miles per hour,* 5
mimoso/a *affectionate,* 6
el minuto *minute,* 2
mirar *to watch, to look at,* 4; mira *look,* 1; **mirar la televisión** *to watch television,* 4
mismo/a *same,* 3
el misterio *mystery,* 1
la mochila *book bag; backpack,* 2
el modelo *example, model,* 1
el modo *way, mode,* 2
la montaña *mountain,* 5
montar *to ride;* **montar en bicicleta** *to ride a bike,* 4
morado/a *purple,* P
moreno/a *dark-haired, dark-skinned,* 3
el motoesquí *jet-ski,* 5
el movimiento *movement,* 6
la muchacha *girl,* 3
el muchacho *boy,* 3
mucho *a lot,* 1
mucho/a *a lot (of),* 2; **Mucho gusto.** *Nice to meet you.,* 1
muchos/as *many, a lot of,* 2; **muchas veces** *often,* 5
muerde *bites,* 6
la mujer *woman,* 6
el mundo *world,* P
municipal *municipal, city* (adj.), 4
el mural *mural*
el museo *museum,* 3
la música *music,* 1; **escuchar música** *to listen to music,* 4; **la música clásica/pop/rock** *classical/pop/rock music,* 1; **la música de...** *music by . . .,* 1

muy *very,* 1; **muy bien** *very well,* 1; **(muy) mal.** *(very) bad,* 1

nada *nothing,* 5
nadar *to swim,* 4
nadie *nobody,* 5
el náhuatl *Nahuatl (language),* 4
la naranja *orange,* 6
la natación *swimming,* 1
necesitar *to need,* 2; **necesita** *he/she needs,* 2; **necesitas** *you (familiar) need,* 2; **necesito** *I need,* 2
negro/a *black,* 6
nevar (ie) *to snow;* **Está nevando.** *It's snowing.,* 5; **Nieva.** *It's snowing.,* 5
ni *nor,* 6; ni... ni... *neither . . . nor . . .,* 6
la niña *child (female),* 2
el niño *child (male),* 2
los niños *children,* 2
el nivel *level,* 4
no *no,* 1; **¿no?** *isn't it?,* 3; **No es aburrido/a.** *It's not boring.,* 3; **No es cierto.** *It isn't true.,* 6; **No me gusta...** *I don't like . . .,* 1; **No sé.** *I don't know.,* 2; **No te preocupes.** *Don't worry.,* 3
la noche *night;* **Buenas noches.** *Good night.,* 1; **de la noche** *in the evening* (P.M.), 3; **por la noche** *at night,* 5
el nombre *name,* P; nombre completo *full name,* 6; nombres comunes *common names,* P
normal *normal,* 5
normalmente *normally,* 2
el norte *north,* 1
norteamericano/a *of or from the U.S.,* 1
nos *we, us,* 5; **Nos gusta** + infinitive *We like to . . .,* 5; nos juntamos *we get together,* 4
nosotros/as *we,* 4; **nosotros/as** *us* (after preposition), 5
las noticias *news,* 5
notificar *to notify,* 1
la novela *novel,* 3
noventa *ninety,* 2
noviembre (m.) *November,* 5
nublado/a *cloudy,* 5; **Está nublado.** *It's cloudy.,* 5
nuestro/a *our,* 6

nueve *nine*, 1
nuevo/a *new*, 3; **nuevos amigos** *new friends*, 2
el número *number*, 1; el número secreto *secret number*, 1
numeroso *numerous*, 6
nunca *never, not ever*, 5

o *or*; **Más o menos.** *So-so.*, 1
o ... o *either . . . or*
el oceanario *oceanography institute*, 2
el océano *ocean*, 5; océano Atlántico *Atlantic Ocean*, P; océano Índico *Indian Ocean*, P; océano Pacífico *Pacific Ocean*, P
ochenta *eighty*, 2
ocho *eight*, 1
octubre (m.) *October*, 5
el oeste *west*, 1
la oficina *office*, 4
oír *to hear, to listen to*, 4; **¡Oye!** *Listen!*, 3
los ojos *eyes*, 6; **Tiene ojos verdes/azules.** *He/She has green/blue eyes.*, 6
la ola *wave*, 5
olímpico/a *Olympic*, 5
once *eleven*, 1
operar *to operate*, 5
la oración *sentence*, 6
el orden *order* (sequence), 6
las órdenes *orders*; a sus órdenes *at your service*, 5
organizado/a *organized*, 6
organizar *to organize*, 2
el orgullo *pride*, 3
el oro *gold*, 4
oscuro/a *dark*, P
el oso *bear*, P
el otoño *fall*, 5
otro/a *other; another*, 4
¡Oye! *Listen!*, 3

el padrastro *stepfather*, 6
el padre *father*, 6
los padres *parents*, 6
el padrino *godfather*, 6; los padrinos *godparents*, 1
la página *page*, 4
el país *country*, 4
el palacio de gobierno *town hall*, 4
la papa *potato*, 5; **las papas fritas** *french fries*, 5
el papá *dad*, 6
la papaya *papaya* (fruit), 2

el papel *paper*, 2
el par *pair*, 5
para *for, to*, 4; **para +** infinitive *in order to*, 4
el parador *roadside stand*, 6
el parking *parking lot; parking garage* (Spain), 4
el parque *park*, 4; **descansar en el parque** *to rest in the park*, 4
participar *to participate*, 5
el partido de... *game of . . .* (sport), 3
el pasado *past*, 6
el pasaje *fare; passage*, 3; *passageway*, 4
pasar *to pass; to spend (time)*, 4; **pasar el rato con amigos** *to spend time with friends*, 4; **pasar la aspiradora** *to vacuum*, 6
el pasatiempo *hobby, pastime*, 1
el paseo *walk, stroll;* 4
el paso *step*, 1
pasó *happened;* lo que pasó *what happened*, 4
pata: ¡Hola, pata! *Hey, man!* (slang: Peru), 4
patinar en línea *to in-line skate*, 6
la pecera *fishbowl*, 2
los peces *fish* (sing. el pez), 2
la película *movie, film*, 4; **ver una película** *to see a film*, 4
pelirrojo/a *redheaded*, 6
el pelo *hair*, 6
la pelota *ball*, 6
pequeño/a *small*, 3
la pérdida *loss*, 1
perezoso/a *lazy*, 6
el periódico *newspaper*, 5
el permiso *permission, permit*, P
pero *but*, 1
el perro *dog*, 6
personal *personal*, 2; anuncios personales *personal ads*, 4; estilo personal *personal style*, 2
la personalidad *personality*, 1
pesado/a *heavy*, 2; ¡Qué pesado/a! *How annoying!*, 2
pescar *to fish*, 5
¡Pésimo! *Terrible!*, 2
el peso unit of currency in Mexico (and other countries), 2
el pez *fish* (los peces), 2; el pez de colores *goldfish*, 6
el piano *piano*, 4
¡Piénsalo! *Think about it!*, 2
el pincel *paintbrush*, 2

pintar *to paint*, 4
la pintura *paint*, 2; *painting*, 4
la piña *pineapple*, 2
los Pirineos *Pyrenees (Mountains)*, 1
la piscina *swimming pool*, 4
el piso *apartment*, 2
la pizza *pizza*, 1
la pizzería *pizzeria*, 2
la placa *license plate*, P
planchar *to iron*, 6
el planeta *planet*, 5
la planta *plant*, 2
la plata *silver*, 4
el plátano *banana*, 6
el platero *silversmith* (f. la platera), 4
el plato *dish*, 6; lavar los platos *to wash the dishes*, 6
la playa *beach*, 5; **por la playa** *along the beach*, 5
la plaza *town square*, 4
la pluma *ballpoint pen*, 2
poco *a little*, 6; un poco de todo *a little bit of everything*, 4; **un poco gordo/a** *a little overweight*, 6; pocas veces *not very often*, 5
el poema *poem*, 5
policíaco/a *police* (adj.), *detective* (adj.), 3
el pollo asado *roasted chicken*, 6
poner *to put, to place*, 2; Me pongo a estudiar. *I start studying.*, 3; **poner la mesa** *to set the table*, 6
por *at*, 3; *by*, 5; *in; around*, 4; **por eso** *that's why, for that reason*, 4; por favor *please*, P; **por fin** *at last*, 3; **por la mañana** *in the morning*, 5; **por la noche** *at night, in the evening*, 5; **por la playa** *along the beach*, 5; **por la tarde** *in the afternoon*, 5; por lo general *in general*, 4; **por teléfono** *on the phone*, 4
¿Por qué? *Why?*, 3; **¿Por qué no...?** *Why don't . . .?*, 3
porque *because*, 3
la portada *cover* (of a book or magazine), 2
posible *possible*, 5
practicar *to practice*, 4; **practicar deportes** *to play sports*, 4
el precio *price*, 4
precioso/a *beautiful; really nice*, 5; Hace un tiempo precioso. *It's a beautiful day.*, 5
la pregunta *question*, 3

preliminar *preliminary*, P

el Premio Nóbel *Nobel Prize*, 3

preocuparse *to worry;* **No te preocupes.** *Don't worry.*, 3

preparar *to prepare*, 4

preparatorio/a *preparatory*, 3

presentable *presentable, well dressed*, 6

presentar *to introduce*, 1

la **prima** *cousin (female)*, 6

la **primavera** *spring*, 5

primero/a *first*, 3; **el primero** *the first (of the month)*, 5

el **primo** *cousin* (male), 6

los **primos** *cousins*, 6

la princesa *princess*, 4

la **prisa** *haste;* **¡Date prisa!** *Hurry up!*, 3; **Tengo prisa.** *I'm in a hurry.*, 3

el prisionero *prisoner* (f. la prisionera), 3

probar (ue) *to try, to taste*, 6

el **problema** *problem*, 6

el **profesor** *teacher* (male), 3

la **profesora** *teacher* (female), 3

el **programa** *program*, 3; el programa de televisión *television program*, 3

el pronóstico del tiempo *weather report*, 5

el protagonista *protagonist, main character*, 2

próximo/a *next*, 5

la prueba contra reloj *time trial*, 4

la psicopedagogía *educational psychology*, 3

ptas. abbreviation of **pesetas**, currency of Spain, 2

pueden *(they) can*, 2

puedo *I can*, 2

la **puerta** *door*, 2

pues *well . . .*, 2

punto: en punto *on the dot*, 3

el pupitre *student desk*, 2

que *that, which, who*, 4; **Dice que...** *He/she says that . . .*, 6

¿Qué? *What?;* **¿Qué clases tienes?** *What classes do you* (familiar) *have?*, 3; **¿Qué fecha es hoy?** *What's today's date?*, 5; ¿Qué hacemos? *What shall we do?*, 4; ¿Qué hacen? *What are they doing?*, 4; **¿Qué haces después de clases?** *What do you*

(familiar) *do after school?*, 4; ¿Qué hay? *What's up?*, 1; **¿Qué hay en...?** *What's in . . .?*, 2; **¿Qué hora es?** *What time is it?*, 3; ¡Qué horrible! *How terrible!*, 2; ¿Qué hubo? *What's up?*, 1; ¡Qué lío! *What a mess!*, 3; ¿Qué onda? *What's up?*, 1; ¡Qué padre! *How cool!*, 2; ¿Qué pasa? *What's happening?*, 1; ¡Qué pesado/a! *How annoying!*, 2; **¿Qué tal?** *How's it going?*, 1; **¿Qué te gusta hacer?** *What do you* (familiar) *like to do?*, 4; **¿Qué te gusta?** *What do you* (familiar) *like?*, 1; **¿Qué tiempo hace?** *What's the weather like?*, 5

los **quehaceres domésticos** *household chores*, 6

querer (ie) *to want*, 2

querido/a *dear*, 6

el quetzal *Guatemalan bird, Guatemalan currency*, P

¿quién? *who?*, 4; **¿quiénes?** *who?* (plural), 5

Quiere... *He/She wants . . .*, 2; quiere decir *means*, 4; **Quieres...** *You* (familiar) *want . . .*, 2; **Quiero...** *I want . . .*, 2

la química *chemistry*, 3

quince *fifteen*, 1

la **radio** *radio*, 2

rápido/a *quick, fast, quickly*, 5

el raspado *snowcone*, 4

real *royal*, 1

recibir *to receive*, 5

el recorrido *tour*, 4

el recuerdo *souvenir, remembrance*, 1

el **refresco** *soft drink*, 4; **tomar un refresco** *to drink a soft drink*, 4

el regalo *present*, 4

la **regla** *ruler*, 2

regresar *to return, to go back, to come back*, 4

Regular. *Okay.*, 1

la reina *queen*, P

la religión *religion*, 3

el **reloj** *clock, watch*, 2

remar *to row*, 4

el remo *paddle, oar*, 5

el repaso *review*, 1

el reportaje *report*, 5

los reptiles *reptiles*, 2

respondes *you answer*, 1

responsable *responsible*, 6

la respuesta *answer, response*, 2

el **restaurante** *restaurant*, 4

el retrato *portrait*, 6

la reunión *meeting, reunion*, 6

reunirse *to gather, to meet*, 6

la **revista** *magazine*, 2

el rey *king*, 6

el río *river*, 5

el ritmo *rhythm*, 5

roer *to gnaw*, 6

rojo/a *red*, P

romántico/a *romantic*, 4

la **ropa** *clothing*, 2; **lavar la ropa** *to wash the clothes*, 4

rosado/a *pink*, P

rubio/a *blond(e)*, 3

el **sábado** *Saturday*, 4

saber *to know (information);* **No sé.** *I don't know.*, 2; **Sé.** *I know.*, 2; No saben. *They don't know.*, 6

¿sabías? *did you know?*, P

el sabor *taste*, 4

el sacapuntas *pencil sharpener*, 2

sacar *to take out*, 4; **sacar la basura** *to take out the trash*, 4; sacar buenas/malas notas *to get good/bad grades*

la **sala** *living room*, 6; la sala de clase *classroom*, 4

salgo *I go out*, 5

salir *to go out, to leave*, 6

el salón *hall*, 4

saludar *to greet*, 3

el saludo *greeting*, 1

salvar *to save*, 2

el salvavidas *life jacket*, P

la sandía *watermelon*, 2

el **sándwich** *sandwich*, 5

santo/a *saint*, 1

Se llama... *Her/His/Your name is . . .*, 1

Se ve joven. *He/She looks young.*, 6

sé *I know*, 2; **No sé.** *I don't know.*, 2

el secreto *secret*, 1

seguidamente *immediately afterward*, 5

segundo/a *second*, 1

seis *six*, 1

el semáforo *traffic signal*, 5

la **semana** *week*, 4; los días de semana *weekdays;* 4;

los días de la semana *the days of the week*, 5; **fin de semana** *weekend*, 4

el semestre *semester*, 3

señor *sir, Mister*, 1; **el señor** *the (gentle)man*

señora *ma'am, Mrs.*, 1; **la señora** *the woman, the lady*

señorita *miss*, 1; **la señorita** *the young girl; the lady*

el sentido *sense, faculty of sensation*, 5

septiembre (m.) *September*, 5

ser *to be*, 1; **¿Cómo es?** *What's he/she/it like?*, 3; **¿Cómo son?** *What are they like?*, 3; **¿De dónde eres?** *Where are you* (familiar) *from?*, 1; **Es de...** *He/She is from . . .*, 1; **Es la una.** *It's one o'clock*, 3; **No es cierto.** *It isn't true.*, 6; ser unido(s) *to be close-knit*, 6; **somos** *we are*, 3; **Son las...** *It's . . . o'clock.*, 3; **soy** *I am*, 1; **Soy de...** *I'm from . . .*, 1

serio/a *serious*, 5

el servicio *service*, 1

sesenta *sixty*, 2

la sesión *session*, 4

setenta *seventy*, 2

si *if*, 4

sí *yes*, 1

la sicología *psychology*, 1

siempre *always*, 5; **casi siempre** *almost always*, 6

siento *I regret;* lo siento *I'm sorry*, 1

la siesta *nap; afternoon rest*, 3

siete *seven*, 1

el siglo *century*, 4

siguiente *following*

la silla *chair*, 2

simpático/a *nice*, 3

sin *without*, 3; sin determinar, *undetermined;* 4

la situación *situation*, 1

sobre *about, on*, 5

el socio *member, associate* (f. la socia), 1

la sociología *sociology*, 1

el sol *sun*, 5; **Hace sol.** *It's sunny.*, 5

sólo *only*, 5; **sólo cuando** *only when*, 5

el sombrero *hat*

somos *we are*, 3; **somos cinco** *there are five of us*, 6

son *(they) are*, 3; **¿Cómo son...?** *What are . . . like?*, 3; **Son las...** *It's . . . o'clock.*, 3

el sonido *sound*, 1

la sopa *soup*, 1

soy *I am*, 1; **Soy de...** *I'm from . . .*, 1

Sta. abbreviation of **santa** *(saint)*, 1

Sto. abbreviation of **santo** *(saint)*, 1

su(s) *his, her*, 2; *their, your (formal)*, 6

el sucre unit of currency in Ecuador, 2

el suéter *sweater*, 5

la sugerencia *suggestion*, 2

el supermercado *supermarket*, 4

el sur *south*, 1

T

tal: **¿Qué tal?** *How's it going?*, 1

el taller *shop, workshop*, 1

la tamalada party to make *tamales*, a Mexican dish, 6

el tamaño *size*, 5

también *too, also*, 1; **Yo también.** *Me too.*, 1

las tapas *hors d'oeuvres* (Spain), 1

la taquilla *ticket office*, 4

tarde *late*, 3; **Es tarde.** *It's late.*, 3

la tarde *afternoon*, 3; **Buenas tardes.** *Good afternoon.*, 1; **de la tarde** *in the afternoon* (P.M.), 3; **por la tarde** *in the afternoon*, 5

la tarea *homework*, 1

la tarjeta *card;* **tarjeta postal** *postcard*, 5

te *(to, for) you*, 1; **No te preocupes.** *Don't worry.*, 3; **¿Te acuerdas?** *Do you remember?*, 5; **¿Te gusta...?** *Do you like . . .?*, 1; **te gustan** *you like*, 3; te presento a... *I'd like you to meet*, 1; te toca a ti *It's your turn.*, 2

el teatro *theater*, 1

la tecnología *technology*, 1; tecnológico/a *technological*, 3

la tele *TV*, 3

el teléfono *telephone*, 4; **por teléfono** *on the phone*, 4

la telenovela *soap opera*, 3

la televisión *television*, 4; el programa de televisión *television program*, 3;

mirar la televisión *to watch television*, 4

el televisor *television set*, 2

tenemos *we have*, 3

tener (ie) *to have*, 2; **Bueno, tengo clase.** *Well, I have class.*, 1; **¿Cuántos años tiene?** *How old is (he/she)?*, 1; **¿Cuántos años tienes?** *How old are you* (familiar)*?*, 1; **tengo** *I have*, 2; **Tengo ... años.** *I'm . . . years old.*, 1; **Tengo prisa.** *I'm in a hurry.*, 3; **Tengo que irme.** *I have to go.*, 1; **tiene** *he/she has*, 2; **Tiene ... años.** *He/She is . . . years old.*, 1; **Tiene canas.** *He/She has gray hair.*, 6; **Tiene ojos verdes/azules.** *He/She has green/blue eyes.*, 6; **tienes** *you* (familiar) *have*, 2

el tenis *tennis*, 1; **las zapatillas de tenis** *tennis shoes* (Spain), 2

tercero/a *third*, 1

terminar *to end, to finish*, 5

la terraza *balcony*, 4

el terror *terror*, 2

ti *you* (emphatic); **¿A ti qué te gusta hacer?** *What do you* (emphatic) *like to do?*, 6

la tía *aunt*, 6

el tiburón *shark*, 6

el tiempo *weather, time*, 5; **(en) el tiempo libre** *(during) free time*, 4; **Hace buen tiempo.** *The weather is nice.*, 5; **Hace mal tiempo.** *The weather is bad.*, 5; Hace un tiempo precioso. *It's a beautiful day.*, 5; pronóstico del tiempo *weather report*, 5; **¿Qué tiempo hace?** *What's the weather like?*, 5

la tienda *store*, 4

tiene *he/she has*, 2; **Tiene ... años.** *He/She is . . . years old.*, 1; **Tiene canas.** *He/She has gray hair.*, 6

tienes *you* (familiar) *have*, 2

la tierra *Earth*, 2

las tijeras *scissors*, 2

la tilde *tilde,* (diacritical mark over the letter ñ), 1

tímido/a *shy*, 6

el tío *uncle*, 6

típicamente *typically*, 5

típico/a *typical, characteristic*, P

el tipo *type, kind*
las **tiras cómicas** *comics,* 5
el tocador de discos compactos *CD player,* 2
tocar *to touch, to play;* **tocar un instrumento** *to play an instrument,* 4
todavía *still, yet,* 5
todo/a *all, every,* 5; todo el mundo *everyone, everybody,* 4; todo el tiempo *all the time,* 5; **todos los días** *every day,* 5
tomar *to drink, to take,* 4; **tomar el autobús** *to take the bus,* 5
el tomo *volume, tome,* 2
la toronja *grapefruit,* 6
la tortilla *omelet* (Spain), 1; *corn cake* (Mexico)
los tostones *fried green plantains,* 6
trabajador/a *hard-working,* 6
trabajar *to work,* 4; **trabajar en el jardín** *to work in the garden,* 6
el **trabajo** *work, job,* 4
el trabalenguas *tongue twister,* 2
tradicional *traditional,* 6
las tradiciones *traditions,* 6
transportado/a *transported,* 2
el transporte *transportation,* 1
travieso/a *mischievous,* 6
trece *thirteen,* 1
treinta *thirty,* 1
tremendo/a *tremendous, incredible,* 5; ¡Hace un frío tremendo! *It's incredibly cold!,* 5
tres *three,* 1
el trivia *trivia,* 1
tú *you* (familiar), 1
tu(s) *your (familiar),* 2
el tubo *tube,* 4
tuvo *he/she had,* 4

un *a, an,* 2; **un poco gordo/a** *a little overweight,* 6
una *a, an,* 2
la una *one,* 3; **Es la una.** *It's one o'clock.,* 3
único/a *only, unique,* 1
unido/a *close-knit,* 6
el uniforme *school uniform,* 2
uno *one,* 1
unos/as *some, a few,* 2
usar *to use,* 5
usted *you,* 4

ustedes *you* (pl.), 4; **a ustedes** *to you,* 5
útil *useful,* P
la utilización *use,* 1
la uva *grape,* 4

va *he/she goes,* 5
las **vacaciones** *vacation,* 5
el vals *waltz,* 4
vamos a... *let's...;* vamos a escribir *let's write,* 3; vamos a leer *let's read,* 1; **¡Vamos!** *Let's go!, we go,* 3
las variedades *varieties; variety section* (of a magazine or newspaper), 6
varios/varias *various, several,* 3
varonil *men's* (adj.), 4
vas *you* (familiar) *go;* **¿Adónde vas?** *Where are you going?,* 4
las veces *times* (sing. **vez**); **a veces** *sometimes,* 5; **muchas veces** *often,* 5
veinte *twenty,* 1
el velero *sailboat,* 5
la velocidad *velocity, speed,* 5
venezolano/a *of or from Venezuela,* 2
vengo de *I come from,* 1
la **ventana** *window,* 2
ver *to see,* 4; **ver una película** *to see a movie,* 4
el **verano** *summer,* 5
¿verdad? *don't you?, right?,* 3
verde *green,* 6
el vertebrado *vertebrate,* 2
la **vez** *time, turn, occasion, occurrence;* de vez en cuando *once in a while,* 5; **a veces** *sometimes,* 5; **muchas veces** *often,* 5; tres veces por semana *three times a week,* 5; una vez *once,* 5
el **viaje** *trip,* 6; **hacer un viaje** *to take a trip,* 6
el video *video,* 1
la videocasetera *VCR,* 2
el **videojuego** *videogame,* 3
viejo/a *old,* 6
viene de *comes from,* 4
el **viento** *wind,* 5; **Hace (mucho) viento.** *It's (very) windy.,* 5
el **viernes** *Friday,* 4
el violín *violin,* 4

visitar *to visit,* 6
las visitas *visitors,* 6
vivir *to live,* 6
vivo *I live,* 1
vivo/a *alive,* 6
el vocabulario *vocabulary; glossary,* 1
volar cometas *to fly kites,* 5
el **voleibol** *volleyball,* 1
vosotros/as *you (familiar plural),* 4
votar *to vote,* 4
voy *I go* (from **ir**), 3
el vuelo *flight,* 3
vuestro/a *your* (pl., Spain), 6

y *and,* 1; **y cuarto** *quarter past (the hour),* 3; **y media** *half past (the hour),* 3; ¿**Y tú?** *And you (familiar)?,* 1
ya *already,* 2
el yate *yacht,* P
yo *I,* 1; **Yo también.** *Me too.,* 1

la zapatería *shoe store,* 4
las **zapatillas de tenis** *tennis shoes* (Spain), 2
el **zapato** *shoe,* 3
el zócalo *main square* (Mex.), 4

ENGLISH-SPANISH VOCABULARY

This vocabulary includes all of the words presented in the **Vocabulario** sections of the chapters. These words are considered active—you are expected to know them and be able to use them. The number after each entry refers to the chapter in which the word first became an active part of your vocabulary.

Longer phrases are listed under the English word you would be most likely to look up. If a Spanish verb is stem-changing, the change is indicated in parentheses after the verb: *querer(ie)*. To be sure you are using the Spanish word in the correct context, refer to the chapters in which they appear.

a/an *un, una,* 2
aerobics *los ejercicios aeróbicos,* 5
a few *unos, unas,* 2
affectionate *cariñoso/a,* 6
after *después,* 3; *después de,* 4
afternoon *la tarde,* 3; **in the afternoon** *de la tarde,* 3; *por la tarde,* 5
afterward *después,* 3
a little *un poco,* 6
all *todo/a, todos/as,* 5
a lot *mucho,* 1
a lot of; a lot *mucho/a, muchos/as,* 2
almost *casi,* 6; **almost always** *casi siempre,* 6
along *por,* 5; **along the beach** *por la playa,* 5
already *ya,* 2
always *siempre,* 5
American *americano/a,* 1; *norteamericano,* 1; **American football** *el fútbol norteamericano,* 1
amusing *divertido/a,* 3
and *y,* 1; **And you?** *¿Y tú?,* 1
April *abril,* 5
art *el arte,* 3; *las artes* (pl.)
at *a, por,* 3; **at last** *por fin,* 3; **at night** *por la noche,* 5; **At what time . . .?** *¿A qué hora...?,* 3
attend, to *asistir a,* 5
August *agosto,* 5
aunt *la tía,* 6
autumn *el otoño,* 5

backpack *la mochila,* 2
bad *malo/a,* 3
ballpoint pen *el bolígrafo,* 2
baseball *el béisbol,* 1
basketball *el baloncesto,* 1; *el basquetbol,* 3
be, to *ser,* 1; *estar,* 4;

to be in a hurry *tener prisa,* 3
beach *la playa,* 5
because *porque,* 3
bed *la cama,* 2
before *antes de,* 4
belt *el cinturón*
beneath *debajo de,* 4
bicycle *la bicicleta,* 4
big *grande,* 3
black *negro/a,* 6
blond *rubio/a,* 3
blue *azul,* 6
book *el libro,* 2
book bag *la mochila,* 2
bookstore *la librería,* 2
boring *aburrido/a,* 3
boy *el chico,* 5
break *el descanso,* 3
brother *el hermano,* 6; **brothers and sisters** *los hermanos,* 6
brown *de color café,* 6
bus *el autobús,* 5
but *pero,* 1
buy, to *comprar,* 2
by *por,* 5
'bye *chao,* 1

C

cafeteria *la cafetería,* 1
calculator *la calculadora,* 2
camp, to *acampar,* 5
car *el carro,* 4
cat *el gato,* 6; **to take care of the cat** *cuidar al gato,* 6
chair *la silla,* 2
children *los hijos,* 6
Chinese food *la comida china,* 1
chocolate *el chocolate,* 1
chores *los quehaceres domésticos,* 6
class *la clase,* 1
classical music *la música clásica,* 1
classmate *el compañero* (male)/ *la compañera* (female) *de clase,* 3
clean, to *limpiar,* 6; **clean the**

kitchen, to *limpiar la cocina,* 6
clever *listo/a,* 6
clock *el reloj,* 2
close-knit *unido/a,* 6
closet *el armario,* 2
clothing *la ropa,* 2
cloudy *nublado,* 5; **It's cloudy.** *Está nublado.,* 5
cold *frío;* **It's cold.** *Hace frío.,* 5
color *el color,* 6
Come along! *¡Ven conmigo!,* P
comical *cómico/a,* 3
comics *las tiras cómicas,* 5
companion *el compañero* (male), *la compañera* (female), 3
computer science *la computación,* 3
concert *el concierto,* 3
cousin *el primo* (male), *la prima* (female), 6
cut, to *cortar,* 6; **to cut the grass** *cortar el césped,* 6

D

dad *el papá,* 6
dance *el baile,* 3
dance, to *bailar,* 4
dark-haired *moreno/a,* 3
dark-skinned *moreno/a,* 3
daughter *la hija,* 6
day *el día,* 4; **every day** *todos los días,* 5; **a day off** *un día libre,* 3
December *diciembre,* 5
delighted *encantado/a,* 1
desk *el escritorio,* 2
dictionary *el diccionario,* 2
difficult *difícil,* 3
dinner *la cena,* 4
disagreeable *antipático/a,* 3
do, to *hacer,* 2
dog *el perro,* 4; **to walk the dog** *caminar con el perro,* 4
dollar *el dólar,* 2
door *la puerta,* 2
downtown *el centro,* 4
draw, to *dibujar,* 4

drink, to *tomar,* 4; *beber,* 5
during *durante,* 5

easy *fácil,* 3
eat, to *comer,* 5; **to eat
  breakfast** *desayunar,* 5;
  to eat dinner *cenar,* 6
education *la educación,* 3;
  physical education *la
  educación física,* 3
eight *ocho,* 1
eighteen *dieciocho,* 1
eighty *ochenta,* 2
eleven *once,* 1
end *el fin,* 4
English class *la clase de inglés,* 1
eraser *la goma de borrar,* 2
especially *especialmente,* 5
evening *la noche,* 5; **in the
  evening (P.M.)** *de la noche,* 3
every *todo/a, todos/as;* **every
  day** *todos los días,* 5
exam *el examen,* 3
excellent *excelente,* 1
exercise *el ejercicio,* 5;
  to exercise *hacer ejercicio,* 5
eyes *los ojos,* 6

fall *el otoño,* 5
family *la familia,* 6
fantastic *fantástico/a,* 3
far *lejos,* 4; **far from** *lejos de,* 4
father *el padre,* 6
favorite *favorito/a,* 3
February *febrero,* 5
few, a *unos/as,* 2
fifteen *quince,* 1
fifty *cincuenta,* 2
find, to *encontrar (ue),* 2
first *primero/a,* 2
fish, to *pescar,* 5
five *cinco,* 1
folder *la carpeta,* 2
food *la comida,* 6; **Chinese food**
  la comida china, 1; **Italian food**
  la comida italiana, 1; **Mexican
  food** *la comida mexicana,* 1
football *el fútbol
  norteamericano,* 1
forty *cuarenta,* 2
four *cuatro,* 1
fourteen *catorce,* 1
free time *el tiempo libre,* 4
French *el francés,* 3
french fries *las papas fritas,* 5
Friday *el viernes,* 4
friend *el amigo* (male), *la amiga*
  (female), 1; *el compañero* (male),

la compañera (female), 3
from *de,* 1
fruit *la fruta,* 1
fun *divertido/a,* 3
funny *cómico/a,* 3

game of . . . (sport) *el partido
  de...,* 3
garden *el jardín,* 6
geography *la geografía,* 3
get to know someone, to
  conocer a, 2
girl *la chica,* 5
go, to *ir,* 2; **to go out** *salir,* 6;
  to go to the mall *ir al centro
  comercial,* 2
good *bueno/a,* 3; **Good
  afternoon.** *Buenas tardes.,* 1;
  Good evening. *Buenas
  noches.,* 1; **Good morning.**
  Buenos días., 1; **Good night.**
  Buenas noches., 1
Goodbye. *Adiós.,* 1
good-looking *guapo/a,* 3
grandfather *el abuelo,* 6
grandmother *la abuela,* 6
grandparents *los abuelos,* 6
grass *el césped,* 6
gray hair *las canas,* 6
great *excelente,* 1; *estupendo,* 1
green *verde,* 6
guitar *la guitarra,* 4
gym *el gimnasio,* 4

hair *el pelo,* 6 **He/She has gray
  hair.** *Tiene canas.,* 6
half brother *el medio hermano,* 6
half past (the hour) *y media,* 3
half sister *la media hermana,* 6
hamburger *la hamburguesa,* 5
have, to *tener (ie),* 2; **to have
  breakfast** *desayunar,* 5;
  to have to go *tener que irse,* 1
he *él,* 2
heat *el calor,* 5
Hello! *¡Hola!,* 1
help at home, to *ayudar en casa,* 5
her *su(s),* 2
here *aquí,* 4
high school *el colegio,* 2
his *su(s),* 2
home *la casa,* 4; **at home** *en
  casa,* 4
homework *la tarea,* 1
horrible *horrible,* 1
hot, to be *hacer calor,* 4
hour *la hora,* 3
house *la casa,* 4

how? *¿cómo?,* 1; **How are you?**
  ¿Cómo estás? (familiar), 1
how many? *¿cuántos?,
  ¿cuántas?,* 2
how much? *¿cuánto/a?,* 2
how often? *¿con qué
  frecuencia?,* 5
How old are you? *¿Cuántos
  años tienes?* (familiar), 1
How's it going? *¿Qué tal?,* 1
hundred *cien, ciento,* 2
hurry *la prisa;* **Hurry up!**
  ¡Date prisa!, 3; **I'm in a hurry.**
  Tengo prisa., 3
husband *el esposo,* 6

I *yo,* 1
in *en, por,* 5; **in order to** *para +
  infinitive,* 4; **in the afternoon
  (P.M.)** *de la tarde,* 3; *por la
  tarde,* 5; **in the evening (P.M.)**
  de la noche, 3; *por la noche,* 5;
  in the morning (A.M.) *de la
  mañana,* 3; *por la mañana,* 5
intelligent *inteligente,* 3
interesting *interesante,* 3
iron, to *planchar,* 6
isn't it? *¿no?,* 3
Italian food *la comida italiana,* 1
It's cold. *Hace frío.,* 5
It's cool. *Hace fresco.,* 5
It's hot. *Hace calor.,* 5
It's raining. *Está lloviendo.,* 5;
  Llueve., 5
It's snowing. *Está nevando.,* 5;
  Nieva., 5
It's sunny. *Hace sol.,* 5
It's windy. *Hace viento.,* 5

January *enero,* 5
jazz *el jazz,* 1
job *el trabajo,* 4
juice *el jugo,* 5
July *julio,* 5
June *junio,* 5

K

kitchen *la cocina,* 6
know, to *saber,* 2; *conocer,* 2

L

lamp *la lámpara,* 2
late *atrasado/a,* 3; **to be late**
  estar atrasado/a, 3
later *más tarde,* 7
leave, to *salir,* 6

less *menos*, 6
letter *la carta*, 5
library *la biblioteca*, 4
like, to *gustar*, 1
likewise *igualmente*, 1
listen, to *escuchar*, 4;
  to listen to music *escuchar
  música*, 4
little, a *un poco*, 6
live, to *vivir*, 6
living room *la sala*, 6
lot, a *mucho*, 1
lunch *el almuerzo*, 3

ma'am *señora*, 1
magazine *la revista*, 2
make the bed, to *hacer la cama*, 6
mall *el centro comercial*, 2; **to go
  to the mall** *ir al centro
  comercial*, 2
many *muchos/as*, 2
March *marzo*, 5
mathematics *las matemáticas*, 3
May *mayo*, 5
me too *yo también*, 1
Mexican food *la comida
  mexicana*, 1
mile *la milla*, 5
mischievous *travieso/a*, 6
miss *señorita*, 1
mister *señor*, 1
Monday *el lunes*, 4
money *el dinero*, 2
month *el mes*, 5
more *más*, 1
morning *la mañana*, 5; **in the
  morning** (A.M.) *de la mañana*,
  3; *por la mañana*, 5
mother/mom *la madre/mamá*, 6
movie *la película*, 4
movie theater *el cine*, 4
Mr. *señor*, 1
Mrs. *señora*, 1
music *la música*, 1; **classical
  music** *la música clásica*, 1;
  music by . . . *la música de...*, 1;
  pop music *la música pop*, 1;
  rock music *la música rock*, 1
my *mi*, 2; *mis*, 6

named, to be *llamarse*, 1; **My
  name is . . .** *Me llamo...*, 1
near *cerca de*, 4
need, to *necesitar*, 2
never *nunca*, 5
new *nuevo/a*, 3; **new friends**
  los nuevos amigos, 2
newspaper *el periódico*, 5

next to *al lado de*, 4
nice *simpático/a*, 3
Nice to meet you. *Mucho gusto.*, 1
night *la noche*, 1; **at night** *por
  la noche*, 5; **Good night.**
  Buenas noches., 1
nine *nueve*, 1
nineteen *diecinueve*, 1
ninety *noventa*, 2
no *no*, 1
nobody *nadie*, 5
nor *ni*, 6
not *no*, 1
notebook *el cuaderno*, 2
nothing *nada*, 5
novel *la novela*, 3
November *noviembre*, 5
now *ahora*, 3
number *el número*, P

October *octubre*, 5
of *de*, 2
often *muchas veces*, 5
okay *regular*, 1
old *viejo/a*, 6; **older** *mayor*, 6
on *en*, 3; **on the dot** *en punto*,
  3; **on top of** *encima de*, 4
one *uno*, 1
only *sólo*, 5
organize, to *organizar*, 2
ought to, should *deber*, 6
our *nuestro/a*, 6
overweight *gordo/a*; **(a little)
  overweight** *un poco gordo/a*, 6

paint, to *pintar*, 4
pal *el compañero* (male), *la
  compañera* (female), 3
paper *el papel*, 2
parents *los padres*, 6
park *el parque*, 4
party *la fiesta*, 3
pencil *el lápiz*, 2; *(pl. los lápices)*
physical education *la educación
  física*, 3
piano *el piano*, 4
pizza *la pizza*, 1
pizzeria *la pizzería*, 2
play an instrument, to *tocar un
  instrumento*, 4
pop music *la música pop*, 1
postcards *las tarjetas postales*, 5
poster *el cartel*, 2
post office *el correo*, 4
potato *la papa*, 5
practice, to *practicar*, 4
prepare, to *preparar*, 4
pretty *bonito/a*, 3

problem *el problema*, 6
put, to *poner*, 2

quarter to (the hour) *menos
  cuarto*, 3
quite *bastante*, 6

radio *la radio*, 2
read, to *leer*, 5
receive, to *recibir*, 5; **to receive
  letters** *recibir cartas*, 5
recess *el descanso*, 3
redheaded *pelirrojo/a*, 6
rest, to *descansar*, 4; **to rest in
  the park** *descansar en el
  parque*, 4
restaurant *el restaurante*, 4
return, to *regresar*, 4
ride, to *montar*, 4; **to ride a bike**
  montar en bicicleta, 4
right? *¿verdad?*, 3
rock music *la música rock*, 1
room *el cuarto*, 2
ruler *la regla*, 2
run, to *correr*, 5

salad *la ensalada*, 1
Same here. *Igualmente.*, 1
sandwich *el sándwich*, 5
Saturday *el sábado*, 4
say, to *decir*, 6
science *las ciencias*, 3
scuba dive, to *bucear*, 5
seasons *las estaciones*, 5
See you later. *Hasta luego.*, 1
See you tomorrow. *Hasta
  mañana.*, 1
semester *el semestre*, 3
September *septiembre*, 5
set the table, to *poner la mesa*, 6
seven *siete*, 1
seventeen *diecisiete*, 1
seventy *setenta*, 2
she *ella*, 2
shopping mall *el centro
  comercial*, 2
short *bajo/a*, 3
should *deber*, 6
sing, to *cantar*, 4
sir *señor*, 1
sister *la hermana*, 6
six *seis*, 1
sixteen *dieciséis*, 1
sixty *sesenta*, 2
ski, to *esquiar*, 5
small *pequeño/a*, 3

smart   *listo/a,* 6
snow   *la nieve,* 5; **It's snowing.**
   Nieva., 5
soccer   *el fútbol,* 1
social studies   *las ciencias*
   sociales, 3
soft drink   *el refresco,* 4
some   *unos/as,* 2
something   *algo,* 6
sometimes   *a veces,* 5
son   *el hijo,* 6
so-so   *más o menos,* 1
Spanish   *el español,* 1
speak, to   *hablar,* 4
spend time with friends, to
   pasar el rato con amigos, 4
sports   *los deportes,* 1
spring   *la primavera,* 5
stepbrother   *el hermanastro,* 6
stepfather   *el padrastro,* 6
stepmother   *la madrastra,* 6
stepsister   *la hermanastra,* 6
still   *todavía,* 5
store   *la tienda,* 4
strict   *estricto/a,* 3
study, to   *estudiar,* 4
subject   *la materia,* 3
summer   *el verano,* 5
Sunday   *el domingo,* 4
supermarket   *el supermercado,* 4
swim, to   *nadar,* 4
swimming   *la natación,* 1
swimming pool   *la piscina,* 4

table   *la mesa,* 2
take, to   *tomar,* 4
take a trip, to   *hacer un viaje,* 6
take care of, to   *cuidar,* 4; **to take**
   care of your brother/sister
   cuidar a tu hermano/a, 4
take out the garbage, to   *sacar*
   la basura, 4
take the bus, to   *tomar el*
   autobús, 5
talk, to   *hablar,* 4; **to talk on the**
   phone *hablar por teléfono,* 4
tall   *alto/a,* 3
teacher   *el profesor* (male),
   la profesora (female), 3
telephone   *el teléfono,* 4
television   *la televisión,* 4
television set   *el televisor,* 2
tell, to   *decir,* 6
ten   *diez,* 1
tennis   *el tenis,* 1; **tennis shoes**
   (Spain) *las zapatillas de tenis,* 2
Thanks.   *Gracias.,* 1
that   *que,* 4
that's why   *por eso,* 4
the   *el, la,* 1; *los, las,* 3

their   *su(s),* 6
then   *luego,* 3
there   *allá,* 4
there is, there are   *hay,* 2
these   *éstas, éstos,* 6
they   *ellas, ellos,* 3
thin   *delgado/a,* 6
thing   *la cosa,* 2
thirteen   *trece,* 1
thirty   *treinta,* 1
this   *ésta, éste,* 1
three   *tres,* 1
Thursday   *el jueves,* 4
time   *la hora,* 3; **to spend time**
   with friends *pasar el rato con*
   amigos, 5
to   *a,* 4; **to the** *al (a + el), a la,* 4
today   *hoy,* 3
together   *juntos/as,* 5
tomorrow   *mañana,* 3
too   *también,* 1
too much   *demasiado/a,* 6
trash   *la basura,* 4
Tuesday   *el martes,* 4
twelve   *doce,* 1
twenty   *veinte,* 1
two   *dos,* 1
typically   *típicamente,* 5

ugly   *feo/a,* 3
uncle   *el tío,* 6
under   *debajo de,* 4

vacation   *las vacaciones,* 5
vacuum cleaner   *la aspiradora,* 6
vacuum, to   *pasar la aspiradora,* 6
very   *muy,* 1; **very bad** *muy*
   mal, 1; **very well** *muy bien,* 1
videogame   *el videojuego,* 3
visit, to   *visitar,* 6
volleyball   *el voleibol,* 1

walk, to   *caminar,* 4; **to walk the**
   dog *caminar con el perro,* 4
want, to   *querer (ie),* 2
wash, to   *lavar,* 4
watch   *el reloj,* 2
watch, to   *mirar,* 4; **to watch TV**
   mirar la televisión, 4
water   *el agua,* 5
we   *nosotros/as,* 4
weather   *el tiempo,* 5; **The**
   weather is bad. *Hace mal*
   tiempo., 5; **The weather is**
   nice. *Hace buen tiempo.,* 5
Wednesday   *el miércoles,* 4

week   *la semana,* 4
weekend   *el fin de semana,* 4
Well . . .   *Bueno...,* 2
what?   *¿cuál?,* 3; *¿qué?,* 3
What are . . . like?   *¿Cómo son...?,* 3
What color is . . . ?   *¿De qué*
   color es...?, 6
What do you like?   *¿Qué te*
   gusta? (familiar), 1
What do you like to do?   *¿Qué*
   te gusta hacer? (familiar), 4
What is today's date?   *¿Cuál es*
   la fecha?, 5
What's . . . like?   *¿Cómo es...?,* 3
What's the weather like?   *¿Qué*
   tiempo hace?, 5
What's your name?   *¿Cómo te*
   llamas? (familiar), 1
What time is it?   *¿Qué hora es?,* 3
when   *cuando,* 5
when?   *¿cuándo?,* 3
where   *donde,* 1
where?   *¿dónde?,* 4; **Where are**
   you from? *¿De dónde eres?,* 1
where (to)?   *¿adónde?,* 4
which   *que,* 4
which?   *¿cuál?,* 3; *¿qué?,* 1
who   *que,* 4
who?   *¿quién?,* 4; *¿quiénes?,* 5;
   Who likes . . . ? *¿A quién le*
   gusta...?, 4
why?   *¿por qué?,* 3
wife   *la esposa,* 6
window   *la ventana,* 2
winter   *el invierno,* 5
wish, to   *querer (ie),* 2
with   *con,* 4; **with me** *conmigo,* 4;
   with you *contigo* (familiar), 4
work   *el trabajo,* 4
work, to   *trabajar,* 4; **to work in the**
   garden *trabajar en el jardín,* 6
worry, to   *preocuparse,* 3; **Don't**
   worry! *¡No te preocupes!,* 3
write, to   *escribir,* 5

year   *el año,* 5
yes   *sí,* 1
yet   *todavía,* 5; **not yet** *todavía*
   no, 5
you   *tú, vosotros/as* (familiar), 4
you   *usted, ustedes* (formal), 4
young   *joven,* 6; **He/She looks**
   young. *Se ve joven.,* 6
younger   *menor,* 6
your   (familiar) *tu,* 2; *tus,* 6;
   (formal) *su,* 2; *sus,* 6

zero   *cero,* 1

GRAMMAR INDEX

Page numbers in boldface type refer to **Gramática** and **Nota gramatical** presentations. Other page numbers refer to grammar structures presented in the **Así se dice, Nota cultural, Vocabulario,** and **¿Te acuerdas?** sections.

A

a: see prepositions
accent marks: 7, **30**
adjectives: agreement—masculine and feminine **78, 127;** agreement—singular and plural **78, 127,** 271; demonstrative adjectives—all forms 271; possessive adjectives 76; all forms **237,** 271
adverbs: adverbs of frequency—**siempre, sólo cuando, nunca, todavía, todos los días, muchas veces** 195; **una vez, de vez en cuando, todo el tiempo, cada día, a menudo** 209; adverbs of sequence—**primero, después, por fin** 110; adverbs of time—**por la mañana, por la tarde, por la noche** 209
affirmative expressions: **algo, alguien, alguno (algún), alguna, o ... o, siempre** 272
al: contraction of **a + el** 163, 270
-**ando:** see present participle
-**ar** verbs: see verbs
articles: see definite articles, indefinite articles

C

commands: 122, 125
comparisons: with adjectives using **más ... que, menos ... que, tan ... como** 272; all comparatives, including **tanto/a/os/as ... como** 272
con: see prepositions
conjunctions: **pero** 43, 152, 255; **y** 29, 76, 85, 149; **o** 31, 203; **porque** 129; subordinating conjunction: see **que**
conmigo, contigo: 155
contractions: see **al** and **del**
cuánto: agreement with nouns **78,** 236

D

dates (calendar): **213**
days of the week: **174**
de: 121; used with color 245; see also prepositions
deber: all present tense forms **255**
definite articles: **el, la 46,** 270; **los, las 109,** 270
del: contraction of **de + el 121,** 270
demonstrative adjectives: all forms 271
demonstrative pronouns: see pronouns
diminutives: 247
direct object pronouns: see pronouns
doler: all present tense forms 273
durante: see prepositions

E

e → ie stem-changing verbs: 273
el: see definite articles

empezar: 273
en: see prepositions
encantar: all present tense forms 274
-**er** verbs: see verbs
estar: 31, 161, **162,** 273

F

frequency: adverbs of—**siempre, sólo cuando, nunca, todavía, todos los días, muchas veces** 195; **una vez, de vez en cuando, todo el tiempo, cada día, a menudo** 209

G

gender of nouns: 270
giving the date: **213**
gustar: to express likes and dislikes 43, 129, 149, 203; all present tense forms 274

H

hacer: 85, 248; all present tense forms **249,** 273; **hacer** with weather 216, 217; preterite 274
hay: 76, 236

I

-**iendo:** see present participle
imperatives: see commands
indefinite articles: **un, una 66, 68,** 270; **unos, unas 68,** 270
indirect object pronouns: see pronouns
infinitives: **86**
informal commands: see commands
interrogatives: see question words
-**ir** verbs: see verbs
ir: all forms **172,** 273; preterite 274
irregular verbs: see verbs

J

jugar: all present tense forms 273

L

la: see definite articles, see pronouns
las, los: see definite articles
le, les: see pronouns, indirect object
lo, la: see pronouns, direct object

M

más ... que: see comparisons
me: see pronouns, indirect object

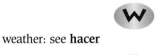

GRAMMAR INDEX

CREDITS

PHOTOGRAPHY

Abbreviations used: (t) top, (b) bottom, (c) center, (l) left, (r) right, (i) inset, (bkgd) background. All other locations are noted as "other".

All pre-Columbian symbols by EclectiCollections/HRW. All photos by Marty Granger/Edge Video Productions/HRW except:

FRONT COVER: (bl), Townsend P. Dickinson/Comstock; (br), Dallas and John Heaton/Westlight; (bkgd), © Robert Fried; (c), Joe Viesti/Viesti Associates, Inc.

TABLE OF CONTENTS: Page vii (r), Andrea Booher/Tony Stone Images; viii (tl), Sam Dudgeon/HRW Photo; ix (tr), David Phillips/HRW Photo; (br), Christine Galida/HRW Photo; xi (br), Sam Dudgeon/HRW Photo; xii (tr), David Young-Wolff/PhotoEdit; (br), Sam Dudgeon/HRW Photo; xiii (tr), Bachmann/ProFiles West, Inc.; (bl), Daniel J. Schaefer; xv (tr), S. Howell/Gamma Liaison; xvi (bl), Linc Cornell/Stock Boston, Inc.

PRELIMINARY CHAPTER: Page 2 (cl), Superstock; (bl), Index Stock Photography; 3 (br), Sam Dudgeon/HRW Photo; 4 (tr), Steve Crandall/New York Yankees; (cl), Culver Pictures, Inc.; (cr), HRW/File Photo; (bl), Bettmann Archive; 5 (tl), Bettmann Archive; (cl), Viacom/Shooting Star; (cr), S. Howell/Gamma Liaison; (br), Simon Bruty/Allsport USA/PNI; 8 (other), (a) Stephen Dalten/Animals Animals; (other), (b, ch, d, e, f, g, j, l, ll), Sam Dudgeon/HRW Photo; (other), (c), F. Mons/Allsport USA; (other), (h) Superstock; (other), (i), Animals Animals; (other), (k), Image Bank; 9 (other), (m, n, ñ, p, s, t, u, v, x), Sam Dudgeon/HRW Photo; (other), (o), Johnny Johnson/Animals Animals; (other), (q), Michael Fogden/Animals Animals; (other), (r), C. Prescott-Allen/Animals Animals; (other), (rr), Robert Maier/Animals Animals; (other), (w), Michelle Bridwell/Frontera Fotos; (other), (y), Superstock; (other), (z), Bob Pizaro/Comstock; 10 (tr); 11 (tr); 14 (t) Michelle Bridwell/Frontera Fotos.

LOCATION OPENER - SPAIN: Page 16–17 (bkgd), Macduff Everton; 18 (tr), Danilo Boschung/Leo de Wys; (c), David R. Frazier Photolibrary; (br), Zoom/Vandystadt/Allsport USA; 19 (tl), David R. Frazier Photolibrary.

CHAPTER ONE: Page 20–21 (bkgd), Scott Van Osdol/HRW Photo; 21 (bl), Bill Bachmann/Photo Network/PNI; 28 (br), Christine Galida/HRW Photo; 32 (cr), John Langford/HRW Photo; 35 (b); 36 (other), (0, 2, 3, 4, 5, 6, 7, 8), Sam Dudgeon/HRW Photo; (other), (1, 9), Mavournea Hay/Frontera Fotos; (other), (10) Laurie O'Meara/Frontera Fotos; 39 (tr), John Lei/Stock Boston, Inc.; 43 (cl), Nathan Bilow/Allsport/PNI; (c), Roy Morsch/The Stock Market; (cr), Scarborough/Shooting Star; (bl), Superstock; (br), Peter Van Steen/HRW Photo; 46 (bl), David R. Frazier Photolibrary; (cr), Leif Skoogfors/Woodfin Camp; (br), Aaron Haupt/David R. Frazier Photolibrary; 47 (all), Sam Dudgeon/HRW Photo; 48 (tr), Simon Bruty/Allsport USA; 55 (br), John Langford/HRW Photo; 57 (br), Aaron Haupt/David R. Frazier Photolibrary.

CHAPTER TWO: Page 58–59 (bkgd), Scott Van Osdol/HRW Photo; 59 (bl), John Langford/HRW Photo; 61 (tr), (other), (clock, 10:00, clock, 10:30) Sam Dudgeon/HRW Photo; 62 (tl), Michelle Bridwell/Frontera Fotos; (cr), Sam Dudgeon/HRW Photo; 64 (cr), Michelle Bridwell/Frontera Fotos; 70 (all), M. L. Miller/Edge Video Productions/HRW; 71 (all), Christine Galida/HRW Photo; 72 (t), Michelle Bridwell/Frontera Fotos; 77 (c), John Langford/HRW Photo; 78 (tr); 79 (cl), (cr), Michelle Bridwell/Frontera Fotos; 80 (tl), (cr), (cl), (tr), Sam Dudgeon/HRW Photo; (bc), David Phillips/HRW Photo; (i), Stock Editions/HRW Photo; (br), John Langford/HRW Photo; (bl), Image Copyright © 1996 Photodisc, Inc./HRW; 84 (tl), Michelle Bridwell/Frontera Fotos; (tr), Sam Dudgeon/HRW Photo; 86 (tl), (tr), (cl), (cr), Michelle Bridwell/Frontera Fotos; 88 (all), Sam Dudgeon/HRW Photo; 91 (bl), Stock Editions/HRW Photo; 91 (br), (cl), (cr); 92 (cl), Image Copyright © 1996 Photodisc, Inc./HRW; 94 (all), Michelle Bridwell/Frontera Fotos; 95 (c), John Langford/HRW Photo.

LOCATION OPENER - MEXICO: Page 98–99 (bkgd), Tony Stone Images; 100 (tr), Marie Ueda/Leo de Wys; (br), Jorge Nuñez/Latin Focus; 101 (tl), Tony Freeman/PhotoEdit; (b), Melinda Berge/Bruce Coleman, Inc.

CHAPTER THREE: Page 102–103 (bkgd), Scott Van Osdol/HRW Photo; 102 (b), Jeff Greenberg/PhotoEdit; 104 (br); 108 (cr), Michelle Bridwell/Frontera Fotos; 112 (all), Peter Van Steen/HRW Photo; 114 (cl), © Robert Fried; (c), Robert Brenner/PhotoEdit; (cr), Michelle Bridwell/Frontera Fotos; (bl), (br), Christine Galida/HRW Photo; (bc), Michelle Bridwell/PhotoEdit; 115 (tr), Robert Brenner/PhotoEdit; 119 (cl), Michelle Bridwell/HRW Photo; (c), David Phillips/HRW Photo/HBJ; (cr), Russel Dian/HRW Photo; 120 (tl), (tc), (tr), (cl), Sam Dudgeon/HRW Photo; (c), Michelle Bridwell/HRW Photo; (cr), Image Copyright © 1996 PhotoDisc., Inc./HRW; 128 (c), Michelle Bridwell/Frontera Fotos; 131 (i), Sam Dudgeon/HRW Photo; 135 (br), Stuart Cohen/Comstock; 136–137 (b); 137 (all), Image Copyright © 1996 Photodisc, Inc./HRW; 140 (t), Peter Van Steen/HRW Photo; (other), (Yolanda) Michelle Bridwell/Frontera Fotos; (other), (Gabriela) Kent Vinyard/ProFiles West, Inc.; 141 (tr), Image Copyright © 1996 PhotoDisc., Inc./HRW; (c), Sam Dudgeon/HRW Photo.

CHAPTER FOUR: Page 142–143 (bkgd), Scott Van Osdol/HRW Photo; 142 (c), David Young-Wolff/PhotoEdit; 153 (tl), Robert Brenner/PhotoEdit; (tc), Lawrence Migdale/Stock Boston, Inc.; (tr), (cl), (cr), Michelle Bridwell/Frontera Fotos; 154 (tl), Chip & Rosa María de la Cueva Peterson; (tc), Index Stock Photography; (tr), (cr), Michelle Bridwell/Frontera Fotos; (cl), Bob Daemmrich; (other), (refresco, helado), Peter Van Steen/HRW Photo; 155 (cr), Sam Dudgeon/HRW Photo; 157 (tr), Ron Davis/Shooting Star; (br), Richard Hutchings/HRW Photo; 158 (t), Michelle Bridwell/Frontera Fotos; 174 (cr), Melanie Carr/Zephyr Pictures; 176 (tl), Paul Rodriguez/Latin Focus; (tr), Sam Dudgeon/HRW Photo; (cl), Latin Focus; (cr), Suzanne Murphy-Larronde; (br), David Simson/Stock Boston, Inc.; 177 (tl), Reuters/Jeff Vinnick/Archive Photos; (tc), Rick Stewart/Allsport USA; (cl), Paul J. Sutton/Duomo Photography; 178 (cl), Image Copyright © 1996 Photodisc, Inc./HRW.

LOCATION OPENER - FLORIDA: Page 184–185 (bkgd), Jim Schwabel/Southern Stock/PNI; 186 (tr), Tony

Arruza; (b), Steve Ferry/P & F Communications; 187 (tl), Steve Ferry/P & F Communications; (cr), Latin Focus; (bl), David Phillips/HRW Photo.

CHAPTER FIVE: Page 188–189 (bkgd), Scott Van Osdol/HRW Photo; 189 (tr), Lisa Davis/HRW Photo; (bl), David Young-Wolff/PhotoEdit; 190 (all); 191 (all); 192 (all); 193 (bc); 194 (tl), M. L. Miller/Edge Video Productions/HRW; 196 (br), David R. Frazier Photolibrary; 197 (bl), (bc); 203 (all); 204 (all); 208 (tl), (tr), (cl), (c), Michelle Bridwell/Frontera Fotos; (tc), HRW/File Photo; (br), Stuart Cohen/Comstock; (cr), Sam Dudgeon/HRW Photo; 211 (c), David R. Frazier Photolibrary; 215 (tr), Steve Ferry/P & F Communications; 216 (other), (frío) Randy O'Rourke/The Stock Market; (other), (fresco) Leon Duque/Duque Múnera y Cia; (other), (nieva) Linc Cornell/Stock Boston, Inc.; (other), (llueve) Mary Kate Denny/PhotoEdit; (other), (viento) Michelle Bridwell/Frontera Fotos; (other), (calor) Peter Van Steen/HRW Photo; (other), (nublado) Weston Kemp/Bentley-Kemp Corp.; 220 (br), Robert Frerck/Odyssey Productions; 221 (tr), Jack Kurtz/Impact Visuals/PNI; (bl), Index Stock Photography; 222 (cl), Image Copyright © 1996 Photodisc, Inc./HRW; 223 (t), Michelle Bridwell/Frontera Fotos; (br), (tr), Comstock; (b), David R. Frazier Photolibrary; 224 (tr), Superstock; (cl), David Young-Wolff/PhotoEdit; (c), Susan Van Etten/PhotoEdit; (cr), Michelle Bridwell/Frontera Fotos; 226 (all), Michelle Bridwell/Frontera Fotos.

CHAPTER SIX: Page 228–229 (bkgd), Scott Van Osdol/HRW Photo; 228 (c), Sam Dudgeon/HRW Photo; 235 (tl), (tr), Michelle Bridwell/Frontera Fotos; (cl), Bachmann/ProFiles West, Inc.; (cr), David Young-Wolff/PhotoEdit; 237 (cr), Daniel J. Schaefer; 239 (br), Nik Wheeler/Westlight; 241 (bl), Image Copyright © 1996 Photodisc, Inc./HRW; 242 (t), Michelle Bridwell/Frontera Fotos; 244 (br), Image Copyright © 1996 Photodisc, Inc./HRW; 245 (bl), (cr), M. L. Miller/Edge Video Productions/HRW; 249 (cl), (bl), Michelle Bridwell/Frontera Fotos; (cr), HRW/File Photo; (br), Robert Frerck/Woodfin Camp; 250 (c), *Billiken Almanaque 1997,* December 30, 1996, p. 34. Reprinted by permission of Editorial Atlántida S.A.; 251 (all), Sam Dudgeon/HRW Photo; 255 (all), Michelle Bridwell/HRW Photo; 265 (tr), John Langford/HRW Photo; 266 (all), Natasha Lane/HRW Photo.

ACKNOWLEDGMENTS

For text acknowledgments, see page ii.

ILLUSTRATIONS AND CARTOGRAPHY

Abbreviated as follows: (t) top, (b) bottom, (l) left, (r) right, (c) center. All art, unless otherwise noted, by Holt, Rinehart and Winston.

FRONT MATTER: Page viii, Elizabeth Brandt; ix, Precision Graphics; Fian Arroyo/Dick Washington; xiii, Fian Arroyo/Dick Washington; xvii, GeoSystems; xviii, GeoSystems; xx, GeoSystems; xxi, GeoSystems; xxii, GeoSystems; xxiii, GeoSystems.

PRELIMINARY CHAPTER: Page xxiv–1, GeoSystems; 3, GeoSystems; 4, Annette Cable/Claire Jett & Associates; 5, Annette Cable/Claire Jett & Associates; 12, Deborah Haley Melmon/Sharon Morris Associates; 13 (tc), Boston Graphics; 13 (c), Eva Vagretti Cockrille; 15, Precision Graphics.

CHAPTER ONE: Page 17, GeoSystems; 25, Boston Graphics; 27 (tl), Precision Graphics; 27 (br), Boston Graphics; 28, Edson Campos; 30, Boston Graphics; 31, Precision Graphics; 37, Manuel García/Richard Salzman; 40, GeoSystems; 44, Eldon Doty/Pat Hackett; 45, Eldon Doty/Pat Hackett; 49, Fian Arroyo/Dick Washington; 50, Boston Graphics; 52, Eldon Doty/Pat Hackett; 55, Boston Graphics; 57, Precision Graphics.

CHAPTER TWO: Page 65, Elizabeth Brandt; 66, Elizabeth Brandt; 67, Mauro Mistiano; 75, Antonio Castro/Cornell & McCarthy; 76, Boston Graphics; 79, Eldon Doty/Pat Hackett; 82, GeoSystems; 85, Eldon Doty/Pat Hackett; 87, Elizabeth Brandt; 93, Michael Morrow; 96, Eva Vagretti Cockrille; 97, Elizabeth Brandt.

CHAPTER THREE: Page 99, Geosystems; 109 (br), Boston Graphics; 109, Deborah Haley Melmon/Sharon Morris Associates; 113, Michael Morrow; 116, GeoSystems; 121, Holly Cooper; 123, Meryl Henderson; 125, Elizabeth Brandt; 126, Holly Cooper; 129, Michael Morrow; 130, Holly Cooper; 134, Precision Graphics; 135, Michael Morrow; 138, Deborah Haley Melmon/Sharon Morris Associates; 141, Deborah Haley Melmon/Sharon Morris Associates.

CHAPTER FOUR: Page 146, Eva Vagretti Cockrille; 149, Edson Campos; 151, Ignacio Gomez/Carol Chislovsky Design, Inc.; 156, Boston Graphics; 159, Elizabeth Brandt; 161, Lori Osiecki; 161, Ignacio Gomez/Carol Chislovsky Design, Inc.; 164, Manuel García/Richard Salzman; 165, Deborah Haley Melmon/Sharon Morris Associates; 167, Ignacio Gomez/Carol Chislovsky Design, Inc.; 168, Precision Graphics; 177, Michael Morrow; 181, Bethann Thornburgh/Lindgren & Smith; 182, Edson Campos; 183, Edson Campos.

CHAPTER FIVE: Page 185, GeoSystems; 194, Edson Campos; 198 (bl), Boston Graphics; 198 (tr), Edson Campos; 199, Edson Campos; 200, Geosystems; 204, Deborah Haley Melmon/Sharon Morris Associates; 206, Meryl Henderson; 209, Edson Campos; 212, Fian Arroyo/Dick Washington; 213, Edson Campos; 214, Bethann Thornburgh/Lindgren & Smith; 217, Precision Graphics; 218, Fian Arroyo/Dick Washington; 225 (tr), Boston Graphics; 225 (cl), Precision Graphics; 227, Edson Campos.

CHAPTER SIX: Page 236, Edson Campos; 238, Lori Osiecki; 246, Meryl Henderson; 256, Ignacio Gomez/Carol Chislovsky Design; 257, Fian Arroyo/Dick Washington; 260, GeoSystems; 267 (tc, bl), Edson Campos; 267, Ignacio Gomez/Carol Chislovsky Design, Inc.